Dominican
Republic

Other Places Travel Guides

Dominican Republic
Katherine Tuider & Evan Caplan

Published by
OTHER PLACES PUBLISHING

First edition
Published January 2012

Dominican Republic
Other Places Travel Guide

Written by: Katherine Tuider & Evan Caplan

Cover designed by: Carla Zetina-Yglesias
Cover photograph and photograph of family on mule on back cover by: Katherine Tuider
Photograph of boy in tree on back cover by: Darien Clary

Published by:
Other Places Publishing
www.otherplacespublishing.com

The Authors

Katherine Tuider

Katherine attributes her love of travel to a one-way ticket to Buenos Aires that evolved into a two-month adventure around South America. Since then she has explored Vietnam by motorcycle, led medicinal tours in Ecuador and traveled to every corner of the Dominican Republic while serving as a Health Extension Volunteer for Peace Corps. After three years of experiencing the island's rich culture and history, eating its soul-warming food and creating lifelong friendships with the incredibly warm and generous Dominicans, she decided to share the country she loves with others by becoming a travel writer.

Evan Caplan

Evan hails from just outside the quaint and bucolic locale of New York City. After graduation, he heard the calling of the Peace Corps, serving in an equally rural village of 400 in the central valley of the Dominican Republic. He subsisted off of plantains, rice, and local brews as he worked with his local counterparts to implement appropriate and sustainable projects, from raising rabbits to teaching business skills. At the end of his service, sitting in the trunk seat of a nine-passenger car and marveling at the setting sun over a nearby precipice, Evan realized he wanted to inspire others to embark on this same journey.

Acknowledgments

Katherine and Evan would like to thank all of the following friends and colleagues for providing support, *bolas*, humor, *amistad*, adventures, assistance and "a buen tiempos":

Peace Corps DR (Sandy Santana, Jennifer McGowan, Romeo Massey), Lynne Guitar, Tatiana Fernández, Patricia Grassals, Annett Rieger, Chichi Reyes, José Carlos Oviedo, Carla Campos, Ruben Torres, Manuel Bolos, José Miguel Font, Carmen Espinosa, Jerson Mateo Taveras, José Duluc, Darien Clary, Stephanie Brewer, Dilana Pickett, Cheryl Holub, Rebekah Powell, Victor Galvan, Alanna Hughes, Derrick Lewis, Linsey Longstreth, Carla Campos, Megan Moore, Henry Fernández, Sandy Reyes, Justin Kersey, Ben Hulefeld, Elizabeth Black, Aaron Arnoldy, Genaro "Cayuco" Reyes, La Secretaria de Medio Ambiente (Yesenia Saud, Benedicto Maceo, José Ramón Martínez Batlle, Pedro Rodríguez), Laura Baetscher, Trina Mintern, Clayton Rotuno, Bailey Gamble, Tod Haggard, Ruth Schlotman, Charlie Seltzer, Kate Wallace, Ann Smyntek, Jennifer Bailey, Justin Lee, Amy Martin, Taylor Joyal, David Garfunkel, Todd Schweitzer, Joan Perreault, Neal Riemer, Keane Bhatt, Leticia Hinojosa, Cassidy Rush, Shannon Alston, Ali Bujanovich, Magee McDonald, Renata Sancken, Lily Mendelson, Regina Cruz, Kelly Connors, Peter Boberg, Asahi Wada, Marite Pérez, Ben Simasek, Jenie Barker, Alissa Karp, Mica Jenkins, Rob Gradoville, Pam Schreier, Arya Zarrinkelk, Andrea Montague, Stephanie Garry, Iris Padilla, Rosalba Gillardi, Noemi Araujo, Altagracia Ramírez, Checo Merette, Rafi Vazquez, and Yomidis Disla Rodríguez. A special thanks goes to the entirety of 517-07-02, as well as the communities of El Puente, El Rifle, Las Aromas, and our various host families.

In addition, we say *muchísimas gracias* to the Sustainable Tourism Clusters of: Constanza (Johnny Tactuk), Puerto Plata (Rebeca Urena, Alberto Khoury, Rosa Tavarez), Jarabacoa (Alida, Carmen), Montecristi (José Luis Bornigal, Neris de Almonte), Barahona (Dreidy Smith), Samana/Altagracia (Katia Rios), and Romana-Bayahibe (Gemma Fontanella).

Katherine would like to extend a special thanks to her father, for always supporting her crazy ideas.

Evan would like to do the same to his family, for whom he finally gets to write down his helpful hints; his roommates of 1854, who dealt with typing at all hours; and those special people who knew that positive thinking could get him to the end.

Contents

Introduction 11

The Basics 43

Santo Domingo 65

The East 119

The North Coast 175

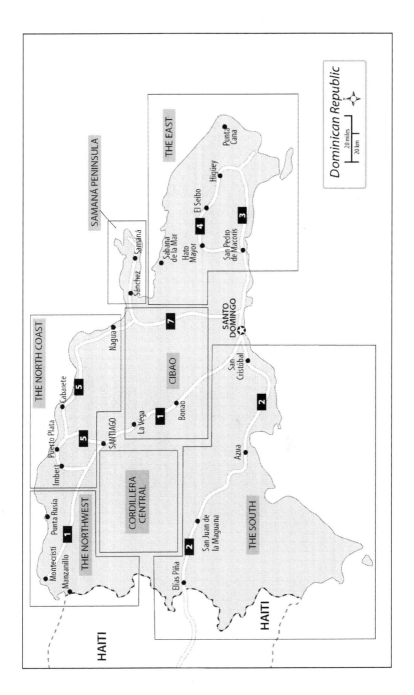

Quick Reference

Official Name – República Dominicana

Official Language – Spanish, though English and Haitian Creole are spoken among certain populations

Location – The eastern two-thirds of the island of Hispaniola, shared with Haiti

Size - 48,734 sq km

Climate – tropical, with wide variations across altitude

Terrain – rugged mountainous interior and coastal lowlands

Lowest Point – Lago Enriquillo -46 m

Highest Point – Pico Duarte 3,175 m

Population – 10 million

Capital – Santo Domingo

Ethnic Groups - Mixed 73%, White 16%, Black 11%

Religion – 90% Catholic; 10% Evangelical or Afro-Caribbean Syncretism

Government – republic

Administrative Divisions – 31 Provinces and a Federal District

GDP - $51.6 billion (2010)

GDP per capita - $8,900 (2010)

Life expectancy - 77

Time Zone – UTC -4

Literacy Rate – 87%

Poverty Rate – 40%

Business Hours – Businesses are generally open 9am – 12pm and 2pm – 5pm Monday – Friday, and many open Saturday morning as well. Almost all businesses are closed on the Sunday. Many restaurants are open only for dinner.

Currency:

The prices in the book are in Dominican pesos (RD$).

Exchange rates as of publication:

  1 USD = RD$37

  1 Euro = RD$50

  1GBP = RD$58

  1 AUS = RD$38

Phone numbers: Dial the ten-digit number as you would in the U.S., by first dialing "1" followed by the area code, the the 7-digit number. (829) and (849) prefixes are generally cell phones.

National holidays:

  1 January: Año Nuevo/New Year's Day

  6 January (observed 9 January). Día de los Santos Reyes/Three Kings Day

  21 January: Día de Nuestra Señora de la Altagracia/Our Lady of Altagracia Day

  26 January (observed 30 January): Día de Duarte/Day of Duarte

  27 February: Día de la Independencia/Independence Day

  6 April: ViernesSanto/Good Friday

  8 April: Pascua/Easter

  1 May (observed 30 April): Día del Trabajo/Labor Day

  7 June: Corpus Christi

  16 August: Día de la Restauración/Restoration Day

  24 September: Día de las Mercedes/Our Lady of Mercedes Day

  6 November (observed 5 November): Día de la Constitución/Constitution Day

  25 December: Navidad/Christmas Day

Book Icons

⬛ Indicates a sustainable tourism establishment or service.

✎ Author recommended spot or activity.

Introduction

From the first indigenous arrivals in canoes to Christopher Columbus and his crew to the modern tourist, no one has left the Dominican Republic (DR) the same as when they arrived. The DR has defied expectations for more than five centuries as a country of movement, discovery, and adventure. At once acting as a seaside haven and a mountainous getaway, dotted with gleaming beachside hotels and tiny wooden houses, and home to lush cloud forests and sun-baked scrubland, the DR continues to amaze travelers from across the globe. It is now the biggest tourist destination in the Caribbean, as millions each year visit its shores. Yet this country's offerings go much farther than manicured beaches. The DR challenges us to explore and experience the land, the people, and its rich history.

Sharing the picturesque island of Hispaniola with its neighbor Haiti, the Dominican Republic boasts extraordinary geographic diversity, from deserts to pine-covered slopes and coral reefs to humid mangrove forests. The highest peak, tallest waterfall, and lowest lake in the Caribbean are all located within its borders. Endangered mammals numbering just a few dozen share turf with fan-favorite flamingos and crocodiles, while migratory birds and humpback whales gather here for a winter respite. Though environmental degradation has taken its toll, today, protection and preservation of natural resources have become paramount goals, illustrated by the many ecotourism opportunities highlighted in this book.

The DR is described as warm for another reason besides the climate: the people. The unique Dominican culture draws on indigenous, African, and European roots to produce a multi-ethnic landscape of friendly, welcoming people proud of their heritage and homeland. This is where the Old and New World collided, and the resulting pan-hemispheric cultural fusion continues to make waves today. Wherever they are, visitors are always kept on their toes: swaying to the syncopated beats of the music, preparing a traditional family meal, or even cheering along with hot-blooded fans at a baseball game.

Beyond experiencing home life, no trip is complete without sampling the endless outdoor activity. National parks stretch from coast to coast, showcasing breathless vistas and vast undersea beauties. Take in the infinite seascapes from the imposing cliffs of El Morro. Feel the rush of adrenaline while rafting down the rivers of Jarabacoa. Steep yourself in the history of intercontinental trade and agriculture deep in a hilly coffee forest.

Just as every region of the Dominican Republic is markedly different, each trip offers distinct challenges and opportunities. A vacation to the DR is all about the journey, enjoying the resonant, unhurried experience of personal interaction and appreciation for the surroundings. Here, sharing is not just a virtue, but a way of life.

History

ORIGINAL INHABITANTS

The history of the Dominican Republic "officially" began in 1492, when Christopher Columbus tripped over the Bahamas and stumbled onto Hispaniola. For thousands of years before European arrival, indigenous peoples inhabited the island and its mountains, valleys, forests, and shores. Successive waves of migration from Central and South America brought over diverse groups of settlers. Over time, cultural and linguistic mixing in the relative isolation of this island resulted in the evolution of the Taíno people, who spoke an Arawak language related to those of other nearby Caribbean islands and the northern coast of South America.

In the 15th century, various groups of Taínos were spread across the Caribbean basin, with an approximate population of 500,000 on Hispaniola, or "Quisqueya," an indigenous name for the island. The Taínos of Hispaniola organized themselves into political units, headed by leaders called *caciques*. Taíno society was matrilineal, composed of small villages with central squares, around which cultural and family life was organized. They were an agricultural people, farming *yuca* as a staple crop, among others like sweet potatoes, beans, squash, and tobacco. The dugout canoe was a primary mode of transport, which was used to move between the various Caribbean islands.

All but wiped out by newer, more aggressive foreigners, the Taínos bequeathed a subtle legacy on Hispaniola. Few remnants are left from their centuries of civilization on the island. However, a few pertinent Taíno bits of vocabulary remain in the Spanish language: *arepa, barbacoa, canoa, hamaca, huracán,* and *yuca* (corn cake, barbecue, canoe, hammock, hurricane, and cassava, respectively). Popular Dominican culture harkens back to mythologized indigenous ancestry, though the contemporary population has little real connection with the original inhabitants of the island. Contemporary presence of Taínos on Hispaniola can be found in cave drawings, petroglyphs, museum artifacts, and in the collective historical memory of Dominican society.

COLONIZERS

Christopher Columbus (Cristóbal Colón, in Spanish) and his crew – who were explorers, but perhaps not the best navigators – landed on the north coast of the island of Hispaniola in December of 1492. A curious local population is said to have reacted warmly to their visitors. Only a few days later, one of the flotilla's ships ran aground on a nearby reef. The sailors built a fort from the wreckage and christened it La Navidad for its Christmas construction date. Columbus then left 39 members of his party to man the settlement as he made his way back to Spain to spin tales about his incredible discovery and the potential for immense wealth. Those who stayed at the fort fared poorly; vicious infighting took a bloody toll, and the sailors provoked the ire of the local Taínos by taking indigenous women back to La Navidad. Columbus returned in 1493 to find the sailors dead and the fort in ruins.

Ever industrious, Columbus and his new band of adventurers established what was to be the first European colony in the New World, named Isabela after the Spanish queen. This settlement on the north coast served as the first base for the

Spanish exploration and exploitation of Hispaniola and surrounding islands. The first peaceful interactions between visitor and local became violent and vengeful as sailors turned into conquistadors, wielding technology, war, disease, and the subjugation of the Taíno population. Spanish landowners used the Taínos as forced labor in short-lived gold mines and later, on agricultural plantations. Little gold was discovered, but the forced labor on farms continued, contributing to the demise of the Taíno population. While Columbus moved on to explore other territories, his brother Bartholomew traveled to the southern part of the island to establish a new city, and later the capital, Santo Domingo de Guzmán, in 1496. This city grew in importance as Spain's new colony flourished. According to the accounts of Fray Bartolomé de las Casas, famous for his written critique of the Spanish treatment of the indigenous people, the Taíno population dropped to less than 50,000 by the first decades of the 16th century. Within 50 years, they had entirely disappeared. Overwhelmed by hunger, disease, and exhaustion, the Taínos took to suicide and fled to remote parts of the island. Various ill-prepared Taíno leaders defended themselves valiantly, but were considerably over-matched by the Spaniards. The last great Taíno rebellion (and the most successful) was led by Cacique Enriquillo in the mountains of the southwest, near present-day Bahoruco. Enriquillo and his followers coaxed a treaty out of the Spaniards in 1534 after a decade of insurgency. Land-hungry Spanish settlers soon broke the treaty, burned the Taíno town, and ran the inhabitants into the ground.

With the Taíno population quickly dying off, Spain began importing slaves as early as 1501. Serving as labor on the colonial *encomienda* plantation system, the number of African slaves exploded, growing cash crops like sugarcane for export. Columbus, meanwhile, ended up as a more adept adventurer than administrator. Though named as first governor of the island, a set of powerful elites came to resent his overbearing authority and in 1499, sent him back to Spain. Nicolás de Ovando took his place, and oversaw Santo Domingo become the economic and administrative center of Spanish colonial designs.

ENCROACHMENT

As the colony of Santo Domingo flourished, so did the envy of neighboring imperialists, France and England. English pirates plied the Caribbean Sea and picked fights for decades along the north coast with small towns that the Spanish crown could not easily defend; even Santo Domingo was briefly captured by English marauder Francis Drake, who was knighted by the Queen for his conquests. The French, however, were much more successful in actually settling the island, establishing an outpost on the western end of Hispaniola, and creatively naming their side of the island Saint-Domingue. A greatly unbalanced ratio of African slaves to French colonists began working on enormous sugarcane plantations radiating from the coast. Soon, the small Spanish population was greatly outnumbered by the French settlers. In a nod to pragmatism after being frayed by skirmishes on the island, war in Europe and further exploration in the rest of the Americas, the Spanish agreed to officially demarcate a border between the two colonies with the Treaty of Ryswick in 1697. During the 18th century, Santo Domingo floundered as the Spaniards found more lucrative territory in Central and South America, and France's Saint-Domingue flourished as the wealthiest colony in the New World.

THE SECOND FREE COUNTRY IN THE WEST

French domination on Hispaniola was not destined to last forever. Enlightened by the French Revolution across the pond, slaves and mulattoes (those of mixed African and European ancestries) in neighboring Haiti took to arms in rebellion against their colonial overseers in 1791. Spain hesitatingly supported the rebellion against its neighbor-adversary, but this proved more difficult when the former slave and Jacobin revolutionary general Toussaint L'Ouverture changed loyalties back to the French side in 1794, after France abolished slavery in its colonies. Meanwhile, in 1795, Spain lost its continental war to France. The peace treaty that concluded the war required Spain to give up its Hispaniolan colony. Under the gifted leadership of L'Ouverture, and ignoring official French policy against an armed invasion of its new possession, the French-Haitian forces entered Santo Domingo, declaring the end of slavery on the entire island. Spanish settlers, however, were loath to leave their homes and land, so the majority stood their ground. L'Ouverture and his revolutionary followers then turned on the French, sacking cities and towns across both sides of island in an effort to create a homeland of their own. The Haitian fighters declared independence in 1804, as the second country to have done so in the New World, and as the first black republic in the hemisphere.

INDEPENDENCE, ANNEXATION & THE RESTORATION OF INDEPENDENCE

The Spanish soon retook control of Santo Domingo, reestablished slavery, and continued in uneasy coexistence with their new, restive neighbors to the west. Less than ten years later, in 1821 and alongside many other Spanish colonies, the Dominican Republic declared independence. The new country petitioned to become a part of Gran Colombia, the short-lived political alliance that encompassed today's Colombia, Ecuador, and Venezuela.

Before they could move on that claim, the powerful Haitian army swept across the island in 1822 and renewed its control over the infant country. Conquering Haitian authorities again abolished slavery and allowed few liberties to their Spanish-speaking subjects, giving rise the bitter currents of Dominican resentment that run fast and deep, even today. Dominicans chafed under foreign occupation by a foreign people, institutionalizing the ethno-cultural tension that continues to divide the two nations today.

After 22 years, Dominican forces under immortal leader Juan Pablo Duarte, considered the father of the Dominican Republic, finally threw off the hated Haitian rule and proclaimed independence on February 27, 1844, which is today celebrated as the Dominican Independence Day. Duarte is known in Dominican lore as a third of the "Trinitarios," or triumvirate of heroes of independence; the other two are Francisco del Rosario Sánchez and Matías Ramón Mella.

Though established as a presidential republic, the Dominican Republic underwent the same fate as many of its former Spanish colonial contemporaries, suffering under a series of *caudillo*-style leaders that looked to consolidate power and enrich themselves through elaborate clientelist systems while neglecting the development of the broader economy and society. The military junta dictators, in 1861, presented with a state in financial ruin, a threatening neighbor, and an increasingly violent revolt on their hands, turned to an eager Spanish government to reannex their country. Spanish forces arrived on the island to confront a seething populace unhappy with the recent turn of events. Disorganized rebels clashed with Spanish troops, battling over four bloody years until the Queen finally declared the annexation annulled in 1865. Dominicans celebrate this date, March 3, as the *Restauración de la República*: the Restoration of the Republic.

DICTATORSHIPS AND U.S. INVOLVEMENT

Although the country was reestablished as a republic, elections occurred infrequently and just a small cadre of elites – bitterly divided along regional lines – in the capital and Santiago controlled political power. In 1882, General Ulises Heureaux was elected president, expertly wielding his political power to control the country for the following two decades. Familiarly called Lilís, Heureaux ruled as either an outright dictator or through a series of puppet presidents. He presided over industrial modernization through the procurement of massive international loans and investment but aroused the ire of merchants who were not pleased with his machinations – nor the economic decline associated with his defaulting on many of the loans. Having accumulated enormous personal wealth and becoming increasingly oppressive, Lilís was assassinated in 1899 in Moca, leading to an enormous power vacuum that ended in further violence and fiscal insolvency.

Padres de La Patria

As part of the fight for independence from Haitian rule, three men came to the forefront, today known as the Padres de La Patria, or Founding Fathers. The first, and most famous, is Juan Pablo Duarte. Born in 1813 in Santo Domingo, Duarte became involved in politics after seeing firsthand the ideological upheaval in Europe and the U.S. In 1838, already as a well-known personality in Dominican politics, he founded an underground organization called the Trinitaria, which espoused liberal, reformist doctrines under the banner of "God, Country, and Liberty," and worked towards the independence of the Dominican Republic. Because of his subversive actions, Duarte was exiled in 1843. The next year, on February 27, his compatriots in the fight for freedom declared independence. Duarte returned to the DR with a hero's welcome, and assisted in drafting the new Constitution. He was then nominated for the Presidency, but conservative actors led by General Pedro Santana blocked his accession. Fearful of his more republican leanings, these military leaders sent him into exile again. He died in Venezuela in 1876.

The second Padre de la Patria is Francisco del Rosario Sánchez, born in 1817. Second in command of the Trinitaria, Sánchez took over the organization when Duarte was exiled and wrote much of the document that declared independence from Haiti. Sánchez himself proclaimed independence in Santo Domingo's Puerta de Misericordia on February 27, 1844, raising the new Dominican flag for his countrymen. Like Duarte, Sánchez was exiled by the powerful Santana government. He was later allowed back into the country, and then led the fight against re-annexation to Spain. For this work, Santana's pro-annexation forces executed him in 1861.

The last Founding Father was Ramón Matías Mella, born in 1816. Heading up the military wing of the independence fight, Mella defeated Haitian forces in the north before marching on and taking Santo Domingo. Mella, too, was exiled under Santana, but returned to the DR soon after. He worked with the anti-annexation forces as well, organizing troops for the War of Restoration. He died in 1864.

European nations clamored to receive a return on their loans, threatening invasion. The U.S., therefore, acting under the new Roosevelt Corollary to the Monroe Doctrine, positioned itself strongly to oversee the improvement of the Dominican financial and political situation by taking over the administration of Dominican customs.

Another series of leaders and coups d'état left the country in shambles and in a state of near-civil war. Demanding political stability, the American government under President Wilson required the warring factions to shape up or get invaded. The threat of force was not compelling. United States forces entered the DR in 1916 (after having earlier invaded Haiti), restoring order and protecting American economic interests in Dominican agriculture and real estate. American authorities helped kick-start some basic reforms: formation of an educational system, beginning basic tax collection, and the creation of a national army. Such reforms also included market economy liberalization, opening the DR to foreign, and especially American, investment. After World War I, the U.S. was ready to conclude its occupation, and under new leadership, Dominicans retook control of their country in 1922.

EL JEFE: TRUJILLO

Peaceful elections were held after the U.S. vacated the island, leading to a democratically and fairly elected presidency, though it would be the last fair election for a generation. After but one uneventful term, political instability returned. The strengthening National Army, commanded by one Rafael Leónidas Trujillo Molina, took advantage of an unpopular administration and economic instability caused by the Great Depression. Trujillo, a son of the lower class rural South, had joined the Dominican National Guard – formed by the American government after it invaded the DR in 1916. The U.S. approved of his muscular leadership skills, and left him as the commander of these forces upon the American departure in 1924. Trujillo formed his own political party, called the Dominican Party, and stood for the presidential election in 1930. Through strong-arm tactics and the threat of violence, Trujillo was elected president in 1930 with an astounding 95% of the votes. *Trujillismo* had begun.

Trujillo moved quickly to consolidate absolute political power through the enormous expansion of the *Guardia Nacional*, as well as several secret intelligence agencies that fanned out across the country, seeking and destroying subversive elements of society. Trujillo promoted a personality cult: he renamed Santo Domingo "Ciudad Trujillo," (old manholes and plumbing grates still bear this name around the Colonial Zone) and the West Indies' highest peak, Pico Duarte, "Pico Trujillo" (p296). Among other self-serving edifices, he had constructed a monument in Santiago (p245) dedicated to his own glory. Trujillo and his national army crushed political opposition as well as civil society, while controlling major economic output for his own personal ends. He was a modern-day *caudillo*, modeling himself after these past generations of other Latin American strongman dictators. Trujillo's ruthless efficiency in rooting out resistance and creating a stranglehold on power well surpassed the authoritarian apex of previous Dominican leaders. While accumulating a personal fortune, Trujillo presided over general improvement of the Dominican Republic's economy, since political stability through utter repression let the economy open and grow.

Beyond sowing fear and anxiety among Dominicans, Trujillo orchestrated one of the most egregious and bloody attacks on a specific group of people by a state government. In 1937, after decades of increased Haitian migration to serve as plantation labor, Trujillo declared a cleansing of his country. In October of that year, Trujillo ordered an execution of any Haitians living in the Dominican Republic. The machete-wielding Dominican army then slaughtered over 20,000 Haitians, turning the river that forms the border red, giving it a new name that it still holds today: Río Masacre. Over his tenure, Trujillo implemented various anti-Haitian and racist policies called *blanquismo* (whitening), focusing his politics towards his personal understanding of Dominican history. Trujillo oriented his country to Europe, and away from Africa. In concerted efforts, he grandly welcomed Republic refugees from the Spanish Civil War and Jewish refugees of the Holocaust. Trujillo also elevated the status of the merengue style of music and dance, which he claimed was modeled after traditional European dances.

For much of Trujillo's rule, the U.S. remained open to working the Dominican dictator. Sensing an opportunity, Trujillo eliminated the Dominican Communist Party, taking a strong anti-red stance to shore up support from the West. However, by the late 1950s, Trujillo had reached his domestic and international limit. The economy flagging and deeply unpopular abroad, Trujillo finally met his end when underground rebels, covertly supported by the CIA, assassinated him as he drove along Santo Domingo's seaside promenade on May 30, 1961. The site is marked by an awe-striking black and gold mosaic sculpture, "Monumento 30 de mayo," by Dominican artist Cristian Tiburcio.

BALAGUER & THE DOCENA

The political succession after Trujillo's assassination went less smoothly. Joaquín Balaguer, Trujillo's second in command, held onto his post just long enough to be sent into exile by the fractured, though more reformist, government. In 1962, free elections were finally held and the people selected Juan Bosch of the newly founded *Partido Revolucionario Dominicano* (PRD, or Dominican Revolutionary Party) as president. His intellectual style and left-leaning politics disturbed the economic elites who had prospered under the previous conservative regime, as well as Communist-fearful Western governments. The army engineered a coup that overthrew the democratically elected government less than a year after Bosch was elected, again throwing the country into chaos. A military junta held tenuous power through April 1965, when pro-Bosch forces toppled it. The country descended into civil war as the conservative military fought back in the capital city. United States President Lyndon Johnson, leery of the uncertainty in his island neighbor and seizing a chance to control regional politics, sent a force of over 20,000 troops to restore order in the Dominican Republic.

Under American guidance, new elections were held in 1966. While in exile in New York, Balaguer stoked opposition to the volatile, reformist government. During the invasion maelstrom, Balaguer returned home to stoke support from his elite conservative base. This time, Balaguer, as the candidate representing a return to stability, was elected president. Balaguer, a perceptive student of Trujillo, won re-election in 1970 and 1974, leading for twelve consecutive years. Balaguer used the national army to curtail opposition through coercion and other extra-democratic means, deft echoes of *Trujillismo*.

In the 1978 elections, the opposition PRD candidate Antonio Guzmán Fernández seemed headed for victory, but the army refused to allow vote counting to continue. Balaguer, however, bowed to international pressure, and let Guzmán assume the presidency. Another PRD candidate, Salvador Blanco, won high office in 1982. Balaguer, phoenix-like, rose to win the presidency back in 1986. Irregularities and violence marred the 1990 elections, which Balaguer won yet again. In 1994, 88 years of age and blind, Balaguer claimed victory in an internationally denounced fraudulent election process. The opposition candidate Peña Gómez met with Balaguer to discuss possible solutions; the president served the first two years of his final term and then held elections in 1996 in which he did not run. Under Balaguer, the DR saw similar economic transformation as under Trujillo: a more open market, macroeconomic expansion, and increased foreign investment. The poorest and most underserved, however, saw little of the new wealth.

FREE AND FAIR TO LEONEL

The electoral process thereafter, beginning in 1996, saw a series of free and fair elections. Leonel Antonio Fernández Reyna, with Balaguer's support, defeated Peña Gómez. Fernández served out his four-year term and was voted out of office in 2000, when voters chose Hipólito Mejía. Though Fernández had continued economic liberalization, Mejía found support in those who were displeased with alleged corruption in the Fernández regime and looking for more support for the poor. However, Mejía presided over a destabilizing drop in the Dominican peso, bankruptcy of major Dominican financial institutions, and a general economic decline. Mejía also amended the constitution to allow for sequential terms in office, vowing not to run in 2004. Mejía broke his promise, but was soundly defeated by Leonel Fernández. A supportive electorate helped Fernández turn the tables on Mejía's ploy. Fernández ran again in 2008, soundly defeating his opponent. In the same election, his party gained sizable majorities in both houses of Congress. Hi third term is set to end in 2012, and he is not expected to to stand again.

Joaquin Balaguer

Joaquin Balaguer was the nicer, kinder version of Trujillo. Though schooled in the dictator's strongman ways and holding onto power until an octogenarian, Balaguer was both loved and reviled by his countrymen. His funeral flooded the streets with supporters upon his death at age 95, and many still speak with nostalgia of low prices and ironclad political stability. Professorial, bespectacled, and holding a doctorate, Balaguer performed the part of the kindly all-powerful leader, eager to play to the loving masses. Yet he was still able to broadly repress dissention within Dominican society. His electoral victories in 1970 and 1974 came against a weakened and boycotting opposition. For the two terms he was not in power, Balaguer continued to cultivate his cult of personality, again winning the presidency in 1986 and then implementing vast public works projects. He held onto power for an additional ten years, pulling in support from both the poor who benefitted from his programs, as well as strong national and international business interests. His authoritarian ways remained until the end, when he rigged the 1994 elections and then only agreed to serve half of his term. Today, Dominican students are steeped in his voluminous works written over seven decades, and his face can be seen plastered on billboards, regally looking out into the sunset over his beloved country.

Politics & Economy

The Dominican constitution establishes the country as a multi-party, representative republic with universal and compulsory suffrage at the age of 18; though members of the police and armed forces are not allowed to vote. The government is based on the classic Western system of separation of powers and checks and balances among the legislative, executive, and judicial branches. The president acts as the head of state, head of government, and head of the armed forces. The executive branch also contains a cabinet selected by the president. The president and vice-president are elected on the same ticket for a four-year term. The president must win 50 percent plus one of the votes to avoid a second-round runoff between the first and second place candidates.

The legislative branch is composed of a bicameral *Congreso de la República* (Congress). The Senate has 32 elected members, one from each province and the capital district. The Chamber of Deputies has 178 members, elected from the provinces according to proportional representation. Members of Congress are also elected to four-year terms, without limitations. The judicial branch is led by the Supreme Court, which has 16 justices. The justices are chosen by a complex procedure involving the president, representatives of major political parties, and the president of the Supreme Court.

POLITICAL PARTIES

The current political party system dates only to the post-Trujillo era, although short-lived parties existed over various times during electoral or leadership struggles. The Dominican Liberation Party (*Partido de la Liberación Dominicana*), or PLD, was founded in 1973 by a disaffected Juan Bosch of the PRD. It was a leftist party, but has since moved to the center-right. The PLD is the party of the current president, Leonel Fernández, and holds a large majority in both houses of Congress. Its political color is purple.

The Dominican Revolutionary Party (*Partido Revolucionario Dominicano*), or PRD, was originally a Trujillo opposition party. Its foundation was leftist, socialist, and reformist, though it has become much more centrist in recent elections. It is a broad-based, moderate party, but still draws support from rural and lower classes. Its distinguishing color is white.

Joaquín Balaguer founded his own party in the 1960s, which he then folded into the Social Christian Reform Party (*Partido Reformista Social Cristiano*), PRSC, in 1985. It began as a conservative and right wing populist party, but has evolved into a more populist movement without an ideological core. The PRSC leader is the engaging, though slightly eccentric, Amable Aristy. Its distinguishing color is red.

> In the 2008 presidential election, Fernández of the PLD won 54 percent of the vote, Vargas of the PRD gained 41 percent, and Aristy of the PRSC just 5 percent.

The DR passed a new constitution in 2010, the 32nd in its history (any time there is a change to the constitution, a new one is promulgated, leading to the high number). Many of these constitutions were passed and soon abolished or ignored. This most recent document is intended to strengthen government institutions and guarantee rights. A new ministry of the public defender was created to protect citizen freedoms. Election of the president, always a knotty issue, was declared to be one four-year term without consecutive re-election, but with the possibility of a later term.

The constitution also sets forth some controversial points. For instance, Dominican citizens are defined explicitly as those who are born to two registered Dominican parents (a clear swipe at the growing Haitian population). To those born to Haitian parents in the DR, even those who have lived in the country for years and speak fluent Spanish, citizenship and all associated rights are denied. Gaining citizenship thereafter is nearly impossible. In addition, the constitution strictly defines marriage as a union between a man and a woman. The document also applies one of the most stringent bans on abortions in the Western hemisphere, even in such instances as rape and incest. Finally, the constitution now allows for the privatization of public beaches. Representatives from the major political parties met and agreed on the constitution, which was then voted on by Congress. It was not put up for public referendum, prompting several protests in the capital. Popular disagreement could be seen on bumper stickers, graffiti, and through social media. One Gallup-Hoy poll showed that only 14 percent of the population agreed with constitutional regulation of abortion.

ECONOMY

Because of the Dominican Republic's tropical location, proximity to the U.S., and relatively low labor costs, the service sector, including tourism and manufacturing, has become the top employer and largest contributor to the national economy. Large Free Trade Zones (known as *Zonas Francas* in Spanish), especially of textiles, are major components in manufacturing, though they have seen a decline after the DR-CAFTA agreement passed in 2007.

GDP (2010) – US$51.6 billion

Real GDP growth (2010) – 7.8%

GDP per capital (2010) – US$8,900

Poverty rate (2009) – 40%

Income inequality – Richest ten percent produces 40% of GDP and bottom ten percent produces 1.5%.

·The IMF estimates that the informal economy makes up almost half of GDP.

DR-CAFTA Agreement

The DR-CAFTA agreement reduces most tariffs on exports and imports, decreasing the market niche of the FTZs. While the agreement officially opens up the vast American market to Dominican products, few have been able to take advantage. The American government subsidizes many agricultural products, the industry in which many of the poorest Dominicans are employed, and therefore can introduce cheaper goods in both the domestic and international markets. Anticipated drops in prices for poor consumers of many goods never materialized. In addition, DR-CAFTA eased barriers for investment for American companies in large infrastructure in tourism, communications, and manufacturing, creating jobs, though mostly low-paid, unskilled positions. The agreement also promotes good labor and environmental practices, whose enforcement may be lax because of a lack of funds. In the first year of DR-CAFTA implementation, American exports to the DR grew, while Dominican exports to the U.S. fell.

The Dominican Republic also relies heavily on cash crop agriculture exports. Agriculture accounts for 15 percent of the labor force and 12 percent of GDP. The DR was once extremely reliant on the sugarcane crop, shuddering under its extreme price fluctuations. However, as the economy has undergone diversification, the economy no longer plunges with a drop in sugar prices. Still, sugar represents the largest agricultural export. Other important crops include coffee, tobacco, cacao, bananas, and rice. Raw materials and natural resources also account for some exports, including gold, silver, and nickel. The U.S. is by far the DR's biggest trading partner, where over 60 percent of exports are sent, principally agricultural products, minerals, and textiles. Remittances also comprise a significant portion of GDP. Imports include food, clothing, oil, and consumer goods.

Remesas

With over 1.5 million Dominicans abroad, remittances (*remesas*) are a major factor in improving the lives of friends and family living in the DR. Nearly US$3 billion in remittances are sent to the DR annually; 70 percent from the U.S. and almost 30 percent from Europe. Remittances provide an important safety net for daily purchases and household improvements, but only a small percentage goes towards savings or investment. Upwards of 40 percent of Dominican households receive some sort of remittances.

People & Culture

DEMOGRAPHY

The approximately ten million inhabitants of the Dominican Republic live in a country of 48,734 square kilometers (18,816 square miles) slightly smaller than West Virginia. Thirty percent of the population is under 14 years of age, and only 6 percent live to reach the age of 65. With a high population density of 537 people per square mile, the DR continues to see growth, though the rate has slowly declined

---

Dominican Hospitality and Culture

If there is one thing that may be generalized about the people of the Dominican Republic, it is that they extend warmth and hospitality to friends and strangers alike. Regardless of economic situation, there is always enough food (and coffee) for everyone to share. A common Dominican refrain is that "when two are eating, a third can join." This sharing and conviviality may extend well beyond the dinner table, such as sharing room in a small bus seat or the back of a motorcycle; there is always space for another. Though it may feel as if personal space has been invaded, this is just an aspect of people helping each other. Whether it comes to lending a hand to a neighbor or friend, Dominicans are always *"a la orden,"* ready to help. Dominicans can be especially forward, sometimes seemingly quite eager, in attempting to please or give guidance to foreigners.

Dominicans are also very confident, and are proud of their national identity. Even as a relatively homogeneous society, socio-economic stratification sharply splinters the Dominican population. Skin color, gender, geographic location, and heritage all play a part in social mobility, access to services, and employment. While feeling a strong sense of unity, cooperation, and affection among themselves, Dominicans tend to frown upon deviation from norms like family unity and gender roles.

over the past couple decades.

The Dominican Republic maintains an agricultural psyche; its symbols and myths are based on an idealized *campo* and Taíno nostalgia lifestyle. In 1950, 75 percent of the Dominican population lived in rural areas. Yet urban centers have undergone near exponential growth since that time. The urbanization rate is currently at 3 percent, but topped 6 percent during parts of the last century. In a complete reversal, 70 percent of today's Dominican population lives in cities. Almost a quarter of the country's population resides in and around the capital of Santo Domingo. This rural flight can be attributed to the potential of salaried, sustained employment in urban areas, as the unstable income of farmers has declined. Social services, almost nonexistent in the *campo*, have a much stronger presence in large centers of population.

MIGRATION

Migration in the Dominican Republic is both a longstanding and explosive issue. Even with a growing population, the DR has a net emigration rate of two people per thousand. There is no stigma for Dominicans to leave their country. In fact, the ability to immigrate, especially to the U.S., is highly sought after and many thousands of Dominicans join the waiting list for a visa each year. It is estimated that 1.5 million Dominicans live in the United States, and at least 10 percent do so without papers. Most Dominican émigrés end up in New York, though there is large network in other areas, including Boston, Philadelphia, Miami, Chicago, and Puerto Rico. Outside the U.S., Western Europe is the other major destination for Dominican emigration, especially since the language barrier is less of an issue in Spain, and access to jobs can be easier. A small amount travel to other Latin American countries, and a few stay within the Caribbean.

Emigration to neighboring Puerto Rico, however, is in a class of its own. To reach that island, one well-known, though dangerous, method of entry is across the Mona Passage, a 70-mile strait separating the DR from Puerto Rico. Successfully landing in Puerto Rico signifies access to the U.S. mainland since travel to and from the island does not require a passport. However, the crossing, undertaken in rough-hewn boats called *yolas*, is treacherous and expensive, costing each passenger up to RD$80,000 (just over US$2,000). One estimate puts failed crossings at 40 percent, including both boats that were able to turn back to the Dominican Republic and those that were not. It is possible that upwards of 50,000 Dominicans, both legal and undocumented, live in Puerto Rico. Once there, many find that employment opportunities are not as great as hoped, and they end up living in impoverished conditions.

Immigration to the DR is much more nuanced. While over several centuries the likes of Spanish, Germans, Italian, Dutch, Chinese, Japanese, Middle Eastern, and Jewish immigrants have arrived on the island, by far the biggest immigrant population comes from movement much closer to home: the migration of Haitians over the land border the two countries share. Reliable data on the Haitian population in the DR is scarce; various estimates place the number between 500,000 and 1 million. An additional 250,000 were born in the DR to Haitian parents. The vast majority of this population lacks formal papers, even those who were born on Dominican soil. Haitians, fleeing poverty, often find work in informal, low-paying jobs and live in menial conditions, carving out marginal space without access to government services. While Dominicans celebrate their kin living abroad, they often revile Haitians living among them. Discrimination is rampant and institutional, though slowly easing through the work of quiet advocates. The issue of Haitian population is controversial, and ignites the ire of many. Tread lightly in related discussions with Dominican hosts and counterparts.

Ethnic Makeup

The Dominican Republic is nothing if not a crossroads of global backgrounds, dating back to the pre-Columbian era. However, through the hard work of Spanish colonizers and successive administrations, the DR today is much more culturally homogeneous than its population's diverse antecedents would suggest. For centuries, Arawak populations from across the Caribbean and mainland arrived on the island, mixing with local Taíno and other indigenous populations. Beginning with European colonization, generous melding between European immigrants and African slaves resulted in a large mulatto population, which persists as the largest ethnic group today. The few indigenous survivors quickly assimilated into this entirely new ethnic group. Today, 16 percent of the population is considered Caucasian, 11 percent black, and 73 percent mixed. There is also a small, but significant and growing, Chinese population in Santo Domingo that makes up a fractional percentage of the overall population.

RACE & IDENTITY

Dominicans take great pride in their ancestry and heritage, though emphasizing certain aspects of their history while glossing over perhaps more undesirable features. Racial identity, identified principally through skin color, is tightly associated with social class and economic power. Broadly, those with darker skin tend to be poorer and are less socially mobile. Dominican society is oriented towards other Latin American countries and their common Spanish and indigenous roots, shying away from the Caribbean and their shared African progenitors. This attitude is especially prevalent toward their Western neighbors. While Haitians do have darker skin, so do many Dominicans; an especially harsh insult is using "Haitian" as an epithet.

Eschewing the white/black racial dichotomy, Dominican society breaks down skin color in a more nuanced way. Those with any type of brown skin are called "*indio*," so named after the former indigenous population. Classifications run from the paler *indio claro* (light), to *indio canela* (cinnamon), and *indio oscuro* (dark). Other words associated with skin color include *moreno*, meaning brown, and the condescending *prieto*, literally translated as burnt, but in practice meaning black. No matter what the shade of skin, most Dominicans ascribe to this schematic when describing themselves – a complex and uniquely Dominican understanding of racial identity.

LANGUAGE

The national language of the DR is Spanish, introduced by the former colonial power. The Haitian population also speaks Haitian Creole. English is taught in schools, though it is not widely spoken except in areas with heavy tourist traffic. While written Dominican Spanish varies little from standardized Spanish, when spoken it may seem like a different language. Dominicans speak quickly, clipping words and changing consonants. One of the most common signifiers of Dominican Spanish is dropping vowels at the beginning of words, as well as the letters *s* and *d* in the past participle: *está* becomes *tá*, *buscar* becomes *bucar* and *acostado* becomes *cotao*, leading to the indicative example of *"Paco tá cotao"* (*Paco está acostado* – Paco is lying down).

In addition, there are distinct regionalisms within the country. In the north, the letters "r" and "l" becomes an "i" (*amor* is spoken as *amoi*, *capital* as *capitai*) and in the capital region, "r" becomes "l" (*amor* as *amol*). In the south, the letter "l" sounds like an "r" (*capital* as *capitar*). Many of these quirks are holdovers from colonial-era Spanish that has evolved out of the spoken language in Spain, but remains in the DR.

When meeting someone, be sure to use the formal *"usted"* form, and not the informal *"tú,"* as a sign of respect, especially towards elders. In addition, recognition of positions of power, seniority, and titles are very important – for example, refer to someone in charge as *"Señor"* or *"Señora."* *"Don"* may be used for a man as well, though slightly more informally, and *"Doña"* is a term of respect reserved for mothers and female heads of household, but rarely in professional settings.

Flag

The Dominican flag is a white cross on a background of alternating blue and red squares featuring the Dominican coat of arms in the center with a banner that reads, "God, Country, Liberty." First conceived during the War of Independence against Haiti by founding father Juan Pablo Duarte, it was ironically borrowed from the French and Haitian flags. The color blue represents liberty; the white, salvation and sacrifice; and the red, the blood of those who died for country.

FAMILY

Dominican life is centered on *la familia*, for many the most significant aspect to their daily, and lifelong, social interaction. Large, extended families live in close proximity, and rely on each other for social protection as the state has traditionally provided a poor safety net. Because the government was, for so long, far removed from the people and subject to violent upheaval, the situation dictated that dependence and solidarity belonged at home, with the family.

Business and social ventures require deep trust and confidence, called *"confianza,"* among stakeholders and participants. Even during this current era of immigration, family is still incredibly important; a large family represents safety, support, and labor, especially in rural areas. Filial duty is supreme: immigrants to urban areas and abroad return home whenever possible, and almost universally send home remittances. In rural and poorer areas, various members of extended families will sleep in different houses than their immediate family because of convenience, monetary incentives, and space constraints, and some children may be sent to live with more urban or affluent relatives. In addition, marriage may also be more loosely defined and practiced in rural areas. Weddings are expensive, so a marriage is often signified simply by cohabitation.

WOMEN & GENDER

Traditional gender roles dictate that men are sole breadwinners, as agricultural, industrial, or commercial laborers, while women hold ground at the home to tend to the household or small plots of land. While traditional gender roles have always been a part of Dominican society, recent economic development, modernization, and opportunities for education have changed these rules, especially in urban areas.

Today, an increasing number of women seek employment outside the home. In fact, in many factories, including the *zonas francas,* women make up a large majority of employees. Women tend to be paid less than men, and may also be hired and fired more easily. Once a woman marries or has children, it becomes much more difficult for her to work or attend school, as she is expected to spend her time at home. However, female students now have a higher attendance and graduation rate from both secondary and higher education.

PASTIMES

Dominos

In a category of its own, dominos is an activity close to the heart of the Dominican psyche, dominating the rural and urban street corner as well as the furnished patio social scenes, more often than not accompanied by beer. Children grow up around the domino set, learning how to play as soon as dexterity affords them the ability to pick up the tiles. The game can be fiercely competitive or a relaxed affair, played by the young and old, men and women, family and friend. Dominos, requiring four players and usually gathering a crowd, brings people together for hours as they play under a shade tree during the day or by single candlelight at night. Involving intricate strategy, math, and counting skills, the game is deceptively simple, but mastery takes years of practice. Sitting down to a game is a ticket to immediate integration with a family or community, and a great way to get to know people through a national leisure activity. Nearly every *colmado* has a spare set of dominos, a wooden dominos table, and plastic chairs. Ask the attendant to borrow them and invite friends and locals to play, who are often happy to join.

Cockfighting

There is nothing like a little blood lust and flaring tempers to forge cultural bonds. Cockfighting in the DR, as a major social activity, can be a bit more edgy – and dodgy – than the others. Men spend years grooming specially-bred roosters for the big day at the *gallera* (cockfighting ring). Grooming techniques range from weekly vitamin injections to the outlandish cleansing of the rooster's backside accomplished by spitting a steady stream of water at the rooster's bottom. Attracting alcohol, gambling, and mostly men, cockfighting is popular across the entire country. Even without formal structures, the smallest villages have packed-dirt floors at which to watch the fight.

The roosters are coddled and trained, their lower feathers removed for increased aerodynamics and efficiency, and spikes can be placed on the roosters' trimmed spurs. Cockfighting represents themes of *machismo* and competitive culture running through Dominican history and society. Though animal rights activists cringe, Dominicans defend cockfighting as part of their tradition and heritage, brought from Europe during the earliest of Spanish voyages. The sport is also a source of employment for thousands of Dominicans.

The fight ends when one rooster kills another, though a draw can be called when one is wounded or the fight lasts for an extended period of time. A rooster who runs from a fight brings intense shame to his owner.

To experience a cockfight firsthand, see p108 in Santo Domingo or p314 in Las Matanzas, Baní, or be on the lookout for *galleras* present in every Dominican town.

ETIQUETTE & FORMALITY

Home is not only where the heart is, but also where casual is. Ripped sweatpants and the stained Aerosmith t-shirt from middle school doesn't cut it outside the house. Dominicans are particular and place high importance on appearance, formality, etiquette, and respect.

Even among the poor, clothing that is clean, pressed, and smart is the norm for any activity outside the home, even just for a trip down the street to the *colmado* or a neighbor's house. Dominicans are fashion-flashy: a mix of tropical and European. In the DR, you'll find tight, trendy jeans with intricate embroidery on the back pockets and up and down the legs. Women's jeans tend to be more elaborate, affixed with sparkles and rhinestones. Women sport brightly colored tops, often glittered and be-jeweled. Hair is straightened as a status and fashion symbol. Natural, Afro-style hairdos are uncommon, worn principally by Haitian women or those who cannot afford the process. Men sport collared, polo, or button-down shirts with jeans or slacks over recently shined shoes. Shorts and sandals are reserved for children, the beach and the river, and the backyard. You might also notice that men cut their hair very short. Facial hair, when worn at all, is also short and neatly trimmed into a goatee or a thin beard (known as a "chinstrap"). Since overall appearance is very important, first impressions make a world of difference. Dominicans believe that care must be shown as a sign of respect for yourself, your family, and whomever you are meeting.

The same rule applies to personal effects. Young people are beginning to lose regional accents for fear of sounding uneducated. Across the country, the façades of homes and businesses will be brightly painted in warm, tropical colors, coordinated with trim on the doors and windows. In rural or poorer areas, however, the other sides of the house are often unpainted, unadorned, and bare. Windows are replaced by aluminum sheets or wooden slats. Inside, a TV and refrigerator may stand on a dirt floor. Similarly, a Dominican's mode of transport, whether motorcycle or car, will always be clean and sparkling. Carwashes and riverbanks are full of people maintaining the sheen of their vehicles, especially after a muddy or long drive.

Meeting schedules, however, are less rigid. Punctuality, while nice, is not enforced; arriving a half-hour late can be considered right on time. Of course, you should be there on time, but it may be a good idea to bring some reading material. As in any interaction, whether at a hotel or someone's home, begin with appropriate greetings, pleasantries, and small talk inquiries.

If you are lucky enough to be invited into someone's home, be kind in accepting or rejecting the offer. You will likely be offered a meal or a drink, especially coffee, and will be expected to eat or drink almost everything you're given. It is custom to leave just a little on your plate to show that you ate well and are full. If you eat all your food, it might mean that you were hungry and you were not served enough. If you decide not to eat for whatever reason, it is best to say that your stomach hurts or you just ate, rather than that you didn't like what is being served. It is common to share food and drinks, though as a guest, you'll probably receive your food first and separately. Often, just a spoon is used, though a fork and knife might be present for meals with meat. Dominicans tend to eat and drink quickly, but it is best to linger and always, always comment on your enjoyment of the meal.

Buen Provecho

If you come upon someone eating, say *"buen provecho,"* which is similar in meaning to *bon appétit*. He will respond with *"a buen tiempo,"* (to good timing) and might offer you some of his rice and beans. Likewise, if someone happens upon you while eating, say *"a buen tiempo,"* though be prepared to give a taste of what you're having.

EDUCATION

Education in the Dominican Republic is free and mandatory from age five to fourteen, which is considered primary education. After eighth grade, students are consolidated into public secondary schools, or *liceos*, or their family can pay for a private secondary school, or *colegio*. Upon graduation from high school, the degree conferred is called *bachiller*. The university system is dominated by la UASD (pronounced "wazz"), or Universidad Autónoma de Santo Domingo. It is the oldest university in the Americas, founded in 1538, and now has branches in most major cities across the country. More recently, other public and private universities have been founded to meet the growing need of an increasingly educated populace.

> UNESCO estimates that 89 percent of the Dominican population over the age of 15 is literate.

MEDIA

Freedom House categorizes the Dominican Republic as "Partly Free" in terms of press freedoms, ranking 82nd in the world. Dominican laws protect press freedoms, but national media are controlled by a few powerful organizations. The state owns two of the seven major TV stations, but there are over 200 radio stations that play a variety of Dominican and foreign music, or are focused on news or religious programming. National daily newspapers include *El Caribe, Hoy, Listín Diario, Diario Libre,* and *El Nacional*. Each of these outlets now has a website.

> Visit dr1.com for an English alternative for the news and extensive travel resources.

MUSIC & DANCE

It is impossible to speak about Dominican music without discussing dance, its seamlessly intertwined other half. The two developed alongside one another, drawing from the same Taíno, European, and African influences. Little evidence remains of any written music from the colonial era, most likely due to Sir Francis Drake's burning of the city in 1586. Prior to the fervor and inspiration brought by independence, music was a pastime among slaves and free mulattoes, who blended the instruments of areíto Taíno, African rhythms brought in the 16th century, and the melodies of European string instruments. It was not until the Independence era in the mid-19th century that the first vestiges of Dominican musical institutions, such as merengue, began to take shape.

In 1855, José Francisco Quero and Fermín Bastidas started one of the first formal music schools in Santo Domingo, cultivating musical talents in European instruments such as the violin, guitar, and flute; which would give rise to a number of other music schools. Though heavily European-influenced music dominated the popular music scene throughout the late 19th and early 20th century, Dominican musicians began to incorporate the countryside's staccato and organic rhythms such as *zapateo*, *sarambo*, and *mangulina*. When European immigrants brought the accordion in 1870, merengue started to rise from the heady fusion that had been simmering. In 1918, Juan Francisco García brought merengue to the upper echelons of society by presenting it in Santiago. Once accepted by the Dominican wealthy, aided by Trujillo's cooptation of merengue as a campaign tactic in 1930, the music and dance were firmly established in the national psyche. Merengue legends include Toño Rosario & Los Hermanos Rosario, Sergio Vargas, and Johnny Ventura – all of which are part of the "Golden Years" of merengue in the 1980s.

Developed during the early 20th century, *bachata* was not embraced by Trujillo or the wealthy and therefore was not even recorded until the fall of the dictatorship in 1961. This was the year José Manuel Calderón recorded "Borracho de Amor," making him the first recorded bachata artist. With rural influences both lyrically and musically, bachata continued to be looked down upon by the mainstream until the

---

Dance

Areíto Taíno: An indigenous form of music and dance used to transmit Taíno history orally and visually through words, movements, and melodies. The themes of the songs varied greatly from the amorous, to bellicose, to religious. Instruments used included maracas made of gourds (*higüeros*), tamboras made from hollowed out trunks, and flutes made of sugar cane or bones, accompanied by the percussion of shells adorning the dancers. This art form was particularly important in the transmission of culture and history from generation to generation, as the Taínos did not have a written language.

Merengue A typical style of music and dance born in the countryside of the Dominican Republic. Merengue generally involves the accordion, bass guitar, *güira* (a metal percussion instrument resembling a cheese grater that is played by rubbing a wire comb against its jagged surface), guitar, tambora (a two-sided drum laid across the lap and played with a stick on one side and the hand on the other), and brass instruments including the saxophone and trumpet. Merengue is danced on a two-four beat causing dancers' hips to move in a fluid figure eight. This motion has also been compared to that of an eggbeater, which may have given rise to the music's name meaning meringue, whose stiff peaks are the results of an eggbeater's frenzied motion.

Merengue Típico or Perico Ripiao Merengue *típico* and *perico ripiao* are nearly interchangeable terms that refer to an up-tempo, more instrumental version of merengue popularized in rural communities of the Cibao in the late 19th century. The sometimes-suggestive lyrics and related body movements were seen as offensive by the upper classes, and so it remained a pastime of the countryside, where it continues to flourish in its most authentic form. Trujillo elevated the music to national popularity during his rule, and it became more widely accepted. The term *perico ripiao* means "ripped parrot," possibly referring to a house where this music was played. *Típico* bands use a guitar, guira, tambora drum, accordion, and, more recently, saxophone.

Bachata From the same influences that merengue arose came *bachata*, a four-count rhythm characterized by an upward flick of the hips on the fourth beat as if a puppeteer's string was plucking them in the air. *Bachata* employs a lead guitar, rhythm guitar, electric bass guitar, bongos, and *güira*. It is traditionally favored among rural populations, but has gained broad popularity in the past decade, especially with the band Aventura.

1980s when established artists – such as Luis Segura, El Chivo Sin Ley (Ramoncito Cabrera), and Antonio Gómez Salcero – were able to reach larger audiences. Grammy-award winning Juan Luis Guerra was the first to sneak bachata into the musical repertoire of the upper-middle class with his smooth renditions sometimes confused for merengue. Aventura, a Dominican New York-based pop bachata sensation, catapulted bachata onto the iPods and into the hearts of young Latinos across the world after performing at the Grammy's and even at the White House for U.S. President Barak Obama. Other popular bachata artists include Anthony Santos, Zacarias Ferreira, and Frank Reyes.

Mambo callejero or *mambo violento*, merengue's street-smart urban cousin, employs accelerated counts accompanied by the style and lyrics of rap. Artists such Omega, El Sujeto, Julian y Oro Duro, and El Jeffrey are among the better known artists winning over Dominican youth with their pelvic-thrusting rhythms. Another brainchild of Dominican urbanity is reggaeton, Latin America's response to hip hop, though the true pioneers of this genre hail from Puerto Rico. Dominican hip-hop, which employs a crude blend of Caribbean rhythms, is slowly taking root as well with such artists as DKano, El Lapiz Consciente, Del Patio, and Mozart La Para y Villanosam.

An area of Dominican music that is challenging to fit into one genre due to its numerous influences can best be described as World Music. Standing on the backs of giants, young Dominican bands are drawing from their Caribbean roots to create fun and authentic fusions. Calor Urbano, formed in 2002, mixes Caribbean rhythms with soul, hip-hop, and a pinch of pop to create an immediately pleasing sound that has earned a significant following. Rita Indiana, a published author and former model, along with her band, Los Misterios, has taken on and incorporates reggaeton, electronic, meringue, and everything in between to create something that is authentic, but simultaneously has broad appeal. Lesser-known fusion bands such as the percussion–heavy rhythms of Batey Cero, El Batey, and ConCon Quemao are strongly influenced by *palos*, a percussive style of music born in the sugar cane communities (*bateyes*) throughout the country. At the heart of the Dominican folklore-world music movement are living legends such as Xiomara Fortuna, José Duluc, Irka Mateo, and Patricia Pereyra.

Dominican rock 'n' roll is one of the few genres that has drawn less upon Caribbean roots, but has rather looked to the U.S. and Europe for influences. Dominican rock's humble beginnings grew from such bands as The Masters in the 1970s, followed by Empiphis and Cahobazul formed in the mid and late eighties. Another band formed in eighties by the undeniably influential musician, Luis "El Terror" Díaz, was Transporte Urbano, a unique product of Díaz's return to Santo Domingo after being thrown into the mix of New York's punk rock scene. The 1990s were the true renaissance of the *rockeros* in the Dominican Republic. During this period, bands such as Toque Profundo, Arcangel, Tribu del Sol, and Tabu Tek came to the forefront providing an unapologetic response to the homogenous music scene dominated by merengue. Spain-based JLS (Jodio Loco Sucio or "Screwed Crazy Dirty"), a heavy metal band started up by former Toque Profundo member Leo Susana, has achieved an international following. Also popular is New York-based Aljadaqui, whose pop rock sounds are indicative of the more palatable rock taking over the music scene today. However, the heavy metal of the nineties continues to be received by loyal fans in smaller Santo Domingo venues like Cinema Café (p105) and Hard Rock Café, where Toque Profundo celebrated their 20th anniversary in 2010.

ART

Painting, Drawing & Sculpture

Despite its pre-Colombian roots, authentic Dominican fine art was late to bloom. Unlike in other Latin American countries, early Dominican art did not draw strongly from its antecedents such as the pictographs and ceramics of the Taínos. Rather, Spanish conquest and Catholic fervor inspired the typical religious and patriotic scenes up until the mid-19th century. Stunted by war, dictatorships and isolation, the bona fide Dominican art movement did not begin until the 1920s.

Following the declaration of independence in 1844, the beginnings of authentic, local Dominican art began to develop, and by 1890 Santo Domingo hosted the first "Gran Exposición," featuring landscapes, still lifes, and portraits. Dominican art historian Emilio Rodríguez Demorizi purports that the European vestiges of primitivism, classicalism, romanticism, and impressionism melded together into one movement throughout the late 19th century in the DR. These styles did not have the space to develop independently and completely as their own movements due to the tumultuous state of politics and society. Opportunely, this merging of styles gave rise to one that was uniquely Dominican demonstrated by such artists as Alejandro Bonilla (1820-1901) or Luis Desangles (1861-1940), who is known for his historical depictions and portraits.

As European artists were throwing out all the rules with abstraction, Dominican artists stayed within the safe confines of romantic portraits and landscapes in the early 20th century. By 1920, realism, which advocated objective, unembellished depictions of daily life, and neoimpressionism, long made famous in Europe by the pointillist paintings of Seurat, became protagonists in Dominican style. Pastoral depictions were among the most common of this period, seen in the country parties and amapola trees of Yoryi Morel, whose impressionistic style won him a gold medal in 1939 at the International Art Exposition in San Francisco. Those that were fortunate enough to study in Europe, such as Jaime Colson who spent his formative years in Paris, brought back cubism and neoclassicism with his Picasso-inspired figures. One of the first women to establish herself during this period was Celeste Woss y Gil, daughter of Dominican President Alejandro Woss y Gil. Celeste, strongly influenced by the impressionist movement, is known as the originator of the "modern nude" for her depictions of black and mulatto women.

World War II marked a new era for Dominican painting as Europeans sought exile from the tyrannies of Franco and Hitler by most ironically fleeing to the dictatorship of Trujillo. Nonetheless, they were able to cultivate an inspiring fusion drawing from their European training mixed with the heat, lush surroundings, and culture of the Caribbean. Those that established roots in the Dominican Republic include Josep Gausachs, José Vela Zanetti, Manolo Pascual, Eugenio Fernández Granell, and Jorge Hausdorf. These were among the founders of La Escuela de Bellas Artes, the country's publically funded art school, in 1942. This year also marked the first Bienal Nacional de Artes Plásticas, one of the country's most prestigious art competitions along with the E. León Jiménez Art Contest, which began two decades later funded by the tobacco fortune of the Jiménez family.

By 1960, unrest rampant, the Dominican population was clamoring for a return to democracy after thirty years under Trujillo. The vigor and rebellious nature of this time manifested itself in a generation of distinctively Dominican styles including the blue and orange figures of Cándido Bidó, the ethereal women of Elsa Nuñez, and the moody abstractions of Ramón Oviedo and José Rincón Mora. Though a period of creativity, the turmoil of the 1960s impeded the implementation of the national art contest, El Bienal Nacional de Artes Plásticas, which did not begin again until 1972. The 1970s were an important era for Dominican art institutions, resulting in the establishment of several art schools: El Colegio Dominicano de Artistas Plásticas, La Galería de Arte Moderno, and Altos de Chavón (see La Romana, p144). Associated with the Parsons School of Art in New York, Altos de Chavón continues to be the country's most prestigious art school. These institutions gave the support and encouragement that artists needed to turn art into a respected profession.

Abstraction and antagonism towards convention marked the 1980s, epitomized by El Colectivo Generación del 80 (The Collective Generation of the '80s). Sculpture, installations and prints began to take on a larger role. International critics started to notice these achievements, marked by Alonso Cuevas as first Dominican to be awarded in the International Festival of Cagnes-sur-Mer, an annual painting festival held in Provence, in 1985. That same year, Santo Domingo hosted the first Ibero-American Symposium of Sculpture. Prior to this symposium, lack of resources, academic instruction and appreciation for public art stunted the development of sculpture and ceramics as serious art forms. Sculptors, such as Luichy Martínez Richiez, whose elongated wooden sculptures employ fantastical Afro-Caribbean influences, were able to establish Dominican sculpture as a fine art.

Unrestrained channels of inspiration resulting from technological advances of the 21st century have allowed for a greater exchange among Dominican artists and their international counterparts, resulting in parallel trends. One thread common throughout them all is the vibrant use of color and expressionism employed by modern Dominican artists. Carlos Goico embodied this vibrant style with his stream of consciousness paintings and drawings of diabolic Carnaval masks and colorful though often disturbing portraits. From the same generation came Yuly Monción, whose paintings have won several awards in the E. León Jiménez Art Contest and are part of the Banco Popular collection. Sculptors, such as Genaro Reyes, have given artisan work newfound distinction, with his recycled material sculptures. A younger generation of artists continues to use expressionism as a vehicle to put to paint the passions, myths and magical realities of life on this Caribbean island, including the unbridled swaths of color, harsh charcoal lines and evocative subjects of Chichi Reyes or the abstractions of Ney Díaz, where aggression and elegance hang in a precarious balance.

SPORTS

Baseball

Baseball in the Dominican Republic is the equivalent of soccer in much of the rest of the world: it is baseball that holds fast the hearts and minds of every Dominican citizen. This sport is the focus of time, energy and money. A longstanding national joke is that the official religion of the DR is not Catholicism, but *pelota* (ball).

Baseball has deep roots in the DR. Its introduction likely came from immigrant Cubans fleeing turmoil at the end of the 19th century who had learned the sport from Americans involved in the sugar trade in the 1860s. As baseball grew in popularity, professional teams were organized by the beginning of the early 20th century.

The DR currently supplies the highest number of international players active in Major League Baseball (MLB), as over five hundred have made it to the big leagues. Dominicans dutifully follow homegrown talent playing professional baseball in the U.S.; sports highlights on local and national news programs include teams with significant numbers of or particularly popular Dominican players. Famous Dominican MLB stars include Ozzie Virgil, who began the Dominican player onslaught in 1956, Juan Marichal, Pedro Martínez, Sammy Sosa, Vladimir Guerrero, Miguel Tejada, and even a manager, Omar Minaya of the Mets.

The DR hosts the professional-level *Liga Dominicana de Beísbol Invernal* (LIDOM), also known as Winter League, played from October through January. Here, Dominican baseball players find the path to international stardom begins at home. MLB teams also send rookies or other players to fill roster spots in the Winter League to gain additional professional experience. The six teams play 50 games during the regular season, and four teams advance to the 18-game round-robin playoffs. The top two teams play a best-of-nine championship series. The winner of these games then goes on to play in the Serie del Caribe (Caribbean Series), played since 1949 in various iterations. Today, the Caribbean Series involves teams from the Dominican Republic, Puerto Rico, Venezuela, and Mexico. The DR has won 18 times, more than any other competitor. LIDOM teams include:

Team Name	English translation	Location
Tigres (also called Licey)	Tigers	Santo Domingo
Leones	Lions	Santo Domingo
Águilas	Eagles	Santiago
Gigantes	Giants	San Francisco de Macoris
Toros	Bulls	La Romana
Estrellas (Azucareros)	Stars (Sugar farmers)	San Pedro de Macoris

If you are visiting the DR during baseball season, attending a game is a must. The quality of play is high, and you will likely catch a glimpse of a future all-star that you still haven't heard of. Baseball games are raucous, rowdy affairs, especially between Santiago's Aguilas and Santo Domingo's Tigres de Licey. Some liken the two teams to the Yankees and the Red Sox, with diehard fans and a long and fierce rivalry. Games are especially raucous during the playoffs, when fans make liberal use of not only beer, but also various noisemakers like thundersticks and plastic horns resembling vuvuzelas, the cacophonous instruments made famous in the 2010 World Cup. The stadiums are modern and spacious, resembling the feel and atmosphere of minor league stadiums in the U.S.

Trujillo & Baseball

Trujillo himself got involved in baseball, hiring Negro League players for his preferred team in Santo Domingo for the 1937 season. His team had lost in the year prior; in 1937, his team won. He built a large, modern stadium in 1955 in the capital, creating momentum and building popular support for the sport that carries through today.

Basketball

The Dominican Republic also has a well-regarded professional basketball league (La Liga Dominicana de Baloncesto, LIDOBA). Basketball is played across the country, though it is especially popular in the capital and the northern Cibao region. While not nearly as popular as baseball, basketball enjoys a significant fan base, and the DR national team is represented well in international competitions. In addition, there are semi-professional municipal leagues in both Santiago and Santo Domingo. Current Dominican players in the NBA include Charlie Villanueva and Al Horford.

Team Name	English translation	Location
Metros	Metropolitans	Santiago
Reales	Royals	La Vega
Tiburones del Atlántico	Atlantic Sharks	Puerto Plata
Indios	Indians	San Francisco de Macorís
Cañeros	Sugarcane farmer	La Romana
Cocolos	Afro-Caribbean descendants	San Pedro de Macorís
Leones	Lions	Santo Domingo
Titanos	Titans	Santo Domingo

Soccer

Overwhelmed by baseball's immense popularity, soccer does not have the clout or support that it does across the rest of the globe. Soccer did have a following here until the mid-20th century, when baseball took off, promoted by Trujillo and a closer political and cultural alignment with the United States. Several local teams formed a domestic semi-professional league, which played to varying crowds between the 1950s and 1970s, including teams from universities. This league is no longer in existence, though small soccer schools still service the sport. As of publication, the Dominican national team ranked 184 out of 202 in the FIFA rankings, and has never played in the World Cup.

Adventure Sports

Caving: Not all of the Dominican Republic's outdoor activities take place on a sunny beach. Exploring the extensive networks of caves, hidden among the many hills and cliffs across the country, provides a fascinating look into both geology and history. Many of these caves were inhabited or used by the indigenous Taínos, whose petroglyphs and pictographs still grace the walls of many a cave. The best way to visit these caves is with a guide, so as to best understand and protect the fragile underground monuments. A few of the most popular Dominican caves include Cueva de las Maravillas outside La Romana (p144), El Choco caves near Cabarete (p196), and the various caves of Los Haitises National Park (p131). Santo Domingo's Mirador del Este Park (p89) has a trio of easy-to-explore caves right in the city.

Paragliding: This low-impact activity is a great way to see the sights from a different perspective: hundreds of feet up in the air. There are a number of paragliding spots around the country. Contact Caribbean Free Flying (caribbeanfreeflying.com), which has a dozen sites around the country, KiteExcite (p202) in Cabarete, or Tony Fly (p289) in Jarabacoa.

Hiking: While Pico Duarte is the most famous of all hiking trips in the country, there are other less strenuous and less time-consuming trekking, hiking, and mountain climbing spots. National Parks are the best places to find the perfect hikes, like Parque Nacional del Este (p159), Jaragua (p343), El Choco (p196), Pico Duarte (p296) and the spectacular hike to Playa Fronton in Samaná (p215).

Kayaking and white-water rafting: There are some spectacular spots on Class II-V rapids in and around Jarabacoa on the Río Yaque del Norte and other rivers. It is best to go during the rainy season (winter months), as the rivers may run very low in the dry season. A number of tour companies run trips, including Iguana Mama in Cabarete and Rancho Baiguate or Rancho Jarabacoa in Jarabacoa. While rafting is only possible on the Yaque, kayakers have much broader possibilities on other waterways in the Cordillera Central. Sea kayaking, though much less developed, is possible at Monte Cristi, Punta Rucia, La Caleta, and Los Haitises.

Kiteboarding/Kitesurfing: Cabarete is home to the best location in the country, and one of the best in the world, for kiteboarding. There is a beach reserved for just this sport, called Kite Beach, to the west of Cabarete. Many operators and guides run out of the area; check around for the ones that fit what you are looking for. The best beach in the South for kiteboarding is at Las Salinas, near Baní.

Canyoning: This hard-to-define sport takes it all in: climbing, jumping, hiking, swimming, and more, through a river cut into a canyon. Jarabacoa in the Cordillera Central provides several spots for a day of canyoning (as well as cascading, involving waterfalls), but the most famous – and popular – location is the 27 Charcos in Damajaguas, outside of Imbert (p188).

Mountain biking: With a good portion of the country's surface covered in rugged topography, the Dominican Republic is a mountain biker's dream. Biking up, over, and through any of the various mountain ranges can provide stunning views and exciting challenges, like over the Cordillera Septentrional to Moca, or around the valley towns of Jarabacoa, Constanza, or San José de Ocoa. Ridges along the coast have some of the best rides that end at sandy beaches such as Cabarete, Playa Grande, and Playa Rincon. It is possible to rent bikes in Santo Domingo, Santiago, and Cabarete. Look out for extreme biking races in these towns during your stay. Both Iguana Mama (p201) and Rancho Baiguate (p288) offer mountain biking rentals and tours.

Snorkeling and scuba diving: The hundreds of miles of diverse coastlands in the Dominican Republic makes nearly any spot a good one for snorkeling: strap on some goggles and peer under the surface to witness tropical waters teeming with life. There are several natural and artificial reefs all along the northern and southern coasts. Sosúa is a hotspot because of its sheltered bay and calm waters. It has a number of dive centers for rentals, lessons, and excursions, but can therefore get overcrowded. Quieter locations include Samaná, Punta Rusia, Montecristi, and Bahia de las Aguilas, by Pedernales. Look out for shipwrecks surroundings the island including around Bayahibe, Montecristi, and Juan Dolio.

Surfing: Catching that elusive, perfect wave might be a challenge elsewhere, but look no further than Playa Encuentro, near Cabarete, as the surfing capital of the Dominican Republic. Oceanic and atmospheric conditions combine to make that beach a surfer's playground, and the beach is dotted with places to rent boards and get lessons. Good breaks can be found along the entire north coast, from Sosúa Bay through Cabarete, to Playa Grande and Samaná. On the southern coast, breaks tend to be shorter, although they can be just as high. The best bets here are Paraíso and Ojeda. The closest surfing to the capital is at Playa Caribe by Juan Dolio.

RELIGION

One of the most indelible legacies of Spanish colonialism is the strength of Catholicism the Dominican Republic. Though not enshrined in the constitution as the legal religion, the Catholic Church is granted special status and advantages that other religions do not have, including the ability to utilize public funds for religious buildings, activities, and economic activity. Dominican law provides for freedom of worship and forbids discrimination on grounds related to religion. Though vibrant and politically active, the Catholic Church does not have the commanding authority it did during most of the history of the DR. Apathy and the emergence of other faiths have lessened the force of the church, even as 90 percent of Dominicans still claim to be Catholic. Mass is not highly attended as the population takes a more relaxed understanding of Catholicism. Still, Catholic holidays are treated as national holidays with work and school canceled. Each town and city also has a patron saint, for which an eight-day long celebration occurs, called *Patronales* (see Festivals & Holidays, p62). There is a chapel or church in nearly every small village, and most cities' place their churches prominently in central squares, serving as not only centers of religion, but also community and society. These churches also often provide important social services that may not be available from the state.

Evangelical Protestantism, spurning elaborate worship and alcohol consumption among other supposed vices, is developing a significant presence in Dominican society. Protestantism arrived on Dominican shores in the 19th century, but did not become a force until the middle of the 20th century. Groups like Seventh-day Adventists, Pentecostals, Jehovah's Witness, Mormons, and the Assembly of God have active and growing movements. While Protestants live openly and freely, and relations with Catholics are peaceful, there is some underlying resentment from the Catholic Church about the undermining of their authority and popularity.

Many of these and other forms of spirituality comprise a unique fusion of European, indigenous and African elements in popular religion. Witches and healers, though no longer as widespread, were once common in rural areas. Haitian immigrants have also introduced their own religious beliefs in the country, one of the clearest examples of syncretism in the DR. If practiced, it is often done in private, away from those who denounce it as foreign and pagan. African-Catholic syncretism can be seen in various iterations among the Haitian-Dominican populations across the island. Some co-opt Catholic saint worship into traditional African religions, while others involve African-inspired *palo* music and dance into Catholic or other community ritual. A common form of syncretism among Haitian-Dominicans and their descendents is called *gagá*, or sometimes *rara*. It is a broad category, encompassing worship of many different spirits, both benevolent and malevolent. The worship also draws on Catholic and African influences and the historical plantation culture from which many Haitian-Dominican descendents draw. *Gagá* is noted for its highly festive nature – *gagá* celebrations are large and exuberant affairs. The largest celebrations are held around Easter, involving wooden or metal drums, maracas, *güiras*, trumpets, and other often improvised instruments including plastic tubes used as horns. The term *gagá* is also used to describe just the music and dancing of these celebrations. In fact, all across the south, *fiestas de palo* are very popular at community gatherings and occasions, though celebrants might deny the African influence of this music and dance. Several cultural centers today are trying to bring socio-historical education to the Dominican public about these issues (See

El Centro Cultural de España in Santo Domingo, p104, or El Centro Cultural Bomaná in La Romana, p144).

The Dominican Republic is also home to a tiny Jewish population of about 300 people. It is likely that some of the earliest explorers and settlers of the island were, in fact, Jewish. In 1492, the Spanish crown began the Inquisition, driving the large and vibrant Jewish and Muslim populations underground out of the country entirely. Similarly, the few émigré Jews from Spain or other European countries quickly assimilated into Dominican society, both because no organized community existed, and due to the constant presence of anti-Semitism. In the 1940s, Trujillo opened his doors to Jews fleeing Europe, eventually accepting about 700 refugees. These unlikely immigrants settled in Sosúa (p191) as dairy and cattle farmers. Today, the Jewish community conducts prayer services at the Centro Israelita de la República Dominicana in Santo Domingo. This synagogue was built in 1958, and serves both locals and expatriate Jews. In an effort to sustain the Jewish community, a Chabad cultural and religious center opened in 2008 in Santo Domingo.

Similar to the Jewish Dominican community, the Muslim community in the DR is small, but with a long history that dates to the colonial era. Islam arrived on the island in the 1500s, practiced by African slaves and their descendents. Colonial authorities did not allow the slave populations to worship freely, requiring conversion to Catholicism and repressing traditional culture and customs. A unique Muslim slave rebellion took place in 1522, checked only through violent suppression by a local militia. During the 19th century, small numbers of Lebanese and other Middle Eastern immigrants came to the Dominican Republic. Later, the arrival of immigrants from the Indian subcontinent bolstered the community, which now numbers about 1000. The Centro Islámico de la República Dominicana mosque in Santo Domingo provides a place to worship for Dominican Muslims.

Geography

The Dominican Republic stands on two-thirds of the Caribbean island of Hispaniola, sharing a border of 360 kilometers with its only neighbor, Haiti. Its land area is 48,734 square kilometers (18,816 square miles), the second-largest country in the Caribbean basin after Cuba. The DR also boasts 2,073 kilometers, or 1,288 miles, of stunning coastline.

Though unnoticeable from its famous white sand beaches, the Dominican Republic hosts an incredible diversity of geographic formations, microclimates, and plant and animal species. The tallest mountain in the Caribbean is located in the Dominican Republic, called Pico Duarte (p296), which stands at over 3,000 meters (10,000 feet). The country is also home to the largest lake in the Caribbean, Lago Enriquillo (p346).

The Dominican landscape is something of a topographical roller coaster, dominated by four mountain ranges, and supported by the valleys that separate them, running in a northwest-southeast direction across the island. Along the north coast is a thin ribbon of coastal plain, stretching from Monte Cristi in the west to Nagua in the east. The narrow plain is flanked by gorgeous sandy beaches on one side and the hills of the first of these ranges, the Cordillera Septentrional, whose highest peak is Diego de Ocampo, at 1,250 meters (777 feet). Meaning "northern mountain range," this Cordillera is cool and rainy, with a climate and altitude ideal for growing coffee and cacao. South of this range is the Cibao Valley, colloquially known as "El Cibao," a broad, fertile plain that serves as the breadbasket of the Dominican Republic. It is here that many of the staple foodstuffs are grown, including plantains, yuca, and rice. Tobacco is also farmed in the Cibao region.

On the other side of the Cibao's fecund valley is the rugged and extensive Cordillera Central, home to Pico Duarte. Sometimes called the Dominican Alps, the Cordillera Central can often feel like those European peaks, as temperatures drop to near freezing in the winter months. This towering range leaves the southwestern Dominican Republic in a rain shadow – the majority of precipitation that falls south of these mountains comes from tropical disturbances during the hurricane season. A small spur of the range dives directly south, called the Sierra de Ocoa, surrounding the Valley of Ocoa.

On the other side of the Cordillera Central is the semi-arid San Juan Valley. To the south is the Sierra de Neiba, overlooking the Neiba Valley, also called the Enriquillo Basin. This valley is home of Lago Enriquillo, and the hottest and driest lands in the country. Some elevations in the valley drop to more than 40 meters (131 feet) below sea level, including Lago Enriquillo and its salt flats and crocodiles. Finally, beyond the low-lying hills of the Sierra de Bahoruco, which in some places ends in cliffs at the ocean's edge, stretches the southern coastal plain, with small-pebbled beaches facing the Caribbean Sea.

The eastern region of the country, including Santo Domingo, is composed a flat plateau that slowly rises into small hills called the Cordillera Oriental that runs along the southern coast of the Samaná Bay. These lands, dry and grassy, are perfect for large plantations raising sugarcane and cattle. Ringing the eastern and southeastern coasts lie the famous and picturesque coconut palm-flecked beaches, including the resort areas around Punta Cana. Located off the southeast coast is Isla Saona, home to one of the prettiest beaches in the country.

In the Dominican Republic's northeast is the geographical quirk of the Samaná Peninsula, once an island but now attached to the rest of the country by a small isthmus. Jutting out into the Atlantic, Samaná's spine is called Sierra de Samaná, an extension of the Cordillera Septentrional. This series of rugged hills gently slope into the sea on the northern side of the peninsula, but just as often end abruptly in vertigo-inducing cliffs at the azure waters.

Environment

With such vast geographic and climatological diversity, it is no surprise that the Dominican Republic is home to a huge array of species – both invasive and endemic. Because of its insular nature, Dominican biodiversity is characterized by a high incidence of endemism, but because of human encroachment, it also suffers significant destruction of habitat. Upwards of 95 percent of Dominican reptiles and amphibians are endemic, while almost 40 percent of plant species are endemic. There are only two extant endemic mammal species alive today – eighteen became extinct after the European colonization. Interestingly, though a tropical island, there are no poisonous animals in the country.

FLORA

The Dominican Republic is home to over 5,600 plant species, 1,800 of which are endemic, dispersed across a wide array of forest zones. The DR is also home to over 300 species of orchids. A third of Dominican land is forested, most of it now in protected areas; only 10 percent of original-growth forest, however, is still standing. This contrasts to about one percent in neighboring Haiti, which has suffered from the vast usage of slash-and-burn farming techniques and the removal of trees for lumber and coal, resulting in erosion and the further depletion of valuable soils.

In the highest elevation zones of the Cordillera Central are coniferous forests. Towering Creole pine trees are at home throughout these cold and rainy mountains. In lower, more humid areas of the Cordilleras Central and Septentrional are the broad-leaf cloud forests and rainforests, where coffee and cacao are grown. Subtropical forests are found on the humid valley floors, most of which have been converted for intensive agricultural use. Here, palms, mahogany, muskwood, and cedar are common.

Finally, in the arid South and Southwest is a thornbrush ecosystem, dominated by cactus and other desert vegetation. The emblematic royal palm, tall and slender, was once threatened, but is now protected and is being replanted. Interestingly, the coconut palm, so celebrated on Dominican beaches, is native to the Indian Ocean basin, even as the tree has graced the country and postcards for many years. Island flora is not without vibrant color: look out for the white and purple flowers of the jacaranda, and the brilliant red flowers of the aptly-named *flamboyán* tree, also called the Royal Poinciana or amapola.

Deforestation and concomitant erosion are two of the biggest threats to the ecological hearth of the Dominican Republic. Deforestation had an enormous impact on the health of the environment, as can be seen in the bare hillsides of Haiti. Erosion causes degradation in soil productivity, reduced water retention and increases flood risks, which increases the size of arid, unusable land. The UN estimated that in the 1990s the DR was losing 20,000 hectares annually of forest cover. In recent years, the use of slash-and-burn activities to convert cropland from forest has decreased as rural populations decline. The government has introduced programs incentivizing reforestation, land conservation, and protection. It also focused on urban growth and industrialization, which, while having its own environmental problems, has decreased pressure on the use of rural lands for agricultural use. Though widespread in the past, the practice of removing live trees to make charcoal has decreased significantly.

FAUNA

Mammals

Hispaniola, and the Caribbean in general, is not very hospitable to land mammals. There are just two endemic land mammal species in the Dominican Republic. The first is the solenodon, which resembles a large rat with a very long snout and tail. The solenodon can grow up to two feet long, and is known for screeching and biting without provocation. The second is the hutia, also a small groundhog-like rodent that feeds on insects and worms. Both of these species are highly endangered, and are rarely, if ever, seen in the wild. They are restricted to protected parks in heavily forested mountainous regions, including the Reserva Loma Quita Espuela in the

Cordillera Septentrional, as well as Parque Nacional del Este and Parque Nacional Los Haitises. Closely related species that once populated the island, like the Marcano's solenodon and Montane hutia, are extinct. Other mammal species living in the country were all introduced by European colonizers including domesticated animals like cats, dogs, pigs, and cows. Several bat species also live on the island, making their homes in various cave systems, especially in the southern and southwestern regions of the country.

While it is more difficult to classify marine mammals as native to an island, the DR is home to two popular well-known animals: the humpback whale and manatee. The warm waters on the Dominican Republic's eastern shores, especially Samaná Bay, play host to important wintering and breeding grounds for the humpback. Upwards of 5000 whales call these waters home from January to March to mate and give birth. Whale watching excursions in Samaná (p219) provide some of the most extraordinary visions of humpback activity. Less graceful, but no less beautiful, is the manatee. Manatees are lumbering herbivores that prefer warm, quiet, and sheltered bays and estuaries. In the DR, they are most commonly found around Punta Rusia, Samaná, and Parque del Este. Though once widespread across the Caribbean and Gulf of Mexico, they are now highly endangered. Several species of dolphins also make the invitingly warm, tropical waters around the Dominican Republic home.

Birds

The Dominican Republic has become an increasingly popular birding hot spot. Strategically situated in migratory pathways and home to hospitable tropical forests, 296 bird species are found in the country, 26 of which are endemic – more than any other Caribbean island. Fourteen bird species are endangered. The Dominican national bird is the *cigua palmera* (palmchat), a small songbird that nests in the emblematic royal palm tree. In the mountainous regions, species like the hummingbird, papagayo, white-necked crow, and green-tailed warbler are common. Found in the many lagoons, mangroves, and estuaries that line the Dominican coast are egrets, pelicans, herons, ibis, and flamingos. Other important endemic bird species include the Hispaniolan Woodpecker, Hispaniolan Parrot, Hispaniolan Parakeet, Broadbilled Toady, and Stolid Flycatcher. The South is known for its especially high bird species diversity, as over 100 bird species have been found in Parque Nacional Jaragua and adjacent areas. One interesting bird is the Bicknell's thrush, which, like many Dominicans, travels between New York and the DR. While it spends most of its time in hilly Dominican retreats, the thrush migrates to the mountains of New York to mate and nest during the summer.

Reptiles & Amphibians

Though there are only about 200 reptile and amphibian species in the Dominican republic, over 95 percent are endemic. The majority of these species are lizards and snakes, most of which are small in size, as the larger animals have been hunted to extinction or faced insurmountable loss of habitat. Only in the arid southwest at Lago Enriquillo do large reptiles still flourish. The most famous is the American crocodile. Hundreds of crocodiles live in and around the saltwater lake, one of the largest wild populations of the species. Male crocodiles can grow to upwards of 12 feet, and females over 8 feet. Though the population is not yet endangered, the increased salinity of the lake is a potential threat to the existence of the crocodiles, as they need sources of fresh water to survive. Lago Enriquillo is also home to the two types of iguanas on the island, both endangered, the ricord and rhinoceros iguana.

The rhinoceros iguana can grow three to six feet in length. On its head are three horns, as well as a helmet-like pad. They can only live in the hot, dry conditions of the southwest, but because of encroachment, have now settled in just the protected areas of Enriquillo and Lago Oviedo.

There are also four types of sea turtle that live in and around the coast of Dominican Republic. All four are threatened, both by hunting and the loss of land-based habitat necessary for hatching and nesting, and marine habitats like coral reefs for feeding. While the turtles spend most of their time in the ocean, they come ashore to lay and hatch their eggs. In the DR, they are found around the islands and lagoons of Parque Nacional Monte Cristi, Parque Nacional del Este and Parque Nacional Jaragua, as well as along other parts of the southwestern coast. The largest of the turtles is the leatherback, which does not have a shell but rather hard, leathery skin. The hawksbill is critically endangered because of its highly prized and quite striking shell, fancifully colored in golden brown, with orange, red, and black streaks. In 2009, the Dominican government began a major crackdown on the sale of hawksbill products, with the hopes of decreasing demand and reducing hunting. The logger-head turtle actually spends much more time on land than the other turtles, which only come ashore to lay eggs, so its habitat is especially endangered. Finally, the green sea turtle is also threatened, due to hunting for its usage in cooking, especially soup. Smaller, more abundant freshwater turtles are found in various spots across the island, especially in the southwest.

Lizards and geckos are ubiquitous across the island – don't be surprised if you find them surreptitiously crawling along bedroom walls hunting for flies and other small insects. There are dozens of species of lizards in the DR, ranging in size, shape, coloration, and length. The smallest lizard (and also smallest reptile, amphibian, mammal, or bird) in the world was discovered in 2001 on Isla Beata off of the southwestern coast. Called the Jaragua lizard, at just over a half-inch long, it can fit comfortably curled on a dime. In addition, there are almost 200 species of fish that live in and around the Dominican Republic.

MARINE LIFE

A defining feature of the Dominican Republic is its extensive and diverse coastline and marine life. The coastal regions vary from dunes and sandy beaches that are the foundation of the tourism industry, mangrove forests at the base of river deltas, and coral reefs, home to incredible biodiversity that supports, maintains and replenishes marine life around the island. These colorful reefs support the small-scale fishing industry, as well as diving and other forms of tourism.

The growth of the tourism industry is a significant challenge to the fragile coastal ecosystems. Although tourism provides needed economic support and employment opportunities, unchecked growth has resulted in serious environmental consequences, include beach and dune erosion, degradation and destruction of sensitive habitats and over-exploitation of potable water resources. Damage to coral reef ecosystems is especially severe, impacting fishing stocks and the loss of critical marine species. The World Resources Institute estimates that 80 percent of Dominican coral reefs are at risk and threatened by human activity. The most significant threats are overfishing, which throws fragile ecosystems out of balance, and pressure from highly developed coastlines, including Punta Cana-Bavaro and Boca Chica. Dominican coastal regions also serve as key turtle and waterfowl nesting regions, also threatened by human encroachment. Only very recently have national and local governments begun to partner with conservation organizations and business to protect fragile areas.

ENVIRONMENTAL PROTECTION

In 1980, there were just nine protected areas in the Dominican Republic. Today, as the government has become more cognizant of the importance of defending its remaining natural resources, there are dozens of these areas. These include 22 national parks, 10 scientific reserves, 10 panoramic viewing areas, and 9 national monuments, covering 18 percent of the Dominican Republic's land surface. There are also marine natural parks and reserves for aquatic habitat. These areas include much of the remaining virgin forests, habitats of the most highly endangered species, and isolated but vulnerable and ecologically important regions.

The protected areas are still new and underdeveloped. As of 2009, only eight provided visitor infrastructure and 26 had paid staff, though this number is changing. As a nation of scarce financial resources, the Dominican Republic has had trouble allocating funding for these areas, but has been active in promulgating public policy for environmental protection. The DR has in place a sustainable tourism development policy and various national plans for sustainable environmental development, implemented to varying degrees. One-hundred and thirty NGOs are active in the environmental sector in the DR. Several international development organizations, including USAID, are heavily investing in more environmentally sustainable projects and programs across the country, with both private and non-profit institutions. An innovative program begun by USAID created regional tourism

---

Organics

Responding to demand from Europe and the United States, farmers in the Dominican Republic began production of organic agricultural goods for export in the early 1990s. Today, organic production plays an increasingly important role in the growth of Dominican agriculture and therefore has very relevant macroeconomic impact. In 2000, organic exports stood at $21 million, and by 2009 reached $200 million. By far, the largest organic export is bananas, but also includes, coffee, cocoa, oranges, mangoes, lemons, pineapples, cherries, coconut, and even sugarcane.

Organic agriculture is also changing the face of small producer production. Over the past ten years, the number of cooperatives and associations has exploded, as an increasing number of small farmers are working together to take advantage of economies of scale in inputs, production, transportation, and marketing. Organic and fair-trade certification is a difficult and lengthy process, and requires specific use of resources and methodology. These cooperatives charge each member farmer a small fee, and then assume responsibility for macro business elements of production. Many small farmers already produce "organically" because they cannot afford synthetic pesticides, but by following the required protocol, they are positioned to take advantage of the organic products premium of up to of 10 percent above normal pricing. Still, many of these groups are poorly organized and lack funding. Into this need have stepped the Dominican government and international organizations from the World Bank to smaller NGOs. With their support, small producer groups are able to expand to fill the growing demand of organic products that benefit not only the earth, but the producer as well.

clusters involving local governments, NGOs, businesses, and hotels to more efficiently manage natural resources and the economic growth potential that tourism plays in the development of the Dominican economy. The DR is also party to various international and regional treaties and agreements for the protection of the environment, including the Convention on International Commerce Governing Endangered Flora and Fauna, the Framework Convention to Combat Desertification and Drought, and the Conference on Climate Change.

The Basics

When to Go

With enormous variations in climate and topography, the Dominican Republic is not a typical tropical island. Average temperatures across the island do not vary much, rising to 27°C (81°F) in August and falling to 24°C (75°F) in January. That being said, wide variations do exist across geography and altitude. Locations along the coast, especially in the north, enjoy the sea breeze, while central valleys are hot and humid almost the entire year. As rookie climatologists know, higher altitudes are the coolest, and hilltop towns and villages may see temperatures drop below 10°C (50°F) in the winter. The southwest is the hottest and driest region of the country, as parts of it lie below sea level. Temperatures there can reach over 38°C (100°F). Extremes notwithstanding, there is still no bad time to visit the country.

The winter months, December to March, are generally the dry season for most of the country, as humidity readings are much lower and nighttime becomes very comfortable. Summer, from May through October, brings with it high humidity, heat, and hurricanes, and makes for sticky evenings. Locals expect afternoon rains nearly every day in the late summer days, especially in the northern valleys and mountain ranges where the rainy season can extend through the end of the year.

High travel season comes in two distinct waves. During the summer and Christmas holiday months, many émigré and urban Dominicans often return to

---

Hurricanes

As the Dominican Republic anchors the middle of the Caribbean, it sometimes seems to function as an unfortunate bull's-eye for hurricanes and tropical storms. Hurricane season officially extends from June through November, but historically, the DR tends to get hit the most often in August and September. Storms bring with them high winds, heavy rain, and unforgiving destruction. Meteorological forecasting and disaster prevention and mitigation have seen great improvements of late, but tragedies still occur. On August 31, 1979, Category 5 Hurricane David struck the Dominican Republic, making landfall just outside Santo Domingo. It caused over 2,000 deaths, left at least 200,000 homeless, and caused $1 billion in damage. Dominicans today talk about where they were when David hit and the destruction it wrought across the country. Unruly children born in the '80s were nicknamed "David" in honor of the storm's disastrous effects. Several other storms, including Georges in 1998 and Noel in 2007, are also remembered for their devastating power. If the forecast calls for hurricane landfall, it is imperative to seek shelter that can withstand the winds and rain over a number of days. Always pay attention to news reports about the potential for hurricanes during your stay.

extended families' homes in rural areas and visit local attractions, especially lakes and riversides. In addition, Semana Santa, or Holy Week, is the biggest travel week of the year, as people flock to the beach for days of fun in the sun. Crowds can swell to the unmanageable, and it is advisable to avoid the popular beaches this week. Prices also increase December through February and June through August.

Packing

The Dominican Republic is a tropical country, but varying weather and social situations require well more than sandals and a bathing suit. Public appearance is very important. Dominicans tend to wear relatively formal attire, donning jeans and tight, brightly colored tops, even if it's to the neighbor's house. You will quickly be taken as a foreigner in khaki shorts and floppy straw hats, so try to avoid those if possible, as thieves or others may look to take advantage of tourists unaccustomed to local ways. A trip to the DR may include visits to the beach, the city, and the mountains. Be aware that on the coast it will be hot, but the higher elevations are cooler, especially at night and in the winter. Also, once outside of urban centers, the personal items used at home are scarce or expensive, so be sure to bring extra supplies and toiletries in case you run out.

For the beach: The t-shirt, bathing suit, and flip-flops look is acceptable here. Bring a quick-dry towel, sun protection, and insect repellent (both sunscreen and repellent are expensive in the DR).

For the city: The best is comfortable and casual, yet neat clothing. Wear jeans, shoes or sneakers, and a short-sleeved shirt.

For the hills: Roads are rocky, so have shoes with sturdy soles handy. Bring long pants, a long-sleeved shirt, and a jacket or sweatshirt for nighttime. Sport sandals like Tivas are a good option.

Miscellany:

✓ Fancy electronics don't perform well in high heat and humidity and may attract unwanted attention. Protect your valuables by leaving them at home or in a hotel safe.

✓ A small, sturdy, waterproof backpack for day trips

✓ It can rain at any time: have on hand a travel-sized umbrella

✓ Because of the heat and difficulty of finding potable water, a reusable water bottle like a Nalgene is important

✓ Money clip or belt to carry passport and cash

✓ Antibacterial hand wipes or hand sanitizer

Here are some ways you can get extra protection on your visit:

Sun protection: sunscreen, sunglasses, hat

Disease and injury: small medical kit, sturdy hiking boots or sneakers

Insect protection: repellent, long pants, close-toed shoes

Haplessness protection: flashlight, pocketknife/multi-tool, matches, umbrella, Spanish phrasebook

Organizing your trip

There are a wide variety of tourist groups running around the Dominican Republic offering an array of travel options. Thoroughly check out each one before using their services. Getting around the DR, especially to the bigger towns and tourist areas, can be fairly easy, and quite cheap. Using tours, especially those based out of large chain hotels, could be a waste of money. Backpacking and taking public transportation (or even renting a car) is a much more economical option. It is a good idea to put together a rough travel itinerary, and to have some accommodations booked ahead of arrival. Organized tours, however, do offer the possibility of seeing places that might not otherwise be accessible on your own. They can also organize many activities in few days, if time on the island is limited.

Getting There and Away

ENTRY REQUIREMENTS

All visitors to the Dominican Republic must present a passport valid for at least six months after the end of the trip. Citizens of Australia, Canada, the EU, New Zealand, the US, and the UK do not need a visa to visit. However, they must purchase a tourist card when entering the country at a cost of US$10, allowing the holder to stay for 30 days. The card may also be obtained at the Dominican Embassy in home countries in advance of the trip. Staying beyond the 30 days will require payment of additional fees upon leaving the country. A departure tax of US$20 may also be charged at the airport upon leaving the country. However, most air carriers and tour groups include this tax in their fees.

Dominican Embassies Abroad

Australia *343A Edgecliff Road, Edgecliff, New South Wales 2027; +61-2-9363-5891*

Canada *130 Albert Street, Suite 418, Ottawa, ON K1P 5G4; 613-569-9893*

United Kingdom *139 Inverness Terrace, Bayswater, London, W2 6JF; 020-7727-6285*

United States *1715 22nd Street Northwest, Washington D.C., 20008; 202-332-6280*

Consulates & Embassies in DR

While overseas, it is important to register with your embassy of citizenship in case of emergency. This way, the embassy might contact citizens immediately.

Canada *1099 Av. Winston Churchill, Torre Citigroup in the Acrópolis Center, 18th floor, Ensanche Piantini, Santo Domingo; 809-262-3100; sdmgo@international.gc.ca*

France *42 Calle las Damas, Zona Colonial, Santo Domingo; 809-695-4300; ambafrance@ambafrance-do.org*

Germany *33 Calle Rafael Augusto Sánchez, corner of Av. Lope de Vega, Condominio Plaza Intercaribe, 5th floor; Naco, Santo Domingo; 809-565-8811*

Haiti *33 Av. Juan Sánchez Ramírez, Santo Domingo; 809-686-5778; amb.haiti@codetel.net.do*

Italy *Calle Rodríguez Objio 4, Gazcue, Santo Domingo; 809-682-0830; visti.santodomingo@esteri.it*

Spain *1205 Av. Independencia, Santo Domingo; 809-535-6500; embespdo@mail.mae.es*

United Kingdom *Av. 27 de Febrero, No. 233, 7th and 8th floors, Corominas Pepín building, Santo Domingo; 809-472-7111; brit.emb.sadom@codetel.net.do*

United States *Calle Cesar Nicolas Penson at Av. Máximo Gómez, Santo Domingo; 809 221-2171; 809-731-4292; Fax 809-686-7437; acssantodom@state.gov*

U.S. Consulate in Puerto Plata *Calle Villanueva at Avenida John F. Kennedy, 2nd floor; 809-586-4204*

AIR

Virtually all visitors enter the Dominican Republic on an airplane. As the country has become a popular tourist destination, customs and immigration are easy to navigate and generally hassle-free. The five international airports are built with the foreign traveler in mind: they are bright, spacious, and orderly. Flights to Santo Domingo, Santiago, and Punta Cana are the cheapest for solo travelers, but if visiting areas not especially close to these cities, it may be worthwhile to check out other airports for convenience once on the ground. Visit aerodom.com (in Spanish) for updated information on all airports and carries related to the Dominican Republic.

The best way to find a well-priced ticket is through an internet travel company like Expedia, Travelocity, Orbitz, and Kayak. If you are planning a trip to an all-inclusive resort, package deals are definitely worth some research, as they often include flights, transportation, and hotel for a lower price.

International Airports

Puerto Plata: Aeropuerto Internacional Gregorio Luperón (POP; 809-586-1992) Serves the north coast and its beaches.

Punta Cana: Aeropuerto Internacional Punta Cana (PUJ; 809-959-2473) Serves the eastern part of the country and the many resorts found there.

La Romana: La Romana International Airport (LRM; 809-556-5565) Serves the southeast, especially Casa de Campo.

Samaná: Aeropuerto Internacional El Catey/Juan Bosch (AZS; 809-338-0094) Serves the peninsula of Samaná.

Santo Domingo: Aeropuerto Internacional Las Américas (SDQ; 809-947-2225) Serves the central and southern regions.

Santiago: Aeropuerto Internacional Cibao (STI; 809-581-8072) Serves the interior, but is also easily accessible to the north coast.

Offices of Major Airline Operators

American Airlines Bella Vista Mall, 6 Ave. Sarasota, corner Calle de los Arrayanes, 3rd level, Bella Vista Mall, Santo Domingo; 809-542-5151; www.aa.com

Continental/COPA Ave. 27 de Febrero at Ave. Tiradentes, Santo Domingo; 809-472-2672; www.continental.com; www.copaair.com

Delta Plaza Comercial Acropolis Center, First Floor NW Corner, Corner of Av. Winston Churchill and Calle Andres Julio Aybar, Santo Domingo; 809-955-1500; www.delta.com

Iberia Av. Lope de Vega at Av. Kennedy, Santo Domingo; 809-508-0288; www.iberia.com

JetBlue Plaza Las Americas II, Corner of Avenida Winston Churchill & Paseo de los Locutores, 2nd Floor, Suite Y-B, Santo Domingo; 809-947-2220; www.jetblue.com

Spirit 54 Av. Gustavo Mejía Ricart, Torre Azar, Naco, Santo Domingo, 809-381-2003; www.spiritair.com

USAir 54 Av. Gustavo Mejía Ricart, Torre Azar, Naco Santo Domingo; 809-540-0505; www.usair.com

LAND

Given that the Dominican Republic is an island, entering by land takes a bit of effort. This is especially the case seeing as its only neighbor, Haiti, has poorly developed infrastructure and the border region is relatively inaccessible. Traveling to Port-au-Prince simply to see the Dominican Republic makes little sense. Still, a visit to Haiti can provide a very rewarding journey as part of your visit to Hispaniola. The best way to cross the border is by bus traveling directly through the border region. You may also take a bus to the last stop on one side, cross the border on foot, and hop another bus on the other side. It is not advisable to cross in a private car. Rental companies will not allow drivers to traverse the border in their cars, and even with a privately-owned vehicle, permission from the Dominican government is required, which can take months to receive, and is a frustrating, expensive process.

Immigration and customs officers at border stations are more discerning than those at the airports, so even at these dusty outposts, crossing the border may prove to be a time-consuming task. Officials are much more concerned in dealing (at times, not especially kindly) with the Haitian population, but it is best to be courteous and patient regardless of nationality.

The most commonly used border station is in the south at Jimaní/Malpasse, on the Santo-Domingo–Port-au-Prince highway. In the north, on the Santiago-Cap Hatien highway, is the Dajabón/Ouanaminthe crossing. The border is also open to travel at the Elías Piña/Belladere crossing, but no major bus line uses this isolated location, as it is very difficult to access and roads are in poor condition. See Jimaní (p358) and Dajabón (p240) for more information.

Costs

The charge to leave the DR is US$10, and US$10 for the tourist card if travelers do not already have one. On the other side, Haiti charges a departure tax of up to US$25. Note that this fee may change without warning, and it may be required to pay it in the Haitian currency, called gourdes. Check with the bus company to make sure you have all the required forms and cash on hand, in the three currencies, to make the crossing smooth. Carry enough for all of these fees in both pesos and dollars, since in the end your fate is up to the discretion of a disgruntled border guard.

Transportation

The Dominican Republic is a relatively small country, but variable road conditions can lead to unexpected delays. Four wide, modern highways run leave Santo Domingo: north through Santiago to Puerto Plata, northeast to Samaná, east through La Romana to Bavaro, and southwest to Azua. Upon leaving these highways (called *autopistas* or *carreteras*) however, most smaller roads become narrow and strewn with potholes – and many are not be paved at all. While there is rarely large vehicle volume on the highways away from urban areas, cities and towns are often choked with traffic due to bottlenecks, accidents, and endless roadwork.

Bus

Traveling the country by bus (*guagua*, in Dominican Spanish) is the best way to get to know the country, and is the cheapest, most efficient option for those on a budget. Buses are consistent and run regularly to destinations across the country. Bus is the only way that locals travel long distances, and they are often happy to share a seat and discuss weather, politics, and the beauty of the country and its people. Buses range from luxury to the ancient, and therefore some are quiet and have A/C, while others are cacophonous and uncomfortably warm. The most expensive journey on a coach bus tops out at around RD$400, while the majority of *guagua* routes run between RD$100 and RD$200. Major bus lines include:

Caribe Tours Caribe Tours is the most trusted and popular Dominican bus company. These bright yellow coach buses run from Santo Domingo to fifty destinations across the country, as well as to Port-au-Prince. Boasting a gleaming, modern terminal in the middle of downtown Santo Domingo, Caribe Tours is any traveler's best bet for inter-city travel. There are also small offices at each of the local stops, where tickets can also be purchased. Caribe buses often show old movies you didn't know existed, and blast the A/C fit for a meat locker. *Av. 27 de Febrero, at Av. Leopoldo Navarro, Santo Domingo; 221-4422; www.caribetours.com.do*

Metro Tours A similar, though slightly more expensive coach bus company than Caribe, Metro travels from Santo Domingo to Santiago and six other cities in the north. *Av. Winston Churchill at C/ Francisco Pratts Ramírez, Santo Domingo; 566-7126; http://www.metroserviciosturisticos.com/*

Terrabus Terrabus operates only to Santiago and Puerto Plata. *Av. 27 de Febrero at Av. Máximo Gómez, Santo Domingo; 472-1080*

Javilla Tours Javilla runs smaller buses that also ply the highway from Santiago to Puerto Plata, and multiple stops in between. It is the perfect choice for local trips along that corridor. The central station is in Santiago; otherwise, just flag the bus down when it passes by. *118 Av. Colón at La Rotonda, Santiago; 261-3340*

Expreso Bavaro This bus company runs four departures daily between the resorts of Bavaro and Punta Cana and Santo Domingo. Arrive at least an hour early, as the bus sells out quickly and the company does not take reservations. *In Santo Domingo, 31 C/ Juan Sánchez Ramírez (there is usually a bus parked outside) by Máximo Gómez ;682-9670. In Bavaro, find it by the Texaco gas station, also known as the Friusa or Sitrabapu bus stop; 552-1678.*

Expreso Vegano This company has colorful buses that travel between Santo Domingo and La Vega, and is slightly cheaper than Caribe Tours. *35 Av. 27 de Febrero at Av. San Martín, Santo Domingo*

The *Guagua*

Beyond the relative luxury of coach buses, the *guagua transport* system is how Dominicans get around, running to every town and village in the country. The term *guagua* is applied to anything from pickup trucks to old minivans to 20-person minibuses – pretty much anything that picks up passengers. Some are clean, have A/C and run on schedules, others look to be mid-century relics and run whenever the driver decides to come back from lunch. *Guaguas* pick up and drop off passengers whenever anyone asks. This is convenient, but often causes the journey to take longer than those of coach buses with limited stops. To catch a *guagua*, stand on the side of the road and hold out your arm, punctuated by a vigorous wave and wrist flick when a bus appears. A man (or rarely, a woman) stands in the doorway of bus – this is the *cobrador*, or the bus fare collector, who also yells out destinations. Speak with the *cobrador* to make sure he knows where you're headed. *Guaguas* are a fascinating part of Dominican culture, full of life, excitement, rice sacks, and the occasional animal.

Car

Renting a car is surely the most convenient method of getting around the country, especially if you are headed to smaller or remote locales. While the major highways are paved, many smaller roads are just dirt and stone, so be sure to rent a car that can withstand some shocks. A car is also important to reach off-the-beaten-path locations in the hills or on isolated beaches. Note that gasoline prices are high, hovering above $4 a gallon. Gas stations, called *bombas*, can be found in many big towns and along major highways. The most secure place to find a rental car is at the airport, especially in Santo Domingo. Use a well-known company that offers insurance, which is strongly recommended. A valid international driver's license is required. Only those over 21 may rent a car.

Hertz *La Romana airport, 813-9351; Santo Domingo airport, 549-0454; Santo Domingo C/ José María Heredia, 221-5333; Santiago airport, 233-8555.*

Avis *Las Americas airport, 549-0468; Santo Domingo 517 Av. George Washington, 535-7191*

Europcar *Santo Domingo airport, 549 0942; Santo Domingo 8 C/ Gustavo Mejía Ricart, Ensanche Piantini, 565-4455; Santiago airport, 233-8150; Puerto Plata airport, 586-0215; Punta Cana airport, 686-2861*

National, Thrifty, and Dollar also have locations at the major airports.

Motorcycles

Motorcycles, or *motos*, are very common in the Dominican Republic as a very cheap and efficient alternative to cars. Travel by *moto* is convenient and sometimes the only public option in rural areas, as the motorcycles act as taxis where cars are not able to go. Often, a gaggle of motorcycle drivers (called *motoconchistas, conchistas,* or *conchos*) will badger passengers debarking from buses on the side of the road. However, be aware *moto* travel can be dangerous, as drivers travel at high speeds, routinely ignore traffic regulations, and are lax towards safety in general. It is also important to wear a helmet as a precautionary measure. Avoid *moto* travel in large cities if at all possible.

Motos can also provide entertainment: a great game is to spot the greatest number of people on a motorcycle; the authors have seen six.

Taxis

When in doubt, take a taxi. Cab companies are safe and reliable to get across town, and are plentiful in big cities. Always agree on a price and destination before you start moving, or the driver may decide to up the fare without warning. A taxi within downtown Santo Domingo should not cost more than RD$200, and in Santiago, RD$150.

The Road Heavily Traveled

Getting around the country should be relatively easy, but a traveler should take necessary precautions. While some roads are quite nice, others are not. Road rules are followed on an as-needed basis, and are seen as more like suggestions. The driving scene may therefore resemble something like organized chaos, with an emphasis on chaos, especially in large urban areas. A crush of cars, buses, trucks, motorcycles, and other vehicles will fondly accompany you on your journey across the city. Watch out for motorcycles weaving heedlessly through traffic, and *guaguas* that stop without warning on the side of the road. Traffic lights exist in few intersections, but are generally adhered to only in big cities. Always be aware of what your fellow drivers around you are doing; it is probably best to follow their lead. Enjoy the ride!

Subway

President Leonel Fernández inaugurated the first metro system in the Caribbean with much fanfare in January of 2009. Boasting 16 stations and a 100,000 average daily ridership, the metro offers an impressively clean, quiet, and efficient method of getting around Santo Domingo. It currently has only one line, but construction is ongoing for the second line, with grand plans for four more. Each ride is just RD$20, the same price as careening *carros públicos*. However, its construction was not without controversy. Costs of the first line topped US$700 million, a hefty sum in a country where basic infrastructure does not yet reach many citizens. Still, traffic in the capital is often unbearable, and though it may seem somewhat out of place, the metro is worth at least a glance.

Hitchhiking

For many locals in the Dominican Republic, hitchhiking is a useful transportation alternative. We can't entirely condone the practice as it can fall askew of playing it safe.

Catching a *bola*, or free ride, is something of an art. For safety, it is best to hit-chhike in small, mixed-gendered groups, and never at night. Look for pickups or other large trucks that may be more amenable to picking people up than motorcycle drivers. To get that *bola*, stand on the side of the road, and flap your arm and wrist, much like hailing a *guagua*. Give a little holler or yell "una bola!" when your target vehicle drives by. With any luck, you'll be on a ride in no time.

Health

As far as exotic tropical diseases go, the Dominican Republic has few. Therefore, the most common illnesses, especially for travelers, tend to arise from less-than-clean food and water. Take necessary measures before and during any stay to ensure the optimum travel experience. While seeing the inside of a Dominican hospital may be educational, it is not fun, as they suffer from regular blackouts, unsanitary conditions, and long waits. In major cities, modern, private medical facilities are available, and are listed in their respective sections. If possible, seek medical care there instead of at a public clinic or hospital.

PRE-DEPARTURE

A visit with a doctor or medical professional is highly recommended one to two months before heading to the Dominican Republic. Discuss with the doctor all of the relevant and updated information on illness and injury prevention involved in traveling to the DR. A timely consultation is especially important so that vaccines have time to take effect. Both the Center for Disease Control (CDC, www.cdc.gov) and the World Health Organization (WHO, www.who.int/en/) have great resources and information for the itinerant traveler. It may also be a good idea to research international health insurance plans and talk to your provider regarding its policy for international coverage. Travel insurance may also cover theft and baggage, so it can be a good investment.

Vaccinations

Since some vaccinations and medication only become effective a few weeks after they are given, be sure to begin any dosage well before leaving your home country. While no vaccinations are required to visit the DR, those listed below are recommended by the United States Center for Disease Control (CDC):

Hepatitis A: For all travelers, at least two weeks before departure. Hepatitis A is a liver infection caused by exposure to contaminated food or water sources.

Hepatitis B: For everyone not previously vaccinated for this disease. Hep B is a liver infection, acquired through exposure to infected blood or other body fluid contact, including those present during sexual activity. It is also important for those who may undergo medical treatment while abroad.

Typhoid: For travelers who plan on leaving large hotels or resorts. Typhoid fever, as it is also known, is contracted through contaminated water, including from food prepared with contaminated water or by someone with the disease.

Rabies: For those who are going to spend a lot of time outdoors or around animals. Rabies is contracted from contact with saliva of infected animals; in the DR, it is most common in wild street dogs and mongooses. A bite from any animal should be treated with urgency: clean with soap and water, and then contact a doctor for information about the necessary rabies booster shot.

Tetanus-diphtheria: For those who have not received an immunization in the previous ten years. Infection also comes from contaminated water.

Measles-mumps-rubella: For those who have not received two doses.

DURING YOUR VISIT

Various communicable diseases are present in the Dominican Republic, Always take necessary precautions against contraction of any of these illnesses and understand the risks of traveling where they are prevalent.

Malaria: Malaria is a mosquito-borne disease found in tropical and subtropical regions, including the DR. Malaria is one of the most widespread illnesses in the world, with over 300 million new infections reported annually. The disease is present in the entire country, except in Santo Domingo, and is most prevalent in the western border regions. Malaria-carrying mosquitoes bite only at night, so sleeping under a mosquito net is very important. While the risk to foreign travelers is low, there are some precautions you can take to ensure that you do not contract malaria. The CDC recommends taking malaria prophylaxis such as chloroquine, administered weekly and begun two weeks before departure. Side effects are minimal, including nausea and abnormally vivid dreams. The CDC also approves atovaquone (Malarone), mefloquine (Lariam), and doxycyline as acceptable prevention drugs. See below for mosquito bite prevention.

Symptoms include cyclical fevers, body aches, nausea, and diarrhea, and can occur from a week to a year after being bitten by an infected mosquito. Malaria can cause anemia, jaundice, kidney failure, and death. Because there are several strains of malaria, treatment varies widely, but usually includes the usage of the drugs listed here.

Dengue Fever: Dengue fever, also known as breakbone fever, is another mosquito-borne infectious disease. Dengue fever infects 50 million people a year, and is endemic to the Dominican Republic. Interestingly, the mosquitoes that carry dengue feed during the daytime, contrary to malaria-carrying mosquitoes. Dengue infection results in generic flu-like symptoms, but is characterized by intense body pains, especially behind the eyes, and a full-body rash. There is no vaccine or specific treatment for dengue besides rest and hydration. Drugs like acetaminophen are administered, though not pain relievers that tend to thin the blood, such as aspirin and ibuprofen, because severe dengue can result in hemorrhaging.

Leptospirosis: This disease is a bacterial infection contracted through the urine of infected animals, usually through the consumption of food or water that had been contaminated or come into contact with an infected animal. A large outbreak of the disease took place after hurricane-related flooding in 2007, when many people were exposed to contaminated water. Leptospirosis is dangerous in that it, too, produces "flu-like" symptoms, which can then progress and cause serious kidney, liver, and nervous system damage. There is no vaccine, and is treated with antibiotics. Be aware if there have been reports of the disease in your area.

Conjunctivitis: Yes, this is pink eye. It is not nearly as serious as other illnesses listed here; it is just unsightly and highly contagious. In 2008, there was an astonishing outbreak, affecting over 40,000 people across the country, your authors included. Prevent infections through general cleanliness practices, especially of the hands and face.

HIV/AIDS: UNICEF estimates that the prevalence of HIV/AIDS in the Dominican Republic is 1.1%, and that the infection rate has stabilized. The incidence of HIV is highest in urban areas and among sex workers. Be thoughtful before engaging in any activity that might put you at risk for infection.

Cholera: Cholera in the DR was almost nonexistent until recently, when the outbreak in Haiti crossed the border in late 2010. It is now increasingly important to make sure that water intake is from a clean, potable source, and that visitors wash their hands and face at frequent intervals, and with soap and water. Cook food well, keep it covered, and peel fruits and vegetables. The cholera vaccine, however, was not required as of publication.

The most common form of health problems of visitors to the Dominican Republic is intestinal distress accompanied by **diarrhea**. To avoid this entirely un-fun illness, a good rule of thumb is to steer clear of drinking water from unknown sources. Tap water, rainwater, well water, river water – don't drink it. Restaurants almost always serve potable water, but ask first. If in a rural area or someone's home, ask if the juice or water being offered is bottled. Even if water is free of disease, it may still contain elements or particles that your body is unaccustomed to ingesting, causing irritation.

Boiling water for at least one to three minutes is the most effective method of purification, leaving any particles to settle at the bottom. Coffee is probably safer than juice because it is heated almost to a boil. If boiling is not an option, iodine tablets are a good alternative, though not for long-term use. Many rural families use regular, unscented bleach to purify water, and this is a recommended option for travelers as well. The approximate ratio to purify water is eight drops of bleach per gallon of water. Portable water filtration systems are not as effective, because the pores are often large enough for tiny viruses or other contaminants to move through them. You should avoid foods like fresh fruit and salads that haven't been washed with potable water, and be wary with street food, as its origin and state of cleanliness is often questionable at best. In the DR, a country with a hot climate, moderate refrigeration capabilities, and blackouts, foods tend to sit out for long periods of time. Therefore, be aware of a food's source, especially when consuming seafood, meat and dairy products.

Money & Costs

Because the Dominican Republic sees its fair share of foreigners, the euro and dollar are increasingly used in tourist-heavy locations on the beaches and resorts. The DR tends to run on a cash-based economy, and it is a better idea not to use credit cards even if the option is available. Many small- and medium-sized businesses, most as part of the informal economy, only accept cash. The Dominican currency is called the peso, symbolized as in this book as RD$.

Coins come in one, five, ten, and twenty-five peso denominations, and notes in 20, 50, 100, 200, 500, 1000 and 2000. Bills in ten peso denominations float around but are no longer in production, and if you get your hands on one it might disintegrate in your pocket.

BANKS, ATMS, & CASH

There are multiple foreign banks with branches in Santo Domingo and Santiago, like Citibank and Scotiabank. Other major banks include Banco BHD, Banco del Progreso, Banco León, Banco Popular, and Banreservas. At least one branch or ATM of local banks is present in nearly every town. ATMs are generally secure, though it is best to use machines that are physically in the banks themselves, instead of ones on the street. Also, try to use ATMs at which cards are swiped, instead of being inserted, to avoid getting the card stuck in the machine. Of course, it is best to take out cash during the day in populated areas and not on isolated street corners at night. Additionally, using credit cards and travelers' checks tend to incur an extra surcharge.

As of publication, the exchange rate was about 38 Dominican pesos to the U.S. dollar (USD), 54 pesos to the Euro (EUR), 61 pesos to the British pound (GDP) and 40 pesos to the Australian dollar (AUD).

Banks are generally open from 9am until 4pm, and some smaller branches close for lunch. In addition, small change can be hard to find, so always take advantage of larger businesses such as grocery stores and coach bus terminals to break large bills. In lieu of providing a few pesos as change, small stores such as *colmados* might offer candies or mints instead of smaller denominations of pesos.

Exchanging money is easy, though there are better places to do it than others. Change booths at airports, businesses, resorts, and hotels are secure, though they will not give you the best rates. Banks and independent exchange booths will present the most equitable rates. In the capital and beach towns, there will be small change booths on the street. These are always a better option than guys on the street flashing about wads of cash for exchange (and often, lottery tickets). The money they have isn't going to be counterfeit, but it doesn't make sense to take the chance when there are plenty of other, more secure options. They often claim they do not have small change, meaning customers lose out. Restaurants and bars may charge more for using foreign currency over pesos. Therefore, it's best to use pesos when possible.

TAX & TIPPING

The DR has a difficult time collecting duties on goods and services to maintain the government. Therefore, expect to pay high taxes at many establishments, as tourism is a reliable source of income for the state. A base 16 percent tax called ITBIS (pronounced ee-TEH-bis) is levied by most businesses. An additional ten percent service charge is placed on the check at hotels and restaurants. Tipping on top of this ten percent is not strictly necessary, though is certainly appreciated as service wages are very low, and this tax may never reach your server or the other staff. In other service transactions like taxis and hotel staff, you should add an appropriate tip of at least US$1. If you receive a service from someone on the street, he is going to expect a tip. For example, men with soapy rags will accost your car if you are stopped in an intersection, froth your windshield, and ask for change. Try to wave then away before the suds obscure your view of the road.

COSTS

Though the Dominican Republic may not specifically cater to the budget traveler, it is still an affordable place to travel and stay if you seek out the right places. The DR can also be quite expensive, all depending on activity and location. A locals' bar in a small town, for example, might charge RD$40 for a bottle of beer, while the same bottle may go for US$160 at a bar in downtown Santo Domingo or the popular beach towns.

Highest costs will probably be lodging, since hostels are rare. The cheapest rate you can find is about RD$300 a night, but luxury hotels will run to hundreds of dollars. This very wide range also goes for food and drink prices. Sit-down restaurants with service are only patronized by well-off Dominicans and tourists, so expect to pay at least RD$500 per person for meals there. However, you can find very inexpensive food at more informal eating locales, like *cafeterías*, and at small general stores (*colmados*). Shopping at grocery stores and local markets to make your own food, or even finding families with whom to eat a couple meals, are great alternative options.

As discussed earlier, public transportation is very inexpensive, especially for longer rides. The most you will pay on a long route is RD$400, and a ride through the city will break the bank at RD$25. Taxis run RD$100-300.

Urban areas like Santo Domingo and Santiago, as well as beach towns like Sosúa and Cabarete, are going to be more expensive than smaller places without an overwhelming tourist presence. Of course, Punta Cana, Bavaro, and fine hotels and resorts will also be more expensive.

Safety and Security

The Dominican Republic is not known to be especially threatening for foreigners or locals, so travelers should feel safe moving about the country. General violence and civil unrest are rare. During hurricane season, be aware of the dangers of storms. Violent crime is almost unheard of, though petty theft is common, especially in tourist areas.

STRIKES

Though the Dominican Republic has suffered under the rule of various foreign military interventions and a series of oppressive dictatorships, it has enjoyed peaceful transitions of government over the past half-century, and democratic institutions are slowly strengthening. Nevertheless, widespread poverty, economic stagnation, and a lack of political participation by many sectors of society can result in episodes of planned or spontaneous civil unrest. These most often take place in poor neighborhoods experiencing water or electricity shortages. Transportation and other industry strikes are common forms of protest that can bring the country to a standstill; these may also result in clashes between police and protesters. While rare, hotspots for such incidents are universities and public buildings, as well as the cities of Barahona, Licey, Navarette, San Francisco de Macorís, and Santo Domingo.

During election season, politicians and their followers are on the street in full force, creating immense traffic headaches. The vast majority of these gatherings are peaceful, and the best protection is patience and a sense of humor.

NATURAL DISASTERS

Hurricanes represent the most precarious and unpredictable element of any visit to the Dominican Republic. If possible, move to an urban center and find lodging in a sturdy, modern hotel. While strong winds are not usually an issue, even without a hurricane, heavy rainfall and serious flooding are major concerns in rural and urban areas. Urban drainage is often poor at best, and saturated grounds during the rainy season can cause swollen rivers to overflow their banks. While these problems will usually not present themselves during your stay, if you plan on river or ocean adventures, be aware of recent or possible rains and flooding.

Earthquakes are also a significant presence, as Hispaniola sits on the boundary of the Caribbean and North American tectonic plates. On January 12, 2010, a destructive magnitude 7.0 earthquake hit Haiti, and was felt as far away as central Dominican Republic. Previous earthquakes have struck the DR during its history, causing significant damage, including one that leveled the city of La Vega in the 16th century. The dangers of an earthquake, though rare, should not be ignored.

OUTDOOR ACTIVITIES

Outdoor and water-related activities are part of the allure of a Dominican Republic vacation, but take necessary precaution when frolicking in the ocean. Currents and riptides around the island can be strong and unpredictable. Except at resorts and large tourist destinations, there are no lifeguards on duty. There have been several incidents of drowning by those unprepared or taken off guard by such currents. We highly recommend surfing, kiteboarding, swimming, and rafting in the DR, but make sure you refresh yourself on water safety first and ask locals about areas of strong currents.

The Dominican Republic can also get very hot, especially under the strong Caribbean sun. It is best to wear sun protection when you are outside for any length of time, even if you aren't at the beach. Many Dominican women take to using umbrellas during the sunniest of days: both as a safety precaution and as fashionistas. Take a cue from the locals. Wear a hat, sunglasses, long pants, and sunscreen, and try to avoid being outside too much during the hottest part of the day, from noon to 4pm. Always have a water bottle, as heat and sunstroke can hit tourist unaccustomed to the tropical climate.

CRIME

Though rural areas are generally safe, crime can be a problem on the streets of larger towns and cities, especially after dark and in tourist destinations. Petty theft and burglary, including pickpocketing and muggings, are not infrequent occurrences in places areas such as markets, parks, festivals, public transportation, and other popular locations. Avoid wearing ostentatious jewelry or clothing, and try not to lug around a big travel backpack. Try not to have too much cash, and hold it securely. Carry wallets in the front pocket, especially when on public transportation, or use a money belt for more security. Women, avoid carrying a large or flashy purse – over-the shoulder bags that can be kept close to the body are better. Remember to keep purses or bags on the side of the body opposite to the street, because a common tactic is for thieves to ride up along an unsuspecting pedestrian on a *moto* and pull or cut the strap loose, then speed away.

Never walk alone late at night along poorly lit passageways or in isolated areas. Be especially aware in Santo Domingo's *Zona Colonial*. Simple precautions like these and a general awareness of surroundings will prevent any incidents from reducing the fun factor of your trip to the DR.

In addition, credit and debit card fraud has been on the rise in the DR. Try to avoid using your plastic, especially at ATMs on the street, except at resorts and large hotels. Contact your bank about your visit so that you and they can stay vigilant about suspicious movement in your account.

DRIVING

As mentioned in the Transportation section, driving around the DR takes a mix of courage and creativity. While traffic laws are similar the US, they are poorly enforced and rarely adhered to; aggressive and unpredictable driving seems to be the norm. Take special precaution during the summer, Easter, and Christmas, as drunken driving peaks at these times.

DRUGS

Drug laws are harsh and strongly enforced in the DR. All drugs, except those with a prescription, are illegal. While drugs on the street are not very common, they may have more of a presence in tourist-heavy beach towns. It is best to steer clear of any illicit substance while in the country.

FEMALE TRAVELERS

Traveling as a woman, especially alone, can present unique hazards, but in no way can inhibits the ability to enjoy everything the DR has to offer. In fact, women will probably be treated better and garner much more attention on many occasions than male friends or travel partners. The DR presents a fascinating mixture of misogyny and chivalry, depending on the time, location, and opinion. The most widespread complaint by women travelers is of sexual harassment. Dominican men tend to be very vocal and active in their display of opinion towards women. Catcalls, called *piropos*, are frequently tossed at women, whether local of foreign. Men see these as complimentary, not adverse attention. Women's fashion, especially eveningwear, may dictate more provocative dress than found in the US, including sparkles, sequins, and tight-fitting clothing. Because foreign women are seen less often, they will probably attract more attention. It is common enough now for women to walk around alone and speak with men. However, to ward off unwanted advances, whether verbal or otherwise, it may be best to wear a ring or speak of a boyfriend or husband, or even travel with other male companions. Men who wish to dance with women generally ask permission of the potential dance partner's male companions.

Rural areas are more conservative than big cities, and for that reason, it is best to act accordingly. Women, especially, are seen to have a more traditional place in society: as mothers, in the home, and single women rarely go out by themselves. Remaining decorous, including refraining from drinking heavily and from wearing revealing clothing, in rural country is a safe bet.

Communication

PHONE ACCESS

Landlines are well established in urban areas and major commercial centers across the country, though connection quality is variable. Phone booths are rare and poorly maintained. Landlines, however, do not exist in rural areas, and with increased cell coverage, are not going to be installed any time soon. In general, cell phones (called *móviles* or *celulares*) are much more commonly used. Cell service is nearly ubiquitous across the DR, except in swaths of rural or mountainous regions of the country. On an interesting note, many people own phones but leave little or no credit on their phones, leading to a practice called *bipeando* (from the English, to beep), or calling people and hanging up after one or two rings so that the receiver calls back the first person without incurring costs. Minutes cost about RD$10, and the tendency is to use prepaid minutes instead of plans with contracts. Popular cell phone providers include Orange, Tricom, Vivo, and Claro. Phone numbers in the DR begin with the area code (809), and some cell phones have a newer codes, (829) or (849). Always dial 1, then the area code, and the seven-digit number from any phone for domestic calls. To call the US, simply dial the area code and number, as if you were in the US. Phone cards can be purchased at any store, small or large, anywhere in the country. It is also possible to bring a GSM phone and get a local card.

INTERNET

Internet access is spottier than cell services, though is experiencing similar, considerable growth. According to INDOTEL, the state information telecommunication agency, 30 percent of Dominicans have internet access, not including the thousands of internet cafés. Even most small towns have at least one business with internet availability. Hourly rates run between RD$50 and RD$75. Free internet is available at INDOTEL centers in large cities. Internet cafés also offer copies, faxes, and photo printing, as well as international calls at considerable discounts from cell phone prices. Electronic viruses have followed their more organic cousins to the DR, so be wary of downloading information onto removable drives or disks. Wi-Fi is also increasingly common in parks and public spaces, but pulling out laptops in the central plaza is never a good idea. Instead, find a restaurant that offers Wi-Fi service. These places usually have A/C, too, which is always nice.

MAIL

The postal system is less reliable than cell phones or the internet. Sending a postcard home to mom is more dependable than writing a long letter, stuffed in an envelope that will get lost in the tropical ether. Send mail through hotels, if it offers this service, or at the central post office in Santo Domingo at Centro de los Heroes. There are post offices in other cities, but again, better to send an email. Mail can take weeks to arrive (if at all) at its intended destination.

Tourist Information

The Dominican Republic Ministry of Tourism maintains offices or kiosks in the international airports, in 16 towns and cities across the country, and in Europe,

South America, North America, and Japan. The Ministry also publishes a very informative website, www.godominicanrepublic.com, in six languages. It is a great supplement to this book for the most updated information on events and activities. The site provides pretty pictures and videos and helpful trip planning advice, including a "Cool Stuff" page. Wherever you happen to be, information about the DR is not too far off. In Santo Domingo, find the Ministry at the Oficinas Gubernamentales on the corner of Av. México and Av. 30 de Marzo, Bloque D. 221-4660.

Accommodation

Finding a great spot to rest your head, drop your bags, and sleep mosquito-free is an important part of your trip. One of the most critical pieces of information to know about traveling in the DR is that there is a discernible lack of backpacker-friendly lodging. Traditional youth hostels are almost nonexistent in the DR. Therefore, with the economical traveler in mind, the authors have endeavored to list lodging that is safe and wallet-friendly. Of course, the country itself is still cheap – travel, food, activities, beer – so finding a place to sleep that won't break the bank is not impossible. Expect to pay at least RD$350 to RD$550 per night per person at many of the hotels listed. We have also included a few splurge-worthy hotels that might warrant spending some extra cash, because of something special or significant that they provide. All of these locations provide beds, sheets, towels, and plumbing, unless noted.

As hostels are not terribly common, neither is camping. There are few organized camping locations, and spending the night alone on a deserted beach is not a good idea for safety's sake. Camping is most common in national parks or on long hikes, such as on the route to Pico Duarte, where there are rustic shelters for sleeping bags (Pico Duarte, p296). Otherwise, there are precious few camping shelters. Note that there were a couple official campgrounds as of publication within the national parks themselves, but the Ministry of Environment has increased its efforts to equip camping sites throughout the country. Currently, a pass must be purchased from the Ministry of Tourism to be able to camp in national parks (RD$50; 472-4204). When camping is a viable option, it will be discussed in the relevant chapter. Responsible and environmentally friendly lodging will also be highlighted as we look to respect our surroundings as we travel.

Food & Beverage

Dominicans work hard to eat well. A common compliment is to tell someone how *fuerte* he or she looks; *fuerte*, meaning strong, here acts as a euphemism for plump. A nation's cuisine speaks volumes about its culture, and the Dominican Republic is no exception. Dominican food shares basic commonalities with its immediate Caribbean neighbors, which draw from a mélange of European, African, and traditional foodstuffs and preparation styles to form a unique cuisine. The biggest meal of the day is lunch, while breakfast and dinner tend to be lighter affairs. Meat can be served at every meal, which might make life difficult for the vegetarian. However, it is easy enough to find a substitution, and even a meal of just rice and beans without chicken is hearty enough. The Dominican meal is not complete without a starch and a protein; if one is missing, the meal is called *vacío*, or empty. One staple of the Dominican diet is the *vívere*, or starchy vegetable. The most common include *plátano* (plantain) and *yuca* (cassava root), but others include *batata* (a kind of sweet potato), *tayota* (chayote), *yautía* (taro root), and *auyama* (yam). *Víveres* are served most often boiled or fried.

Breakfast

In some parts of the *campo*, breakfast may consist of nothing more than a small piece of bread and hot chocolate or liquid oatmeal. However, breakfast is usually a two-fold affair. The first half involves a serving of *víveres*. The second is played by one of a trio of fried delicacies: *huevos* (eggs), *queso* (cheese), or salami, topped off with some of the frying oil. *Arenque*, or salted cod, might be used as the protein on rare occasions. Breakfast is taken with a small cup of strong, sweet coffee. Another popular breakfast dish is *mangú*, made from mashed boiled plantains. It is can be topped, along with boiled plantains or *yuca*, with red onions marinated in vinegar then fried.

Lunch

The midday meal is by far the heaviest and most involved in terms of preparation and consumption time. Women in the *campo* often spend the entire morning, and some of the previous evening, putting together this meal. Lunch features *la bandera dominicana,* or the Dominican flag, because of the food trio on the plate parallels the trifecta of colors on the flag. Dominicans are clearly as patriotic about their homeland as they are about their food. This tripartite meal features a base of *arroz*, or white rice, topped with *habichuelas rojas*, or red beans, and *carne*, or meat, (usually chicken). The beans used may vary depending on the season, like *habichuelas negras*, or black beans, and *guandules*, or pigeon peas. *Cerdo, res*, or *chivo* (pork, beef, or goat) can be used in place of chicken, but the big bowl of rice is the one constant. Beyond traditional white rice preparation, the rice may also be cooked directly with other ingredients. One variant on the rice-and-beans dish is called *moro*, in which the beans and rice are cooked together in one pot. Corn may be substituted for beans, which is called *moro de maíz*. The various meats may be prepared together with rice as well, in a dish known as *locrio*. For a well-balanced meal, a small salad or vegetable sides like eggplant, potato, avocado, or okra accompanies the *bandera*.

Dinner

The evening meal mirrors breakfast: small, with a carbohydrate and protein component. Boiled *víveres* are again paired with fried eggs, cheese, or salami. Oatmeal may also be served in cooler months.

DESSERT

The Dominican Republic is not Italy or Greece; delicate, flaky treats are uncommon. Still, anyone eating in the DR, home of the endless sugarcane plantation, would be remiss without a sweet ending to a savory meal. Dessert may be simply a heavily sugared cup of coffee, or a piece of *dulce* (literally, sweet) made with milk, sugar, and boiled fruit. In restaurants, you'll find international dessert flavors like flan, bread and rice pudding, and *tres leches*, a dish made with three iterations of dairy product. Coconut, when available, is popular in postprandial sweets, made into cookies or biscuits called *coconetes*. Coconut is also often used in the corn pudding-like *majarete*, popular across the Caribbean.

SPECIALTIES

Mealtime in the Dominican Republic usually means eating with a large group of people: close family, relatives from out of town, friends, co-workers, other visitors, and any number of household animals. Dominicans therefore know how to cook for big crowds. One of the most popular dishes for such times is *sancocho*, a hearty stew prepared with several kinds of *víveres*, a multitude of other vegetables, and various kinds of meat. The stew simmers for hours over an open fire, serving dozens and making everyone happy. Even more filling is *asopao*, a meat and *vívere*-filled stew prepared with rice. Simpler soups prepared with fewer ingredients, and the addition of noodles, is called *caldo*.

At Easter, a popular dish is *habichuelas con dulce*, a pudding-like dessert made from a base of beans, along with sweet potato, condensed milk, and cinnamon. It is usually served with small milk cookies.

Tostones
Tostones are the French fries of the Dominican Republic. What better to do with unripe plantains, found in abundance across the country, than twice-fry the big guys and serve with every meal? To make *tostones*, plantains are sliced less than an inch thick, flattened, fried, then flattened again, and finally fried for a second time. They are ubiquitous and delicious, found in every fancy restaurant and roadside stand. When in doubt, order *tostones*.

FRUIT

A Caribbean island, the DR features dozens of sweet and colorful tropical fruits. Some fruits grow all year and are available for your enjoyment, while others have a short growing season, and arrive by the truckload. Two of the most popular fruits that have specific seasons are *aguacate* (avocado), in the fall, and mango, in the spring and summer. Also try *limoncillo* (resembling a lychee), around in the late summer. These fruits will appear in abundance on the street and in the home, dropping in price and increasing in tastiness. Year-round, enjoy *lechosa* (papaya), *guineo* (banana), *china* (orange), and *toronja* (grapefruit).

STREET FOOD

If you are looking to take your taste buds (and digestive system) on an adventure, try sampling some of the food from roadside stands. Of course, it is important to be cautious: Make sure your street meat hasn't been sitting out in the sun for too long. Much street food has been fried into oblivion, so in the short-term, you should be fine; a cholesterol check-up once you return home might not be a bad idea. That being said, be sure to stop by any of the fried food stands called *frituras* to try out famed *tostones*, *chicarrón* (fried pork skin), *arepitas* (fried balls of cornmeal), *quipes* (a fried wheat dumpling with a ground meat center), *yaniqueques* (savory dough that is stretched, then fried) and the ubiquitous *empanada*, sometimes called a *pastelito*, depending on the filling. More established joints selling Styrofoam bins of fried chicken called *pica pollo* can be found every few blocks in any town, usually the cheapest meal around, and often paired with fried rice as a nod to the small but growing Chinese population on the island.

DRINKS

Dominicans are very fond of their *jugos naturales*, or natural juices, perfect as an afternoon treat under the hot Caribbean sun. Skip traditional flavors in favor of tropical *chinola* (passionfruit), *tamarindo* (tamarind), *pera-piña* (pear-pineapple), and *cereza* (Barbados cherry). Just as popular are *batidas*, thick fruit smoothies made with ice, sugar, and condensed milk. Must-try varieties include *zapote* (sapote, a blood orange-colored fruit with a brown skin), *lechosa* (papaya), and *guanábana* (soursop, with a rough green exterior that protects this fruit's soft creamy white flesh and large black seeds).

Despite the heat, tea is also popular, especially around Christmas when *té de gengibre* (ginger tea) is served at meals and cultural gatherings. As mentioned above, hot chocolate and liquid oatmeal are very popular as more economical, in terms of time and money, alternatives for breakfast and dinner.

As the Dominican Republic is a tropical country, it is a good idea to drink lots of water (see Health, p50, for more water information). However, tap water is not potable, even in Western hotels. Only drink bottled or treated water. Most hotels and restaurants will serve bottled or treated water with the meal, but it is best to ask first before taking a sip. A few rivers high in the mountains, like those on the way to Pico Duarte, are potable.

Two drinks that are always potable are beer and rum. Social gatherings are not complete without one of these two Dominican favorites. The most popular national beer, plastered on billboards everywhere, is Presidente Especial. Its main competition is Bohemia (produced by the same parent company as Presidente) and the Brazilian beer Brahma, which tend to be cheaper, but not necessarily of lesser quality. All three of these beers are pilsners. To date, the only widely available dark beer is Ambar. Just as ubiquitous as Presidente is Brugal, the favored hometown Dominican rum. Take it straight out of the bottle, as is done in the countryside, or play it cool by mixing it with Coke and ice. Urban Dominicans turn to Barceló, a smoother and more expensive brand of rum. Other lesser-known brands include Siboney and Macorix. Rum generally comes as both white (*blanco*) and dark, of which there are three kinds: the cheapest and most pungent, *dorado*; a mid-level variety, called *añejo*; and the longest-aged, most expensive, and highest-quality, *extra viejo* or *extra añejo*.

Presidente Beer

Presidente is the most popular drink in the Dominican Republic, and has roots just as lofty. Cervecería Nacional Dominicana (CND), a company that distributes most of the beer and several other drinks available in the DR, is the current owner and producer of Presidente. The beer was first brewed in 1935, with permission from Trujillo to bestow his title on the beverage. Presidente became increasingly popular, and in 1986 CND was taken over by the large Grupo León Jimenes, of museum and cigar fame. The beer itself is a pilsner, with an alcohol content of about five percent. Presidente beer is a true Dominican icon. The brand supports various cultural and artistic events, fairs, and concerts, including a vacation cruise and the Carnaval festivities in La Vega.

Coffee

Even more than beer and rum, coffee is the drink of choice for every citizen across the country. Coffee accompanies every family conversation, midday meal, business meeting, and first date. In the DR, the coffee is distinctive: hot, strong, and exceedingly sweet. Served in small, espresso-sized cups, coffee in the home is often called a *cafecito*, or little coffee. Sugar, another Dominican agricultural star, is added in liberal amounts, but *café con leche* (coffee with milk) can only be found in restaurants. At home or in small shops, coffee is served black, called *solo* or *negro*.

Coffee forms an integral part of the Dominican history and economy. Brought over from Africa in the early 18th century, coffee has become one of the DR's major exports. Cultivation of the sublime bean takes place all across the Dominican highlands, in both the north and the south. Visiting a small farm to see where that *cafecito* came from is well worth a visit to experience a taste of *campesino* life.

Festivals & Holidays

The Dominican Republic is nothing if not a celebratory country. Seemingly every other week a public holiday pops up, releasing the school kids in the streets and parents from work. The entire summer, all of December, and half of March are considered vacation.

For a list of national holidays, see the Quick Reference on page 10 .

Parties and festive occasions are well worth your attendance to get a sense of Dominican way of life. Participate in the festivities, but also be aware that they might not be the safest places.

Fiestas Patronales

Fiestas Patronales represents one of the most raucous celebrations in the country. Patronales is the commemoration, lasting up to nine days, of a specific location's patron saint; every tiny village and big city celebrates Patronales. Music, alcohol, dancing, mass, and midnight processions meld, if somewhat uneasily, during the week. Municipalities plan for months in advance for the most exciting affairs. These include big-ticket live music acts and country-fair style rides, games, and food, usually in the central square. Attending Patronales festivities is fun and informative on Dominican religious and celebratory culture.

Christmas

Snow and tinsel don't make an appearance, but this doesn't mean Christmas in the DR isn't festive. The Christmas season lasts from the beginning of December through the first couple weeks of January. December 24 is when the real celebrations take place, while December 25 tends to be a quieter day where gifts are only exchanged among wealthier families. Very early in the morning on Christmas Eve (called *Noche Buena*) one or more pigs are slaughtered and slow-roasted over an open fire as other food and drink preparations are made. Large, extended families sit down to a big meal, with dancing and drinking to follow. Additional celebrations happen on January 6 for Three Kings Day, supposedly the day that the Three Wise Men visited Jesus, when presents can also be exchanged.

Semana Santa

The Holy Week leading up to Easter (*Pascua*) is another time for big gatherings. Dominicans celebrate by visiting relatives or taking vacation to the beach or river. While this week is the holiest week of the year for practicing Catholics, Dominicans put their own Caribbean twist on the week, combining the pious with the Bacchanalian. Church groups, family reunions, and school field trips all take place this week, as the entire population is on the move. In a nod towards "better safe than sorry," the Dominican government has banned motorized water sports during the week, given that half of the country is in the water at any given time, at times with rum and Coke in hand. Of course, party week has its downside: beaches are packed and hotel rates skyrocket, pricing out many would-be revelers.

Independence Day

Unlike most other former Spanish colonies, the Dominican Republic does not see Independence Day as they day they freed themselves from the yoke of Spanish imperialism, with which the state has had a distinct love/hate relationship. Instead, Independence Day is celebrated February 27, the day that the DR won independence from its neighbor Haiti after a 22-year occupation. As with any independence day, it is packed with carousing and general revelry. Dominicans love parades, and this day is no exception, as parades and their proud participants march along main thoroughfares across the country. It also represents the last, and most boisterous, day of Carnaval festivities.

The Basics

Responsible Travel

The Dominican Republic is blessed with geographic diversity and cultural bounty, where travelers are met with endless options inside the island's shores. For the survival and protection of these assets, we must be reminded that a visit to the DR is much more than a plane ride, hotel reservations and a beach chair. There are many potential, unintended consequences of traveling to a developing country. Therefore, the authors of this book are committed to responsible tourism. We encourage positive interactions with Dominicans and their culture, and work with our readers to ensure the most enjoyable visit possible for both you and the people of the Dominican Republic. We advocate a responsible tourism concept that was set out by the Cape Town Conference as part of the World Summit on Sustainable Development in 2002. Responsible tourism, as decreed by the Conference:

- Generates greater economic benefits for local people and enhances the well-being of host communities, improves working conditions and access to the industry;

- involves local people in decisions that affect their lives and life chances;

- makes positive contributions to the conservation of natural and cultural heritage, to the maintenance of the world's diversity; and

- is culturally sensitive, engenders respect between tourists and hosts, and builds local pride and confidence.

Responsible tourism is reflected in the cooperation between businesses, government, communities, and travelers. We have undertaken to include businesses that reflect, as much as possible, these guidelines, and encourage our readers to do the same. While the expansion of tourism and foreign investment in the Dominican Republic is vitally important to macroeconomic growth, it also represents possible damaging consequences to the environment and society. For the visitor, responsible tourism could mean nothing more than common sense and good manners. Here are some easy ideas as to how to be a responsible traveler:

- Try to pick up some Spanish before leaving, and be understanding when people do not speak English.

- Learn about and be respectful of local culture and practice.

- Patronize businesses that are smaller and locally run.

- Use public transportation when possible or accessible, as a nod to the environment and as an opportunity for cultural exchange.

- Respect local traditions, rules, and laws.

- Dress and act modestly when in rural areas.

- Ask permission to take photographs.

- Purchase locally made products.

- Try to pay the local prices that are provided in this book to avoid creating inflation for locals.

Taking part in responsible tourism is simple, and can improve experiences and livelihoods for everyone involved.

Santo Domingo

In its infancy five hundred years ago, Santo Domingo was the capital of the New World – a launching pad for the transformation of history and a clash of civilizations that today's social scientists could only dream of. Over its storied history, Santo Domingo has been invaded, defeated in battle, and burned to the ground. Nevertheless, a resilient local population never gave up, and Santo Domingo has grown into a proud daughter at the melding of worlds. The capital city's historical apex might have come in the early 1500s, but today it is as vibrant as ever.

Without an understanding of Santo Domingo's long and colorful history, we are lost as to its significance, which led UNESCO to declare this lively city a world heritage site. To truly appreciate Santo Domingo, visitors must immerse themselves in its grand patrimony.

History

Santo Domingo's founding came about only because Christopher Columbus and his crew had failed twice in finding a suitable location to settle. First, the men he left at La Navidad in 1492 fought with local Taínos and were killed; later, the men living at La Isabela were growing restive (and dying at an alarming rate) in an inhospitable and unfriendly locale. Bartolomé, Christopher's brother, led a group of explorers down the middle of the island and set up a fort in 1496 when he reached the southern coast, on the eastern bank of the Río Ozama where it meets the Caribbean Sea. He called the fort Santo Domingo de Gúzman, and though he named the neighboring settlement La Nueva Isabela, the colonists stuck with the name of the fort, shedding the bad memories of the original Isabela.

> The Spanish crown officially recognized Santo Domingo as a city in 1498.

Christopher Columbus quickly ran afoul of powerful interests on two continents. He was removed from his post as governor and replaced by Nicolás de Ovando in 1502. After a destructive hurricane, Ovando moved Santo Domingo to the opposite side of the river, which is where the remains of the colonial city are found today. It was also under Ovando that Santo Domingo began its ascent to New World prominence. Exploration and energy radiated from this city oriented towards discovery and conquest. The Spanish crown established its colonial headquarters here, creating a building boom reflective of the late medieval period – imposing forts of stone and wood and grand, arching cathedrals. Many of the famous Spanish conquistadors spent time in Santo Domingo, planning their journeys, raising funds, and hiring explorers. By 1509, Ovando was gone, replaced by a familiar face, that of Diego Columbus – Christopher's son. Over the course of just a few decades, Santo Domingo came to be the proving ground of many men who set off to claim lands and conquer peoples in the name of the Crown: Ponce de León hopped to Puerto Rico and Florida; Diego Velázquez set off for Cuba; Hernán Cortéz vanquished Mexico; and Vasco Nuñez de Balboa landed on Panama, crossed its isthmus and glimpsed the Pacific for the first time by a European.

Santo Domingo, as the first New World capital, came to be known as the city of firsts. It was home to the first American cathedral, university, paved road, convent, hospital, and factory, among other distinctions. Santo Domingo as a seat of power and prestige, however, was not to last. New and exciting lands farther south drew people and resources away from Hispaniola. The English and French, covetous of Spain's colonial supremacy, moved to take their share. A valiant colonial government built walls and forts to protect the city, but in time Santo Domingo fell, both physically and in importance. In 1586, Santo Domingo sunk to its nadir, as the pirate and English nobleman Sir Francis Drake invaded and sacked the city. He held it for ransom, pillaged with vigor, and left half of Santo Domingo in ashes. The Spanish colony did not recover for many years. France also took advantage of the powerless Spanish authorities by landing on and then claiming the western third of the island, calling it Saint Domingue (present-day Haiti). Santo Domingo itself came under French colonial rule in 1795 as part of a peace treaty between France and Spain.

Six years later, Toussaint L'Ouverture and his revolutionary Haitian army crossed the colonial border and captured Santo Domingo. After the Haitian rebels declared independence from France in 1804, they eventually ceded back to Spain its former colony. The Dominican Republic declared independence from Spain in 1821, with Santo Domingo as its capital, but fell back under Haitian rule from 1822 until 1844. During the repeated invasions, Santo Domingo suffered ignominiously, its buildings torched and inhabitants driven from their homes.

Dominicans finally saw victory in 1844, when independence forces led by Juan Pablo Duarte drove out the Haitian army for the last time. The Dominican Republic became an independent state, and Santo Domingo took its rightful place as a national capital. Of course, this lasted just until 1861, when the feckless military government under General Pedro Santana allowed Spain to re-annex the country. The rest of the country, displeased, supported a rebellion, which then threw off the unwanted neo-colonial yoke in 1865. The city then became home to a restive population under constant threat from outsiders and endured endless political intrigue.

While European prominence in the Caribbean declined, the United States moved in to claim regional supremacy. Ostensibly for the sake of peace and security, the U.S. invaded and occupied the Dominican Republic from 1916 through 1924. Rafael Trujillo, having been trained by Americans with the new Dominican army, soon rose to power, humbly renaming Santo Domingo after himself – calling it Ciudad Trujillo. Under the dictator, the city experienced industrialization and modernization while being stifled under political and cultural repression. The Trujillo regime built businesses and infrastructure, and Santo Domingo attracted a flow of migrants from rural areas. After Trujillo's fall, the U.S. again invaded to quell political instability and protect against a supposed potential communist threat, sending tens of thousands of marines into Santo Domingo in 1965.

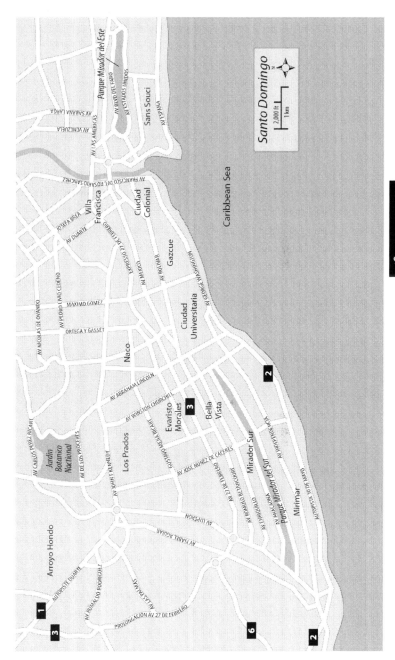

Over the past half-decade, the Dominican capital city has experienced enormous growth, doubling in size several times over. The tight grids of la Zona Colonial have morphed outwards into large, traffic-choked avenues lined with gleaming skyscrapers and trendy bars and restaurants directly alongside horse-drawn carts and vendors hawking everything under the hot Caribbean sun. Endlessly jumbled suburbs to the east, north, and west provide homes for the city's three million inhabitants. Santo Domingo, bursting at its seams, is back in action, thrilling, energetic, and alive.

Transportation

AIR

All international flights to the capital come into **Aeropuerto Internacional Las Americas** (SDQ) (549-0328; 947-2225), located 22 kilometers (14 miles) east of the city on the Caribbean Sea. Licensed taxis from the airport to the center of Santo Domingo cost around RD$1,600, but hotels often offer airport transport; check on this when making reservations. Taxi drivers will try to flag down passengers and give them similar prices, but there is a taxi office immediately to the left when walking outside with a printed price list. A trusted taxi driver used by Peace Corps Volunteers is named Wilson, a friendly character who can pick up passengers in his weathered yet dependable station wagon for prices

Airlines servicing SDQ
Air Canada
Air France
American Airlines
British Airways
Continental
Copa
Delta
Iberia
Jet Blue
KLM
Spirit
U.S. Airways

well below the going rate at the airport (494-7935). Try to call him the day before arrival to arrange for pick-up (Spanish only).

To catch a *guagua* from the airport, go upstairs to Departures. Step outside, turn to the left and walk to the end of the building. This is where the *guaguas* pick up passengers. The vehicle should have a *carro público* seal on the doors. The *guagua* enters downtown through C/ 27 de Febrero, continuing towards C/ Duarte and C/ Paris, which is a major transfer point to pick up *carros públicos* heading towards la Zona Colonial, Gazcue, and other neighborhoods. Tell the driver where you are trying to go, and he will direct you to the best place to get off and transfer.

To get to the airport from Santo Domingo using public transportation, take the bus that leaves from Av. Sabana Larga in Santo Domingo del Este, on the east side of the Ozama River. To get there, catch a Corredor 27 bus anywhere along Av. 27 de Febrero, and then get off at Av. Sabana Larga. Look for the Airport Terminal route, a yellow bus that goes directly to the airport (there is a sign painted on a small corner building, though not easily visible from the street). Be sure to double check with the driver about his route (RD$50).

Another option, albeit a bit more expensive, is to take a Boca Chica bus that generally does not stop at the airport (only a few go to the airport in the morning and afternoon), so you'll have to hop off at the entrance to Route 66 (Sammy Sosa highway) and catch a *motoconcho*. It's not as cost effective as the Sabana Larga route because the *motoconcho* is generally RD$300 and up.

Located in Higüero, Santo Domingo, **Aeropuerto Internacional Dr. Joaquin Balaguer** (AZS – formerly Aeropuerto La Isabela) replaced Aeropuerto Internacional La Herrera in 2006. Still sometimes known as La Isabela, this airport was renamed after former Dominican President Dr. Joaquin Balaguer. Domestic flights, and those to Port-au-Prince, Haiti, depart from this airport. *Located north of Parque Mirador del Norte at the end of Av. Presidente Antonio Guzman Fernández in El Higüero; 826-4019 ext. 112/826-4003*

Airlines servicing AZS
Aerodomca
Air Century
Helidosa
Servicios Aéreos Profesionales (SAP)
Volair

RENTAL CARS

Numerous rental car companies have offices in the Dominican Republic. The best way to find a good deal is to do a simple search on orbitz.com, priceline.com, or any other preferred rental company's direct site.

See the Transportation section (p47) in the introduction of this book for major rental car companies and more information on driving in the Dominican Republic.

BY BUS

As described in the Transportation section (p47), the entire country is well connected by both private bus companies and *sindicatos de guaguas* or bus unions. Below are some of the major private companies that connect Santo Domingo to towns and villages across the DR, as well as important bus stops where *guaguas* congregate before heading to their respective destinations.

Caribe Tours Offering the most comprehensive coverage in cool comfort, Caribe Tours runs bus routes across the entire country, as well as one to Port-au-Prince, Haiti. Check out the website or visit the station in Santo Domingo for destinations and departures times. Prices range from RD$50 to RD$350. The bright, busy, but highly functional central terminal is located on the corner of Av. 27 de Febrero and C/ Leopoldo Navarro. *221-4422; www.caribetours.com.do*

Metro Tours Slightly cleaner, more organized, and more expensive than Caribe Tours, Metro services several cities in the north, including Santiago and Puerto Plata. *Av. Churchill at C/ Francisco Prats Ramírez; 227-0101; www.metroserviciosturisticos.com*

Transporte Espinal Espinal is an additional, though not as highly regarded, coach bus service that runs from Santo Domingo north to Bonao, La Vega, Santiago, and Puerto Plata. In Santo Domingo, buses depart from the downtown terminal (69 Av. Paris between C/ Juana Saltipopa and C/ Dr. Betances), and also at Kilómetro 9, every twenty minutes from 5am to 8:40pm. Prices are similar to the above two lines. *689-9301 or 560-1463; www. transporteespinal.com*

Expreso Bavaro runs a direct coach bus service between the capital and Bavaro, with a stop in La Romana. Departure times in both directions are 7am, 10am, 2pm and 4pm. Arrive early, as the buses tend to sell out quickly, and the company does not sell tickets in advance. *RD$400; Corner of C/ Juan Sánchez Ruíz & Av. Máximo Gómez; Santo Domingo: 682-9670; Bavaro: 552-0771*

Santo Domingo

MAJOR BUS STOPS

Kilómetro 9 (also simply called "Nueve")

Located on kilometer nine of Autopista Duarte north out of Santo Domingo, buses leave every 15 to 30 minutes (except to Cotuí) for the Cibao from this "terminal," which is best described as a loud, chaotic cluster of *guaguas* and street vendors. To get there, all cab drivers know where Kilómetro 9 is and many *carro público* routes service the terminal. In private vehicle, it is located where Autopista Duarte and Av. Luperón meet. *Guaguas* leave Km 9 to the following destinations:

Bonao: (on the Tarea Bus company) RD$115; 1hr; 560-7779

Cotuí: RD$170; leaves every hour; 2hrs

Moca: RD$180; 2hr 15min

San Francisco Macorís: RD$220, 2hrs15min

Santiago: RD$220, 2hr 45min

The same bus services: **La Vega** (RD$150, 1hr 30min), **Villa Tapia** (RD$180, 1hr 45min), **Salcedo** (RD$200, 2hrs), and **Tenares** (RD$200, 2hr 15min).

Parque Enriquillo

Parque Enriquillo is another hub for long-distance *guagua* departures, mostly to the East. Numerous bus collectives are tucked around the surrounding blocks of the park, so the best way to find yours is by asking a local. An important distinction to keep in mind is that nearly all locations offer an *expreso* and a *voladora/caliente*. *Expresos* generally go straight to the location clearly labeled on the windshield, with a few stops in major towns on the way. *Voladoras/calientes* stop wherever a *doña* wishes, so unless traveling to a particular rural area or small town, take the *expreso* and save time. A/C is generally available on the buses, but it's often hard to notice on those packed with passengers' packages and the occasional animal. If you get stuck standing, it may be worth asking when the next bus leaves and wait it out, or else you might be standing for the entire trip.

Baní: RD$85; every 15 min, 5am-10pm; 1.5hrs

Boca Chica: RD$70; *caliente* every 15 min, *expreso* hourly, 6am-8pm; 45min

El Seibo: *Caliente/expreso* RD$160/175; 6am-5:30pm; 2.5hrs; *guaguas* leave from Parque Enriquillo on C/ José Marti between C/ Ravelo and C/ Caracas

Higüey: *Caliente/expreso* RD$150/170; *caliente* every 20 minutes, *expreso* hourly, 6am-7pm; 2.5hrs

Juan Dolio: RD$80; every 30 minutes, 6am-9:30pm; 1hr

La Romana (with stops in Juan Dolio and Boca Chica): *Caliente/expreso* RD$150/160; *caliente* every 20min, *expreso* hourly, 5am-9pm; 2hrs; on C/ Ravelo between C/ Duarte and C/ 19 de Marzo.

Las Galeras: RD$325; 6am, 7:30am, 12pm, 5pm; 4hrs; (see Samaná below for location)

Las Terrenas: RD$285; 8:30am, 9:30am, 11am, 1:40pm and 3pm; 3.5hrs; (see Samaná below for location)

Samaná: RD$275; every 30min 6am-5:30pm with some exceptions in the morning; 3hrs; 129 C/ Barahona near Parque Enriquillo across from the Plaza Lama parking lot

San Cristóbal: RD$90, every 30min, 6am-10pm; 45min; along C/ Duarte

San Pedro de Macorís: RD$90; every 30min 6am-9:30pm; 1hr; along C/ José Martí

Sosúa: RD$320; nine departures 6:30am-3:30pm; 5hr

Pintura

Named for the adjacent paint factory, Pinturas Popular, Pintura is the final departure point for all *guaguas* leaving for the Southwest. Most of them originate in Parque Enriquillo or near Parque Independencia along Calle Bolívar, but all pass through here. Generally the *guaguas* are full by the time they arrive to Pintura and so to ensure a seat, it's best to hop on one closer to their origin. There is no terminal, but rather a jumble of buses waiting for passengers while zealous vendors jump on trying to sell passengers cakes, cheese puffs, and rainbow lollipops the size of a child's head. Pintura is located just west of the Plaza de la Bandera (flag) when traveling along Avenida 27 de Febrero near the entrance to the Highway 6 de Noviembre, which eventually unites with Highway 2/Sánchez. Some of the *guaguas* that pass through Pintura include Azua, Baní, Barahona, Jimaní, Pedernales, San José de Ocoa, and San Juan de la Maguana.

INTRAURBAN TRANSPORT

The motley public transport system in Santo Domingo is comprised of *guaguas* (run by *sindicatos* or unions), green government OMSA (Oficina Metropolitana de Servicios de Autobuses) buses, the new underground Metro, *carro públicos*, and *motos*. Below are some tips to make sense of this organized chaos. Favorite travel stories often find their roots in public transport, so don't be shy, and as Dominicans say, *pégate como anoche* (press yourself [against someone] like last night)!

Ten "Must Know" Dominican Phrases

Pégate como anoche – Press yourself (against someone) like last night: get real close

Anda el Diablo – The devil walks: whoa, damn, that's crazy

Dique (diz que) – It is said: supposedly, I heard people say

Qué lo que? – What is what: what's up?

Ya tú sabe – You already know: You know (what I mean), no need to explain

Y entonce?: So, what do we do?, What's up?, What's going on here?

Bueeeno: Well (then), hmm…: Used as a way to agree or disagree without involving or implicating oneself. For example, if Neighbor A says to Neighbor B, "I think José is stealing mangos from my tree," Neighbor B can respond, "Bueeeno," to participate in the conversation without having to actually agree or disagree.

Dime a ver – Tell me to see: What's up?

Pero ven acá! – But come here!: Oh, come on!, really?!

Ah po' tá bien – Ah well it's fine: OK or you'll see (I'll get you back)

LOCAL BUSES

Known in the Dominican Republic as *guaguas*, these vehicles can be anything from minivans to minibuses to large buses. A trip to Santo Domingo would not be complete without sharing a three-person seat with four others as *bachata* music roars, the *cobrador* yells catcalls to bystanders, and passengers swap *chisme* (gossip) of the day. *Sindicatos de guaguas* (bus driver unions) connect the entire city, but the routes are not posted, so the best way to learn them is by asking a local, who are always eager to assist. *RD$20-40 per trip*

SHARED PUBLIC CARS – *CARROS PÚBLICOS*

Japan's auto trade agreements with the Dominican Republic have resulted in a vast sea of Toyota Corollas in various states of disrepair that make up the *carro público* brigade. The *carros* are easy to spot because of their distinctive green or yellow-painted roofs, the signs affixed to the roofs displaying their route and the windshield and door stickers denoting them as an official *carro público*. *RD$20-40 per trip*

Piratas

Be wary of *piratas* (pirated cars), which function as *carros públicos* but are not registered with the union. *Piratas* often have the same painted roof, but lack the route sign and registration sticker. Unfortunately, robberies can occur in *piratas*, during which the passengers and driver are all in on the plot and demand money and valuables. Don't let this deter you from using *carros públicos*. They are a fast and inexpensive way to get anywhere in the city, and like *guaguas*, give you a unique perspective on the daily lives of Dominicans. Just be sure to look for the official *carro público* insignia.

Public Transport Hand Signals

A key element to understanding the public *guagua* and *carro público* routes are the drivers' hand signals, which are always made outside their left-hand window. These signals often take the place of destination banners or signs on the windshield of these vehicles, though most do have some type of signage. The following signals describe which route that vehicle is taking, how far they will travel and if they are full:

Finger point left or away from the driver: Routes that cover that direction of the city, depending upon which direction the vehicle is heading. For example, if a *carro público* is heading west along Av. Bolivar and the driver points left, he will be turning left/south at some point along his route.

Finger point right or towards the driver: Using the same ideology as the left point, the right point means the vehicle will eventually turn the direction that is to the right of the driver at some point in the route. For example, if a *carro público* is heading west along Av. Bolivar and the driver points to the right, he will be turning right/north at some point along his route.

Finger point straight: this vehicle will continue straight (*derecho*) on its current street for the majority of the route.

Similarly, many savvy Dominicans will use these hand signs to signal to the *carro público* drivers which car routes they want to catch and the drivers will stop in response.

Another key thing to remember is *carro público* etiquette. That front seat may have a seat belt for one, but it is meant to hold two. This means the passenger closest to the driver must negotiate between the emergency break and the remaining bit of seat left by the other passenger. In order to fit four in a three-seater, the rule for the backseat is the third person from the right door must slide forward. Don't worry about forgetting – the driver or the other passengers will scoot any newcomers into place.

OMSA (OFICINA METROPOLITANA DE SERVICIOS DE AUTO-BUSES)

These government sponsored lime green buses are the cheapest travel option (RD$10-15) around the city, but coverage is limited. Stops can be found on major thoroughfares signaled by covered benches. Try to avoid them at rush hour because they get dangerously packed. For route information, visit www.omsa.gob.do.

METRO

The infamous brainchild of President Leonel Fernández is a sleek and silent subway system that puts other lines to shame, at least if rated on aesthetics alone. Currently, there is but one north-south line with few stops, with rides costing RD$25. The metro therefore is rather useless, especially to visitors, until the longer east-west line running from Los Alcarrizos to San Isidro is completed. Construction for this line began in 2009, at a cost estimated above US$1.5 billion. It is not scheduled to be completed for several years. See Transportation (p47) for more information.

TAXIS

For a break from the initially confusing public transport system or for night travel, call up one of the many cab companies in the city. In the name of safety and to prevent getting ripped off, always call a trusted cab company. Do not flag them down on the street. Taxis do not have meters, but rather charge a flat rate of around RD$150. A taxi should never cost more than RD$200, unless the ride reaches outer neighborhoods. Avoid taxis parked near the Conde, as they charge nearly double the going rate. Taxis located

> **Motoconchos**
> Though available to ride in Santo Domingo, the risks far outweigh the benefits. Take public transport or a taxi and leave riding on a motorcycle for the countryside.

at major hotels can charge up to triple the local rate because they claim that other companies are unsafe, which is not true. Be sure to ask the dispatcher the fare to avoid any misunderstanding with the driver before setting out.

One the oldest and most dependable taxi companies, **Apolo Taxi** is available 24/7 (537-0000).

Other trustworthy companies are **Aero Taxi** (686-1212; 829-688-1212) and **Amarillo Taxi** (620-6363; 368-3333).

Gas Stations

Gas stations (called *bombas*) can be found throughout the city. Some of the ones that may come in handy are the Texaco Station on Máximo Gómez across from the Teatro Nacional in Gazcue and the Texaco Station across from Parque Independencia in the Colonial Zone.

Santo Domingo

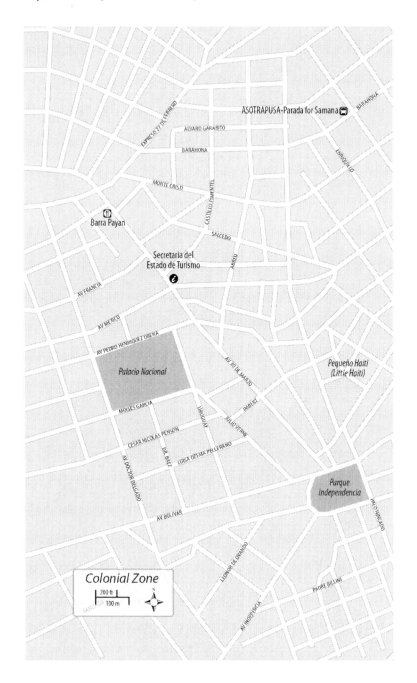

Santo Domingo

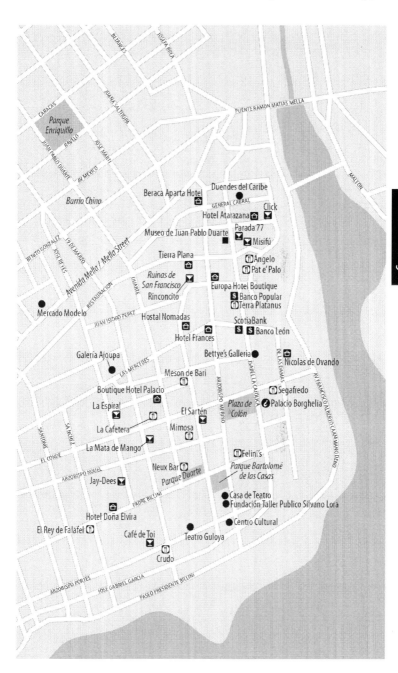

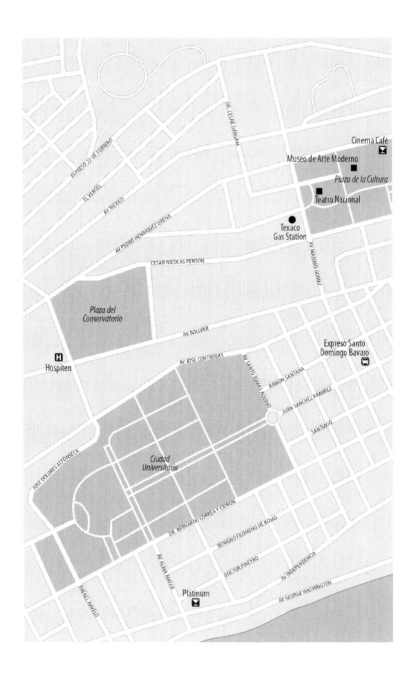

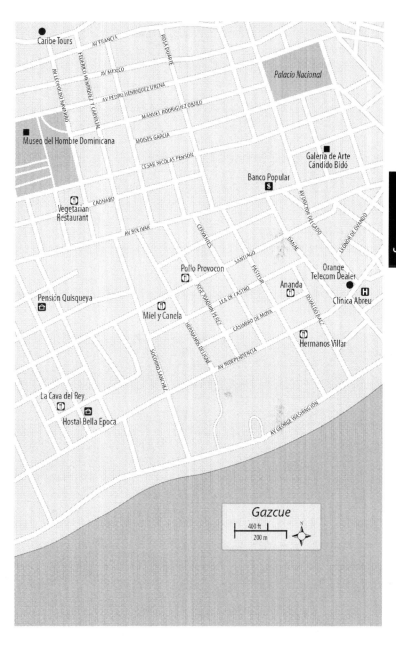

Caribe Tours

AV FRANCIA

ROSA DUARTE

AV MEXICO

AV LEOPOLDO NAVARRO

FEDERICO HENRIQUEZ Y CARVAJAL

AV PEDRO HENRIQUEZ UREÑA

MANUEL RODRIGUEZ OSUJLO

Palacio Nacional

Museo del Hombre Dominicana

MOISES GARCIA

CESAR NICOLAS PENSON

Galería de Arte
Cándido Bidó

Banco Popular
S

Vegetarian
Restaurant

CAONABO

AV DOCTOR DELGADO

LEONOR DE OVANDO

AV BOLIVAR

CERVANTES

Pollo Provocon

SANTIAGO

DANAE

Orange
Telecom Dealer

Ananda

PASTEUR

Pensión Quisqueya

JOSE JOAQUIN PEREZ

LEA DE CASTRO

Clínica Abreu **H**

Miel y Canela

HERMANOS DELIGNE

CASIMIRO DE MOYA

OSVALDO PAEZ

Hermanos Villar

SOCORRO SANCHEZ

AV INDEPENDENCIA

La Cava del Rey

Hostal Bella Epoca

AV GEORGE WASHINGTON

Gazcue

400 ft
200 m

Medical & Emergency Services

Peace Corps Volunteers and embassy employees living in the Dominican Republic use the following centers. English is spoken at these locations and many of the doctors were trained in the United States.

HOSPITALS

Clínica Abreu *Corner of C/ Beller 42 and Av. Independencia; 688-4411; www.clinicaabreu.com.do*

Hospiten *Corner of C/ Alma Máter and Av. Bolívar; 541-3000 (Consults: ext. 2500); Fax: 1 (809) 381-1070; santo.domingo@hospiten.com; www.hospiten.es*

Doctors

Dr. Fernando Contreras *45 C/ Rafael Augusto Sánchez (near C/ Lincoln); Edificio Medical Net; 6th floor; 567-1815; Mon and Tue 9:30am-12:30pm and 3:30pm-6:00pm; Thu 9:30am-6pm*

DENTISTS

Dr. Hector Read *7 C/ Rafael Augusto Sánchez; Naco; 566-7892; Mon, Wed, and Fri, 9am-5pm.*

Dr. Ursula Maratos *8A Pablo Casals, Piantini; 549-3108; Mon- Fri, 9am-5pm.*

Dr. Fauato Gonzalez de Chavez *Av. Winston Churchill and Paseo de los Locutores; Plaza las Americas II, 3rd level suite 6C behind Metro bus station.; 732-9106.; Mon, Tues, Thurs. 9:30am-1:30pm and 3-7pm; Wed and Fri 9:30am-1:30pm*

PHARMACIES

Small pharmacies (*farmacias*) can be found throughout the Zona Colonial and Gazcue, especially concentrated around Clínica Abreu. For a wider selection and later hours of operation, try the following chains with locations throughout the city.

Farmacia Carol There are multiple branches with one in Gazcue at 251 Avenida Bolívar. *689-6000; gazcue@farmaciacarol.com; www.farmaciacarol.com*

Farmacia Farmax's Gazcue branch is located at the corner of Av. Independencia and Dr. Delgado. *333-4444; info@farmax.com.do; www.farmax.com.do*

POLICE

The occasionally helpful tourism police station, **Politur**, is located on the corner of El Conde and C/ José Reyes (689-6464).

The central **National Police** station is located in Gazcue on C/ Leopoldo Navarro between Av. Francia and Av. México. For emergencies, dial 911. *National Police: 682-2151/685-2020; info@policianacional.gob.do; www.policianacional.gob.do*

Banking

Santo Domingo has numerous bank options to serve its growing international population and business industry. Check with your personal bank to see if it has any affiliates in the Dominican Republic to avoid international charges, ATM fees, and to ensure the best exchange rates. Each of the following banks has multiple branches and ATM locations. Below is a list of full service branches in the Zona Colonial and Gazcue; take a quick look at bank websites to locate other ATMs outside this area.

Banco BHD *Corner of Av. Máximo Gómez and C/ Santiago; 243-5516; www.bhd.com.do*

Banco del Progreso *Corner of Av. Independencia and C/ Socorro Sánchez; 378-3212; www.progreso.com.do*

Banco León *65 C/ Isabel La Católica by C/ Las Mercedes, Zona Colonial; 476-2000; www.leon.com.do*

Banco Popular *357 Av. Bolivar, Gazcue; 682-2343; or C/ Isabel Católica and C/ Hostos, Zona Colonial; www.bpd.com.do*

BanReservas *201 C/ Isabela la Católica, Zona Colonial; 960-2000; www.banreservas.com.do*

ScotiaBank *(reciprocal relationship with Bank of America) C/ Las Mercedes and C/ Isabel la Católica, Zona Colonial; 689-5151; 689-5152; www.scotiabank.com/do*

Wells Fargo *Representative Office: Torre Piantini, Suite # 702; Avenida Abraham Lincoln and Gustavo Mejía Ricard Ensanche Piantini; 412-0557; www.wellsfargo.com*

Communication

Below are the nearest offices or kiosks for each cell company in the Zona Colonial and Gazcue or their central headquarters. See Communication section (p57) for more details.

TriCom (Codetel) *www.tricom.net; Comercial Office Lope de Vega; Lope de Vega, no 95, Naco; 476-6000; Mon – Fri: 8:00am - 6:00pm; Sat: 8:30am - 1:00pm; Teller Services: Mon– Fri: 8:00am - 7:00pm; Sat: 8:30am - 2:00pm*

Claro (Verizon) *www.claro.com.do; Claro: Bella Vista Mall; Av. Sarasota, Bella Vista Mall, 2nd floor; Mon-Fri: 8am- 8pm; Sat: 9am-8pm; Sun & Holidays: 10am- 2pm; Claro: Acrópolis; Av. Winston Churchill, Plaza Acrópolis; Mon-Fri 9am-9pm; Sat: 10am- 9pm; Sun & Holidays: 11am-6pm*

Orange *www.orange.com.do; Orange: El Conde; 688-8101; 829-723-8901; Corner of El Conde and Av. Duarte, Supermercado Jumbo; Orange: Zona Colonial; 221-3997; 829-770-2823; 402 C/ Arzobispo Nouel (near corner of Pina); Panadería Colonial Antigua, Casa Pérez; Gazcue; Corner of Av. Independencia and Dr. Delgado, Farmax.; 412-8434*

Viva *www.viva.com.do; Call Center: 503-7500; Toll-free: 1-809-200-7500; Viva Winston Churchill; 73 Av. Winston Churchill near Max Henríquez Ureña, Piantini; Mon-Fri: 8am-7pm; Sat: 9am-6pm*

INTERNET

This website has a great list of universities, plazas, restaurants, and cafés with free Wi-Fi: http://duarte101.com/2007/06/26/wi-fi-gratis-en-santo-domingo-hotspots/

Here are some free Wi-Fi favorites:

Centro Cultural de España (see p104) Also has computers. *Calle Arzobispo Meriño & Calle Arzobispo Portes; Colonial Zone; 686-8212*

Segafredo (see p83) *El Conde & C/ Las Damas; Colonial Zone*

Thesaurus (see Bookstores, p109) *Ave. Abraham Lincoln & C/ Sarasota; 508-1114*

POST OFFICE

Below are post office locations in and around the Colonial Zone, as well as the central office. For all locations, visit: www.inposdom.gob.do (Spanish).

Santo Domingo, Central Office *C/ Héroes de Luperón at C/ Rafael Damirón; 534-5838; 533-1407*

Ciudad Nueva *510 C/ Arzobispo Portes at C/ El Número; 333-6987*

Zona Colonial *103 C/ Isabel la Católica*

If mailing something valuable or time sensitive, try these mail couriers:

Mail Boxes Etc. *10 Ave. Tiradentes, Naco; 333-2002; Fax: 809-412-2442*

UPS Dominicana, S.A. *Km 25 Autopista Las Americas; 549-2777; 1-809-200-5177 (toll free); Fax: 809-549-9561*

UPS Customer Centers *Plaza Andalucia II, Local 47-A, Ave. Abraham Lincoln*

Tourism Offices

Secretaría del Estado de Turismo *Av. Mexico & 30 de Marzo; 221-4660; www.dominicana.com.do; Weekdays: 9am-4pm*

Palacio Borghelia, Office of Tourism *103 C/ Isabel la Católica, Parque Colón; 686-3858; Weekdays: 9am-3pm*

For more information about Santo Domingo, visit the Santo Domingo Sustainable Tourism Cluster's website at www.gosantodomingo.travel or contact their office by calling 687-8217.

Eat

Dining out in Santo Domingo runs from styrofoam trays piled high with rice and beans, to fine-dining, multi-course meals. On the surface, the city's culinary options may appear to be dominated by the Dominican starchy staples, but the city's diverse expat population, as well as some inventive locals, has contributed to a tremendous variety of restaurants.

The "Eat" Section is divided by both price (Plato del Día, Inexpensive, Mid-Range, Upscale) and location (Zona Colonial, Gazcue, El Centro) to accommodate all travelers' wallets and tastes. Though the city is peppered with restaurants, the Zona Colonial, Gazcue, and El Centro have the most diverse and quality representations of what Santo Domingo has to offer. Steep competition due to the tremendous volume of food options helps maintain the high quality and ingenuity of dining establishments in Zona Colonial. These attributes, along with the stunning and romantic backdrops of the colonial city, particularly in the evening, make la Zona Colonial a requirement for all visitors.

Just a short walk or ride west from la Zona Colonial is the bordering residential neighborhood of Gazcue. Shady tree-lined streets and Trujillo-era mansions mixed with tasteful middle class homes contribute to Gazcue's charm, making it a lovely place to take a stroll while contemplating its few (but solid) casual or upscale dining options.

Further west, from Avenida Tiradentes and on, is the area the writers have loosely defined as "El Centro." El Centro incorporates various *ensanches* or neighborhoods, including Piantini and Naco, which have exploded in the last few decades with high-rises and chic restaurants. Though there are some affordable food choices in El Centro, the majority of the restaurants cater to the wealthy clientele that live in these neighborhoods and so the menus – and the prices – seem imported. For those who want authentic Dominican food, El Centro is certainly not the place to start, but it is perfect for a dressy night on the town amongst Santo Domingo's rich and beautiful.

TOP PLACES FOR A *PLATO DEL DÍA*

The *plato del día* is a set lunch special that revolves around the much-loved *bandera dominicana*: rice, beans, and chicken. Many places also have options that include other meats and side dishes; all for an established price, starting at around RD$100. *¡Qué rico!*

Zona Colonial

Esquisiteces Virginia Seafood salad, stewed eggplant, and empanadas are among the mouthwatering accompaniments to the consistently delicious *plato del día* served at this inviting neighborhood joint. Come hungry, because there is a case full of irresistible baked goods to end the meal. *RD$70-250; 102 C/ Santomé and C/ Arzobispo Portes; 333-9001*

Mimosa Family-owned-and-operated for 31 years, Mimosa serves up a solid *bandera dominicana* well as other Dominican favorites such as *arepitas* (fried cornmeal fritters). The menu also includes some international options. *RD$130-250; 51 C/ Arz. Nouel between Calles Duarte and Hostos; 866-0911; Mon-Sat 10am-7pm*

Gazcue

Pollo Provocón Ask any local – this is the best rotisserie chicken in town. Golden brown on the outside, moist on the inside, and with a splash of the special *wasakaka* sauce makes this *pollo* a nationwide favorite. The midday hours are packed with locals taking advantage of a superb meal deal that includes all of the classics: either dark or white meat, a choice of *moro* or rice and beans, a side of boiled bananas or *yuca*, a small salad, and on good days, *arepitas*, or fried sweet plantains. Meals here are not complete without a rich papaya *batida* or a fresh squeezed tamarind juice. Provocón also has branches in other major cities like Santiago and Puerto Plata. A top choice for lunching locals is the outlet in Gazcue because of the large, breezy patio seating under a leafy canopy of beautiful trees. *RD$100-200;C/ Santiago and C/ José Joaquín Pérez, Gazcue; 238-5125*

Miel y Canela Miel y Canela adds a gourmet twist on the typical plate of the day. This popular lunch spot for professionals has a varied menu offering fish, chicken, and meat, as well as delicious side items like ripe plantain casserole or lasagna, and a great selection of vegetables and salads. Don't forget to order a freshly squeezed glass of passion fruit or another bright tropical juice. *RD$100-200; C/ Santiago 302, Gazcue; 682-1204*

INEXPENSIVE

Zona Colonial

Neux Bar This closet-sized restaurant uses its space and diners' pesos efficiently. Serving up a simple Mexican menu on ping-pong paddles, this local favorite is perfect for grabbing a cheap bite while admiring the owner's Dali-inspired clock paintings. If there is no space on the benches, order to go and enjoy the filling burritos or quesadillas next door in Parque Duarte. *RD$100-200; C/ Duarte 53 between C/ Padre Billini and C/ Arzobispo Nouel; 6pm-12am Mon-Thu, 6pm-2am Fri-Sat*

 Barra Payan It's tough to get any more local than this 24-hour diner serving up hot-pressed sandwiches, freshly squeezed juices, and *batidas*. Try a *pierna con gouda* sandwich (shredded pork with Gouda cheese) or a *derretido* (grilled cheese with tomato) alongside a *batida* with "Ca," which is Payan's shorthand for Carnation milk. If arriving in a car, roll down the window and a waiter comes by 1950s-style, minus the roller skates. *RD$ 100-200; C/ 30 de Marzo 140; Colonial Zone; 689-6654; Everyday 24 hours*

La Cafetera Follow the aroma of freshly ground coffee into this watering hole for Dominican artists, philosophers and lovers of debate. Sound like a regular and order a *medio pollo* (espresso with steamed milk) or a grilled ham and cheese sandwich with a juice or *batida* made before your eyes. *253 El Conde at C/ Duarte; no phone; Mon-Sat 8am-11pm, Sun 10am-5pm*

Gazcue

 Hermanos Villar This busy and celebrated deli, bakery, and restaurant offers several dining areas: the hustle and bustle of a diner in the front, a quiet and relaxed environment in the back, and dining al fresco in the gazebo. They all offer the same menu, but service is fastest in the front. Try the *sancocho* (meat stew) or their rotisserie chicken with *pastelón de berenjena* (eggplant casserole). Finish off the meal with a *cafecito* and a treat from the bakery such as *dulce de coco y leche* (coconut and milk candy). *RD$100-300; 312 Av. Independencia at C/ Pasteur; 682-1433; Mon-Sun 8am-12am*

Ensanches and Barrios

When asking for directions in Santo Domingo, it is always helpful to know both the neighborhood and streets' names because locals generally know places by geographical markers or neighborhoods verses the official address. *Ensanche* and *barrio,* both meaning neighborhood, are used to describe locations because the same streets names are often used more than once or are not terribly memorable or descriptive, such as the commonly used Calle A or Calle 1. The word *ensanche* is typically used for the newer and often wealthier neighborhoods in the center and western parts of the city like Ensanche Piantini or Naco, whereas *barrio* has a more humble connation and its residents tend to share a more collective spirit.

El Centro

Los Huaraches Los Huraches offers the surprisingly hard to find combination in Santo Domingo of authentic Mexican flavor and reasonable prices. With vegetarian options to tacos or burritos filled with succulent *ropa vieja* (pulled beef) or well-seasoned chicken, this place is sure to please any crowd. *RD$150-300; C/ David Ben Gurion near Winston Churchill, Paraíso; 566-4023; Mon-Sun: 4:30pm-11:30pm*

Baladi Located in the owner's casual home in Ensanche Julieta, this Lebanese restaurant is by far one of the most authentic in the city, serving halal meat butchered by the owner himself and imported Lebanese wines, beers and other specialty products like shanklish – a tangy fermented goat cheese – or Arak – a traditional grape-based aperitif. The Baladi Mix – an assortment of hummus, baba ghanoush, shanklish, labneh (a yogurt herb dip), and pita – is perfect for sharing. The chef features weekly specials based on the fish or vegetable of the season, but the regular offerings are consistently delicious, such as the lamb shawarma – succulent, marinated cubes of lamb dressed with yogurt, tomatoes, parsley and onions and wrapped in a warm pita. *RD$150-320; 19B C/ David Masalles, Ens. Julieta; 567-0070; baladirestaurant@gmail.com; Tues-Sun 12pm-12am*

 La Cuchara de Madera Decadent and irresistible, this café with two locations in the neighborhood of Piantini is known for its sumptuous desserts such as Marifer cheesecake with Oreos, pralines and Nutella, or mango and passion fruit mousse. The ten-layer chocolate avalanche cake, with rich chocolate ganache and covered with whipped cream and white chocolate, curbs any craving and the fresh-squeezed juices or espresso drinks are the perfect pairing. *RD$60-350; 63 José Amado Soler and Federico Gerardino; 683-6544; or 86 Freddy Prestol Castillo near Max Henríquez Ureña, Piantini; 566-2420; info@lacucharademadera.com.do; lacucharademadera.com.do; Mon-Sat 8am-7:30pm, Sun 10am-5pm*

La Vecindad This small Mexican restaurant quickly developed a loyal following for its traditional and artisanal tacos. Though the menu is varied, offering interesting combinations such as quesadillas with squash blooms or Caldo Loco (a beef and shrimp soup), patrons cannot leave here without trying a few tacos stuffed with an array of ingredients from ribs or chorizo to fish. *RD$150-350; Corner of Ave. Tiradentes and Cub Scout, Plaza Damaso, Naco; 633-2121*

MID-RANGE

Zona Colonial

El Rey de Falafel This charming Middle Eastern restaurant has come a long way from its roadside stand roots. The Israeli owner gutted an old colonial home, knocked down the ceiling and created a terraced, open-air dining room. Its walls are painted a crisp white, adorned with Haitian and Dominican metal sculpture. Dine under the stars on falafel or grilled kebabs while enjoying a local brew. The restaurant also has a full-service bar and a gallery supporting local artists on the second floor. *RD$200-450; 352 C/ Padre Billini and C/ Sánchez, Colonial Zone; 688-9714; Sun-Thurs. 5pm-12am, Fri-Sat 5pm-2am*

Segafredo Whether it's for Segafredo's thin crust pizzas, simple but flavorful pastas, or the daily two-for-one happy hour, patrons regularly flock to this Italian restaurant/bar. During the day, this is one of the few spots that allows lovers of café culture to read while sipping an espresso in the umbrella covered outdoor tables. Owning facing buildings along El Conde, the northern building extends out into a softly lit patio with chez lounges and arching tropical plants great for a romantic evening rendezvous or a spirited group of friends. *RD$200-500; 54 El Conde near C/ de las Damas; 685-4440; Facebook: Segafredo Caffe' Zona Colonial; info.segafredo@gmail.com; daily 11am-12am and until 2am on weekends.*

El Centro

Aka In a city where plantain and chicken wrapped in seaweed is called sushi, this Japanese restaurant is a godsend for sushi purists. Try the sashimi platter featuring a variety of fish along with conch shell and scallops or any of the traditional rolls. *RD$200-400; C/ 50 Max Henríquez Ureña near Av. Lope de Vega, 2nd floor; 732-9502; www.red.com.do; Sun-Thurs 12pm-12am (until 1am Fri-Sat)*

Chino de Mariscos With over two decades in business, this Cantonese restaurant has won loyal customers with its authentic and flavorful cuisine such as hot pots with tofu and seafood or baked lobster with ginger and scallions. On Sunday, Chino de Mariscos features dim sum, including a large array of dumplings, eggrolls and other delectable Chinese finger foods. *RD$70-480; 38-A Av. Sarasota, Bella Vista; 533-5249; Thurs-Sun 11am-12am and Fri-Sat 10am-1am*

La Dolcerie Pastels and Victorian accents bedeck this upper crust café and bistro serving international fare including pastas and sandwiches along with French pastries and desserts. A sweet and savory special is Natilie's Favorite Crepe with goat cheese, dates, prosciutto, four-cheese sauce, toasted nuts, arugula, and truffle oil. The over-the-top salads – such as the Lady Blue with blue cheese, grilled chicken, bacon, and mandarin oranges dressed with truffle and passion fruit vinaigrette – are big enough for a meal. For the especially hungry, try one of the generous entrees such as the Volcán Mixto, a juicy filet of beef paired with grilled chicken and blue cheese mashed potatoes. *RD$195-595; 20 C/ Rafael Augusto Sánchez, Piantini; 338-0814; ladolcerie@gmail.com; Everyday 7:30am-12am*

UPSCALE

Zona Colonial

Angelo Offering one of the best rooftop views in the La Zona Colonial, Angelo is perfect for sipping a refreshing glass of pinot grigio as the sun sets over the Río Ozama – or for an authentic Italian feast. Angelo's thin crust pizzas are a delicious, economical alternative to the pasta and meat dishes. While a bit overpriced, this place is worth visiting simply for their wacky décor of baroque style furniture, crystal chandeliers, zebra-patterned upholstery, and bold color scheme. *RD$400-700; 21 C/ Atarazana; Zona Colonial; 686-3586; Sun-Thurs 12pm-12am, Fri-Sat 12pm-2am*

Café Bellini A candlelit tropical garden gives way to this whimsical Italian restaurant specializing in handmade pasta, such as the Tris di Ravioli della Casa, pumpkin, beet and spinach raviolis harmoniously brought together in a vine-ripe tomato sauce. Take time to peruse the Italian owner's impressive modern art collection ranging from a gargantuan, mirrored sculpture of Italy, doubling as a wine rack to the equally quirky yet functional light fixtures. The Filete alla Bellini – an impeccably prepared cut of beef served in a truffle cream sauce – is beyond decadent especially when followed by a chocolate flan soaked in Amaretto. *RD$450-980; Corner of C/ Arzobispo Meriño and C/ Padre Billini in Plazoleta Padre Billini; 686-3387; Tues-Sat 12pm-12am, Mon dinner only, closed Sun*

Mesón de Bari Known for its *cangrejo a la criolla* (Dominican-style crab) or *chivo guisado* (stewed goat), this restaurant marries down-home Dominican cooking with a fine dining atmosphere. The walls are covered with splashes of color, adorned with numerous paintings by local artists. For a more intimate dining experience, go straight to the second floor. Or stay on the first with the elegant yet lively locals. Lucky diners can catch a live band playing Cuban *son* music, usually on Thursday evenings after 9pm. *RD$300-600; 302 C/ Hostos and C/ Salome Ureña; 687-4091; Everyday 12pm-12am*

La Bricola Though its enchanting setting in a colonial coral and brick home softened by tropical plants and twinkling lights may have played a role in this Italian restaurant's long-term success, the artfully prepared food is what keeps patrons coming back for decades. Details such as the herbed butter served with the fresh baked bread before a timbale of crawfish, frisée greens, avocado and orange sections are what set this restaurant apart from other upscale Italian restaurants. Delighting the senses are such second courses as the Ravioli Agnolloti – hand-rolled ravioli delicately stuffed with minced sirloin in sage butter and a red wine reduction – or the Risotti Briciola – shrimp and arugula folded into creamy risotto. *RD$450-1200; Corner of Arz. Meriño and Padre Billini; 688-5055; labricola@codetel.net.do; www.labricola.com.do; Mon -Sat 12-3pm and 6pm-12am*

Pat e' Palo Soak up the ambience of Plaza España and enjoy the international fare of this pirate-themed restaurant that offers a range of salads and pasta, as well as meat and fish dishes. If dining on a Friday evening, sit outside and enjoy the free music and dance performances in Plaza España. *RD$400-700; 25 C/ Las Atarazanas, Plaza España; Sun-Thurs 12pm-12am, Fri-Sat 12pm-2am*

Gazcue

La Cava del Rey This quaint French restaurant is tucked away in a quiet, upper-middle class residential neighborhood. Try one of the reasonably priced and delicious pastas or crepes, or splurge on a filet mignon paired with cabernet sauvignon. Around the corner is a French bakery with excellent *pan au chocolat*, paninis, fresh-squeezed juices, and espresso, as well as a few specialty items like French wines, homemade pasta, and pâté. *RD$300-500; C/ Pedro Ignacio Espaillat and C/ Abelardo Rodríguez Urbaneta; Gazcue; 412-7918; Everyday 6pm-12am*

El Centro

Caffé Milano After embracing the brassy décor exemplified by the red Porsche showcased in the entrance window and photos of supermodels toying with cigars plastered around the bar, this exquisite Italian dining experience begins. Inventive combinations – like homemade pasta made with cacao sautéed with mussels, zucchini, and coconut or red bell pepper tagliatelle served with rabbit, olives, and tomatoes – make this restaurant anything but the run of the mill Italian cucina. *RD$400-995; 11 Av. Tiradentes; 540-1572; 540-3000; caffemilano@codetel.net.do*

Mesón de la Cava Featuring an international menu of hearty seafood and meat dishes such as juicy rib eye steak or Spanish paella and an extensive wine list, Mesón de la Cava's patrons flock here not only for the food, but also for its unique setting in an underground cave. Locals and tourists have enjoyed the restaurants' atmosphere since 1967, but the cave enjoys a rich history. It has supposedly been utilized by several groups: Taínos; buccaneers hiding out before sacking colonial Santo Domingo; guerillas (known as *gavilleros*) fighting against the foreign occupation in 1930; and troops with the Organization of American States, who used the cave as a warehouse during the U.S. occupation of 1965. *RD$400-800; 1 Av. Mirador del Sur, Bella Vista; 533-2818; www.elmesondelacava.com; Daily 12pm-12am*

Cane Cane's lively happy hour (weekdays 5pm-8pm) featuring the best mojito in town, and sleek yet island influenced interior draw Dominican young professionals looking to unwind after work. Nibble on delicious Latin fusion finger foods such as fried plantain cups topped with juicy *ropa vieja*, or try the indulgent main plates like the Napoleon layered with creamy shrimp and crab or the beef filet encrusted with macadamia nuts. *RD$300-700; 1059 Av. Abraham Lincoln, Piantini; 368-2200; Sun-Thurs 12pm-1am, Fri-Sat 12pm-3am*

Marocha One of the only places serving an authentic brunch in the city, expats and well-traveled Dominicans alike frequent this international bistro to join in the weekend tradition of make-your-own omelettes, eggs Benedict, and buttermilk pancakes for lunch. Weekdays, young professionals take advantage of the two for one bottles of Cava until 8pm while sharing the house bruschetta – a mozzarella-filled calzone topped with bruschetta – followed by one of their world tour entrees from Pad Thai to Moroccan glazed chicken breast or braised short ribs. *RD$225-800; 124 Av. Gustavo Mejía Ricart and Manuel de Jesús Troncoso, Piantini; 473-4191; marocha.rd@codetel.net.do; Daily 7am-12am*

 Gallo Pinto Restaurante & Bar Upon entering this gourmet Latin-inspired restaurant, the first thing to catch the eye is a wall-sized chalkboard illustrated with the bar's latest cocktail creations including the popular Ron Romero, a refreshing cocktail with rum, ginger, lemon juice, and honey, garnished with rosemary. Red industrial fixtures mix with slim black furniture and wood paneling create a casual yet funky atmosphere to enjoy some *antojos* (appetizers) like duck taquitos or an inventive salad like chicken with artichokes, avocado, pistachios, and strawberries. Or try some of the main plates, like beef tenderloin and gnocchi tossed in pistachio pesto. *RD$225-795; Plaza Dorada, Corner of C/ Manuel de Jesus Troncoso and Roberto Pastoriza, Piantini; 567-4345; gallopintofood@gmail.com*

VEGETARIAN

Crudo Crudo is an organic vegetarian restaurant and natural products store. The restaurant prepares salads, juices, and vegetarian dishes, including a reasonably priced *plato del día*. The store carries natural remedies, vitamins, incense, and aromatherapy oils that waft outside into the street. Dr. Felix F. Casas, doctor of holistic medicine, owns and operates the establishment. *RD$150-250; 152 C/ Arzobispo Portes near C/ 19 de Marzo, Colonial Zone; 689-0796; Mon-Sun 12pm-7pm*

Delicias Integrales at El Instituto de Medicina Inovativa y Bioquímica Funcional Though the selection is limited at this doctor-owned restaurant, the daily options are always quality. Try the *plato del día*, which generally comes with brown rice, beans, salad and a side such as vegetarian lasagna or veggie meatballs for RD$140. Beverages are not served save for hot anise tea, but there is a small health food store next door that sells juice and water. If a hint of cinnamon wafts through the air, ask for the delectable cinnamon bread (*pan de canela*), generally sold out within minutes of leaving the oven. *RD$140-200; 31 C/ Caonabo between Calles Felix M. del Monte and Leopoldo Navarro, Gazcue, 947-8312; Mon-Fri, lunch only*

Ananda Vegetarian Restaurant/Centro Cultural Yoga Devanand This tucked-away yoga studio and vegetarian eatery offers a large variety for reasonable prices. Meals are charged per item, so take a minute to check out the options in the buffet line before being shuffled along by the working professional crowd that frequents the spot. Vegan options are available, as well as yoga and vegetarian cooking classes. *RD$100-200; 7 C/ Casimiro de Moya, Gazcue; 628-7153; Open for all meals Mon-Sat until 10pm and Sun until 3pm*

Raíces An unlikely spot to find an excellent variety of vegetarian-only options, this Seventh-Day Adventist Church has a cafeteria open to all. There is no sign, so keep a look out for people entering through the glass doors in the middle of the complex. There's also a health food store on the far right of the church that is open weekdays and on Sundays 9am to 1pm. *RD$80-150; C/ Juan Sánchez Ramírez near the corner of Av. Máximo Gómez, in the Adventist; Church complex around the corner from the Supermercado Nacional and across from the Embassy of Haiti; Mon-Fri 8am- 3pm, Sun 11am-3pm, Closed Sat*

Jardín Verde This organic, Chinese-vegetarian restaurant offers a pleasant patio to sip on inventive Eastern teas infused with tropical fruits and flowers while waiting for one of Chef Suzuki's meat-free creations, such as chontz, a savory rice-based pastry stuffed with Chinese mushrooms and garnished with peanuts. Handmade noodles served with tofu, bok choy, and carrots in a flavorful brown sauce serve as an excellent way to follow any of the scrumptious starters, which include fried mushrooms or vegetable eggrolls. *RD$150-300; 18A Salvador Sturla, Naco; 565-2084; Mon-Sun 11am-10pm*

Sleep

BUDGET

Gazcue

Pensión Quisqueya Located on a residential street, this hostel is the cheapest accommodation that can be found in the city, and therefore not the classiest. The shared bedrooms have fans, which help scare off swarms of mosquitoes. Some private rooms have A/C and occasionally hot water. There is a common area with a TV where guests will often find Peace Corps Volunteers and the occasional traveler congregating. But other than that, this is a place strictly to rest your head at night. *RD$275 per bed or RD$1200 and up for private rooms; C/ 201 Cayetano Rodríguez at C/ Juan Sánchez Ramírez, Gazcue, 687-6037*

 Hostal Bella Epoca This white stucco and Spanish tile house-turned-budget-hotel offers clean, comfortable rooms of varying sizes just a few blocks south of Pensión Quisqueya. A communal kitchen and water cooler makes this a popular place for a convenient, affordable, and comfortable stay in the capital. The hotel has both indoor and outdoor courtyards that are brightly painted and full of natural light – perfect spots for an afternoon coffee or late-night chat. *RD$1000-1500; C/ 3 Cayetano Rodríguez, Gazcue; 221-1271; www.hostalbellaepoca.com Amenities: A/C, hot water, TV, Wi-Fi*

Hotel Residence This budget hotel has free Wi-Fi and relatively consistent hot water (a difficult commodity to find among budget hotels), not to mention roof access to enjoy the night sky. If the hotel is at capacity, there are two other similar budget hotels across the street, all of which are a quick walk to the Zona Colonial and the Plaza de Cultura. *RD$600-1200; 62 C/ Danae between Calles Santiago and Castro, Gazcue; 412-7298; www.hotelresidencia.com*

Zona Colonial

Bettye's Galleria Offering shared dorm-style rooms as well as a beautifully decorated private room, this budget hotel pays attention to detail and design. American art dealer and hotel owner Bettye displays her varied collection in each of the rooms, covering the colonial walls with bright Dominican and Haitian artwork. Be sure to check out the adjoining gallery for unique souvenirs. Rates include tax and breakfast. *RD$800 for dorm beds RD$1500 for private rooms; 163 C/ Isabel La Católica by C/ Luperón, Plaza Toledo; 688-7649*

MID-RANGE

Zona Colonial

Tierra Plana Owned by a hip Spanish and Dominican couple, this hotel, with clean and modern décor, lends an enchanting contrast to the ruins of San Francisco located directly across the street. Head up to the roof for an aerial view of the ruins and the Zona Colonial. Room rates include continental breakfast. *US$35-50; 357 C/ Hostos, across from Las Ruínas de San Francisco and down the stone pathway from the Colmado de Rinconcito; 686-0120; 444-4452 (cell); tierraplanacoolhostal@hotmail.com; www.tierraplana.com*

Hostal Nomadas Located on historical Calle Hostos, a backdrop for movies depicting mid-20th century Havana, this hostel offers reasonably priced private rooms on a unique street. A hookah bar serving Middle Eastern fare is set up on the roof. Try hibiscus iced tea and a falafel sandwich or share a mixed platter including hummus, baba ganoush, falafel, and tabouleh. *US$28-85; 299 C/ Hostos near C/ Las Mercedes; 689-0057; info@hostalnomadas.com; www.hostalnomadas.com; Amenities: A/C, fan, hot water, fridge, Wi-Fi, safe in reception, security guard, camera surveillance*

Europa Hotel Boutique Boasting an excellent view of the Zona Colonial from its rooftop bar and restaurant, Europa Hotel Boutique's rooms have maintained the original ornate tiled floors dating from the 19th century contrasting the hotel's modern décor. The majority of the rooms are small, making an upgrade worthwhile, especially to the corner rooms, which have private balconies and are significantly more spacious. *US$70-150; Corner of Arzobispo Meriño and Hostos, Colonial Zone; 286-0005; europahb@hotmail.com; www.europah.com*

LUXURY

Zona Colonial

Hotel Atarazana Designed with impeccable taste and a sense of whimsy, Hotel Atarazana is a true boutique hotel. Each bathroom is a work of art, incorporating handmade fixtures and thoughtfully selected tiles of coral, marble, and shells. The German owners designed and carved the wooden bed frames, giving each room an individual and creative touch. The back patio, lush with tropical plants and the sound of a gurgling fountain, is a lovely spot to enjoy one of the bar's rum drinks or in a hammock on the rooftop deck with a view of Plaza España and the Río Ozama. *US$80-100; 19 C/ Vicente Celestino Duarte; 688-3693; info@hotel-atarazana.com; www.hotel-atarazana.com; Amenities: hot water, A/C, fan, Wi-Fi, computer with internet, bar, solar panels, breakfast included*

Hotel Doña Elvira This hotel, housed in a 16th century colonial home, has 15 comfortable rooms, some with exposed brick walls, surrounding a stone patio with a century old mango languidly shading the pool. The reception area encapsulates the hotel's charm with original mahogany beams supporting the vaulted ceiling and warm-toned floor tiles decorated with Alhambra-inspired stars and embellishments. *US$90-170; 207 Padre Billini, Colonial Zone; 853-1113; reservations@dona-elvira.com; www.dona-elvira.com; Amenities: A/C, fan, hot water, TV, restaurant, Wi-Fi, pool, Jacuzzi, laundry service, 24-hr security, room service, massage, breakfast included*

Hotel Frances Also located in a 16th century colonial home, this UNESCO World Heritage site overflows with character and charm. Dine on decadent international fare or sip exquisitely mixed drinks in the romantic central courtyard lit only with twinkling white strands and candles in the evening. The small hotel with just 19 rooms is enchantingly Old World in a New World setting. *US$150-200 (see website for online specials); C/ Las Mercedes & Arzobispo Meriño, 685-9331; H2137-GM@accor.com; hotel-frances-santo-domingo.com; www.mgallery.com; Amenities: A/C, Wi-Fi, cable*

Boutique Hotel Palacio Occupying the former residence of Dominican President Buenaventura Báez Méndez, Boutique Hotel Palacio draws from the building's colonial origins, using period pieces throughout and decadent furnishing such as red velvet curtains, iron chandeliers, and grand portraits of conquistadors and their bejeweled spouses. *US$65-114; 106 C/ Duarte at C/ Salome Ureña; 682-4730; hotelpalacio@codetel.net.do; www.hotel-palacio.com; Amenities:A/C, TV, café, bar, Wi-Fi, computers in suites, laundry service, safe, minibar, parking garage, gym, spa, sauna*

 Hotel Nicolás de Ovando Hotel Nicolás de Ovando is poshest hotel in Zona Colonial, with its sleek and modern rooms, the beautiful people lounging by the pool overlooking the Río Ozama, and the delightful courtyard restaurant. This watering hole for the glamorous combined the adjacent colonial homes of Nicolás Ovando and the Dávila family. Though a relatively large hotel with 104 rooms, its colonial brick-and-stucco arched pathways contrasted with modern art, gardens, and a bar serving fine Dominican cigars and rums create an intimate and inviting feel. *US$ 250 (Check website for online specials); C/ Las Damas between Las Mercedes and El Conde; 685-9955; h2975@accor.com; www.accorhotels.com*

APARTMENTS

Beraca Aparta Hotel If planning a longer-term stay, the Beraca offers fully furnished studio apartments with cable, Wi-Fi, and utilities included. In addition, kitchenettes allow visitors to save on dining costs. The bathrooms require some renovation, but the rooms are brightly painted and breezy, offering stunning views of la Zona Colonial. *US$300-400/month, US$45-60/night; Corner of Arzobispo Meriño and C/ General Cabral, Santa Bárbara (next to Zona Colonial); Contact owner Carmen Espinosa: 829-881-3150; caresmia@hotmail.com*

Aparta Hotel Drake Located in the quiet, upscale neighborhood of Piantini, Aparta Hotel Drake offers weekly and monthly rates for long-term travelers. Rooms come with one or two beds, private bathrooms, and kitchenettes perfect for preparing simple meals. The hotel is within walking distance of the city's best malls and chic restaurants, and has a large and secure parking lot for guests. *RD$1235-1950; 29 C/ Agustín Lara and C/ Gustavo Mejía Ricart, Ensanche Piantini, 567-4427; info@apartahoteldrake.com; www.apartahoteldrake.com*

Sights & Culture

PARKS

Mirador del Sur

A slender sliver of green running for several kilometers just a few blocks north of the Caribbean Sea, this park is a popular gathering spot for well-heeled residents of the nearby neighborhoods, as well as athletes from all over of the city who take advantage of its bike paths and jogging trails. There are baseball diamonds and basketball courts for pickup games, playgrounds for the little ones, and limestone caves in which to explore, one of which doubles as the Guácara Taína nightclub (p106). Natural rock walls on the perimeter of the park are popular among rock-climbing enthusiasts to practice their sport. *Bordered by Av. Luperón on the west, Av.*

Moya on the east, Av. Anacaona on the north and Av. Cayetano Germosen on the south.

Mirador del Norte

The Parque Mirador del Norte is a vibrant, sprawling expanse of park well-suited for relaxation and recreation on rolling terrain set along the northern bank of the Río Isabela. Authorities like to claim that Mirador del Norte is the lung of the city, and as the biggest park in Santo Domingo at 40 square kilometers (15 square miles), it probably is. Guides are available for the many kilometers of walking trails through nature preserves showcasing rare and endemic wildlife. An artificial lagoon offers paddle boating and lakeside picnicking alongside the many resident species of colorful tropical birds. There are also monuments to the cultural patrimony of the city, as well as a restaurant and medical center. *Bordered by Av. Presidente Azar on the west, Av. Máximo Gómez on the east, Av. Mirador Norte on the north, and Río Isabela on the south; 926-9022; www.parquemiradordelnorte.com; Tue-Sun 9am-9pm*

Mirador del Este

Mirador del Este hosts several of the major attractions of Santo Domingo and is therefore more of a tourist attraction than natural urban oasis. The Faro a Colón, Olympic training facilities, and Los Tres Ojos (below), among others, comprise the park grounds. *Bordered by Av. Boulevard del Faro on the north, Av. Iberoamericano on the south, and Expreso Las Americas on the east.*

Faro a Colón

Based on the vainglorious winning design of Scotsman Joseph L. Gleave, construction of this monument in honor of Christopher Columbus did not begin until 1986, 55 years after it was originally conceived. The enormous cement structure lies in the shape of a cross, supposedly entombing the remains of Christopher Columbus. From the beginning, it has been nothing if not a lightning rod of controversy, costing over US$70 million for its construction. The monument displaced hundreds of poor families when construction caused the razing of an entire neighborhood. The monument is known as a "lighthouse" (*faro*, in Spanish), because it sends out a cross-shaped beam of light into the night sky. It therefore consumes an exorbitant amount of energy to power this beacon, seen from up to 50 miles away, including in the surrounding neighborhoods that suffer from chronic blackouts. Meanwhile, Havana, Cuba, and Seville, Spain, also claim to have Columbus's remains in their possession. Despite it all, multi-term President Balaguer was determined to finish construction in honor of the Columbian Quincentenial in 1992 and it was indeed completed on time, inaugurated by the Pope himself. The museum inside the cold stone walls includes displays from each country that supported the monument's construction in a forced entreaty to cross-cultural unity. *RD$100; Av. Mirador del Este; East Santo Domingo; 591-1492; Tues-Sun 9:30am-5:30pm*

Los Tres Ojos

These actually four – not *tres* – underground pools referred to as *ojos* are all connected through a cave system used by Taínos for religious ceremonies and as a temporary refuge from both hurricanes and Spaniards. As much as the enthusiastic guides may insist, Taínos never actually inhabited these caves. Stairs lead down to cement paths connecting each of the pools and an optional boat ride transports visitors to the fourth pool used in the filming of Jurassic Park. *RD$50; Expreso Las Americas, Parque Mirador del Este; Mon-Sun 9am-5pm*

El Aquario

Not too many aquaria can count on a backdrop against the sea, but this one beckons with well-manicured grounds set on cliffs overlooking the coast that often attract just as much attention as the creatures behind the glass. Santo Domingo's aquarium can get crowded, but during a quiet hour, it provides an otherwise impossible view of manatees, giant sea turtles, and other underwater wonders. Though the complex has been open for over twenty years, signage is still unfortunately sparse and even then, just in Spanish. The most exciting section is an underwater Plexiglas tunnel that allows visitors to stretch their necks in gazing up and around at the fishes. *RD$50 for foreigners/RD$30 for Dominicans; Av. 26 de Enero and Av. España; Tues-Sun 9am-5:30pm*

El Jardín Botánico

El Jardín Botánico Nacional Dr. Rafael Moscoso is the largest botanical garden in the Caribbean at over 2 million square meters, showcasing the lush flora of the island, including a spectacular collection of orchids. The park's centerpiece is a tranquil and meticulously manicured Japanese Garden, along with a flower clock that once was counted as the largest in the world. The Botanical Gardens also hosts special exhibitions and activities like the National Flower Festival, so it's a good idea to check out the website before heading over. Naturalist Kate Wallace (see Tody Tours, p353) offers bird-watching tours of this refuge for a number of endemic bird species such as the country's national bird (the palm chat), and black-crowned palm tanagers. *Price for foreigners is US$5, which includes access to the tram that runs across the gardens. Av. de los Próceres between Av. de Argentina and Av. Jardín Botánico; 385-2611; www.jbn.gob.do; Mon-Sun 9am-6pm*

El Parque Zoológico Nacional

El Parque Zoológico Nacional, as this wildlife sanctuary is officially known, is fun and educational for the kids, but otherwise, the exhibits and the animals' living conditions may underwhelm visitors. Zoo admission is cheap, and includes unlimited tram rides as well as screaming students running around in blue shirts and khakis. The petting zoo is great for family-friendly entertainment, featuring farm and exotic animals and lots of room to run and play. *RD$100; Paseo de los Reyes Católicos just west of Avenida Máximo Gómez; Tues-Sun 9am-5pm.; www.zoodom.gov.do*

MUSEUMS

Museo de Juan Pablo Duarte

The birthplace of the founding father, this museum now houses memorabilia from Duarte's childhood, as well as from the Independence era, including documents and photographs. As an adult, Duarte and his compatriots held clandestine meetings here in preparation for independence from Haiti. It was also

For museums in the la Zona Colonial, see Zona Colonial Walking Tour starting on page 94.

in this modest wooden home that María Trinidad Sánchez toiled over her creation of the first Dominican flag, raised on February 27, 1844. *308 C/ Isabel la Católica, between Calles Restauración and Duarte. 9am-5pm Tues- Fri, 9am-12pm Sat*

Casa de Salomé Ureña

Next to the home of Duarte is the birthplace of Salomé Ureña, a renowned Dominican poet. Ureña is also known for her promotion of female education, opening an institute of higher education for women called El Instituto de Señoritas in 1881. Author Julia Alvarez wrote a novel titled *In the Name of Salomé* loosely based on the poet's life. *C/ Isabel la Católica between Restauración and Duarte; Tues-Fri 9am-5pm, Sat 9am-12pm*

Plaza de la Cultura

The Plaza de la Cultura is a large, leafy expanse containing several important cultural attractions dotting the pleasingly landscaped park. This complex covered with amapola trees contains the following four museums, as well as Cinema Café (p105), the Cinemateca, and the National Library (under renovation at the time of research), along with attractive classical and modern sculpture. The green space is a welcome reprieve from the congestion of the surrounding streets, even if the museums on its grounds don't always amaze. In addition, each May, La Feria Internacional del Libro (International Book Fair) takes place in here, drawing energetic school kids from across the country for the range of exhibits on science, art and history and, of course, dozens of tents filled with books and other literary paraphernalia. Each day of this two-week fair features an honored guest, such as the celebrated Dominican-American Junot Díaz, author of *The Wondrous Life of Oscar Wao.* Visit www.ferilibro.com for dates and exhibit information. *Plaza de la Cultura is located in the residential neighborhood of Gazcue, flanked on the north and south by C/ César Nicolás Pensón and Av. Pedro Henríquez Ureña, and Av. Máximo Gómez and C/ Felix M. del Monte to the west and east.*

El Museo del Hombre Dominicano

The second floor of the Museum of the Dominican Man has a remarkable collection of Taíno pottery, but the exhibit is poorly labeled and described, so prior knowledge or a great imagination are important to appreciate the artifacts. Many of the pieces on display were for daily use, such as the stone pestle and mortars used to grind

---

Salomé Ureña

Ureña, renowned for her progressive work in women's education, was also an ardent patriot. She wrote an epic poem on the Taíno chieftess Anacaona, and a poem called "A La Patria" – to the Fatherland – the last stanza of which is below:

¡Oh Patria idolatrada! Ceñida de alta gloria
prepárate a ser reina del mundo de Colón:
tu rango soberano te guarda ya la historia,
la fama te presenta tu lauro y tu blasón.

Oh, adored Fatherland! Tied to the highest glory
Ready to be queen of the world of Columbus:
Your sovereign rank guards you for history
Fame presents you your laurels and your flag.

starchy roots into flour and ceramic water jugs in the shape of deities. Others had purely spiritual functions, such as the Taíno god statues with a platform on their heads (a resting place for the hallucinogenic powder used during religious ceremonies), or the triangular-shaped pieces adorned with faces of deities, which were buried with crops as an offering to the gods. The third floor features Carnaval costumes and a half-baked exhibit on rural Dominican culture, but both lack accurate and descriptive labeling. *RD$50; Plaza de la Cultura, Gazcue; 687-3622; Tues-Sun 9am-4:30pm*

El Museo de Arte Moderno

A rather disappointing display of modern Dominican art, the Museum of Modern Art appears to cater more to the child artists of the elite than truly representing the diversity and talent of local modern artists. The museum's permanent collection does have some impressive works by local masters including Ramón Oviedo and José García Cordero, who came out of La Escuela de Bellas Artes in Santo Domingo. *RD$50; Plaza de la Cultura, Gazcue; Tues-Sun 9am-4:30pm*

Museo Nacional de Historia y Geografía

The Museum of History and Geography offers an underwhelming look at several periods of Dominican history, the most interesting of which is dedicated to Trujillo and his personal effects like his wallet placed tastefully near the makeup kit he used to whiten his face. Other rooms depict the post-independence era until the Restoration, and then post-Restoration until 1916. There is an additional display that looks at historical cartography. *RD$50; Plaza de la Cultura, Gazcue; 686-6668; Tues-Sun 9am-4:30pm*

Museo Nacional de Historia Natural

Jet through the solar system in the Museum of Natural History, followed by a section focused on regional and worldwide geological formations. Other exhibits scale down to Hispaniola's delicate marine and terrestrial ecosystems, which are educational, but not particularly impressive in presentation. *RD$50; Plaza de la Cultura, Gazcue; 689-0106; Tues-Sun 10am-4:30pm*

Museo Bellapart

This fifth-floor museum explores modern Dominican art through the past two centuries, beginning with the post-independence renaissance of creative forms. Featured artists include Yoryi Morel and Jaime Colson. Other spaces display the work of the European expats who fled 20th century dictatorships for the Dominican Republic, followed by their disciples, who reaped the benefits of the Escuela de Bellas Artes, established by a group of these exiles. Bellapart is privately held but open to the public, and the owners and curators have clearly given great thought to their beloved Dominican subjects and *audience. Free entry; Av. Kennedy and Dr. Peguero, Edificio Honda; 541-7721; www.museobellapart.com; Mon-Fri 10am-6pm, Sat 9am-12pm*

THEATER

El Teatro Nacional

The National Theater hosts a diverse array of both national and international acts covering the cultural gamut from musicals, film festivals, dance, and drama. With two theaters, the principal one seating up to 1,600 spectators and a stage accommodating 250 performers, the Teatro Nacional is the premier locale for big-ticket events. *Prices vary, RD$200-2000; Plaza de la Cultura, Gazcue; Ticket Office: 682-7255*

El Palacio de Bellas Artes

Recently renovated, this Roman-inspired edifice is a place of both education and entertainment, with classrooms for students of the performing and visual arts and expansive gallery spaces. With a theater hosting acts as diverse as Dominican comedy musicals,

Works by Picasso and Botero have been on display at the Palace of Fine Arts.

to string quintets and ballet, the Palace of Fine Arts will add a little culture to any itinerary, without wearing through a budget because many of the art exhibitions and performances are free to the public. *Corner of Máximo Gómez and Av. Independencia, Gazcue, 687-0504; dgba.do@hotmail.com; dgba.do@gmail.com; www.bellasartes.gov.do*

Casa de Teatro

Casa de Teatro is the best place to find quality events in Santo Domingo. Featuring a small theater, outdoors stage, screening room, two art galleries, and a bar and restaurant, works by all the great Dominican artists have graced the walls or stage of this establishment. The screening room offers international film showings every weeknight at 8pm for RD$50. The galleries exhibit Dominican painting, drawing, and photography, but international artists are occasionally featured as well. Nearly every night there is either free live music or reasonably priced jazz and world music concerts. *Prices vary, RD$100-500; 110 C/ Arzobispo Meriño, Zona Colonial; 689-3430; www.casadelteatro.com*

Teatro Guloya

This intimate theater, named after the festively clad dancers and musicians of San Pedro de Macorís, is one of the only venues featuring experimental theater and dance, often leaving visitors with more questions than answers – but in a good way. Check the theater's website for current productions including children's theater, generally on Sunday afternoons. *Free-RD$500; 205 C/ Arzobispo Portes, Zona Colonial; 685-4856; www.teatroguloya.org*

La Cinemateca

Located within the Plaza de la Cultura, this small movie theater has three showings on weekdays (5:30pm, 7:30pm, and 9:30pm), and two on weekends (6:00pm and 8:30pm), of foreign and domestic independent films. It regularly sponsors film festivals by country or genre so check out the website to see what's playing next. *Plaza de la Cultura, enter on Avenida Pedro Henríquez Ureña; 689-6102; www.cinematecadominica.org*

NEIGHBORHOODS OUTSIDE THE COLONIAL ZONE

Barrio Chino (Chinatown)

A city can't be called a city without a Chinatown. Within walking distance of the Colonial Zone, Barrio Chino is small but packed full of family-run, inexpensive restaurants that provide some needed culinary diversity. Renovated in 2006, a traditionally inspired decorative arch (at C/ Mexico and C/ Duarte), as well as samurai and turtle bronze casts, clearly marks the center of this *barrio*. Chinatown hosts an interesting variety of shops selling medicinal teas and oils imported from across the Pacific.

A favorite restaurant in Chinatown is **Dragon I**, serving both Chinese and Japanese fare. Brahma beer is cheaper than water here and don't forget to ask for complimentary hot tea. *Dragon I: RD$90-300; 28 C/ Duarte, near corner of C/ Mexico, second floor; 687-0230*

Avenida Mella

This area is full of oddball shops selling electronics, hats, and cheap clothes, as well as an open-air food market. Sacks of spices, wood blocks piled high with chicken innards and mountains of fruit and vegetables provide an interesting backdrop for the aspiring photographer. This is a great place to practice Spanish with the vendors, but don't spend all your time in the *Mercado Modelo* here. This market was once a true indoor market where the *capitaleños* bought daily provisions, but the market slowly transformed into what it is today: a tourist trap full of cheap and tacky souvenirs, many of which are not even made in the Dominican Republic. Upon entering, overzealous vendors pounce, steering visitors toward stalls overflowing with mass-produced trinkets. Do take a peek at the *botánicas*, inside and dotted around the perimeter the *Mercado Modelo*. These little shacks are full of voodoo scented oils that promise a lover's return, male virility, or revenge against enemies. On the second floor in the far southern corner is one art dealer that actually knows about art and has a few hard-to-find gems by Dominican artists.

Little Haiti

In the same general area is Pequeño Haití (Little Haiti), which got its name from the Haitian population that moved in to sell their wares. Like Av. Mella, this area is full of sights like Dominicans negotiating over piles of used cell phones, generators, and computer parts while sipping on coconut water. Pequeño Haiti, however, should be avoided at night.

The Zona Colonial Walking Tour

For many independent travelers, the idea of being herded like cattle around Santo Domingo in a shiny air-conditioned bus, while a tour guide glosses over names of historical buildings and makes painfully cheesy jokes, is a fate worse than death. Not to fear! This do-it-yourself walking tour is designed for travelers to indulge in quirky historical details, stroll the narrow, balcony-lined streets hung with laundry, and make leisurely stops to imbibe and refuel. The walk can take anywhere from two hours to two days, depending upon the pace and interests of the traveler. The goal is not to see everything as quickly as possible, but to promote a multisensory experience: step back in time and take in the stunning architecture, the smell of the sea intermingled with freshly cut pineapple, the sound of *bachata* blasting from a corner barber shop, the feel of polished stones meant to keep away the evil eye, and the taste of an earthy *mamajuana*.

With beautifully restored colonial edifices dating back to the early 16th century, the Zona Colonial conjures up the days when conquistadors roamed the cobblestone streets, Spanish monks were busy converting the "heathen" Taínos, and genteel Spanish ladies fanned themselves during their afternoon strolls. Today, each has its modern equivalent: the conquistadores have been replaced by male *tigueres* scheming their next female conquest; Evangelicals now take to the streets with megaphones in this predominantly Catholic nation; and women of all ages strut along the Conde while peering through the shop windows for the latest fashions.

Parque Independencia, La Puerta del Conde & Fuerte La Concepción

Begin the tour in the heart of downtown Santo Domingo, where old meets new, and history springs to life. To defend against pirate attacks in the early 16th century, the Spanish decided to build a thick wall of stone around the city, starting on the western and eastern sides. Construction began in 1543, but lack of laborers stalled progress until a crew of African slaves arrived in 1547. **La Puerta del Conde** was one of the original entrances to the walled city. Ironically, Sir Francis Drake used this entrance when he pillaged the city in 1586. Entering the La Puerta leads into **Parque Independencia**, home of the **Altar de la Patria** where the remains of Founding Fathers – Duarte, Mella, and Sánchez – reside. *Free; open every day 8am-6pm or sunset.*

Santo Domingo

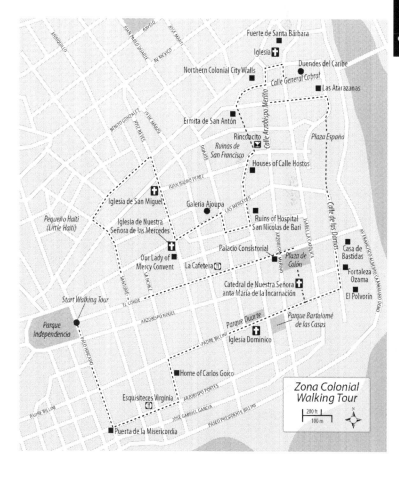

Puerta de la Misericordia

Heading south along Calle Palo Hincado is **La Puerta de la Misericordia**, where Dominican patriots led by Sánchez fired the first shots that signaled Dominican independence from Haiti on February 27, 1844. Heading east along Calle Arzobispo Nouel is the fine bakery and restaurant **Esquisiteces Virginia** (p81), a great spot to pick up fresh pastry or a home-style Dominican meal followed by a hot and sweet *cafecito. Corner of C/ Arzobispo Nouel and C/ Santomé.*

Home of Carlos Goico

Turning left on C/ Sánchez, before reaching the corner of Calle Padre Billini, is the former home and studio of expressionist painter Carlos Goico (1952-2009). The owner of a nearby falafel restaurant and admirer of Goico's work lent the space to Goico, who could be seen toiling over a canvas, slathering on paint to form faces with bulged eyes or Carnaval masks. Living simply in this closet-sized space, Goico would search his surroundings for anything that produced color when inspiration hit, even licking his brush when he lacked water. He was known for giving away his paintings, placing more importance on sharing his creations than the money that they could bring. Though the space is closed to the public, it has quickly become an important cultural monument for what was created there. It is denoted by a small, multi-colored tile painted with faces and "Goico" on the east side of Calle Sánchez.

Quinta Dominica

After Goico's artistic energy infuses the senses, the Quinta Dominica on C/ Sánchez and Duarte is the perfect complement. This Dominican art center showcases paintings, drawings and photography with an emphasis on local artists, and also has an enchanting garden with chairs and tables to enjoy the peace of the surroundings.

Parque Duarte & Iglesia de los Dominicos

Legend has it that this peaceful park by day and bohemian hangout by night was where Nicolás de Ovando ordered that Anacoana, the legendary chieftess of two of the most important Taíno provinces, be hung in 1503. Across C/ Padre Billini is the Dominican Church, completed in 1532, with additions in 1732 that include the stone ceiling and baroque accoutrements around the main entrance. On this site in 1511, Dominican Friar Antonio de Montesinos gave a speech condemning the severe Spanish *encomienda* plantation system that enslaved Taínos, which influenced Bartolomé de las Casas to do the same.

Parque Fray Bartolomé de las Casas

On the corner of Calles Padre Billini and Hostos is the former site of the Bartolomé de las Casas' home, which was built in the mid-16th century. Known for his efforts to abolish the *encomienda* system, his grand solution to replenish the labor lost was to increase the number of African slaves brought to the island. He soon became opposed to both, for fear of the damnation of his soul. In 1552, his seminal *Brevísima Relación de la Destrucción de las Indias* (Brief Account on the Devastation of the Indies) was published, regarding the mistreatment of the indigenous population. De las Casas' reflective figure is immortalized in the center of the park in a sculpture by Juan de Vaqueros. On weekends, the park fills with artisans and their wares, taking on a lively atmosphere.

Calle de las Damas

The first paved road of the New World, Calle de las Damas, was originally called Calle de la Fortaleza in honor of Fortaleza Ozama at its southern end. This changed in 1509 when María de Toledo, Diego's Columbus's wife, arrived on the scene with her ladies-in-waiting. María, accompanied by her coterie, needed a place to stroll in the cool afternoons, and so the road was extended and became known as the "Street of the Ladies."

Fortaleza Ozama

Standing two hundred meters from where the Río Ozama meets the Caribbean Sea is La Fortaleza Ozama. Along with Fortaleza Santo Domingo on the eastern bank of the Río Ozama, Fortaleza Ozama was constructed to protect the river's mouth from ravenous buccaneers. Built in stages beginning in 1505, the Fortaleza's first structure was El Torre de Homenaje (Tower of Homage), making it the oldest standing European stone building in the Americas. The original entrance gate on Calle de las Damas was built in 1608. Known as the Prevention Gate, the foundation of its original Roman towers peeks through the looming stone walls built over it a century later. To the southwest of the main fortress is the Santa Bárbara Powder House (known locally as El Polvorín), buttressed by ten feet thick walls to protect its highly explosive former contents. Observing from on high is a Juan Vaquero statue of Gonzalo Fernández de Oviedo y Valdéz, who was in command of the fortress from 1533-1557, but is better known for his opus, General and Natural History of the Indies. Serving a number of uses including as a military jail and later as a holding center for political dissidents under Trujillo, the space now hosts various and more benign cultural activities. *Entrance RD$50; every day 9am-5pm*

Casa de Bastidas

This colonial building was the home of an accountant-explorer from Seville named Rodrigo de Bastidas who came with Nicolás de Ovando's fleet in 1502 to start a trade

Santo Domingo

Protector of the Indians

For his work in defense of the doomed indigenous population, Bartolomé de las Casas received the official title of Protector of the Indians in 1516. Because of his somewhat subversive activities, the title was revoked in 1520 and given to another friar. The Crown named several men to this post in its other colonies, but the title became irrelevant, and it soon ceased to exist.

De las Casas left Santo Domingo in 1520, traveled to other Spanish possessions, and eventually returned to Spain in the 1540s. In what was likely the first act in the anti-slavery movement, De las Casas entered into the celebrated Valladolid debates – presided over by the King of Spain Charles V in 1550-1551 – against the scholar Juan Ginés de Sepúlveda. While Sepúlveda argued that the indigenous inhabitants could not be classified as people and Spain was therefore justified in using war, subjugation, and forced Catholic conversion in their conquest (supporting the *encomienda* system in place), de las Casas countered that, according to natural law, the native populations were rational and free men, if slightly less civilized, and should be dealt with in peace, including persuasive conversion to the Christian faith. Both orators claimed victory, but although the *encomienda* system was indeed weakened after the debates, violent colonization continued, and the real losers were those who had no representative at the debate: the indigenous population.

business with new clients. A savvy businessman, Bastidas capitalized on the Catholic Church's wholehearted campaigns of conversion by importing wheat and wine (elements crucial for communion), as well as underwear to dress the "heathen" Taínos. He also participated in the slave trade, but a pang of guilt and fear of fiery afterlife propelled him to join forces with Bartolomé de las Casas to establish the Santa Marta (in Colombia) and Coro (in Venezuela) settlements, designed for Spaniards and Indians to live in harmony. Located next to La Fortaleza Ozama, the residence took on a number of military uses. Today, it serves as the Trampolín children's museum.

Casa de Francia

Known as the House of France (since the French embassy and Alliance Française began occupying the space in 1999), it was originally built by Nicolás de Ovando. As discussed above, Santo Domingo was the lively stomping grounds for nearly every Spanish conquistador, and many lived in this very home. In fact, before waging his campaign against the Aztecs, Hernán Cortés rented the home from Ovando. He was followed by Francisco Pizarro, conqueror of Peru, and Alonso de Ojeda, a particularly ruthless explorer, who focused his pillaging energies on Venezuela and Colombia. Spanish Baroque painter Diego Velázquez, known for his portraits of the Royal family, including his magnum opus, *Las Meninas*, also took up residence here.

Residencia del Gobernador Nicolás de Ovando

Ovando constructed many houses that he eventually rented to other colonists, but it was here – in one of the first stone buildings in the Americas – that he rested his head at night. After several renovations, the French hotel company Accor joined Ovando's massive, gothic-inspired home with two others, including that of the wealthy Dávila family, to fashion this luxury hotel with 125 rooms. Even before its official conversion, the house saw some honored guests. In 1504, Ovando invited Columbus to his home to recover from his shipwreck in Jamaica on his fourth and final voyage to the Americas. In the mid-19th century, the first Dominican president, General Santana, took up residence here. Across from the hotel is the **Plazoleta María de Toledo**, named for Diego Columbus's wife. The Roman arches at the plaza's eastern entrance are all that remain of the monastery originally built on site.

Iglesia de los Jesuitas/Panteón Nacional (Jesuit Church/National Pantheon)

Though the building's foundation was laid in 1702 on the former site of another of Nicolás de Ovando's numerous houses, the Jesuits did not finish construction of the former church for another 50 years. Shortly after completion, King Charles III of Spain kicked the Jesuits out of the New World and claimed the church, which then took on such uses as a tobacco warehouse, a theater during the independence era, government offices, and eventually what it is today: a mausoleum. True to form, Trujillo envisioned the church as his own personal mausoleum, where the masses could worship his legacy. However, after his death in 1961, the idea of Trujillo's body entombed on national soil appalled Dominicans, so his remains were shipped to Paris. The building, along with the neighboring ivy-covered House of the Jesuits' School, was remodeled in the 1970s and converted into a mausoleum for all of the important players in the Dominican

House of the Jesuits' School is also known as the House of the Gargoyles for the stone guardians perched on the outer walls. Locals swear the Jesuits took these from the Cathedral Primada de las Americas.

Republic's development, including writers, former presidents, and social reformers. The Pantheon is adorned with some rather loaded memorabilia from Trujillo's cronies such as the iron chandelier, a friendly offering from Franco, and the iron grates that form the shape of swastikas on the upper level, apparently a gift from Hitler.

Capilla de los Remedios (Chapel of Remedies or Chapel of Divine Help) or Capilla Dávila (Dávila Chapel)

Francisco Dávila, a wealthy sugar plantation owner, built this chapel as a private place of worship for his family, but invited the other Spanish elite to join in worship here until the main Cathedral was completed in 1540. Having undergone remodeling in the 1880s after a fire, followed by another restoration in 1970, the building now hosts small artistic performances. An image of the Virgen de los Remedios (a statue of Mary brought to the New World by Spanish conquerors) resides inside the chapel, giving the building its name. Behind the chapel on the cliffs overlooking Río Ozama is the Dávila House, which has now been incorporated into the Nicolás de Ovando Hotel.

Museo Casas Reales & Reloj del Sol

What appears to be one giant house was once two edifices (distinguished by the shape of the windows on the second floor), until they were joined during a restoration following earthquake damage in 1673. Built in 1512, the house on the northern end was originally the home (*casas reales* – royal homes) and office of colonial governors and captains-general. Another part of the building was dedicated to the

> Outside the museum is the Reloj del Sol, installed in 1753 so that during meetings city officials could keep time by looking out the windows of Las Casas Reales.

Real Audiencia, or Royal Court, where most major decisions and judgments regarding early Spanish colonial exploits were made. The Royal Treasurer Cristóbal de Santa Clara occupied the second floor of the southern end, erected in 1508, while the first floor was used as the House of Trade and Royal Treasury. In 1976, President Balaguer and Spanish King Juan Carlos I dedicated the museum that exhibits artifacts from the Hispanic era through the 18th century. Pieces of particular interest include Trujillo's private weapons collection and medical equipment used in Hospital San Nicolás de Bari. *RD$30; 682-4202; Tues-Sun 9am-5pm; museodelacasar@verizon.net.do*

El Alcázar de Colón

After five years of construction, the second Admiral and third Governor of the Indies, Diego Columbus, and his wife María de Toledo moved in to this Mudéjar-style mansion in 1515. Even with their twelve children, this three-story, twenty-two-room home was extravagant. By 1770, the house was abandoned, and it was not until the 1950s that it was restored as a two-story building, most likely to cut costs off the nearly US$1 million expense. The building houses the Museo Alcázar de Colón, which showcases art and artifacts from the era, including a large display of tapestries. The museum also features period shows on Saturday nights, where actors dressed in colonial threads wander among spectators interested in catching a glimpse of 16th century life. In its refurbished stone glory, El Alcázar peers over the Río Ozama to the east and Plaza España to the west. *RD$20; 9am-5pm Mon-Sun; 686-8657*

Plaza España

What was once a small Taíno farm, the Spanish quickly turned into a Plaza de Armas where colonial troops massed and trained. Today, this grand square is Plaza España, and remains an area of perpetual activity. The southern section was originally separate, when it was known as the Plaza del Contador (Accountant's Plaza) and served as a public market. Warehouses for shipping and trade bordered the expanse, one of which still remains and is now used as the ticket office for Casa de Colón. The cacophony of clanking iron from the adjacent Calle Los Herreros (Blacksmith's Street), has now been replaced with soft music and lively conversation coming from the chic restaurants that now line the cobbled street. At the center of it all is a statue of Nicolás de Ovando looking down upon his master scheme of gridded thoroughfares and organized chaos. In the evenings, locals and tourists gather for open-air concerts and festivities against the striking colonial scenery.

Calle La Atarazana

Heading north and downhill from Plaza España is Las Atarazanas, or the Drydocks, where traders stored their goods. One of the former warehouses now functions as the Museo de las Atarazanas Reales (Museum of the Royal Shipyards), full of coins, ceramics and other trinkets retrieved from the numerous shipwrecks around the island. The museum is located in front of **Plaza de Retiro**, the site of an immense public market during colonial times where slaves were auctioned and then hauled off to the **La Negreta** building.

Calle Arzobispo Meriño to Fuerte de Santa Bárbara and Iglesia Santa Bárbara

Originally known as La Calle de los Pateros (Silversmith Street) or Calle las Canteras (Quarry Street), Calle Arzobispo Meriño was once home to candle makers, blacksmiths and occupations associated with shipping from sail makers to stevedores. This neighborhood, known as Santa Bárbara, has maintained its working-class atmosphere, but these colonial occupations have been replaced with printers and tailors. The street also was once called Calle La Moneda for the Casa de Moneda (358 Arzobispo Meriño), where Charles V mandated the minting of silver coins. The building, also known as La Casa de Medaliones (House of the Medallions), now houses the Dominican Philatelic Society. These stamp-collecting enthusiasts hold meetings every Sunday morning until about noon, and are always eager to share their knowledge of postage and the history it represents.

Iglesia Santa Bárbara was built in 1537, but fell victim to a hurricane, several earthquakes, Drake's fires, and other calamities. Its present state, therefore, is a fascinating jumble of architectural dissonance. Of note, Juan Pablo Duarte was baptized here.

Directly abutting the church is the fort of the same name, part of the series of defenses raised by colonial authorities to protect the city. It is one of the few remaining fortifications visible today.

Break for Art: Duendes del Caribe

While in barrio Santa Bárbara, stop along the southernmost block of Calle General Cabral to revel in the local paintings and artisan wares of this truly original gallery and workshop. See Art Galleries (p108) for more details.

Calle General Cabral to Ermita de San Antón (Hermitage of San Antón)

Walking west (uphill) around the curve of Calle General Cabral, the original northern city walls can be observed amidst the comparatively new row of houses. This portion of the colonial walls was not constructed until the late 17th century, which is why the stone is in excellent condition compared to the western and eastern walls, erected over a century earlier. At the top of the hill, the road curves down to the left; find to the right a picturesque plaza with Ermita de San Antón (Hermitage of San Antón) at its crown. Governor Ovando decreed the building of this church in 1502, but in 1586, Sir Francis Drake let loose his pyromaniacal techniques on the charming stone edifice. Having undergone a number of restorations, the church took another hit in 1930 from Hurricane San Zenón, after which it has remained closed. Victims of the hurricane used the debris to build ramshackle homes along the plaza, which still stand today, though the owners have made some upgrades.

Las Ruínas del Monastario de San Francisco de Asís

Run by the Franciscan Order of monks, the elegant San Francisco monastery and church was borne of the sweat and toil of African and Taíno slaves. In this respect, the Franciscan and Dominican monks, who fought to abolish the *encomienda* system, differed greatly, with the Franciscans allying themselves with the Spanish elite. Though construction of the monastery, at the highest point in the city, began in 1544, official inauguration did not take place until 1664.

The grassy expanse to the west of the ruins served as a cemetery, where Bartolomé Colón and conquistador Alonso de Ojeda are buried. The monastery was left to decay following the order for all Franciscans to evacuate in 1795, and fell into further disrepair when its stone walls were used as building materials during the Haitian occupation. In 1885, Padre Billini turned the remnants into an insane asylum until 1930, after which it was used as a refuge for Spanish artists during the Spanish Civil War and World War II. An old man, the gatekeeper to Las Ruínas, occasionally waits by the locked gate, and he is always happy to show curious passersby around. Though his historical knowledge is not particularly abundant, he is full of anecdotes about the ruins' modern day uses such as weddings, photo shoots, and playing dominos.

If a break is in order, the *colmado* at the curve of Calle Hostos, **El Rinconcito de Don Guillermo**, has icy-cold Presidentes flowing freely around the umbrella-covered tables with the ruins creating a surreal backdrop.

Las Ruínas del Monastario de San Francisco de Asís

As this was the city's tallest elevation, Santo Domingo's first aqueduct was also installed here, using gravity to feed water down to the Cathedral in the main square. Remnants of the original water wheel and reservoir still serve as reminders of its history and importance in colonial life.

Calle Hostos & Ruínas de Hospital San Nicolás de Bari

Head down Calle Hostos, where quaint wooden homes line this gorgeous, steep cobblestoned street. The highest point of this road offers a panoramic view of the Zona Colonial.

After this stroll, cross Calle Mercedes to the ruins of Hospital San Nicolás de Bari. Though considered the first European hospital in the Americas, this hospital was actually the third built on this site. The earliest hospital was a simple wooden building from 1502, and the second, a small stone edifice built between 1512 and 1519. Hospital San Nicolás de Bari was constructed over twenty years, from 1533 to 1556, and remained in use until the early 20th century, when it was declared structurally unsound, and its façade collapsed. The adjoining church of San Nicolás de Bari was torn down during the building of the Iglesia Nuestra Señora de Altagracia (on the southeast corner of Calles Mercedes and Hostos), but La Concepción, the church's inner chapel dating from the 1540s, was restored and is protected within La Altagracia. Architecturally stabilized to further prevent decay, the ruins now serve as a backdrop for cultural events and throwback photo ops.

Break for Art: Galería Ajoupa
Mix in some modernity with this spectacular Haitian art gallery featuring fantastical interpretations of rural life and modern religious depictions swathed in bright bold colors. *255 C/ Mercedes*

Iglesia Nuestra Señora de las Mercedes
Rodrigo de Liendo, whose famous works include the Cathedral and Monastery of San Francisco, designed this stone church that ties in Romanesque and Moorish influences into its stunning bell tower as well as the slender Gothic structure in the interior. The church was built so delicately that in 1635 the roof caved, though it was subsequently repaired. The church's baroque altar is still used to split the Eucharist on Sundays, the best day to catch the church doors open. Next to the church on C/ José Reyes is the Our Lady of Mercy Convent, where Spanish friar Gabriel Tellez briefly took up residence. Using the nom de plume Tirso de Molina, he authored *El Burlador de Sevilla y Convivada de Piedra* (The Trickster of Seville and the Stone Guest) in 1630, the first written reference to the legendary Latin libertine Don Juan.

Iglesia de San Miguel
Heading north along Calle José Reyes towards Avenida Mella is the Iglesia de San Miguel, a simple church originally built of straw, then later in stone, and still in use today. The Plaza de la Restauración, in honor of the country's second independence from Spain in 1865, is located directly across the street, and has welcoming benches to take in the scene of men gathered around a game of dominoes and frolicking children.

Avenida Mella
Enterprising immigrants from Europe and the Middle East turned this neighborhood into a principal shopping district where locals flock for deals on clothing, house wares and fabric. Built around *El Mercado Modelo*, the area has declined in the past years since its golden era in the 1970s and 1980s as the shiny new malls have won over consumers' hearts. (See Malls, p111)

El Conde, Refuel: La Cafetera
Knowledge alone cannot quench thirst, though some may beg to differ after observing the regulars at La Cafetera debate for hours while nursing a tiny coffee. Balmy days in the city send locals and visitors alike to sip one of La Cafetera's freshly made juices and *batidas*. (See Eat, p80)

Palacio Consistorial

Once the site of the old City Hall (hence its other name, Antiguo Ayuntamiento), this building was torn down after the Haitian occupation, and the newer adaptation of the current "Town Hall Palace" was constructed in 1920. The building's signature clock tower rises tall above Plaza Colón, the highest edifice in the area. Though rarely used today beyond occasional special events, the Hall is open to the public providing the opportunity to admire José Vela Zanetti's murals adorning the interior walls. *Open weekdays, allowing visitors to wander through the main wings.*

Plaza de Colón & Catedral de Nuestra Señora Santa María de la Incarnación (Cathedral of Our Holy Lady Mary of the Incarnation)

It was another three decades after Diego Columbus placed the cornerstone of the Cathedral in 1510 that the first section would be completed. After overcoming construction delays, in 1546 Pope Paul III deemed it "Primada de las Indias," or "Supreme Cathedral of the Indies," a highly esteemed position. Entering through the Gate of Pardons on the northern end of the Cathedral gives way to the repeated Gothic arches and twelve side chapels, well worth exploring as each has its own subtly unique history and style of construction. Exiting through the southern door, the Geraldini Gate, leads to the Priests' Alley, draped with bougainvillea, and eventually to Calle Arzobispo Nouel. The Cathedral was the final resting place for Columbus and his son, Diego, but in 1992, an urn of Columbus' presumed ashes was relocated to the Faro de Colón. *Open 8am-5pm daily.*

Plaza de Colón began as the governing and religious heart of the colonial city, a central square of sorts, with administrative offices built on the northern end and the imposing Cathedral to the south. Not wanting to miss out on the action, the wealthy built their mansions on the eastern side of the plaza, conveniently located to the outlet of the colonial era's aqueduct that began at the Monastery of San Francisco and piped water directly to the plaza. Galleries, restaurants and cigar shops replaced the government offices, formerly located on the northern end of the plaza, after the Presidential Palace was built in 1940 in Gazcue.

Nightlife & Entertainment

From sophisticated lounges with bottle service to dancing at the corner store next to plastic chairs, the vibrant Santo Domingo city life never disappoints – especially after dark. The primary areas to revel in the evening's many offerings are la Zona Colonial, Gazcue, El Centro, and "Aquel Lao," each of which are described in more detail below.

ZONA COLONIAL

La Zona Colonial offers more bars and restaurants within a short walk than any other district of Santo Domingo. Venues range from chic with modern architectural lines and fancy cocktails to artsy cavernous spaces featuring live music, performance art, and expositions. Though recent law has imposed a midnight closing time for all bars and restaurants, many owners have found loopholes to keep their establishments open until as late as 4am on weekends. As a result, there is always a place open to keep the party going. As in any city in the world, visitors must take certain precautions; crime rates have increased significantly with the rise of tourism and foreigners moving into the area. Though violent crime is not common, petty theft and muggings can occur. For damage prevention, only take the necessary amount of cash, but no important documents (bars do not check IDs) or credit cards, as most bars do not accept them anyways. These precautionary suggestions should by no means taint the atmosphere or deter visitors from enjoying the area's vibrant and diverse nightlife, full of characters and adventures.

 Café de Toi Also known as La Resistencia, this after-hours bar is the place to see and be seen with the artists and musicians of Santo Domingo. The proprietor, Odalis, has turned part of her home into an underground late-night haven. Using her mysterious ways of persuasion, she has managed to keep this bohemian hangout open very late despite its post-curfew hours. Each room is full of plush lounge furniture, paintings by local artists, and a whimsical décor reminiscent of a Toulouse-Lautrec painting. The bar has a great selection, but prices are a bit steep because it is the only bar within blocks open until the wee hours of the morning. *C/ Arzobispo Portes between C/ Sánchez and C/ 19 de Marzo*

El Centro Cultural de España The Spanish government continues to fund projects in the Dominican Republic, including the Centro Cultural de España, which regularly hosts cultural events free to the public. On most evenings, El Centro will have exhibitions, performance art, or concerts, oftentimes with complimentary wine or beverages. Or, escape the heat of the day in the air-conditioned library, complete with free Wi-Fi. *C/ Arzobispo Meriño and C/ Arzobispo Portes; 686-8212*

 La Espiral The former site of Ocho Puertas Bar (and, therefore, sometimes referred to as such), this restaurant/bar has character bursting from its colonial walls from the psychedelic mural in the Spanish outdoor patio, to the Islamic style wooden panels on the doors and dreadlocked staff. This venue hosts unique acts ranging from *gagá* (percussion-based music with Voodoo roots), electronic and spoken word, along with Capoeira during the day. Try a fresh watermelon or passion fruit caipirinha while dancing and mingling with the young, artsy crowd. The kitchen also puts out delicious fusions as well as sushi, sandwiches, salads, and Dominican sweets like *coco horneado* (baked coconut). *Drinks RD$100-250; food RD$150-300; 107 C/ José Reyes and Salomé Ureña; Facebook "La Espiral"*

Misifú A haven for the young, hip, and beautiful, this tiny bar with outdoor patio is a trendy weekend hangout. Tapas and other light fare are offered, but this is more a place to drink and chat while being surrounded by the outrageous furnishings involving converse sneakers, Papa Smurf, crystal chandeliers, and alluring dark walls and upholsteries. *1 C/ Restauración by C/ Atarazana; 685-7166*

Parada 77 The walls of this alternative bar are covered with graffiti, murals, and modern art composed by its patrons. Late on Friday nights, this is the place to dance because of its extended hours (3am) and the lively bohemian crowd that it draws. Dance the night away to a mix of contemporary and *merengue* or *bachata* music, or better yet to one of the generally free live acts on weekends. *C/ Isabel La Católica 255; parada77@gmail.com; www.parada77.com*

Cacibajagua Known by some regulars as the "rock 'n' roll bar" for its incredible selection of rock music, this tiny bar with exposed brick walls, cozy dark corners, and spectacular paintings by such artists as Chichi Reyes, has great energy, but with an intimate feel. Patrons pack the bar on Thursday nights, taking advantage of the late closing time of 4am. *201 C/ Sánchez; 333-9060; Facebook: Cacibajagua; Tues-Wed 8pm -1am; Thurs. 8pm-4am; Fri-Sat 8pm-3am*

 Rinconcito Every Sunday starting around 5pm, El Grupo Bonye gets together in the shadows of colonial ruins to give lovers of *merengue* and *son* their weekly dose of live music and dance. This Dominican group has been performing in Rinconcito ("little corner," which refers to this cobblestoned corner among the colonial ruins) since 2008. Although the event has increased tenfold in size and popularity, it still remains a primarily locals' event. Pick up a beer or bottle of rum from a nearby *colmado* and watch as the experienced dance couples sweep the floor with passionate Cuban dances like *bolero-son*. Or get in on the action with a *merengue* when the whole crowd joins in for this fast-paced favorite. *C/ Hostos, in front of the ruins of San Francisco*

El Sartén Those who want to keep the night going after Rinconcito head to El Sartén to rub shoulders with old school dance professionals. Although it is open seven days a week, Sundays after 10pm is the time to go. Impeccably dressed *damas* and *caballeros* show the young folk how a *son* is done. Grab one of the few tables and order a service of Cuba libre while watching generations of Dominicans show off their masterful *merengue* skills. Ladies, don't be afraid to make eye contact with one of the gentlemen standing around the perimeter of the shotgun dance floor. They love to share their knowledge with others, and these are some of the best teachers on the island. *153 C/ Hostos; 686-962; Sun-Wed 8pm-12am; Thu-Sat 8pm-2am*

Patio de Lucia Open only on Thursday and Saturday, this spacious outdoor dance hall attracts passionate lovers of Latin dance. Live musicians crank out everything from hip-flinging merengue to soulful boleros and sultry Cuban *son*, while waiters sling bottles of rum and buckets of ice to eager patrons seated around the plant-covered patio. *203 Hostos; Thu and Sat 8pm-1am*

GAZCUE

Being primarily an upper middle-class residential neighborhood, Gazcue has few spots that contribute to the city's active nightlife. There are several standouts, however, close to nearby hotels, and a nice walk or short cab ride from la Zona Colonial. Admittance is generally free unless there is a performance, and drink prices run in the RD$100-200 range.

Platinum With live acts nearly every weekend and regular ladies' nights, this bar is a popular university student hangout. *Av. Independencia near C/ Alma Mater*

Cinema Café This bar and concert venue runs a different theme every night, involving such varied acts as oldies tributes, 80s bands, and poetry readings. Cinema Café also hosts live performances by popular Dominican musicians like Toque Profundo and Calor Urbano. A favorite (and potent) drink special is the caipirinha, served in a fishbowl. The kitchen dishes out a selection of Spanish and Dominican tapas and sandwiches. During the weeknights, Cinema Café is a low-key place to catch up with a friend, whereas on the weekends it turns into a packed playground for 20-somethings. *Plaza de la Cultura; enter plaza on C/ Pedro Henríquez Ureña; located next to the Cinemateca; 221-7555; www.cinemacafe.com.do; Mon-Thu 4pm-1am, Fri-Sat 4pm-3am, Sun 5pm-1am*

Terraza Olímpica (Teleofertas) Located just north of Gazcue, this open-air dance floor is both a blast and down-to-earth. Only in the DR can drivers pass the time while getting their cars washed by dancing bachata and drinking beer. Weekends are the best time to soak up the neon-lit atmosphere with locals circled in plastic chairs bopping to loud beats as waitresses in jaw-dropping short skirts serve up Cuba Libres. Of course, a good time is guaranteed any day of the week. *Av. Gómez between Av. 27 de Febrero and Carretera Kennedy; no number; Open every day until 12am and at least 2am on weekends*

EL CENTRO & BEYOND

The establishments clustered around El Centro tend to draw a young professional crowd, especially those located along Av. Winston Churchill and Av. Lincoln, which there are major thoroughfares that bisect the wealthier neighborhoods full of high-rises. As a result, prices can be a tad more expensive than those found in La Zona Colonial or Gazcue; prices start at RD$200 for a mixed drink.

Cinnamon Depart from the bohemian hangouts of the Zona Colonial and mingle with the urbane young professionals of Santo Domingo at this outdoor bar located in the city center. While most of the patrons tend to come in groups, there is definite potential for socializing. Surrounding the bar is a plaza with a variety of restaurants including Mexican, Japanese, Italian, and international to grab a bite with new friends. *Corner of Av. Winston Churchill and Francisco Carias, Plaza Orleans, Ensanche Paraíso; 683-6510*

Jet Set This popular nightclub is the premier place for dancing to local favorites with some house music mixed in, featuring live music on Mondays. *RD$300 cover on weekends; 533-9707; 2253 Av. Independencia*

Guácara Taína Rave in a cave! Playing mostly techno and international music, this club built in a cave of the Parque Mirador del Sur offers multiple dance floors and bars spread across the subterranean dance paradise. More recently, it has drawn a younger and smaller crowd, but it is a rare opportunity to party in a grotto. *Ave. Mirador Sur, Parque Mirador del Sur; 533-1051*

SANTO DOMINGO DEL ESTE OR "AQUEL LAO"

A lively neighborhood known as Avenida Venezuela centered on the street of the same name has emerged over the last couple years as a center for some of the best dancing the city has to offer. For those looking for authentic Dominican nightlife, Avenida Venezuela is the destination, where foreigners are a rare sight and social pretense is left at home. Located on the eastern side of the Río Ozama in Santo Domingo del Este, this entire region of the city is colloquially referred to as "*aquel lado*," meaning "that (far) side." The ideal time to go is late night (after 11pm) on weekends, though decent nightlife can be found every night of the week. Arrive in a cab because throngs of cars choke the avenue, and parking is scarce as eager dancers flood the scene. Newcomers are bound to find a spot that suits their style after perusing the drags of Av. Venezuela and Av. San Vicente de Paul, but the locations below are among the most popular.

La Barrica With live music acts, karaoke, ladies' nights, sultry dance shows, and DJs spinning Dominican and international favorites, this bar, also known as "mega-colmadón," has raucous entertainment every night of the week. After working up a sweat from singing and dancing, La Barrica also offers tasty fried and grilled bar food to accompany the generous pours. *19 Av. Venezuela; 333-9188; superbarrica@gmail.com; www.labarricasportbar.blogspot.com*

La Nave Under neon lights, dancers grind out the latest *mambo callejero* and reggaetón hits in this bar/dance club, while icy Presidentes and Santo Libres are shared – and flow freely – among friends. *17 Av. Venezuela, 699-2856; lanavesport@hotmail.com*

Tráfico Located on the second floor directly across from La Nave, Tráfico is similar in feel with hot bodies packed into a dimly lit space as couples get down to the musical bounty of Santo Domingo's streets. *16 Av. Venezuela*

GAY BARS

The gay scene in Santo Domingo is small but strong, with several underground establishments. Acceptance of homosexuality has a long way to go in the Dominican Republic, though there are human rights groups actively working to promote wider acceptance. The exteriors of these bars are generally quite understated to prevent negative attention, but their interiors range from relaxing bars to high-energy dance clubs attracting patrons of all sexual persuasions. While hate crimes are not common, it may be best to err on the side of safety and avoid public displays of affection in order to avoid unnecessary risk, especially late at night.

Jay-Dees Jay-Dees provides a non-stop dance party complete with 1960s-inspired gargantuan daisies and enough glitter to blind. All are welcome, but the crowd is predominantly gay men of a wide age range. The main floor stays packed with gyrating bodies, while the second floor includes a small viewing room featuring gay films. *Cover RD$100-200; 10 C/ José Reyes, Zona Colonial; 333-5905; Thu and Sun 8pm-1am, Fri 9pm-3am, Sat 9pm-4am*

Amazonia This longstanding lesbian bar provides a laid-back and safe atmosphere. The owners are rather choosey about who is allowed entrance so as to avoid characters with less-than-honorable intentions. Poetry readings and expositions are among this bar's artistic offerings. *71 C/ Dr. Delgado, Gazcue; 412-7629*

CHA Opened by the renowned Dominican drag queen Chacita Rubio, this gay dance club welcomes all, offering late-night dance parties, drag shows, and strippers. *165 Av. George Washington between Máximo Gómez and Lincoln); www.chaclub.ning.com; Open Fri 9pm-4am, Sat 9pm-3am and Sun 9pm-1am*

Click With its regular drink specials, this new gay bar attracts a diverse crowd. The space is dark and cavernous, with multiple rooms for those looking for a more lounge-like atmosphere. *11 C/ Atarazana, Zona Colonial; click.nightclub@hotmail.com; Thurs.-Sat 9pm-1am; Sun 9pm-12am*

Sports & Outdoor Activities

There is no end to the available opportunities in and around the city: baseball, cockfights, basketball, biking, hiking, diving, climbing – the list goes on. With modern sports venues, shops carrying equipment for every passion, and an active community, sports fans and athletes will have a harder time deciding which sports to choose rather than where to find them.

ESTADIO QUISQUEYA

This stadium represents baseball fever at its highest pitch – don't miss a game between Licey and Escogido, Santo Domingo's rival teams. Aided by rum, beer, and booty-shaking cheerleaders, the energy is contagious when these two teams play head to head. Avoid driving because the stadium parking lot gets chaotic before and after the games. The Metro also runs here, so it would be a good way to give it a try. For game times, check local papers or the website; the season runs November through February. *Av. Tiradentes and C/ San Cristóbal; 540-5772/ 616-1224; estadioquisqueya@gmail.com; www.estadioquisqueya.com.do;*

Palacio de los Deportes is the home of the city's professional basketball team and other sporting events, besides hosting big-ticket musical acts like Juanes. Built in 1974 for the Central American and Caribbean Games, the arena is part of the sporting complex that houses the **Estadio Olímpico** (another popular venue for concerts), tennis, basketball and volleyball courts, baseball diamonds and a cycling track. Check local newspapers for upcoming concerts at both the Palacio de los Deportes and Estadio Olímpico. *C/ Ortega y Gassett and Av. 27 de Febrero*

COCKFIGHTING

To see another side of popular Dominican culture, head to the Coliseo Gallístico Alberto Bonetti Burgos (also, see Cockfighting, p25). The action can be fierce, and emotions run high, as money, beer, rum, and roosters flow freely. It may be best to keep a low profile in the farther reaches of the ring to evade calling attention to yourself. A rogue hand signal, for example, could signify a bet of a few thousand pesos, which might not endear you to your fellow participants. *Av. Luperón across from Aeropuerto de Herrera; 565-4038*

SCUBA SHOPS

There are a numerous scuba shops throughout the island, but here are two that are guaranteed to be up-to-date with their equipment safety checks.

Gus Dive Center With over 30 years of diving experience, owner Gus Torreira and his friendly staff offer SSI, NAUI, PADI, PDIC, IANTD, and SDI certifications from the most basic scuba courses to instructor certification. Courses are given in English as well as Spanish, French, Italian, and German. This aquatic sports center also offers dive trips for those already certified to amazing dive destinations around the island, including an all-inclusive catamaran trip to Isla Saona or Bahia de las Aguilas. *356 C/ Roberto Pastoriza, Plaza Lira II; 566-0818; www.gusdivecenter.com*

Golden Arrow Dive Center Owner Denis Bourret offers PADI or IANTD systems of education for a variety of certifications including Cave Diving, Technical, Recreational, Instructor, and DAN, all of which are available in English. *C/ Mustafa Kemal Ataturk No. 10, Local No. 1, Naco; 566-7780; 886-7777; denis@cavediving.com.do; www.cavediving.com.do*

BIKING

For mountain bikes, tune-ups, and gear, head to **Planet Bike** (535-2152; 103 Calle G. Polanco), **Aro & Pedal** (483-1912; 1 Prolongación Charles de Gaulle), or **Bici Centro** (397 Av. Rómulo Betancourt; 533-4404, 533-2783; www.bicicentro.com.do and in Santiago, 25 Av. Bartolome Colón, Centro Comercial Jorge, 582-4146). Bici Centro has two locations that sell and rent a wide selection of bikes and gear, as well as provide maintenance and repair services certified by Barnett Bicycle Institute. Check out the website for upcoming races and events.

SHOPPING

A vibrant painting, a smooth hand-rolled cigar, and a precious piece of larimar are among the unique, authentic gifts to best remember a visit to the DR. From narrow, locally owned boutiques to gargantuan malls, Santo Domingo's shopping scene can quell even the most tenacious shopaholics. If character is important to the shopper, stick to the small shops of the Zona Colonial located off El Conde, or peruse the quirky outdoor vendors and shops stuck in an older era on Calle Mella. For art lovers, peruse the Zona Colonial's galleries, replete with Dominican artists' lively, bright, and occasionally haunting styles. Those looking for fun international shops and a break from the noise of the city, try one of Santo Domingo's numerous air-conditioned malls, complete with food courts and movie theaters.

Art Galleries

Bettye's Galleria American owner Bettye has a high quality selection from Dominican and Haitian artists, but be sure to barter while she is there because her prime location drives her prices up quite a bit. Her gallery features smaller souvenirs like brightly painted metal work, antique jewelry, and small affordable paintings, as well as paintings by Dominican masters such as artists from the Oviedo family. *163 C/ Isabel La Católica; Plaza de María de Toledo; 688-7649; Wed-Mon 9am-6pm*

 Duendes del Caribe Combining quality with reasonable prices, this gallery and artists' workshop is the best place in the capital for gifts and authentic souvenirs. Skip all the tourist traps of El Conde and head straight to Santa Bárbara, the adjoining neighborhood to the Zona Colonial. Manuel Bolos, the owner, hand picks each of the artisan crafts and paintings done by both Haitian and Dominican artists. Visitors will have a hard time deciding between the rustic Haitian metal sculptures, brightly painted papier mâché, and range of painting styles. Look for the row of whitewashed buildings with Bolos' signature blue shutters. *17 C/ General Cabral; Santa Bárbara; 686-5073; www.duendesdelcaribe.blogspot.com*

Galería Ajoupa One of the only galleries in the country that features strictly Haitian paintings, Galería Ajoupa also hosts Haitian cultural events and presentations on such topics as Voodoo. *255 C/ Mercedes, Zona Colonial*

Fundación Taller Público Silvano Lora A space dedicated entirely to the artist Silvano Lora (1931-2003), this art gallery showcases Lora's most recent mixed media works that utilize flattened pieces of scrap metal and tin cans to form moving pieces representing the struggles of the disenfranchised. Fundación Silvano Lora aims to keep alive Lora's revolutionary spirit and desire to unite Dominican society through presentations, discussions, expositions, film festivals, and concerts. *104 Arzobispo Meriño near C/ Arzobispo Portes, Zona Colonial, 689-9835 fundacionsilvanolora@hotmail.com; www.silvanolora.org*

Galería de Arte Cándido Bidó This gallery is difficult to miss, painted in Cándido Bído's signature orange with blue accents. Works of Bidó, known for his paintings of local women, birds, and nature in bold blues, reds, yellows, and oranges, are displayed throughout the first floor. Cándido Bidó, born in 1936, is internationally recognized, having won multiple prizes in the El Bienal Nacional and El Concurso de Arte de León Jimenez art contests. *5 C/ Dr. Baez, Gazcue; 685-5310; www.grupointeractivo.com/bido*

Feria Artesanal Navideña Every year in early December, artisans travel from all corners of the country to participate in this weeklong festive gathering in the heart of the city. Started in the back patio of the Peace Corps office by a group of determined volunteers in 2001, the event has grown to be the largest artisan fair in the country, utilizing the entire Plaza de Colón in front of the Cathedral. Crafts and products include organic cacao, coffee, handmade jewelry, hand-woven *macutos* (bags), ceramic dolls, lanterns and other items intricately carved from *higüero* gourds, and various styles of painting. Along with the products for sale, organizers put on courses, exhibitions, workshops and displays of music, dance, and theater. Check local papers in the fall for exact dates.

Feria de Artesanía Every weekend in Parque Bartolomé de las Casas, Casa del Teatro sponsors an artisans' fair featuring handmade jewelry, paintings, hand-rolled cigars and other handicrafts. *Corner of C/ Meriño and C/ Padre Billini*

Bookstores

Bookstores are rare, even in the capital city. Be sure to bring books from home because English books are especially scarce and expensive. For great books in Spanish, as well as a few in other languages, try the following:

Librería La Trinitaria Named after the trinity of Dominican founding fathers, this small, family-owned bookstore sells a range of mostly Spanish-language books. Dominican historical and political classics are featured, including works by such heavy hitters as Juan Bosch, or books about immortalized Dominican revolutionaries like Francisco Caamaño Deñó. *160 C/ Arzobispo Nouel and C/ José Reyes, Zona Colonial; 682-1032/ 686-6110; Mon-Sat 9am-6pm*

Librería Cuesta One of the largest bookstores in Santo Domingo and in the country, Librería Cuesta offers a respectable selection of books in English as well as smaller Dominican publications about Dominican culture, music, politics and history that are difficult to find outside of the country. *Av. 27 de Febrero and Abraham Lincoln; 473-4020; www.cuestalibros.com; Mon-Sat 9am- 9pm; Sun and holidays 10am-3pm*

Thesaurus Thesaurus' collection spans a diverse range of genres from esotericism to decorating. Peruse a good find in the Wi-Fi-enabled café nibbling on tasty finger food, one of the few places in the country to find frozen coffee drinks. *Av. Abraham Lincoln and Sarasota; 508-1114; www.thesaurus.com.do; Mon-Sat 9am-9pm. Sun 10am-3pm*

Cigars

If you don't have time to visit some of the rolling factories in the Cibao, such as in Santiago (p255), Santo Domingo's cigar stores are the next best option.

Along El Conde, there are two cigar shops worth taking a gander for their impressive selections and optimal storage, which extends the life and flavor of the cigars. Keep a look out for Davidoff, La Aurora (Connecticut wrapper), La Flor Dominicana, and Cohiba, which all regularly score high in international rankings.

Boutique El Fumador *109 El Conde; 685-6425; Mon-Sat 9am-7pm and Sun 10am-3:30pm*

Museo del Tobaco *101 El Conde, 689-7665; Mon-Sun 9am -8pm*

Megastores

La Sirena The original Dominican superstore, La Sirena is a cheap place to get photos developed, pick up a bathing suit, or load up on food for a road trip. Most even have food courts. There are almost 20 La Sirena outlets across the country, with half in the capital city. *Multiple locations: the closest to the Zona Colonial is on Calle Mella and Duarte, but a larger and much nicer store is located on Av. Winston Churchill at C/ Angel Severo Cabral; 472-4444; Mon-Sat: 8am-10pm; Sun and holidays: 9am-8pm; www.tiendalasirena.com*

Carrefour Carrefour is France's upscale response to Wal-Mart. While a bit pricier than its superstore competitors, this place has all the imported specialty foods a Francophile could ever want, along with a slew of items that give Carrefour its superstore reputation. *Autopista Duarte Km 10 ½; 412-2333*

El Conde

This famous pedestrian thoroughfare of the Zona Colonial marks the center of tourism in Santo Domingo, bursting with movement, color, and life. Although the street at times exudes over commercialized tackiness with its chain restaurants and cheap shops selling imported souvenirs, it's a must-see for a few key stores, local haunts, and Zona Colonial characters. A couple small jewelry shops sell quality amber and larimar pieces here, but it's a good idea to barter a bit because the tourist traffic inflates prices.

Calle El Conde was a principal thoroughfare in the colonial era, and was probably just as crowded as it is today. The famous street went through a half-dozen name changes until it settled on El Conde ("the Count") named for Count Peñalba, who defended the city from British attacks in the 1650s. It is the only pedestrian thoroughfare in the capital city.

MALLS

Acropolis If there is a strong need for an air-conditioned escape or a hankering for Häagen-Dazs or Cinnabon, this American-style mall – one of the largest buildings in the country – provides

> All malls listed here are located in El Centro

a nice respite. Hosting stores such as Zara, Mango, and Nine West, Acropolis is a four-level multiplex that could be confused for the set of "Housewives of Santo Domingo," as it is consistently populated with well-heeled Dominican women (and men). It also has a food court and movie theater showing (somewhat delayed) Hollywood flicks. *Av. Winston Churchill and C/ Rafael Augusto Sánchez*

Plaza Central This mall's rather worn exterior distinguished by an large red apple shouldn't deter prospective shoppers, because it is full of international retailers, such as United Colors of Benetton, as well as various stores selling clothes, shoes, and art. *C/ 27 de Febrero and C/ Winston Churchill; 541-5929; Mon-Sat 9am-7pm*

Bella Vista Mall Posh, modern, and the shopping home for the beautiful and stylish, this mall hosts a variety of mid-level and high-end shops. Its modern stadium-style movie theater features Hollywood exports, but annually hosts international film festivals for less than RD$250 per viewing. Check out the show times at www.uepa.com. *62 Av. Sarasota at C/ de los Arrayanes, Bella Vista; 255-0664/0665*

Blue Mall The newest entry in Santo Domingo's burgeoning mall craze, Blue Mall is a cut above the rest with its sleek architecture and exclusive stores, including Louis Vuitton and Salvatore Ferragamo. Proclaiming Blue Mall as a symbol of "progress and modernity," President Fernández, accompanied by the First Lady, inaugurated the upscale shopping center in August of 2010. *Corner of Av. Winston Churchill and C/ Gustavo M. Ricart; bluemall.com.do; 955-3000; 8am-2am Mon-Sat, 12pm-12am Sun*

Tour Operators

⚡ Anti-Tour Started by co-author Katie Tuider, this adventure travel company is for the intrepid traveler who is bored by the structure of traditional tours, but doesn't have the time to take off for months to discover the hidden gems of a culture and country. Anti-Tour cuts out the wrong turns, tourist prices, and regrettable cultural misunderstandings. Members experience the bohemian hangouts, local eateries, and charming back roads of the Dominican Republic. Tours range from four to fourteen days, but Anti-Tour also offers specifically designed tours for groups. While the anti-tours have basic itineraries, each is flexible, based on the interests of its participants. Anti-Tour supports small, local businesses, community-based eco-tourism, and development projects by incorporating them into its adventures. *See website for prices; www.antitourdr.com; theantitourdr@gmail.com*

⚡ Explora Ecotour Explora Ecotour offers guided tours by bilingual guides to national parks and other natural and cultural attractions with an emphasis on educating others about the unique ecosystems and rural culture they encounter. *See website for packages and prices; Gustavo Mejía Ricart No.43 Suite 209, Naco; 567-1852; http://exploraecotour.com*

Courses

DANCE CLASSES

Escuela de Baile Ritmo 70 This dance school offers classes in classic Latin dance, merengue, bachata, and salsa, as well as less-traditional styles such as gagá, hip-hop, modern ballet, and belly dancing. Classes are available in various experience levels, including exercises classes like yoga and capoeira. *261 C/ Mercedes near José Reyes, Zona Colonial; 829-733-0279; 829-638-3595 ritmo.70@hotmail.com; www.ritmo70.blogspot.com*

LANGUAGE CLASSES

Tom's Atelier Friendly native French speaker Tom teaches French, Spanish, and English to small groups of all levels right out of his home. *6 Av. Leopoldo Navarro and C/ Caonabo, Gazcue, 545-9426*

Instituto Cultural Dominico Americano With more than 60 years of experience, this centrally located language school has a reputation for being one of the best in Santo Domingo. The school offers Spanish language classes at set times in small groups, or private lessons based on the student's schedule. *For more information and prices, contact the school at 535-0665, ext. 3202/3240. idiomas@icda.edu.do.*

Academia Europea Offering a number of languages including Spanish, French, Italian, Portuguese, and German, the Academia Europea courses were initially designed to teach languages in a minimal amount of time, and so they are ideal for

---

The Son Circuit

Though not originally from the Dominican Republic, *son*, the music and dance originating in the early 20th century from Cuba, has gained a respectable following in Santo Domingo. Every night of the week, there is at least one spot where the often lively, other times melancholic, but always sultry rhythms of *son* can be heard throughout the barrio. Typical instruments include a Cuban guitar called the *tres* (with three double strings) and trumpet, with a strong emphasis on percussion. Such percussion includes a double bass or *marímbola* (a bass box with metal plates that are plucked to create a resonating sound reminiscent of a xylophone), claves (two wooden dowels struck together for percussion), maracas, and bongos.

For those new to dancing son, **El Club Nacional de Soneros** (www.soneros.org; info@soneros.org) frequently offers free dance classes to the public in la Sede del Club (Club headquarters, 3 Baltasar de los Reyes, near C/ Dr. Betances, Villa María).

Seven Days of *Son* in Santo Domingo:

Sunday: Rinconcito (Ruínas de San Francisco) with el Grupo Bonyé, 6-10pm

Monday: Trovas Tapas Bar (6 C/ Leopoldo Navarro, Gazcue, 688-8466)

Tuesday: El Secreto Musical (corner of C/ Baltasar de los Reyes and Pimentel, Villa Consuelo) is open from 6pm, but the dancing heats up after 9pm until 12am. Be sure to arrive and leave in a taxi and with a group as this neighborhood can be dangerous after dark.

Wednesday: D'Niño Siempre Fría (corner of C/ Yolanda Guzmán and C/ Osvaldo Basil, Villa María) is a newer spot for *son* enthusiasts hosted by the Chino Méndez, a dedicated and well-known Sonero. Also known for being *caliente* or dangerous after dark, so arrive and leave in a taxi and preferably with a group.

Thursday: La Casa de Lucía is open from 8pm with live musicians playing *son* and merengue beginning at 10pm.

Friday: Havana Café (corner of Palo Hincado and Padre Arz. Nouel, Zona Colonial) is a new addition to the *son* line-up with the live act el Grupo Bonyé. A more dependable locale for *son*, merengue, and salsa would be El Sartén.

Saturday: Check out Casa de Lucía and El Sartén.

students passing through and those interested in functional language learning. *8 C/ Gracita Álvarez and Presidente González, Ens. Naco; 227-3687, 549-7231*

UNAPEC Escuela de Idiomas Along with its diverse academic tracks such as law, business, art, engineering, and computer science, this university also has short-term Spanish language classes for foreigners as well as a variety of other languages, generally lasting a semester long. *Campus Principal Dr. Nicolas Pichardo, 72 Av. Maximo Gómez; 686-0021 ext 2268/2269, 2292/2294; escueladeidiomas@adm.unapec.edu.do; www.unapec.edu.do*

Entrena Entrena offers intensive, high-quality Spanish language immersion courses of two or four weeks in duration. The company is well regarded in international circles, and trains such clients as Peace Corps volunteers and MLB employees. The programs include six hours of language training per day, plus a homestay that provides meals and laundry. Entrena also offers personalized classes and programs on an hourly or daily basis that can include lessons and field trips. Hourly rates begin at US$15. *23 Av. Lope de Vega, Edificio Progreso Business Center, Suite 601, Naco; 567-8990; entrena@entrenadr.com*

Cultural Centers

Centro Cultural Brasil-República Dominicana This cultural center, sponsored by the Brazilian embassy, will make any Brazilian or Lusophile feel at home. Its calendar is full of performing arts events, including theater, live music, and capoeira performances. Brazilian Portuguese language courses and classes with the capoeira group Alemar also add to the cultural diffusion. *52 C/ Hermanos Deligne, Gazcue; 682-1128/1192; admcentroculturalbrasil@gmail.com*

Centro Dominico Alemán With monthly gourmet food markets selling beer, sausage, and other delicacies, as well as free German movie screenings and cultural events, this German-Dominican cultural center always offers interesting and economical entertainment. The center is sponsored by the German embassy and is tied to other international German cultural centers. To find out the week's activities, stop by the center in the evening or check them out on Facebook "Centro Dominico-Aleman Santo Domingo." *212 Isabel La Católica, Zona Colonial; centrodomaleman@gmail.com*

Alianza Francesa The French Alliance offers excellent, regular (four hours per week) and semi-intensive (eight hours per week) French language classes starting around US$120 per trimester. A proponent of both French and Dominican culture, the French Alliance supports a diversity of art and artists. It works with local talent, like Cayuco Reyes, as well as French artists from street circus acts to concert pianists. The Mediatec, a quiet, air-conditioned, and Wi-Fi-equipped library, is open to all for work and study. And for a small annual fee (RD$400), members can check out French books and music. *103 C/ Horacio Vicioso; Centro de los Héroes; 532-2844/2935; alianza.francesa@afsd.net; www.afsd.net/es*

Beaches Near Santo Domingo

LA CALETA

This beach is relatively quiet, used by fisherman and favored by locals, but the real reason to visit is for the exquisite diving. Hosting the unique Parque Nacional Submarino ("Undersea National Park"), La Caleta offers excellent cave diving and opportunities to see shipwrecks and thriving coral reefs up close. It is therefore is considered one of the top places to dive in the country.

Of the three sunken boats in the park, the most visited is the Hickory shipwreck, which was installed in 1984 to foster the growth of coral reef and other marine life. Fish and invertebrates flock to the ship's dark corners and corals and sponges affix themselves to the undersea walls; a perfect example of the synergy of environmental stewardship and tourism. The Hickory, a U.S. Coast Guard steamboat built in the 17th century, was later converted to scour the Caribbean waters for treasures left behind by pirates. The ship has now become a treasure itself. Divers of all skill levels can explore above and below the deck, enjoying the great visual stimulation that the coral reefs surrounding La Caleta afford.

Diving at La Caleta

Several fishermen of La Caleta formed a fishing and tourism cooperative, La Cooperativa de Producción y Trabajo de Pescadores y Prestadores de Servicios Turísticos de La Caleta (COOPRESCA), in order to meet the demand in tourism for la Caleta's underwater national park. For prices and scheduling, contact the secretary of COOPRESCA, Johanna Rosado (Spanish only) at 829-372-1334 or Gus Dive Center (p108) for excursions, including equipment and pro diving instructors, who speak English.

BOCA CHICA

Boca Chica is the archetypal Dominican beach – tawny sand, warm waters, and a lively atmosphere. Boca Chica ("little mouth") is the closest beach to the metropolis of Santo Domingo, and for that reason is probably the most popular beach on the island. It is easily accessible – just east of the international airport and a half hour drive from Santo Domingo. The sea is smooth and reverentially calm, perfect for families and casual beach frolickers coming in from the big city. Boca Chica caters to a wide audience, and for that reason there are few all-inclusive hotels, but much in the way of affordable lodging and eating establishments surrounding the blocks by the water. While it is not nearly the cleanest or prettiest beach on the island, and is no longer the luxury retreat it once was during its midcentury heyday, Boca Chica's infectious energy, especially at night and on the weekends, makes for an entertaining, proximal, and budget-friendly beach trip from the capital.

Though the town is bisected by the Autopista, there is nothing for the visitor on the north side, so stick to the southern part by the beach and the main drags of Av. Caracoles running south to Av. Duarte, also known as the *malecón*, along the beach.

Info

The **Shell gas station** is located on the highway at Av. Caracoles, the main entrance to Boca Chica. For cash, find **Banco Popular** by the water at Av. Juan Bautista Vicini and **BanReservas** at Av. San Rafael and C/ Juanico García. For groceries, a block south is the **Supermercado Boca Chica** at Av. Duarte (the *malecón*) and C/ Juanico García. The **Tourism Office** (523-5106) and **Politur** are on the same block on C/ Juanico García between the Malecón and Av. San Rafael.

Eat

No popular Dominican beach is complete without fried fish stands. This is where to get a cheap, fresh meal topped off with a frosty Presidente, just as the locals do. Otherwise, Boca Chica has a few decent restaurants, from beach casual to beach classy.

Neptuno's Club The god of the sea would be pleased enough to get his fill of tastefully plated fresh grilled seafood at this waterside establishment, set on a wooden terrace overlooking the Caribbean. The stylish décor speaks to a more formal night out, not a casual lunch, and reservations are recommended. The menu is expansive, and can be expensive. *RD$500-1000; 12 C/ Duarte, east of Av. Caracoles*

Sleep

Don Paco Cheap and easy, but not in the bad way. Don Paco is just a couple *tostones'* throw from the beach, and within reach of a budget while still providing tidy and comfortable rooms, sufficient security, and a soothing garden patio. *RD$800; 523-4816; C/ Duarte and C/ Vicini*

Calypso Beach Hotel With bright and clean rooms with kitchenettes, a pool and a breakfast buffet, Calypso Beach Hotel provides a nice escape from the city or a convenient place to stay before or after flying as it is only ten minutes from the airport. Though not located directly on the beach, the hotel is a short walk from the water. *US$45-87; Corner of Calles Caracol and 20 de Diciembre; 523-4666; info@calypsobeachhotel.com; www.calypsobeachhotel.com; Amenities: A/C, safe, hot water, TV, phone, restaurant, Wi-Fi*

Diving in Boca Chica

Protected by a barrier reef, the waters of Boca Chica are filled with shipwrecks promoting further coral reef growth and fascinating caves of ranging diving difficulties. Of the shipwrecks, the Ocean Spring is excellent for beginners and underwater photographers as it is located only 8 to 14 meters (24 to 42 feet) under the sea. The Captain Alsina wreck is the deepest man-made attraction in the area, located at a depth of 40 meters (120 feet), attracting green eels and other interesting sea life.

For diving trips, **Treasure Divers** (523-5320; watersports@donjuanbeachresort.com) is located within the Hotel Don Juan Beach Resort in Boca Chica (687-9157; www.donjuanbeachresort.com). Giving CMAS and PADI certified courses, this shop offers dives at 8:30am, 10:30am, 1:30pm, and 3:30pm, as well as a night dive.

PLAYA CARIBE

Cradled between rock walls, this tiny beach attracts local surfers and body-boarders for the intense waves. Besides the few vendors selling beer and snacks, bathers have the beach to themselves. To get a spot on a lounge chair, tip the *muchacho* in charge about RD$100 when leaving; otherwise, just claim a spot in the sand. Exert caution here, because the waves can get very strong and there is no lifeguard on duty. *To reach Playa Caribe via public transportation, grab a guagua in Parque Enriquillo heading to La Romana. Make sure it is a caliente, not an expreso, because the expreso does not stop here. Ask the cobrador to leave you at Playa Caribe or the local name "Embassy" after about a 30-minute ride east.*

PLAYA GUAYACANES

Next to Playa Juan Dolio, Guayacanes is a small beach community with a smattering of restaurants and hotels. Before leaving this clean white-sand beach, take time to explore Calle Principal, where an artisan named Julian has lived and worked since the late 1940s. A carpenter and fisherman by trade, Julian carves model sailboats, rustic bowls, and sculptures inspired by the natural gnarls of the oak and almond trees. A few houses down on the main street is **Les Ateliers de Chantal** (526-3077; solaidom@yahoo.com), where French owner Chantal and volunteers train local youth in ceramics, painting, and artisan crafts, providing them with a creative outlet and a vocation. The beautiful creations are for sale in the workshop's storefront, the proceeds of which support educational programs. *Playa Guayacanes is located between Playa Caribe and Juan Dolio east of Santo Domingo along Av. Las Americas.*

Eat

Salitre Restaurante serves generous portions of seafood paella and grilled fish with a passion fruit glaze amidst a seafaring-inspired atmosphere, complete with colorful murals and installations of driftwood. The inventive cocktails such as the Blue Salitre and Chinola Fiesta paired with the unobstructed beach view provide for a splendid afternoon. *C/ Central, Los Guayacanes; 526-1969; 829-521-6070*

Sleep

Les Ateliers de Chantal rents a comfortable and colorfully decorated room above the library with kitchen access for RD$1,000 a night, or as low as RD$300 a night for week-long stays. Two smaller rooms are available free of charge for volunteers willing to teach languages, art, or a craft of the volunteer's choice to local youth. *C/ Central; 526-3077; solaidom@yahoo.com*

PLAYA JUAN DOLIO

Located 52 kilometers (32 miles) east of Santo Domingo, the white sand beach and placid aquamarine water at Juan Dolio is close enough to the capital to make for an excellent day trip. Most of the beach, though bordered by walled vacation homes, is pleasingly quiet, allowing sunbathers to enjoy it unobstructed.

Info

The **Gift Shop Mini-Market Naito** sells everything from snacks to blow-up toys. **SITRADUSA** (526-3507/2227) offers taxi service around the area. Both of these along with **Soriano's Casa de Cambio** (money exchange) are located on the Calle Principal. Leaving town toward the highway from Gift Shop Mini-Market Naito and turning left is **Cyber Leonardo**, which offers internet access by the hour (green façade; Carretera Santo Domingo-San Pedro de Macorís).

Eat

Pepek Narmonick With tables directly on the beach, this Russian-owned seafood restaurant offers international fare in an elegant but casual setting featuring wicker chairs, a respectable wine selection, and a naturally-treated wooden bar. Start with one of various salads such as the iron-rich Ensalada Popeye, followed by filet mignon with Roquefort or grilled shrimp. *RD$295-650; C/ Principal Plaza Perla Mar I; 526-1890; info@pepeknarmonikjd.com; www.pepeknarmonikjd.com*

Luca's Ristorante Italiano This Italian kitchen opened in 2005 and specializes in seafood spaghetti, crisp pizzas, and, of course, seafood. Check out Luca's list of Italian wines, best enjoyed at one of the waterfront tables. *RD$200-800; C/ Principal; 526-1311*

Restaurante El Sueño On the weekends, this Italian-owned, open-air restaurant with an ocean view is bustling with Italian expats and *capitaleños* pining for steaming plates of pastas, thin crust pizzas, and succulent seafood dishes. Try the arugula and prosciutto pizza or the ravioli stuffed with lobster, and finish the meal with cool, smooth gelato. *RD$380-630; C/ Principal*

Sleep

A gloomy economy and changes in local tourism have revamped Juan Dolio's hotel scene, causing many hotels to go out of businesses while condominium complexes sweep up the desirable real estate. As a result, there are few decent hotels left, but if planning a long-term stay, it is worth doing an internet search of apartments for rent, especially in the low season when prices are quite affordable.

Hotel Fior di Loto Bridging her love for India and the Dominican Republic, the Italian owner Mara started this hotel and yoga studio in order to support her charitable efforts in India. The incense-infused common area of the hotel is like stepping into an Indian tea house, covered in mirrored tapestries and intricately embroidered cushions that invite visitors to lounge while sampling the hotel café's sandwiches or fresh juices. The rooms are more understated, with basic amenities and white walls decorated with bright Indian-inspired accents. When she is not traveling, Mara offers free yoga and chakra classes in the hotel's gym. Proceeds support the Fundación Fior di Loto India. *RD$500-1,500; 517 C/ Principal; 526-1146/3332; hotelfiordiloto@hotmail.com; hotelfiordiloto@yahoo.com; www.fiordilotohotel.com; Amenities: cable, hot water, generator, gym, Jacuzzi, Wi-Fi.*

Coop Marena Beach Resort This massive and rather run-down all-inclusive resort attracts Dominicans looking for a low-budget vacation. Occupying a large area both on the beach and the northern side of the main road, the resort boasts 210 rooms, a disco, three pools, conference rooms, restaurants, a game area, and typical resort activities. *RD$2,500 and up (all-inclusive; check for low-season deals); C/ Principal; 526-2121; 689-9048; coopmarena@hotmail.com*

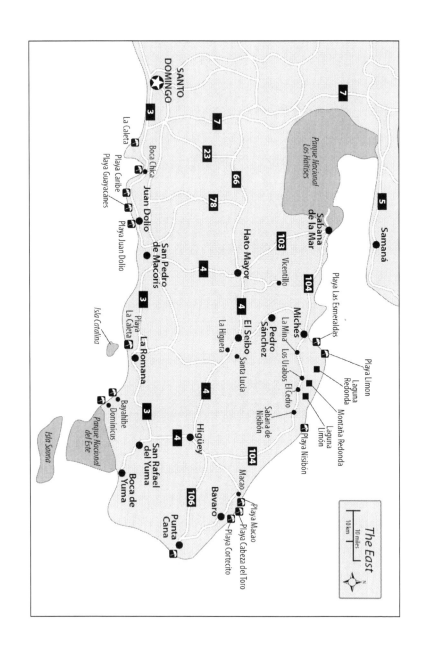

The East

Moving east out of Santo Domingo, flat, scrubby plains (*llanos*, in Spanish) dominate the landscape, reaching beyond the horizon shimmering in midday heat. These grassy expanses begin at the Caribbean Sea and slowly rise in elevation moving northward toward the coast of the Samaná Bay. This environment has provided for the tremendous development of the region's two bedrock industries – sugarcane production and livestock ranching.

Just south of the bay is the Cordillera Oriental mountain range, also known as the Sierra de Seibo, where the forested peaks can reach over 800 meters (2,600 feet). The East is also home to two spectacular, can't-miss national parks, Los Haitises and Parque Nacional del Este (National Park of East). The warm waters and lengthy coastline – including the picture-perfect Isla Saona, the biggest offshore island in the country – create a welcome atmosphere for marine animals and an impressive diversity of plants and birds, as well as for the intrepid visitor seeking outdoor adventure.

The tropical vacation destination of Punta Cana at the eastern tip of the island far outdraws any other area in the region. The many all-inclusive resorts attract millions of tourists a year to the white sand beaches and turquoise waters. The less prominent, but more impressive, beaches (often requiring four-wheel drive and a good sense of direction) are located along the southern coast of Samaná Bay between Miches and Macao. Lack of accessibility has allowed these stunning areas to remain untrammeled and underappreciated, with the only accommodations being the shade of a palm tree. Towns in the East, with the exceptions of La Romana and San Pedro de Macorís, are small and quiet, subsisting on agriculture: sugarcane and ranching across the plains, rich organic cacao farming in the hills around El Seibo and Hato Mayor, and fishing in Boca de Yuma, Sabana de la Mar, and Miches.

San Pedro de Macorís

Though San Pedro de Macorís is a town of many monikers, the provenance of its actual name is not known – most likely, it is probably simply named for a popular Spanish saint and a common Taíno word that was also given to a nearby river. San Pedro's history is unique to the Dominican Republic, for it was not a colonial city, but founded by exiles fleeing the Cuban independence wars of the late 19th century.

The first nickname San Pedro goes by is appropriately the "City of Firsts," referring to the many events and inventions that came out of the city, much like Santo Domingo. Among the achievements that San Pedro claims are the first telephone, firefighters, and hydroport in the country. When Cuban cane workers immigrated to the San Pedro, they brought with them baseball (see below), turning San Pedro into a pioneering town of this ever-popular pastime. Other sports, such as cricket and horse racing, continue to compete at the country's first hippodrome.

These early advancements were the result of the wealth emanating from the sugarcane industry that came to define San Pedro. Sugar production began in 1879, and sparked an economic revolution that was to produce almost three quarters of the country's GDP at the turn of the 19th century. The demand for sugar and its derivatives (namely, rum) increased the need for labor both on the plantations and in related industrial manufacturing. Italians, Dutch, Chinese, Arabs, Puerto Ricans and other Latinos, and *Cocolos* (see p123) arrived in droves to the city's port. San Pedro also attracted wealthy European traders and patrons, transforming the city into a cosmopolitan center of international commerce. This golden era led to other nicknames for San Pedro, like "the Cup of Gold" and "Sultan of the East." Unfortunately, every cane stalk must come down, and so did the price of sugar in latter half of the 20th century. San Pedro has fallen hard, but is slowly recovering with the help of a diversified economy, more stable prices, and a nascent tourism industry.

> Which of these MLB Players hail from San Pedro de Macorís?
>
> Manny Alexander
> George Bell
> Robinson Cano
> José Offerman
> Tony Peña
> Julio Santana
> Sammy Sosa
> Fernando Tatís
>
> *Answer: All of them! 80 MLB players hail from San Pedro.*

Another nickname, "The Cradle of Baseball," is a result of the region's biggest sports obsession. Dozens of professional baseball players call San Pedro home, and several MLB teams run intensive training camps around the city. Ask the average San Pedro boy what he wants to be when he grows up, and his response will almost undoubtedly be ballplayer. Besides an evening of fun, baseball represents the oft-elusive ticket out of an otherwise dreary local economy. Dominican youth and their families dream big, hoping that MLB money will build them a mansion resembling Dominican baseball giant George Bell's, in San Pedro's center. Catch a boisterous game in this baseball-crazed town at Estadio Tetelo Vargas (see p124) during the winter season.

TRANSPORT

To Santo Domingo: RD$90; 5am-7pm, every 20 minutes; 1hr; there are two companies that travel between San Pedro and Santo Domingo, ASOTRASANP and ASTRAPU. **ASOTRASANP** (930-7883) is located across from the *Mercado* on the corner of C/ Francisco Caamaño Deñó and Ramón del Castillo and **ASTRAPU** *guaguas* leave from C/ Caamaño near C/ Gómez.

From Santo Domingo: RD$90; 5am-7pm, every 20 minutes; 1hr; **ASTRAPU** *guaguas* leave from C/ José Martí a half block south of Parque Enriquillo toward C/ México; **ASOTRASANP** *guaguas* leaves from C/ Caracas and C/ José Martí in front of Parque Enriquillo.

Heading southeast and northeast (La Romana, Hato Mayor, El Seibo, Higüey): All these *guaguas* pass about every 30 minutes through San Pedro and can be hailed on the Autopista del Este (Highway 3).

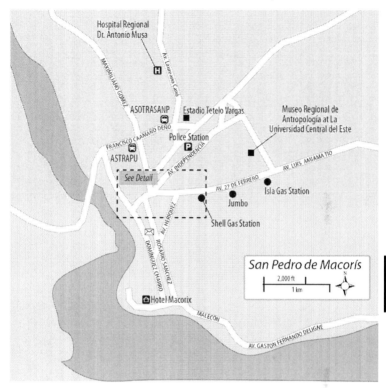

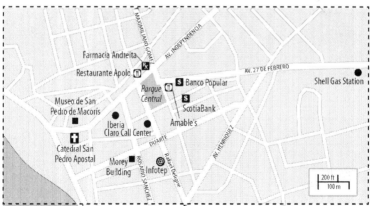

The East

INFO

Medical Attention

Farmacia Andreita is located on the northeast corner of the Parque Central. For emergencies, the public **Hospital Regional Dr. Antonio Musa** (529-1022) is located on Av. Laureano Canó and C/ Libertad.

Communication

Infotep has computers with internet for RD$30/hour across from what remains of the 1883 Fundación Logia building (C/ Rafael Deligne between C/ Mella and Duarte). **Claro Call Center** is located on C/ Deligne one block south of the Parque Central. The **Post Office** is located on the corner of C/ 10 de Septiembre and Domínguez Charro (529-2029; 910-1875).

Banks

There is a **Banco Popular** on C/ 27 de Febrero near the east side of the Parque Central (C/ Cabral), a **ScotiaBank** at 15 Alejo Martínez and **BanReservas** is located 39 C/ General Cabral near C/ Bermúdez, all of which are open Mon-Fri 8:30am-4:30pm and Sat 9am-1pm.

Police

The **Police Station** is located on Av. Independencia across from the high school, Liceo José Joaquín Pérez near C/ Sergio A. Beras.

Gas

There are multiple gas stations located in town including the **Shell Gas Station** located on Av. 27 de Febrero and C/ Dr. Joaquín Ruíz or there is the **Isla Gas Station**, also located on Av. 27 de Febrero, but closer to Av. Francisco Alberto Camaaño Deñó.

Grocery Stores

In terms of size and selection, the top grocery stores in town are the large chains **Jumbo** and **Iberia**. Iberia has everything from house wares to clothing and food, as well as a pharmacy and a **Banco Popular** ATM (C/ Sánchez and C/ Independencia). **Jumbo** is a nationwide superstore owned by Wal-Mart that sells every human necessity, including a food court and a branch of **BanReservas** (104 Av. Luís Amiama Tió; changes to Av. 27 de Febrero).

EAT

The options for eating out in San Pedro are rather limited. Though the scene is sparse, the following restaurants are longstanding local favorites.

Amable's Both delicious and cheap, this bright and casual restaurant with A/C is famous across the East for its *pasteles de hoja* (mashed plantain, yuca or cornmeal stuffed with meat or vegetables and boiled in a banana leaf). The *pasteles* come in three sizes for the adventurous to mix and match flavors., It's always a good idea to accompany a meal with a fresh squeezed juice or *batida*. *RD$30-70; C/ General Cabral, in front of Parque Central; 529-4500*

Restaurante Apolo For a slightly more upscale meal, try this San Pedro tradition, open for more than 50 years. The variety in food from Chinese to European to Dominican speaks to the multitude of ethnicities that converged in San Pedro during the heyday of the cane industry. *RD$200-400; in front of Parque Central on corner of C/ Deligne and Independencia*

SLEEP

Due to San Pedro's proximity to **Juan Dolio** (p116), there is little sense in staying the night when there are a number of inexpensive and charming hotels on the beach less than a 30-minute *guagua* ride away. There are cheap hotels in San Pedro, but they either fall into the pay-by-the-hour cabaña category, or are pretty grim.

Hotel Macorix There is a one surprisingly nice option in town, the seaside-situated Hotel Macorix. Operated by the same owner as the Universidad Central del Este, this hotel is well equipped with 170 rooms, a pool, tennis courts, a disco, and two restaurants. *RD$1,664-3,175; C/ Malecón at C/ Deligne; 339-2100; info@hotelmacorix.com; www.hotelmacorix.com; Amenities: A/C, hot water, TV, internet*

DO

Museo de San Pedro de Macorís

This museum is the result of proud locals uniting to preserve the rich history of San Pedro. Located in a grand home built over a century ago, the museum has a collection of photos and artifacts that portray the many "firsts" for which San Pedro is famous. There also are a number of cases with knickknacks, period pieces, and furniture dating from the early 20th century. *Admission is RD$20 for Dominicans, US$1 for foreigners; 529-1078; museo_historia_sanpedrodeMacorís@hotmail.com; open Tues-Sat 8am-12pm and 3pm-6pm*

> When the weekend rolls around, start a party on the seaside *malecón* with a few Presidente Jumbos after the sun goes down.

Cocolos

"Cocolo" is a term in the Spanish-speaking Caribbean used to describe people of African descent from the other non-Spanish speaking Caribbean islands. In the DR, the word specifically refers to those immigrants who came to work in the sugar industry in San Pedro and other nearby towns in the late 19th century. Today, the definition of *cocolo* has broadened, with more of a cultural significance (and less island-specific meaning), though it can be seen as derogatory if used in an insulting manner by an outsider.

Early 20th Century Architecture on Calle Duarte

Heading toward the water from the Parque Central on C/ Duarte, there are a number of relics from the golden era of San Pedro when sugar cane money flowed freely. Built in 1917, the **Morey Building** is among the most famous, said to be the first three-story cement building in the country. Its turret can be seen from Parque Central, and the colorful stained glass windows and moldings are a pleasure to see after blocks of poured concrete buildings that predominate downtown. When it was still open, the building went through a number of uses, including as a hardware store and a rented space for the adjacent Hotel Saboya. Sadly, it is now a boarded-up monument of better times.

Continuing in that direction is **Catedral San Pedro Apóstol** (C/ Colón between C/ Anacaona Moscoso Puello and C/ Independencia), which was finished in the 1920s, and is one of the few well-preserved buildings from the era. The building was completely reconstructed in a French neo-Gothic style after a gas lamp that illuminated the exterior clock led to a devastating fire. Today, the cathedral's beautiful white façade and crowning bell tower (sans flammable gas lamp) are prized monuments of the city.

The East

Estadio Tetelo Vargas

Home to the Estrellas Orientales baseball team, this stadium carries the name of the Dominican baseball legend. The park is small, holding up to 8,000 crazed fans, guaranteeing a decent view of the game from any seat. The cement structure looks rather shabby despite a renovation in 2007, but it has a down-home feel and attracts droves of diehard Estrella fans hoping against all odds that this is their team's year (it probably isn't). Bring your rally caps and a hundred-peso bill to pick up a necessary rum on the rocks in a styrofoam cup and watch the action go down on the diamond. Remember: root, root for the home team, for if they don't win, it's a sad day in Mudville. *Av. Circunvalación; for tickets, call 529-3618 or buy tickets at the box office for RD$100 or less.*

Tetelo Vargas

Born Juan Esteban Vargas in 1906, the man nicknamed Tetelo became one of the pre-eminent Dominican baseball stars of the early 20th century, playing in the US, the DR, Cuba, Mexico, and Puerto Rico. After beginning his career at home with the Licey Tigres, he moved to New York to play with the Cuban Stars Negro League team in 1927, because while he was Dominican, American baseball classified him as a black man. He played with this team over several seasons until 1944, and was lauded as one of the fastest players in his era. He then moved to Puerto Rico, where he had occasionally played in the off-season winter leagues during his tenure on U.S. mainland teams. Vargas continued his career there for the next ten years, until his retirement from professional baseball in 1954.

Museo Regional de Antropología at La Universidad Central del Este

Open on weekdays by appointment, this museum houses a number of Taíno artifacts as well as the colorful Carnaval costumes of the *Cocolos*. Though the museum is open to the public, visitors must either call ahead or ask someone at the university office on the bottom floor of the library to open the building. *Carretera La Romana and Av. Circunvalación; 529-3562 (ext. 319)*

Hato Mayor

The long version of the city's name is Hato Mayor del Rey (the Grandest Herd of the King), named for the grazing grounds kept by the royal family in this livestock-heavy region. A settlement here grew up only much later, comprised of the landholder's descendants. Today, the dusty streets of Hato Mayor roar with the drone of *motos* that fill its thoroughfares. Compounded by the lack of attractions within the town, visitors rarely

---

Los Colmadones

Across the Dominican Republic, *colmadones* pull out massive speakers and turn into dance halls where the liquor is cheap and the music is loud. They are found in every neighborhood of San Pedro and are enjoyed as an inexpensive and convenient way to spend the weekend. Any given day of the week, men can be seen sitting in plastic chairs nursing a *cerveza*, while catching up with friends or playing dominoes in silent intensity. Weekends, especially Sunday, *colmadones* fill with preening couples showing off bachata skills with incredible coordination despite the consumption of bottles of Brugal. Due to the volume of the music, conversations are short. Revelers have little need to engage in serious conversation, tapping their feet to the tempo and utilizing the many hand signals integral to Dominican communication. Ask any *motoconchista* to take you to his favorite *colmadón* on a weekend night.

spend much time amidst the urban racket. However, the surrounding countryside has much to offer: clean, crisp rivers that invite a cool dip, charming small villages, lush mountains perfect for adventurous hikers, and fascinating agro-tourism projects.

TRANSPORT

Guaguas leave for the following destinations every 20-30 minutes:

To El Seibo: RD$50; 6am-7pm; 30min; leaves from Carretera Mella near the Texaco Gas Station

To Higüey: RD$110; 6am-9pm; 1hr 15min; leaves from Carretera Mella near the Texaco Gas Station

To Sabana de la Mar: RD$100; 6am-5pm; 1hr 15min; leaves from the bus stop at the entrance of the Hato Mayor-Sabana de la Mar Highway

To Santo Domingo: RD$140 (*caliente*) or RD$150 pesos (*expreso*); RD$60 for **San Pedro de Macorís**, a stop along the way; 5am-7pm; 2hrs; from C/ San Antonio across from the Shell Gas Station

From Santo Domingo to Hato Mayor: RD$140 (*caliente*) or RD$150 (*expreso*); 5am-7pm; 2hrs; Parque Enriquillo, Av. Duarte

INFO

Medical Attention
Clínica Harache on the corner of Av. Libertad and C/ Santiago Silvestre is the nicest private clinic in town with 24-hour emergency attention. **Clínica Mercedes** is another option in case of an emergency, but not as a modern as Harache (located on the highway to Sabana de la Mar, near Iberia).

There are five pharmacies in town, but **Farmacia Torres** (C/ Duarte and C/ Mercedes) and **Farmacia Independencia** (C/ Duarte and Av. Independencia) have the largest selections.

Communication
For internet, **D'Mauricio Center,** located near Iberia Supermarket, has cheap and relatively fast internet as well as phone booths (C/ Palo Hincado and C/ Ramírez Curro).

Or, **Reytel Internet** is located at C/ 27 de Febrero and C/ Melchor Contín. Wi-Fi is also available at **Miguelina's B&B** (see Eat) or **El Conuco Restaurant** (see Eat). The **Post Office** is located on the corner of C/ Palo Hincado and 27 de Febrero (553-3570).

Banks
BanReservas is located on C/ San Antonio and C/ Palo Hincado and **Banco Popular** is located on C/ Mercedes between C/ Palo Hincado and C/ Duarte.

Gas Stations
There is a **Shell Gas Station** on Carretera Mella near the Santo Domingo bus stop, a **Texaco** Gas Station by the stop for El Seibo on Carretera Mella near the corner of C/ Julio Lluberes and an **Esso Gas Station** on the corner of C/ Duarte and Padre Pena.

Grocery Stores
Iberia Supermarket is on the corner of Duarte and Pedro Guillermo (or Quintina Peguero) and **Mota Supermarket** is on C/ Padre Meriño and Av. Melchor Contín.

EAT

Limited to casual open-air restaurants serving Dominican staples, Hato Mayor would not be a vital stop on a gourmet culinary tour through the DR. However, at these places the portions are plentiful, the flavors are authentic, and the prices are friendly toward all budgets.

El Conuco El Conuco combines cheap and scrumptious Dominican and American classics. Order the *plato del día* or the hamburger for a wallet-pleasing RD$100. *RD$ 100-250; C/ Mercedes, by the park; free Wi-Fi when functioning*

Conuco

The word *conuco* is loosely translated as "farm," but its real significance is more nuanced. A *conuco* is a small, usually family-owned-and-operated farm geared toward individual consumption or local commerce. Popular food crops and consumables, rather than plantation goods for export like sugar, are grown on *conucos*.

El Coral Try Hato Mayor's specialties at this roadside restaurant: *longaniza* (sausage) and *mondongo* (tripe). There are also healthier options, like grilled chicken breast with vegetables. *RD$100-250; Corner of C/ Mercedes and C/ Duarte*

Colinas del Rey A restaurant or perpetual pool party? Ponder this and other life questions while dining either poolside or a bit more removed from the aquatic merriment under a breezy thatched roof. Tuck into Dominican or Italian classics such as stewed goat or spaghetti carbonara. Be sure to bring your bathing suit to partake in the fun at the massive pool outfitted with speakers blasting bachata and merengue. *RD$175-390; Km 1½ Carretera Hato Mayor-San Pedro de Macorís; 553-1039; 917-6429*

Organic/Fair-Trade Cacao

Often overshadowed by the immense commercial cacao production in African countries like Kenya and Ghana, the cacao industry in the Dominican Republic is unique and critically important: the DR is the number one country in terms of organic cacao export. A large portion of cacao farmers are organized under CONACADO, (Confederación Nacional de Cacaocultores Dominicanos, or National Confederation of Dominican Cacao Farmers), which promotes these farmers' commercial and agricultural interests. The CONACADO regional office, called Bloque 3 (there are seven nationwide) represents Hato Mayor and nearby El Seibo, and includes 2,000 associated cacao farmers and over 3,000 more indirect members. Cacao farmers in this region began to organize in 1985 and were officially registered in 1988. By 1991, the region was completely organic.

CONACADO has provided tremendous benefits to the cacao farmers across the country, enabling them to enter the fair trade market. The coordinator of Bloque 3, Romero, claims that the lives of cacao farmers have noticeably improved after becoming licensed as fair trade. The farmers are no longer subject to the dramatic fluctuations of larger market prices, and are generally guaranteed a higher price through the fair trade premium. Today, with the development of cacao eco-tourism options (See Cacao Tour Vicentillo, p127, and Los Botados, p142), the farmers have another way to support their families. In addition, local women's associations now play a greater role by manufacturing artisanal cacao-based products such as cocoa, chocolate wine, and marmalade.

SLEEP

Miguelina's Bed & Breakfast This pretty three-room B&B wins the "best bang for your buck" award. Miguelina's is the nicest and most affordable place to stay in the Hato Mayor and El Seibo area. Having grown up in the nearby village of Vicentillo, owner Miguelina spent many years in Canada and the U.S. and recently moved back home to start her comely business. At check-in, Miguelina greets guests with a glass of freshly squeezed juice or a mug of local, shade-grown coffee. After spending the day in the *campo* or on the cacao tour, this is a peaceful place to enjoy the creature comforts of home and Miguelina's warm company. The B&B also offers meals, travel arrangements, and other tour services on request. *US$35 per night; 21B C/ José Francisco Papaterra near the corner of C/ Ramírez Curro behind the Ayuntamiento; 553-4135; miguelinafranco51@hotmail.com; Amenities: A/C, TV, internet, laundry service*

Parque Acuático Colinas del Rey Colinas del Rey is not the best place for a good night's sleep because of its proximity to gargantuan speakers pumping out an all-day dance party. For a late-night pool party with the locals, however, this complex delivers, complete with seven double rooms to crash in after the festivities have ended. (See Eat section for more details.) *RD$1000; Km 1½ on Hato Mayor-San Pedro highway just outside Hato Mayor; 553-1039/917-6429; josiasab@hotmail.com; info@colinasdelrey.com; www.colinasdelrey.com; Amenities: A/C, TV, hot water*

Hotel Burgos has a variety of reasonably priced sleeping options, from bunk beds to double rooms and apartments. Located on the main highway through town, this standard cinderblock hotel lacks some charm, but makes up for it in convenience and cost. *RD$600-900; Carretera Hato Mayor-San Pedro near Colinas del Rey; 553-3013; Amenities: A/C, hot water, TV*

DO

Cacao Tour Vicentillo

Leaving at 9am from Hato Mayor, this community-based tour started by the local branch of CONACADO is both a treat to the intellect and to the taste buds. The half-day local adventure includes all the relevant pieces in the cacao production process, and includes some rich chocolate treats when it's done. The tour begins at a cacao plantation to experience the intricacies of the farming process, including planting, crop maintenance, and harvesting, with a stop by a farming family's home. The tour next pays a call to the local growers association, founded to protect local agricultural interests. There, facilitators lead a demonstration on the fermentation and drying of cacao, and then discuss the fair trade export market, and how such commercialization benefits the community. The tour's final stop is at the women's association, where members illustrate the production of various cacao products, including wine, cocoa, and marmalade, followed by a tasting. Here, the tour concludes with a traditional Dominican lunch. Proceeds from the tour benefit both the women's association and local cacao farmers. Visitors short on time looking for a true cultural experience should consider this tour as a perfect way to get a taste of *campo* life in the East. *US$30 or RD$1,100 (p/p); Tour begins at El Bloque No. 3 de CONACADO on the Carretera Hato Mayor-Vicentillo, Km 1, Hato Mayor; Transportation is available for small groups (four or fewer), but providing your own transport is requested. Book at least 24 hours in advance; Romero: 838-8882 or 829-760-1153 or Office Tel: 553-2727; tourdechocolate@hotmail.com; hromerom@hotmail.com; http://www.paseo.nu/dominican-republiC/*

The East

Cowboys & Pilgrimages

During the month of August, Hato Mayor's small-town feel transforms into a raucous religious scene complete with real cowboys. As part of the pilgrimage in honor of the Virgen of Altagracia, families decked out in cowboy threads ride into town on horseback for the Fiesta de Toros (Festival of the Bulls). The procession continues on to the community of La Guayaba, where the riders eat, drink, and make merry thanks to the exhilarating beats of an all-night *fiesta de palo* (p62).

Cueva Fun Fun & Rancho Capote

This daylong outdoor adventure tour marries one of the largest karst caves in the country with a functioning cattle ranch for a unique, active look at the Eastern countryside. The morning starts with a bounty of colorful tropical fruit at the Rancho Capote farm, followed by a leisurely horseback ride through the ranch's tropical forest. Then, the real excitement begins with a hike to Cueva Fun Fun. After rappelling 20 meters down into the cave, take in the mesmerizing Taíno petroglyphs, towering stalagmites and stalactites, and the underground river teeming with fish and other marine life. After a few minutes of getting used to the subterranean atmosphere, listen for the slow but constant chirp of bats nestled in corridors and entryways. The tour slowly winds its way through the labyrinthine caves. After nearly an hour inside the earth, admiring a bat's eye view of the underground world, the tour eventually leads back out into natural light. Stroll back to the ranch and then enjoy a well-deserved spread of hearty *campo* food. The tours are pricey, but very professional, employing requisite safety measures. *US$120; 12 C / Duarte, Barrio Puerto Rico, Hato Mayor del Rey. Take the Carretera Hato Mayor-Yerba Buena-Las Claras-Capote west of Hato Mayor toward Sabana de la Mar for 20 kilometers until arriving at the Rancho Capote entrance; 553-2812 / 2656; 299-0457; info@cuevafunfun.net; www.cuevafunfun.net*

NIGHTLIFE

If you are looking for nightlife, **Mambo Discoteca** is a popular weekend spot for bachata and merengue lovers (C/ 27 de Febrero and C/ Duarte). There are also a number of **colmadones** on the Hato Mayor-San Pedro highway that fill with *motos,* especially on Sundays. A favorite is **El Cochinito**, which during the day functions as a *comedor* then unleashes *perico ripiao merengue* on weekends for a its loyal throng of patrons (located on main Highway coming from San Pedro de Macorís on the left; look out for the sign with a jovial pink pig).

Sabana de la Mar

Beyond serving as an entry point for Parque Nacional Los Haitises, Sabana de la Mar is a rather shabby fishing village with few options for even the most imaginative of travelers. Home to around 15,000 residents, the city trudges along on subsistence fishing and agriculture. The town also plays reluctant host to activity associated with illicit drug and people trafficking on *yolas* (see below) to Puerto Rico. The city's most curious characteristic is its idolization of Señorita Elupina Cordero, a devout Catholic who performed miraculous acts of healing. Followers continue to recognize her with mass every June 4, the date of her death.

TRANSPORT

Bus

The following routes leave every 30 minutes (Miches) or hour (Hato Mayor and Santo Domingo) from the corner of the Hato Mayor-Sabana de la Mar highway at Av. Los Heroes and C/ Salomé Ureña.

To Miches: RD$120; 7am-6pm; 2hr

To Hato Mayor: RD$100; 6am-6pm; 1.5hrs

To Santo Domingo: RD$260; 4am-6pm; 3.5hrs

From Santo Domingo to Sabana de la Mar: RD$275; 8:15am, 8:30am, 11:00am, 12:50pm, 2:15pm, 4:00pm, 5:30pm; 3.5hrs; *guaguas* leave from Parque de los Fuentes; C/ José at C/ Paris (near the Duarte Bridge). Call ahead to confirm times as schedule occasionally changes: 682-0744.

Boat

To Samaná: RD$150; 7am, 9am, 11am, 3pm, 5pm; 2hrs; east of the Parque Central on C/ José García.

INFO

Medical Attention

Farmacia Cánada is on the corner of Av. De los Heroes and C/ 16 de Agosto (556-7656).

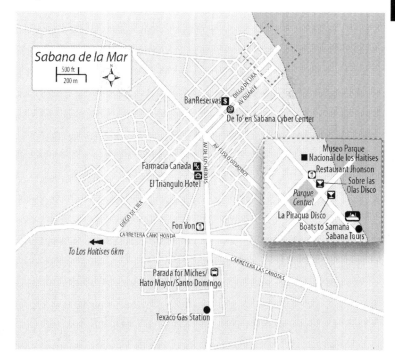

Communication

For internet use **De To' en Sabana Cyber Center** (RD$15/30 min; C/ Duarte; Mon-Sat 8am-10pm), and for calls there is a **Claro Call Center** next to Farmacia Cánada on Av. De los Heroes (556-7366).

Banks

Find **BanReservas** on C/ Diego de Lira near C/ Duvergé. A **Western Union** is located next to Farmacia Cánada on Av. De los Heroes.

Gas

There is a **Texaco Gas Station** at the southern entrance of town along Av. de los Heroes.

EAT

Restaurant Jhonson The cooking is better than the spelling at this eatery, the better of the two open-air restaurants by the Parque Central. This one specializes in seafood, especially octopus, lobster, and conch shell fresh from Samaná Bay, which also provides a spectacular view from the restaurant. *RD$180-500; 5 Paseo Elupina Cordero; 556-7715; 829-820-6291*

Fon Von Chow down on some chow fan (fried rice) or try more traditional Dominican specialties. Share the smoked pork chops or stewed crab with local *sabaneros* at this simple, but solid eatery. *RD$90-315; 60 Av. De los Heroes; just past the turn for Caño Hondo toward the water; 556-7332/967-5150; fonvonrestaurant@hotmail.com; http://fonvonrestaurant.blogspot.com; Mon-Fri 11am-11pm, Sat 11am-11:30pm, Sun 11am-12am*

SLEEP

El Triángulo Hotel For geometry buffs, this triangle-shaped edifice is the only decent option in town, and an economical alternative if Paraíso Caño Hondo is too pricey. The two-story hotel has clean, no-frills rooms with TVs. It is a convenient 15-minute drive from the boat launch where tours leave for Los Haitises. *RD$400-800; 24 Av. De los Heroes at C/ Conrado Hernández; 556-7264; Amenities: A/C or fan, hot water, cable*

 Paraíso Caño Hondo An impressively arranged convergence of man and nature, this hotel is tucked in the rural community of Caño Hondo, just outside Los Haitises National Park. All the hotel's structures are seamlessly incorporated into the lush vegetation, rivers, and pools that make up the serene grounds. There are a total of 28 rooms located in the two eco-lodges on the property, where horses, birds, and

---

Yolas

Yolas are small motorboats infamous for transporting illegally emigrating Dominicans to Puerto Rico. Survivors tell tales of disappointment and danger, sustaining cramped conditions and choppy seas, and paying thousands of dollars under the table. After arriving, many migrants are often simply sent back home by Puerto Rican authorities. Others make it safely and are more successful in attempting new lives on the island. Unfortunately, a few souls each year never arrive back on dry land.

When in Puerto Rico, jobs available to these unofficial laborers are scarce, poorly paid, and off the books, ranging from factory workers to domestic positions. Horror stories of *yola* captains extorting female passengers for both money and sex (or even throwing them overboard if they are menstruating for fear of attracting sharks) are not uncommon. The *yola* business continues to thrive in this area, even with all of the inherent physical and political hazards.

dogs roam freely. Check out the various scenic hiking trails on the premises, and ask the concierge about horseback riding, hiking, and boat tours of Los Haitises. See Eat in Los Haitises (p 131) section for the restaurant description. *RD$1350-3700; 15 minutes outside of Sabana de la Mar in Caño Hondo (look out for a Caño Hondo sign near the guagua stop for Miches), a moto from the guagua stop to the hotel will be RD$150-200; 248-5995; 889-9454; info@www.paraisocanohondo.com; Amenities: fan, hot water, restaurant, pool*

DO

Museo Parque Nacional de los Haitises

Though an unremarkable museum, it's still a good place to get some background information and interesting ecological and geological factoids about Los Haitises (see following section) and Hispaniola in general, presented on low-budget informational boards in both Spanish and English. *Free; located just west of the park on Paseo Elupina Cordero; the museum itself is open every day, but office staff is generally there Mon-Fri 9am-4pm.*

For nighttime fun, there are two discotecas, **Sobre las Olas** and **La Piragua**, located around the Parque Central. Just keep your eye out for pickpocketing.

Sabana Tours

This locally run operator from Sabana de la Mar offers boat tours of Los Haitises, as well as to various locations around Samaná Peninsula, like El Limón Waterfall (p224), Las Galeras, (p225) and Las Terrenas (p221). The guides, all of who are fishermen from Sabana de la Mar, also provide whale-watching tours during mating season in Samaná. *Tours start at RD$1500; Parque Central, C/ José García; 829-419-0570*

Parque Nacional Los Haitises

Characterized by its immense mangrove and humid forests, Los Haitises National Park is 826 square kilometers (313 square miles) of untouched jungle, spread across the provinces of Hato Mayor, Monte Plata, and Samaná. Los Haitises, from the Taíno word *haitis*, meaning mountain, is best known for its classic karst topography. This unique terrain is composed of small, nearly identical hills, dotted with sinkholes and caves formed by subterranean drainage that slowly dissolved the bedrock to create this spectacular scenery.

All visitors of the National Park pay a RD$100 entrance fee, which goes toward the maintenance and protection of the park. For more information, check out the National Park's website: www.visitaloshaitises.com

The vast subtropical forest and complex estuary system, much of the only virgin and protected lowlands left in the country, provide a welcome environment for several endemic animals, like the highly endangered Hispaniolan Hutia and Solenodon (p37). Avian species, including Stygian and barn owls, perch in the predominant Cupey trees, alongside stands of cigar-box cedar, West Indian mahogany, and grandleaf seagrape. Fashionably adorning the trees are wild orchids, which colorfully thrive in the humid temperature and rocky soil. Along the swampy coast, brown pelicans dive-bomb for fish while the Frigate bird, identified by its impressive wingspan, inky black body, and the male's red inflatable flirting device, waits intently to steal their catch. Marine mammals like humpback whales and dolphins make seasonal appearances in the park's waters to escape chilly North Atlantic winters.

Organized boat tours that slowly navigate the mangrove canals are the best way to experience Los Haitises, because the majority of the park that is open to visitors is accessible only by boat (See the following Tour Operators section). Hiking through the humid forest is another option, allowing visitors to better appreciate the flora and fauna up close, but the blanket of mosquitoes can be thick, so be sure to bring insect repellent.

DO

Caves

Because of its geological composition, Los Haitises is full of caves. Many contain excellently preserved pictographs of Taíno gods and local fauna, such as those found in **Cueva de Arena**. Other subterranean highlights include **Cueva de la Línea** or **Cueva del Ferrocarril**, named for the 19th century railroad line that connected Santo Domingo with the bay (used primarily to transport bananas to the coast for export). The original dock posts (called **Punto de los Aves**) still stand, and have become a gathering area for the pelicans and seagulls scoping out their next meal. Nearby, the **Cueva del Desprendimiento** is so named because at its entrance, the rock has been naturally split in two, yet somehow remains structurally sound.

The Legend of the Ciguapa

From the Cueva de la Línea sprung one of the many versions of the legend of the Ciguapa, longhaired mythical females, whose feet are inverted making them appear to walk backwards. As the legend goes, the Taíno Cacique Caonabo had a lover and confidant, Onaney, a Ciguayan princess from Samaná. In an effort to promote peace between the Spaniards and the Taínos, Onaney encouraged Caonabo to reach an agreement with the Spanish, who seized the opportunity to kill the notorious Taíno leader. Overcome with sorrow and guilt, Onaney, relinquished herself to the Cueva de la Línea along with her ladies in waiting, all of whom walked backwards in order to confuse Spanish troops as to their whereabouts. For another version of the Ciguapa, see page 295.

The Threatened Forest

The ecological gem of Los Haitises, though officially protected by the National Park in which it sits, is nevertheless constantly under threat. In 2009, the government approved the construction of a cement factory on the edge of the park by Grupo Estrella, a large industrial conglomerate. Authorities green-lit the project over the protests of the environmentalists, the UN Development Program (UNDP), and much of the Dominican population. The state finally capitulated and cancelled its plans, however, after several anti-construction protests across the country displayed the ability of diverse groups within civil society to unite in a coordinated campaign .

Nevertheless, the same year saw the completion of a major highway connecting Samaná with Santo Domingo, which cuts directly through the national park. While the highway dramatically reduces travel time between the two cities, it also has the potential to cause significant damage through increased development and transit in protected areas.

Trails

Though the majority of the protected area is closed to visitors, there are a few hiking trails that take anywhere from a half hour to a half day. All paths pass through the remarkable humid forest, which is best enjoyed with a trained local guide who can point out the plants, animals, and other relevant information found along the way.

Beaches

One of the few small beaches located around the perimeter of Los Haitises will most likely be a stop on a tour throughout the park. Many, such as Playa de los Uveros, are located within protected alcoves, making their waters calm and shallow.

TOUR OPERATORS

Tin Tours A trusted guide named Tin picks up his guests in Sabana de la Mar and takes them to the Paraíso Caño Hondo hotel for a very reasonable price. He offers an excellent tour that includes a narrated boat ride through the thick mangrove forest, stops at several caves, and a hike through the humid forest with descriptions of the medicinal uses of plants. Tin lets his customers spend as little or as much time at each destination allowing them to explore at their own pace as opposed to the more commercial tours, which shuffle larger quantities of people through under tight time constraints. *RD$1500-2000; 225-0535/0517; Spanish only*

> **Sabana Tours** on page 131 is another recommended tour operator.

Brigada Verde A youth-run environmental awareness and guide association based in Sabana de la Mar, this "Green Brigade" was developed by Peace Corps Volunteers in an effort to create a source of income for youth as trained guides, as well as to promote environmental education and consciousness among community members. The knowledgeable guides provide eco-tours by boat or foot to all of the major attractions within Los Haitises. Having grown up in the area, the guides are well-informed about the flora and fauna, but because they are young, the group is in a state of flux as members leave for university or other employment. Previous projects of Brigada Verde include mangrove rehabilitation efforts and protecting endangered hawk species. *RD$1500-2000; Contact Brigada Verde's president, Kelvin: 829-846-7927 or guide, Luis: 847-5375; Spanish only*

The Guayiga Massacre

Found throughout Los Haitises is guayiga (Zamia pumilis), a low-growing dark green plant resembling a hearty fern. After carefully soaking the root of this plant to remove toxins, Taínos would dry and then grind this root into flour for their staple unleavened bread. Among guayiga's other common uses were starch for clothes and rat poison. Faced with famine in 1809, inhabitants of Santo Domingo opted for this pervasive root to quell their hunger, but instead ended up poisoning themselves because they did not know the proper preparation methods.

SLEEP & EAT

Because Los Haitises is a National Park, the closest accommodations and food options are in Sabana de la Mar. There is also Restaurante "El Cayuco," which is part of Paraíso Caño Hondo (p130) and is open all day. Ask for the catch of the day (*pesca del día*) in coconut sauce or try crabmeat *a la criolla*. *RD$150-370*

Miches

When Christopher Columbus entered the Bay of Samaná in January 1493, the notoriously bellicose indigenous population greeted him with a volley of arrows. Although they were accustomed to marine attacks from their neighbors, especially the Caribes of Santa María de Guadalupe, this testy brand of Taínos was soon wiped out by disease and colonial repression.

In the early 19th century, families from nearby El Seibo were lured by the abundant fishing available in what was then known as the "Costa de los Uveros" due to the abundance of *uveros* (beachgrape trees) there. The new arrivals began cultivating cacao, coconut palms, and rice.

In the 1970s, the coastline provided another source of income and also disrepute for the small town, as it emerged as a major launching point for Dominican immigration to Puerto Rico. Miches soon became known for little more than the *yola* trade. The town itself offers little diversion besides an endearing central plaza bedecked with murals and set above the sea, perfect for a sunset stroll. However, its gorgeous beaches, two magical lagoons (Redonda and Limón), and surrounding mountains have recently caught the attention of tourists and international developers.

The Future of Tourism in Miches

The Venezuelan Grupo Cisneros and its sister foundation Fundación Tropicalia are capitalizing on the outstanding potential for tourism in the Miches area, with plans to carefully develop the virgin coastline. Fundación Tropicalia has made efforts to involve and prepare the community for the anticipated surge of tourism. Projects such as capacity building among the fisherman are in early stages, but it is still unclear if this work will result in the type of sustainable tourism Grupo Cisneros has in mind.

TRANSPORT

The following routes leave about every 30 minutes (Miches, Sabana de la Mar, Santo Domingo, El Seibo) or hour (Hato Mayor, Higüey):

To El Seibo: RD$110; 6:35am-5:50pm; 1hr; leaves from 29 Carretera de Miches; 457-4151

To Hato Mayor: RD$100; 6am-5pm; 1.5hrs

To Higüey: RD$170; 4:20am-5:20pm; 2hrs; 2 Juan Sánchez Ramírez (corner of María Trinidad Sánchez) just before crossing the bridge; 553-5742

To Santo Domingo (with stop in El Seibo): RD$275, RD$120 (El Seibo); 4am-3pm; 3.5 hours; SITRAMICHES *guaguas* leave from near the park at 12 C/ San Antonio; 553-5738

To Sabana de la Mar: RD$120; 7am-6pm; 2hrs; 20 C/ Mella; 476-1460

INFO

Medical Attention
The pharmacy with the best selection is on the road to El Seibo, next to the *parada* for Sabana de la Mar. For medical attention, go to either **Consultorio Médico San Antonio De Padua** (2 C/ 16 de Agosto and C/ San Antonio; 553-5780; 8:30am-12pm and 2pm-5:30pm) or **Consultorio Médico Dr. Aneuris Mota Jiménez (Dr. Nazara)** (11 C/ Miguel Pérez; 829-347-4235).

Communication
PYP Cyber Café is the most reliable place for internet. Corner of C/ Juan Sánchez and C/ María Trinidad Sánchez by Isla Gas station; 553-5748; cybercafepyp@gmail.com

Banks
There is a **Banreservas** on the corner of General Santana and Deligne. For wiring money, there is a **Western Union** on C/ Mella between Anicento Cedán and Rosa Julia de León. To change money, there is a **Caribe Express** on the corner of C/ Mella and General Santana.

Gas Stations
Isla Gas is located across the street from the *parada* for Higüey on C/ Juan Sánchez Ramírez right before the bridge.

Grocery Stores
Appropriately named, **Casa Dulce** is a large *colmado* owned by a *dulce* (sweet) family, and is the best in town in terms of service (corner of C/ Juan Sánchez Ramírez and C/ M. Pérez). **Supermercado Duarte** is conveniently located if you are headed to Playa Arriba, as it is immediately after the bridge on C/ Juan Sánchez Ramírez (553-5296; 829-342-5296).

EAT

Hotel La Loma Dine on pasta and fresh seafood dishes while enjoying the breathtaking view of Miches, including Montaña Rotonda and Playa Esmeralda (see Sleep section). *RD$200-400; follow sign for Hotel la Loma atop the hill overlooking Miches before entering town from the west; 980-7903/7903; lalomamcihes@yahoo.de; jumbomiches@yahoo.de; open for lunch and dinner*

Pico Pollo Marcos You'll still be licking your fingers long after trying Marcos's decidedly fried chicken and *tostones*. *RD$100; near the Parque Central on C/ M. Pérez between C/ Deligne and Mella; open for lunch and dinner*

Comedor Paulina Owner/chef Paulina cooks and serves Dominican mainstays with lots of love. Her modest eatery always has a plentiful and cheap *plato del día*; customers especially like the *moro* with stewed beef or chicken. *RD$100-200; located in an unmarked peach and white wooden house; 56 C/ Juan Sánchez Ramírez; lunch only*

Hotel Coco Loco Head to this hotel's spacious outdoor restaurant located right on Playa Arriba for exquisite thin crust pizzas in varieties like *quattro estaciones* with artichokes, ham, olives, and mushrooms. The menu also includes other wallet-friendly meat or seafood dishes like conch shell *al ajillo* or fresh whole fish in coconut sauce. With a name like Coco Loco (crazy coconut, in English), the restaurant would be lost without its full-service bar. Go at sunset and enjoy a drink while the ocean breeze caresses your face. *RD$180-320; Hotel Coco Loco, Playa Arriba; 886-8278; 974-8182; Closed Thursdays; Restaurant open for dinner only after 5pm; snack bar offering a limited menu open all day*

SLEEP

Hotel La Loma Perched on top of a hill overlooking Miches, the hotel can be seen from any point below. The majority of the apartments are privately owned by Swiss expats, but there are select rooms with spectacular mountain views available to visitors. Actually arriving is a bit trickier due to the conditions of the road, which is best traversed with 4WD. *Motoconchos* will take passengers for RD$50 from the center of town. Ask Swiss hotel manager Andrea Weiersmuller about horseback riding out to Playa Esmeralda (includes lunch). See restaurant's description in "Eat" section. *US$45; Located on top of a hill marked clearly from anywhere in town; 553-5562; Amenities: A/C, TV, restaurant*

Coco Loco Located directly on Playa Arriba, Coco Loco's simple cabins accommodating up to four guests are scattered throughout a grassy fields dotted with coconut palms. The hotel also offers a number of tours to Playa Esmeralda, Playa Las Minas, Playa Limón, and Laguna Limón, and a trip to Samaná's Playa Bonita by catamaran. See the Coco Loco restaurant description in "Eat" section. *US$15-25 (includes breakfast); located on Playa Arriba; follow C/ Pedro A. Morel de Santa Cruz toward the coast and then make a right at the beach; 886-8278, 974-8182; Amenities: fan, 24-hour water and electricity*

Bahía del Este The drab cement rooms have few redeeming qualities, but Bahía del Este is centrally located, inexpensive, and the pool is certainly welcome on hot days. *RD$500-RD$750; C/ Deligne and San Antonio; 553-5834; Amenities: A/C or fan, restaurant, pool*

Hotel Comedor Orfelina Hotel Comedor Orfelina provides cozy, quaintly decorated rooms in a central location facing the ocean. The hotel is appropriately named after its in-house restaurant, which is a great place to grab a hot breakfast like *mangú* and fried eggs with coffee for RD$115. *RD$300-1000; 71 C/ Duarte; 553-5233; Amenities: A/C or fan, restaurant open 9am-9:30pm*

DO

Ceyba Park

Whale-watching season is the time to visit the natural grounds and water views of Ceyba Park. Eden Tours operates whale-watching trips out of the park with stops at the area's gorgeous natural attractions such as Playa Esmeralda. Outside whale-watching season, the park is still well worth a visit, as it hosts a refreshing set of swimming holes – one freshwater and two saltwater – to enjoy year round. There is also a restaurant in the park, though it's not known to be well-stocked. *Located on the Sabana de la Mar-Miches highway just outside Miches. For Eden Tours, contact Jumbo: 980-7903; jumbomiches@yahoo.com; www.hotel-limon.com*

Dive Academy

Recognizing the untapped potential of scuba diving in Miches, an English couple founded this dive shop around the time of research. Prior to opening the shop, the owners were actively engaged in reef conservation and research activities in Miches; profits from their business helped to sponsor continuation of this work. In addition to scuba diving and snorkeling, they offer tailored excursions by land and by sea to fit any need and interest. *Located just outside of Miches in Ceyba Park on the highway connecting Sabana de la Mar and Miches; 327-0292; info@diveacademy.org; www.diveacademy.org*

Playa Arriba (Playa Miches)

Located on the eastern edge of Miches, this beach cannot compete with La Costa Esmeralda in terms of beauty, but it is fine for swimming and remains relatively trash-free. It is also quite social, as there's almost always a game of pickup beach baseball alongside area families enjoying the waves. Avoid the beach after dark for safety reasons.

Costa Esmeralda

The placid aquamarine waters that gently lap virgin white sand catapults this beach to among the top in the country. Accessible by boat, horseback, or scenic drive, the beach is set in a protected bay, leaving the water smooth and clear with few waves. Development has yet to touch the pristine sands of this beach, meaning Esmeralda has no accommodations. The Marina de Guerra (Coast Guard) is stationed at Playa Esmeralda, so don't be alarmed if well-armed military personnel approach beachgoers. The soldiers are open and friendly, and will welcome a break in boredom to chat and chop open coconuts. There are no stores or restaurants nearby, so bring your own snacks and rum for a taste of a real *coco loco!*

To reach the beach by foot from Miches, walk east along the beach and ask a local to show you the footpath that cuts through the forest to the other side of the point seen to the East of Playa Arriba. The walk takes about an hour and a half. Arrive in a group and don't carry valuables, because the trail is isolated and the occasional mugging has been reported. By car, drive east toward the town of La Mina for about 8.8 kilometers (5.5mi). Just beyond La Mina, find the turnoff to Playa

The East

Genaro "Cayuco" Reyes

Behind his intense stare and calming demeanor, the artist Genaro Reyes, called "Cayuco," has a seemingly endless flow of creativity and vision. Upon entering his home, a fantastical ever-changing work of murals, sculptures, and mosaics, guests feel immediately inspired.

Born in Miches, Cayuco fostered his artistic talent after spending hours alongside the artisan Cristino de la Cruz Linares (known as Chinsito). A fisherman by trade, Chinsito began to carve boat models later in life when old age prevented him from fishing. Cayuco, encouraged by both Chinsito and a Peace Corps volunteer, continued to hone in his skills, exploring a number of different media. He settled on sculpture with wood and found objects, as well as painting. After moving to Santo Domingo, Cayuco was able to exchange ideas with a diverse group of artists, continuing to develop his rustic, raw style. He eventually moved back to Miches, where he built his home, which functions as workshop, classroom, and gallery for visitors. There, he produces a variety of carved and brightly painted wooden sculptures depicting daily life in Miches, including his signature *cayucos* (canoes) full of passengers, and other items like saints and crèches. In his spare time, he teaches artistry to local youth, passing along his passion and encouraging a blooming industry in Miches. With the support of Cayuco and Artemiches, a number of youths have won national awards for their creations, including those prizes given during the Feria Navideña in Santo Domingo. *To contact Cayuco: 713-1100; cayuco666@gmail.com; www.cayuco.info*

Esmeralda, marked by a Brugal sign. Follow the dirt road and go left at the fork until the road runs parallel to the beach (veer right). Continue until reaching the far eastern end of the beach, which is the best section for swimming. This area is just past the Marina de Guerra office. Boat and horseback riding trips to Costa Esmeralda are also available through Coco Loco Hotel.

Montaña Redonda

With a 360-degree view of the coast, two lagoons, verdant surrounding hills, and electric green rice fields, this mountain is definitely worth the trip. The turnoff is located about 17 kilometers (11 miles) east of Miches, right after the village of Los Urabos, and then a short but rocky 20 minute drive to the top. For those without a private vehicle, take the Higüey *guagua* and ask the driver to leave you at "*la entrada para Montaña Redonda*" (the entrance for Montaña Redonda), which has no signage, but has a wooden post splashed with red paint as a marker. You can also see a red and white cell tower on the top of the mountain. The relatively challenging hike takes about an hour and a half from base to peak. After reaching the top, find a lush, grassy space perfect for a picnic, as well as a small hut and a bathroom installed by the gracious landowner.

Playa Limón

Heading 20 kilometers east from Miches, beach enthusiasts come upon Playa Limón, another gorgeous, wild, and isolated beach boasting miles of empty sand. Turn north off of Highway 104 at the village of El Cedro down a bumpy dirt road to arrive at the beach. In the spring, look out for sea turtles, once widespread across the country, that still lay their eggs on the shores of Playa Limón. Be aware that the currents can be dangerously strong at Playa Limón – take extra caution while in the water.

Laguna Limón & Laguna Redonda

Adjacent to Playa Limón are two astounding lagoons: Redonda, larger and brackish to the west; and Limón, smaller and freshwater to the east. Their cerulean, placid waters abound in tropical wildlife, teeming with tropical birds like herons and egrets. The lakes have been placed under the care of a Scientific Reserve for protection and research, so there is a RD$100 entrance fee. Make reservations in Miches at your respective hotel, or with locals at either lake, for a boat tour (See **Rancho La Cueva** below).

Playa Nisibón

This beach is a bit farther away, but also worth the trip. Continuing east from Miches and after Montaña Redonda, pass the quiet communities of El Cedro, Laguna Limón, and Los Guineos along the Miches-Higüey Highway. Finally reach the town of Sabana de Nisibón, where there is a difficult stretch of road that leads to the wild, untouched Playa Nisibón. A river dyed by the tannins of the mangroves feeds into the crystal clear water of the ocean, creating a beautiful churn of color and movement in the bay. The beach has some large rocks in the water, but there are plenty of places lined with soft white sand to swim. The only way to get there is with 4-wheel drive, and when it rains, the road fills with water, and so only the locals know how to avoid the water-lodged potholes. Therefore, it's best to convince someone with an all-terrain vehicle from Sabana de Nisibón to take you for a couple hundred pesos. Ask for Danilo, *el pescador* (fisherman), who owns a surprisingly dependable junker of a truck, to get to Sabana de Nisibón, instead of risking getting stuck in the mud. The trip from Miches lasts at least an hour. An arduous trip is soon forgotten after the cattails and low vegetation along the plain open into a soothing vista of endless white sand and coconut begging to be cracked open.

Rancho La Cueva

Located about 45 minutes east of Miches on Playa Limón, this eco-tourism outfitter offers excursions on horseback or in a truck or boat to Playa Limón, Laguna Limón, and La Montaña Redonda. Rancho La Cueva also provides comfortable sleeping facilities, as well as a cafeteria for guests. *US$30 and up; El Cedro, Miches; 470-0876; Walter: rancholacueva@gmail.com; rancholacueva.com*

◢ Artemiches

Headed by artisan Sélvido Candelario, this community-based artisan association provides a wonderful outlet for budding and professional artisans in Miches. The association runs an active youth painting school and organizes a Cultural Week every June with exhibitions and activities including theater, music, guest speakers, and artisan workshops. To see some of the artisans' unique wooden sculptures, contact Sélvido via email at Artemiches@gmail.com, who is happy to open his home to visitors.

Pedro Sánchez

If en route to Miches from El Seibo, take time to stop off at this budding eco-tourism destination in the heart of the hills of the Cordillera Oriental. This small community's tremendous potential has been developed over the years by Peace Corps Volunteers and is finally ready for public enjoyment.

The community of Pedro Sánchez, having rebranding itself as "The Treasure of the East," presents unique community-based sustainable tourism options that include trails to stunning waterfalls, natural springs, and subterranean caves run by ◢ **Ecoturísmo Pedro Sánchez**. There are two excursions, which can be done on foot or horseback, and are led by trained guides from the community (in Spanish only). The first excursion is the Cave Package, which winds through the forested mountain of El Grumo to four caves with impressive mineral formations, root systems, and Taíno pictographs. This tour stops by La Cueva de la Chiva, where U.S. troops supposedly corralled and killed the East's famous guerilla warriors during the American occupation of 1916-1924. The second option is the Waterfall Tour, which follows the riverbed to either La Cascada Blanca and El Salto Grande or the Salto Cucuyo. Each tour culminates with a rejuvenating dip in the river that runs through town.

Tours end with hearty servings of homemade Dominican specialties like *moro con coco* (rice and beans simmered in coconut milk) followed by an organic coffee or organic hot chocolate, both of which are made from locally grown crops. Be sure to wear sturdy and waterproof shoes, because parts of the trails are steep, narrow, and muddy. *US$26-36 depending on transport and food. Pedro Sánchez; eco.pedroSánchez@gmail.com; https://sites.google.com/site/ecotourismpedroSanchez/*

Basic lodging in Pedro Sánchez is available at either of the town's two hotels: **Hotel Santa Clara** (RD$300-350; 9 C/ José Chireno; 498-3021; Amenities: fan) and **Hotel Pura Plaza** (RD$300-500; located on main road behind Pura Plaza clothing store; 829-435-9961; 422-2615; Amenities: fan, private bathroom). There is also a typical country wooden home nestled on the mountainside available through Ecoturísmo Pedro Sánchez (eco.pedrosanchez@gmail.com).

TRANSPORT

From El Seibo: RD$60; 6:30am-5:50pm every 30min; 20min; *guaguas* leave from la Rotonda en route to Miches with a stop in Pedro Sánchez.

El Seibo

Founded in 1502, El Seibo was not only one of the original colonial settlements, but also one of the original provinces created by the Constitution of 1844. While the province of El Seibo (sometimes spelled El Seybo) is home to waterfalls worth an exploratory dip, caves dripping with stalactites perfect for spelunking, and serene, gurgling rivers, the town itself, officially titled Santa Cruz de El Seibo, has few attractions. However, its kind people and slow tempo may be welcome after experiencing other, more tourist-ridden towns of the East. Even if there isn't much to do on its dusty streets, stick around for the area's waterfalls, caves made for spelunking, and serene, lazy rivers.

El Seibo proudly claims as former residents such historical figures as Alejandro Woss y Gil, briefly president of the Dominican Republic in 1903, and Manuela Diez Jiménez, mother of the founding father Juan Pablo Duarte. Despite its noteworthy children, there are few monuments to mark El Seibo's rich past. The only remaining edifice dating back to the colonial era is the Basílica de la Santísima Cruz, constructed in 1556.

While in El Seibo, be sure to try *mabí*, a refreshing drink made from the roots or bark of the *behuco de indio* tree, plus cane juice, which is then fermented. Its flavor profile resembles a lost but pretty love child of root beer and lemonade. For more than 100 years, *mabí* has been a staple drink in El Seibo.

Mabí

Mabí, though consumed across the Caribbean, is not widely commercially available in the Dominican Republic, especially outside El Seibo. Instead, the drink is most often produced and consumed locally. Therefore, find *mabí* in recycled bottles of other soft drinks in *colmados*. Other spices can be added to homemade *mabí*, like anise and vanilla. Incidentally, several bottlers manufacture *mabí* abroad, including in the United States and Trinidad and Tobago.

TRANSPORT

Bus

El Seibo, though small, is a major travel hub for the East, with access to nearly all major cities in the region. The *guaguas* run from about 6am to 6pm, depending on the route, and depart every half hour or less.

To Hato Mayor: RD$50; 25min; the stop is on the main road across from Shell Station near La Rotonda. Connect to guaguas for **Sabana de la Mar** in Hato Mayor.

To Higüey/La Romana: RD$100; 1hr/1.5hrs; *Guaguas* leave from the stop on Av. Manuela Diez across from the Centro de Capacitación and Producción Progresando

To Pedro Sánchez and Miches: RD$50/100; 20min/90min; large vans leave from La Rotonda.

To Santo Domingo: RD$160 (*caliente*); RD$175 (*expreso*); 2.5hrs; Transporte Seibano (552-3341) is located at 4 Av. Manuela Diez and also makes stops in Hato Mayor and San Pedro de Macorís.

From Santo Domingo: *caliente/expreso* RD$160/175; 6am-5:30pm; 2.5hrs; *guaguas* leave from Parque Enriquillo on C/ José Marti between C/ Ravelo and C/ Caracas

Public transport within El Seibo is reliant upon *motoconchistas*, who will take passengers anywhere in town starting at RD$20.

INFO

Medical Attention
There are a number of pharmacies located throughout town such as **Harolt**, near the Higüey bus stop. The business is connected to a deli and a *colmadón* that get hopping on Friday nights. Otherwise, try the **Super Farmacia Canepa** (Mon-Sat 8am-8pm) located next to the Parque Central on Av. Manuela Diez; it also has a money exchange booth.

> **Centro Médico del Este** Skip the large public hospital on the road toward Higüey in favor of the superior medical attention at this 24-hour private clinic. *C/ Nuestra Señora del Rosario near Av. Manuela Diez; 552-2737/5505*

Communication
PC.com is an internet café located next to the Fiscalía de Menores and near the *Fortaleza* (military post) on Av. Manuela Diez. For calls, head to the **Claro Call Center** just off Av. Manuela Diez on the left side of C/ Libertad (the road to Villa Guerrero).

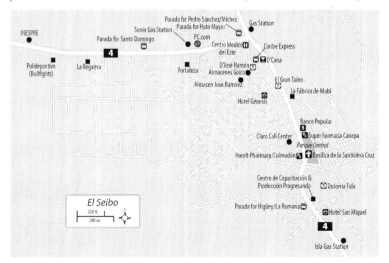

The East

Banks

Find branches of **Banco Popular** and **BanReservas** on the main road (Av. Manuela Diez) near the Parque Central. To change money, use the **Caribe Express** on C/ Nuestra Señora del Rosario near C/ Julio Dalmasi (behind the *Ayuntamiento* and next to D' José Ramón).

Gas Station

The **Shell** station is located at La Rotonda when entering town from Hato Mayor, and an **Isla Gas** Station is across from the Hospital. There's also a **Sunix** across from the Fortaleza.

Grocery Stores

INESPRE, a government-funded supermarket with slighter lower prices, is located on the left side of the main highway when entering town from Hato Mayor (Calle Manuela Diez, next to the Polideportivo). The *Mercado Municipal* is the place to buy fresh produce brought in from the surrounding *campos*, but it's best to get there in the morning before the stalls have been picked over. Most *Seibanos* buy their food at the *almacen*, a sort of supermarket-*colmado* hybrid. **Almacen José Ramírez** and **Almacenes Goico** located near the *Mercado* have the best selections.

EAT

D'José Ramón Delicious pulled chicken sandwiches, as well as a flavorful array of fresh juices, *batidas*, and other drinks are among José Ramón's specialties. Try a *completo* sandwich (pulled chicken, ham, and cheese) with a *batida* de *granadillo* or be more adventuresome with a *remolacha con avena* (beet with oatmeal) juice. *RD$100-160; C/ Nuestra Señora del Rosario near Av. Asomato and next to Caribe Express; 552-5155*

El Gran Taíno For a reasonably priced sit-down meal, this garden restaurant tucked away from the main road serves *criollo* specialties like grilled *mero*, conch shell, and pork chops under a thatched roof bordered by broadleaf tropical plants. *RD$200-300; Av. Manuela Diez*

SLEEP

Hotel Génesis Simple and safe, this hotel painted brightly in yellow and peach is nestled away from the buzz of motorcycles. *RD$400-600; Av. Asomanto between C/ Nuestra Señora del Rosario and C/ Tomas Otto; 552-3024; Amenities: A/C or fan; cable, overnight security guard*

In case Hotel Génesis is full, the less pleasant alternative is **Hotel San Miguel,** of simple cement rooms with fans and cold water. *C/ Deligne near Av. Manuela Diez, by the Centro de Capacitación y Producción Progresando; 552-3684*

■ **La Casa Familiar "Los Botados"** To experience a little more *campo* life after the cacao tour (below), the fair trade farmers of CONACADO provide a simple zinc roof and cinderblock home with two double rooms, dormitories with bunk beds and a common area with the new *campo* must-have – a flat-screen TV. *RD$350-RD$400 or RD$6,000 for whole house; 30min outside Pedro Sánchez in the community of Los Botados. 838-8882; 553-2727; tourdechocolate@hotmail.com, hromerom@hotmail.com; www.conacado.com.do; http://www.paseo.nu/dominican-republiC/ ; Amenities: fan, hot water, kitchen*

DO

■ Cacao Tour "Los Botados"

The tour starts at CONACADO's Bloque 3 headquarters, just outside El Seibo. Following a short history of the co-op and a visit to its modern drying facilities, the tour heads for the hills to experience a cacao farm in the village of Los Botados. At the farm, cacao specialists will head up an informative discussion about planting and harvesting the valuable crop. After farmers explain their traditional fermentation and drying methods, listeners are rewarded with a simple, yet rich hot chocolate brewed on the spot. The tour's last stop is the Women's Association center, at which hungry visitors sit down to an impressive spread of *comida típica* (Dominican food) followed by some of the group's famous sweets. This tour is a slightly more commercialized version of the one offered in nearby Vicentillo. However, this program also offers a night's sleep, as well as a weeklong home stay program, in which visitors spend time with local families to best get a feel of life as a cacao farmer. *$30USD or RD$1,100; Transportation is available for small groups of four or fewer, but providing your own transport is requested. Book at least 24 hours in advance; closed Tuesday; Coordinator Romero: 838-8882/829-760-1153; Office: 553-2727; tourdechocolate@hotmail.com; http://www.paseo.nu/dominican-republic/*

Buenas Noches
Seibanos flock to this location along a river just outside of town during Semana Santa, lugging blackened pots to cook up *moro de bacalao* (rice with salted dried cod). The river is 20 minutes toward Higüey between the communities of Santa Lucia and La Higuera. *By motoconcho RD$50*

Piedra Rodonda
Another swimming hole that comes alive during *Semana Santa*, this one is conveniently located right in town under the bridge on the way to Higüey. *By motoconcho RD$25*

Dulcería Tula
Tula started her famous sweets shop in El Seibo and now sells *dulce de leche* all over the East and as far away as Santo Domingo. Despite its success, the *dulcería* is still housed in a small room on the bottom level of the owner's home. This sugar store offers several variations on the original *dulce de leche*, mixing it up with orange, guava, and cashew fruit infusions. Check out the refrigerated section for local

The East

Corrida de Toros

A tradition unique to El Seibo is the *corrida de toros*, or running of the bulls, the only one in the Dominican Republic. The action takes place in a bullfight-style ring like those found in Spain, but the animals are toyed with – not physically harmed – during delicate dances between the bull and the *torero*. At least five fights take place every afternoon during *Patronales* when El Seibo celebrates its patron saint Santa Cruz, from May 1 through 10. In fights later in the week, the golden-clad *toreros* often welcome the friendly help of alcohol-infused youths who jump into the ring to assist in tormenting the bull. Once the bull tires, the crowd screams, a new bull is brought out, and the fight starts anew. In a fine show of public safety, EMS and hospital services are out in full force all afternoon.

On the first day of the *corrida*, be on the lookout for luminaries in the stands, from local politicians to the Queen of Patronales in her bejeweled crown. Arrive at the ring by 3pm, because prices go up after the fights start and seats become scarce. Festivities after the *corrida* is over, like in all Patronales celebrations, last well into the night. *Free for standing room; VIP seats RD$50; Polideportivo; fights start at 4pm* favorite *dulce de coco con batata* (shaved coconut, milk, and sweet potato). *RD$30-100; 48 C/ General Santana, near C/ Rafael Zorilla; 552-3808*

La Fábrica de Mabí
Known as the champagne of El Seibo, *mabí* is a heralded specialty enjoyed since Taíno times. Production of the popular drink continues in the original factory built in 1883 by Antonio Duvergé, who, according to the hyperbole-prone current owner and Duvergé descendent, was responsible for the first ice factory, the first motorcycle, and the first appearance of electricity in El Seibo. Stop by to ask for a free tour of the premises. *RD$15/bottle; Av. Manuela Diez near BanReservas*

Centro de Capacitación and Producción Progresando
A project sponsored by the Office of the First Lady and the European Union, this community center offers courses in a number of artisan trades. The students' creations are for sale in the store, proceeds from which directly support the community members who make them. *Av. Manuela Diez across from the parada for Higüey / La Romana*

Basílica de la Santísima Cruz
Named for the patron saint of El Seibo, this colonial monument built in 1556 is all that remains of the of the town's Spanish roots. Although other buildings have long since disappeared, the church has been well maintained, and priests still celebrate mass here every Sunday. Rare images and icons of gold and silver in the interior of the church also date from the colonial era. *Located in the Parque Central on Av. Manuela Diez*

La Reguera
Every Tuesday, a large plot of dirt transforms into a bustling flea market, covered with makeshift tents and tarps with clothes, toiletries and every possible use of plastic, from chamber pots to hair rollers. *Near entrance of town coming from Hato Mayor; Tues 9am-5pm*

NIGHTLIFE

During the week the **Parque Central** is simply a nice place to relax, but on Sunday evenings, Seibanos congregate in the park in honor of a *bien fría* (a cold one). Friday nights, **Harolt Colmadón** on Av. Manuela Diez and C/ General Cabral is the hangout of choice, and then on Monday, step up to a hip-energizing *perico ripiao*, the *campo*-style merengue, at **D'Cana** (Av. Manuela Diez).

La Romana

With a population of more than 250,000, La Romana is the largest and most developed city of the East. The origins of the La Romana's name are disputed; some claim it comes from an ancient word for scale, while others believe it comes from the Taíno word for the nearby Río Dulce, which they called Bomana. Attracted by precious lumber, the first modern inhabitants settled along the banks of the Río Salado (a Río Dulce estuary), which eventually meets with the Caribbean Sea. This aquatic confluence made La Romana a perfect site for a port, which was built in the middle of the 19th century. Tremendous growth here over the last century, however, can be attributed to the sweet and simple: sugar.

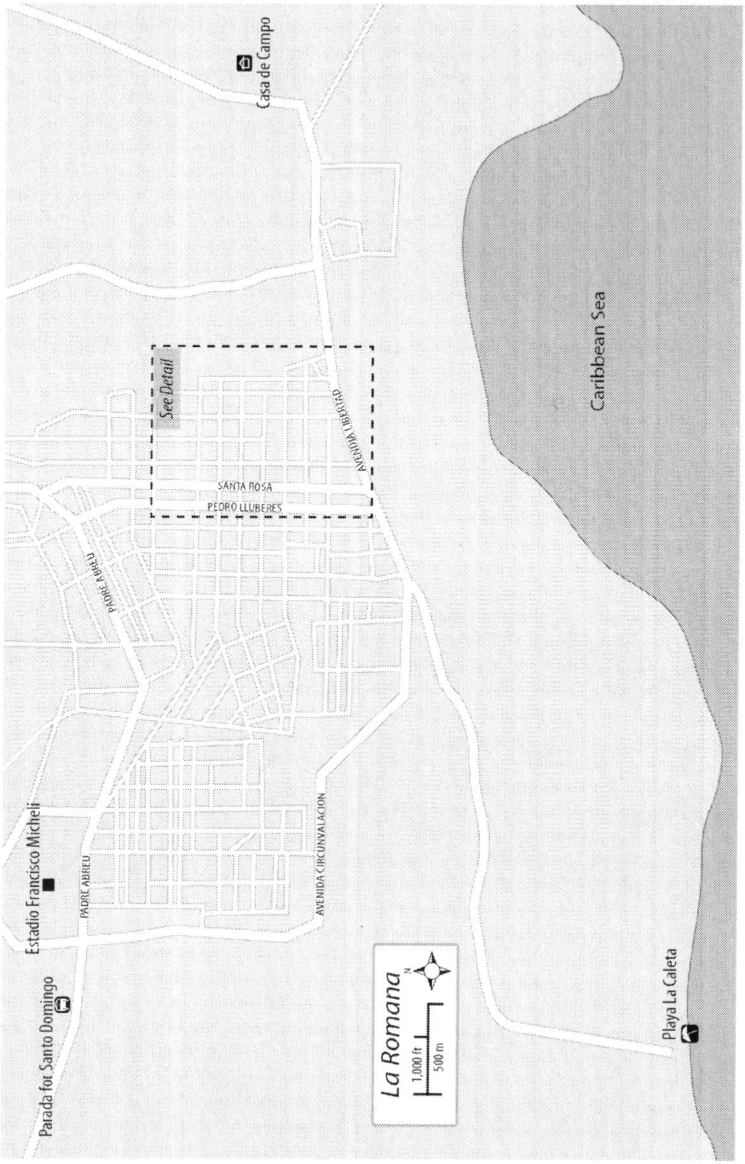

La Romana

1,000 ft
500 m

Casa de Campo

Caribbean Sea

See Detail

AVENIDA LIBERTAD

SANTA ROSA

PEDRO LLUBERES

PADRE ABREU

AVENIDA CIRCUNVALACIÓN

PADRE ABREU

Estadio Francisco Micheli

Parada for Santo Domingo

Playa La Caleta

The East

The South Puerto Rican Sugar Company jumpstarted La Romana's fortune with the construction of the city's first sugar mill in 1917. Sugar operations changed hands in the 1960s when Gulf and Western swept up the massive processing complex called Central Romana. Then, after acquiring the U.S. Consolidated Cigar Corporation in 1968, Gulf and Western moved its center of operations to La Romana. Gulf and Western processed its sugar alongside rollers that churned out highly popular and lucrative cigars such as Romeo & Julieta and Montecristo.

Gulf & Western

Gulf and Western was also responsible for building the island's first and most comprehensive resort, Casa de Campo (p149), in 1975. Casa de Campo fulfilled the "if you build it, they will come" philosophy, as a wave of tourism arrived when construction completed and has yet to abate. This breathed life into La Romana's economy, needed especially after the drop in sugar prices. Gulf and Western made its grand exit after selling off Casa de Campo to the Cuban-American Fanjol family in the 1980s, and the company has now ceased to exist (its remnants are owned by Viacom) after creating such enormous influence in the city.

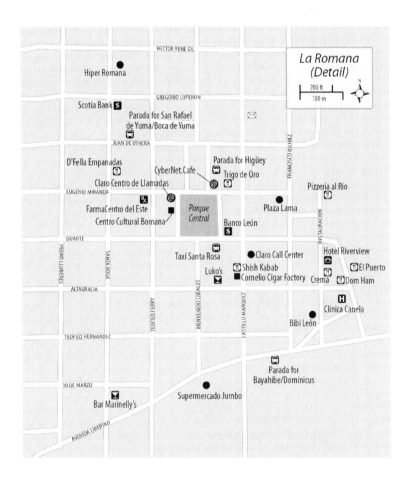

Today, brushing aside the economic old-timers of sugar and cigars, tourism has become the driving force in local economy, having expanded to the nearby towns of Bayahibe and Dominicus.

More of an industrial and commercial center than anything else, La Romana hosts few sites of interest beyond several pretty Victorian homes and the mural-covered obelisk. As in many Dominican towns, there is a pleasant Parque Central, this time crowned by the Iglesia de Santo Rosa de Lima. It does have a decent nightlife on weekends, as well as some culinary highlights, but hotels are scarce and overpriced, making it more suitable as a day trip from Bayahibe or quick pass-through to or from Santo Domingo.

TRANSPORT

Guaguas provide regional transport to the following locations and leave every 20-30 minutes:

To Higüey: RD$90 *caliente*; RD$100 *expreso*; 5:30am-10pm; 2.5hrs; 550-0880; the SITRAIHR bus company *parada* is located near the Parque Central across from the west side the Catholic Church, Santa Rosa de Lima

To Bayahibe/Dominicus: RD$50; 6:20am-7:20pm; 30min; the *parada* is located near the obelisk

To San Rafael de Yuma: RD$80; 5:30am-7pm; 1hr; C/ Juan de Utrera between C/ Santa Rosa and C/ Teofilo Ferry, near the *Mercado*

To Santo Domingo: RD$150 *caliente*; RD$160 e*xpreso*; 5am-6pm; 2hrs; free buses take passengers from the Parque Central to the SICHOEM bus company's Santo Domingo stop, and pass every 15 minutes, or take a taxi for RD$150. The stop itself is located at the entrance to La Romana if coming from the west on C/ Padre Abreu, near the intersection of Av. Nueva

From Santo Domingo: RD$150 *caliente*; RD$160 e*xpreso*; 5am-6pm; 2hrs; *guaguas* leave from Parque Enriquillo

Local transport around the city is either by *motoconcho* (RD$20-30) or taxi (starting at RD$75). Two respected taxis companies are **Dino Taxi** (550-5060) and **Taxi Santa Rosa,** whose hub is located on C/ Duarte just off the *Parque Central*. Smaller *guaguas* also occasionally give lifts around town en route to one of the surrounding bateyes (See the box on the Sugarcane Industry, p338)

INFO

Medical Attention

Approved for Peace Corps Volunteers, **Clínica Canela** is a private clinic with a 24/7 Emergency Room (44 C/ Libertad by C/ Benito Monción; 556-3135). The pharmacy **FarmaCentro del Este** is located on C/ Teofilo Ferry and C/ Miranda between the Parque Central and the *Mercado* (556-5259).

Communication

CyberNet.Café (cybernetcafe@hotmail.com) is located on C/ Eugenio Miranda near C/ Trinitaria. A **Claro Centro de Llamadas** and internet café is located across from the Parque Central on C/ Diego Avila. Another **Claro Call Center** is located on C/ Castillo Marquez between C/ Duarte and C/ Altagracia. The **Post Office** is at 71 C/

Castillo Marquez (556-3060, 910-4854). There is a **FedEx** in the Turinter Office on C/ Eugenio A. Miranda just west of the Parque Central between C/ Diego Avila and C/ Teofilio Ferry.

Banks

Scotiabank is located at the corner of C/ Gregorio Luperón and Santa Rosa. On the southeast corner of the Parque Central on C/ Duarte is a full-service **Banco León**. Both are open Mon-Fri 8:30am-4:30pm and Saturday 9am-1pm.

Gas

There is a gas station on C/ Santa Rosa and another on C/ Padre Abreu by the Polideportiva and the *parada* for Santo Domingo.

Grocery Stores

The **Jumbo** megastore is located on Avenida Libertad, near the entrance to Central Romana. **Plaza Lama** is between C/ Castillo Marquez and C/ Francisco Richiez Douvrey.

EAT

Pizzeria al Río So aptly named is this restaurant that it is possible to both dine on superb wood-fired oven pizza (and some decent pasta dishes), while also overlooking the river. *RD$200-400; 43 C/ Restauración; 550-9109*

Restaurant El Puerto El Puerto acts as a door to a culinary world tour, featuring delicious *criollo*-style grilled halibut, Italian pasta, Spanish *paella,* and Thai curry. The location overlooking the Río Salado provides a delightful ambience under the sun or at night, when flickering candles illuminate the restaurant. The Italian and German proprietors also own the Terminal Nautica Marina, where the high rollers of La Romana dock their yachts. *RD$340-600; 11 C/ Benito Monción; 847-8853/550-8156; nauticaterminal@hotmail.com; Open every day 4pm-12am*

Trigo de Oro At this restaurant meaning "golden wheat," find flaky French baked goods like pastries and tarts, as well as light meals such as quiche Lorraine, chicken Caesar salad and a variety of sandwiches. *RD$50-260; 9 C/ Eugenio A. Miranda; 550-5650; trigo_de_oro@hotmail.com; Mon-Sat: 7am-9pm; Sun 7am-1pm*

Dom Ham Hailed as the best burger joint in the city, this open-air restaurant also offers German beers on tap like weihenstephan, in case you've had enough (gasp!) of Presidente. *RD$125-150; C/ Benito Monción and C/ Altagracia; 550-9220*

Crema This small, chic bakery is capable of sating any sweet tooth with its flourless chocolate cake, *tres leches,* or *coco horneado* (baked coconut cake). *RD$50-75; 15 C/ Restauración; 813-2103/2110/2140; foodconsulting@codetel.net.do*

Shish Kabab Adding to the cultural diversity of the city, this Lebanese restaurant has been around since 1969. Though a bit expensive, it has the ambience and service to account for the markup. A more reasonably priced item and the one for which the restaurant is famous is the simple yet delicious *quipe*. Starters include hummus, grape leaves (waraf-inab) and baba ganoush. Don't leave without trying the namesake shish kabob dish, made with chicken or beef. *RD$50-600; 32 C/ Castillo Marquez; 556-2737; jgiha@hotmail.com*

D'Fella Empanadas Fella makes one thing, and she makes it well. Step out of the empanada comfort zone and taste a specialty empanada like crab or conch shell, or go for one of the classics like chicken or cheese. *RD$20-35; 75 C/ Santa Rosa de Lin across from the Honda dealership; 813-2547*

SLEEP

Unfortunately, travelers will be hard-pressed to find inexpensive, quality lodging in La Romana. Although tourists do come to the city, they rarely stay overnight (except for those at nearby Casa de Campo; see below), creating the feeling of tourism and therefore inflated prices, but not the actual revenue to support decent hotels. Among the options are **Hotel Riverview**, clean and conveniently located in the center of town, but a bit pricey and has no river view to speak of (RD$1200-RD$1350; C/ Restauración; 556-1181/813-0984; Amenities: A/C, hot water, cable TV, telephone, mini-fridge, Wi-Fi, computer with internet in lobby). A more economical option would be **Hotel Olympo,** which is on par with the Riverview for slightly less (RD$1000; C/ Pedro Lluberes and C/ Padre Abreu).

On the other end of the spectrum is **Casa de Campo**, an exclusive luxury resort that is internationally renowned for being the location of Michael Jackson and Lisa Marie's wedding in 1994, as well as the vacation destination for such celebrities as Oprah, Shakira, and the Clintons. Among other attractions, the resort offers a hotel, villas, a private beach, an Italian-inspired shopping piazza, the faux-European art village Altos de Chavon (p150) an airport, heliport, a marina, and world-class golf courses. *Rooms start at US$295/night in the off-season, and can run up to US$1300/night for suites during the winter holiday season. Reservations outside the DR: 1-800-877-3643 or (305) 856-5405; within the DR: 523-3333/8698; res1@pwmonline.com; reserva@ccampo.com.do; www.casadecampo.com.do*

DO

Playa La Caleta

This quintessential Dominican beach experience combines fresh seafood, a cold Presidente beer, and surround sound merengue. The beach was also the site of a major archaeological dig that uncovered artifacts left behind by pre-Hispanic populations. Its proximity to La Romana makes La Caleta a great spot to swim and party with the locals, but for the pristine white-sand beaches, head farther east. *Guaguas* to La Caleta leave from the Parque Central.

Estadio Francisco Micheli

The 2011 Dominican national baseball champions Toros del Este (formerly known as the Azucareros, or sugar farmers) play their lively and physical version of pelota at this stadium during the Dominican winter league season. With a logo and color scheme strikingly similar to those of the Texas Longhorns, games here are not to be missed by fans of any sport. Indeed, ex-president George W. Bush donned a Toros cap during his 2011 spring break at Casa de Campo. Tickets are cheap (RD$200 and less) and even if baseball is not your thing, the beer and rum flow freely, and Toros fans are a constant source of entertainment. As they say, "aquí, to' somos Toros" – here, we're all Toros. *C/ Abreu and C/ Luperón; 556-6188; www.torosazucarerosdeleste.com*

Centro Cultural Bomana

This gem sponsors art and culture events across the city, including jazz in the park, theatrical productions, in-house art classes, and cultural education in the city's schools. Among other goals, the center aims to preserves the country's rich Afro-Caribbean culture, including the music and dance of *gagá. Housed in the former Don Quijote restaurant on C/ Diego Avila across from the Parque Central; 556-2834; Bomana@gmail.com*

The East

Parque Central

The city's central plaza is an expansive, green oasis, always alive with activity as *motoconchistas* call for customers at every corner, and children play around the massive iron sculptures of bulls and horses by the local artist El Artístico. High-school sweethearts take cover from the hot sun on the shady benches while enjoying passion fruit and coconut Skim Ices – the Dominican RD$5 version of ice pops. The traditional cement gazebo at the center of the park is home to the occasional concert sponsored by the Centro Cultural Bomana. Grab a cold refreshment from one of the surrounding *colmados* and take it all in. *C/ Duarte and Deligne*

SHOPPING

Cornelio Cigar Factory

Try a cigar rolled before your eyes in this shoebox of a store. Ask to see the small selection of Dominican cigars in the back and look out for the store's own specialty brand, Estrella Punta Cana. *C/ Castillo Marquez near C/ Altagracia; 444-4279*

Bibi León

Stunning hand-painted functional art with designs inspired by the island covers this boutique situated in an unassuming white house. The matching sets of wooden bowls, plates, and other housewares make unique and beautiful gifts. *2 C/ Restauración; 550-8393; bibileon@hotmail.com; www.bibileon.com*

Concerts & Shopping: Altos de Chavon

A Grecian-style amphitheater offering seating for 5,000 is one of many attractions in Altos de Chavon, a 1970s replica of a medieval Mediterranean village overlooking the Río Chavon. The complex includes the Altos de Chavon School of Design, affiliated with Parson's School of Design in New York. The movie-set atmosphere, imagined and constructed by the president of Gulf and Western Charles Bludhorn in the 1970s, is complete with restaurants, boutiques, and a disco. The amphitheater was inaugurated in 1982 with a performance by Frank Sinatra and has since hosted such international acts as Sting, Gloria Estefan, Spyro Gyra, and Julio Iglesias. Beyond historical whimsy, the complex hosts a real archaeology museum called El Museo Arqueológico Regional that displays a small but impressive exposition of Taíno artifacts (9:30am-5:00am; free). *Altos de Chavon is part of the Casa de Campo resort complex (p149). If you are not a guest at the hotel, there's an entrance fee of US$25. www.altosdechavon.com*

BARS & NIGHTLIFE

Bar Marinelly's Marinelly's is an upscale bar and dance club featuring 80s-style light and fog machines. It is one of the only in town that charges a cover, giving it a whiff of exclusivity, but also importantly dissuades prostitutes from frequenting the club. *RD$50 females; RD$100 males; C/ Santa Rosa between C/ 30 de marzo and Av. Libertad*

Luko's This relatively new club appeals to a wealthier clientele with themed nights like "White Party." *C/ Altagracia near C/ Francisco Castillo Marquez; open quite late Thurs.–Sun*

Bajo Mundo Locals find this a great spot to dance the night away to reggaeton, merengue, and bachata. As with all discos in La Romana, women revelers should err on the side of caution and arrive with a group, as some Dominican men can be aggressive when they see a female unaccompanied. *C/ Pedro Lluberes near C/ Santa Rosa*

Guerrero Mega Drink The name here says it all – no translation required, just a willingness to dance and throw back some cool Presidente. On weekend nights after 10pm, this *colmadón* dims the lights and transforms into a disco as couples break it down to bachata and merengue. *Located on the road toward La Caleta; arrive and leave in a taxi because the road is dark at night.*

Dominicus (Americanus)

Unlike its coastal neighbor Bayahibe, Dominicus was founded as a specifically tourist-oriented development under the auspices of the Dominicus Americanus Project. An American investor named Wayne Fuller bought up the land in the 1970s and then sold it off piecemeal to the various all-inclusive resorts that now dominate this tiny town. Though the name Bayahibe is often used to refer to both the town of Bayahibe and Dominicus, the two are distinct, both geographically and culturally. Nearly all of the businesses and residents here are Italian, and so there are few cues that Dominicus is actually in the Dominican Republic at all.

Because the majority of visitors go directly to all-inclusive hotels and leave only for the airport, the few businesses that exist are kept afloat by the expat-filled housing developments, also part of the Dominicus Americanus Project.

TRANSPORT

From Santo Domingo: See La Romana Transport on page 144. Once in La Romana, get off at the *parada* for Bayahibe, located near the obelisk. Take the *guagua* to Bayahibe (RD$50; leaves every 20 minutes 6:20am-7:20pm; 30 min), which first passes through Bayahibe and then continues on to Dominicus.

By car: Take the East highway (officially, Highway 3) to La Romana and continue southeast, following the signs toward Bayahibe when leaving La Romana. The road then forks to either Dominicus or Bayahibe.

INFO

Medical Attention
In Plaza Pino, there is a pharmacy and clinic (Dr. Rafael Veter: 803-5628; 318-5109).

Banks
BanReservas is the only bank in town and is located on the Pedestrian walkway (Open Mon-Fri, 9am-4pm). To change money, **Rovisa** is located on Av. Eladia in Plaza Pino, Local 2 (868-7125). To receive or send money, **Western Union** is also located in Plaza Pino.

Spa
La Belleza del Espíritu This unisex spa is the only one of its caliber located outside of the hotels in the area and offers a number of treatments such as hair care, waxing, massages, aromatherapy, and hydrotherapy. *Cayuco Village, Villa 32; 829-758-3602; Open Tue-Sat 9am-6pm*

EAT

Rancho El Paso Don't let the American Wild West decorations fool the unsuspecting diner – this restaurant is pure Italian. The menu offers a wide selection of meats, pastas, and authentic Italian pizzas such as the Bavaria with gorgonzola and bacon. *RD$180-500; C/ Los Corales; 833-0197; 980-8254*

El Mundo Bar-Restaurant The only place in town where you can get a *plato del día* for RD$150, as well as a selection of inexpensive Italian food such as the Roman favorite piandine, which is similar to a frittata made with prosciutto and brie or mozzarella. Pasta, of course, is among the other offerings, as well as paninis and risotto. *RD$150-500; C/ Peatonal; 829-410-7241; info@el mundo-dominicus.com; www.elmundo-dominicus.com*

 Tracadero Beach Club and Restaurant An elegant hotel and yacht club where white linens sway in the ocean breeze and soothing music floats through the air. Soak up the relaxing ambiance in either the salt or fresh water pools, or try one of the restaurant's Italian-influenced offerings such as lobster linguine or a glass of wine from the bar's diverse wine list. *RD$400-700; end of C/ Los Corales; 906-3664; info@tracadero.it; www.tracadero.it*

Heladería Fragola Pistachio The homemade gelato served here, with flavors such as chocolate hazelnut, coconut, and tiramisu, is a superb way to cool off the afternoon. *RD$100; C/ Wayne Fuller*

SLEEP

Cabanas Elke The most economical option in town with some of the perks of Viva Wyndham Dominicus Resort, as guests have access to its beach and restaurants if they buy a pass. The rooms and apartments are comfortable and clean and located right on the beach. *US$30-90; C/ Los Corales next to Viva Wyndham Dominicus; 689-8249; 860-4845 www.viwi.it; Amenities: fan, hot water, restaurant bar*

Hotel Eden One of the only non-inclusive hotels in the area, and is therefore perfect for the unexpected visit. Sleeping options vary from double to quadruple rooms as well as apartments and bungalows with well-equipped with cable TV, A/C and kitchens. *Low season US$50-90, high season US$60-100; 10 Av. La Laguna; 833-0856; www.santodomingovacanze.com; Amenities: A/C, fan, cable TV, restaurant, bar, safe, disco, pool*

All Inclusives

There are four all-inclusive resorts in Dominicus, all of which need to be booked in advance through their respective websites. Of the bunch, the Iberostar Hacienda Dominicus and Viva Wyndham are the most affordable, but prices vary tremendously depending on the season and the online deals each one may be offering. All provide similar carefree experiences with endless bounties of food and drink.

Viva Wynham and Viva Wynham Dominicus Palace: *Both found on www.vivaresorts.com*

Catalonia Gran Dominicus: *www.cataloniagrandominicus.com*

Iberostar Hacienda Dominicus: *www.iberostar.com*

Be Live Caribe (formerly Oasis Canoa): *www.hotelesoasis.com*

Rentals

There is also **Cadaques Caribe,** a pricey non-inclusive hotel and condominium complex designed to resemble a Mediterranean village. The first phase of development was modeled after the Spanish town of Cadaques, with its white stucco walls and orange Spanish tiles. The Italian owner then sold a portion of the property to a Dominican, who has continued to expand the hotel, shifting the focal point from the quaint Mediterranean chapel to a purple dragon that wraps around a tangle of water slides. *5 Boulevard Dominicus Americanus, 237-2000; info@cadaquescaribe.com; www.cadaquescaribe.com*

DO

If you are in Dominicus, you are most likely staying at one of the all-inclusive resorts, which offer a number of activities, such as snorkeling, sea kayaking, and excursions to the Parque Nacional del Este (National Park of the East, p159). If this is not the case, or you simply want to get out of the confines of the resort, there are a number of tour operators in town.

A good place to start your search is at the **Centro de Información Turística** (Tourist Information Center) located on the pedestrian walkway. The Sustainable Tourism Cluster of La Romana-Bayahibe sponsors the center, and so it's great for advice about activities in the area. *Gemma Fontanella: 829-520-7390; Mon-Fri 9am-12:30pm; 3-7:30pm, Sat 9:30am-12:30pm; Sun 3-7:30pm*

TOUR OPERATORS

Rancho El Paso (p151) offers horseback riding around the National Park and is the only licensed tour operator that can enter the **Padre Nuestro Trail** (p159).

The following tour companies offer similar packages to the Parque Nacional del Este, such as boat excursions to Isla Saona and Catalina, as well as hiking to the caves located within the Park. As competition is fierce, the best strategy is to contact each one and see which package suits your interests and budget.

Baya Tour Unlike other tour operators, the Italian owner Stefano is the one actually running the tours, saving the middleman fees. *Plaza Pino #2; 710-7336; 833-0048; stefbay2000@yahoo.it; www.villabayahotel.com*

Seavis Tours Seavis is an independent tour operator specializing in eco-tours and snorkeling. Unlike the booze cruises that spill out onto Bayahibe's dock en route to Isla Saona, Seavis Tours takes small groups away from the crowds to appreciate the natural beauty of Parque Nacional del Este. Not only does it have a strong environmental focus, but proceeds also benefit the small fishing community of Mano Juan on Isla Saona. Some of the tours include Saona Crusoe VIP, which takes visitors to remote parts of Isla Saona, or the 2-Island 2-Ocean Tour, which goes to Isla Catalinita bordering both the Atlantic Ocean and Caribbean Sea. There's also the so-called Hookah Snorkeling, which is a safer alternative to scuba diving, but allows for deeper dives than traditional snorkeling. *US$49-95; 4 C/ Eladia; 829-714-4947; seavistours@yahoo.de; seavisbayahibe.com*

ECO REP DOM is a tour operator group with seven partners throughout the country. In Dominicus, **Mariposa Tours** is the affiliate company, which offers a number of excursions around Bayahibe, as well as regional transport and hotel reservations. *Jean Pierre Albert: 829-878-6802/828-8602; jp@rd-w.com; www.marposatours-bayahibe.com*

Dominicus Public Beach

Fortunately, some of the pristine coastline in Dominicus is still open to the public. One section is called La Laguna, and is impeccably clean due to its international "blue flag" status. This requires that a beach meet certain environmental management and safety standards including the cleanliness of the beach, water, and facilities. There are a few tasty seafood restaurants such as the Italian owned **Los Lagos** (978-5538), located right on the beach.

NIGHTLIFE

Besides the restaurant bars, nightlife in Dominicus is centered around the **Casino Diamante Dominicus** located on Blvd. Dominicus. Alongside Lady Luck and a band

The East

of jovial Italian expats, spin out a fortune on the roulette tables or dance it out at the disco. Don't forget to stop by the casino's tourist information center for tour ideas.

Restaurant Eden Antichi Sapori This Italian restaurant specializing in seafood distinguishes itself from the others for its spectacular happy hour. Starting at 6pm, there are discounted mixed drinks and wine paired with a free buffet of finger foods and heartier dishes such as meatballs, eggplant Parmesan, and lump crabmeat. Be sure to try one of their homemade desserts such as tiramisu or strudel. In the evenings, they screen classic black and white Italian films. *10 Av. la Laguna; 833-0856; info@edencxa.com; www.santodomingovacanze.com*

SHOPPING

There are a number of tacky gift shops hawking the same overpriced Dominican Republic souvenirs and "artisan" crafts that are mass-produced and made nowhere near the Caribbean. If you are interested in authentic Dominican art and are willing to make an investment, **La Bottega de Cadaques,** located in Cadaques Caribe, features Dominican artists, many of who studied at the school at Altos de Chavon (p150). Gemma Fontanella, the owner, displays a variety of styles and media, from oil paintings to photography and sculpture. *Cadaques Caribe, Blvd. Dominicus Americanus. If not a guest of the hotel, call Gemma to get into the complex; 847-3553; arte.la.bottega@gmail.com; Open Sat and Sun*

Bayahibe

The small but quite lively fishing town of Bayahibe is located on the edge of the Parque Nacional del Este, making it an excellent place to overnight while enjoying the islands, caves, and trails of the beautiful park. The attractive town meanders around the placid bay, offering a number of attractions: an archaeological dig with artifacts dating back over 4,000 years, shallow fresh springs with unique character, locally-run jewelry and art workshops, and historical sailboats still in use today.

Despite the influx of all-inclusive resorts, the people of Bayahibe continue to be warm and welcoming, while aware that they need to preserve the remaining land and beachfront that have not been bought up by foreign developers. For this reason, concerned residents put together various community efforts to foment sustainable forms of tourism. Such programs include the La Punta Ruta Cultural (The Cultural Tour of La Punta) and La Rosa de Bayahibe, an artisans' association. Resort guests and other travelers will also enjoy the annual regatta of antique sailboats on the Saturday of Easter Week. The regatta sails from the cove of Bayahibe to Isla Catalina, proudly displaying fine craftsmanship.

Besides tourism, fishing was and continues to be a primary source of income for many in Bayahibe. Fishermen use both the antique sailboats as well as small, rough-hewn motorboats to venture out into the waters filled with fish, lobster, and shrimp. During the late afternoon, onlookers can observe the fishermen cleaning their daily catch before selling it to local restaurants.

TRANSPORT

To/From La Romana: RD$50; leave every 20 minutes, 6:20am-7:20pm; 30 minutes; *Guaguas* leave La Romana for Bayahibe near the obelisk, and leave Bayahibe for La Romana across from the Super Colmadón Bayahibe.

INFO

Medical Attention

For emergencies, see the **El Centro Clínico Bayahibe** on the corner of C/ Juan Brito and C/ de Domini (829-361-0903/265-9485). For medicine, **Farmacia Job** is located on C/ La Bahia. (833-0453; Mon-Sat 8am-9pm; Sun 8am-1pm)

Communication

There are two internet cafés along C/ Juan Brito, one of which is located across from the tiny park after entering the town, and the other is located inside **Bayahibe Color** across from the basketball court.

Banks

BanReservas is the only bank in Bayahibe and is located on C/ Juan Brito. To change money, use the **Caribe Express** on C/ Juan Brito. To receive or send money, there is a **Western Union** next door. Both are located across from the basketball court.

Grocery Stores

La Defensa is the only supermarket in town, carrying a good amount of international brands. It is centrally located next to **Super Colmadón Bayahibe**, which itself is handy for snacks and cold drinks.

Buying Seafood

Buying fresh seafood directly from the fishermen who catch it is an excellent way to support the local economy without throwing out the budget. A store-bought lobster cannot compare to flavor and texture of one straight from the ocean. This tradition of fishing, upon which the town of Bayahibe was built, is one that the local population has fought to preserve, even as overfishing and tourism interests threaten their livelihood. Overfishing is a serious issue across the country, but lack of effective environmental education has created a perceivable tension between the Ministry of the Environment that tries to restrict fishing, and fishermen, who simply see their income as being threatened by overbearing restrictions. Complicating the fishermen's situation, corporate hotel interests do not want fishermen trolling the waters in front of their resorts (ruining the view!) or docking boats in the waters that surround the resorts. Growing up with this trade, the fishermen of Bayahibe have been placed in an increasingly difficult situation, especially because the economy provides few other job options. Visitors can do their part for both the environment and the fishermen by staying current on which species are not in breeding season and only buying regulation-size fish and lobster.

EAT

Restaurante La Punta A community institution for more than 20 years, this seafood restaurant is known for its collaborative community spirit. it continues to support local projects like Fundemar's efforts (p156) to protect and study marine mammals off of the coast. *RD$150-600; C/ La Bahia and C/ Yirardy; located toward the Point near the tour bus parking lot; 833-0080*

Restaurante Mare Nostrum Nearly all restaurants in Bayahibe offer the catch of the day, but this one offers it prepared either as carpaccio or delicately cooked in such sauces as cream and fresh tomato. Other specialties include vegetable tempura and lobster ravioli. Once a month on Friday, there are themed prix-fixe buffet dinners such as lobster night or "Favorites from the Orient." *RD$350-800; C/ Juan Brito; 833-0055; www.web-dominicana.com; closed Mondays, Tues open at 4pm*

The East

Capitán Kidd With an unobstructed view of the ocean, this restaurant has enjoyed success for generations (including under its previous name, La Bahia), due to its simple yet exquisitely prepared seafood. *RD$200-600; C/ Juan Brito; 350-1977/313-1629*

Cafecito de la Cubana One of the most affordable and quality eating options, this beach hut is perfectly situated under the shade of grand old trees with a view of bobbing boats. The *ropa vieja* is a house specialty, or try cheaper options such as the *plato del día*. Alternately, tuck into any of the fresh seafood dishes, which is always of legal size because one of the restaurant's partners is a marine biologist for the environmental NGO Fundemar. *RD$125-350; Located near the tour bus parking lot, on the beach; 757-9601/350-2203; anasotoca@yahoo.es; Facebook: "el cafecito de la cubana"; Open every day except Tues, 11am-11pm*

Barco Bar Barco Bar has seen many owners, many of whom were Italian, that have maintained the restaurant's quality and popularity. It is a favorite spot to watch the sun set over the bay while enjoying a drink. Beyond the Italian menu, Barco Bar adds to the town's nightlife with bachata contests and theme parties, which draw a European and local crowd. *RD$125-350; Located at the end of C/ Juan Brito after Captán Kidd but before the baseball field; info@barcobarbayahibe.com*

Snack Shops

Near the parking lot where tour buses disembark for Isla Saona, there is a row of small wooden snack shacks. Among them is **La Jungla**, perfect for drinks (locals claim it would win a *batida* contest) or a quick sandwich. Also try **Mamma Mia**, specializing in pizza and as authentic a gelato as possible in the Caribbean.

SLEEP

Hotel Bayahibe This hotel is both well managed and reasonably priced for this tourist-infused town. All rooms come with two double beds and a balcony; be sure to ask for one with a view of the sea. Put down a few extra pesos for the continental breakfast, served on a balcony overlooking the bay. *RD$1300-2000; C/ Principal, 833-0159/0045; hotelbayahibe@hotmail.com; www.hotelbayahibe.net; Amenities: A/C, fan, hot water, cable, fridge, Wi-Fi, 24/7 electricity and water; restaurant for breakfast; computer w/ internet in lobby*

Cabanas La Bahía The oldest cabanas in town, these stone and zinc-roofed huts have the charm that their competitors lack. Two of the ten cabins are located right on the beach between Mare Nostrum and Capitan Kidd. To save some pesos, request the other cabanas tucked within the community on C/ de los Manatiales near the natural aquifer of Manatial La Cueva. *RD$800-RD$1200; 710-0881; Amenities: fan, A/C, kitchen*

Both **Cabañas Trip Town** and **Cabañas Maura** are centrally located between the coastline and the Super Colmadón Bayahibe, and are similar both in price and Amenities. Cabañas Trip Town is slightly more aesthetically appealing with Spanish tile roofs and white stucco walls, and each room comes with a double and single bed, making Trip Town ideal for groups. Neither offers kitchens, so these are better for shorter stays. *RD$800-1000; Cabanas Trip Town: C/ Juan Brito; 833-0082; Amenities: A/C or fan, hot water, fridge*

DO

☑Volunteer with FUNDEMAR

Fundemar was founded in 1991 by the renowned Dominican marine biologist Idelisa Bonnelly. Fundemar established a presence in Bayahibe when the water amusement park Manatee Park captured dolphins off the town's coastline. The event created a stir among locals in Bayahibe and marine activists on an international level. The

NGO Amigos de los Delfines (Friends of the Dolphins) provided funding for the first study of the dolphins inhabiting the waters between Bayahibe and Isla Saona. By 2007, Fundemar was able to obtain the funding necessary to launch a two-year study that aimed to catalogue and track the dolphins' social patterns, using GPS and a computerized fin scan program. Fundemar also studies the manatees and sperm whales that call these warm waters home.

In addition to efforts to protect marine life, Fundemar plays an active role in the community of Bayahibe, supporting such projects as the Artisan's Association La Rosa de Bayahibe and the Cultural Route La Punta.

Fundemar offers housing in Bayahibe to volunteers of all skill backgrounds, from marine biologists to web designers to those with business experience. Volunteers are responsible for personal expenses and transport. For more information, contact Rita Sellares, Director of Fundemar in Bayahibe: *833-0481; 829-714-0616; rsellares@gmail.com; www.fundemar.org*

◪ Artecuseco de Benerito

Located in the small, poor community of Villa Padre Nuestro (See Padre Nuestro, p159) in Benerito, this artisan group sprung from a few simple courses offered through IDDI, a government educational organization (Instituto Dominicano de Desarollo Integral, or Dominican Institute of Comprehensive Development). The local women's association formed the artisan group in 2007, and has advanced tremendously in terms of skill and design through the efforts of a Peace Corp volunteer and outside artisan teachers. The women use natural material such as seashells, seeds, cow horns, wood, gourds (*higüeros*) and coconut shells to make rustic yet lovely jewelry. The pieces make excellent gifts not only for their originality, but also because the sale of such items goes directly into the pockets of the women who make them. At the time of research, the women were in the process of securing funding and land to construct a permanent workshop, but until then, the best way to see their creations is to contact them directly to visit one of their homes. *RD$100-250 earrings and RD$250-800 for necklaces; Contact Esmeralda, 829-741-3507 or Ani, 829-741-3509; artecuseco@gmail.com*

◪ Asociación de Artesanos La Rosa de Bayahibe

This artisan association in the town of Bayahibe is composed of individual artists who use local and recycled materials such as driftwood, seeds and shells to make jewelry, dolls and miniature sailboat replicas. In 2008, a Peace Corps volunteer helped the group form an association and begin marketing to the tourism industry. The group's creations are on display in the center of Bayahibe, outside the Super Colmadón Bayahibe.

Several members of the association maintain their own workshops, where visitors can see the artisans at work. Try catching the artists known as Gauba and Negro working on model boats of the traditional Bayahibe sailboats, or Leni creating her signature dolphin necklaces. If in town for Patronales, be sure to stop by the artisan booth, where artisans from Bayahibe as well as from Padre Nuestro's Artecuseco in Benerito display their wares. Find the group on Facebook under the name "La Peresquía de Bayahibe" *833-0017/829-520-9154; larosadelbayahibe@gmail.com*

◪ The Cultural Route "La Punta Bayahibe"

One of Bayahibe's hidden treasures is the Ruta Cultural La Punta, a tour highlighting the historical, cultural, and environmental heritage of the town. The tour begins at

La Iglesia Santa María de Nazaret on the small peninsula called La Punta that bisects the bay of Bayahibe. On La Punta is the only known forest of the endangered and indigenous *Pereskya quisqueyana* plant, known to the locals as "La Rosa de Bayahibe." The tour winds around the schoolyard on the seashore, offering spectacular views of both the town and the bay where Bayahibe's traditional sailboats are docked. Midday tours might catch fishermen unloading their haul after a long morning at sea. Of particular interest is the archaeological site that was discovered in 2004 while constructing the school. The remains of a former inhabitant along with other items have been dated at more than four centuries old. The tour then takes a pause at a series of *manantiales*, or small aquifers, each with a unique past. The closest aquifer to La Punta is alive with green turtles that greet onlookers as they approach the water. Community members conduct all tours in Spanish, and proceeds benefit the upkeep of the route and community organizations. *For tours, contact Eliani "Leni" Herrera 829-520-9154; rutalapunta@hotmail.com; or Yulissa Reyes cafejulissa_8@hotmail.com (Spanish only)*

◪ Wild Ranch

This environmentally and socially sustainable adventure outfitter offers four-wheel excursions, zip-lining, and kayaking in the Río Chavon. The company directly supports residents of a local community called Santa Cruz del Gato by donating livestock and houses, as well as creating a source of employment for residents. *Located just outside of Bayahibe and 25 minutes from la Romana; 330-4339; wild_ranch_rd@yahoo.com; www.wildranchcanopy.com; www.wild-ranch-canopy.blogspot.com*

Scuba Diving

Bayahibe is a popular launching point for scuba divers. Shore dives launch from the public beach (past the baseball field in the eastern part of town), and it's also possible to go out on a dive excursion in a catamaran or motorboat.

> **Casa Daniel** Offering excursions to Isla Saona, Catalina, Catalinita, the St. George Wreck, as well as other points of interest around the Parque Nacional del Este, this German-owned dive shop accepts all internationally recognized certifications. If planning on staying awhile in Bayahibe, consider one of the PADI certification courses. *833-0050; Casa-daniel@gmx.net; www.casa-daniel.com; free hotel shuttle*

> **Scuba Fun** American-owned, this dive shop offers excursions to all major dive sites in the National Park of the East. It is also authorized to offer all levels of PADI certification courses. As the name suggests, enjoy yourself. *28 C/ Principal; 833-0003; 763-3023; info@scubafun.info; www.scubafun.info*

> **Gus Dive Center** (p108) in Santo Domingo offers a high-quality and moderately priced diving package for groups to Isla Catalina. The package includes transportation to and from Santo Domingo, a catamaran ride from Bayahibe to Isla Catalina, dive gear rentals, lunch, and drinks. *Prices start at RD$1,500*

NIGHTLIFE

Super Colmadón Bayahibe brings together locals and tourists who share a love for cold Presidentes and loud reggaeton. There is nothing particularly unique about this colmadón, but it manages to attract a large crowd from the late afternoon until about 10pm, at which point the party shifts to the **Discoteca Coco Rico** near La Defensa Supermarket.

Parque Nacional del Este

The beautiful and geographically diverse Parque Nacional del Este is comprised of a stretch of mainland east of Bayahibe plus three islands: Isla Saona, Isla Catalina and Isla Catalinita. Covering both land and sea, the Park has an immense array of flora and fauna, as well as a number of important archaeological sites. Stony coral reefs composed of over 75 species like Elkhorn and brain coral foster a thriving environment for the 120 species of tropical fish that inhabit the reefs. Brilliantly colored parrotfish live among stingrays, hawksbill turtles, and the occasional nurse shark. Marine mammals such as manatees, dolphins, and humpback whales make seasonal appearances in the warm Caribbean waters. Of the 14 terrestrial mammals found throughout the park, two are endemic and nearly extinct – the hutia and the solenodon. Pelicans swoop down to meet them in search of a fresh catch for lunch. Parrots and the red-tailed hawk (*Buteo jamaicensis*) are among the few endemic birds found in the area, though the Park is home to approximately 144 different species.

Note: there is no public transportation to the islands. Tourists usually arrive via private tour operators. It is possible, though not easy, to negotiate a *bola* (ride) in a local's boat if you get to the boat launch early, at around 7am

DO

Padre Nuestro Trail

A community-led trail on the edge of the National Park, this route is easily accessible by public transport or car from Bayahibe and Dominicus. Guides take visitors through what was formerly their community but is now a densely vegetated area with cactus, the *guáyica* plant, and squat trees like the Vera. The flora and terrain made of sea rock indicate the land's submerged past. The area's rather tumultuous recent history, on top of the unique landscape, makes for a truly interesting experience.

In 2001, when the area was still inhabited, the Hotel Association of Bayahibe began the process of relocating resident families, because they were supposedly damaging the aquifers used by the hotels in Bayahibe. Contracts were drawn and by 2003, nearly the entire community of Padre Nuestro was relocated to Villa Padre Nuestro in Benerito, a community about 10 minutes east of Bayahibe. The Dominican government built houses for displaced community members, and installed electricity, a water treatment plant, an aqueduct, and roads. However, neither of the surrounding municipal governments has taken responsibility for the community. A few families still remain in the old Padre Nuestro, either because they are paid to manage the water plant and aqueduct for the hotels, or have refused to leave the annexed land.

Despite the questionable auspices under which the project began, the trail now provides a source of income for community members who once lived there. On the hour-long hike, guides discuss endemic medicinal vegetation such as *guáyica*, a plant whose roots were used by the Taínos to make flour. This starchy root continues to be used by older generations to make a specialty *arepa* (salty dense cake) and *ojalda* (sweet *arepa*), especially during Easter week. The tour will also stop by a *horno de carbón* (coal oven) where the guide explains how the community used wood from the Vera tree to make coal. The tour ends at two famous subterranean *manantiales*

The East

(aquifers), accessible through caves.

One of these underground aquifers, called Manantial de Chicho, is particularly impressive. Bats chirp from their nestled ceiling locations as visitors take a refreshing dip in the pool below. The local dive shops in Bayahibe provide opportunities to cave dive here as well. (See Dive Shops in Bayahibe, p154). *RD$200; located off the Romana-Higüey highway, just after the Dominicus-Bayahibe fork. Look for the Padre Nuestro sign just past the fork on the right if heading in the direction of Higüey. Contact guides Lilia or Lucia 829-520-9155 or 829-718-0399; www.rutpadrenuestro.com; open every day 7am-5pm*

Isla Saona

Measuring 22 kilometers (14 mi) in length and about 5 kilometers (3 mi) in width, Isla Saona is the largest of the National Park's three islands and the largest island off the coasts of the Dominican Republic. Besides the few remaining families in Padre Nuestro, Isla Saona is the only inhabited portion of the park. The islanders are descended from a dozen families that Trujillo relocated there in 1944 from the mainland. The entire population lives in the small fishing community of Mano Juan.

Taínos originally inhabited Isla Saona; their pictographs can be seen in the Cave of Cotubanamá. After the Spaniards destroyed the local Taíno population, the island was only intermittently inhabited during the 16th and 17th centuries, functioning both as a lookout point for enemy ships as well as a safe haven for pirates. In 1855, General Pedro Santana began to exploit the island's rich deposit of mahogany, only to lose government permission the following year. Currently, Isla Saona only hosts day tourists that come with the various operators to enjoy the island's pristine beaches. One favorite beach is Playa Palmilla, dotted with bright wooden houses along the blindingly white sand. Sinkholes on the island have led to the creation of three saltwater lagoons, including the picturesque Los Flamencos. Surrounding the island are a number of coral reefs at multiple depths, providing a veritable playground for divers of all skill levels.

Future Plans for Isla Saona

Some exciting projects are underway under the guidance of the Ministry of Environment, like bike routes that traverse the small island. The people of Isla Saona in Mano Juan are mitigating the environmental threats that come with the tourism, having created a turtle conservation center, which was still under construction at the time of research. The center will allow for turtle-gazers to observe incubating eggs, and perhaps even sneak a peek at the adorable little baby turtles during hatching season.

Isla Catalina

Located a few miles off the coast of La Romana, the tropical island nirvana is accessible through tour operators in either La Romana or Bayahibe. After exploring the beautiful white-sand beaches and thick palm forest that remain intact today, Columbus named the island in honor of Catalina de Aragon, daughter of the Spanish Queen Isabela. At less than 25.9 square kilometers (10 square miles) of sand dune and mangrove, the island is without any man-made structures. Isla Catalina is best known for its extraordinary dive sites, as it is surrounded by a stunning coral reef bursting with color and life.

Isla Catalinita

Covered with billowy grasses and swaying palms, Isla Catalinita is located just north of Isla Saona in the Catuano Canal. The former Taíno inhabitants left behind a tremendous collection of conch shells, which still remain after over 1,000 years. Make for a stroll amidst the beach grape trees while watching out for tropical birds, and follow it up by a dip in the shallow waves. It is the rare and lucky tourist who is able to arrive at this tiny deserted isle, so try to make it part of any package when visiting the Parque Nacional del Este.

Hiking from Bayahibe to Dominicus

Aside from Parque Nacional del Este and Padre Nuestro Trail, there is another beautiful, short hike in the area, which connects Bayahibe to Dominicus in about 45 minutes. The trail begins on C/ Juan Brito, just after the baseball field in Bayahibe. Follow the road to reach a woodsy trail that hugs the shoreline. The trail is mostly sand, but turns into asphalt near the Dominicus end. Once in Dominicus, the road turns into Av. Eladia, the heart of Dominicus, and ends at the lovely La Laguna Beach.

More Local Tours

Fun yet professional, **Carlos Jambrina** is an eco-tourism guide for commercial outfitters like Seavis. As a certified PADI instructor, he also designs independent scuba diving and hiking excursions in

Also see Tour Operators based out of Dominicus on page 151.

El Parque Nacional del Este. Fluent in English, Spanish, and French, Carlos can also organize fishing, kiteboarding, and surfing trips to various locations throughout the country. *829-884-9142; carlosjambrina@hotmail.com*

San Rafael de Yuma

Known simply as Yuma to the locals, this area caught the interest of Spanish explorer Ponce de León in 1503 because of its proximity to the navigable Río Yuma. León played a key role in subjugation of the local Taínos, for which he was rewarded with the title of Governor in this region of the colony.

Today's Yuma is a minor town with no attractions beyond the Casa Museo de Ponce de León. The basic essentials are here, but there are no hotels worth mentioning; the closest overnight options are located in nearby Boca de Yuma.

TRANSPORT

Guaguas for all of the following locations leave near the Parque Central every 20-30 minutes:

To Higüey: RD$50; 5:30am-8pm; 1hr

From Higüey: RD$50; 5:30am-8pm; 1hr; leaves from Polideportivo in Higüey

To Boca de Yuma: RD$40; 6am-6pm; 15min; Mini-buses coming from Higüey pass along the main road through town along the Parque Central and then continue on to Boca de Yuma.

To La Romana: RD$80; 5:30am-7pm; 1hr; Parque Central

From La Romana: RD$80; 5:30am-7pm; 1hr; C/ Juan de Utrera between C/ Santa Rosa and C/ Teofilo Ferry, near the *Mercado*

INFO

Medical Attention

There is a small **pharmacy** on Av. Libertad near La Avenida Sports Bar.

Communication

Jenny Cyber (551-0259) is located in front of the Parque Central near La Iglesia Parroquía San Rafael y Ntra. Sra. del Carmen, at the corner of Av. Libertad and C/ Jorge Mota). To make calls, visit **Centro de Llamadas Claro** on the corner of C/ El Carmen and C/ Teodulo Guerrero in front of Parque Central.

Banks

The only bank in town is **Coopcentral Banco** located just off the Parque Central on the corner of C/ San Rafael and C/ Escolático Rondón.

Grocery Stores

Colmados are the name of the game here but **Supermercado Pitufa** on C/ San Rafael and C/ Escolático Rondón offers a wider selection.

Gas

There is a gas station located on the highway to La Romana (4) near C/ Duarte.

EAT

Eating options are slim in Yuma, but **D' Niki Cafeteria** next to the *parada* for La Romana offers the standard *plato del día*, while a *colmado* just a block west off the Parque Central serves up some satisfying BBQ chicken in the afternoon hours.

DO

Casa Museo de Ponce de León

Renovated and then re-opened to the public on March 26, 2010, the Casa Museo was the home of the intrepid Ponce de León. He built it in 1503, after arriving by way of the Yuma River. With his wife and three daughters, León lived in the home for four years before he continued on to Puerto Rico, where he became governor in 1509. Convinced that he was closing in on the fountain of youth, León sailed to Florida in the spring of 1513 when the flowers were in bloom, inspiring the state's name from the Spanish word for flower – *flor*.

It was not until 1972 that the Dominican government under President Balaguer restored the León home. At that point, the roof and second floor had rotted and caved in. After touch-ups, the museum now houses artifacts and furniture used by León, such as his sword, armor, and ornately carved desk. Notice the slotted convex windows designed to let in sufficient light, but also to protect against Taíno attacks. For this same reason, the walls are also extremely thick, at 1.35 meters (4.4 feet) on the first floor and 0.70 meters (2.3 feet) on the second. *Entrance RD$50; to arrive, when entering the town of Yuma, veer left at the fork and turn left on Carretera Los Jobitos just before the cemetery, where there is a sign for Casa Museo de Ponce de León. Follow the road about a 3 kilometers (1.9 miles) down and the museum will be on the right; Mon–Sat 7am–5pm*

Boca de Yuma

The sleepy fishing village of Boca de Yuma has yet to attract the wave of tourism found in other coastal towns of the East, which may make it more attractive to the independent traveler. This does not mean that Boca de Yuma has anything less to offer in terms of beauty and charm, spectacularly set on tremendous cliffs overlooking the sea. Though the nearest beach is not easily accessible, local fishermen are happy to take passengers there by boat, as well as to nearby caves and up the Río Yuma. Within the town itself, there are a handful of delicious fish-fry shacks, but little more, so be prepared to wind down to a slower pace of life.

TRANSPORT

The *guagua* route that services Boca de Yuma leaves Higüey from the Polideportivo. It passes through San Rafael de Yuma at the Parque Central every 30 minutes, continuing on to Boca de Yuma, and then again in reverse (RD$40).

INFO

Communication

There is no call center in town but there is **Chando Internet Café** located in Barrio La Piedra on C/ Proyecto in front of Colmado Milian.

EAT

Along the coastline there are a number of huts, such as **Doña Carmen** or **Restaurant Don Biembe,** serving up fried or grilled seafood caught fresh that day. See "Sleep" for information on the restaurant at **Hotel El Viejo Pirata.**

> **Bahia Azul** Located atop a precipice above the Yuma River, Bahia Azul offers a casual dining experience surrounded by the beauty of the outdoors. Plentiful plates of fried whole fish or grilled octopus marinated in garlic, pepper, and cilantro pair splendidly with a savory *moro* or crispy *tostones. RD$160-475; Follow sign for Bahia Azul on the left side of the main road leading to Boca de Yuma just before entering the town; 846-4409; Iankel, the owner: 877-3529*

SLEEP

> **Hotel El Viejo Pirata** Essentially the only sleeping option in town, this newly remodeled hotel with an ocean view has clean, bright rooms, as well as an Italian-Dominican restaurant. Try the catch of the day prepared *a la muyaya* (breaded and then simmered in butter and lemon) or one of their more traditional Italian offerings. *RD$1200; When the main road through town ends at the coast, turn right at the hotel's sign, after which the hotel will be on the right; 780-3236/804-3151/780-3464; nancy.felix@hotmail.com; hotelelviejopirata@hotmail.com; www.modna.com/vp/pirata_do.html; Amenities: A/C, hot water, breakfast included, laundry service*

DO

Malecón Tours

This unofficial tour provider is composed of fishermen from Boca de Yuma, who give motorboat tours (Spanish only) up the Río Yuma. The tours include stops at the Pirate Cofresi Cave, Playa Blanca (or Borinquen), and at natural aquifers. The entrepreneurial fishermen also provide full or half-day fishing trips (and even a money back guarantee if customers come back empty-handed). Because the group is not legally organized, price negotiations may be necessary, but the advantage is that they know the waters better than anyone else. *Excursions start at RD$1500; contact Longo for details: 829-268-0764, or ask around for him at the fish-fry shacks*

Higüey

With a fast-growing population of 150,000, Higüey is a bustling town that plays host to flocks of religious pilgrims once a year. The city is otherwise ignored, seen only through the bus windows by tourists passing through on their way to the resorts and beaches on the far coast. Formerly a rather unpleasant city of concrete jumble, the municipal government of Higüey commenced an ambitious beautification campaign, resulting in many more green spaces and trees across the city center. Each January 21, the city bursts at the seams with religious pilgrims visiting the Basílica de Nuestra Señora de la Altagracia (see below) for the feast celebration of the Virgin of Altagracia, the patron saint of the Dominican Republic. During the celebrations, transport and lodging are nearly impossible, and so it's best to avoid the city until the masses disperse.

An increasing number of residents here are employed by the Punta Cana and Bavaro resorts. Higüey is the closest town to the resort area that is able to provide affordable housing and plenty of amenities, while being near enough for a palatable commute.

TRANSPORT

The following *guaguas* leave every 15-30 min:

From Santo Domingo: RD$200; 6am-6pm; 3hrs; *Guaguas* leave Parque Enriquillo from the SICHOPROLA bus comapnay's *parada* at 92 C/ Ravelo; 686-0637

To Santo Domingo: RD$200; 6am-6pm; 3hrs; *parada* located near the corner of C/ La Altagracia and C/ Hermanas Trejo across from the Basílica.

To El Seibo: RD$90; 1hr; *parada* located on C/ La Altagracia across from the Basílica.

To Bavaro/Punta Cana: RD$100; **Bavaro** 5am-10:30pm; **Punta Cana** 5am-8pm; 1hr; *Guaguas* leave from the same SITRABAPU bus company stop on C/ Juan Julio Fao (Higüey-Punta Cana Highway) near the Shell Gas Station before the bridge.

To La Romana: *caliente* RD$90; *expreso* RD$100; 5:30am-10pm; 1.5hrs; SITRAHIR *parada* located across from Basílica on C/ Hermanas Trejo; 554-1177

To San Rafael de Yuma/Boca de Yuma: RD$50; 6am-6pm; 1hr; leave from the Polideportivo in Higüey

INFO

Medical Attention

Super Farmacia Altagracia is located on C/ Augustín Guerrero in front of the Parque Central (554-2274). For 24-hour emergency attention, the public Hospital Nuestra Señora de la Altagracia (554-2661) is located on C/ José R. Payan and C/ Juan XXIII.

The East

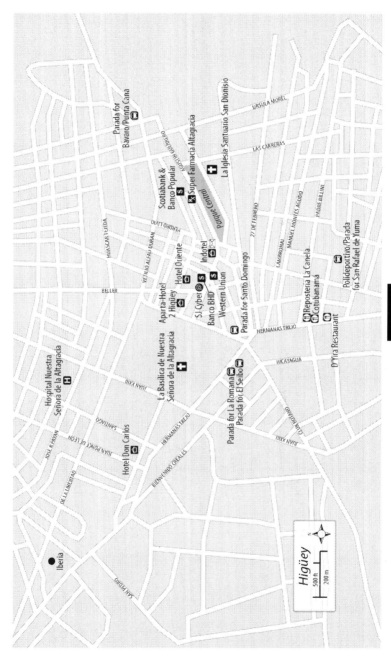

Parada for Bavaro/Punta Cana

Scottiabank & Banco Popular

Super Farmacia Altagracia

La Iglesia Santuario San Dionisio

URSULA MOREL

LAS CARRERAS

Parque Central

27 DE FEBRERO

MANUEL MONTES AGUDO

PADRE BELLINI

LAMBRONAL

AGUSTIN GUERRERO

FLORIDO LIVIO

Hotel Oriente

Indotel

Aparta-Hotel 2 Higüey

SJ Cyber

Banco BHD

Western Union

Parada for Santo Domingo

Repostería La Canela

Cotubanamá

Polideportivo/Parada for San Rafael de Yuma

HUASCAR TUEDA

VETILIO ALFAU DURAN

BELLER

HERMANAS TREJO

D'Yria Restaurant

Hospital Nuestra Señora de la Altagracia

La Basílica de Nuestra Señora de la Altagracia

JUAN XXIII

HICAYAGUA

Parada for La Romana

Parada for El Seibo

MARIA AUXI..?

SANTIAGO

JUAN PONCE DE LEON

Hotel Don Carlos

HERMANAS TREJO

BIENVENIDO GREALES

JUAN XXIII

GURABO VIEJO

DE LA LIBERTAD

Iberia

SAN PEDRO

Higüey

500 ft

200 m

N

Banks
Banco BHD is located on Augustín Guerrero near C/ Colón. Across from the Parque Central are branches of **Scotiabank** and **Banco Popular** located on C/ Augustín Guerrero. All banks are open Mon-Fri 8:30am-4:30pm and Sat 9am-1pm. There is also a **Western Union** (Mon-Sat 8am-6pm) on the corner of C/ Augustín Guerrero and C/ Antonio Váldez (hijo).

Communication
SJ Cyber internet café is located on Augustín Guerrero next to Banco BHD or there is always the government sponsored, but less reliable (and free!), **Indotel,** on C/ Duvergé and C/ Augustín Guerrero next to the **Post Office.**

Grocery Stores
Iberia (554-4444) food superstore has produce, clothing, a pharmacy, a food court, and ATMs. *Located on main road when entering Higüey from the west.*

EAT

Cotubanamá Specializing in steak and seafood and boasting an impressive wine selection, this restaurant also doubles as a karaoke bar on the weekends. Splashed with oranges and yellows and decorated with flowers and fabric tablecloths, this air-conditioned establishment has an upscale look, but is well within the reach of budget travelers. *RD$350-RD$450; 87 Av. Hermanas Trejo, Plaza Mario 2nd floor; 554-3506/223-2661; pcotubanama@hotmail.com; 11am-12am, closes 2am on weekends; karaoke Fri-Sun*

D'Yira Restaurant *Mofongo*, the mashed and fried plantain delicacy, is the name of the game here. Try the *mofongo* with shrimp or ask for *el pozito de la virgen*, which is mofongo with sauce on the inside and the meat on the outside, an example of Dominicans' not especially subtle sexual humor. *61 Av. Hermanas Trejo; 554-1962; RD$300-790*

Repostería La Canela Be naughty after your soul-purifying pilgrimage to the Basílica. This air-conditioned bakery carries a variety of freshly baked pastries and just-squeezed juices, as well as cakes slathered in creamy *dulce de leche* and meringue. *RD$30-100; Av. Hermanas Trejo below Cotubanamá Restaurant; 746-0241*

SLEEP

Hotel Don Carlos Perhaps the best bet in town, Hotel Don Carlos gets crowded in high season but otherwise provides a suitable place to sleep. It is just slightly run down enough to give it some character while still being a quality place to spend the night. *US$ 35-40; C/ Juan Ponce De León and C/ Sánchez; 554-2713*

Hotel Oriente This hotel is merely a place to rest. It has cramped rooms and private bathrooms, but is located away from the roar of the street and rooms have balconies to enjoy the breeze. *RD$500-RD$700; C/ Esquibel between C/ Colón and Beller; 554-0040*

Aparta-Hotel 2 Higüey Located between the Basílica and the Parque Central, this hotel is well-situated for sightseeing, and covers all the essentials of A/C and TV. The restaurant connected to the hotel only sold drinks at the time of research. *RD$595; 228-7312; C/ Cece Catrina*

DO

La Basílica de Nuestra Señora de la Altagracia
The Basílica is one of the most important houses of worship for Catholics in the country and across Latin America, and likely the most visited site for religious

pilgrims on the island. The Basílica was dedicated in 1972 after almost two decades of construction. Built in the contemporary-utilitarian Dominican style of architecture (that is, entirely of cement), its parabolic arches representing a modern, unique twist on the typically gaudy Catholic cathedrals. The emblematic 75-meter high arch reigns over the others, standing proud in its vaunted position in front of the church. Exterior lighting installed in 2002 creates lively color and shadow at dusk, dramatically brightening the concrete cathedral.

The altar echoes nature, with leaf-like wooden carvings, backlit by multicolored panes of stained glass that mimic magnified plant cells. These organically inspired elements are beautifully contrasted with the repeating cement arches that lead up to the altar. At the top is a glass-encased image of the holy Virgen de la Altagracia. The Basílica turns into an enthusiastic mess of religious fervor during Semana Santa and around the celebration of La Virgen de Altagracia on January 21. As it is a place of worship, beach attire is not appropriate inside. *Entrance located on C/ Arzobispo Nouel between C/ La Altagracia and Av. De la Libertad; 554-4541; 5am-7pm*

La Iglesia Santuario San Dionisio

Erected in 1512, this chapel was one of the first in the Americas and was the original destination for pilgrims making the journey to Higüey. The simple church and its single nave have withstood the tests of time, a silent witness to the other colonial buildings that have fallen victim to earthquake, hurricane, or invading army.

The simple whitewashed outer walls of this small church belie the ornate decoration within. Many of the original murals and décor have faded, but a few original elements remain. Visitors can especially appreciate the Baroque altar with golden cherubs and roses adorning the cupola, alongside colorful tiles covering the walls and floors of the side chapels. *Parque Central; C/ Augustín Guerrero*

El Pozo de la Virgen

Outside of the church of San Dionisio sits the miraculous El Pozo de la Virgen, or Well of the Virgin Mary. The legend of the well pronounces that many years ago, a fire threatened the holy building, its flames licking the edifice walls. From the well, a surge of water spontaneously emerged, quelling the flames that threatened the chapel. The well is located just behind the church, but has yet to sprout water again.

NIGHTLIFE

Like all Dominican pueblos, nightlife revolves around the *colmadones*, where the Presidente is *bien fría* and fun is measured in decibels. Find the *colmadones* around the Parque Central or the Basílica. Also check out weekend karaoke at Cotubanamá (see Eat above).

Punta Cana

In the late 1960s, the Dominican Republic was hardly a vacation destination. Within that decade, Trujillo was assassinated, American troops occupied the island, and the political and economic future of the island was insecure, even for the most optimistic. Despite the turmoil, a group of American investors, including attorney Theodore W. Kheel, decided to buy 48 square kilometers (19 square miles) of land on the eastern tip of the island in 1969. When the investors arrived to investigate their purchase with the help of a young Dominican pilot named Frank Rainieri, they found infertile land stunted by limestone outcroppings and sand patches. Besides a few small farms, the area was an undeveloped jungle.

Mr. Kheel, rather disappointed with his purchase, asked his 23-year old Dominican pilot Frank Rainieri, what he would do with the land, to which he replied, "tourism." Today, this may seem like a rather obvious answer, but taking into account the political environment of the DR at the time, this answer seemed outlandish at best. Despite the inherent difficulties, the American investors began to develop their lot in 1971. Their first try was the construction of the Punta Cana Club, which could accommodate up to 40 guests and included employee living structures, a power plant, and a basic runway. The Club struggled along until 1978 when the Club Mediterrané of Paris bought up a piece of beachfront property from the Punta Cana Group, and began construction of a 350-person hotel – known today as Club Med.

As the nearest airport was located in Santo Domingo more than five hours away via a dusty, unpaved highway, transportation to Punta Cana for international visitors became a concern. Initially, the Punta Cana Group approached the Dominican government in an effort to build an international airport. After eight years struggling through negotiations, the Punta Cana Group ended up financing the entire project with the permission of the state. Lacking resources for a project of this magnitude, Kheel approached an architecture student at Pratt University named Oscar Imbert to design the airport, with a few stipulations. Kheel required that the architect use local materials, and that he could not pay him for his design. Recognizing an opportunity to boost his resume, Imbert accepted, and the first limestone was broken in 1982. The airport officially opened in 1984 with arrival of a propeller plane from Puerto Rico. Today the airport receives more flights than any other airport on the island.

The Punta Cana Group forever changed the face of tourism in this part of the

---

La Virgen de la Altagracia

No one is able to give an account of the actual origin of this image of the Virgin, as its provenance is shrouded in mystery. As one popular legend goes, the daughter of a rich colonial merchant in Higüey asked for a picture of the Virgen de la Altagracia from her father, though he had never heard of this particular saint. On a trip to Santo Domingo, the merchant searched everywhere, but was unable to find his daughter's present. On his return journey, he stopped at a friend's house for the night. As the merchant recounted his story of empty-handedness, an old, bearded man appeared at the home. The old man unrolled a canvas and produced nothing less than this very picture. By morning, he had mysteriously gone, leaving behind no trace but the image.

The miracles continued after the merchant returned home. While his happy daughter placed the image on their mantle, the next day, they found it outside under a tree – a process that repeated itself several times. They eventually put the image in a church for safekeeping, and it is this image that graces the altar of the Cathedral today.

The saint's day of January 21 was also the date of an important early battle success against foreign armies. On January 21, 1691, Spanish settlers defeated a small French force outside of Higüey, preventing the city from invasion. This providential coincidence deepened the worship of the Virgen de la Altagracia.

Visit the Basilica and speak with the worshippers or pilgrims to hear about other miraculous stories of the origin and history of the Virgen de la Altagracia. After doing so, it will be easy to understand why she is the patron saint and spiritual mother of the Dominican Republic.

island. Hotel corporations from around the world have bought up immense tracts of beachfront, producing an explosion of resorts spanning from Macao in the northeast all the way to Cap Cana in the south. This represents at least 65 kilometers of an almost non-stop line of high-rise, luxury development.

The transformation has gone inland, too. Before the turnoff for Bavaro and Punta Cana, the highway passes through the growing sprawl of a place called Verón. This mess of a town is a product of the tourism boom on the East coast and lacks any sense of planning. Recognizing the instability that this settlement presented, the Punta Cana Group has financed a number of projects in Verón, including a public school, clinic, career training center, and police department. The Dominican government's lack of involvement also caused the Group to finance basic infrastructure, such as electricity, water, sidewalks, and roads.

TRANSPORT

Air

Flights to the far eastern coast arrive at the private Punta Cana International Airport (PUJ). Designed with the tropics in mind, the open-air terminals receive almost 4 million passengers a year, making it the busiest airport in the country; further growth is expected as tourism continues to increase. The airport serves both domestic and international airlines. *Find the airport on Carretera Aeropuerto, at the southern end of the Boulevard Turístico del Este, and south of most resorts. www.punta-cana-airport.com*

Int'l Airlines serving PUJ
Air Canada
AirTran
American Airlines
British Airways
Continental
Delta
JetBlue
KLM
Spirit
United
USAir

Ground Transport

From the airport, *guagua* service is irregular, and is used almost exclusively by support staff, so transport might not reach tourist-specific destinations. Some hotels offer transportation, so check with them first. Taxis leaving the airport charge between US$20 and US$50, depending on the distance to the hotel. Renting a car is another option, though having a vehicle at most all-inclusive resorts is usually not necessary. **Avis** (688-1354; avis.com), **Budget**, (480-8153; budget.com), and **National** (595-0434; nationalcar.com) have a desk at the airport. Be sure to book before arrival.

Within Punta Cana

Taxi prices are extremely inflated and often quoted in U.S. dollars ranging from US$20-40 (in Santo Domingo the same distance is in the US$4-5 range). *Motoconcho* prices should be between RD$40 and RD$50 for short rides, but you will have to negotiate down from RD$100. Longer rides such as from Bavaro to the Cruce de Verón – the transportation hub – start as high as RD$500, in which case it's best to take a *guagua*.

The following *guaguas* leave every 15 to 30 minutes:

To Higüey: RD$100 *caliente*; RD$110 *expreso*; Bavaro 5am-10:30pm; Punta Cana 5am-8pm; 1hr; SITRABAPU bus company *guaguas* leave from the *parada* near the Cruce de Verón; 552-1678/682-9670

From Higüey: RD$100 *caliente*; RD$110 *expreso*; Bavaro 5am-10:30pm; Punta Cana 5am-8pm; 1hr; *Guaguas* leave from the same SITRABAPU *parada* on C/ Juan Julio Fao (highway for Punta Cana) near the Shell Gas Station before the bridge.

To Santo Domingo: RD$200; 7am-4pm; 4hrs; SITRABAPU *guaguas* leave from the *parada* on the main road through Verón (Highway 106) near the Shell Station

From Santo Domingo: RD$200; 7am-4pm; 4hrs; SITRABAPU *guaguas* leave Parque Enriquillo for Higüey at which point passengers must board a different *guagua* for Bavaro or Punta Cana.

Local Public Transport

SITRABAPU *guaguas* coming from Higüey take passengers from the Cruce de Verón to Bavaro or Punta Cana for RD$40-50 every 30 minutes. To catch the *guaguas* that go to **Punta Cana**, wait in front of the Shell Gas Station along Highway 104 at the Cruce de Verón. To go to Bavaro and Cortesito, wait along Avenida Barceló near the Cruce de Verón. After 7pm, *motoconchos* and taxis are the only options.

INFO

Because Punta Cana is a set of closely guarded compounds, all practicalities are available in Verón, many of which are concentrated around the Cruce de Verón (also known as the turn-off for Punta Cana or Bavaro).

Medical Attention

Hospiten, a modern hospital built to support the influx of tourists, is located on the Higüey-Verón Highway before the Cruce de Verón.

Communication

Ciber Café y Llamadas is an internet and call center at the Cruce de Verón.

Banks

Branches of **Banco Popular** and **BanReservas** are located at the Cruce de Verón on the road to Bavaro.

Gas

At the Cruce de Verón, there is a **Shell Gas Station** (and **Burger King**).

Grocery Stores

Supermercado Mansanillo is located east of the Cruce de Verón toward Punta Cana.

SLEEP

Punta Cana Hotel One of the few non-inclusive hotels in the area, the upscale Punta Cana Hotel is the only one besides Club Med that can officially claim to be located in Punta Cana (many resorts have adopted the name despite being located in Bavaro proper). The hotel is situated within the compound owned by the Punta Cana Group. Guests have access to a number of amenities including tennis courts, swimming pools, three freshwater swimming holes, combed white-sand beaches, a dive shop, and a number of restaurants ranging in price and selection. In order to enter the compound, guests must make reservations beforehand, which can be arranged through the hotel's website. Besides the hotel, there are numerous vacation homes on the property, including that of Julio Iglesias, who is a partner in the Punta Cana Group. House styles range tremendously, from the multi-million dollar mansion of Señor Iglesias, which has its own private beach, to eco-friendly clusters of cottages. There is a shuttle service that provides transport around the immense property, but a private vehicle is recommended because taxis outside the property are pricey. *US$96-360; 809-959-2262, or toll free from the U.S. and Canada at 888-442-2262; info@puntacana.com; www.puntacana.com*

DO

The possibilities offered at these resorts are endless, from lounge chair exercises to daylong, high-adrenaline excursions. Underwater entertainment, including scuba diving and snorkeling, are obviously very popular, but the sand dunes also offer their own excitement through horseback riding trips and sojourns in dune buggies and jeep safaris. Depending on the season, whale-watching and other marine life trips are also attractive options. Check at your respective hotel for the incredible variety of sports, trips, and on-site entertainment, and reserve early, as the activities get booked up quickly.

Punta Cana Village
This is an outdoor shopping center with a variety of chain and nominally ethnic restaurants. There are also a number of clothing boutiques and a salon in the complex. The Village is owned by the Punta Cana Group and a shuttle service is available between it the Punta Cana Hotel & Club.

Fundación Ecológica Punta Cana
Though on the premises of the Punta Cana complex, this foundation sponsors numerous environmental conservation projects and studies. Grupo PUNTACANA founded the organization in 1999 to foment corporate responsibility among the hotels and other business of Punta Cana. In its decade of existence, it has worked to promote, protect, and respect social and environmental resources. Special programs include beekeeping, protecting Carey turtle hatchlings, and farming organic vegetables sold to the nearby resorts.

The foundation accepts short-term volunteers, especially those with a science or environmental background. The foundation also offers guided tours to ecological sites in the area. *959-9221; FEPC@puntacana.com; www.puntacana.org*

Bavaro & Cortesito

A two-lane road lined with all-inclusive resorts, Bavaro is the northern anchor of Punta Cana, and hosts not much more than these sun-drenched hotels, pools, and tawny sand. The heavily guarded compounds inhibit the development of any other sort of commerce, so few guests leave the resorts outside of planned excursions.

Despite the fact that all beaches by law are public, the resorts make beach access nearly impossible, posting guards and chasing away anyone without a neon resort bracelet. The only beaches with public access are **Playa Macao, Playa Cortecito,** and **Playa Cabeza del Toro**. Macao and Cabeza del Toro give a taste of why millions flock to the East's beaches each year, but Playa Cortesito is usually scattered with trash.

Despite the less desirable beach, **Cortesito** is one of the few areas of Bavaro that has not been scooped up by the all-inclusive model and has a few good restaurants and hotels.

TRANSPORT

See Transportation section in Punta Cana, p167.

To Cortesito and **Bavaro**: RD$40-60; 7am-7pm; 20min; in Verón wait along the road to Bavaro in front of the Police Station and across the street from BanReservas. SITRABAPU *guaguas* and (often-unmarked) larger buses heading to Bavaro can take you. The best strategy is to ask one of the locals waiting or just flag down every bus that passes until one stops.

INFO

In Cortesito, on C/ Pedro Mir next to Capitán Cook, there is a **Western Union** and a pharmacy, **Farmacia Soamar** (552-1526). **La Marqueta Supermarket** is located on Av. Barcelo in Bavaro.

EAT

Playa Cortesito

Capitán Cook Mr. Cook probably didn't eat here, but surely he'd enjoy the smell of grilled lobster that greets diners at the door. The casual beachfront atmosphere, friendly staff and impressive variety of fresh seafood and meat combine to make a truly enjoyable experience. Go with a group and enjoy the decadent *parillada de mariscos* (mixed grilled seafood). *RD$300-1500; C/ Pedro Mir; across from Cortesito Inn; 552-0646*

Noir Beach Lounge A sophisticated oasis located on Cortesito Beach, Noir's eclectic menu offers a number of creative and luscious options, such as the soft puff pastry topped with smoked salmon and caviar, or bacon-wrapped shrimp with sherry sauce. *RD$250-900; C/ Pedro Mir, El Cortecito; at the junction of Av. Francia and Av. Alemania take the road into Cortecito. At the T-junction turn right, go past Capitan Cooks on the left, follow the road to the end where there is a set of black iron gates. 552-1466; noirbl@hotmail.com*

SLEEP

In Bavaro, there is a plethora of all-inclusive resorts, many of which are owned by the Spanish corporation Barceló, such as the Barceló Bavaro Beach Resort. Other all-inclusive resorts include NH Arena Real, Carabela Beach, and Grand Paladium Punta Cana. They all offer very similar packages of unlimited food and bottomless drinks. To work off the inevitable gluttony that results from partaking in all-day buffets, there are a number of beach sports offered, from kayaking, snorkeling, and scuba diving to banana-boats and hiking. Don't miss the water aerobics, an activity that is often more fun to watch than in which to participate.

Playa Cortesito

Cortecito Inn One of the few non-inclusive options in town, this hotel is rather pricey considering that many of the all-inclusive resorts start at US$50. However, it is handy if you arrive to the area without reservations. *US$50-80; C/ Pedro Mir; 552-0646; Amenities: A/C, cable, hot water, pool, parking lot*

DO

As housing developments have sprung up around the area, a number of restaurants and shopping areas have moved in as well. One of the larger ones in Bavaro is the shopping center that houses a movie theater, international retail shops, and chain restaurants like Hard Rock Café. Dance away the hot tropical nights at the bar/club Mangú. The center is located on the right side of the main road, Avenida Barceló, upon entering Bavaro. *Palacio del Cine*

Conscience vs. Convenience

It is important to be aware of the consequences from the development of this stretch of mega-hotels. While much of the area was uninhabited jungle before development, a few small fishing villages dotted the coast. Massive construction displaced the residents, forcing them to move inland, and denying them access to the water. Resorts have attempted to keep the fishermen away, but they still return to the waters, leading to continuous struggle between the two groups.

Coastal development has also caused serious environmental damage. Many beaches surrounding the resorts have been dredged, removing the natural sediment and mangroves that acted as wave breakers to prevent erosion. The beaches are now reinforced with cement and then covered with combed sand to create tidy, unobstructed views. Due to the high volume of guests that occupy resorts each year, water pollution, trash disposal, and energy sources are threats to the area's already-strained infrastructure.

Of course, the resorts also offer direct and indirect employment to many thousands of Dominicans; most residents in the area are somehow involved in the tourism industry. Stable work and better compensation make resort work quite coveted. While the allure of the beach is strong, the positions far from home can break up families and drain small towns of young labor.

If you are interested in the all-inclusive experience, a simple internet search of Bavaro and Punta Cana will come up with dozens of options. It's best to book early, as prices are unpredictable, and are certainly cheaper than simply arriving without a reservation. Many also offer packages that include airfare and transportation.

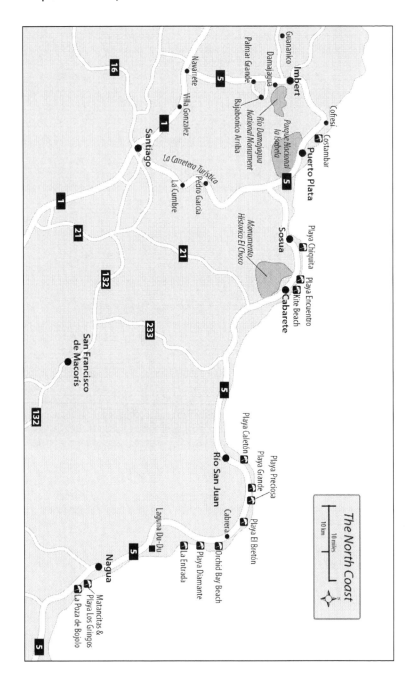

The North Coast

Much more than successive ribbons of beautiful sand, the Northeast Coast is the budget traveler's beach-going paradise. Each of the major towns in this popular destination has its own unique flavor: Puerto Plata's bustling movement and history; Sosúa's mature, European atmosphere; Cabarete's youthful and trendy vibe; and Río San Juan's quiet authenticity. Beyond them are some of the world's best beaches, where people come from all over the world to surf, kiteboard, and spend languid days under the tropical sun. While some of these beaches in urban areas may be more crowded than a dance floor during the night's last merengue song, many spots (especially farther east) will see no more than a few bathers each day. The Cordillera Septentrional is just a short drive south, full of hiking, camping, and other eco-friendly opportunities. In some places, like at Cabo Frances Viejo, these same hills end in rocky cliffs that collide spectacularly with the sea. From upscale resorts to tiny cottages, nightlife havens to private getaways, there is a place – and a beach – for everyone.

Puerto Plata

The humming center of North Coast commercial activity, Puerto Plata is the largest city in the region, a bustling jumble of a cityscape with 150,000 inhabitants with. Though it might take some polish and elbow grease to uncover the sheen of this "Silver Port," underneath the grunge is a city with 500 years of history and character. Puerto Plata has been through its ups and downs. Having been fortified, ambushed, abandoned, and repopulated, the town has seen a lot, and there is still a lot to see. Puerto Plata is still energetic, but has fallen since its 1980s heyday in the spotlight of Dominican tourism. Today, many people arrive in the city, only to leave it again in haste, overlooking Puerto Plata on the way to the resorts outside of town.

Puerto Plata is a showcase of a thriving city unsure how to handle its own success. At once catering to tourists, it must still provide for its people. Puerto Plata's central location on the coast means that it is accessible to the area's top destinations, and even Santiago is a quick bus ride away; it also offers fully stocked supermarkets and modern amenities. Though you will undoubtedly be on your way to the beaches nearby, take some time to wander around the vibrant old city streets, stroll the *malecón*, and see what the city has to offer.

Downtown Puerto Plata, bounded by centuries-old buildings, is centered on the Parque Central (or Independencia), which features a novel two-story Victorian gazebo built in 1919. In fact, a number of old Victorian "gingerbread" houses dot the old city (called Centro Histórico), pretty relics of the construction boom in the late 19th century. The old town's bustling, narrow lanes run to the coast, full of activity and an almost Continental feel to it, with its strong historical European influence. The newer neighborhoods spread farther south and up the hills bounding the city, growing in irregular patterns as migrants from rural areas move in seeking economic opportunities.

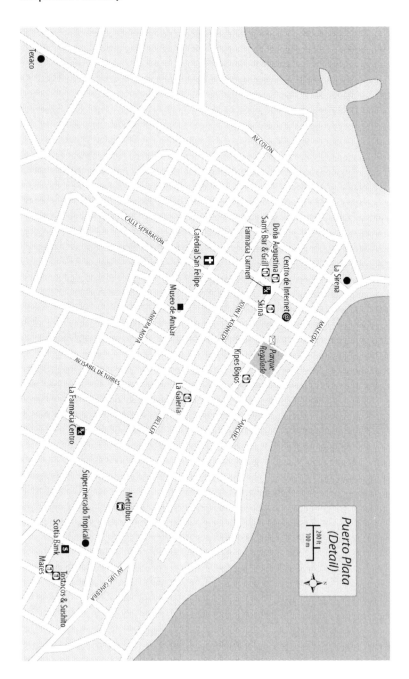

Texaco

AV COLON

CALLE SEPARACION

Catedral San Felipe

Farmacia Carmen

Sam's Bar & Grill

Doña Augustina

Centro de Internet

La Sirena

MALECON

Skina

Museo de Ámbar

JOHN F. KENNEDY

Parque Regulado

ANTERA MOTA

Kipes Bojos

AV ISABEL DE TORRES

La Galería

BELLER

La Farmacia Centro

SANCHEZ

Supermercado Tropical

Metrobus

Scotia Bank

Mares

AV LUIS GINEBRA

Tostacos & Sushito

Puerto Plata
(Detail)

200 ft
100 m

N

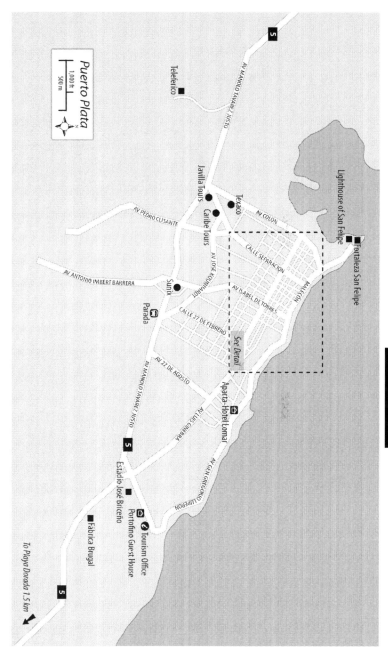

Puerto Plata

1,000 ft
500 m

N

Teleférico

Javilla Tours

Texaco

Caribe Tours

AV MANOLO TAVÁREZ JUSTO

AV COLON

AV PEDRO CLISANTE

CALLE SEPARACIÓN

Lighthouse of San Felipe

Fortaleza San Felipe

AV JOSÉ KÚNHARDT

AV 12 DE JULIO

AV ISABEL DE TORRES

AV ANTONIO IMBERT BARRERA

Sunix

Parada

CALLE 27 DE FEBRERO

See Detail

AV 27 DE AGOSTO

AV MANOLO TAVÁREZ JUSTO

AV LUIS GINEBRA

Aparta-Hotel Lomar

AV GRAL GREGORIO LUPERÓN

Estadio José Briceño

Tourism Office

Portofino Guest House

Fábrica Brugal

To Playa Dorada 1.5 km

The North Coast

HISTORY

It was not too far to the east of Puerto Plata that Columbus and his crew built La Isabela, the first settlement on Hispaniola (see History, p12). The origin of Puerto Plata's name (meaning Silver Port) is uncertain, though silver mining is certainly not one of them. It is said that when Columbus first saw the bay, he declared that it looked like shimmering silver coins under the sea; others claim that Columbus decided that the mist-shrouded mountain behind the bay had a silver-like appearance; and still others are certain that Columbus named the port after the silvery sparkling of the leaves from a distance of the local trees. Nevertheless, it was not Columbus, the intrepid confounder of etymologists, who built a settlement in the protected port. Rather, this task was left up to Nicolas de Ovando, a Spanish nobleman who arrived in 1502 with the specific intent of colonizing and populating the island. Ovando became a major player in urban and agricultural planning across the Spanish colony, and he was one of the first to import African slaves to work in houses or plantations. Puerto Plata quickly became the most important port on the north coast, dominating trade between Spain and the colony. In 1541, the Spanish built Fortaleza San Felipe for the defense of the city. However, the rise of Santo Domingo on the southern coast as the administrative and economic colonial center signified the decline of Puerto Plata. By the middle of the century, the port was being pestered by swashbuckling English pirates, much too far from the capital for the Santo Domingo colonial authorities to guard. In a policy repeated across northern sections of the island, the Spanish crown ditched the city altogether in 1605. Unable to make the expenditure of protecting the settlement, the weak authorities were powerless to prevent the entrepreneurial buccaneers from making serious inroads with the local colonists.

After remaining without much in the way of government or inhabitants for over a century, Puerto Plata and the surrounding regions were repopulated by the forced settlement of Canary Islanders, among others. This time, the crown, with more resources, moved to fortify its holdings in the area and repel incursions by foreign nations, especially the French. Through resettlement, Spain could better defend its colonial holdings. The fort was rebuilt, and the city began to grow again. The city did not fare well under Haitian rule of 1822-1844, and was almost entirely destroyed during the War of Restoration against Spain in 1863. After the war, however, Puerto Plata regained prominence as a major port for the new nation's international trade. Products from the fertile Cibao valley and across the region flowed from its harbor, including coffee, cacao, and tobacco, assisted by railway linkages to Santiago and La Vega (these no longer exist today). Immigration from Europe, especially Germany, recharged the export industry. Though the city experienced some growth, its prominence declined as investment and industrialization were refocused on Santo Domingo under Trujillo. However, with his death, Puerto Plata reemerged not as an agricultural port town, but as a center of tourism. By the 1990s, income from the tourism-related service sector eclipsed all other industries in Puerto Plata. Today, the city serves as a gateway to the north coast and its array of tropical beaches, nightlife hotspots, and undiscovered opportunities.

TRANSPORT

Caribe Tours (586-4544) is located on C/ Camino Real and C/ Eugenio Kunhardt.

To Santo Domingo (through **Santiago**): RD$300; 5:15am, hourly 6:20am to 6:20pm at: 20 past the hour; 3.5hrs.
To Sosúa: RD$50; hourly 6am to 7pm; 30min

The air-conditioned **Javilla Tours** *guaguas* leave from the entrance of town to Santiago, and can drop you off at transfer places such as Maimón, Imbert, Altamira, Navarrete, the entrance to Guananico, and or anywhere else – just tell the driver. Prices range from RD$20 (Maimón) to RD$110 (Santiago), depending on the distance. *Guaguas leave every 15 to 20 minutes from 5:10am to 7:50pm. 261-3340; C/ Camino Real and Av. Colón*

Metrobus Metrobus (586-6061/6062) is located at C/ Beller and 16 de Agosto. Because it stops less, Metro shaves off a few minutes on the trip to Santo Domingo as compared to Caribe Tours.

> **To Santiago and Santo Domingo**: RD$150/RD$300; 6am, 7am, 9am, 11am, 2pm, 3pm, 4pm, 6:30pm; 45min/3.5hrs

The only direct service to Samaná, **Transporte Papagayo** is an easily spotted maroon minibus. There is one departure at 6:45am, taking at least three hours. *Av. Manolo Tavares Justo in front of the municipal hospital (749-6415).*

Local Transport
Guaguas to Playa Dorado, Sosúa, and points east leave from Parque Central, from 6am to 6pm. They can also be hailed along the main highway through town, called Av. Manolo Tavarez Justo, or officially (but not colloquially), Highway 5.

Motoconchos are clearly designated by their brightly colored vests. Rides within town range from RD$25 to RD$40.

INFO

Medical Attention
La Farmacia Centro is located on C/ Antera Mota and Dr. Zafra, next to **El Centro Médico Dr. Bournigal**, which is a decent private clinic for emergencies. Also find **Farmacia Deleytte** on C/ Profesor Juan Bosch.

Communication
The **Post Office** is on C/ Margarita Mears, by C/ Padre Castellanos.

Banks
Scotiabank is on C/ 27 de Febrero by C/ Presidente Vázquez and **Banco León** is on C/ John F. Kennedy and C/ 30 de Marzo.

Police
The **Police Station** is located on Av. Luis Ginebra by the Polideportivo sports complex.

Gas
Sunix Gas Station is on Av. Manolo Tavarez Justo at Av. Isabel de Torres and **Texaco** is on C/ Treinta de Marzo by Caribe Tours.

Grocery Stores
La Sirena is located on Av. Malecón and **Supermercado Tropical** is on C/ 27 de Febrero and C/ Beller.

Tourist Info

The **Tourism Office** is on Av. Hermanas Mirabal at Av. Malecón, offering maps and other information in English and Spanish. *9am-6pm; 586-4393*

EAT

Sam's Bar & Grill This casual restaurant is a favorite expat hangout and watering hole with English-speaking staff and English-language TV on repeat. Sam's serves hearty American fare in welcoming, diner-style atmosphere. Take a second to look at the architectural styling of the building, constructed in 1896. A hotel is on the higher floors. *RD$100-400; C/ José del Carmen Ariza, by C/ Kennedy; 586-7267*

Kipes Bojos A local hot spot for an afternoon snack of quipes and empanadas, this small eatery is run out of the owner's bright, peach-colored gingerbread home. *RD$50-100; Mon-Sat 4-7pm; 51 C/ Margarita Mears*

Tostacos & Sushito The popular Puerto Plata restaurant Tostacos recently expanded both in size and in palate. It is now joined by Sushito, and serves up burritos, sashimi, mofongo, and burgers to those who just can't figure out what to eat or who want it all. The upgraded restaurant is brightly festooned, and gets originality points for the extensive menu. *RD$100-300; Mon-Sat 12pm-3pm and 7pm-11pm; 3 Av. Presidente Vásquez*

La Galería A solid *plato del día* joint housed in a charming yellow Victorian home facing Parque Luperón. Note that it is on C/ Juan Bosch, which is alternately called C/ Kennedy. *RD$100; lunch only; 79 C/ Prof Juan Bosch*

 Skina Natural and rustic, this unruly garden restaurant is frequented by Puerto Plata's intellectuals and artists. The plates are as creative as the conversation in the air, using Dominican staples to make original and witty combinations. Try the specialty dishes: *Caviar de la Crisis* (salt-cured cod over tostones, a sly comment on difficult times) or *Barquito de Plátano Choriqueso* (chorizo with tomato and basil served in a plantain boat). The experience is complete with soft Latin jazz playing in the background; the setlist is handpicked by the owner, a talented percussionist. *RD$95-400; Corner of C/ 12 de Julio and C/ Separación; 979-1950*

 Mares Eating outside can be uncomfortable under the hot Caribbean sun, but this spot is all about cool patio dining on some of the most creative dishes on the island. Personable chef/owner Ramón Vázquez is known to leave his post cooking up culinary magic and converse pleasantly with his patrons, locals and foreigners who delight in his inspirational Dominican dishes, like the mashed guinea hen confit on crispy yuca with guinea hen breast in a wine reduction and avocado salad. Vázquez visited Epcot Center in 2010 to demonstrate his international – Dominican fare at Disney's Food & Wine Festival, where he cooked a goat-breadfruit cake with a Brugal rum reduction sauce. Diners take their time eating on the serene open-air terrace, set among lush tropical plants is a welcome respite from the heat of the city. *RD$200-800; 6pm-12pm Wed-Sat; 6 C/ Francisco J. Peynado; 261-3330 or 224-1998; info@maresrestaurant.com; www.maresrestaurant.com*

Cariatides Cariatides is Greek in name, but global in character, serving some of the best food in the area. Dishes include steak, pasta, seafood, pizza, and salads, and a smattering of Mediterranean food, too. With a fun atmosphere, and better service than most Dominican restaurants, it is well worth the small trip. *RD$300; 11am-11pm; highway to Luperón Km 3 ½; 320-1410*

Doña Augustina A sweets shack known by all Puertoplateños (Puerto Plata residents) for its sugary delights, such as *dulce de coco* and bread pudding, and its delicious juices. *Two blocks north of the Parque de la Independencia on C/ José de Carmen*

El Manguito Right before Playa Dorada, El Manguito ("the little mango") serves excellent meat and seafood – try the *chivo guisado* (stewed goat) and *cangrejo guisado* (stewed crab). The carnivorous offerings are the best here, though there's always the classic rice and beans for vegetarians. The kitschy thatched roof adds some serious Dominican atmosphere. Look out for the sign on the side of the road. *RD$250-500' Mon-Fri 11am-11pm; highway to Sosúa Km 5; 586-4392*

Provocón IV This national chain delights customers from all over the country – and is well worth a visit from the international traveler. Provocón is consistently jammed with hungry locals, firing up the best *pollo al carbón* (rotisserie chicken) made with the specialty "salsa wasakaka." Pick and choose your chicken and side combos like fried plantains, rice and beans, or boiled yuca. Add a *batida* for RD$50, and you've tasted the Dominican Republic. Try either the location listed below or the one next to the college campus of the UASD (the local public university) on the highway. *RD$100-200; 8am - 2am; corner of C/ Gustavo Mejía Ricart and C/ Lorenzo Despradel, en La Castellana; 970-1200; provocon4to@hotmail.com*

SLEEP

Hotel Castilla Reliably cheap, though certainly small, Hotel Castilla is located in one of Puerto Plata's old Victorian homes, decked out in red-trimmed white clapboard. The hotel sits above Sam's Bar & Grill, so don't expect a dull moment, or too much quiet either. Some of the nine rooms have TV and a bathroom; others are just a bed, fan, and four walls. There are also weekly and monthly rentals available, as well as a separate apartment with a private bath and full kitchen. *RD$150-200; 34 C/ José del Carmen Ariza, by C/ Bosch; 586-7267; sams.bar@codetel.net.do*

Portofino Guest House Portofino is off the main drag, but well within walking distance of the *malecón* and the heart of the city – convenient, but not noisy. The hotel has 18 rooms, plus a patio and uniquely designed pool with a separate children's area. There is an open-air pizzeria and restaurant inside the hotel. *RD$700-900; 12 C/ Hermanas Mirabal; 586-2858; Amenities: A/C, cable TV*

Aparta-Hotel Lomar Located right on the *malecón*, Lomar occupies some prime real estate for the Puerto Plata social scene. The hotel has a number of ocean-facing rooms with private balconies, and a bar that livens up in the evening. *RD$800-950; Av. Malecón; 320-8555; Amenities: cable TV, A/C*

 Tubagua Plantation Eco Village The open-air cabins at this environmentally friendly lodge are set in the hills of Yásica and offer a spectacular view of Puerto Plata. With "walls" made of canvas and palm-thatched roofs, the sleeping arrangements bring guests closer nature, enjoying the cool, clean air and sound of the jungle, while also providing modern amenities. Bathrooms are communal and strategically positioned for a view of a precipice covered with taro root and avocado trees. Having lived more than 25 years in the DR, the Canadian owner is a great resource on places to visit as well as for interesting stories. *US$25-35; located just after the "U" in the road of Yásica; 696-6932; www.tubagua.com; Amenities: pool, restaurant, breakfast included*

DO

Malecón

The *malecón*, a mainstay of coastal Dominican cities, is a seaside boulevard and a center of local and visitor life in Puerto Plata. At about four kilometers long, it traverses the city's entire coastline, packed with small bars and restaurants and vendors selling golden fried plantains and tropical fruit. People bring speakers and drinks down to the seaside on weekend evenings, and socialize late into the night.

The city's municipal beach is at the *malecón*, though swimming is not recommended because of the high pollution factor.

An annual merengue festival is held on the boulevard in October. The street is opened to pedestrian traffic, and crowds throng to dance to the enchanting beats of live bands all day and late into the night.

Teleférico & Cristo Redentor

Opened in 1975, the *teleférico* (cable car) transports passengers up a rainforested hillside track to the summit of Loma Isabel de Torres, the mountain Columbus supposedly spotted with a shimmering silver color. The *teleférico*, the only one on the island, rises 779 meters (2,555 feet) above sea level over an eight-minute journey. Its glass sides afford a dramatic view of the mountain, city, and water below. A statue of Christ the Redeemer, in the style of Río de Janeiro, greets the visitor at the summit. On occasion, the mountain is actually shrouded in mist, dampening viewing possibilities, but providing that rare but ethereal head-in-the-clouds experience. Unfortunately, the *teleférico* has been known to run on its variable and unpublished schedule, and was out of service for a few years in the early 2000s. Still, it has its own generator, important in a country where the power supply is intermittent at best. The mountain itself is a nationally protected Nature Reserve, with a 135,000 square-foot botanical garden featuring gurgling streams and vibrant flora. The breezy mountaintop also has a gift shop and restaurant. It is easily accessible by car or makes for an invigorating half-day jaunt through the mountainside (see Oscar López below for guide information). *RD$350; 8am-5pm; Turn-off clearly marked with sign off of Av. Manolo Tavares Justo heading west just after leaving the city center*

Fortaleza San Felipe

At the western end of the *malecón*, on a promontory that juts out into the Atlantic, rises Fortaleza San Felipe. In 1577, the Spanish completed construction on the fort in order to protect its settlement and trade from pirates and other sea thugs, strategically locating it at the mouth of the port for which the city is named.

Oscar López, "Vigia de la Montaña"

After braving a ride on the *teleférico* up the lush mountainside, a number of eager vendors attempt to entice visitors with cheap souvenirs. Among the bunch is Oscar **López**, self-proclaimed "Vigia de la Montaña" (Guardian of the Mountain). Oscar first climbed Loma Isabel de Torres in 1959, taking shelter in a cave for the night. Since then, Oscar has made the mountain his home and his livelihood. As the area evolved from farmland to a scientific reserve, Oscar found his niche as the official contact for the Ministry of Environment, cell phone companies who have installed towers there, and various branches of the military and law enforcement.

A poignant moment in Oscar's endless list of odd jobs was when a Cuban plane crashed into the mountainside in 1992. Oscar was the first to arrive, a bit drunk but with his senses enough intact to scuttle up the dark mountain-side and locate the bodies. Two years later, a significant portion of the mountain came crumbling down and Oscar was at the center of action, informing the proper authorities of this shocking geological occurrence. When Oscar is not acting as a one-man rescue team, he offers guided tours up the mountainside from the center of Puerto Plata. After more than 50 years of finding his way through the jungle covering the peak, Oscar can find his way up blindfolded. To contact Oscar, call 809-204-7605.

Surrounded by a moat, the fort is the only standing monument from the first century of Spanish colonization in the city. The fort's eight-feet thick stone walls proved useful when serving as a prison for dissidents or political opposition, which it did for much of its existence after the importance of warding off invaders waned. The fort has housed at least one famous prisoner – the country's founder, Juan Pablo Duarte, was held here after displeasing the early government of General Pedro Santana. The fort is great for a pretty walk from the *malecón* with views of the port, city, and sea. A small museum displays 18th and 19th century sometimes-musty military artifacts, and has a gift shop. *RD$50; 261-6043 or 708-5354; Sun-Fri 8:45am-4:45pm*

El Faro

At the same site as the fort stands a lighthouse, which guided mariners coming across the Atlantic. Constructed in 1879, it climbs 24.4m high on a six-meter base. Together, the lighthouse (*faro*, in Spanish) and the fort comprise a designated national monument site. The cast-iron lighthouse, one of few on the continent, has had its entire interior worn away by the fury of nature, and the outer support structure suffered significant oxidization. The World Monuments Fund declared the lighthouse endangered, and aided local agencies in a large restoration beginning in 2002, including improvements to the spiral staircase and electrical signaling.

Brugal Factory

The largest and most prominent producer and provider of rum in the Dominican Republic is Brugal. The company was founded in Puerto Plata, where the elixir of the people is still processed and bottled. Even if only to have the ability to see where a much-consumed Dominican resource gets it start, head over to the distillery for a tour, which includes a video and short walk through the bottling area. Free samples are proffered at its conclusion, along with time for browsing in what might be a glorified, though informative, gift shop. *Free; Mon-Fri 9am-12pm, 2pm-5pm; Av. Tavarez Justo*

Museo de Ambar

Much respect goes out to the creatures stuck in the golden resin seen in this impressive museum; they have been around and entirely intact for quite a number of years. Though simple tree sap, amber is actually considered to be semiprecious. The

The North Coast

Victorian Architecture

Puerto Plata is home to some of the most spectacular and well-preserved Victorian architecture in the country. Waves of immigrants from English colonies like the Bahamas, St. Thomas, and other Antilles islands brought this style of brightly painted "gingerbread" houses here in the 19th century.

Some of the best examples can be found around the perimeter of Parque de la Independencia, such as the white Victorian that now serves as an evangelical church on the corner of C/ Beller and C/ José del Carmen Ariza. At the same corner across the street, look for the three-story baby blue Victorian with a rust-red roof, originally a pharmacy called La Botica San José. The building was later bought and restored by an Italian developer, Aldo Costa, and is now maintained by the Costa Foundation.

In the blocks surrounding the Parque de la Independencia, there are also numerous handsomely decorated warehouses dating from the 1870s to the 1940s. Serving as depots for goods coming in and out of the port, business owners obviously believed in both functionality and beauty.

museum, set in a nicely restored Victorian mansion, has an impressive collection and provides guided tours in multiple languages so curious visitors can learn just how many million years old that lizard is. One special piece with an encased mosquito was immortalized in Jurassic Park. A gift shop is available so you can put history on your wrist. *61 C/ Duarte; Mon-Sat 9am-6pm; 586-2848*

Catedral San Felipe

Though there has been a church on this site since 1502, the current building with its dual towers was constructed in 1871 of wood and zinc. The church was renovated in 1929, covering its exterior in whitewashed cement after much of the original wood burned down. Since then, it has undergone two additional renovations, in an attempt to preserve original artwork and the Italian stained-glassed windows. *9am-5pm; Parque Central*

Parque Regalado

Named after Padre Francisco Regalado, a philanthropist from Puerto Plata, this pleasant park built in 1801 is surrounded by a number of architectural gems with regards to their historical significance. Along Calle Margarita Mears is the former site of the home of General Ulysses Urroz, a president-turned-dictator. While the original home no longer exists, the original iron fence still protects the replacement. On the west side of the park is a neoclassical pink and white building that once served as the headquarters in town for Trujillo's political party, "El Partido Dominicano", and is now used by ministry of public health (SESPAS). Buildings similar to this one can be seen in various towns around the country, all of which served the same purpose of maintaining ultimate control under the Trujillo's iron fist.

Amber

Most commonly found in the Cordillera Septentrional, this precious fossilized tree resin called amber (*ambar*, in Spanish) is formed when tree resin dries and hardens. Insects, particularly bees, would become trapped in the sticky resin, encasing themselves in a future piece of jewelry or a specimen in a paleontologist's prized collection. Less common inhabitants of these golden tombs, such as frogs and lizards, can be sold for tens of thousands of dollars. The amber in the DR is rare for its variety of different shades, from light yellow to dark brown to the rare blue. Amber's color is more than a source of beauty, because it's also identifier of its age, with darker shades originating in older deposits. What is found within the amber, such as plants and invertebrates, plays an important role in understanding past climates and the evolution of ecosystems. Amber samples have been collected in the DR dating back 15 to 20 million years, with some as far back as 45 million years, providing invaluable sources of information on the flora and fauna from earlier ages.

Light and plastic-like to the touch, amber is easily falsified. Only buy it from a trusted source or use the following techniques to determine its authenticity:

- Carry a black light or request one from the seller, who should have one on site, if he is legitimate. If the amber glows under the light, it's authentic.

- Bring a piece of wool and a credit card or ATM receipt ripped into small pieces. Rub the wool against the amber and if then if the amber attracts the pieces of paper, it's authentic.

Estadio José Briceño

Though Puerto Plata does not host a baseball Winter League team, it does have a large stadium that is set to undergo renovations. The stadium has seen better days, but it's still possible to find pickup games being played on the grounds. The stadium is most often used as a venue for top artists and other entertainment, like the traveling circus. Check with your hotel to see if there are any shows during your visit. Ticket prices vary widely. *Av. Hermanas Mirabal by Av. Luís Ginebra*

AROUND PUERTO PLATA

Seafood in Maimón

On the way to Imbert from Puerto Plata, the roadside seafood restaurants of Maimón are not to be missed. On weekends, these various restaurants are full of visitors savoring fresh fish served with *moro* or *tostones*. All the restaurants serve essentially the same *criollo*-style seafood, usually fried or *al ajillo* (sautéed in garlic and olive oil), so pick the one that draws your attention and enjoy an inexpensive, authentic Dominican meal.

Playa Dorada

Playa Dorada means "Golden Beach" in English, and it does have something of a Midas touch. The expansive complex represents one of the heaviest concentrations of all-inclusive resorts on the island, hosting over a dozen low-slung luxury hotels curled around a horseshoe-shaped road along the beach. For convenience, the complex is also equipped with a full golf course and a mall. Its exclusivity is highlighted in its isolated nature, away from both the highway and the city. The beach at Playa Dorada is open to the public, but the *guagua* drops off passengers on the highway, leaving beachgoers with at least a 15-minute walk to the water. For information about each hotel, including rates and amenities, visit www.playadorada.com.do.

Cofresí

Cofresí is a quiet expat beachside development of houses and apartments available for short- and long-term rent about five kilometers west of Puerto Plata. Within the development are a number of restaurants such as the Mexican-style **Charros** or **Chris and Mady's,** catering to the foreign jet set with its international/American fare. All practicalities such as a mini-market and even rooms for rent (contact 829-855-7190 about rooms) can be found at the Plaza Taína complex (970-7504) on the road running along the beach. Cofresí is designed more for the long-term visitor, usually from Europe, rather than those on shorter vacations. It also hosts **Ocean World**, a large animal park (and casino) with opportunities for encounters with marine wildlife.

Costambar

Closer in to Puerto Plata is Costambar, with the best, most accessible beach in the area. Like Cofresí, much of the development is in the form of condos or longer-term rentals, but it is a very quick ride from downtown Puerto Plata. The beach is wide, sandy, clean, and generally peaceful, much quieter than Sosúa and Cabarete. Dominican families arrive on the weekends and holidays, while European expats take charge the week. There are a number of restaurants directly on the beach serving standard Dominican fare like fresh fish and the *plato del día*, which at night turn into bars serving standard Dominican drinks like Presidente and Brugal.

The North Coast

Yasika Adventures

If cruising 300 feet above the forest floor at up to 30 miles per hour on a rope sounds like fun, it might be a good idea to check out Yasika, whose Adventure means zip-lining. Not for the faint of heart or slim of wallet, Yasika's zip line is a thrilling, though pricey, half-day activity, though the fee does include refreshments and transport from Puerto Plata hotels. The center is located about a 30-minute drive south on the *carretera turística*. *US$84; Mon-Sat 8am-5pm; 650-2323; reservation@yasikaadventures.com; www.yasikaadventures.com*

∎ El Chocal

Located in Bajabonico Arriba, a village in the mountains south of Puerto Plata, this entirely women-run chocolate factory and community-run bakery has significantly improved area employment opportunities for both men and women. The local women's association (REMURA) offers a tour called "Cacao, Chocolate, y Aventura," taking visitors through the process of turning cacao into chocolate on a daylong adventure. The tour begins with how the cacao is grown through the production process, and is followed by sampling the cacao in its various forms, from wine to liquor

---

La Familia Reyes, Kings of Carnaval

A narrow alley in Puerto Plata opens up into the home of the Reyes family, legends of Puerto Plata's Carnaval. Each addition to their two-story cinderblock home, complete with an entire loft dedicated to a costume workshop, represents a proud moment in the family's history when their designs won them prizes for their outstanding costume designs. The head of the family, Simeon Reyes, recalls that he used to make fun of his wife, Aida Rodríguez de Reyes, when they were children for the elaborate costumes she and her family carefully constructed. After getting over his juvenile flirting techniques, Simeon began to participate in Carnaval with Aida and her family and then discovered a hidden talent. Since the early 1970s, the Reyes family has won prizes for both individual costumes, which consists of a group of one to three people, and *comparsa*, which refers to a group of more than three.

In Puerto Plata, the official identity for Carnaval is the Taimascaro, an elaborate costume incorporating Spanish, African, Taíno, and Dominican culture. The sleeves of the Taimascaro are adorned with seven scarves, each color representing a different saint worshipped in Dominican syncretism. The puffy sleeves and breast scarf of the shirt pay tribute to Spanish colonial dress. The pants, covered in seashells, are representative of Puerto Plata's proximity to the ocean, and produce a sound that distinguishes the Taimascaros from other Carnaval personalities. On the back of the cape is a Taíno-inspired drawing along with feathers, sequins, and beads leaving a lasting impression as Taimascaros march away. Each *"tribu"* (tribe; or group of participants in this case) creates its own take on the Taimascaro costumes. Greater variations can be seen in the individual costumes, which generally draw influences from Dominican countryside, like Simeon's award-winning coconut tree or chicken costumes.

Starting as early as September, the Reyes home is covered with wire frames and cardboard waiting to be covered in fabric and shells and transformed into iconic costumes. After participating in the success that their parents' hard work has rendered, Jairo Reyes and his sister, Kendra, became zealous participants. In 2010, Jairo decided to break out on his own, designing his own *comparsa*. With strong leaders holding the reins, the Reyes may continue to be the "Kings of Carnaval" for yet another generation.

to truffles. For an extra cost, the community's Atabales music group fills the air with the contagious beat of drums and soulful voices in a mesmerizing performance. Lunch and a visit to a swimming hole are included. It is also possible to stay overnight with a hiking excursion for US$40 per person, including dinner and breakfast. *US$20-40; to arrive in public transport, take Javilla Tours from Puerto Plata or Santiago (RD$50-70) and get off at Quebrada Honda. From there, take a motoconcho to "Chocal" in Bajabonico Arriba (RD$50); asoproconcacao@hotmail.com, fundelosa1@hotmail.com; Tours start around 9am and last until about 3pm*

Parque Nacional la Isabela (El Castillo)

The National Park contains the oldest remnants of European civilization in the Western Hemisphere. Unfortunately, the park is a bit disappointing, considering its immense historical significance. As one of the only informative signs in the park states, La Isabela was where Christopher Columbus put down anchor on his second voyage in 1493, establishing it as the first European city in the New World. Of course, he had previously landed at La Navidad on the Haitian side of the island, but that attempt ended in disaster, with all of the sailors perishing before Columbus could return to them. On the grounds are several pieces of the ephemeral outpost: an unidentified graveyard of Spanish colonialists, scarce ruins of Columbus' house, the first church, and other buildings; foundational cornerstones marking these edifices are haphazardly protected by palm shelters. There is also a museum displaying other artifacts as archeological excavation, begun in the 1950s, continues on the site.

Directly preceding the National Park, stop by **Templo de las Americas** (free entrance; 8am-5pm), a replica chapel built in neo-colonial style to commemorate the 500th anniversary of Columbus' landing on Hispaniola. Note the colorful stained glass windows in the otherwise unadorned church. At the entrance of the National Park (also called El Castillo), take a moment to speak with the artisans, who hand carve sculptures from *guayacán* wood. Picking through the more desperate attempts to cater to foreigners, there are a few interesting pieces like representations of Taíno gods with small platforms on their heads for hallucinogenic powder, or wooden pieces used to induce vomiting, both of which were utilized during Taíno religious ceremonies. At the edge of the park is Playa Isabela, a relatively untouched expanse of sand and sea.

En Route to La Isabela

On the road to the park, there are a number of sites that reveal elements of Puerto Plata's rural culture and history. Sugarcane fields give way to the community of Saballo, a product of nearby Ingenio Amistad ("Friendship Sugar Refinery"), known for its tremendous *gagá* celebrations. Continuing on towards La Isabela, dairy cows munch on tall grasses in small communities like Angostura and La Escalerita, where aluminum jugs of milk for sale line the roadside. In La Escalerita, be sure to stop at one of the small stores selling yogurt; *queso de hoja*, a fresh moist, white cheese; and *bombones*, small sweet flat cakes baked with molasses. *RD$100; 7am-5pm; 829-298-4979; to arrive in public transport to La Isabela, take Javilla Tours from Puerto Plata to Imbert (RD$35) and then take a guagua to La Isabela.*

The Arts in Puerto Plata

A rare element of Puerto Plata unseen in many other Dominican towns is the quantity and quality of artists that this city has produced. Since its founding as a major port, immigrants helped cultivate a social consciousness and appreciation for the arts. Some of the country's most renowned artists such as Doña Mercedes Coco, who dominated the realms of music, literature, and visual art, honed their skills in this cultured city.

Modern artists such as Rafi Vázquez, known for his richly textured oil paintings of nature and elegant watercolor portraits, have achieved international recognition. A new vanguard of artists and artisans is also emerging. Visual artist Checo Merette established himself as one of the city's budding artists in 2000 with his controversial and sensual series "Puerto Plata All-Inclusive." His expressive style can be appreciated at Puerto Plata's airport counters, which are decorated with his designs. In an effort to beautify the *malecón*, Checo and a team of ten local artists painted the massive tanks of the Electric Corporation of Puerto Plata (CEPP, in Spanish) with whales using Checo's fluid, chaotic strokes. Alberto Khoury, who dominates a number of mediums including drawing, painting, and ceramics, was one of the contributing artists to this project. Khoury is also active with Puerto Plata's art association, Artístas y Artesanos Unidos de Puerto Plata. The artisans' ceramics, leatherwork, and paintings are available in the former Palacio de la Justícia, where visitors can watch the artisans at work. Puerto Plata is also known for its love of merengue *típico*, the rural, traditional form of merengue. The annual merengue festival in October is a wonderful time to experience this music, or simply visit one of the many bars and restaurants in the old city and along the *malecón* that hosts performances.

To see the paintings of Rafi Vázquez (and possibly meet the artist himself, since he often stops by), head to the **Centro de Arte Rafi Vázquez** located in Rafi's childhood home, at 3 C/ Profesor Sertad, by C/ Presidente Vázquez.

Imbert

Imbert originally gained importance as the last major stop on the narrow-gauge railroad that ran between Puerto Plata and Santiago. A small but influential merchant class came to Imbert, and it developed as a commercial hub to transport sugarcane and other crops from the surrounding region to the coast for export. It then became much larger and wealthier than other villages in the region. Today, Imbert is a small town of 20,000, the last of any substance on the way to the coast. A few of these original merchant families still make Imbert their home, as seen in several large homes around the highway.

There are two exciting places of interest around Imbert: an incredible river adventure called the **27 Charcos**, and an artisan association working with petrified wood. Both serve as recommended day trips from Santiago or Puerto Plata.

TRANSPORT

Caribe Tours
Note that Caribe only offers service to Imbert from the capital; it does not pick up passengers in the town.

From Santo Domingo: RD$330; hourly 6am-9pm; 2.5hr

Javilla Tours
At the Texaco station, flag down this company's signature white minibuses going south toward Santiago (RD$55; 30min) or north toward Puerto Plata (RD$40; 20min), from 7am to 7pm. If you're not using Caribe, this is how to get in and out of Imbert.

INFO

Gas

The large **Texaco Station** marks the entrance to the town. It also doubles as a local hotspot/bar/disco at night, when locals blare car stereos before heading off to **Rancho Típico** (below), the real bar two blocks down. Snacks and beer are available at the convenience store inside. A pop-up car stereo music competition in the Texaco parking lot comes alive on Sunday.

EAT & SLEEP

If you're spending any more time in town outside of the Charcos, visit **Rancho Típico Imbert,** a sprawling indoor-outdoor café and dance hall located on the opposite side of the bridge from the Texaco. It transforms into the center of activity on Sunday nights, when youth from all over the region converge to dance away the hot Dominican night to traditional merengue and bachata.

Due to Imbert's proximity to Puerto Plata, there are few reasons to stay overnight in Imbert, and there is no suitable lodging.

DO

☑ 27 Charcos, Damajagua

A stunning set of pools and waterfalls two kilometers south of Imbert in the village of Damajagua, 27 Charcos is a required stop on any trip to the northern half of the country. Aside from the gorgeous, protected surroundings and adrenaline-pumping adventure, the Charcos also represent the good that can come from local and international cooperation to create a community-focused, environmentally conscious, and, just as important, profit-making enterprise to benefit its workers. Arrive early in the morning to take advantage of the best weather conditions, and before the oversized safari tours arrive with hordes of tourists. The visitors' center also has bathrooms, lockers, and a gift shop. Tour guides, helmets, and life jackets are provided and mandatory. The trek is akin to canyoneering, involving hiking and climbing through quiet pools, sheer cliffs, and rushing mini-canyons, and then jumping and swimming back down the same route. Bring close-toed shoes, which are also required to participate. Tours can include all 27 waterfalls, or up to the 12th or 7th waterfalls. The lower falls take less time and cost less, but the real adventure and best action takes place at the top. To be able to do all 27, you must leave the Visitors' Center before noon. *RD$250-460; 8:30am–4pm; info@27charcos.com; www.27charcos.com*

To reach 27 Charcos, take the *servicio corto* (local service) Javilla Tours bus from Puerto Plata or Santiago and ask to be let off at the 27 Charcos, or ask for the *cascadas*, meaning waterfalls (RD$50). The path to the center is off to the east side, under a huge Brugal rum billboard; follow the path through the sugarcane for a few hundred meters. There is a parking lot. It is also possible to pick up the *guagua* from Imbert itself (RD$15).

☑ Asociación de Artesanos de Madera Petrificada de Imbert (ASOARTEP)

Since the late 1960s, artisans from Imbert have worked the petrified wood found in abundance across the Imbert area. Papito Ramos Clase was the pioneer of this craft, training others in the process of mining, shaving, and polishing the wood into elegant sculptures. Papito's nephew, Cecilio Clase Francisco, carries on the tradition, apprenticing under his uncle since the age of nine. Now middle-aged, Cecilio's designs are representative of the skill and creativity that his years of experienced have cultivated. The artisans belonging to the association produce everything from animals to jewelry to chess sets, sold throughout the country. *Take Javilla Tours to Imbert and then a moto to the artisan's workshop in the neighborhood of Barrabas; 250-2327; artesanos.imbert@gmail.com*

⬛ Hacienda Cufa

Located in the village of Guananico, this cacao farm has been in the Mercado family for over 100 years. Having left the village at the age of 13 for Santo Domingo, current owner Sarah Mercado Luna went on to earn a Master's degree in environmental science and worked in the area of environmental protection for decades until she decided to turn her family farm into a both an environmental education and a relaxing retreat center. While there are guest rooms that can accommodate up to 20 people for an overnight stay, Hacienda Cufa also works as a day trip. A typical visit to Hacienda Cufa begins with a cacao tour, in which participants learn how cacao is planted, picked, and then elaborated into gleaming balls of cacao ready to be melted down into rich hot chocolate. Afterward, you'll take a dip in the Río Canao, which

---

27 Charcos

One of the most popular adventure spots on the north coast, 27 Charcos is part of the Río Damajagua National Monument, a park protected by the government for its ecological significance and natural beauty. Otherwise an unobtrusive mountain stream, these waters have carved an intricate, serpentine path through the rocky foothills of the Cordillera Septentrional to create the 27 Charcos, meaning 27 Pools (though the site is known in English as the 27 Waterfalls). Adventure-seeking tourists began arriving in the mid-1990s as word of mouth spread that a hidden gem of a river sat just outside Imbert.

To meet the growing visitor presence, men from local communities acted as impromptu guides, and began leading tours up the river. Word spread to the hotels and tour companies in Puerto Plata, who brought truckloads of tourists to visit the river. The local guides offered their services, but as the tourists had already paid to be driven to the Charcos, the guides lived off sparing tips, and there was little regard for the environmental sensitivity of the area.

In 1998, these enterprising men formed the Asociación de Guías Salvavidas del Río Damajagua (AGRD – Guides Association of the Damajagua River), but accomplished little beyond gaining a title, still disorganized and without proper compensation. In 2004, the guides group received its first of three successive Peace Corps Volunteers, who partnered with local leaders, international donor agencies, and the Secretary of the Environment to strengthen the Guides Association through trainings and capacity-building activities and construction of a visitor's center. Together, they transformed the river into a protected region and drove investment returns back into local communities. Monies from the structured entrance fee furnish guide salaries, park protection, and a community fund that provides funding for educational scholarships, technical trainings, micro-credit loans, and a permanent community endowment. The Charcos now accepts a limited number of guests a day, which defends the sensitive regional watershed and provides direct and indirect income and funding for thousands of people in the surrounding communities.

runs along the property. The stream is full of rich clay beds, so be sure to bring a bathing suit for a do-it-yourself full body clay treatment and refreshing dip. A hearty country meal featuring local favorites like *yuca* bread with *chicharrón* (fried pork rinds) and freshly ground hot chocolate finishes off a pretty pastoral Dominican day. The price includes the daylong tour, lunch, and swimming. *US$25; tour times are flexible, but generally begin at 10am and end by 5pm; to arrive in public transport, take a carro público to Guananico (RD$50) until the entrance of the river at the Colmado de Pedro; ask for "La Familiar Mercado" from where you will be directed towards the Río Canao, then turn right at the river where you will see the entrance of the hacienda; 756-4806; www.haciendacufa.com*

Sosúa

More tranquil than Puerto Plata and Cabarete, but still with its unique sense of coastal charm, Sosúa attracts a slightly older and less rowdy crowd than its frenzied neighboring cities. The city center and the beaches are small, and therefore the city is easily navigable on foot. Playa Sosúa connects Sosúa's two distinct barrios: Los Charamicos in the west, less developed and with very few foreigners, and the now-ironically named El Batey, the "downtown" and more tourist-oriented section of Sosúa.

Sosúa's short history has a fascinating origin. Its founding is a bright asterisk in the tragedy of mid-century Europe that came from an unlikely source: Rafael Trujillo. In 1939, at the Evian Conference was held to determine what to do with the

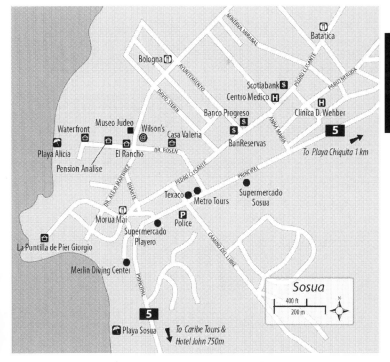

The North Coast

flood of Jewish refugees fleeing Nazi Germany. Trujillo opened the doors of his country for three years, from 1940 to 1942 – the only state in the Americas that agreed to do so unconditionally. Though he agreed to accept up to 100,000 people, only about 700 were afforded the opportunity to make the journey to the Dominican Republic. Upon their arrival, the government settled them in the tiny rural village that Sosúa was at the time. Though originally expected to bring farming expertise and develop the region's agriculture, these new Dominicans founded the most successful local dairy and meat enterprise to date in the country, Productos Sosúa. A small town soon grew around this bustling economic activity. Sosúa underwent a boom after being connected to the national highway network, hastening additional development from beachside tourism in the 1980s. The Jewish community is almost entirely gone, having not ever felt terribly welcome. The vast majority has intermarried or moved to the capital or the US, but the town's international nature lives on. Today, the European expat community is a strong and growing presence, as tourism is now the engine of commerce. Pack your Babel fish next to your towel when you head to the beach, where French, German, and Italian are heard more than Spanish.

TRANSPORT

Caribe Tours
The station is at C/ Principal (Highway 5) at C/ Eduardo Brito in Los Charamicos. Buses leave for **Puerto Plata** (RD$35; 30min), **Santiago** (RD$150; 1.5hrs), and **Santo Domingo** (RD$300; 4hrs), at 5:15am and then hourly from 6:20am to 6:20pm every hour at :20 past the hour. *571-3808; www.caribetours.com.do*

Metro Tours
The station is at C/ Principal (Highway 5) and C/ Dr. Rosen in El Batey. Buses leave for **Puerto Plata** (RD$40; 30min), **Santiago** (RD$150; 1.5hrs), and **Santo Domingo** (RD$300; 4hrs) at 8:20am, 10:20am, 1:20pm, 3:20pm and 5:20pm. *227-0101; www.metroserviciosturisticos.com*

Guaguas
Guaguas and *carros públicos* officially run 24 hours, though most reliably from sunrise to sunset. One route goes west, ending at Puerto Plata, and another goes east, ending at Río San Juan. Flag one down on the side of the road, or visit the stand on C/ Principal and C/ Dr. Rosen, and then get dropped off at any spot along the way. The ride will cost from RD$15 to RD$40, depending on the destination.

INFO

Medical Attention
Both of the following are foreigner-friendly clinics: the **Centro Médico** is located in Plaza Médico, on C/ Pedro Clisante (571-4233; 945-0120) and **Clínica D. Wehber** is on C/ Pablo Neruda by C/ Gabriela Mistral (571-2029; 454-4258).

Communication
Wilson's Internet & Calls & Exchange is on C/ Dr. Alejo Martínez.

Banks
Scotiabank is C/ Pedro Clisante near the corner of C/ Gabriela Mistral and both **BanReservas** and **Banco Progreso** are on C/ Pedro Clisante, on either side of the Ayuntamiento.

Police
The **National Police** office is located on C/ Principal (Highway 5), by Supermercado Playero.

Gas
Texaco is on C/ Principal (Highway 5) at C/ Dr. Rosen.

Grocery Stores
Supermercado Playero is the largest and best-stocked grocery on the North Coast east of Puerto Plata, at C/ Principal (Highway 5) at the western side of El Batey. There is a smaller branch at C/ Duarte and C/ Pedro Clisante. **Supermercado Sosúa** is a close second, located on C/ Principal (Highway 5), by C/ Dr. Rosen.

EAT

Batatica Finding authentic local eats right by the beach can be tricky. Luckily, there is Batatica ("small sweet potato"), named after a Sosúa native who went by that unique nickname. Tucked off the main drag, this spot draws a purely Dominican crowd. The conch shell and fish are fresh specialties, and the prices are the best in town, with the *plato del día* starting at RD$125. Note that the restaurant is actually located on a side street off C/ Pedro Clisante marked with a large sign; every *motoconchista* knows where to find it if you are unable to. *RD$ 125-175; 133 C/ Pedro Clisante; 571-1558*

Casa Valeria The Casa Valeria restaurant, inside the pleasant hotel, claims a locally sourced menu using all-natural ingredients. The dining room is a little tacky, but its bright colors and friendly confines makes this spot a good place to eat, especially if staying at the hotel. *RD$200-500; 8am-11pm; 28 C/ Dr Rosen; 571-3565.*

 Waterfront Restaurant Budget traveler, be not intimidated. The fancy awning, upscale décor, and bluff-top location shouldn't scare, but welcome. Waterfront is classy, to be sure, but the charming owner complemented his upscale fare with half-price daily specials, overflowing salads (including a labor-intensive, tableside-prepared Caesar) and smaller items for less than RD$200, as well as a generous happy hour from 5pm to 7pm. Tantalizing and unique dishes include calamari in ink over black rice, or the extravagant *plato de cinco mares* with shrimp, crayfish, conch shell, calamari, and fish. *RD$100-600; 1 C/ Dr. Rosen (where the street ends); 571-3024; 829-755-6068; sainz.andres@gmail.com; Free Wi-Fi*

Bologna Ristorante Italiano A twin restaurant and chic café, it's no surprise a place called Bologna dishes out authentic Italian cuisine like Parmesan beef medallions on arugula and homemade cannelloni. Save room at the end for the baked-daily desserts and a feisty Italian espresso to perk up for evening activities. *RD$220-750; 33 C/ Alejo Martínez; 571-1454/1144; ristobologna@hotmail.com*

Morua Mai Tropical-classy, Morua Mai is a breezy, open-air restaurant splashed with bold primary colors and warm wicker furniture. The menu spans the globe – filet mignon, salads to share, and ahi tuna with avocado, cilantro, and saffron rice. *RD$250-700; 5 C/ Pedro Clisante; 571-2966/2503; free Wi-Fi.*

La Puntilla de Piergiorgio With a breathtaking view of the ocean, and fountains and gardens gracing the grounds, this restaurant is splurge-worthy for the ambience alone, splashed with pink bougainvillea and a tiered fountain (take a look at the Piergiorgio Palace Hotel, founded by an Italian fashion designer). La Puntilla's food is just as nice – salmon-stuffed ravioli or shrimp in Pernod sauce and salads big enough for a meal. Pair your grilled lobster with a choice from the extensive wine list for a romantic Caribbean evening. *RD$320-950; 571-2626/2786; piergirorgio@codetel.net.do; www.piergiorgiopalace.com*

SLEEP

Casa Valeria Valeria's accommodations are colorful and have plentiful amenities, though the windows are a mite small. The owner-managers are European expats, so communication shouldn't be a problem. Wi-Fi is available and usually reliable. *RD$1500-2000; 28 C/ Dr Rosen; 571-3565; hotelcasavaleria@gmail.com; Hotelcasavaleria.com*

Pensión Analise At press time, this little German-owned spot with ten rooms was changing management and undergoing renovations. When open, it was one of the best value budget hotels in town, so be sure to check it out and see if it's still up to par. *US$15-55; C/ Dr. Rosen; 571-2208; analise.pension@codetel.net.do*

Hotel El Rancho Tacky isn't a problem unless you make it one, so don't mind its presence here, where kitsch equals fun. El Rancho offers 17 comfortable poolside rooms with tropically bright interiors. Groups and those with a larger budget ought to look out for the apartments kitchens and the sweet penthouse. Check out the casual snack bar, serving fast food and drinks, located in the lobby. *Rooms US$45-55; Apts. US$70-155; 36 C/ Dr Rosen; 571-4070; www.hotelelranchososua.com/3.html; Amenities: A/C, fan, safe, fridge, hot water, some with kitchenette*

Piergiorgio Palace Hotel Assuredly the most charming hotel in Sosúa, this hotel was built in the Dominican image of the neo-Victorian style, right on water's edge. Rooms are well-lit, with a view of the ocean. They are elegantly simple, compared to the grandeur of the rest of the hotel: perfectly manicured gardens, leafy trees, gurgling fountains, and multiple white balconies peering over the seawall. Visit the restaurant for a meal overlooking the water. *US$85-105 for low season and US$95-115 high season; 571-2626/2786; piergirorgio@codetel.net.do; www.piergiorgiopalace.com; Amenities: A/C, hot water, TV, Wi-FI, laundry service, safe, breakfast included*

Hotel John Simply named, simply decorated, simply run. Note that it is located not in the center of town, but in Los Charamicos, and so is a bit out of the way, even though it is quite cheap. The building is brightly festooned in orange and blue, but at RD$300 a night, don't expect much more. *RD$300; C/ Dr. Moje (downhill and left from the Caribe Tours stop); Barrio Los Charamicos, no phone.*

DO

Museo Judío

Small in size but long on chutzpah, the Museo Judío in Sosúa documents the fascinating history of the spirited group of Jewish refugees who, through luck and mettle, slipped through the grasp of Hitler's Europe and thrived in a strange, foreign environment. The museum is shaped like an oval, with pictures, artifacts and articles in a half-dozen languages curving along the walls of the building. Many pieces are old, yellowing, and difficult to read, but also give these stories depth and charge. The Sosúa Jews are long gone, but their footprint remains; the city would not be what it is without their influence. The synagogue used by the community still stands, warm with wood and earthy colors; ask the guard to open it for a short, self-guided tour. There are prayer services on select holidays. *RD$100; Mon-Fri, 9am-1pm and 2pm-4pm, Sat 9am-1pm; C/ Alejo Martínez by C/ Dr. Rosen; 571 1386;*

Playa Sosúa

Brash, loud, and full of expats and loquacious vendors, Playa Sosúa is the archetypal Dominican beach. Though not very broad, the beach stretches for almost two kilometers, connecting the two major barrios of Sosúa, and bringing in the tourists, merchants, and locals to enjoy sand and sea. As it curves inside a bay, the water is calm, perfect for a leisurely swim. Snorkeling is therefore especially popular, as the reef reaches almost to the shore, providing a haven for marine life and a boon for those who are fortunate enough to peek below the water's surface.

The beach pitches steeply up to a stone walkway crammed with small shops, restaurants, and bars, full of life and different languages. Many are nice, and afford the beachgoer to snack on wurst or schnitzel and pick up postcards, but be wary of overpriced places geared toward the unsuspecting tourist.

Playa Alicia (Playa Santa)

This cozy beach isn't much more than short landing of sand at the water below steep and rocky cliffs. At about 300 meters (1,000 feet) long, it is smaller and much quieter than Playa Sosúa, and therefore appreciated for its tranquility. It is most accessible from a rocky staircase through the Waterfront Restaurant, offering stunning views of the sea from on high. The beach spontaneously (and mysteriously) appeared in 2002, when an underwater earthquake supposedly moved a sand bar, causing the ocean to recede and leaving this tidy little beach in its wake. Before the shifting sands episode, locals dove into waters more than 10 meters deep from the beachside cliffs, now a significant distance from the tide.

Playa Chiquita

Away from the tourists (and the amenities), is this aptly named little stretch of sand in Los Charamicos. Few foreigners make it to this side of Sosúa and therefore miss this beach, somewhat grimier than its flashy Playa Sosúa neighbor.

Merlin Dive Center

For beginner scuba divers and snorkelers, a lesson is a must to take advantage of the wealth of tropical underwater beauty. Merlin offers both intro classes and trips and dives for all levels of expertise, as well as daylong to weeklong certification packages. Guides fluent in English, German, and Spanish give divers nearly 20 spots to choose from in the Sosúa area. *Las Caobas, at the beginning of Sosúa beach; 545-0538; info@merlin-diving.com; juergen@Divecenter-Merlin.com; merlin-diving.com*

NIGHTLIFE

For better or worse, Sosúa has earned the reputation of being the red light district of the North Coast. This city probably has the most overt prostitution in the country, as everything happens in the open, unlike in Santo Domingo where it might be more discreet. That being said, where there is prostitution there is bound to be free-flowing booze and decent nightlife. The center of town is full of bars and restaurants, especially along C/ Dr. Rosen, C/ Alejo Martínez, and C/ Pedro Clisante along the beach. Take care in poorly lit areas, but downtown Sosúa is generally safe.

Cabarete

Just 2 kilometers (1.2 miles) long, Cabarete is a thriving, thumping seaside destination – the Miami Beach of the Dominican Republic, with more plantains and less electricity. A far cry from the sleepy fishing village it once was just a couple short decades ago, Cabarete today shines as the destination for independent tourism on the north coast. Hugging a simple two-lane highway are thousands of hotel rooms, dozens of cafés, bars, restaurants, and a wide expanse of palm tree-studded sandy beach. This little town never rests: Days in Cabarete are bustling, warm, and sunny; and its nights are nothing but hot.

Cabarete was transformed in the late 1980s after area beaches were discovered to have ideal conditions for windsurfing and kiteboarding. The town is now a haven for these new adventure sports. Cabarete hosts numerous competitions throughout the year, bringing in an additional level of excitement to the already booming beach. Various tour outfits and adventure sports businesses have descended here to take advantage of the impressive array of options within a very short distance. Beyond niche oceangoing activities, Cabarete is also minutes from the famous surfing spot at Playa Encuentro. There are nearby opportunities for other, land-based sports, including biking, horseback riding, and hiking. Of course, lounging on a reclining beach chair with a drink in hand is a perfectly respectable way to pass time on the sandy expanses.

The beach itself is pretty, though not spectacular. Because of the high density of foreigners here, hawkers buzz like sand flies, selling everything from "Cuban" cigars to *mamajuana* to hair-braiding services. A nice, but firm, "*no, gracias*," should be enough to send them along, unless their wares interest you. There are also plenty of yellow and blue beach chairs to rent for about RD$50.

TRANSPORT

Oddly, the large coach bus companies do not serve Cabarete. Instead, you'll have to contend with the *carro público* routes along the highway. For **Sosúa** (RD$20, 20min), catch anything headed west, and to continue on to **Puerto Plata** (RD$50, 40min), you might have to switch at Sosúa, the terminus for some routes. For **Río San Juan** (RD$50, 30min), hop on anything going east. Although these routes run 24 hours, they become infrequent after dusk and more so after midnight, when a taxi is advisable.

To get to **Santiago** and **Santo Domingo**, take the *carro público* to Sosúa and then catch Caribe Tours.

INFO

Medical Attention

Farmacia Cabarete is located at the eastern side of town near Janet's Supermercado. *8am-11pm; 571-0983*

The **Servimed Clinic** is open for consults and emergencies, and conveniently takes some international insurance as well as credit cards. *Casa Laguna Shopping Center on C/ Principal; 571-0964; servimed@gruporescue.com; www.gruporescue.com*

Cabarete

N

400 ft
200 m

Texaco

Politur

5

Casa Blanca

Claro

Janet's

Ban Reservas

Hotel Alegria

Hotel Sans Souci

Café Pitu

Voy Voy

Bambú Bar

José O'Shays

Lax

Banco BHD

Iguana Mama

Hotel Kaoba

Banco Popular

Aloha Surf Café

Supermercado Cabarete

El Rincón Goloso

Esso

5

To Kite Beach Hotel &
Extreme Kite Beach 1 km

The North Coast

Banks

Most major banks have an ATM at the beach: **BanReservas** is outside Janet's on the eastern end of C/ Principal next to the Western Union; **Banco Popular** is on the south side of C/ Principal in the shopping center at the western side of town across from Ocean Dream Hotel; and **Banco BHD** is north side of C/ Principal at the beach walkway by Lax Restaurant.

Gas

There is an **Esso Gas Station** at the western entrance of town.

Grocery Stores

Janet's Supermercado has the largest selection of food and beverage in town. It is pretty much the only thing approximating a supermarket in Cabarete; the other options are all much smaller. *C/ Principal, on the eastern edge of town.*

EAT

The restaurant/bar/club scene in this town is amorphous, as places transform from one to the other as the day turns into night. Most of these places, therefore, double as both eating and drinking locations, unless specifically noted.

 José O'Shays There is no beachside watering hole better known or more perfectly located than José O'Shays. It might be the quintessential Irish pub, except for the fact that its draft beer is Presidente and it serves pitchers of caipirinhas alongside Irish Car Bombs. The sea breeze and crashing waves outside compete with American sports on a half-dozen televisions – all without a hint of irony (OK, but just a hint). For food, nosh on the somewhat pricey American-style bar fare, plus some Irish classics (bangers and mash on the beach, anyone?), all served under palm trees. Happy hour (4pm to 6pm) is a dangerously low RD$200 for bottomless pitchers of Presidente along with appetizer specials. The bar's biggest draw, however, is probably the largest St. Patrick's Day celebration this side of Dublin. José O'Shays sets up a series of billowy tents on the beach that host live Irish music and dance. The day is topped off with, most logically, a parade down the beach, led by a green-hatted man carrying the Irish flag. In more quotidian style, the restaurant owns a number of specially marked blue lounge chairs on the beach for use by patrons. José O'Shay's is a highlight of any Cabarete visit. *RD$100-450; C/ Principal in the center of town; 571-0775; www.joseoshay.com*

Lax Low-slung red chaises beckon under warm orange and yellow lanterns at Lax, one of the better places to start your Dominican evenings. The food is somewhat overpriced, and the service is typically slow. The reason to go is for the atmosphere and great pizza and salad specials at the dinner hour from 6pm to 7pm. Order a couple pitchers of caipirinhas and watch the beach get thick with revelers on weekend nights. Lax is best for a restful – and sexy – seaside cocktail at dusk before the real beach party begins. *RD$100-500; north side of C/ Principal in the center of town; 883-2684*

Gelato Directly behind Lax, on the pedestrian pathway to the beach, is a white gelato stand, serving fresh and flavorful scoops to overheated travelers for RD$70.

Ojo Right by Lax on the beach is Ojo, Cabarete's trendy new hotspot. Look out for the two-story dance hall, with different beats mixing on each level. On most nights, revelers will find Dominican hits on one floor and electronic and house grooving on the other. Every Wednesday is movie night, while other events include body painting competitions and a Miss Cabarete contest. With an exclusive VIP area and a full bar, Ojo is the place to be seen on warm Cabarete nights. *North side of C/ Principal; 829-745-8810; ojocabarete.com*

Café Pitu Dried palm fronds for a roof of a restaurant isn't tacky when the location is beachfront Cabarete, and neither are tropical-orange walls or giant lizards painted on support beams. Busy but cozy, Pitu sits right on the sand, for a nice breeze with quality food – especially when they have some deals going, like two-for-one pizzas on Tuesdays and Thursday's reggae-infused "Rasta Pasta" for RD$99. They also deliver – but why stay at the hotel if you can eat with your toes in the sand and a Presidente in hand? *RD$99-200; 77 C/ Principal; 571-0861; cafepitu@gmail.com; free Wi-Fi.*

Claro Discerning breakfasters delight, for here is where you shall have your fill. Just off the main drag, Claro is open only for the first two meals of the day, serving omelets, pancakes, tropical fruit salads, and a highly-regarded walnut French toast. There is also a 10% discount for people who are volunteering at local NGOs. Not much is better than a quiet poolside breakfast before a long day – or after a long night – on the beach. *RD$100-250; at Hotel Casa Blanca, 50m east of Janet's Supermarket; 889-1406; Tue-Sun 8am-2pm*

 Panadería Dick Much like with their cured meats, Germans don't loaf around when it comes to bread – Panadería Dick is the best bakery and pastry shop in Cabarete. Right in the middle of town, breakfasts run around RD$100 for eggs, toast, and coffee. Skip the protein altogether and sink your teeth into something warm and fresh, like a sweet roll, buttered croissant, apple Danish, banana muffin, animal-shaped loaf of bread, or the classic vacation breakfast standby, triple chocolate cake. *RD$50-100; Thu-Tue 7am-6pm; C/ Principal; 571-0612; panarolfdick@yahoo.com*

Friends More of a casual café than restaurant, Friends is a satisfying eatery on the main road. Friends makes for a good spot for a late-morning or early-afternoon spot to discuss the previous evening's activities over melted croissant sandwiches and filling muesli breakfasts. *RD$100-$300; 7am-5pm; C/ Principal; 677-1016*

El Rincón Goloso If you're looking for a *plato del día* that isn't comprised of rice and beans, El Rincón Goloso serves up some great fish and veggies for the un-Cabarete price of RD$100. Spanish in name, it's really a little Belgian-owned bakery (Rincón Goloso means "sweet tooth corner"), with a distinct Europe-on-the-Caribbean vibe. It's probably the only place in Cabarete to snag real Belgian *gouffres* – and chocolate. *C/ Principal at Plaza Media Luna; Geuenschristine@yahoo.fr; 879-9401 or 829-879-9401*

Voy Voy At the western edge of the beach, Voy Voy is a top spot to start moonlit Cabarete tours. Drink specials are styled as "stupid cheap" – RD$250 pitchers of mojitos from 7pm to 11pm. This is no Cuban art form, but after the first one, it doesn't much matter. The resto also has dinner if you like to eat with your libations, with daily specials running around RD$200. On Wednesday, find live music, but the karaoke is just as much fun, as the international set lands on some interesting song choices. Thursday is funk and soul night, a welcome reprieve from the incessant European house/techno found at the other bars down the beach. There is also a 2-for-1 late-night happy hour. *RD$100-300; 67 C/ Principal; 571-0805; www.voyvoycabarete.com; 8am-2am*

 Bambú Bar A deceivingly quiet restaurant during the day, Bambú cranks up the music after dark, ascribing to the "if you blast it, they will come" philosophy of nighttime entertainment. On weekend evenings, Bambú is as packed as a Santo Domingo *guagua*, except hotter and darker, and with more alcohol. The party spills out of the tiered dance floor onto the beach, where sweaty revelers take breathers and quaff Presidente. It doesn't much make sense to come here during the day, as there are better places to eat and sit by the bar, but for a complete Cabarete night, this is where to find the action. The party lasts until those wee hours in the morning when properly measured decisions never take place. *RD$100-300; C/ Principal; 982-4549; restaurant 9am-11pm, bar until very late*

The North Coast

Aloha Surf Café Patrons of Aloha Surf don't seem to mind straying slightly off the busiest section of Cabarete's main drag, especially on Thursday nights, when Aloha pulls out the stops with a gut-busting buffet and barbecue for a cool RD$200. One of the best food deals in town, given the price and how great the food is – not to mention the fun crowd that happens by. On weekends, there's often live music. *RD$100-300; C/ Principal, behind Ocean Dream complex; 904-7821; 11am-12pm Wed-Sun*

SLEEP

Hotel Alegría On a little side street behind Janet's Supermarket, Alegría is surprisingly quiet given that it is just steps from the sand, complete with a private beach entrance. The hotel has 13 rooms, some with A/C. A top-floor deck has a gym and tepid Jacuzzi sporting views of the sea, while behind reception there is a small bar and restaurant. Don't be afraid of the large and quite friendly dogs that trot around the outdoor lobby. The low-end rooms are nothing special, so opt for the water-view rooms with king-sized beds. *US$30-75; located between Velero and Sans Souci, on the left down the road next to Janet's; 571-0455; reservations@hotel-alegria.com, hotel-alegria.com*

Hotel Sans Souci Spread out over seven different spots along the main road, Sans Souci has 73 rooms and apartments – one of the biggest hotels in Cabarete. The larger suites are great for big groups looking for a reliable, affordable place to sleep. While some lack A/C, all units have fans and a kitchen and are by the beach – a few are just steps from the water. The complex on the south side of the street also includes several shops and a restaurant. *US$12-20 per person, $10 for extra bed; 571-0755 or 571-0613; sansouci@verizon.net.do*

Casa Blanca Cool and Canadian-owned, this budget hotel is the White House's wild recluse cousin, with a splendid tropical garden and delicious pool. There are both rooms and apartments; see about the rooftop pad for 360-degree views of the beach and countryside. *US$20-60; 113 C/ Principal next to Janet's; 571-0934 or 935-0809; Amenities: A/C, fan, hot water, TV, Wi-Fi, fridge, kitchenette*

Hotel Kaoba With almost 70 rooms and separate bungalows right across the street from the beach, Kaoba is a large and pretty hotel adorned with broad-leafed plants and palms arching over the central courtyard and pool. The "deluxe" rooms also include internet. Be very specific about what you're looking for in a room, and ask to see it before you agree to pay. Rates depend on the size of the room and season.*US$30-80; C/ Principal, western end; 571-0300; info@kaoba.com; www.kaoba.com; Amenities: A/C, fan, hot water, bar, restaurant, internet café, gift shop, and laundry, pool*

Extreme Hotel Directly on Kite Beach, this green hotel has solar panels and a wind turbine to power most of its electricity usage (no A/C – the rooms are cool). There are a number of interesting, non-traditional features right on site: a flying trapeze, half-pipe, large beachfront gym, and airy "yoga loft" with classes offered. Though not a budget hotel, it does have the amenities that are worth the price differential if looking for the eco-conscious hotel with the water sports location. There is a two-night minimum, and large parties should look into the three-bedroom penthouse. *US$50; Carretera Sosúa-Cabarete 10.5km; 571-0371; info@extremehotels.com; www.extremehotels.com*

Kite Beach Hotel The upscale Kite Beach Hotel offers spacious accommodations decorated with modern sculpture and paintings. Guests enjoy the on-site pool and restaurant and take comfort in the 24-hour security and gated parking lot. Special rates are available for kite-surfers getting lessons with Kite Camp for as low as US$20, though guests must be willing to share an apartment with other participants. There are eight types of rooms, from standard doubles to luxury three-bedroom apartments, with rates that vary depending on the season. *US$59-US$600; just east of Extreme Hotel; 571-0878; kitebeachhotel@gmail.com; www.kitebeachhotel.com; Amenities: A/C, fan, hot water, restaurant, bar, Wi-Fi, kitchenette, fridge*

DO

Kana Ripai

This store sells bags, clothing, key-chains, and jewelry, but what sets it above the rest is that all of their products are handmade from recycled goods. Many of the artisans live in the *batey* in nearby Caraballo. Take home true Cabarete memorabilia made by locals: a bag made from old windsurfing kites or change purses made from milk cartons. *Located on the pedestrian walkway near Banco BHD*

DREAM Project

The DREAM Project, founded in 2002, is a successful international non-profit that provides educational opportunities to poor youth in and around Cabarete, especially to the children of the workers at tourist establishments. DREAM runs camps, after-school groups, and a preschool, among many other projects. The organization accepts international volunteers for various short- and long-term projects. In addition, visitors and tourists are encouraged to drop off much-needed school supplies for students. Be sure to contact the DREAM office before visiting. *571-0497; info@dominicandream.org; www.dominicandream.org*

⬛ Cabarete Coffee Company (CCC)

A founder of the DREAM Project launched CCC in 2010, hoping to fill the growing niche of environmentally conscious food services and outdoor activities. CCC caters to the responsible tourist, offering full-day coffee (US$100) and cacao (US$75) tours into the mountains. Beyond exploring the intricacies of planting, harvesting, and processing of both crops, the tours also include meals and transport. The cacao tour is local, taking place in the mountains by Cabarete, while the coffee option removes tourists to the Jarabacoa-area farm of Julia Alvarez, author of *In the Time of the Butterflies*. While the tours are pricey for day trips, if you are on a time crunch, they are a good way to see a slice of traditional countryside agricultural life. Besides the travel business, CCC also serves up some good coffee, along with breakfast, sandwiches, juice, and smoothies in a small but colorful and low-key dining space. CCC began Haitian relief efforts after the earthquake, offers internships to local youth, and partners with other non-profits like the Mariposa Foundation, a girls' empowerment organization. *C/ Principal; 571-0919; info@cabaretecoffeecompany.com; www.cabaretecoffeecompany.com*

Iguana Mama

Of the many tour companies in this country, Iguana Mama is one of the best. It offers an impressive amount of services, tours, guides, and opportunities to see the country, especially for those who do not speak Spanish or are short on time. Iguana Mama is well worth a look when in Cabarete, if only to see the many customizable adventure possibilities. The eco-friendly offerings range from mountain biking to diving to whitewater rafting, and allow visits to part of the Dominican Republic impossible to see poolside. Rates run from US$50 to US$500 per person, depending on the duration of the activity. *C/ Principal, across from Scotiabank; 571-0908/0228; info@iguanamama.com; 8am-6pm daily*

Kiteboarding

Quite the sight from happy hour on the beach, the brightly colored kites of boarders across the bay from Cabarete Beach contrast with the deep blue color of the Caribbean waters. Kiteboarding, almost unheard of 15 years ago, is quickly gaining interest and popularity. Conditions at Cabarete are near perfect during

The North Coast

almost the entire year for kiteboarding. Mornings are quieter, better for beginners, and strong, consistent winds emerge around midday and last through dusk. The summers are known for flat water and good wind, while the winter has some higher waves, but still dependable wind. The Kiteboarding World Cup has utilized Cabarete's superlative conditions since 2001, holding weeklong events and competitions for up to $40,000 in prizes. Kiteboarding is centered on Kit Beach, two kilometers west of Cabarete, with the perfect combination of natural conditions for boarding. Bozo beach, between Kit Beach and Cabarete Beach, is also a kitesurfing hotspot; the World Cup has held events there. At least a half dozen agencies offer lessons, courses, and other opportunities for neophyte and professional kiteboarders. *www.cabaretekiteboarding.com*

Kite Excite

Learn how to kiteboard with the original kiteboarding school in Cabarete, consistently regarded as one of the best in lessons and tours. Lessons include eight hours of training over two or three days. Kite Excite uses video training and radio communication as part of instruction: students are filmed while boarding, and the footage is used as part of instruction. Students and teacher are always in contact during the lesson through radio communication inside the helmets. While there, take a peek at the ocean from the sparkling second-story glass-encased observation deck, with unobstructed views of the beach. Kite Excite also gives stand-up paddleboarding lessons, the newest aquatic activity craze. Prices vary based on activity and length of time. *Located at Kitexcite Kite & Surf Center at the western entrance of Cabarete; Stefan (manager) 829-962-4556; www.kitebeachccamp.com*

No Work Team (NWT)

Three happy, friendly Italians founded No Work Team, named for their collective life philosophy. They started a small ocean sports and t-shirt company, which now has ten branches across Europe and the Caribbean. In Cabarete, NWT offers more than 20 options of surfing and kiting group and private lessons, as well as a kiting camp. Rentals are reasonable priced, and everything includes a convenient shuttle back and forth from the office in Cabarete to Playa Encuentro, where the waves are made for water sports. In Playa Bozo, NWT runs the Big Air Kite School. Accommodations can also be arranged. *Bozo Beach Kite Club; 571-0285; 866-1754; info@noworkteamcabarete.com; www.noworkteamcabarete.com*

Windsurfing

Windsurfing appeared in Cabarete in the 1980s as the sport began to experience international growth. The beaches around Cabarete offer that rare environment perfect for windsurfing: good winds and calm surf. Windsurfing season runs from December through April, when waves are the best, and again from June through September, with placid waters. May, October, and November are more variable, but sailors of all levels can find a place in Cabarete, because conditions in the morning are light and quiet, important for beginners to gain traction. By noon, winds begin to pick up and gain steam throughout the afternoon until sunset – perfect for advanced sailing and performing tricks in the waves. Interest in the sport and Cabarete's ideal situation led organizers to hold the Windsurfing World Cup five times in Cabarete between 1988 and 1997. Cabarete Race Week, an international competition in several classes, was held annually in the first half of the 2000s. Various companies offer windsurfing rentals and lessons.

Surfing

While there are more famous destinations for surfing, the Dominican Republic manages to hold its own in a few key locations, offering warm water and consistent breaks. One of the best surf spots in the Caribbean is located just outside of Cabarete at **Playa Encuentro** (p204). Perhaps not as cutting-edge as its sister sports kiteboarding or windsurfing, surfing is less complicated, more accessible, more economical, and no less thrilling. Cabarete surfing is also best practiced from early morning until early afternoon, when breaks are prime. Wave heights run from 0.5 to 1.5 meters, but can reach at least 3 meters, especially if there is a tropical storm out to sea.

Surfing season is during the winter, from November through April, but summer can also produce very ride-able breaks. Though Encuentro is the most popular surfing beach around Cabarete, there are various isolated and more challenging spots nearby, including beach breaks and reef breaks, both west and east of Cabarete. Bozo beach, at Cabarete, can have some good waves during the winter, as well as two swells just to the east of Playa Grande, near Río San Juan.

> **Surfing 321** Surfing 321 is one of the larger and better-known surf outfits in Cabarete. The multilingual staff speaks English, Spanish, German, French, and Russian. Surfing 321 offer many deals and options for all levels of surfers, including rentals, lessons, trips, and the newfangled stand-up paddleboarding. Lessons start at US$45 per day and rentals at US$20; there are also deals for longer usage, as well as a kids' camp. Trips are about US$100, including one that takes surfers to five different beaches along the north coast. Booking online is recommended. *Located at the entrance to the Coconut Palm Resort, continue to the beach and find the TakeOff School; 963-7873; 321takeoff@gmail.com*

> **Pauhana Surfing** Pauhana is another reputable option for surf lessons located on Playa Encuentro. Rates for lessons run from US$45 for a day to US$225 for a week. *902-1212; www.pauhanasurfing.com; surfpauhana@gmail.com*

Monumento Historico El Choco, Laguna Cabarete

Once a cave, always a cave, even if someone decides to drop a nightclub inside of it. The government rescued this cavern from drunken revelers, and turned the surrounding area, including three other caves and a freshwater lagoon, into a national park. Remnants of the club and outdoor bar still remain, but otherwise nature as well as reforestation efforts by the park service and tour operator have returned the area to its original natural splendor. Three tours are available for RD$550 each: horseback riding through the forest; boating to the lagoon; or hiking to the four caves open to the public, including La Cueva de Vudú, where visitors can take a dip in the chilly underground waters. *Located 1 kilometer from the entrance to La Callejón de la Loma when entering Cabarete, turn-off from main road near the Tigermart; Luis (tour guide): 829-201-4363, National Park: 571-0609*

Monkey Jungle

Monkey Jungle is an adventure outfit spread out in the forested foothills above the sea. Swing over for its famous zip line, one of the few in the country. Gliders are provided with all necessary safety features on the course, which runs up and down the hillsides, and a new line that soars through a cave. Intriguingly, transplanted monkeys do actually live here, even though they are not endemic to the country. They join several other tropical creatures in a separate park, who might cast a confused eye at humans flying through the air. All proceeds are donated to the on-site medical clinic, which offers volunteer opportunities. There is also a bar and gift shop for those looking for liquid souvenirs. The entrance is located on a small lane that turns south off of Highway 5, 10 kilometers west of Cabarete (by the Coastal gas station). *Luna Tours and Iguana Mama offer tours here, including transport from Cabarete for US$86; Zip line is RD$2000 adults, RD$1000 children; Monkey Jungle Park fee is RD$700 adults, RD$500 children; 829-649-4555; ritzenchuck@gmail.com; monkeyjungledr.com; daily 9:30am-5pm*

Blue Moon

Blue Moon is just a short drive from the beach, but more of a lush retreat than party center. This retreat center is a peaceful oasis in the northern hills, affording occasional views of the mountains and sea. The property is green and well tended, with a generous dining space, pool, patio, kitchen, bar, and lounge areas. The evening meal, diverse and decadent, is the highlight – an Indian-Caribbean affair served on banana leaves, eaten lounging on plush cushions. A large breakfast is included with the price. *US$40-60 per cabana; In a private vehicle from Cabarete, turn right at the intersection of Sabaneta de Yásica, heading south for 6 kilometers over the bridge in Los Brazos. The entrance to Blue Moon is on the left. If coming by public transport, take a guagua to the Sabaneta intersection. Here, catch another guagua headed towards Jamao al Norte, and disembark at the entrance to Blue Moon, a five-minute walk off the highway up a short hill. Must book prior to arrival. 757-0614, ask for Eneyda; info@bluemoonretreat.net*

Playa Encuentro

Encuentro means meeting or find, and this isolated beach is certainly a gem of a find, bringing together man, his board, and the surf. Playa Encuentro is one of the most highly regarded beaches for surfing, both on the island and worldwide. With five distinct breaks that vary by season, time of day, and atmospheric conditions, Playa Encuentro attracts professional and amateurs from all over the globe to test their mettle battling the classic Caribbean waves. There are also various levels of competitions that take place at the beach throughout the year. Several surf rental and lesson shacks are set up on the beach, so you don't have to bring your own board on the plane. This beach is not great for swimming, as the bottom is lined with sharp coral. Make sure to wear water shoes and a rash guard while surfing, usually provided by the surf shack. It is best to arrive early in the morning, as the breaks are best before noon – after which a nap on the beach or a cold drink (or both) are in order. *Less than 5 kilometers west of Cabarete, accessible by catching a moto or public transport. The entrance to the beach is by the Coconut Palms resort.*

Río San Juan

Farther down the coast lies Río San Juan, a universe apart from the rest of the high-energy north coast cities. Quiet and friendly, the town feels more like it should be in the middle of farming country, with agriculture still a large part of the economy, affording a welcome reprieve from the buzz of tourism. Yet Río San Juan is still worth its salt: the small, compact town sits just a quick ride from some of the most stunning beaches in the country. The town also hosts a unique Carnaval celebration, taking cues from its maritime location. Río San Juan is a perfect place to spend a couple nights as a base to explore these beaches and relax in a welcoming, unpretentious community. Find most business on Calle Duarte, which runs parallel to the highway.

TRANSPORT

Caribe Tours

The Caribe Tours (589-2644) stop is on the highway, between C/ Duarte and C/ Nelson Antonio López.

To Santo Domingo: RD$330; 6:30am, 7:15am, 8am, 9:30am, 1pm, 2pm, 3:30pm, 4pm; 4hrs

To Nagua: RD$100; 6:30am, 7:30am, 9:30am, 2pm, 3:30pm; 1.5hrs

Guaguas

Smaller *guaguas* ply the coastal route both east (to places like Playa Grande and Cabrera) and west (to Cabarete and Sosúa). They leave from either side of C/ Duarte when it crosses the highway; it is also possible to flag down a passing *guagua* without going to the stop. They depart with frequency from 6am to 6pm. Note that several routes run by, each with different end points, so be clear as to your destination.

Taxi

The taxi stand is at C/ Duarte by C/ Dr. Virgílio García. Though the town is small, taxis may be useful for a trip to the beach or other local destinations, and especially for arranging pickup at the end of the day.

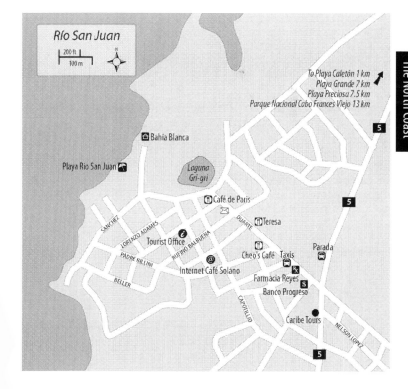

INFO

Find **Farmacia Reyes** on C/ Luperón by C/ Duarte and **Solano Internet Café** at C/ 30 de Marzo and C/ 16 de Agosto. The **Post Office** is located at C/ Duarte and C/ Rufino Balbuena. There is one ATM in Río San Juan, a **Banco Progreso** at C/ Alvarado and C/ Duarte. The **Tourist Office**, variably reliable, is on C/ Mella and C/ 16 de Agosto, open 9am-2pm and 2pm-5pm Monday to Friday (589-2831).

SLEEP

Hotel Bahía Blanca Set above the Caribbean is Hotel Bahóa Blanca, a stately hotel with a tiered façade rising like a bluff over the sea. It has 30 spacious and comfortable rooms, a restaurant and open-air verandas overlooking the water on each floor with whitewashed spiraled staircases leading to each level. The owner is a pleasant woman who speaks English, and the hotel isn't often full, so it pays to ask for a seaside room. The downstairs rooms are a little damp, but are inches from the water – perfect for those who like to awaken to the sound of the surf. Reception is behind the veranda, with a commanding view of the ocean beyond. *RD$450; end of C/ Gaston F. Deligne; 589-2562*

EAT

Cheo's Café Cheo's serves quite a broad menu for an unassuming Dominican-style eatery, good for travelers tired of rice and beans. Modestly decorated and designed, it nevertheless fulfills a need for reasonably priced lunch and dinner. *RD$200-450; 6 C/ Padre Billini; 589-2377*

Restaurante and Repostería Teresa Teresa's food is what quality seaside Dominican food should taste like, with a cheap *plato del día* and other coastal specialties like fish stewed in coconut sauce. Stop by for breakfast or dessert and nosh on delicious pastries and other toothsome baked goods. *RD$100-250; C/ Duarte*

Café de Paris Though not quite like munching on a baguette on the Champs-Elysées, when eating here, it is clear that the French owner of this little spot made an effort to bring a touch of Parisian sensibility to his adopted corner of the DR. The café's breezy terrace overlooks the lagoon, where diners can enjoy dinner, beer, and wine with the view. *RD$200-400; C/ Sánchez at C/ Duarte*

DO

Right in the middle of town is Laguna Gri-gri, a declining mangrove swamp, overpowered by people and pollution. It is still worth a look, however, to catch a glimpse of its natural beauty and see firsthand the consequences of unsustainable tourism. Once brimming with wildlife and trees dripping in green, locals decided to provide unofficial boat tours of Gri-gri. As tours increased, so did pollution, and there seems to be little effort at constraining growth. If unregulated boating continues, the lake could become uninhabitable.

There are opportunities to take a guided boat ride through the lagoon and its mangrove swamp, casting glances at egrets and the occasional crocodile. Ask at your hotel for close companies, or walk up to the southern part of the lagoon, where the boaters hang out, waiting to take people through the dark, mossy waters.

BEACHES

Playa Río San Juan

Small municipal beaches rarely impress, and the one here is no exception, though at least this one is swimmable. Located on the western side of Hotel Bahía Blanca, the gray-sanded beach isn't terribly long or pretty. Still, the water is inviting, and as it is a stone's throw from the hotel – well-positioned for relaxing morning, evening, and postprandial dips.

Playa Caletón

A quick two kilometers east of Río San Juan, Playa Caletón's ochre sand is nestled in a protective cove. The calm and tidy surf is perfect for both children and a lazy ocean swim. This beach is something of a hidden gem, as few foreign tourists manage to visit. On Sunday, the beach transforms from quiet to festive, as families from nearby communities bring food, drinks and work off some tropical energy. Just to the east, notice several sculptures made of white plaster peering out from their black-rock perch, as well as another figure scaling the rock in the middle of the cove. There is also plenty of shade potential and perfect trees for climbing. Caletón is also known for the quality of its snorkeling because of the teeming life in the shallow seabed. The turnoff for the beach is a little hard to see; look out for a small sign across from an open-air restaurant. Boat tours from Río San Juan also stop here. *The guagua ride from Río San Juan is RD$15; to return to town, just stand on the highway and flag down the bus.*

Playa Grande

If there were ever a destination beach, Playa Grande would be it. Consistently rated in the top five beaches of the country, this beach stands apart from its formidable competitors. The expanse of sand is wide, deep, and visually stunning, and though just a short drive from Río San Juan, has a distinct feeling of isolation. Rocky cliffs on either side of the beach set it square against the sea: palm trees behind, the sea up front and buffeted by a constant tropical breeze, the four kilometers of sand and sea make Playa Grande a must-visit. Though it is, in fact, a large beach, it may have received its name because of the deceivingly quiet waves that chomp at its shores. While some days the teal sea is placid, more often than not, the waters erupt into hidden, body-tossing riptides and unseen currents. For this reason, while we do recommend a dip, exercise caution and swim with a buddy.

On the drier side of things, tin-roofed food shacks do a fine send-up of classic Dominican beach food (and cold beer) on plastic tables. Vendors occasionally come by offering massages and cheap jewelry but for the most part, Playa Grande is very quiet. The surrounding area is being developed, as evidenced in the golf course with a view that sits on the hills to the west of the beach. Now, however, Playa Grande shines in isolated splendor. From Río San Juan, catch any of the *guaguas* heading east (RD$25), and make sure to let the driver know you're heading to the beach, as it requires a small detour. To return from the beach, you may have to walk a bit to the main road to catch a passing bus.

Playa Preciosa

Just off to the east of Playa Grande is Playa Preciosa. This bit of sand and rock is much smaller and less frequently visited. Preciosa's waves have more consistent and higher breaks, making it a hit with surfers. It lacks the amenities of Playa Grande, but the short cliffs hewing to the sea and surf give the beach an untamed feel. Because of its more isolated nature, petty theft has become an unfortunate occurrence, so visit with caution and never alone.

Parque Nacional Cabo Frances Viejo

This tiny national park stands tall with its lighthouses that lord over a rocky promontory jutting into the Atlantic Ocean – offering expansive, panoramic views of green and blue. A stone path from the highway leads directly to the lighthouses, another curves right down to the beach of Playa El Bretón. The park, within a humid subtropical forest, was established in 1974 and is poorly maintained; there is a suggested, but not required entrance fee. The lighthouses, one of which is more than a century old, no longer serve their original purpose, but their presence atop the heights of the cliff is monumental. Ruins of an older lighthouse speak to the vastness of the waters and treacherousness of the sea. The park is about four kilometers west of Cabrera, before reaching the small town of Abreu. It is possible to camp in the park, but you must check with a park employee first and the station. The park guards, when around, are friendly and happy to give a tour or answer questions; ask especially about visiting the cave by the beach. Take a *guagua* here along the coastal highway from Cabrera or Río San Juan.

Playa El Bretón

Set at the base of Cabo Frances Viejo, El Bretón provides the quiet charm and isolated beauty of a golden-sand tropical beach, this time buffeted by rocky white cliffs that meet the sea. There is a nearby shipwreck and fanciful fish colonies, making it a good spot for snorkeling. The cacophony of fish shacks and car speakers are absent here – all that can be heard is the pounding of the surf.

Cabrera

Nestled at the northeastern tip of the island, Cabrera is the north coast's tranquil take on Punta Cana. Luxury resorts and villas touting exquisitely designed interiors abound on the beachfront and hills surrounding Cabrera, and many Europeans make Cabrera their permanent home. The large expat population means that many foreign products are available here that are unavailable elsewhere, but prices are also generally higher. Cabrera therefore has a slightly upscale and Continental vibe, but amenities are thin unless staying at one of the grand villas dominating the landscape among coconut palms. The town is a great launching point for Cabo Frances Viejo, and the various beaches running down the shore on either side of Cabrera are as beautiful and diverse as they are numerous.

TRANSPORT

Caribe Tours (589-*7212)* is located on C/ Lorenzo Alvarez.

> **To Santo Domingo**: RD$330; 7am, 7:45am, 8:30am, 10:30am, 1:30pm, 2:30pm, 4pm, 4:30pm; 4hrs

> **To Nagua:** RD$50; 6:30am, 7:30am, 9:30am, 2pm, 3pm; 90min

> **To Río San Juan:** RD$50; 7:30am, 9am, 1pm, 2pm, 3pm; 30min

Local Transport
As with the entire North Coast, travel between Cabrera and the nearby cities and beaches is very easy: Simply flag down a *guagua* on the highway at the edge of town to go west (toward Río San Juan) or east (toward Nagua).

DO

Orchid Bay Beach
South of Cabrera and just to the north of the private driveway for the Orchid Bay housing development is a public dirt road that serves as the entrance to the beach. After about a ten-minute walk, the path passes the Orchid Bay guard station; just say that you're off to swim and the guards will let you by. A short sidewalk and some steep steps lead down to this pretty and quiet length of surf. While swimming may not be the best here – craggy rock and coral lurk just below the water's surface –these conditions do make for optimal snorkeling. The beach is very safe, as the aforementioned guards routinely patrol the area, and you'll never see the crowds or aggressive vendors that populate other beaches. The *guagua* ride from Cabrera shouldn't be more than RD$15.

Playa Diamante
Playa Diamante rises almost imperceptibly from the sea, at the base of a small, rectangular inlet. The vibrantly turquoise waters are placid and shallow, allowing bathers to wade far toward the cove's mouth without the water rising above the waist. Diamante's unique formation has yet to draw large crowds; it still provides a quiet and pleasant seaside afternoon.

La Entrada
La Entrada is the local's local beach. Unlike the more isolated area beaches, there is a Dominican village right on the water's edge here. The dark sand stretches for more than two kilometers, and the water can kick up some quality waves. Besides the allure of being absolutely the only foreigner here, a small river empties into the sea at the center of the beach. Though some worrisome locals say that the stream is a bit dirty, the only time it is unadvisable to swim in it is after a rainstorm. Jumping between the river's cooler, fresh water and the warmer, salty ocean is a unique delight possible at only a couple other spots on the island. Be wary of the bridge that crosses the river, as the river is too shallow to jump into from that height, even if you might see locals doing so. Because it is astride a village (also called La Entrada), there are various *colmados* and cafés at which to find food and drink for a Dominican picnic. This also means the beach can get crowded on weekends and holidays, especially during Semana Santa. To get here, catch a *guagua* south from Cabrera or north from Nagua (RD$50), and ask to be let off at La Entrada. Walk downhill and east directly through the community, soon arriving at the beach.

Laguna Du-Du
Unconventionally named, Laguna Du-Du is a breathtaking freshwater lagoon in an enormous sinkhole. Its neon blue waters reflect the steep, rocky cliffs that rise high above the water. About 40 minutes from Nagua, it works as a fun stop in between there and the north coast towns. The lagoon is so deep that it is possible to scuba dive if you happen to truck around equipment. There is a small visitor's center and gazebo, but otherwise, the park is devoid of people or amenities. From the visitor's

center, take the set of wooden stairs down to the lake and find a rope swing for your enjoyment. The daring sort may try to leap into the lake from the cliffs above, a relatively safe activity since the water is so deep. There is a typical Dominican lunchery on the highway just south of Du-Du, serving a quality midday special of fried chicken, rice, beans, and salad. It is easily accessible via local *guagua* from Cabrera (RD$60) or Nagua (RD$50). *Entrance fee RD$50*

Nagua

Nagua is the easternmost city in the Cibao, where the valley meets the sea in unspectacular fashion. The town serves as both an agricultural trading center, based mostly on rice and cacao production, and as a gateway to the exotic beaches of Samaná and the north coast. At just below sea level, Nagua is hot, dusty, gritty, and not terribly pretty. Though the city isn't often highly regarded, its inhabitants are lively, and proud practitioners (some say inventors) of *merengue típico*, an energetic, accordion-spiced flavor of the national dance music. Nagua's mantra, pasted on billboards outside the city, is *"Entra si quieres y sal si puedes,"* which translates as "come if you want, and leave if you can." Though perhaps slightly misleading, it displays a unique sense of humor – and pride – found among the Naguenses.

There isn't much to do in Nagua, though as of publication, there was an ongoing *malecón* construction project in hopes of bringing in more tourism. A block from the water is Parque Duarte, for what could pass as a downtown. The city is devoid of a swimming beach, but along the coast both north and south are several strategic sand locations, ranging from satisfactory to sublime. It is nearly impossible to get to Samaná without passing through the town of Nagua, even if it offers little to the visitor. If here on a Monday, however, La Poza de Bojolo is an exciting diversion (see p211).

TRANSPORT

Caribe Tours is at 76 C/ Duarte.

To Santo Domingo: RD$320; 7:30am, 8am, 8:15am, 9am, 10am, 10:30am, 2pm, 3pm, 4pm, 4:30pm, 5pm; 3hr

To Río San Juan/Cabrera: RD$100/RD$50; 7:30am, 9am, 1pm, 2pm, 3:30pm; 2hrs/90 min

Guaguas

To San Francisco de Macorís: RD$50 in back, RD$100 in the cab; 7am-6pm; 75min; Av. María Trinidad Sánchez at Parque María Trinidad Sánchez

To Samaná: RD$100; 7am-6pm; 1.5hrs; C/ Julio Lample by the cemetery

EAT

There are a number of options right around Parque Duarte. One of the best is **Nicol's**, rustling up down-home saucy beans, starchy rice, and shimmering fried plantains. *RD$100-250; C/ Sánchez at C/ Emilión Conde*

SLEEP

It isn't recommended to stay in Nagua, as there are much more pleasant options in Samaná and the north coast that aren't too far away. If you must, look into **Aparta Central** at C/ Mella and C/ Emilio Conde, at RD$500 per night.

Matancitas

Southeast of Nagua is the village of Matancitas, named for an earlier village called Matanza that was devastated by flooding after a 1946 earthquake. The beach resembles a wide, gray rainbow of sand, dotted with several small thatched-palm stands to place drinks and hang towels. The village itself has some exciting nightlife for a small town, especially Sunday evenings at the Parque Viejo, where a merengue típico group plays until late. Take the "Ruta B" car (RD$15), or a *motoconcho* (RD$30).

DO

Playa Los Gringos

There are few actual gringos to be seen at this beach in Matancitas. Its dark, fine sand is patronized almost exclusively by locals, who enjoy the beach's cleanliness and tidy waves – important for the area children who spend afternoons and weekends on the beach. Don't miss the perennial beachside lunchtime specialty, fried fresh fish.

La Poza de Bojolo

Beyond Los Gringos, La Poza de Bojolo is another popular local hangout, and can get packed on the weekends as families and couples stroll and swim at the shore. The beach here is a bit narrower, but dotted with leaning coconut palms. On Monday nights, the whitewashed gazebo at the beach explodes with vigor as a live merengue típico band plays from 5pm until at least 9pm. This is not your mother's beachside bandstand: patrons come dressed in their shiny, Monday best, ready to sweat and sway to the energetic beats of music in the salty, sandy air. Drinks are bracing, making dancing easier, but leave room for the freshly caught, and even more freshly cooked, fish; head on back behind the stage to the kitchen and pick out dinner yourself, waiting patiently in waist-high ice chests. Take a "Ruta B" car from Nagua at RD$15 or the *Expreso* Nagua bus from the capital. As transport stops at sundown, arrange a ride home with a taxi or one of the *motoconchistas* who lounge at the gazebo.

The North Coast

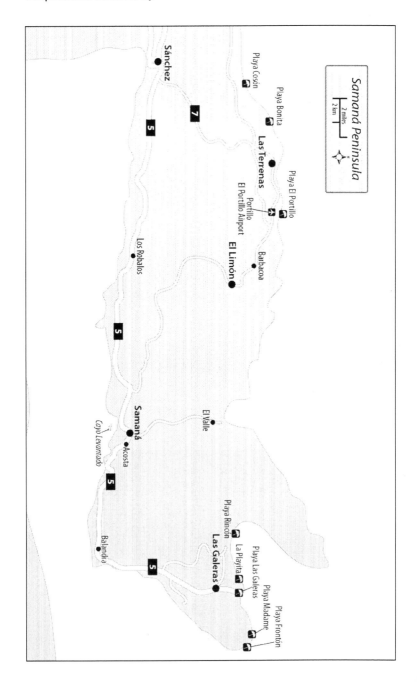

Samaná Peninsula

Like a lobster claw reaching out into tropical waters, the Samaná Peninsula beckons visitors to its isolated shores and emerald hills. Once a separate island cut off from Dominican mainland, Samaná has retained a unique and quirky nature.

Though Columbus passed by the Samaná coast on his second voyage, European presence here was sparse and irregular during the first two centuries of colonialism. Only a handful of runaway Taínos and slaves, as well as English and French pirates and adventurers, ventured into this wild land.

The first official Spanish town on the peninsula was not established until the middle of the 18th century, when the crown put down a fort in what is now the city of Samaná. During the short French occupation of the Spanish side of the island, French authorities settled a few subjects on the peninsula. Later, during Haiti's 22-year occupation of the Dominican Republic, the Haitian government convinced hundreds of freed slaves from Philadelphia to populate the region. Spain, too, coveted the Samaná space: During its reconquest of the Dominican Republic, Spain settled several families in and around the city of Samaná, and built up its military presence in the bay. Until recently, descendants of all of these far-flung populations spoke a mix of English, French, and Spanish, giving the area a distinct melting pot flavor.

Samaná is still thinly populated, but full of a certain mystique not present in the rest of the country. A culinary tour of the peninsula reflects the region's diverse inhabitants, where pizza Margherita or *pain au chocolat* is as common as *la bandera dominicana*. Its residents have been able to maintain a laid-back, independent spirit, seen in the families gathered on stunning virgin beaches, the multiple generations of fisherman in sun-bleached boats looking for dinner, and the all-hours, Euro-influenced nightlife of Las Terrenas.

A well-rounded visit to Samaná must include a hike to the crashing falls at El Salto de Limón, watching the majestic humpbacks in Samaná Bay, and picking up a catch of fresh fish while enjoying the view on Playa Rincón or Playa Cosón. Regardless of where you go, you'll surely leave with a piece of the distinct Samaná spirit.

Sánchez

Once a wealthy, flourishing port, Sánchez now serves primarily as a transit point between Las Terrenas and Samaná to towns on the North Coast. Signs of its golden era can be seen in the deteriorating Victorian-style wooden houses and the rusted train tracks that once connected the peninsula to the central Cibao. The brainchild of Allen H. Crosby, the train was meant to extend from Samaná and Santiago for the transport and export of commercial and agricultural goods from the Cibao. Upon completion in 1888, however, the ties and tresses only extended from Sánchez to La Vega. An international port developed around this trade, contributing to the tremendous economic and political growth that the region experienced in the late 19th and early 20th century. Sánchez became a cosmopolitan center, full of immigrants from across Europe and the Middle East. Named for founding father Francisco del Rosario Sánchez, it represented a bright future for the country at the turn of the century.

This Sánchez, however, was not meant to be. The train ceased operations in 1971, running its last trip to the Cibao in the wake of an economic downturn from which Sánchez has yet to recover. The city, far and lacking infrastructural development, could not compete with the accessibility and privileged location of Puerto Plata, and the decline of the railroad as an economical mode of transport. Even as the rest of Samaná has flourished over the past two decades as a haven for beach-seeking tourists, Sánchez missed the boat. Today, the town subsists on agriculture and fishing.

TRANSPORT

The *parada* in Sánchez for **Caribe Tours** (552-7434) is located on the Sánchez-Samaná highway.

Sánchez to Santo Domingo: RD$300; 7am, 8am, 9am, 10am, 1pm, 2pm, 3pm, 4pm; 2hrs

Santo Domingo to Sánchez: RD$300; 7am, 8am, 9:30am, 10am, 1:30am, 2:30pm, 4pm, 4:30pm; 2hrs

Guaguas
Guaguas for Sánchez leave Santo Domingo from Parque Enriquillo.

To Santo Domingo: RD$250; 6am-5:30pm; 2hrs; *guaguas* originating in Samaná pass through Sánchez along the Sánchez–Samaná highway.

From Santo Domingo: RD$250; 6am-5:30pm; 2hrs; ASOTRAPUSA *guaguas* leave from 129 C/ Barahona near Parque Enriquillo across from Plaza Lama's parking lot.

To Samaná: RD$60; 1 hr; every 15-30min 6am-5:30pm; from the stop on C/ Duarte.

To Las Terrenas: RD$60; every 15-30min 7am-5pm; 45min *Guaguas* leave from the entrance to Las Terrenas along the Sánchez-Samaná Highway. Taxi drivers charge RD$800-1000 for a private vehicle, but unless traveling with a lot of luggage or a group, opt for the *guagua*.

INFO

Medical Attention
Both **Farmacia Altagracia** (#44; 552-7204) and **Farmacia Duarte** (#21; 552-7298) are located on C/ Duarte. For emergencies, the public **Hospital Dr. Alberto Gautreux** (552-7130) offers 24-hour medical attention or there are a number of private clinics such as the **Centro Médico Integral La Gloria** at 15 C/ Prolongación de Duarte (552-7091).

Banks
There is a **BanReservas** at 5 C/ Duarte (552-7402). To change money, **Agente de Remesas Vimenca** is at 7 Carretera Sánchez-Sánta Barbara (552-7819).

Police
The **Policía Nacional** is located at 60 C/ Duarte (552-7255).

Gas
There is a **Texaco gas station** at the fork for Las Terrenas.

Grocery Stores
Supermercado Popular is located on C/ Independencia (552-7236).

EAT

There are two Dominican restaurants located on the main highway that feature a variety of *criollo* favorites, both serving fresh fish caught by Sánchez's fishermen. **El Suave** is located in front of the high school and **Tropical Coco** is next to the Las Terrenas bus stop.

SLEEP

Due to Sánchez's proximity to lovely and reasonably priced hotels around the peninsula, there is little reason to stay in Sánchez, but in a pinch, try **Hotel Patria** (RD$600-700; 24 C/ Santomé; 552-7371/7070; Amenities: fan, TV, parking).

DO

Calle Libertad
Stroll down Calle Libertad to admire what remains of the grand wooden Victorian homes that may prompt nostalgia for Sánchez's heyday. The stately chapel, commissioned in 1924 by Trina de Moya, the wife of Dominican President Horacio Vázquez, is one of the few well-maintained examples of this style of architecture.

BEACHES

The beach in Sánchez is often dirty and polluted. Except for the fisherman, whose job requires such proximity, even locals tend to avoid it.

Samaná (Santa Bárbara de Samaná)

Samaná is a small waterfront town with big ambitions. Flanked by steep mountains, Samaná has grown from a lonesome outpost on the shimmering Samaná Bay into a center for tourism and commerce, spreading its winding streets out into the hills above. Prior to 1756, when the Spanish crown decided to establish a settlement here with families from the Canary Islands, the entire peninsula ran ungoverned, populated by those outside the control of colonial authorities. The city, formally called Santa Bárbara de Samaná, was named for the Queen of Spain at the time of its founding.

The main drag of Samaná runs parallel to the water, with a beautiful *malecón* (promenade walk) wrapping around the harbor. Samaná's generally tranquil nature is turned on its head during whale-watching time in early spring. Visitors flock to the city on buses and cruise ships to witness the majesty of the whales during their breeding and feeding season in Samaná Bay.

Samaná Peninsula

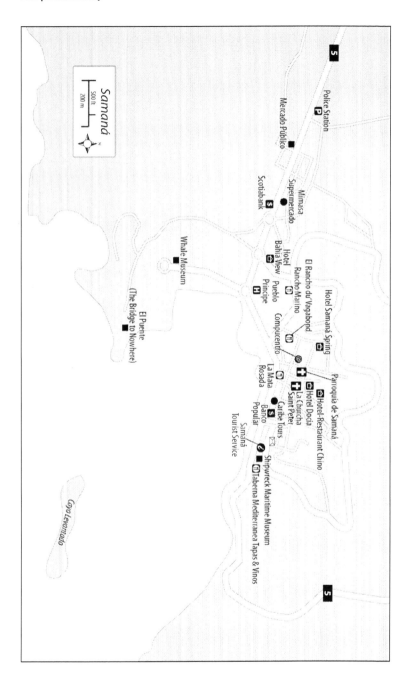

Samaná

500 ft
200 m

N

Police Station

Mercado Público

Mimasa
Supermercado

Scotiabank

Whale Museum

El Puente
(The Bridge to Nowhere)

Hotel
Bahía View

El Rancho du Vagabond
Rancho Marina

Pueblo
Príncipe

Hotel Samaná Spring

Compucentro

Parroquia de Samaná

Hotel-Restaurant Chino

Hotel Docía

La Chuncha
Saint Peter

La Mata
Rosada

Caribe Tours

Banco
Popular

Samaná
Tourist Service

Shipwreck Maritime Museum

Taberna Mediterranea Tapas & Vinos

Cayo Levantado

TRANSPORT

The **Caribe Tours** stop is located on Av. El Malecón facing the port, next to the ice cream shop (538-2229).

To **Santo Domingo**: RD$300; 8am, 9am, 10am, 1pm, 2pm, 3pm, 4pm; 3hrs

From **Santo Domingo**: RD$300; 7am, 8am, 9:30am, 10am, 1:30pm, 2:30pm, 4pm; 3hrs

ASOTRAPUSA Guaguas

From **Santo Domingo**: RD$275; 6am-5:30pm; 2.5hrs; *guaguas* leave from 129 C/ Barahona near Parque Enriquillo across from Plaza Lama's parking lot.

To **Santo Domingo**: RD$275; 6am-5:30pm; 2.5hrs; ASOTRAPUSA *guaguas* leave from the *Mercado Público*.

Guaguas

All small *guaguas* for **El Limón** (RD$80; 5am-5pm; 45min), **Sánchez** (RD$60; 5am-5pm; 45min), and **Santiago** (RD$260; 5am-3pm; 3hrs) leave from El Mercado in Samaná every 30 minutes.

Airports

El Aeropuerto International Presidente Juan Bosch (El Catey-AZS) Opened in 2006, this airport is located between Nagua and Sánchez near the junction point between the Samaná-Santo Domingo highway and the Nagua-Sánchez highway (Km 22). The airport services international flights from all over Europe, Canada, and the U.S. *338-5888; 826-4019*

Arroyo Barril Domestic Airport (DAB) This landing strip services domestic flights from Santo Domingo, Punta Cana, Santiago, El Higüero, and Barahona. *Carretera Sánchez-Samaná Km 12 in Arroyo Barril; 248-2566*

El Portillo (EPS) A small domestic airport located between Las Terrenas and El Limón, it is used primarily by business and private flights. *El Portillo, Las Terrenas-El Limón highway; aerodomep@codetel.net.do*

INFO

Medical Attention

Pueblo Principe has a doctor's office, and both **El Centro Médico Nueva Generación** as well as **El Consultorio Médico Hermanos Olea** are located on C/ Francisco del Rosario Sánchez. For pharmacies, try **Farmacia Bahía** on Av. Circumvalación (538-2236) or **Farmacia Central** on C/ Prolongación Francisco del Rosario Sánchez (538-2122).

Communication

For calls, head to **Dem Communications** on C/ Circumvalación (538-3063). For internet, head to **Compucentro** on the corner of C/ Santa Bárbara and C/ Julio Lavandier. The **Post Office** is located on C/ Prolongación Santa Bárbara (538-2378; 906-0051).

Banks

There is a **Scotiabank** at 11 C/ Francisco del Rosario Sánchez (538-3151/3154) and a **Banco Popular** near Caribe Tours on Av. La Marina and C/ Rosa Duarte. Both are open Mon-Fri 8:30am-4:30pm and Sat 9am-1pm.

Police

The **Police Station** is located on C/ Francisco Rosario Sánchez near corner of C/ del Tanque.

Gas Stations

There is a gas station about 100 meters west of Samaná on C/ Francisco de Rosario Sánchez, as well as one near Arroyo Barril (Km 12 *Carretera Sánchez-Samaná).*

Grocery Stores

Mimasa Supermercado is located at 26 Av. Francisco del Rosario Sánchez (538-2217).

TOURISM SERVICES

Both the **Secretaría de Turismo**, which is part of the government, and the **Tourism Cluster of Samaná** (538-2891), sponsored by various government organizations, have offices in Pueblo Principe. At the time of research both were rather disorganized, but by publication, could be a good spot for free maps and relatively unbiased information. **Samaná Tourist Service**, a tour agency, has informative and helpful employees always willing to assist the indecisive traveler (6 Av. La Marina; 538-2740; 538-2848).

EAT

Rancho Marino This cute little *comedor* serves up a mouth-watering *plato del día.* Pair the *berenjena guisada con queso* (stewed eggplant with cheese) with *moro*, stewed chicken, and salad. *RD$60-RD$250; 13 Av. Trinidad Sánchez; 538-2057; 829-470-1614; ranchomarino@hotmail.com*

La Mata Rosada This open-air Samaná favorite is located right on the *malecón*, specializing in French cuisine and seafood. *RD$170-1000; 5 Av. Malecón; 538-2388; lamatarosada@codetel.net.do*

El Rancho du' Vagabond Wood oven-fired pizzas and delicious pasta dishes are served in an old home's charming patio, bedecked with plants. Don't forget to peruse the South American and Italian wine list to pair with your meal. *RD$165-590; C/ Cristóbal Colón; 12-2pm and 6-11pm*

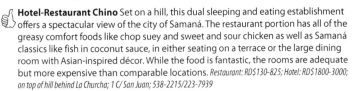 **Hotel-Restaurant Chino** Set on a hill, this dual sleeping and eating establishment offers a spectacular view of the city of Samaná. The restaurant portion has all of the greasy comfort foods like chop suey and sweet and sour chicken as well as Samaná classics like fish in coconut sauce, in either seating on a terrace or the large dining room with Asian-inspired décor. While the food is fantastic, the rooms are adequate but more expensive than comparable locations. *Restaurant: RD$130-825; Hotel: RD$1800-3000; on top of hill behind La Churcha; 1 C/ San Juan; 538-2215/223-7939*

Taberna Mediterranea Tapas & Vinos Tapas, *bocadillos* (sandwiches) and an excellent selection of wines are served in a warm, wood-paneled tavern or on the outdoor deck with a view of the bay. *RD$160-600; Av. Malecón; 829-994-3634*

SLEEP

Hotel Samaná Spring This hotel is the best budget option in town due to its spacious, clean rooms and access to a large kitchen and common area. *RD$1000-1800; C/ Cristóbal Colón; 538-2946; samanaspring@hotmail.com; Amenities: fan, A/C, TV, communal kitchen, laundry service*

Hotel Bahía View Though it no longer boasts a view of the bay due to Pueblo Principe, this brightly painted budget hotel offers clean rooms with balconies in the center of the action – though the rumble of motorcycles might make the stay less than peaceful. *RD$1000-1400; 4 C/ Circunvalación; 538-2186; dgoreyes202@hotmail.com; Amenities: A/C, fan, TV, hot water, restaurant*

Hotel Nilka Nilka is the cheapest option in town, but not necessarily the cleanest. It is, however, on a quiet street conveniently located next to Supermercado Popular. *RD$700-1200; 4 C/ Circunvalación; 538-2849; Amenities: A/C, fan, hot water, TV*

Hotel Docia With bright, tidy, but cramped rooms, Hotel Docia's crowning feature is a view of Samaná Bay from the second floor. *RD$700-1000; Located across the street from La Churcha on the corner of C/ Teodoro Chacerraux & Duarte; 538-2041; 967-2450; hanoymb@hotmail.com; www.hoteldocia.blogspot.com; Amenities: A/C, fan*

DO

Whale Watching

Every winter, from mid-January through mid-March, humpback whales travel to the warm waters of the Caribbean for calving and mating, and a few lucky ones find themselves in Samaná Bay. The male can be heard across the bay attracting his prospective mates with his call or his impressive displays of virility through breaching and creative flipper- and tail-wagging.

One of the most dependable and reasonably priced outfitters is **Whale Samaná**, owned by Canadian Kim Beddall. An animal advocate and conservationist, Kim first arrived to the DR in 1983 and then made a career of her love for these majestic creatures. Trips are conducted on vessels with VHF radio and follow important whale-watching regulations to prevent interrupting mating patterns. If no whales make an appearance during the excursion, Kim will honor tickets for a future trip. Soft drinks, crackers, and anti-nausea medication (necessary in the choppy waters outside Samaná Bay) are included. *US$50; Two trips leave daily at 9am and 1:30pm from the port of Samaná and 9:30am and 2pm from Cayo Levantado*

Patronales

The Dominican dichotomy of *Dios* and debauchery unfolds in the week leading up to December 4, the day of Samaná's patron saint, Santa Bárbara. The city offers carnival rides, food stands, concerts, and mass as requisite components of the celebration, which then sets off the Christmas holiday season.

Cayo Levantado

Known as the Bacardi island, after appearing in the eponymous rum company's ad campaign, this small island in the middle of Samaná Bay has a pristine, white sand beach, as well as a luxury hotel and restaurant. It is possible to get here with one of

The Freed American Slaves of Samaná

The Samaná Peninsula's distinctive history includes a unique chapter tying it closely with the abolitionist movement in the United States. In 1824, the newly installed Haitian authorities worked with American freed-slave groups in Philadelphia to transport hundreds of freed slaves to Samaná. Anglophone, and hailing from across the American South, they and their descendents have flourished in Samaná, and now number in the thousands. Until recently, their unique English-Spanish diction could be heard in isolated communities across the area. Today, they have nearly all assimilated into Dominican culture and society, though vestiges of their past can be seen in the popularity of English surnames, as well as cultural relics like religion, at La Churcha St. Peter, and cuisine, like the Johnny cake, a sweet, cornbread-like coconut cookie.

the many tour operators; most whale watching trips also stop here. Levantado resembles the quintessential tropical island, set amid placid, warm waters, and facing the green hills of mainland Samaná, it is often overrun with tourists on these trips. Visit early in the morning or off-season to steer clear from the crowds.

El Puente
Extending from the Gran Principe Cayacoa Resort out into the sea, connecting through two small islands, this so-called "bridge to nowhere" was part of Dominican President Balaguer's grand plan to turn Samaná into a tourism epicenter. The arches of the cement bridge mimic those found in the architecture of the buildings along the Malecón built in the 1970s as part of Balaguer's plan to cover the town in modern architecture and therefore tearing down all of the historic Victorian homes around the city. Though it provides an excellent view of the city and Samaná Bay, and is still structurally sound, the bridge has not been exquisitely maintained.

Artisans: Centro de Capacitación, Tecnología y Producción Progresando
The first lady together with Norberto Odebrecht, a construction tycoon whose water tanks and other projects dot the Samaná landscape, funded this artisan training facility. Some of the products such as the dolls and jewelry boxes made from coconut are actually quite interesting and expertly crafted. There is also a women's association that sews purses and uniforms, some of which are for Odebrecht's workers. *Av. Circunvalación; Barrio La Mezcla; 854-4427*

Whale Museum
Boasting an entire whale skeleton found in 1993, this museum is worth a look for those interested in learning more about the humpback whale migratory patterns from the East Coast of the U.S. down to the DR. Proceeds go the local NGO, Center for the Conservation and Eco-Development of Samaná Bay and its Surroundings (CEBSE), which formed in 1990 to advocate for and educate locals about environmental conservation. *US$2; located on the dirt road in the direction of the entrance to El Puente; open everyday 8am-3pm*

Samaná for Sale

As foreign powers – Haiti, France, and Spain – spent serious effort coveting and settling Samaná, so too did the United States. After the Civil War, Samaná was nearly annexed by the Dominican Republic's northern neighbor. Newly independent again after its short war with Spain, the DR was looking for both a cash infusion and protection from those aforementioned adversaries. For the US, Samaná represented a strategic Caribbean location for both commercial and military purposes, but it was also far enough from Santo Domingo that the weak state was not able to govern it well. In 1868, President Grant proposed purchasing the peninsula for US$2 million, while at the same time entering into discussions about annexing the entire island. While the latter idea never got very far, the United States Senate rejected turning Samaná into a naval base by just a few votes. The military government then leased Samaná and the bay to an American holding company for 99 years, but the deal caved after the government fell and the company folded. The U.S. government returned to discussions of establishing a base in Samaná for support during the Spanish-American War. After defeating Spain, the U.S. had much more pliable space in newly-annexed Cuba, and finally decided to build its long-awaited Caribbean base at Guantanamo Bay.

Shipwreck Maritime Museum

A small but surprisingly well-curated museum with artifacts from Le Scipion, one of the 20 gunships sent by France to assist in the American War of Independence. After a successful battle against the English in the Chesapeake Bay, the ship then headed south, ending its journey early in the rough waters of the Mona Passage onto Samaná Bay where it met its anticlimactic demise after striking a coral reef in 1782. *Entrance is US$5 for visitors or RD$100 for Dominican nationals; end of malecón towards the road to Las Galeras; open daily 10am-6pm*

Pueblo Principe

A row of Disneyesque candy-colored Victorian-style buildings, Pueblo Principe was built to please the tourists arriving on cruise ships. While a bit contrived, the complex houses a number of handy businesses such as a disco, bank, and doctor's office, all of which are clearly marked in English.

La Churcha Saint Peter

A fascinating piece of early African American history happened here, far from the American South. Freed slaves from the U.S. came to Samaná in 1824, bringing with them the African Methodist Episcopal Church and a cultural diversity whose vestiges can be seen in the English last names common around Samaná. From this movement, La Churcha Saint Peter (from the Spanglish name for a place of worship), was founded in 1899. Services are still conducted today, but only hymns continue to be sung in the original English. *Located behind Pueblo Principe; Sundays 9am-11am*

Another historic religious point of interest is the **Parroquía de Samaná**, the main Catholic Church built in 1885. Beginning in 2009, the church underwent a major facelift and so the original façade has been spackled over, but its structure is from the original design.

Las Terrenas

For decades, French and Italians have been coming to this beachside village. In 1980, a group of Europeans chartered it as a town as part of the municipality of Samaná, though rural Dominican populations had been farming and fishing in the surrounding area for decades prior. Since then, many more of these visitors have made Las Terrenas their permanent residence, giving it a distinctly European vibe, and creating a fascinating melding of cuisine and language. Less conventional cultural exchanges can be seen among older white European men and women seeking the comfort of young Dominicans. Nevertheless, Las Terrenas has the best culinary and nightlife scene on the peninsula, providing food and recreation for those who have come to enjoy the astounding 18-kilometer stretch of gorgeous beaches.

TRANSPORT

From Santo Domingo: RD$285; 8:30am, 9:30am, 11am, 1:40pm, 3pm; *parada* near Parque Enriquillo in Santo Domingo (129 C/ Barahona, across from Plaza Lama's parking lot; 687-1470)

Alternately, take a *guagua* en route to Sánchez (p213) or Samaná (p215) and ask the cobrador to leave you at "la entrada para las Terrenas" (turnoff for Las Terrenas). From there, there are multiple transit options, the best being the

RD$60 *guagua*, which leaves every 15-30 minutes for a 45-minute vertiginous ride through lush mountains that provide a stunning view of Samaná Bay. Pushy taxi drivers will try to convince tourists to pay RD$800-1000 for a private vehicle, but unless traveling with a lot of luggage or a group, opt for the *guagua*.

To Santo Domingo: RD$285; 3 morning departures between 6-12pm and 2 at 2pm and 3pm; 3hrs; *guaguas* leave across the street from Plaza Taína near the wall of murals along the beach; 240-6391/6339

To El Limón: RD$50; 7am-6pm; 30min; leave from Playa Las Terrenas near the mural-covered wall

To Samaná: Samaná is accessible either by taking a *guagua* (RD$60) to Sánchez, which leaves from the parking lot near the mural-covered wall, or from the *parada* for Sánchez at the southern exit of Las Terrenas, then hopping on a *guagua* en route for Samaná. It is also possible to take the *guagua* to El Limón, and then grab a *guagua* from there to Samaná.

Around town, try **Taxi Leo** (860-0849) or *motoconchos* will take passengers starting at RD$25. A common mode of transport around Las Terrenas is also ATVs, due to the many unpaved and narrow roads. Rental companies include **Fun Rental** (C/ Principal 240-6784/360-8771) and **Jessie Car Rental** (C/ Nuestra Señora del Carmen, near the beach; 240-6415).

INFO

Medical Attention
Centro Galeno Integral (242 C/ Duarte; 240-6817) has 24-hour emergency attention and is open during the day for consults.

Farmacia European has a large variety of medications and is located in Plaza Piattini (C/ Duarte); **Farmacia Central** on C/ Prolongación del Rosario Sánchez (538-2122) is also a safe bet.

Tourism Services
The **Secretary of Tourism** (240-6141; Mon-Fri; 8:30am-3:30pm) has its office on the second floor of Plaza Piattini on C/ Duarte and can be a good resource for free guidebooks and maps.

EAT

 La Terrasse This charming French restaurant serves luscious dishes such as langoustines with tarragon butter, or the *entrada variada*, which features an array of appetizers: fried zucchini blossoms, pâté, fish carpaccio, tuna terrine, and zucchini frittata. *RD$280-750; Pueblo de los Pescadores; 240-6730; 12pm-3pm and 7pm-11pm*

Pizza Coco Due to the high concentration of Italians in Las Terrenas, pizza is easy to come by, but this pizzeria is a cut above the rest, with a variety of wood-fired thin crust pizzas at great prices. *RD$200-400; Av. 27 de Febrero, across from Las Terrenas beach; 499-6076*

El Cayuco Restaurant Spanish favorites such as paella and gazpacho are served right on the beach at El Cayuco. The festive colors and prime location near the lively bars make it a great place to start the night. *RD$250-680; Pueblo de los Pescadores; 240-6885; Wi-Fi access*

Boulangerie Française With seating in Plaza Taína, this is a perfect spot for a breakfast croissant or an afternoon café au lait paired with a passion fruit tart or a crunchy, air-light merengue. *RD$25-100; Plaza Taína, C/ Duarte; 240-6677*

Pan de Antes This authentic French bakery's *pain au chocolat* has no rival. Be sure to try the flaky, chewy baguettes and buttery brioche. *Kanesch Business Center; 994-3282; Mon-Sat 7am-7:30pm, Sun 7am-1pm*

La Salsa El Nuevo Ritmo It is easy to get a whirlwind world tour of flavors here, as this seaside restaurant draws its influences from French, Thai, Chinese, and Italian cuisine. Try the fish in curry sauce or seafood risotto while enjoying the picture-perfect view of the beach. *RD$220-650; Pueblo de los Pescadores; 829-719-8060; 240-6805*

SLEEP

 Casa Robinson The best and one of the few budget hotels in Las Terrenas, Casa Robinson has clean and charming rooms to accommodate a single traveler or a whole family. To guarantee a cross-breeze, request a room on the second level or if traveling with a group, ask for the apartment, which is surprisingly lovely and large considering the price, not to mention it comes with a kitchenette. *22-35 Euros; 240-6496; info@casarobinson.it; www.casarobinson.it; Amenities: fan, hot water, café/bar*

Hotel y Restaurante Atlantis This whimsical whitewashed hotel gives a nod to Gaudí with its rounded fantastical roofs and walls. Under French administration for over a decade, the hotel also serves as the French consulate. The superb restaurant features elegant offerings, like shrimp served in guava honey or dorado in champagne sauce, paired with an impressive list of French wines. *RD$440-1050; Playa Bonita; 240-6111/6205; hotel.atlantis@codetel.net.do; www.atlantis-hotel.com.do*

Hotel Casa Nina Breezy rooms decorated with cheery flowers painted on the walls and bright accent pieces make for a cozy and pleasant environment, especially given that the rooms encircle a well-maintained pool just steps from your door. *RD$1500-2000; Av. 27 de Febrero across from Punta Popy; 240-5490; hotelcasanina@gmail.com; Amenities: fan, hot water, pool*

Casa Grande Hotel Restaurant Though the interior designer of Casa Grande may have ran a little too wild with his decorating techniques, the rooms are spacious and some boast ocean views. Just a few steps across a soft, grassy lawn adorned with palm trees and hammocks, is the hotel's beachfront restaurant serving up inventive fusion dishes that incorporate Asian, Dominican and Mediterranean flavors. *US$70-130; 240-6349; casagrandebeachhotel@yahoo.es; www.casagrandebeachhotel.com; Amenities: fan, hot water, restaurant/bar, breakfast included*

DO

18 Kilometers of Beaches

The main beach of **Las Terrenas** is decorated with sloping coconut trees and huts plying drinks and eats to sunbathers. The only downside to these crystalline waters and golden sand is that local vendors are persistent and plentiful, making a relaxing day at the beach a bit of a challenge. Luckily, there are plenty of other options. East of Las Terrenas and just before Playa Limón is **Playa Portillo**, an untouched stretch of beach perfect for an uninterrupted day of sunbathing and swimming. A favorite spot among local surfers and one of the most beautiful beaches on the island, **Playa Bonita** occupies a four-kilometer stretch of sand west of Las Terrenas. Without obscuring the natural surroundings, some of the more luxurious hotels in the Las Terrenas area are located on Playa Bonita. Continuing west is the virtually undeveloped **Playa Cosón**, certified as a Blue Flag Beach for its quality of water and environmental protection standards. As tourism here continues to develop, especially with the construction of the new highway from Santo Domingo, all of these beaches are set to see an increase in people and buildings.

NIGHTLIFE

Nightlife in Las Terrenas is concentrated in the tiny Pueblo de los Pescadores, where there are a handful of bars and nightclubs attracting European expats and Dominicans alike. Somehow escaping national curfew laws, establishments are open as late as 4am, which means nightlife does not start until after midnight, although bars begin service around 6pm.

Boldly decorated in black and red, **El Toro sobre el Techo** (869-7835; xaviermiral@yahoo.fr) has the look of a Spanish bohemian hangout and the feel of a disco, packed with patrons dancing to Latin Caribbean favorites. For electronic and Latin music, head to **Como Tú 'Ta** (781-7822), named for the quintessential Dominican greeting. **El Gaia Club** (240-5133/6832; www.gaiavip.com) is a musical odyssey offering three levels: the first floor features Dominican favorites like mambo and bachata, the second caters to the European expats with house and techno, and the third roof level provides a chill lounge area where high rollers gather around a bottle over ice. For more of a low-key lounge atmosphere with quirky décor, head to **El Mosquito Art Bar** (elmosquitobar@yahoo.com) for mojitos and tapas.

El Salto del Limón

Plunging down from approximately 40 meters (130 feet) in the air, the waterfall at El Limón leaves spectators speechless from the commanding crash of water and the verdant surroundings. Endemic species such as the Royal Palm, the Paradise Tree (Simarouba glauca) and the Doveplum (Coccoloba diversifolia) intermingled with introduced tropical fruit trees such as breadfruit, mango, and soursop.

Whether the journey is by foot or on horseback, the destination is worth the effort. Unless you have been before or speak Spanish to ask for directions, it's best to hike the often muddy and rocky trails with a guide. The four surrounding communities of El Limón, El Café, Arroyo Surtido, and Rancho Español have created paths to access the waterfall, creating a sustainable source of income for the local residents. The trails vary in length and incline, so it is important to discuss your athletic ability with your guide beforehand. There are a number of "tour guides" for El Salto del Limón, but the most legitimate is ◨ **Rancho Santi** (829-342-9976; limónsanti@terra.es), located on the corner of the main intersection of El Limón. Braving the trail on horseback costs RD$750, as well as a tip of about RD$100-150 for the guide. Along with tours to the waterfall, Spanish-owned Rancho Santi also offers canyoning excursions down the river and through the falls. Be sure to wear strong sandals or sneakers and mosquito repellent.

TRANSPORT

El Limón is accessible either through Samaná or Sánchez. If arriving on Caribe Tours, disembark in Samaná, and then get on a mini bus or pickup truck (RD$60) to El Limón, which leaves from *El Mercado*. Otherwise, get off at the "cruce para Las Terrenas," just past Sánchez, and hop on a minibus or pickup truck to Las Terrenas (RD$60). Ask the *cobrador* to leave you at the "parada para El Limón," located in front of the wall with murals near Las Terrenas beach. The *guagua* to El Limón is RD$50.

SLEEP

 ☑ Clave Verde Located in the village of Barbacoa between El Limón and Portillo, Clave Verde offers fully–equipped cabins perched atop a mountain and surrounded by wooded hills that provide a view of the sea in the distance. This family-owned operation has a strong dedication to environmentally-sound practices, as seen in it naturally chlorinated pool, whose pump is powered by solar panels. The modern yet cozy wood cabins range in size to accommodate a romantic getaway for two or a family vacation. *US$ 80-220; 802-1146; noemiaraujo@hotmail.com; Amenities: fan, hot water, pool, kitchen, gym*

Las Galeras

Las Galeras, sitting at the very edge of the peninsula, is a quaint beach town with little in terms of nightlife or restaurants, but it is ideal for nature lovers and those seeking to get far, far away. Las Galeras is an excellent jumping off point for some of the most breathtaking beaches that Samaná – and the island – has to offer, including Playa Rincón, Playa Frontón, and Playa Madame.

La Vieja

Along the 28 kilometer stretch that connects Samaná to Las Galeras, be sure to stop by the roadside bread stand of Albertina Miguel, known to everyone as La Vieja. Taught by her mother, La Vieja has passed down her delicious family recipes to her own daughter. Try the *coconete*, the delicious love child of bread and coconut, or el Brazo de Gitano (Gypsy's Arm), a pillowy loaf made with milk and filled with banana or guava marmalade. Her bakery, called **D'Vieja Pan Inglés**, is located on the Samaná-Las Galeras highway, in the village of Acosta, at the Cruce de Tesón.

TRANSPORT

From Santo Domingo: Take Caribe Tours to Samaná (p215).

From Samaná: RD$80; every 30mins; 7am-6pm; 1hr; from the Caribe Tours office, walk across the street (Av. El Malecón) and hail a pickup truck or minivan marked with Las Galeras. The *parada* is located at *El Mercado* up the hill, so it is also possible to catch it there, before it is full of passengers.

Guaguas also leave directly for Las Galeras from the ASOTRAPUSA *parada* near Parque Enriquillo in Santo Domingo (RD$325; four departures between 6am-5pm; 129 C/ Barahona across from Plaza Lama's parking lot; 687-1470).

To Samaná and beyond: (RD$80; 7am-5pm; 1hr; every 25min) Minivans and pickup trucks leave Las Galeras from La Playita (end of main road) to Samaná, where passengers can hop on connecting guaguas from the Caribe Tours stop or at El Mercado.

To Santo Domingo: (RD$325; 4hrs) There are also few morning and afternoon *guaguas* that leave directly for Santo Domingo from the *parada* at La Playita. Ask for departure times, as they vary widely.

Car Rental

Reyes Picardo Rent a Car also has a Western Union at its office. *Main road; 538-0240; 841-4340; 829-861-4340*

INFO

Medical Attention

They are two small clinics for emergencies, but the hours are irregular, and so it is best to head to Samaná, especially for late-night emergencies. In a pinch, head to **Las Galeras Centro Médico Asistencial** (main road; 963-1633; 910-7936). For pharmacies, **Drug Store Las Galeras** (main road; 538-0103) is located next to Las Galeras Tourist, and **Farmacia Peninsula** is next to Mini-Market Bello at the entrance of town on the main road.

Communication

Las Galeras Tourist Service (964-9555) offers internet access at the rather steep price of RD$30 per ten minutes, but also free Wi-Fi access with a purchase and a convenient money exchange.

Banks

The only bank and cash machine in town is **BanReservas** open Mon-Fri 9am-5pm on the main road.

Grocery Stores

Las Galeras has two grocery stores (generally, only one is open during the low season), **Mini-Market Bello** (538-0152), located at the entrance of town, and **Supermercado No. 1** (538-0091) located closer to the beach.

Gas

There is no gas station in Las Galeras –fill the tank before leaving Samaná. Locals also sell gasoline in Presidente bottles in front of their homes.

EAT

For a cheap eats, head to the **Pollera Pico Blanco**, which sells fried chicken with *tostones* for RD$100 or to **Comedor Rossy**, whose *plato del día* with chicken is reasonably priced.

Pizzeria Restaurant Italian-owned, this authentic thatched-roof pizzeria offers delicious thin crust pizza with a wide variety of toppings, and classic pasta dishes such as spaghetti Bolognese. *RD$200-400; Located just outside the center of Las Galeras on the highway toward Samaná; dinner only*

 Restaurant at El Cabito A member of the Slow Food movement, this restaurant offers a spectacular view while savoring house specialties like bouillabaisse, fresh fish grilled to perfection, or conch shell served with baked papaya. *RD$350-600; located in the hills east of the center of town; turn right at Plaza Lusitania and follow signs toward El Cabito; 820-2263; 829-697-9506*

 Restaurant Plaza Lusitania Using recipes passed down from her Italian grandmother, the owner makes pasta, pizza, and gelato by hand, using fresh ingredients and no preservatives. The fish and meat dishes are healthily prepared, focusing on flavor profiles that don't involve frying. Try the local seafood linguini, and be sure to save room for the chilled *zuccotto* dessert, made with Dominican rum. In Plaza Lusitania, there is also a real estate office, a home décor shop, and art gallery, as well as rooms and apartments for rent on the second floor with breakfast included. *RD$240-480; Plaza Lusitania; 538-0093; www.plazalusitania.com*

SLEEP

 Las Mariposas Part of a community development project sponsored by the Italian government, these charming, brightly painted cabins are highly recommended if traveling in a private vehicle, because they are located just outside the center of Las Galeras, and therefore a sizeable walk to local attractions. Proceeds from the cabins go toward community projects. Surrounded by tropical gardens, the kitchen-equipped cabins accommodate two to six guests each. *RD$1500 and up; located between turn-off for Playa Rincón and the town of Las Galeras; Amenities: fan, included breakfast, laundry service*

 El Cabito Home of the best view in the Samaná Peninsula, El Cabito graces the crest of staggering sea-hugging bluffs a few kilometers outside of town. This self–sustainable, family-run establishment is perfect for the environmentally and socially conscious traveler looking for a beautiful, rustic experience in either the open-air cabins or camping sites. While there, take advantage of the on-site hikes and cliff jumping. Treat yourself to a drink at the bar/restaurant overlooking the sea as the peaks of the cape on which it sits, Cabo Cabrón, swallow up the sun. *US$40 for cabana, US$7.50 for hammocks/camping spots; located 3 kilometers outside of Las Galeras, call the owners for pick up or take a moto up the hill for about RD$100; 829-697-9506/820-2263; www.elcabito.net*

Juan y Lolo The various cabins owned by Juan y Lolo are scattered across Las Galeras, ranging from a duplex with a big deck and featuring a loft (great for big groups) to a house cut into the side of a hill, with natural rock acting as walls. The office, where guests pick up keys, is located on a side street to the left of the main drag. *US$40-175; 313 Calle A; 538-0208; 875 1423; juanylolo@hotmail.com; info@juanylolo.com; www.juanylolo.com*

Casa Por Qué No? This Canadian-owned bed and breakfast is open only when the owners fly south for the winter, from November through April. The two available rooms are airy and bright and the house is set in a lovely garden away from the street noise. Thai-inspired three-course dinners can be arranged upon request, which include shrimp spring rolls, fish in coconut sauce, and chocolate cake, for US$20. *US$50; main road next to Plaza Lusitania near Playa Grande; Amenities: fan, hot water, breakfast included*

Hotel Dorado Hotel Dorado is a bed and breakfast located in a modern, yet warmly decorated two-story home near La Playita. The owners left the hustle and bustle of New York City for the calm and peace of Las Galeras. The large breakfasts are outstanding and vary daily. The owner also offers fishing trips in his 22ft Panga or 28ft Mako boats and will cook up a very fresh catch that evening. *US$75 and up; when entering town, turn left at the Evangelical church and then left at sign for Casa Dorado; 829-221-2493; 829-933-8678; info@casadoradodr.com; www.casadoradodr.com; Amenities: hot water, fan, TV, Wi-Fi, breakfast included, common areas and kitchen; dinner available upon request*

La Isleta The best deal in Las Galeras, La Isleta's beach cabins are backpacker-friendly, as they can fit four or more people and, come equipped with kitchens and porches with ocean or garden views. The peaceful garden features swaying hammocks, a charcoal BBQ, and a hot tub. *RD$1500-2000; A two-minute walk west along the sandy path from Playa Grande; 538-0116; 829-887-5058; www.la-isleta.com; Amenities: fan, hot water, kitchen*

Villa Sirena A charming luxury hotel styled after the former Victorian homes of Samaná, it is far enough from the main road to provide a serene atmosphere, but still within walking distance of all the major businesses. Each room has a balcony with a mesmerizing view of the ocean. Though the prices are on the higher end, they include breakfast, private beach access, kayaks, snorkel gear, and bikes for exploring town. *US$100-150; near Playa Grande; turn left at Plaza Lusitania and follow the road until it dead-ends; 538-0000; info@villaserena.com; www.villaserena.com; Amenities: A/C, fan, hot water, Wi-Fi, laundry service, parking lot, safe, fridge, restaurant, breakfast included, money exchange, pool, massage, excursions*

Todo Blanco Living up to its name, this whitewashed, Victorian-inspired boutique hotel is conveniently located on Las Galeras beach. It offers an ocean view interrupted only by grand palm trees. Each of the eight rooms has two double beds and balconies facing the coast. *RD$1000-1500; Turn right at Plaza Lusitania, take the first left down the dirt road and the hotel will be on the left; 538-0201; 729-2333; info@hoteltododoblanco.com; www.hoteltododoblanco.com; Amenities: A/C, fan, hot water*

Sol Azul This tiny hotel has lofted rooms decorated in earth tones and natural materials. Located just removed from the main drag, it is gated and peaceful, with meticulous, verdant landscaping. *EU$35-EU$50 (owners quote in Euros, but will accept pesos and U.S. dollars as well); turn right at Plaza Lusitania and hotel is on right; Amenities: fan, hot water, pool, BBQ, breakfast included; 829-882-8790; www.elsolazul.com*

DO

Playa Rincón

Accessible by boat, *moto*, or private vehicle, this is easily one of the most jaw-droppingly beautiful beaches on the island. The vast stretch of white sand offers three distinct swimming options: a cool mountain-fed river (to the far left when facing the water); raucous waves for body surfing; and calm, crystalline waters protected by a cove to the far right. There are fish shacks to the far left of the beach for a tasty fried catch of the day served with *tostones* and *moro* (RD$300-$350) or for a few extra pesos, head to the restaurants on the far right for table service.

The beach is noticeably divided between locals and tourists, but don't let this detour you from exploring the area. Enjoying the isolated beauty of Playa Rincón comes with a major caveat: the land surrounding the beach has been bought up from the local community by a massive development company and ominously, rumors of all-inclusives are in the air.

The turnoff for Playa Rincón is located on the left side of the highway before entering the town of Las Galeras from Samaná. Follow the Brugal-sponsored Playa Rincón signs through the small villages that precede the beach. Locals are always happy to give directions, so don't be afraid to ask. *Motoconchos* can take those without private transport, but prices are steep, starting at RD$600, because of the rough condition of the road and the distance from town. Perhaps the best bet is to pay RD$1500 for a motorboat, which can fit a large number of people, and it also includes transport to Playa Frontón and Playa Madame. Boat captains may try to charge more – don't be afraid to barter.

Iguanario Los Tocones

On the way to Playa Rincón, stop by this community project marked by a small blue circular sign that protects and encourages reproduction among the endangered and endemic rhinoceros iguanas. Visitors are invited to observe these scaly adobe colored reptiles, while also enjoying the lush surroundings of mango, coffee, cacao and avocado trees. All proceeds go toward the upkeep of the project. *RD$50; Sociedad Ecológica LOS LAICOS; Los Tocones, Carretera el Rincón, Las Galeras; Contacts: María Altagracia Mirabal and Kathryn Sturman: 771-7661; 637-2489; 829-323-5931; 401-7141; 829-721-6282; ; Maríaalt14@gmail.com; cieloecotur@gmail.com; kathrynroses@gmail.com*

Playa Frontón

This gorgeous thin strip of sand is abutted by a series of arresting black cliffs, attracting adventurous rock climbers. The sheer rock walls also protect the beach from development, as it is only accessible by boat or hiking. Melodramatically arcing coconut trees provide shade for an afternoon nap after exploring the coral reefs surrounding the beach. Other natural treasures such as cactus pears can be found by hiking into the hills. When swimming, take note of the swift current that gathers strength off the point to the left when facing the water. Though swimming can be difficult because of the coral reefs, the underwater views are not to be missed. Pack lunch, snorkel gear, and get ready for an unforgettable day at the beach. *Accessible either by motorboat from the beach at Las Galeras, or ask a local or the hotel about the unmarked trails to access the hike that takes at least two hours.*

Boca del Diablo

An impressive blowhole located just before entering Las Galeras, this natural phenomenon is well worth the trek – especially during whale-watching season as it provides a land-based vantage point to catch those incredible mammals in action. Because Boca del Diablo is on the way to Playa El Frontón, it is a great addition to a day at the beach, combining some decent hiking and a unique geological formation with a lazy day at one of the most isolated and lovely beaches in Samaná. Getting there is a bit tricky as there are no signs and the trail is not well-maintained. The smartest way to get there is to befriend a local to take you or at least show you the entrance to the trail from the Samaná-Las Galeras highway. En route, you will pass through the community of La Cueva, where you can also stop for directions.

Playa Madame

Accessible by boat, this small beach is often covered with a green blanket of vines, accentuated with white and purple flowers. Bring a flashlight to explore the cave located behind the foliage and trees and relish in the beach's isolation.

La Playa de Las Galeras (Playa Grande)

The least impressive that Las Galeras has to offer, but still lovely, this beach is great for taking in the sunset or sunrise due to its close proximity to the hotels and the center of town. Locally, it is known as Playa Grande.

La Playita

Within walking distance from the town of Las Galeras, this beach is clean and picturesque. Most importantly, it won't cost you a peso to get there from Las Galeras. There is also a set of delicious beach restaurants including **Restaurant La Playita**, serving the freshly caught fish with *tostones, moro*, and salad, but be sure to ask for the menu with prices in pesos – the menu in U.S. dollars is inflated, catering to groups of tourists brought by the Da Grand Aparta Hotel.

◪ Grupo de Mujeres del Futuro

A women's group from the community of El Rincón offers horseback riding, hiking, and bird watching, with space for camping. The group also runs a restaurant serving homemade Dominican food. Proceeds directly support the women and their families. At the time of research, the women were still developing their packages, so be sure to ask about them on the way to El Rincón.

Diving in Las Galeras

Las Galeras boasts more than 15 dive spots, catering to all skill levels. Rock walls covered with soft coral plunging deep into the sea, such as **Tibisi**, are popular spots for spear fishing. For cave diving, plan a trip to **Cueva de Chopa**. For the beginner, **Playa Frontón** or **La Playita** offers shallow dives to check out the surrounding coral reefs.

Las Galeras Divers offers scuba rentals, dives, and a range of certification courses.
Plaza Lusitania - Local # 3, C/ Principal; 538-0220; 829-858-44 04; 715-4111; contact@las-galeras-divers.com; www.las-galeras-divers.com

Samaná Peninsula

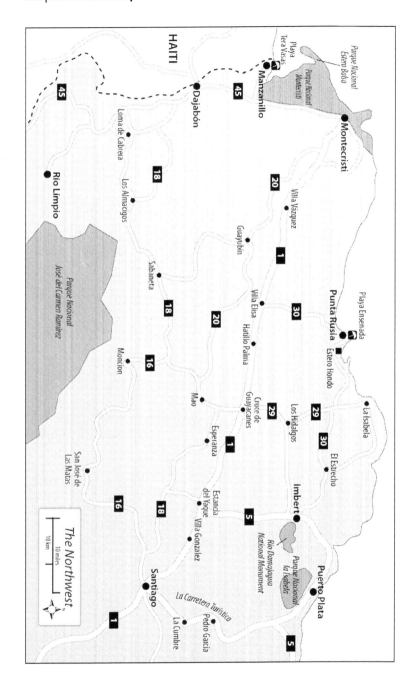

The Northwest

Now a quiet border region of wide vistas and scrubby plains, the Northwest (or "Línea Noroeste," as it is colloquially known) was once a center of commerce and trade. Towns like Manzanillo hosted busy ports to ship exotic and highly sought-after bananas to the U.S. at the turn of the 20th century. Natural hair dyes and precious lumber in demand throughout Western Europe brought in a steady rush of wealth to Montecristi during the same period. Dajabón, separated from Haiti only by the Río Masacre, started as a cross-border trading post, and continues to thrive in this capacity as Haitians are granted passage to the bi-weekly market to ply their wares. The warren of tables piled high with produce, clothing, and appliances, draws people from across the countryside for bargain shopping. Today, rickety frames of Victorian homes and epic tales of sea voyages in the name of patriotism are all that remain of a golden era when this region led the country in exports.

Despite the perceivable economic decline found in the Northwest's towns, the region's beautiful aquatic and terrestrial national parks are reason enough to visit. El Morro, a plateau that is part of the Parque Nacional de Montecristi, offers a stunning view the Atlantic Ocean and surrounding pastures where thousands of cattle graze. The lack of signage and sometimes bumpy roads that connect the Northwest with Puerto Plata and Santiago may be a blessing in disguise, allowing the beaches such as Punta Rusia and Montecristi's Playa Juan Bolanos, to remain relatively quiet and undeveloped. With the exception of major holidays such as Semana Santa, Punta Rusia provides a relaxing respite for those who want to fall off the grid. Lucky visitors come to kayak in the shallow teal waters and enjoy freshly caught seafood both friendly to the wallet and pleasing to the palate. Islands off the coast provide snorkelers and diving enthusiasts colorful views of marine life and bathers a secluded place to picnic and bask in the sun's rays. Don't miss out on regional specialties such as *chivo liniero* (spicy stewed goat) and handmade country cheeses as you step back into the slower pace of life in the Northwest.

Montecristi

With a population of just 123,000, Montecristi is a relatively small province, situated on the periphery of the country both geographically and economically. In 1493, visitor Christopher Columbus waxed poetic in his journal about El Morro, an arresting plateau jutting out over the bay just outside the modern-day provincial capital city (also called Montecristi). He named it Monte-Christy, "Monte" meaning mountain, and "Christy" as a reference to the awe-inspiring power of this geological formation. A town was established shortly after in 1506, under the government of Nicolás de Ovando. A century later, the Spanish throne's interest in Hispaniola began to wane as more lucrative opportunities arose in South America. While Spain exploited natural resources elsewhere, plundering pirates moved in on the northern coast of Hispaniola. At this time, nearly all of the inhabitants of the Northwest fled to Santo Domingo during what became known as "Las Devastaciones de Osorio."

The colonial government repopulated Montecristi at the end of the 18th century, and after the Dominican Republic declared independence from Haiti, peace and prosperity finally arrived. Montecristi experienced unprecedented economic growth in the late 19th and early 20th centuries, establishing itself as a center of commerce through the export of European commodities such as tobacco and hair dye. Signs of this prosperity can be seen in various examples of Victorian architecture and the well-planned streets and parks. Unfortunately, this boom did not last, and many of these historical treasures have been left to decay. The province has since reverted to more traditional economic activities of agriculture, livestock ranching, and fishing. However, this rural atmosphere has maintained the town's quaint charm, making it a restful place to stay while exploring this region. The coasts near town challenges perceptions of the typical Caribbean white-sand beaches, with their dry shrub, jagged ochre cliffs, and chameleon-like waters that seem to change color every hour. Be sure to visit the hulking El Morro, and take a boat trip through the mangrove-studded bay to the tiny offshore islands.

TRANSPORT

The **Caribe Tours** station is located on the corner of Av. Mella and C/ Rodríguez (579-2129), making stops in Santiago, La Vega and Santo Domingo.

To Santo Domingo: RD$350 (with a stop in Santiago RD$180); 6:45am, 8am, 9:30am, 1pm, 2:15pm, 3:15pm; 4.5hrs

From Santo Domingo: RD$350; 6:30am, 8am, 9:30am, 1pm, 2pm, 3:45pm; 4hrs

From Santiago: RD$180; 6:30am, 8am, 9:30am, 1pm, 2pm, 3:45pm; 2.5hrs; Expreso Liniero *guaguas* leave every 20 minutes throughout the day from the Rotunda in Santiago en route to **Dajabón**, with a stop in **Montecristi**. These *guaguas* return to Santiago from Dajabón, and make a stop at the gas station.

From Puerto Plata: Take Javilla Tours to **Navarrete** (RD$100) and then pick up an Expreso Liniero guagua en route to Dajabón (RD$170).

To Villa Vázquez and Dajabón: Small *guaguas* leave during daylight hours from C/ Benito Monción in the center of town for a ride that takes no more than 30 minutes.

INFO

Medical Attention
Super Farmacia María is on the corner of Duarte and Juan de la Cruz Alvarez (579-2315) and **Farmacia Pueblo** is on C/ Duarte and Benito Monción.

Communication
For calls, stop by the call center at **Chic Hotel,** which also has a snack bar serving coffee and *batidas* (44 Av. Benito Monción). **Turbo Service** internet café is at 67 C/ Presidente Henríquez (and C/ Benito Monción).

Banks
BanReservas is at 38 C/ Duarte and a **Banco Popular** ATM is on Duarte. There is a **Western Union** within Comercial Lilo on C/ Juan de la Cruz Alvarez and Presidente Vázquez.

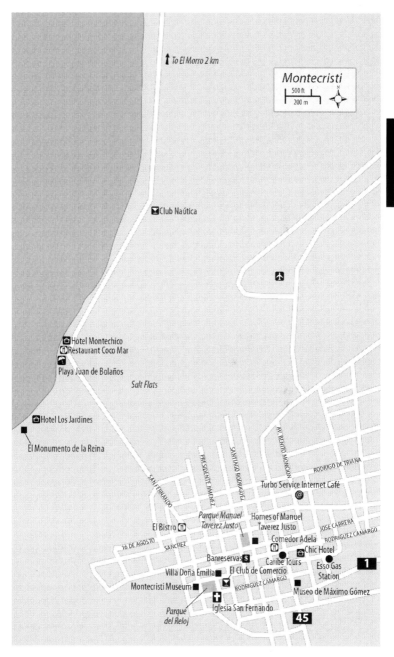

↑ To El Morro 2 km

Montecristi
500 ft
200 m
N

Club Naútica

Hotel Montechico
Restaurant Coco Mar
Playa Juan de Bolaños
Salt Flats

Hotel Los Jardines
El Monumento de la Reina

SAN FERNANDO

PRESIDENTE JIMENEZ

SANTIAGO RODRIGUEZ

AV. BENITO MONCIÓN

RODRIGO DE TRIANA

Turbo Service Internet Café
@

Parque Manuel Taverez Justo
Homes of Manuel Taverez Justo

El Bistro
Comedor Adela
JOSE CABRERA
RODRIGUEZ CAMARGO

16 DE AGOSTO
SANCHEZ
Chic Hotel

Banreservas $
Caribe Tours
Esso Gas Station

Villa Doña Emilia
El Club de Comercio
Montecristi Museum
RODRIGUEZ CAMARGO
Museo de Máximo Gómez

Parque del Reloj
Iglesia San Fernando

45

1

Gas

There is an **Esso Gas Station** on the corner of Av. Duarte and 27 de Febrero.

Grocery Stores

Supermercado Richetti is on the corner of Av. Mella and Duarte and **Comercial Lilo** is on C/ Juan de la Cruz Alvarez and Presidente Vazquez.

EAT

Comedor Adela A cozy restaurant, Comedor Adela feels like grandmother's house. Try the *plato del día* with crab or go decadent with lobster *asopao* (stew cooked with rice). *RD$125-675; 41 C/ Juan de la Cruz; 579-2254*

Restaurant Coco Mar Located on the beach at Juan de Bolaños, this casual eatery with quirky maritime décor serves up succulent lump crabmeat with crispy *tostones* and a seafood *asopao*. *RD$160-300; entrance to Juan de Bolaños Beach next to Hotel Montechico; 579-3354*

El Bistro At this French-inspired seafood restaurant owned by the proprietor of Los Jardines Hotel, ask for the catch of the day to enjoy the freshest of dishes. For a heartier meal, try a tender cut of beef, either grilled to perfection or delicately prepared with traditional French culinary techniques. Don't forget the wine and homemade desserts. *26 C/ San Fernando and C/ Osvaldo Vigil; 579-2091; Open every day from 12pm-12am; www.elbistro.com*

SLEEP

Chic Hotel This is the budget option in town, with rooms that sleep up to four people. At the time of research, the hotel was undergoing a much-needed renovation, adding more rooms, a pool, and gym. *RD$650-1700; 44 Av. Benito Monción; 579-2316/3164/3036; reservaciones@chichotel.net; www.chichotel.net; Amenities: hot water, TV, restaurant, pool, gym, Wi-Fi*

Hotel Montechico Montechico is a reasonably priced hotel located outside of town, though this means that transport can be an issue at night without a private vehicle. It is, however, located right on the beach, providing a lovely ocean view as well as easy access to El Morro. Splurge on the rooms with A/C, or at least the ones facing the bay. The water provides a delicious breeze at night, helping to ward off Montecristi's infamously incorrigible mosquitoes. *RD$750-2500; Playa Juan de Bolaño; 579-3811; Amenities: A/C, fan, TV, hot water*

Hotel Los Jardines Each simple but clean room has its own porch that overlooks a serene garden and the path to the beach. The French owner arranges diving and other excursions around El Morro National Park. If traveling in a group, ask about the three-person room with a loft, and don't forget to sooth those tired muscles in the Jacuzzi after hiking to the top of El Morro. *US$45-US$60; Playa Juan de Bolaños; 579-2091/853-0040; Hotel.jardines@gmail.com Amenities: A/C, fan, hot water, pool, Jacuzzi*

DO

Historic Architecture

Montecristi is home to some dilapidated but nonetheless impressive Victorian architecture, remnants of its fleeting golden era as a major port city. The most striking example is **Villa Doña Emilia**, a gutted Victorian mansion built in 1895. Doña Emilia was a wealthy exporter of campeche, a tree used to produce hair dye. In good fashion, she had the entire house shipped from France and then re-assembled in Montecristi. *A two-story house with baby-blue shingles located across the northeast corner of the Parque del Reloj; C/ Duarte and C/ Federico de Jesus García*

Doña Emilia

Sister of the Dominican President, Juan Isidro Jiménez, Doña Emilia was a formidable and famous businesswoman. However, she also was a benevolent citizen, offering asylum to Haitians in her basement when Trujillo ordered the Operación Perejil massacre. A fearless woman of principal, she was one of the few that resisted Trujillo's relentless courtship methods. At one of Trujillo's parties, after Doña Emilia had already rejected Trujillo's various advances, she finally accepted to dance with him under the condition that she could choose the song. She chose the merengue, "Buche y Pluma" referring to how a rooster puffs his chest and feathers to appear bigger than he actually is. Her choice was an intentional slight to Trujillo, full of bravado, and extremely risky considering the fatal consequences of others who rebuffed him. She, however, was spared Trujillo's wrath to tell her story.

Just across the street is **El Club de Comercio**, built in 1917. Still in use today, this social club was the playground of the elite, and gained fame for denying membership to Trujillo for his lack of blue blood. Miraculously, the club's influential members were able to maintain their operation despite their slight to the dictator, though Trujillo never set aside his disdain for the establishment. *C/ Duarte and C/ Presidente Jiménez*

Continuing west along C/ Duarte, you will come upon **Parque del Reloj**, named after the century-old clock tower imported from France in 1895. The tower, which still keeps good time, provides a 360-degree view of the town and coastline. Benigno Daniel Conde, a wealthy accountant, headed up the project, soliciting the clock and fountains located at each corner of the park. At the south end of the park is the **Iglesia San Fernando** dating back from the same era. *Corner of C/ Rodríguez Camargo and Federico de Jesus García*

Parque Manuel Tavarez Justo and his Childhood Homes

The park serves as a memorial to this revolutionary figure nicknamed "Manolo," a resister of the Trujillo regime. While in law school at the Universidad Autónoma de Santo Domingo, Manolo met his wife, Minerva Mirabal, and became active in student resistance groups. Among his many misdeeds, Trujillo denied Minerva her diploma upon graduation, angering Manolo. One of the founding members of the 14 de Junio movement, he met the same fate as his wife when Trujillo's sons (two years after their father's death) murdered him in 1963.

On Calle Santiago Rodríguez across from the rather modern park are both of his childhood homes. The green wooden home on the corner was his birthplace, and in his formative years, he lived in the canary-yellow house next door. The park supposedly was once a cemetery, and is therefore haunted by tales of ghosts and peculiar occurrences. After dark, people claim to feel strange in the park's vicinity, becoming disoriented or getting lost in their own city.

Museo de Montecristi

Sponsored and operated by the Historical Society of Montecristi and the University of Indiana, this museum helps preserve Montecristi's fascinating and underreported history. The artifacts and displays include exhibitions on Taíno culture and the colonial period up until through the second founding of Montecristi in 1756. Unfortunately, the museum is only open when the American administrator is in

The Northwest

town. *Free admittance; Corner of Av. Duarte and San Fernando; mctaino@aol.com; www.montecristi.org*

Museo de Máximo Gómez

In 1888, the Dominican soldier-turned-Cuban revolutionary Máximo Gómez took up residence in this house. Today, it serves as a museum and historic monument to where he and José Martí, the leader of Cuba's fight for independence, drew up the declaration of Cuba's independence in 1895. In the Dominican Republic, the document is known as the Manifesto de Montecristi. This modest one-story home is sparsely decorated with memorabilia and surrounded by a garden displaying busts of Gómez and Martí. *Mon-Sat 9am-12pm, 2pm-5pm; 39 C/ Mella*

Playa Juan de Bolaños

Juan de Bolaños, named after a city founder, is located beyond the shimmering salt flats that fan out beyond town. The beach, whose water is a calm aquamarine, is impressively clean, unless a storm has just passed through. A handful of hotels and restaurants line the beachfront as well.

Continuing west along the beach, bathers will come across **El Monumento de la Reina del Mar** by the Italian artist "3nrico" (pronounced "Enrico"), whose paintings, sculpture, and furniture have adorned the homes of such famous characters as Michael Jackson. 3nrico's home and workshop is located across the street from the sculpture, so visitors may be lucky enough to talk with the artist himself. The piece, a sort of galactic sea creation, utilizes found objects washed up on the shore, bright orange tiles, and painted stones, all surrounded by prickly plants.

Scuba Diving

The tempestuous waters of the Atlantic off of Montecristi's coast have claimed over 100 ships, more than 20 of which have been excavated and identified, making it a destination for shipwreck enthusiasts. Montecristi's barrier reef, the longest (45 meters, or 148 feet) and widest on the island, forms two distinct diving zones: the calm waters within the reef and then the coral walls outside the reef, plunging deep into the Atlantic. A five-hour boat ride from Montecristi is the Silver Bank, which is likely the only place in the area where it is legal to swim with the humpback whales that visit in January to March. While there are no official dive operators in Montecristi, find them in Cabarete (p196) and Santo Domingo (p107) to rent gear and hire dive masters.

Parque Nacional Montecristi & El Morro

Turning right at Playa Juan de Bolaños and continuing east is El Morro, a sheer rock promontory that seemingly took its cues from the military (or the 1980s) for its flat top. The road to El Morro dead-ends at the ranger station for the Parque Nacional, where park employees are happy to answer questions. Finely layered puff-pastry cliffs cradle a pristine beach, where waves crash and recede over white and ochre pebbles that exhale a cathartic gurgle. After coming out of the pebble-tumbler trance, follow the trail leading to the top of El Morro, which offers a spectacular view of the coast, town, and horizon-spanning arid brush and farmland. At the time of research, the stairs to the trail had fallen into disrepair, so climbing can be a challenge. A second route climbs the mount, though also poorly maintained, which leads to the second-highest peak abutting El Morro. It also boasts a tremendous view.

Las Siete Hermanas & Cabras

These *cayos* (cays) off the coast of Montecristi have become increasingly popular for snorkeling and scuba diving. The live coral reefs around Las Siete Hermanas are teeming with marine life. Shipwrecks with visible cannons lie within three meters of the water's surface. For tours, contact local fisherman Dioni Biliga (Spanish only), or head to the **Club Naútica** where a number of fishermen hang out for an impromptu tour. All-day boat tours to Las Siete Hermanas and neighboring Cabras runs RD$3500. For tours in English, French, or Spanish contact the owner of Hotel Los Jardines (see Sleep).

Punta Rusia

Prior to the newly paved road in 2010, this one-lane beach village seems to have stood still in time. While the occasional tour bus rolls through en route to Cayo Arena, a pristine islet known for its excellent snorkeling, the tourists never stay the night and spend little time in the village itself. Due to Punta Rusia's remoteness, there is little more to do than stroll along the white-sand beaches, go kayaking in the tranquil turquoise waters, and feast on bargain-price lobster. The pace of life may be too slow for some, but after experiencing a starry night or a sunrise on Punta Rusia's quiet beaches, visitors warn that it is difficult to leave.

TRANSPORT

From Puerto Plata/Altamira Area: Take Javilla Tours to Guananico, then catch a *carro público* or *guagua* that says "Puerto Plata-Isabela" (Note: sometimes transport ends at the town of El Mamey. There, simply hop on another *guagua* that goes to La Isabela). Get off at the *motoconcho* stand in La Isabela and the take a *motoconcho* from Isabela to Punta Rusia (RD$200, about 45min).

> From **Santiago** there are two ways to enter Punta Rusia. The faster and almost entirely paved route is via Highway 29 to La Isabela (off Cruce de Guayacanes) and then left to Punta Rusia.

For more of adventure, head west towards Montecristi from Santiago, and then after passing Hatillo Palma, turn right at Villa Elisa (if you reach Villa Sinda, you have gone too far). There is a small sign that says Punta Rusia right before the turn-off at Villa Elisa, along with a *motoconcho* stand with locals happy to take passengers for RD$200. The paved road quickly ends giving way to a rocky, dusty road that bisects dairy farms. The first sign of civilization won't appear again until about 15 minutes into the ride when the road forks, at which point veer to the left. Continue on that same road for 30 minutes and then turn right at El Papayo on Route 30 all the way to Punta Rusia.

From Santiago: At La Rotonda, take an Expreso Liniero (Dajabón-Santiago line) *guagua* going north. Get off at Villa Elisa (RD$150; less than 1.5hrs). Take a *motoconcho* from Villa Elisa to Punta Rusia (RD$200; about 45min)

From Santo Domingo: Caribe Tours en route to Dajabón (See Dajabón p240) may drop passengers off at Villa Elisa (RD$350) on request. There, take a *motoconcho* to Punta Rusia. If the driver will not stop at Villa Elisa, get off at Villa Vázquez and then take a *moto* from there.

INFO

Punta Rusia remains remote and untouched, which is wonderful for relaxing, but also means there are no grocery stores, gas stations, internet, or call centers in town. Spots of cell coverage can be found near Casa Libre on the hill or behind some of the fish shacks on Playa Ensenada.

EAT

Susana's on Playa Ensenada Sandwiched between a series of near-identical fish shacks, the lovely *abuela* Susana, aided by her daughters, grills up garlic-smothered lobster served with fried sweet potatoes or *tostones*. Unlike other vendors, Susana gives the same fair price to all of her customers, and serves each dish with a kind smile. *RD$150-300; midway down the row of food huts on Playa Ensenada; no phone*

Restaurant Damaris One of the few restaurants in the town of Punta Rusia, owner Damaris adds a touch of sophistication to the typical seafood restaurant, offering international wines and attention to detail, while still maintaining a very casual, family-run feel. With more than 15 years in business, Damaris offers American-style breakfasts in the morning, followed by grilled *dorado*, shrimp, or the Northwest's specialty dish, *chivo picante* (spicy stewed goat) throughout the day. *RD$125-600; located on the main road in town just east of the public beach. 829-280-8697*

El Buceador A tiny shack packed with wooden picnic tables, assorted buoys, and a lively crowd on holidays, this seafood restaurant treats customers with the catch of the day and a side of blaring bachata from the monstrous speakers at the bar. Whether it is grouper, lobster, or shrimp, all dishes come with some iteration of rice, beans, and *tostones*. *RD$100-500; Follow signs up the hill off the main road through town; no phone*

SLEEP

 Casa Libre The brightly painted open-air cabins of Casa Libre (also known as Casita Mariposa) are nestled on a vibrantly landscaped hillside with incredible views of Punta Rusia. The amenities are minimal, with only one cold-water bathroom for the three cabins and no cell service, though this certainly adds to the charm of the area. A small path leads to the beach, from where it is possible to walk west to Punta Rusia's main beach or east to Playa Ensenada. The German and French owners, Guertie and Marco, are very helpful and prepare a delicious and healthy breakfast from only the freshest ingredients. *RD$700-900; before entering the town of Punta Rusia from Villa Isabela, just opposite the tire shop, there is a small dirt road leading up to Casa Libre on the right. Coming from Villa Elisa, drive through town and then find the tire shop on your right and the dirt road on your left; 834-5992, 693-5010, 212-8295(Be sure to leave a message as there is no cell signal)*

Hotel La Tortuga A bright orange cement hotel located on the main road leading into town, this inexpensive hotel has an ocean view from its communal balcony. *RD$700; heading out of Punta Rusia east towards Playa Ensenada; 647-1344; 229-6604*

Villa Nadine With such amenities as a kitchen, king-sized beds, a barbecue, and a rooftop plunge pool, this beachfront home fitting up to six is available to rent nightly or weekly. *US$260 for house/night or US$1800 per week; main road of Punta Rusia, directly across from beach; 829-264-0070; www.villanadine.com; Amenities: hot water, internet, TV, breakfast included*

DO

Playa Ensenada

A short walk along the beach during low tide leads to Playa Ensenada, a beach catering to locals. It is packed with dirt-cheap fish shacks and families on the weekends, though it is much quieter during the week. Cradled by cliffs on one side and lined with palms, the beach is clean, and its water warm and brilliant blue.

Diving in Punta Rusia

Cayo Arena, a tiny white-sand islet surrounded by live coral reefs, is a popular diving and snorkeling spot. During high tide, Cayo Arena is nearly submerged, but is surrounded by a sand bar, so the water is always shallow – perfect for lounging around. It's best enjoyed on days when local tour operators are not herding guests from Puerto Plata's all-inclusive resorts. Local fishermen generally are very flexible in terms of the time of departure and return, and the length of stay, so just set up an itinerary that works for you. *Fishermen perched along the beach in town can take interested parties there and back starting at RD$1500; stay as long as the sun is in the sky.*

Located east of Punta Rusia in **Estero Hondo** is a mangrove-lined lagoon serving as a manatee refuge. Dolphins and sea turtles can be occasionally spotted along the entire coast from Luperón Bay to Montecristi. *Ask local fishermen for an impromptu tour.*

The Northwest

Manzanillo

A small port town that was once based entirely on the export of bananas by the U.S.-owned United Fruit Company, Manzanillo has yet to make an economic comeback after Trujillo ordered almost all exports and imports to go through Santo Domingo. At one time, there was an abundance of flamingos in Manzanillo's Laguna La Salina, just east of town, but they are now a rare sight. The nearby **Parque Nacional Estero Balsa** protects an extensive network of mangroves and live coral reefs, popular among divers. Today, the port of Manzanillo continues to function, though lacking the action it saw a century ago. The public beach is hardly worth the trip, but with the help of a local fisherman, the rich marine life of Estero Balsa is just a boat ride away.

> **Navigating Manzanillo**
> Like many small Dominican towns, street names are rarely, if at all, used. Thankfully the town in not big, so getting lost is nearly impossible.

TRANSPORT

Caribe Tours

To Santo Domingo: RD$300 (with a stop in Santiago (RD$90)); 6am, 7am, 2pm, and 3pm; 5hrs; Station located on C/ 27 de Febrero and C/ Restauración; 579-9504

From Santo Domingo: RD$300; 7:15am, 8:30am, 12:30pm, and 2:30pm; 5hrs

From Santiago: RD$90; 7:15am, 8:30am, 12:30pm, and 2:30pm; 2.5hrs

INFO

While there is no private clinic in town, the municipality's public **Hospital Pepillo Salcedo** (no phone) has adequate basic care in the case of an absolute emergency. There are a few internet cafés on the main street of town (C/ 27 de Febrero). Stock up on food at **Supermercado Binorka** and fill up at the **gas station** just outside the entrance of Manzanillo.

EAT

The Coconut, located right on the beach, serves up fresh fried fish and *tostones.* Those taken by the rice and beans fever should stop by **Doña Negra's** (C/ 27 de Febrero), which offers the always-satisfying *bandera dominicana.*

SLEEP

Hotel Manzanillo Though Manzanillo is best suited as a day trip, this place offers rooms for RD$400 a night and comes with a private bathroom and fan. Importantly, there's also an inverter, which comes in handy for blackouts.

DO

Tera Vasas Beach is the local town beach perfect for cooling off during the Northwest's hottest days, but is a bit of a letdown after seeing other area beaches.

Dajabón

The largest border town, with a population of nearly 17,000, Dajabón's proximity to and intimate connection with Haiti has been both a blessing and a curse, always an evocative subject in local dialogue. Spanish Navy Captain José Solano y Bote founded the town in 1776 as a trading post with French colonial holdings while boundary lines between the territories were still being drawn. Abandoned in the 1840s during the War of Independence with Haiti, Dominicans began to re-settle the area following the War of Restoration, which began in the province of Dajabón with the battle "El Grito de Capotillo" on August 16, 1865.

Blood again infamously soaked Dajabón's soil in 1937, when Trujillo ordered his army to destroy the entire Haitian population in the Northwest's frontier region. His proclamation did not discriminate – it required the elimination of both people born in the Dominican Republic accused of being Haitian, and those who had immigrated. Approximately 20,000 people were slaughtered by machete in the course of a few days. This horrific event became known as the Parsley Massacre because in order to "distinguish" between locals and foreigners, Dominican troops forced suspected Haitians to say "parsley" in Spanish (*perejil*) – and their pronunciation decided their fate. The river denoting the border flowed red with blood, from which it derives its present name: Río Masacre, or Massacre River.

After surviving two wars and a massacre, Dajaboneros were finally able to lay down some roots, creating an economy based on bi-national trade, agriculture, and livestock ranching. Goats are a particularly common sight in the region, especially when roasted on a spit at family gatherings. Along with *chivo liniero* (goat from the Northwest Line), be sure to sample the honey produced by the province's growing apiculture industry. Rice patties surround the highway entering Dajabón from the north, and across the province small farms growing staples like yuca, beans, and plantains can be seen throughout the province.

TRANSPORT

Caribe Tours is located on C/ Marcelo Carrasco between Ave. Presidente Henríquez and Calle Beller, 579-8554.

To Santo Domingo: RD$350; stops in **Santiago** (RD$170) and **Montecristi** (RD$55); 6:45am, 8am, 9:30am, 1pm, 2pm, 3:15pm; 5hr

From Santo Domingo: RD$350; 6:30am, 8am, 9:30am, 1pm, 2pm, 3:45pm; 4.5hrs

From Santiago: RD$170; 6:30am, 8am, 9:30am, 1pm, 2pm, 3:45pm; 2hrs

To Santiago and Montecristi: *Guaguas* (*expresos* and *calientes*) leave about every 20 minutes between 5:30am and 6pm and are slightly cheaper than Caribe Tours; the stop is at C/ Dulce Jesús de Senfluer or Autopista 45 at town's entrance

INFO

Medical Attention
For emergencies, the public **Hospital Ramón Matías Mella** (579-7105) is located on Av. Presidente Henríquez and C/ Padre Santa Ana.

Communication
El Café de Internet de Pio is on C/ Marcel Carrasco between Duarte and Ave. Presidente Henríquez. **Café Beller** also has two computers with internet free for customers, as well as Wi-Fi. **Rocafé** also provides complimentary Wi-Fi to guests (see Eat).

Banks
Banreservas is located at 61 C/ Beller (579-8930; Mon-Fri: 8am-5pm, Sat: 9am-1pm). **Banco Popular** and **Scotiabank** are both located on Calle Beller and the corner of C/ Dulce Jesús de Senfleur.

Police
The **Police Station** is located on the corner of C/ Duarte and C/ Dulce de Jesús Senfleur.

Gas
There is a gas station at the entrance of town denoted by a cement arch on C/ Dulce Jesús de Senfleur.

Grocery Stores
The recently renovated **Supermercado Karla** is on C/ Beller and C/ Capotillo.

EAT

Café Beller Don't be deceived by this restaurant's location behind the gas station. Beller is a classy joint, offering fresh salads, sandwiches, and even Mexican food (considered exotic in these parts). Try the mixed fajitas or the grouper wrap. *RD$150-400; located at the Texaco gas station at the entrance of town on C/ Dulce Jesús de Senfleur, alternative entrance on /e Marcelo Carasco between C/ Beller and C/ Manuel Ramón Roca; 579-716; ; free Wi-Fi*

Pollo Beller Offering the solid standbys of fried chicken and a *plato del día*, this casual joint has the added bonus of soft serve ice cream – when the machine works. *RD$100-200; Located at the Texaco gas station at the entrance of town on C/ Dulce Jesús de Senfleur next to Café Beller; free Wi-Fi*

Rocafé Try the Northwest's signature stewed goat at this *criollo* restaurant that also dabbles internationally with some success, serving plates like chicken cordon bleu. *RD$150-400; Above RocaPollo across the street from Ferretería Beller on the corner of C/ Dulce Jesús de Senfleur and C/ Duarte; free Wi-Fi*

SLEEP

Hotel Brisol This favorite for local travelers is conveniently located by the new market, and offers modest, yet tidy rooms with double beds. *RD$500-700; C/ Respaldo Padre Santa Ana*

Hotel Juan Calvo Next to the Parque Central, this establishment offers clean, comfortable rooms with a TV and fan, as well as an on-site restaurant. *RD$400-600; 48 C/ Presidente Henríquez, 579-8285, Amenities: A/C, fan*

Hotel Bonanza With the only swimming pool in Dajabón, this hotel is a popular spot for locals looking to cool off. This family-run hotel has 18 spick-and-span rooms.*RD$500-700; C/ Martín Jufferman, El Centro; 579-8548*

DO

El Mercado

On Monday and Friday mornings from 9am to 4pm, the streets surrounding the border crossing between Haiti and the DR fill with excitement, people, and goods as both Haitian and Dominican vendors cover the sidewalks with their wares under tarps and makeshift tents. Don't expect unique art or priceless antiques – this is a locals' market, selling everyday staples. Items tend toward the practical, such as pots, used clothing, and fresh produce. Personal space is at a premium, as bargain-hunters

---

Post-Quake Policy: Neighborly Gestures or Status Quo?

After the devastating earthquake in January, 2010, the Dominican Republic had an incredible opportunity to assist its neighbor in need. Indeed, many saw it as a potential turning point in the pan-Hispaniola dynamic. Up until this point, the countries had bitter relations, stemming from years of historical enmity (see Independence on page 14 in the History section).

Thousands of Haitians migrate each year, and up to a million people of Haitian descent live in the DR. Many lack official papers, and the Dominican Republic has a policy of deportation of those without papers – even if people have lived in the country their entire lives. Many of the deportees were born in the Dominican Republic, making this policy more about racial and cultural politics than strict anti-illegal immigration programs. Those without documentation, do legally not exist and thus have no access to basic services even as they support the Dominican economy.

After the earthquake, however, the DR was one of the first countries to respond. Schools across the country organized relief drives, and citizens delivered essential materials, even along roads that other international organizations claimed to be impassable. The Dominican government transported food, gas, and supplies, and accepted Haitian patients in the border region and in the capital. The Dominican Red Cross was a strong force in relief efforts.

Today, community-based organizations work against what they perceive to be the restoration of the prior status quo, as deportations resume and cholera has spread to the DR. Organizations like MUDHA (Movimiento de Mujeres Dominico-Haitianas or Movement of Dominican-Haitian Women) and the Jesuit organization, Solidaridad Fronteriza, are attempting to build upon the Dominican public's outpouring of sympathy to push for legal and economic rights for Haitians and Dominicans of Haitian descent. Perhaps with the work of these groups, and the massive support provided by Dominican individuals, cross-border relations can finally improve. *Written with assistance from Keane Bhatt.*

push and argue over everything from tomatoes to sandals. At 4pm, all Haitians without immigration papers head across the border before it closes at 6pm.

Crossing to Haiti

From Dajabón, there are no buses to Haiti. Travelers must cross on foot, and then hop on a public bus on the Haitian side. The fee for leaving and entering the DR is US$10, followed by another US$10 or more on the Haitian side, paid in Haitian *gourdes*. Money-changing peddlers swarm the area, kindly offering to gouge unsuspecting tourists with terrible exchange rates. Depending on the mood of the officials on both sides, crossing the border can be as much as US$50 once you exchange money, give something to the middlemen, and pay off corrupt border officials.

When there is not an epidemic, strike, or other socio-political upheaval, the border generally opens at 8am (Dominican time) and closes at 5pm or 6pm Mon-Sat. On Sundays, it opens later (9am) and closes early (2pm or 3pm). Be aware that Haitian time is an hour earlier.

Río Límpio

Located in an immense valley nestled by mountains, Río Limpio is a haven for the outdoor enthusiast interested in experiencing a small, traditional Dominican village. The surrounding area, declared a national park in 1995, offers great hiking and biking trails, as well as a chance to check out the town's agricultural industries like rice and coffee cultivation. A healthy amount of rain (200-250 inches per year) combined with an ethereal cloud cover, maintains the mountains consistently lush and green.

TRANSPORT

The shortest way to arrive to Río Límpio is via Loma de Cabrera. Caribe Tours will take passengers as far as the town of **Loma de Cabrera**, but the remaining 36 kilometers to Río Límpio are best traversed in a private vehicle with four-wheel drive because of difficult road conditions and inconsistent public transport. For those who do not want to gamble with the finicky *guaguas*, renting an all-terrain vehicle is the recommended mode of transport.

> The dirt roads in Río Limpio are left unnamed, but due to its isolation, the locals are warm and always willing to help. Asking for directions is the only way to get around.

Caribe Tours buses leave from Santo Domingo (RD$350) or Santiago (RD$200) to Loma de Cabrera at 6:45am, 7:45am and 1:30pm.

EAT

The Centro Ecoturístico Nalga de Maco is equipped to serve up to 100 people (though small groups are of course welcome) delicious country-style meals like roasted goat, *asopao* (rice and meat stew) and *sancocho* (hearty stew with multiple meats and starchy vegetables). *RD$100; For reservations and more information, Contact Manager, Margarita Castillo: Río Limpio: 984-5426; Santo Domingo: 221-5566*

Besides a few *colmados*, there are no grocery stores, and so if planning on hiking through the National Park, buy supplies before arriving.

SLEEP

Sleeping options are limited to the community-run **Centro Ecoturístico Nalga de Maco**, which offers cabins and dormitories fitting up to 33 people, as well as camping spaces. *Reservations strongly recommended; Contact Manager, Margarita Castillo: Río Limpio: 984-5426; Santo Domingo: 221-5566; Amenities: solar panel, generator, restaurant*

DO

Agro-tourism

Visit the **Cooperativa de Productores Orgánicos Valle de Río Limpio** or the **Marcelo Guzmán Rice Factory**, where organic rice is processed. Stop by the **Pedro Jacobo Pérez Coffee Factory** to learn how these mountain-grown beans are cleaned and carefully selected. *Across from El Centro Tecnológico, 107 C/ Principal*

Servicios de Guías Ecoturísticos de Río Limpio

Local tour guides lead tours on foot, horseback, and mountain bike through the mountains of Nalga de Maco National Park, which is spread among 280 square kilometers (108 square miles). The mahogany and cloud forests make for beautiful surroundings, as visitors pass through farms and the El Valle and Artibonito rivers. The twin peaks that gave the park its name of Nalga de Maco – Frog's Butt – reign over the lush hillsides. Within the bedrock are several caves, including the highlights of Cueva San Francisco and Cueva Nalga de Maco.

The hike through the park is challenging, but certainly worth the exertion. Come prepared with food and water for two days, in addition to camping gear in case you need to break up the trail with an overnight stay. Before visiting the caves, be sure to discuss your physical capabilities with your guide, as the trail through the underground wonders is strenuous, and only experienced spelunkers should attempt Cueva San Francisco. Also, don't forget to bring proper gear for cold and wet weather, as the peaks are consistently covered with a blanket of fog and temperatures have been known to drop to 10°C (50°F). *After arriving, ask for Máximo Ogando or Juan Antonio Tejada; office located next to La Casa de la Cultura in town.*

For gifts, peruse **Artesanía y Manualidades Guzmán**, a family-run artisan business. The members work with natural materials like seeds, cow horn, and coconut shell to make jewelry, bags, and other island-inspired creations. For more information, ask for Gregoria Guzmán Mercedes, head of the artisans' association. Another native of Río Limpio, Rivera Mora, creates ornate sculptures inspired by his surroundings at his workshop **Arte Mora**. His specialties include immense frogs and lizards scaling trees, created using precious fallen wood found throughout the surrounding forests. He also fashions stunning wooden serving spoons, perfect in size and weight to carry back as gifts. (Rivera Mora; vermora@gmx.net)

Sweets

Famous for her sweets, particularly *dulce de naranja* (sweets made with local oranges), **Doña Iluminada** is one of many characters that adds to the authenticity and uniqueness of this rural mountain village. Ask for her by name.

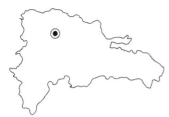

Santiago

The Dominican Republic's other metropolis, Santiago unites the frenetic energies of a city with the laid-back soul of an old agricultural town. Though only a short drive separates Santiago and Santo Domingo, the country's two largest cities couldn't be more different. Santiago is the vibrant soul of the verdant Cibao valley, with thriving agriculture (coffee, cacao, rice, and tobacco), manufacturing, arts, and education. Home to bustling streets and markets, several universities, and the most highly regarded museum in the country, Santiago is certainly deserving of its nickname La Ciudad Corazón – The Heart City.

Santiago sprawls across the banks of the Río Yaque on hilly terrain 175 meters (574 feet) above sea level. For the visitor, it is a gateway to beckoning adventures in the cool, craggy Cordillera Central to the south and east, and peaceful, breezy days in the rolling hills of the Cordillera Septentrional to the north and west. Though not too far from the beaches on the north coast, Santiago has blazed its own trail, and while not a traditional tourism hotspot, the city boasts an intriguing history, thumping nightlife, and many cultural highlights. The most exciting area for visitors is the downtown/old city, including the Monument and Calle del Sol.

History

The official name of the city is Santiago de los 30 Caballeros, a reference to the 30 men of the Order of Saint James (Santiago, in Spanish) who signed the city's founding charter. Santiago was one of the earliest settlements on the island, and therefore lays claim to being the first Santiago in the Western Hemisphere.

In the summer of 1495, having moved inland from their troubled north coast landing, Cristóbal and Bartolomé Colón and their plucky band of Spanish explorers came upon a hilltop by the Río Yaque del Norte. Strategically located and sporting commanding views of the surrounding countryside, this hill was the perfect place to build a fort. Over the next few years, a small settlement grew off to the north, in what is now the village of Jacagua. In 1562, an earthquake leveled this town, as well as many others across the valley. The survivors reestablished Santiago on the banks of the Río Yaque del Norte, where the city has remained ever since. Though Santiago proved attractive at first because of gold found in the river, the precious metal soon ran dry, and gave way to an agricultural economy based on farming and ranching.

As it lies closer to the border and north coast than Santo Domingo, the city was required to defend itself many times from outside forces, including England, France, Haiti, and Spain. In 1805, the city was sacked by the invading Haitian army, fresh from its heady days of throwing off the yoke of French colonialism. It was also here when the Dominican army, chafing under two decades of Haitian rule and just a month after declaring independence, claimed victory in the decisive Battle of

Santiago on March 30, 1844. Dominican forces routed the Haitian army, driving them back towards the border, and eventually out of the country.

Santiago has always maintained an independent streak from the government in Santo Domingo. In the colonial and early independence era, the landed gentry of Santiago resented the growing power of the state centered in the capital. This unease came to a head when the military government allowed Spain to re-annex the country in 1853. Leaders in Santiago refused to recognize this annexation, and occupying Spanish forces leveled the city. The War of Restoration began here with these restive citizens, and after two years, the country regained its independence.

In the 20th century, Santiago has flourished. Railroad and highway connections with Puerto Plata, La Vega, and Moca made Santiago a mercantile and transportation king in the throne of the Cibao Valley. Though these railroads linkages no longer exist, they created the pathways of development for the city. Santiago suffered greatly under the rule of Trujillo, who funneled funding toward his adopted home of Santo Domingo to the developmental detriment of other area. However, after his downfall, Santiago has experienced explosive growth, driven by internal rural-urban migration and a related economic upswing that has not yet ceased. In the last fifty years, Santiago has seen a nearly tenfold increase in population, while coming to grips with urban issues like crime, traffic, and lack of adequate infrastructure.

Transportation

Intraurban transport is dominated by *carros públicos*, like in Santo Domingo, and cost RD$20-25. At least a dozen routes crisscross the main avenues of the city. Situated on the main north-south highways, Santiago is also very well connected with other cities across the north, as well as to Santo Domingo.

Caribe Tours

There are two stops in Santiago: Las Colinas, at Av. 27 de Febrero and Av. Las Americas, and Los Jardines, at Av. 27 de Febrero and C/ Maimon.

To Santo Domingo/La Vega: RD$280/RD$80; every 15-60 minutes from 5:15am to 6:20pm; 2.5hrs/40min

From Santo Domingo/La Vega: RD$280/RD$80; every 15-60 minutes from 6am to 8pm; 2.5hrs/40min

To Puerto Plata: RD$120; hourly 6am-7pm; 75min

To Montecristi/Dajabón: RD$190/RD$200; buses leave at 6:30am, 8am, 9:30am, 1pm, 2pm, and 3:45pm; 2.5hrs/3hr

Metrobus

This additional coach bus option services Santo Domingo and is one block from the Los Jardines Caribe Tours stop, on Av. Juan Pablo Duarte and C/ Maimon.

To/From Santo Domingo: RD$250; buses leave every half hour, 5:30am to 6pm; 2.5hr

The Rotunda

Several reliable transportation companies maintain bus stops across this sprawling intersection at Av. 27 de Febrero and Av. Estrella Sadhala, accessible by both the A and M *carro público* routes. **Javilla Tours** runs local and express minibuses with A/C to Puerto Plata (RD$75). Take the local Javilla *guagua* to any point in between Santiago and Puerto Plata, such as the 27 Charcos. **Espinal** and **Aetrabus** run to the capital for RD$250 every half hour from 6am to 6pm, but the buses are not as nice as those of Caribe Tours. Smaller *guaguas* to Montecristi, Dajabón, Santiago Rodríguez, and other cities leave from the Rotunda as well.

Parque Chachace

One side of this park, at C/ Sabana Larga between C/ Restauración and C/ Independencia, serves as the stop for the *guaguas* to several cities in the Cibao, from about 6am to 6pm. The buses serve **Licey** (RD$30), **Moca** (RD$40), **La Vega** (RD$50), **Salcedo** (RD$60), and **San Francisco de Macorís** (RD$100).

To Samaná: RD$150; 6am-3pm; 3hrs; C/ San Luís and C/ Beller.

Air

The Cibao International Airport is located south of the city on Carretera Duarte. It is the third-largest airport in the country, and serves the US, Turks and Caicos, and Panama, as well as domestic destinations. By public transportation, the airport can be reached by taking the PA car at specified stops: it passes the Fortaleza San Luis, then along Av. Francia, turns at the south side of the Monument, and then out to the highway (RD$35). Leaving the airport for the city, the cars line up across from the parking lot main gates, and come back to the city along C/ Las Carreras on the north side of the Monument. The cars run from about 6am to 6pm. Taxis cost at least RD$400.

Flying to Santiago

Flying directly into Santiago may be a better idea if travelers are planning on spending time on the north coast. The airport is smaller and more manageable than the one in Santo Domingo, and prices for flights are similar. American, Delta, JetBlue, and Spirit all fly from New York, but there are also direct flights from Boston on JetBlue, from Fort Lauderdale on Spirit, and from Miami on American Airlines.

Info

Medical Attention

The Peace Corps-recommended medical center is **Amadita Gómez** in Plaza Comercial Texas, on Av/ Bartolomé Colón and C/ Texas (Mon-Fri 7:30am-6pm and Sat 7:30am-12:30pm; 581-8328). The major hospital is **Centro Médico del Cibao** at 64 Av. Juan Pablo Duarte (582-6661).

Banks

Find branches of **Banco Popular** at the corner of C/ El Sol and C/ Mella and inside **La Sirena**, **Bella Vista Mall**, and **Las Colinas Mall**. T Branches of **Banreservas** are located at 150 Av. Estrella Sadhalá and 82 Av. 27 de Febrero in Las Colinas, and **Banco León is** at C/ del Sol and C/ San Luis.

Communication

The **Post Office** is on C/ del Sol at C/ San Luis (Mon-Fri 8am-5pm, Sat 9am-1pm). The **Centro de Internet Yudith** is located on C/ 16 de Agosto and C/ San Luis, and there is also a reliable internet café at the Hotel Colonial on C/ Salvador Cucurulo, as well as **El Punto Net** a few doors down from Colonial. Also try **Servi-net** on the corner of C/ España and C/ Restauración.

Grocery Stores and Shopping

The **La Sirena** superstore, where almost anything needed is available for purchase, has locations at C/ del Sol by C/ 30 Marzo, and on Carretera Juan Pablo Duarte by Av. Rafael Vidal. There is an additional La Sirena combined with another store called **Super Pola**, to create a giant superstore, on Av. Luperón at Av. 27 de Febrero. Across the street is **Plaza Lama**, which sells clothes and electronics along with food, and has a surprisingly good bakery. **Supermercado Nacional**, another large, full-service store with a bakery and cafeteria, takes up the entire block at Av. Estrella Sadhala and Av. 27 de Febrero.

For outdoor shopping, simply walk down the lower part of **C/ del Sol** (away from the Monument), where there are stands selling everything from sunglasses to mangoes on sticks. These stands continue on the blocks on either side of C/ del Sol as well, including the *Mercado Modelo*, at C/ del Sol and C/ España.

Santiago also manages to have a few malls, with food courts, bank outlets, supermarkets, movie theaters, and upscale shops. Visit **Las Colinas,** which has a **Jumbo** superstore (Av. 27 de Febrero at Av/ Imbert), **Bella Terra** (Av. Juan Pablo Duarte by Av. Estrella Sadhala), and **Plaza Internacional** (just west of Bella Terra mall).

Gas

There are two **Texaco** stations, by Supermercado Nacional (Av. Estrella Sadhala and Av. 27 de Febrero), and across from Centro Médico Cibao (Av. Duarte).

Eat

While Santiago does not offer the wide array of eating establishments that Santo Domingo does, there are still plenty of options for every palate, from mountainside dining to vegetarian-oriented. The restaurants crowded around the Monument area are geared toward tourists, which means that quality, service, and prices will be slightly higher.

Inexpensive

Panadería Cibao Panadería Cibao is a perfect breakfast joint before a day of hoofing it around the city, but also works as an afternoon snack locations. This bakery serves much more than plain Dominican white bread: doughnuts, cookies, brownies, and cakes all fall under Panadería Cibao's purview. *96 C/ Independencia; 247-6318*

Chimi José Just over the bridge in the optimistically named Bella Villa district, Chimi José serves some of the most affordable, authentic, and high-quality Dominican food in the city. For a place with such an unassuming name (*chimi* is a word associated with street food), the top floor of the restaurant offers commanding views of the city and Monument. Favorites include a back-to-the-basics *plato del día* and the overflowing *yaroa* (See Street Food below), as well as a wide selection of juices and *batidas* from carrot to pineapple. *RD$50-200; Av. Emilio Prud'homme and Av. Nuñez de Cáceres*

Pizzeria Ole Downtown, cheap, accessible, and it serves pizza, so this restaurant has something going right. Ole is a nice open-air spot if it's not too hot, as the outdoor terrace presents a view of the park across the street. Sure, Ole is Mexican, and pizza is nominally Italian, but that can be overlooked after eyeing the large menu. *RD$100-500; 10am-1am; 15 Av. Duarte at Av. Independencia; 582-0866*

Pollo Provocón *Pollo al carbón*, perfected. This genius chain has the Dominican *bandera* down better than anywhere else – juicy rotisserie chicken with heaping servings of plantains, *yuca*, and rice and beans. Wash it down with a smooth *batida*. For spot-on, straight-up Dominican food, this is it. *RD$60-150; C/ Restauración and C/ Sabana Larga*

Sushi Ya! and Burger Ya! Santiago is full of US-based fast food joints, including McDonalds, Burger King, and Taco Bell, but for a quality Dominican twist on standard American tastes, try out twin restaurants Sushi Ya! And Burger Ya! Come for the mildly authentic sushi (including a roll called "fiesta shrimp") and specialty burgers like the Atkins burger. *RD$100-300; weekdays 10am-11pm, weekends 11am-2am; Corner of Av. Metropolitana and C/ Sebastián Valverde, Centro Jardines Metropolitanos; 580-1110*

Naturales Tes There aren't many places in this country to get a sweet and relaxing bubble tea, but this Taiwanese tea house is one of them. An oasis of calm, its airy, blue-and-white interior and unique vegetarian fare is gratifying to the eye and stomach. The chefs prepare fresh, inventive *platos del día* that include soups and salads, and vegetables rarely seen on Dominican plates. Plus, it offers free Wi-Fi access. *RD$50-250; C/ República de Israel and C/ D, a block north of Av. Duarte.*

Café Square One Located in the Shell gas station across from the entrance to the PUCMM (pronounced "Pucamaima") university, this café is open 24 hours a day with possibly the best cheesecake in the city. Air-conditioned and serving iced drinks, Square One works at either the beginning or end of your day, which could be at 7am either way. The Wi-Fi here is also exceptionally strong. *RD$100-300; Av. Estrella Sadhala*

Mid-Range

 Il Pasticcio Opened in 1994, Il Pasticcio is one of the best and most authentic Italian restaurants in Santiago, if not the country, perhaps helped by the chef's Italian provenance. The restaurant, which occupies a restored house, feels like a finely decorated period museum, and the charm is apparent – the walls are warmly patterned, and each table is a unique piece of furniture. The eggplant Parmesan, a tower of cheesy delight, is redolent, and perfect for vegetarians in this chicken-heavy country. *RD$170-450; Tue-Sun 12pm-4pm; 7pm-11pm; 3 Av. El Llano, behind Supermercado Nacional; 582-6061*

Puerta del Sol Puerta del Sol is located in the heart of the Monument district. It has a large, open-air terrace with a convivial atmosphere – and its own liquor store. Chow down on a burger with fries for a scant $100 pesos, or other menu items with more average prices. There are also flat-screen TVs to watch your favorite sports games. At night, find a livelier atmosphere, where people go to have a drink, listen to music, and enjoy the occasional karaoke. It is also much more authentic than, say, Kukara Makara next door: While visitors love this place, locals also come here to have a great time at night. *RD$100-500; Mon-Thu 11am-12am and until 2am Fri-Sat; 23 C/ del Sol, at C/ Daniel Espinal*

Kukara Macara Country Western? Yes, please. Sit beside a horseless stagecoach, hanging saddles, and prickly cacti and enjoy one of the quirkier restaurants in Santiago. Directly across from the Monument, there are few better places to take in Dominican nightlife, though clearly catering to outsiders. Stay here well after dinner and sip on cocktails with the fantastically attired wait staff in fully imagined Western regalia. *RD$120-450; 7 Av. Francia; 241-3143; restaurant@kukaramacara.com*

Santiago

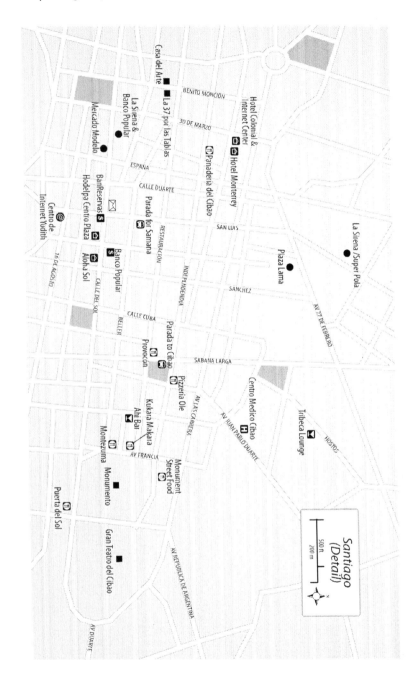

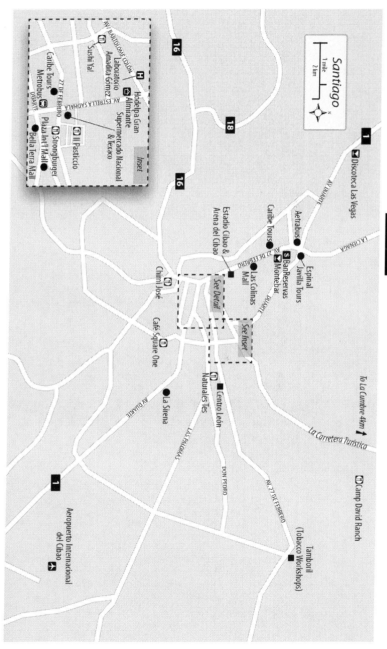

Santiago

Santiago

1 mile
2 km
N

Inset

AV. BARTOLOMÉ COLÓN
AV. ESTRELLA SADHALÁ
Sushi Ya!
Caribe Tours
Metrobus
27 DE FEBRERO
DUARTE
Hodelpa Gran Almirante
Laboratorio Amadita Gómez
Supermercado Nacional & Texaco
Strongburger
Il Pasticcio
Plaza Internacional Mall
Bella Terra Mall

16
18
16
1
Discoteca Las Vegas
AV. DUARTE
LA CIBAO

Estadio Cibao & Arena del Cibao
See Detail
Caribe Tours
Aetrabus
Espinal
Javilla Tours
BanReservas
Montebar
Las Colinas Mall
AV. 22 DE FEBRERO
DUARTE

Chimi José
Café Square One
AV. DUARTE
LAS PALMAS

La Sirena
Naturales Tes
Centro León
DON PEDRO
AV. 27 DE FEBRERO

To La Cumbre 4km
La Carretera Turística
Camp David Ranch
Tamboril (Tobacco Workshops)

1
Aeropuerto Internacional del Cibao

Montezuma Next door to Kukara Macara, the kitsch is slightly less glaring, but it can get just as busy. The open-air restaurant is great for people watching. However, sitting too close to the street is not recommended, as the chances are high of getting harassed by hawkers proffering DVDs and cell phone chargers. There is sometimes live music and karaoke at night. As it is popular with the tourists, Montezuma's food may be a bit overpriced, but chalk it up as an entertainment fee. *RD$200-600; Corner of Av. Francia and Beller, 581-1111*

Upscale

Camp David Ranch Famous businessman José Bermúdez opened Camp David in 1989 as a luxurious retreat on a hillside away from the bustle below, complete with a convenient helipad. He later converted it into an event center and restaurant, and today, it also has 35 hotel rooms. Though the winding road to reach the center can seem lengthy, the stunning views from the restaurant's patio are well worth the drive. During the day, mountains frame the Cibao Valley, and at night, the city lights twinkle. If you're lucky, watch a natural electric lights display as thunderstorms wind their way across the land, feeding off the tropical heat. Personal affects from Trujillo (like his antique cars), Bermúdez, and their contemporaries sprinkle the elegant, well-apportioned halls, lobby, and bar. Wait for a table on the terrace, and perhaps bring along a sweater, as it can get chilly at night in the hills. Many nights, a live band plays ambient music. *US$10-20; Carretera Luperón Km 7 1/2, Gurabo; 276-6400*

Street Food

The late-night scene in the city sees a number of pop-up places for revelers to get their second dinner, but there's no better place than by the Monument. Several carts set up in the parking lot across the street, selling empanadas and other fried and late-night goodies. Be sure to try out the Santiago delicacy called *yaroa*, a sort of steroidal nachos, heavy on the cheese and meat, and light on the salsa.

Strong Burger Really looking for a juicy chunk of America? It comes from a truck, only after sunset, in the form of the Double Bacon Strong Burger (or, and we might have to caution against this for health reasons, the quadruple burger). *RD$50-150; Av. 27 de Febrero, just east of Av. Estrella Sadhala; late night*

Sleep

For such a large city, Santiago does not have the same wide array of places to sleep as it does for eating establishments. All of the options below are located in the general downtown area, ranging from the most affordable to the most expensive.

Hotel Colonial No better deal can be found in a city bereft of decent, economic lodging. Hotel Colonial sits on a quieter side street in the major commercial district of Santiago. The hotel's 67 rooms in two adjacent buildings are sparse but clean, and importantly, a great value. Rooms with A/C are worth the slight increase in price. The hotel is Wi-Fi-capable, and there is also a restaurant and computer center in the lobby. If traveling in a group of three, ask for the special – and only – triple room, located on the roof. There is always someone friendly and helpful at the front desk – the attendants are known to give guests a wink and a nod when arriving back at the hotel in the wee hours of the morning. *RD$300-600; 113 C/ Salvador Cucurullo, by C/ 30 de Marzo; 247-312;, colonialdeluxe@yahoo.com; Amenities: TV, fan, hot water*

Hotel Monterrey Right next to Colonial, it rivals its neighbor in both quality and prices. Rooms are Spartan, but serviceable, clean, and safe. Like Colonial, Monterrey fits well within the scope of a budget traveler's affordability scale. *RD$450-600; 92 C/ Salvador Cucurullo; 582-4558; Amenities: TV, fan, hot water*

Aloha Sol Hotel & Casino Aloha Sol is a very comfortable spot on Calle Sol, for which it is named (though there is nothing much Hawaiian about the hotel, aloha notwithstanding). Its prices are reasonable for the high quality of the lodging: the rooms are nice, the staff highly attentive and bilingual, and the location unbeatable. All eight kinds of rooms, from the standard double to the Honeymoon Suite, come with a fridge, TV, A/C, and pristine private bathrooms. A buffet breakfast with creamy *mangú*, eggs, bread, and fruit is included with the stay. There's also a casino for your gambling enjoyment, with table games and more than a hundred slot machines. *RD$1800-8000; 50 C/ Sol at C/ Sánchez; 583-0090; reservaalohasol@yahoo.es; www.alohasol.com; Amenities: A/C, hot water, cable, microwave, fridge, laundry, business center, conference rooms, included buffet breakfast*

Hodelpa This luxury chain operates three hotels in Santiago (and one in Santo Domingo), all upscale, comfortable places to sleep. The sprawling Gran Almirante has an enormous, popular casino open very late, located downtown. The tidy Centro Plaza is situated next to Aloha Sol in the heart of the old city. Finally, the Garden Court is south of the city by the airport, tailored to business travelers. The hotels work well for those looking to be in the middle of the action, but want a quiet, contemporary oasis at which to lay their heads in the evenings. Prices begin at US$120 per night for rooms ranging from the single to the Imperial Presidential Suite. *Gran Almirante: Av. Salvador Estrella Sadhalá and C/ Sebastian Valverde; 580-1992. Centro Plaza: 54 C/ Mella at C/ Del Sol; 581-7000. Garden Court: Autopista Duarte Km 9; 612-7000. www.hodelpa.com; Amenities: A/C, hot water, TV, restaurant/bar, fridge, safe, iron, phone, radio alarm clock, Wi-Fi, parking lot*

Camp David Upscale, upmarket, uphill. The luxury of the Camp David restaurant is matched only by the hotel upstairs. Enjoy dramatic views of the valley below from the well-appointed rooms, which all have A/C or a fan, cable TV, bathrooms, Wi-Fi and balconies from which to take in the vista. *Rooms start at US$63; See "Eat" for more information on the restaurant and directions*

Do

Monumento a los Heroes de la Restauración de La Republic

A towering spire reigning atop a hill in the heart of the city, the Monumento is a testament to re-imagined history and Dominican society's ability to rebound from horror to pride in united sacrifice. In 1944, the centenary year of the nation, Trujillo ordered construction of an edifice honoring himself as a "Monument to Peace." Prominently displayed around the tower stood bronzes of his family; today, the statues have been replaced by important historical figures. Murals that date from the structure's inception decorate the tower's interior; the artist took some liberties in depicting the struggles of everyday Dominicans and was summarily dismissed from his work for being too provocative. Less offensive life-sized dioramas of important scenes from Dominican history also line the walls. The top floor affords dramatic views of the city, the valley, and the two mountain ranges on the horizon. After Trujillo's death in 1961, the Monument was renamed in honor of the victory in the War of Restoration against the Spanish in 1863. The tower has undergone extensive renovation, newly rededicated in 2007, and now is hailed as a cultural center for visitors to enjoy the fair view, repose-friendly grassy hills, and social atmosphere. Take a short walk on the grounds to see the playful animal sculptures gracing the steps leading up to the Monument. Make sure to visit in the evening, when the Santiago nightlife brings an entirely different atmosphere to the area. *RD$100; Av. Monumental; Mon-Sat 9am-12pm, 2pm-5pm*

Santiago

Estadio Cibao

Baseball is not a sport, it is a passion. There is no greater place to witness emotions running high than a baseball game between the home team Aguilas Cibaeñas against Licey of Santo Domingo in the largest stadium in the country. Attired in yellow and black, rowdy fans cause this 18,000-seat stadium to shake with joy when the beloved Aguilas take the field. Watching from the stands, filled with neighborhood bleacher creatures, is an unbeatable night in the city. Tickets run RD$50-150. Guards sometimes let fans wearing yellow (the team color) in for free to the outfield bleachers.

In the same complex is the brand-new **Gran Arena del Cibao**, with more than 8,000 seats – the largest basketball stadium in the country. The star Santiago team is part of the Dominican professional basketball league that has its season in the spring. Three Dominican basketball players currently play in the NBA, and have been known to show up in low-key tournaments here. Tickets to the games are RD$70. *To arrive, take the A carro público from the city center about one kilometer north along Av. 27 de Febrero toward the Rotunda to Av. Imbert.*

Gran Teatro del Cibao

Located behind the Monument, this theater is Santiago's major performing arts venue, showcasing theater, opera, and concerts. While we cannot promise Broadway quality with the shows, the center does host a fantastic, intimate jazz night every Monday (RD$100), with talented local and visiting artists performing up close to their audience. New York-based Dominican musicians often make this theater a stop on tours of home. *Av. Monumento, 583-5011*

Centro León

Billing itself as a place "where the world comes together," this standout museum certainly comes close. Centro León out-classes any other museum in the country, showcasing a fine permanent collection and relevant, topical rotating exhibits. Centro León was founded by the banking and business León Jiménez family in 1999 as a meeting place of art, culture, and learning, and has succeeded in its valuable mission. The interactive natural history section, with mangrove branches twisting through the exhibit, is a highlight.

The center's grounds include a well-manicured sculpture garden, bird sanctuary, and old tobacco house, where highly skilled rollers churn out the internationally sought-after Aurora cigars. As the men roll, a reader spits off the week's sports scores, along with current events, and occasionally poetry and literature (See the following Tobacco section). A coffee shop and outdoor terrace serves meetings and functions for many in the city. The museum also hosts discussions, classes, and a wide range of events and activities with local and international artists and academics. Entry on Tuesday is free. *RD$70; 146 Av. 27 de Febrero; 582-2315; centroleon@centroleon.org.do; centroleon.org.do; Tue-Sun 10am - 7pm*

Casa del Arte

This art house displays rotating exhibitions in the front rooms and hosts free cultural events several nights a week in the back outside. During performances, there is an optional RD$50 contribution. *Free; Benito Monción at C/ Restauración; 583-5346; Mon-Sat 9am-7pm*

La 37 por las Tablas

Across the street from Casa del Arte, this is space for alternative culture, hosting everything from expositions, speakers, and shows to yoga and meditation. Founded in 1999, the fiercely independent center features events ranging from meditation classes to poetry discussions to local food tastings. Some events are free, while others require a small fee. *37 C/ Benito Monción; 587-3033; la37porlastablas@gmail.com; www.la37porlastablas.blogspot.com*

Tobacco

The production, manufacture and sale of tobacco has a long history in the Dominican Republic, with cigar quality to rival those that come out of the more famous cigar-producing Caribbean country, Cuba. The Cibao Valley is the center of tobacco farming, and the city of Tamboril, just northeast of Santiago, is the home of the cigar creation. Even for those who do not have a subscription to *Cigar Aficionado*, a visit to a cigar rolling factory provides a fascinating afternoon of rural history and wafting aromas. Many offer personalized tours and a free cigar at the conclusion. To get to Tamboril, take Av. 27 de Febrero northeast for about five kilometers. Three of the most popular factories that give tours are: Fábrica Anilo de Oro (85 C/ Real; 580-5808), Los Maestros (299-1702; www.thedominicanrepublic.net/Cigar_Tour/), and Tabacalera Jacagua (13 C/ Capellán; 580-6600). All of them are open weekdays, from 7am to 4pm.

You might also want to visit the **Museo del Tabaco**, housed in a former Victorian mansion-cum-warehouse. The museum displays exhibits detailing the history and craft of tobacco, as well as cigars in the Dominican Republic. *C/ 16 de Agosto and C/ 30 de Marzo at Parque Duarte; Mon-Fri 9am-12pm and 2pm-5pm, and Sat 9am-12pm*

Centro León (see above) also has a small tobacco museum and store where rollers crank out Aurora cigars, housed in a replica building of the family's first cigar factory.

Biking

Situated in a valley between two mountain ranges, Santiago offers beautiful biking treks. Rent bikes and talk about area rides at **Bicicentro** *Av. Bartolomé Colón at C/ 27 de Febrero; 582-4146 or 471-7146; bicicentro@codetel.net.do*

"La Carretera Turística" and La Cumbre

La Carretera Turística is the small highway that runs north out of Santiago, directly up and over the Cordillera Septentrional range (see the regional Northwest map, p231, or the Northeast Coast map, p175, for location). Beyond being a beautiful drive, the road hosts a number of small attractions, though it was probably named a "tourist highway" for purely marketing reasons. Many of these attractions cluster around the village of La Cumbre ("the summit"), situated high atop the Septentrional range. A small sign designates the entrance to the community, which you might also notice when a few roadside stands selling fruit and crafts pop up. Be on the lookout for a little outlet run by elderly ladies selling straw-based products. These women create intricately weaved hats, bags called *macutos*, and other accessories. The area around La Cumbre is home to several amber mines, which is why there are a number of stands selling amber (*ambar*, in Spanish) goods. Because they come directly from the source, handmade amber jewelry here is much cheaper than at any tourist shop in the capital. See Amber in Puerto Plata, for tips on buy quality amber (p183).

It was also just past La Cumbre where the Mirabal sisters took their last, fateful journey. In 2008, the municipal and national governments inaugurated a small monument to the assassinated sisters – as well as their driver – in the place where, 48 years prior, the travelers were apprehended and assassinated by Trujillo's forces. There are plans to convert the area around the monument into an ecological reserve.

If you're feeling peckish after your purchases, or want a break from twisty, vertiginous driving, stop at **Rancho La Cumbre**. Located around the bend from the center of La Cumbre, this restaurant serves traditional and well-prepared Dominican fare with stunning views of the Cibao valley from its deck and terrace (656-1651; open daily 10am-11pm). *The highway leaves Santiago as Av. Bartolomé Colón, then narrows and begins its ascent. This road meets the coastal highway about nine kilometers to the east of Puerto Plata, just west of the town of Montellano.*

NIGHTLIFE

Santiago has a number of options for nocturnal merriment. For concentrated fun, check out the Monument area. There are several *colmados*, restaurants, bars, and general drinking establishments, all of which are good fun – and if one seems slow, just walk next door or across the street. At times, Santiago can rival the capital for evening activities, especially in the live music scene. For shows, there is usually a cover, though less for women (Dominicans claim that chivalry is not dead). Note that many bars and clubs have a dress code much stricter than in the US. No sandals, sneakers, or T-shirts are allowed, especially for men.

Ahi Bar Many of the Monument-area restaurants listed above maintain bars, so they are all good places to check out at night. Ahi is near the Monument, but just around the corner for a slightly more subdued atmosphere. There is dancing on a small floor, but the bar attracts just as many people. Begin your night with a cold Presidente and take in the scene before heading out. *71 C/ Restauración at C/ Tolentino*

Monte Bar Trying to see your favorite merengue/bachata/reggaeton/mambo/salsa musician in concert? Find the hottest acts in Dominican music at Monte Bar, which hosts multiple shows a week in a venue taken straight out of the dance scene in a Latin music video. The cover can reach RD$1000 for famous acts, but the price is worth the music, atmosphere, and company. *Av. 27 de Febrero; 575-0300; www.tipicomontebar.com*

Moma Bar Supposedly named for the museum in New York City, it is one of the more artsy venues in the city. In a cosmopolitan, contemporary atmosphere, the DJs at Moma play decidedly non-Dominican music, like jazz and rock. Women enjoy free drinks on Wednesday. *Centro Plaza Internacional, Av. Juan Pablo Duarte at C/ Ponce; 724-6781*

Discoteca Las Vegas Santiago's glitterati flee the city and its regular folk for the late-night fiestas at Las Vegas. What it lacks in gambling, it makes up for in the sparklingly attired ordering bottle service and hips moving to musicians' thumping beats. Famous singers usually make Las Vegas a stop in touring the country. The only way to get here is by private vehicle or taxi. *Santiago-Puerto Plata Highway; 241-8174*

Tribeca Lounge Tribeca oozes cool in a shimmering space, featuring banquette-lined walls and a crowded dance floor. Here, it's you, the DJ, and 250 of your best-dressed friends. The music shies away from countryside classics and romps towards deep-throated reggaeton, electronic, and top 40 dance hits. There is a cover on the weekend of at least RD$250. *6 C/ Mauricio Alvarez; 724-5000*

Casa Bader Opened 70 years ago, Casa Bader is something of a classic in Dominican social life. The young and old mix easily inside its doors, and it is here you'll see tables of regulars. Head outside to patio for food with a Middle Eastern flair and what some have said are the coldest beers in the country – quite the complement in the land where quality of the brew is rated in both taste and temperature. *75 C/ 16 de Agosto*

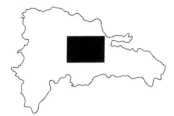

Cibao

The north-central part of the Dominican Republic is a broad, lush valley known as the Cibao. Spreading through the interior from Montecristi in the far northwest through to Nagua in the east, and buffered by mountain ranges to the north and south, the Cibao is the most fertile region of the country. West of Santiago, the population thins and the land turns more arid; this area is called "La Línea Noroeste," or the Northwest Line, and is more suited to ranching. East and south of Santiago, the soils are deep and dark. The rich agriculture lends this part of the valley the name of "La Vega Real," or the Royal Valley. Farming plays an enormous part of economic activity here, as hardy *campesinos* grow plantain, yuca, rice, tobacco, and other staple crops. These farmers tend small personal plots, aided by neighbors and seasonal Haitian workers.

The Cibaeños, as they are called, also have a distinct accent: they replace the letter "r" at the end of words with the letter "i." For instance, the word *amor* (love) is pronounced "amoi."

There aren't many traditional tourist activities in the Cibao as there are on the beach, but this valley is the heart of the Dominican Republic. The quintessential campo music, merengue, is most popular in the villages and towns spread across this valley, where classic merengue *típico* got its start in the early 20th century. In small communities across the valley, live merengue *típico* bands enthrall dancers with their rhythmic, enchanting music.

A slow drive through Cibao country roads provides wide vistas of colorfully painted houses, rolling plains, and silhouettes of purple hills on the horizon. It is well worth spending a day wandering through these vibrant valley towns to get a feel for daily Dominican life.

Bonao

Bonao is the first city on the highway north out of Santo Domingo, about an hour's drive away. It is the capital of the Monseñor Nouel province, bounded on one side by seemingly endless pancake-flat rice paddies, and on the other by the rapidly rising rock of the Cordillera Central. Bonao began, like many other towns, as an outgrowth around a fort; this one built in 1495 by the Columbus expedition. Modern Bonao is a two-industry town: rice production and mining. Falconbridge Dominicana, called Falcondo locally and owned by the Xstrata conglomerate, runs one of the largest extraction operations in the country through several nickel, cobalt, and other mineral mines in the foothills outside of town. The company has had an enormous impact on Bonao, as it employs a plurality of residents, subjecting the local economy – and job prospects – to wild swings in commodity prices, beyond the potential environmental impact of such activities.

Bonao is also home to artist and master painter Cándido Bidó, and there is a fascinating museum here in his honor. Visit www.bonaocityrd.blogspot.com, a local website dedicated to local news, sports, and music, for updates on local happenings in the city.

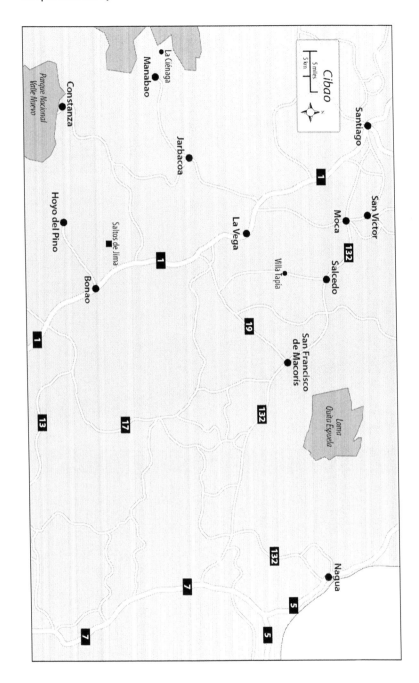

TRANSPORT

Tarea Bus
Tarea is the major line that services Bonao. The price is RD$115, the ride lasts about an hour, and buses depart from 6am to 6pm.

From Santo Domingo: buses leave from the Km 9 depot on Carretera Kennedy.

To Santo Domingo: find the stop on C/ 27 de Febrero and C/ Duarte.

To continue heading head north out of the city, simply stand on the highway and flag down a *guagua*.

Local Transport
Tarea Taxi is located at the Tarea Bus stop (525-3542), and *motoconchos* around town start at RD$20. For places a bit farther away, **Transporte Amarillo** runs along C/ Duarte and offers transport to the surrounding villages, including to Río Masi Pedro and the nearby waterfalls.

INFO

Communication
The internet is fast enough at **Nova & Son Centro de Llamadas & Internet** located on C/ 27 de Febrero near C/ 16 de Agosto (525-8925).

Banks
Banco Popular is on C/ 16 de Agosto and C/ Independencia, across from Parque Duarte (525-4502). There is also a Banco León at 179 Calle Duarte and a **BanReservas** on the corner of C/ 16 de Agosto and C/ Independencia, across from Parque Duarte.

Gas station
A **Shell Gas Station** is located on Av. Libertad near Av. Vargas.

Grocery Stores
Buy supplies and food at **Supermax**, on the corner of C/ Duarte and C/ General Cabral (525-5205).

EAT

Panadería de Miguelina With over a quarter-century in business, owner Miguelina Mirabal continues to make delicious breads and desserts: fruit turnovers, coconut cookies, and cakes covered with fluffy meringue. She has been so successful that she opened a rest stop on Carretera Duarte, which has an even larger selection – and the cleanest bathrooms for miles. *RD$25-200; 126 C/ Duarte near C/ General Cabral; 525-3546*

Plaza Merengue This spacious open-air restaurant throws its doors open for families, but also provides private palm-thatched huts for more intimate dining. Try the specialty rotisserie chicken as part of the *plato del día*, or the specialty steak à la Merengue. *RD$140-495; 52 C/ Isabela Católica; 525-8990/7545; www.plazamerengue.com; free Wi-Fi.*

Vista del Mar Ambitious attempts at swank at this restaurant in the Aquarius Hotel resulted in bejeweled zebra lanterns and white pleather, but the food somewhat redeems the décor. The menu includes a classy *plato del día* starting at RD$120, but the entrées are the big draw, featuring seafood plates like coconut curry shrimp and grouper stuffed with shrimp, as well as other pasta and meat dishes. *RD$120-460; 114 C/ Duarte; 296-0303; raymelgrupoempresarial@hotmail.com; Mon-Thu 5am-11pm, Fri-Sun 7am-11pm*

Caffe Monte Carlo An extra "f" makes all the difference at this destination, where stark black-and-white walls and geometric designs shape the large, multi-roomed dining space. Bonao's upper crust visits Caffe Monte Carlo, as the excellent food draws a stylish crowd. *RD$500-1000; Av. Prologancion Libertad and Autopista Duarte by Típico Bonao; 296-3332*

Típico Bonao This place has been a mainstay on the highway since 1962, even preceding the road's proper paving. Típico Bonao began as traditional as it gets, reveling in fried salami, eggs, and cheese astride mounds of steaming rice and beans – and don't forget the *tostones*. As time has worn on, however, the establishment has matured as well. It now offers more sophisticated fare including the likes of grilled chicken salad and pan-seared grouper. *RD$50-200; Autopista Duarte Km 53; 525-3941*

SLEEP

Hotel Gold Premium Centrally located with a restaurant in the lobby, this is one of the most affordable options in town without falling into the unsavory motel category. All rooms come with A/C and hot water, as well as internet and cable. *RD$1300-2000; 99 C/ Francisco J. Peinado; 296-3838; www.hotelgoldpremium.net*

Aquarius Hotel Hard to miss with a giant lobster scaling the building, this hotel underwent a renovation in 2002, leaving some of the tackier décor in the dust, replaced by the beautiful mosaics of Bonao native Cristian Tiburcio. Rooms range from simple singles to the spacious presidential suite, with all rooms coming standard with king size beds. Attached to the hotel is a popular weekend nightclub hosting live music and a bar open every night. *RD$1800-6000; 114 C/ Duarte; 296-0303; raymelgrupoempresarial@hotmail.com; Amenities: A/C, hot water, TV, restaurant, Wi-Fi, gym, pool*

DO

The city, set astride the gorgeous Cordillera Central foothills, means that there is great outdoor activity around. Bonao also has a strong arts culture, represented by the two museums below.

Plaza de la Cultura Cándido Bidó

Plaza de la Cultura Cándido Bidó is a museum and artistic school dedicated to the Bonao native and master painter for whom it is named. The museum features paintings and sculpture by the artist and his contemporaries. The school is open to all ages and offers a variety of art, music, and dance classes. *Plaza de la Cultura along C/ Independencia, one block from Parque Central; 525-7707; Tue-Sun 9am-5pm*

Cándido Bidó

Probably Bonao's most famous son, Bidó was a celebrated giant of contemporary Dominican art and culture. His vibrant paintings depict his fellow countrymen in quotidian activities, under a signature beaming yellow sun and the brightest of blue skies. Mothers and children, domestic pastoral scenes, and wildlife all figure prominently in his work. Bidó was a professor at the top-tier Escuela de Bellas Artes in Santo Domingo, while holding expositions of his work across the world, and winning several national prizes from artistic foundations. He passed away at age 74 in 2011.

Casa Museo Tiburcio or La Casa de Piedra

Home of the Bonao artist Cristian Tiburcio, along with his wife and three children, the house is made entirely of ceramic and stone mosaics, from the walls, to the beds, and even the blender. Bright tiles form figures like fish and animals, but the house features the artist's signature piece: eyes. Tiburcio uses eyes as a form of self-portraiture, producing an often-overwhelming sensation in its visitors. One particularly impressive area is in the bedroom called Bosque de los Sueños (Forest of Dreams), where the bedroom's toilet is literally a throne covered inside and out with colorful tiles.

The artist studied under Dominican master Bidó, whose influence is apparent in Tiburcio's use of color, especially Bidó's classic hues of blue and orange. The first floor is the only space with white walls, used to display the artist's paintings, sculpture, and mosaic pieces. His home-as-project began in 1998, and continues to be a work in progress with plans that call for an outdoor theater and community park. *12 C/ Los Pinos, Urbanización Falconbridge; contact Cristian at 525-2972 or 304-6510; cristiantiburcio@yahoo.com; www.casamuseotiburcio.com*

Parque de los Amapolas

This small park hosts El Homenaje de los Deportes, a playful and gravity-defying mosaic sculpture of a woman riding a motorcycle while balancing a number of objects with her body and playing the trumpet all at once. A creation of Cristian Tiburcio, the sculpture serves as a symbol of female strength and her ability to juggle all the challenges that life throws at her.

Saltos de Jima

The Saltos de Jima is a series of waterfalls and pools along the Río Jima, including the local favorite Pozos de la Reina, or Wells of the Queen. The waterfalls became part of a protected environmental area in 2009, and are a favorite weekend spot for people from as far away as Santo Domingo. There are trails for exploring the mountain-residing flora and fauna. The falls are located close to a small town called Charco Prieto.

There is no public transportation here, but a motorcycle ride form Bonao does not take long. From the capital, drive north past Bonao until just before Miguelina's Restaurant at a crossing called "Cruce de la Ceiba," where you'll make a U-turn, and then make a right going up the hill for several kilometers. There's a place to park, and a bit of a walk to the falls.

Hoyo del Pino

Seventeen kilometers uphill from Bonao into the deep, piney forests of the Cordillera Central is the small valley village of Hoyo del Pino. In 2004, community members founded a non-profit dedicated to the conservation of the area around a tributary of the Yuna River, one of the largest watersheds in the Dominican Republic. The recently completed **Río Blanco Ecotourism Complex** provides a peek into the wilderness and coffee farms around the village. The center provides hiking treks guided by local experts, birding tours of endemic and migratory species, and visits to mountain-cold swimming holes. Other attractions include one of the highest waterfalls in the country, coffee production demonstrations and tasting, and a stop at a bamboo artisan's workshop. A natural history museum is in the works. The

Cibao

complex has its own kitchen and lodging, and proceeds go to ecosystem preservation efforts and improving economic opportunities for local families around the project area. Guide service, which is required for some activities, is RD$50.

TRANSPORT

Private Car

Enter Bonao from Autopista Duarte, turning onto Avenida Libertad at El Restaurante Típico Bonao, on the west side of the highway. From Avenida Libertad, turn left at the Shell Station onto Calle Aniana Vargas. Remain on Aniana Vargas until it ends (you must make a left and then immediate right when Calle Duarte intersects the street), then turn left at the T-intersection onto Carretera Los Quemados, and then turn right where the road splits in the village of Los Quemados. After passing the high school, turn left at the large *colmado* on the corner. Continue on this road to Blanco. After crossing two bridges and climbing the steep mountain road, arrive in the community of El Cruce de Blanco. Follow the signs for the Complejo Ecoturístico Río Blanco and turn right, descending to Hoyo del Pino, where the complex is located.

Public Transport

At the Tarea Bus station in Bonao, pay a *motoconcho* (about RD$200) or a taxi (prices vary widely, but be aware that the taxi might not be able to make it all the way due to road conditions) to take you to Hoyo del Pino, Blanco, where the complex is located. At the time of publication, there was no reliable *guagua* service.

SLEEP

The **Bamboo Paradise Cabin** offers ten bedrooms – two- or four-person – with private bathrooms and heated water at RD$500 a night per person. The collective lodge has ten bedrooms with bunk beds and shared hot-water bathrooms. Breakfast (RD$80), lunch (RD$150), and dinner (RD$90) are available. Staying with a host family is the most inexpensive (and adventurous) option – the families have extra rooms, and breakfast and dinner with the family is included (RD$400). Note that at press time, these prices were tentative, so to check before booking. Reservations are strongly recommended. *Visit the complex at https://sites.google.com/site/visitacoeturb/home. For reservations, call 204-3279 or 525 8118 and ask for Esteban or email contacto.coeturb@gmail.com. The office is open daily 9am-5pm.*

La Vega

The Brothers Columbus together founded La Vega in 1494, when they ordered the construction of the Fortaleza Concepción to protect nascent trade routes headed toward the coast in 1494. A small market town began to develop around the fort, which gave the town its official name of Concepción de La Vega. The next year, a small band of Spanish troops defeated a much larger Taíno army just outside the city, at what is now Santo Cerro. This achievement is celebrated as a holiday, and thousands of pilgrims visit the site that marks the miraculous victory. The famous writer and defender of indigenous rights, Fray Bartolomé de las Casas, spent time in this church.

Gold, though small in quantity, was discovered in the area in 1508, resulting in further development. However, this boomtown found itself entirely leveled by an earthquake on December 2, 1562. The survivors shuffled their settlement a few miles away, to the city's current location on the Río Camú. Lacking the hoped-for gold supply, the new town remained minor and rural, based entirely on agriculture. However, in 1805, and like many other towns in the Cibao, it was sacked and burned by the Haitian army en route to its capture of Santo Domingo to the south.

Economic opportunity appeared with the arrival of the railroad connecting La Vega to the Samaná Bay and other north coast cities in the early 20th century. Although the tracks no longer exist (a relic engine sits in the median of Av. Rivas on the edge of the city), significant infrastructure and access to a port jumpstarted the city's industrialization. It is now an important center of commerce and transport, closely connected to Santiago and small valley villages. Area production includes both raw materials and manufactured goods, including tobacco, coffee, cocoa, rice, and cattle ranching. The city's population has almost tripled over the past 20 years, owing to rural-urban migration from the surrounding valleys. The population augmentation is a double-edged sword for the city, placing a considerable strain on municipal resources while adding an enormous source of potential economic expansion.

TRANSPORT

Unfortunately, the **Caribe Tours** stop is inconveniently located on a dusty corner by the highway outside of town, so passengers must take public transport or a taxi to access it.

To Santo Domingo: RD$200; 2hrs; 28 daily departures from 6:30am to 7:45pm

To Sosúa (RD$165; 3hrs), **Puerto Plata** (RD$150; 2.5hrs), and **Santiago** (RD$100; 1.5hrs); hourly departures from 6am to 7pm

To Dajabón: RD$150; 3.5hrs; 6:30am, 8am, 9:30am, 1pm, 2pm, and 3:45pm

To Salcedo: RD$60; 30 min; 7am, 10:30am, 2pm, 5:45pm

INFO

Medical Attention

The public **Hospital Luis Morillo King** is on Av. Imbert and Balilo Gómez.

Banks

Banco Popular is located on C/ Colón and C/ Gral. Juan Rodríguez and **BanReservas** is located at C/ Manuel Gómez and José Rodríguez.

Communication

There is an **Indotel** at C/ Mella by Av. Pañal.

Grocery Stores

For your freshest goods, visit the open-air municipal market sprawling out under blue tarps at C/ Nuñez de Caceres and Av. Pañal. Also, a shiny new branch of the **La Sirena** superstore looms large at Av. Rivas and C/ Luis Alberti, with a **pharmacy** inside.

Gas

A **Shell Station** is on at Rivas and Pedro Casado and there are a **Texaco station** and **Isla Gas Station** located on C/ Antonio Guzmán Fernández north of C/ 27 de Febrero.

EAT

Centro Naturista de Orientación Alimentaria Nutrabien Outside of the capital, the vegetarian restaurant pickings are slim, but not so in La Vega with Nutrabien. All of the options are excellent, uniquely bridging Dominican, Caribbean, and pan-Latin cuisine. *RD$100-300; 6 C/ Batista; 277-0044*

Macao Grill There are lots of tasteless places, catering to pilgrims and tourists, ringing the cathedral square. Macao, however, actually fires up some decent pizzas. Besides the requisite rice and beans, it also has other American classics like burgers and cheese-happy nachos. *RD$100-300; 82 C/ Don Antonio Gúzman; 573-2020*

Pollo Restaurant Many eateries in this country fall into the "hole in the wall" classification, but most at least they have some sort of signage. This chicken restaurant has nothing around announcing its existence, but it still cooks up possibly the best bird in town, in addition to all the favorite Dominican sides to go with. Visitors looking for something more authentic away from the central square should make this their lunch destination. *RD$100-150; C/ Luis Alberti and Av/ Rivas, across from La Sirena*

SLEEP

There are not too many options in town, but if circumstances dictate, try **Hotel Familiar San Pedro**. The proprietors are warm and welcoming, and speak some English as they lived in Florida for a few years. The rooms are sparse and without too much character. *RD$400; 87 C/ Núñez de Cáceres; 573-2844*

DO

Carnaval

Carnaval celebrations take place across the world, and the Dominican Republic would never be left out of a good party. In this country, festivities run for the entire month of February, culminating on Independence Day (February 27). The liveliest celebrations happen on Sunday, when parades lasting the entire day, involving thousands of participants wearing elaborate costumes, march along major thoroughfares of every town and city. Each location has its own unique variation, from costumes to music, dance, food, and drink. The most recognizable aspect of the Carnaval tradition revolves around these colorful costumes, topped off by intricately designed masks. The mask and costume are a cooptation of indigenous and African traditions involving warring parties and supernatural, mysterious spirits. Many of the get-ups are representative of diabolical spirits, known as *diablos cojuelos*, probably the happiest-looking devil costumes around. Others include various animal representations or caricatures of well-known figures. Preparations begin a year before the holiday's processions, as groups decide on colors, fabrics, and themes of the costumes. In some cities, neighborhoods and community groups compete against each other for costume prizes. Santo Domingo hosts groups chosen from across the country to have the privilege of marching in its Carnaval parade.

Watching this parade is certainly the best way to participate in Carnaval festivities. Standing too close to the parade route, or anyone in costume, however, will make the jovial onlooker an active participant. One somewhat violent aspect of Carnaval is the wielding of *vejigas*, or inflated pig bladders (though now they are made of synthetic material). The parading costume-wearers flail the devilish *vejigas* at the backsides of unsuspecting spectators and other marchers, resulting in spectacular bottom bruises by the end of the day.

La Vega is the epicenter of Carnaval celebrations. This otherwise inconspicuous city explodes in excitement and revelry from early Sunday morning to very late in the night with a massive parade and enormous celebration running across dozens of city blocks. The party culminates in live music replete with fireworks and lots of food and drink. The biggest celebration comes with the dual party of the last day of Carnaval and Independence Day. Dominicans from across the country visit La Vega at least one weekend in February to take part in these gleeful and spectacular festivities.

La Vega Vieja

Aside from La Isabela, La Vega Vieja represents the oldest remains of European settlement in the New World. On December 2, 1562, a massive earthquake leveled the original La Vega that had grown around Christopher Columbus's Fortaleza de la Concepción. Today, not much remains standing: the fort's foundation, a singular column of the stone Franciscan monastery and church, and various gravesites of both Spaniards and Taínos. Much of the material was carted off after the quake, used as a basis for the new, and current, La Vega. If hungry, there are a few cafeterias on the highway by the ruins. La Vega Vieja was named a Historic National Park in 1977, and excavation and study on the site is ongoing. *RD$50, guided tours in Spanish. Open weekdays 8am-3pm and weekends 9am-4pm. The site is located about 5 kilometers north of La Vega on the main highway, so the easiest way to get there is by taxi. If arriving in private vehicle, look for the large sign noting the exit for site.*

Santo Cerro

Just south of La Vega is Santo Cerro, a small hill with considerable significance. The history of Santo Cerro is shrouded in cultural mythology, but it is an important symbol in Dominican society. Just a year after building the fort, Columbus was met with his first major battle against the local population, who had quickly tired of the Spaniards' shenanigans. Upward of 30,000 Taíno troops fought a much smaller number of European men and a few allied Taínos. After at least a week of fighting, the indigenous army forced the Spanish to retreat to the hill. Before going to sleep, Columbus constructed a small cross from hardy tree boughs and prayed for help. During the night, Taíno troops attempted to burn the cross, but it refused to go up in flames. Soon after, Columbus' personal confessor witnessed a white apparition – now known as the Virgen de las Mercedes – holding a child, descend onto the cross. Miraculously, by the next morning, the Taíno weapons were rendered useless, the army had vanished, and the Spanish were saved. A shrine was later erected on the site of the cross. In 1880, adherents built the white **Iglesia la Mercedes** church that stands there today, which now holds beautiful stained glass windows and a detailed wooden altar.

The cross, of course, is no longer there; all that is left is a hole in the ground, set inside the church (called **Santo Hoyo de la Cruz**). Plenty of entrepreneurial Dominicans, however, are more than happy to sell cheap relics and graphic tees to anyone who passes by. While this might be a bit of an eyesore, the view of the vast greenery of the Cibao Valley from the hill is magnificent. Subtract the signs of civilization, and visualize thousands of displeased Taínos storming across the near view, and it's easy

Cibao

enough to place yourself in Columbus' (probably uncomfortable) shoes. *Free; 8am-2pm, 2pm-6pm*

Catedral Inmaculada Concepción

Like many cities, La Vega has a lively central square, flush with families, vendors, and rumbling motorcycles. This one, however, is dominated by the hulking, postmodern Catedral Inmaculada Concepción. Not unlike its sister Piazza in Venice, the square is pigeon-populated, though in this case, mimicking the Cathedral's joyless gray. While the interior includes pretty images of saints, landscapes, and historical events, the Cathedral's unfortunate cement-and-metal exterior reflects an industrial chic reminiscent of mid-century Soviet architecture. Still, the enormous Cathedral, opened in 1992, represents an important landmark in Dominican culture, as thousands of people arrive in the city each year to pay homage at one of the largest religious centers in the country. *Av. Gúzman and C/ Padre Adolfo*

Moca

Equidistant from Santiago and La Vega, the pretty town of Moca prides itself on being the Cuna de los Héroes – Cradle of Heroes. It was here where rebels hatched the plans to successfully knock off both Trujillo and the 19th century dictator Ulises "Lilís" Heureaux. A small park and vivid mural serves as a monument to the heroes' assassination of Lilís in 1899, at C/ Colón and C/ 26 de Julio. Though it might be famous for taking down dictators, Moca also provided the country with three of its presidents: Horacio Vásquez; Ramón Cáceres, whose own father was killed by Lilís; and Héctor García Godoy.

Among the general bustle around town, Moca's grand Iglesia Sagrada Corazón de Jesus, at Autopista Ramón Cáceres and Av. Duarte, shines through. Built in 1945 and run by the order of the Salesians, the church imported several Italian-crafted stained glass windows, unique among sacred spaces in the country. Mass is performed thrice daily.

Moca is also home to one of the only two public zoos outside the capital. It isn't terribly inspiring, straining under good intentions and limited by a lack of funds, but still important, as it is accessible to those who cannot make it to the capital (C/ Duarte by C/ García Godoy).

TRANSPORT

Unlike the rest of the Cibao towns, Moca is not serviced by Caribe Tours. Smaller *guaguas* run frequently to and from the surrounding towns. Moca is also one of two places besides Santiago to catch a bus up and over the Cordillera Septentrional, one of the most scenic drives in the country.

To Sabaneta de Yásica: RD$100; 90min; 7am-5pm; C/ Antonio de la Maza by C/ Dr Guerrero

To Los Bueyes: RD$150; 2hrs; 12pm and 2pm (the 2pm bus is known to leave as late as 5pm); C/ Presidente Vásquez at C/ Salcedo

To Salcedo: RD$40; 30min; 7am-5pm; C/ Duarte and C/ José María Rodríguez

To Santiago: RD$50; 30min; 7am-5pm; Parque Cáceres at C/ Salcedo and C/ Alfonseca.

There are two options to **Santo Domingo**. The first is **Expreso El Viaducto**, which leaves at García Godoy by the zoo (RD$180; 2.5hrs; 7am, 10am, 2pm, and 5pm). The second is **Expreso Mocano**, which leaves about every half hour from C/ Antonio de la Maza by C/ Caceres (RD$190; 2.5hrs; 6am-6pm).

INFO & EAT

For a quick internet check, visit **Diginet**, at C/ Alfonseca and C/ 16 de Agosto. Other services are available in nearby Santiago.

The hungry visitor should look around the town square, ringed by small cafeterias. One of the best is **Pizzeria Encarnación**, with a good mix between traditional Dominican and American food. It sells a fantastic *plato del día* for just RD$90, pizza for RD$30 a slice, as well as hamburger, hotdogs, salads, cake, and brownies (RD$30-200; C/ Cordoba; 578-0870). For dessert or pastries, visit **La Casona**, a popular bakery downtown. La Casona serves everything crunchy to creamy, including difficult to find birthday cakes. (C/ Córdoba and C/ Presidente Vásquez). Thirsty travelers should stop at **Coffey**, a bar with a rare Dominican happy hour, as well as coffee and snacks (C/ Alfonseca and C/ Cordoba).

Higüerito

The small village of Higüerito lies just northwest of Moca, where an organized and talented collection of ceramic masters calls home. For generations, these artisans have been utilizing the region's unique clay soils to create beautiful ceramic pieces. In 1983, 30 men and women joined together to form the Artisan Association of Higüerito, Moca. The Association, with years of collective production power, markets and sells local, handmade ceramics and pottery in both domestic and international markets.

The signature work of the Higüerito artisans is the faceless doll. The dolls, fashioned in distinct shades and sizes and clad in traditional dress, represent the collectivity of the Dominican spirit. These dolls without facial features tell the story of contemporary Dominican society's diverse origins, united by culture and history. It is worth a visit to experience the artisan workshops firsthand, since Higüerito is very accessible from Santiago. Pass by overpriced shops in the cities and spend an afternoon here, speaking with the artisans themselves and watching them generate their craft.

The artisans also make traditional jars, cooking pots, and wall hangings, loosely basing their work on traditional Taíno designs. Other artisans in Higüerito are metalworkers, creating brilliant painted butterflies inspired by the Mirabal sisters.

TRANSPORTATION

Once arriving at any of the following locations, walk or catch a *motoconcho* (RD$25) to your destination in the village. To return to Santiago or La Vega, simply stand on the highway and flag down a *guagua* going your way; the cost should be no more than RD$40. To Moca, return to the Higüerito entrance to catch the same *carro público*.

From Moca: RD$25; 6am-6pm; 15 min; take a *carro público* located next to the bus station for Santo Domingo to the entrance of Higüerito.

Cibao

From Santiago: RD$10-20; 6am-6pm; 20min Take the green OMSA city bus (routes A, B, or Central) to "la segunda entrada para Ortega," or the second stop for Ortega. It's also possible to catch the *guagua* going to La Vega, and get off at the same road for Ortega. Cross the highway to get to the entrance to Higüerito.

From La Vega: RD$40; 6am-7pm; 20 min; take a *guagua* to Santiago, and ask for the first entrance to Ortega.

Private Transportation

Coming from the south, the highway exit is about 20 minutes past la Vega. Known as the first entrance to Ortega, there is a sign for Veras Supermarket, and a large orange -yellow building. It is also the beginning of Santiago's OMSA bus route, and two entrances before the turnoff for the Santiago airport (helpful if coming from the north). Continue straight and about a mile down you will see a sign for Higüerito, Moca. Make a right at the stop with motorcycles right after the large church on your left. Make a quick left and continue a couple minutes farther to find the Pensión de Elena on your right (a white and pink house with an iron front gate). Two doors down is the Artisan Association building, painted with the name of the Association on the front.

SLEEP & EAT

The artisan association has set up a three-room bed-and-breakfast called **La Pensión de Elena**, run by only the most amiable of its members. Three meals are included in the price. *RD$700; C/ Principal, next to the artisan center; 818-8264 (ask for Elena); radhamescarela@gmail.com*

There are a number of small, local eateries around the village. A new grilled chicken joint is down the street from the Pensión. Also find a stand – located right by Higüerito's baseball field – selling empanadas and *ballas de yuca* (fried yuca fritters) as a tasty nighttime treat.

DO

Artisan Association Tours

The tours last about two hours, but they can be catered to the needs of each group or visitor. Most tours include a peek inside artisan workshops to see ceramics made using traditional techniques, highlighting those making the famous faceless dolls. The tours end at the artisan association headquarters, where artisan products are on sale. Visitors are encouraged to try their hand at making a faceless doll. *Reservations are recommended. Contact Rafael "Nanan" Castaño or Rádhames Carela at 829-967-304; radhamescarela@gmail.com*

Functional Ceramic Creation and Tours

Ask to tour both the Filter Pure (ceramic filter facility) and the stove and oven production. Beyond making dolls, the artisans also make five-gallon ceramic water filters to provide potable water for personal use. Rain or river water is simply poured through the top, filters through the fine layers, and emerges clean enough for drinking. In addition, a few artists specialize in oven making. These ovens, though still using wood as fuel, are cleaner and more efficient than traditional open-air ovens. The ovens are darlings of the appropriate technology movement, which emphasizes affordable, locally sourced technology that fits a community's needs.

Tours last less than an hour, but provide knowledge of the basics of water filtration and of the workings of simple yet critical ceramic ovens. Engineers and those interested in sustainability will be especially interested. *Reservations are recommended. Contact Rafael "Nanan" Castaño or Rádhames Carela at 829-967-3042, radhamescarela@gmail.com.*

San Victor

A small town north of Moca at the foot of the Cordillera Septentrional, San Victor is known for three things: a meditative hillside hike, its large population of painters, and *chicharrón*. While all independent of each other, these three elements combine to make San Victor a good place to stop for a couple hours while driving through the Cibao.

TRANSPORT

From Moca: RD$20; a *carro público* runs here from the corner of C/ Antonio de la Maza and C/ Cordoba in front of Banco Popular

From Santiago: Go to Moca and follow directions above, or take the *carro público* (the line is called "T") that runs along C/ 27 de Febrero to Tamboril to the last stop (RD$30), and then switch on the same road to the *carro público* for San Victor (RD$25).

DO

El Monte de Oración

El Monte de Oración is a conference and retreat center with a meditative walk leading to the top of a small hill. This free hike goes through the 15 stations of the cross, depicting the last hours of the life of Jesus. There are reflection points at each stop. Mass is held on Sunday and holidays. The hike up the hill takes about an hour, including stops at the stations. At the top is a stunning view of Moca, Santiago, the Cibao airport, and the rest of the valley. *The visitor's center is open Mon-Sat, 8am-5pm; 823-0935*

Artist Community

Less famous but just as talented as the sculptors in Higüerito are the painters of San Victor – perhaps there is something about Moca-area villages that inspire. Though not very organized, the artists here are working with the Peace Corps to improve both their craft and business acumen. While many of the artists have only found employment making mass productions sold by street vendors, a few have been able to break out of commercial art, winning domestic and international prizes. Most of the 60 artists who comprise the San Victor community have private workshops, but there are also two loose artisan associations, **Garabato** and **Grupo Primario**. Although neither group has a shared studio, the artists work together and can offer a tour that includes several workshops. Contact Garabato president Alberto Caraballo (829-248-19820) or Grupo Primario representatives Fermin Baret (829-981-4010) or Danilo Peña (829-295-3730), to meet with the artists or buy artwork. The newly reopened **Babeque** art gallery is open to the public for exhibitions and sale of paintings and sculpture. Contact the owner, Raul Geradino (915-9725).

Chicharrón

The farmland around Moca is pig country, so it is no surprise that San Victor lays claim as a center of crunchy, greasy *chicharrón*, or fried pig skin, commonly called pork rinds. San Victor-style *chicharrón* is actually deep-fried pork ribs with a thick, crispy skin layer. At least a dozen *chicharrón* vendors sell their artery-clogging wares along Calle Principal. The largest stand, Parada Eddy, is located at the major intersection, across from the park and gas station. Soldiers from the nearby base, along with travelers headed up the highway to the mountains and coast, stop by and order bagfuls for RD$50 and up of cholesterol-induced fun for breakfast, dinner, or crispy afternoon snack. The servings of *chicharrón* come with sides of boiled green bananas, yuca, or *casabe* (flat yuca bread).

Chicharrón, while hearty, may not actually represent a complete meal, so grab a small bag to snack on and stop at the nearby **Comedor Yaris**. Located on Calle Principal, this local cafeteria serves excellent *platos del día* for RD$80-100. It is open only for lunch, from 10am to 2pm daily.

Los Bueyes

Spectacularly situated atop a ridge of the Cordillera Septentrional, every turn in this tiny village is a verdant mountainscape. Terraced farmlands are sculpted out of the hillside, hefty cows graze on impossibly steep slopes, and swift waterways carve miniature canyons as they rush downhill. Named for the oxen that once carried lumber for export under the American occupation, Los Bueyes is just 35 kilometers from Moca, but it feels worlds away. The only road up is steep and windy, but its conclusion is beautiful.

Almost unprecedented in the Dominican Republic, national and international organizations have teamed up with community leaders and the Asociación de Desarollo de la Provincia de Espaillat (ADEPE, a Moca-based NGO) since 1990 for the promotion and protection of the environment while pursuing sustainable community-based development. By appropriately utilizing the potential of the natural beauty, the organizations work toward quality of life improvements for the community. Though lacking such basic amenities as power lines and running water, the community and its partners have produced a successful environmentally conscious ecotourism park called **Sereno de la Montaña**. The new complex, completed in 2010, offers an array of outdoor activities through the mountains, highlighted by cascading waterfalls, swimming holes, and mountain rivers.

Hiking to Sereno de la Montaña

To throw a hike in the mix, take a *guagua* from the *Mercado Nuevo* in Moca toward Gaspar Hernández and get off at Palo Roto (RD$100), where there is a very clear path through the forest. The trail includes a manageable river crossing (if it hasn't been raining) and it ends directly at Sereno de la Montaña. The walk should take less than an hour.

TRANSPORT

From **Moca**, catch the Los Bueyes *guagua* (RD$150) at the corner of C/ Presidente Vázquez and C/ Salcedo, or catch a *guagua* to Villa Trina (RD$45), and then a motoconcho (RD$200) to Los Bueyes.

If renting a 4x4, take the road to Villa Trina and then follow signs to Los Bueyes. To arrive at Sereno by private vehicle, pass through most of the road that meanders through the village of Los Bueyes, to arrive at the far side of town. There are a few signs, but asking friendly locals always helps.

EAT

The complex houses a restaurant, which serves up breakfast, lunch, and dinner, as well as a bar in which to relax after a day in the outdoors. The *plato del día* is RD$150, and the other meals are a la carte.

SLEEP

Sereno de la Montaña just opened two rustic-chic cabañas running on solar-powered electricity. The cabañas are based on traditional architecture to match their surroundings, and have warm water (if there has been enough sun). Each cabin has five rooms with a total capacity of 50. Reservations are required for lodging, as well as for some activities, for which the prices have not yet been officially set – so ask when making reservations. *Starting at RD$300 p/p; 829-424-7070; serenomontana@gmail.com, www.serenodelamontana.com*

DO

As an ecotourism center, Sereno offers multiple outdoor and educational activities. For the **hikers,** there are four trails, between one and six kilometers in length, through coffee and natural forest, a bird sanctuary, small streams, and rocky mountain passes. Local, trained guides lead the hikes, carrying with them a deep knowledge of the landscape and environment. Those who would rather let a horse do the walking have the option of going on guided **horseback riding** tours, though it's also possible to rent horses by the hour. The tours are the best way to see the countryside, lead by guides that take visitors through adjacent communities with stops at the waterfall and swimming holes. To see the sights while getting wet, Sereno rents **inner tubes** and **kayaks** for trips down a section of the Jamao River.

Finally, those who wish to spend the night outside can bring their own tent and go **camping** in a small plain called La Gloria, right beside the leisurely mountain waters of the Río Jamao. Note that prices for these activities have not yet been set, but vary by number of people and hours of use.

Salcedo

An attractive small town of 12,000 in the middle of the Cibao valley, Salcedo's savvy marketing team has re-branded the city around its claim to fame – the Hermanas Mirabal. These sisters, who grew up on an estate east of town, became martyrs at the hands of dictator Rafael Trujillo, who met his own death just a year later. The city of Salcedo is pleasant and warm, with clean streets and a recently renovated central square featuring brass sculptures and a stately, red-trimmed cathedral.

Over the past five years, the city has undergone a large-scale beautification campaign to paint colorful murals on every empty wall in the city – and eventually the entire province. The murals explore lively pastoral scenes: exploding rainbows of butterflies, bursting cacao pods, and gallivanting children who smile at passersby and motorcycles.

Though Salcedo is named after a hero from the War of Independence, the city's laurels rest on the Hermanas Mirabal, whose presence suffuses the city. In 2007, the province, once also called Salcedo, was renamed Provincia Hermanas Mirabal. The new 200-peso bill, as well as the enormous water tower at the western entrance of the town, prominently features an angelic profile of the sisters. The city has therefore fashioned itself as "Cuna de Las Mariposas, Tierra de los Murales," or Cradle of the Butterflies, Land of the Murals. While Salcedo is not a destination town, it is a convenient and pretty stopover during a drive through the valley. The small downtown is centered on the spruced-up Parque Duarte and its cathedral, worth a look inside. Ice cream, juice stands, and internet cafés line the streets around the park.

The provincial government publishes a monthly magazine and a very informative, if somewhat dry, website, at www.provinciahermanasmirabal.gob.do.

TRANSPORT

Caribe Tours is located on C/ Francisa Mollins at C/ Restauración (577-2414).

To Santo Domingo: RD$230; 2hrs; 6am, 10:30am, 2pm, 5:45pm

From Santo Domingo: RD$230; 2hrs; 7am, 10:30am, 2pm, 5:45pm

Guaguas

To Santo Domingo: RD$180; 2.5hrs; hourly 6am-11am and 2pm-5pm; C/ Hermanas Mirabal and Independencia

To Moca: RD$40; 30 min; 6am-5:30pm; C/ Hermanas Mirabal and C/ Duarte

To Santiago: RD$70; 1 hr; 6am-5:30pm; C/ Hermanas Mirabal and C/ Duarte

To San Francisco de Macorís: RD$60; 45 min; 6am-5:30pm; C/ Restauración and C/ Colón

INFO

Medical Attention

The public hospital here is not advisable. Go to Santiago (p247) for medical services.

Communication

Internet y Copicentro is most reliable internet in town, though prices (RD$20/hr) rise when the electricity goes out and the center uses its gas-powered plant (C/ Hermanas Mirabal and C/ Mella). **Infotep** is a free, public internet center above the library. It has an unreliable schedule, but a good connection when it is open (more or less 9am-12pm, 2pm-5pm Mon-Fri; C/ Hermanas Mirabal and Duarte)

Grocery Stores

Mercado Toribio is on C/ Hermanas Mirabal and C/ Francisca Mollins.

Gas

There are two gas stations on either edge of the city. The first is on C/ Hermanas Mirabal, across from the bus station to the capital, and the other is one kilometer south of the city on the road to the small town of Villa Tapia.

EAT

El Carnero Once the best bet for a good meal in town, sometimes this restaurant does not serve food and just proffers beer. If it's open, it serves generic, but tasty, Dominican fare, along with some Mexican food. Take a table on the patio by the street. Next door is a bustling bar called Punto G, so it can also be great for people watching. *RD$100-200; C/ Doroteo Tapia, between C/ Duarte and C/ Francisca R. Mollins*

Pica Pollo Salcedo This chicken restaurant offers classic *pica pollo* greasy goodness served buffet-style on plastic trays. *RD$50-150: C/ Hermanas Mirabal and C/ Duarte*

El Druño El Druño is popular for business lunches and for that reason, it has the highest quality food in town, serving rice, beans, and chicken on sparkling glass tables. It is also more expensive than other options, and a bit of a walk from the park. *RD$100-400; C/ María Josefa Gómez and Buby Dhose*

SLEEP

Hotel La Casona Gran Imperial Slightly less grandiose than its name implies ("Great Imperial Mansion Hotel"), it is the only decent option in Salcedo. The hotel has 19 quite presentable single-, double-, and triple-occupancy rooms housed in a tropical orange-salmon building dating from 1933. There is a lively open-air bar downstairs. *RD$800-1300; 51 C/ Doroteo Tapia and C/ Francisca Mollins; 577-4468; hotelacasona@hotmail.com, luisramon771@hotmail.com; Amenities: fan, bathroom*

DO

Museo Hermanas Mirabal

The museum is a former home of the Mirabal family, where the famous sisters spent much of their childhood. Surviving sister Dedé serves as caretaker, so lucky visitors might be able to catch her and have the opportunity to chat. The museum provides scant information on their life's work, instead emphasizing the sappy, like family knickknacks, monogrammed linens, heirloom silver, and a lock of hair. Though it

Las Hermanas Mirabal

The four sisters – Patria, Minerva, María Teresa, and Dedé – were born into an affluent family between 1924 and 1935 outside of Salcedo. The first three sisters eventually became activists in the anti-Trujillo Movimiento 14 de Junio resistance group, all also marrying fellow activists. The movement took this name after the day that a group of Dominican exiles met in Cuba to plot a failed coup against Trujillo. Within the group, the sisters were nicknamed "the butterflies," which is why the butterfly image is seen fluttering across the province on walls, literature, and clothing. At different points, the sisters and their husbands were all imprisoned for their activities.

By 1960, underground activism was coming to a head, and Trujillo's iron grip on the country was slipping. On November 25, after visiting their husbands serving yet another prison sentence, the three sisters and their driver were stopped by a cadre of Trujillo henchmen. The party was led into a cane field and summarily executed. To pull off the act as an accident, the perpetrators pushed the travelers' car off of a cliff. The death of the sisters reverberated across the nation, perhaps finally moving the Dominican population and galvanizing public resistance. Only six months later, on May 30, 1961, members of 14 de Junio successfully assassinated Trujillo.

The story of the sisters was known, though not popularly celebrated, after democracy had been painfully restored to Dominican politics. In 1994, Dominican-American author Julia Alvarez took up the mantle of promoting the sisters. She published a historical fiction novel based on the sisters' lives called "In the Time of the Butterflies," adapted into a movie in 2001. An additional movie was filmed on location in the Dominican Republic, with the approval of Dedé herself, under the title *Trópico de Sangre*. It was released in 2010.

Cibao

may resemble a 1950s period piece museum, it is absolutely worth a trip, given the importance of the sisters in Dominican history. The beautiful grounds serve as a memorial to the fallen heroes. *RD$100; 5 kilometers east of Salcedo on the highway toward San Francisco (C/ Doroteo Tapia); 9am-6pm*

Ruta de los Murales

As mentioned above, every empty wall in town is being painted to produce lively murals portraying cultural scenes of families, nature, and historical events. Find a map of the Ruta in the Oficina Técnica, located in the public offices building on C/ Hermanas Mirabal and C/ Independencia, where someone might offer to point out the highlights. It is also easy enough to simply wander around town and marvel at the colors. Though many of the artists involved are local, some have been hired from as far away as Japan to leave their mark on the city.

Feria

Begun in 2007, a biannual artisan fair takes place on November 25, rotating between the three towns (Salcedo, Tenares, and Villa Tapia) in the province. November 25 is the International Day for the Elimination of Violence against Women, as declared by the UN in 1999, on the date that the Mirabal sisters were assassinated. The fair celebrates the bounty of the province, with crafts, paintings, and performances, and serves to remember the work of the Mirabal sisters.

Higüeros

Some of the more interesting pieces for sale at the fair are carved *higüeros*, a kind of gourd. Artisans from the tiny village of Las Aromas , about 7 kilometers south of Salcedo, formed a loose group to market their wares of intricately carved and painted *higüeros*. The artisans fashion such items as cups, bowls, maracas, and specialty güiras – percussion instruments resembling cheese graters used in merengue *típico* performances.

NIGHTLIFE

Citizens of Salcedo enjoy drinking and dancing as much as anyone else. For the biggest party, visit **Orlando Carwash** on C/ Doroteo Tapia, just east of town toward San Francisco. As the most popular car wash in Salcedo, Orlando is also usually the venue of choice for top artists when they come to town. For a more upscale scene, swing by **Ragazzi**, which is a bar in the conventional sense, serving a wide range of mixed drinks without a space for dancing – a rarity in these parts. Carved-wood beams arch over this beautiful-people nightlife spot in town, at C/ Hermanas Mirabal and C/ Independencia. Drinks are pricier, befitting the crowd.

San Francisco de Macorís

San Francisco de Macorís is the largest city in the eastern Cibao, serving as an agricultural, commercial, and transportation center for the surrounding valley. The city's appellation comes from the Franciscan order that arrived with Spanish colonization, paired with the indigenous name for the region. The city is known for its independent nature, political activism, and fiercely loyal fans of the baseball team. Macorís, as it is colloquially known, is home to a large number of university students, giving it a young vibe. The city is also relatively well off, flush with money from agricultural exports and remittances. This wealth manifests itself in the developments full of large houses in the Dominican-gaudy style that spread out away from downtown. The city's central square, called Parque Duarte, features a peeling gazebo and a sprawl of benches, as well as men hawking *frío frío* (shaved ice), cell phone chargers, and animal masks. For a casual, and dance party-heavy view into local life, visit francomacorisanos.com.

The major (and only) east-west highway across the Cibao is Route 132, called Avenida Libertad in town. C/ Castillo runs perpendicular to Libertad downtown, and then turns into the highway that runs south toward Santo Domingo. Many of the cafés, restaurants, and shops are located along these thoroughfares, and especially around Parque Duarte on C/ Castillo.

Be Happy

San Francisco's youth-centered development, especially as compared to other Dominican towns, may be epitomized by Be Happy. This alternative store sells underground literature and sex toys, among other goodies, on C/ Duarte between C/ 27 de Febrero and C/ San Francisco. These are products rarely seen in the DR, even in the trendier student quarters in Santo Domingo. Although the country is still quite conservative, there are some pockets of social progressivism that can be found in establishments like these.

TRANSPORT

Caribe Tours is located on C/ Castillo and C/ Gaspar Hernández in a very large station with a snack bar.

To Santo Domingo: RD$260; 2hrs; 6am-6:30pm every 60-90 minutes

To Samaná (through **Nagua**): RD$140; 3hrs; 7am, 9:30am, 1:30pm, 4pm.

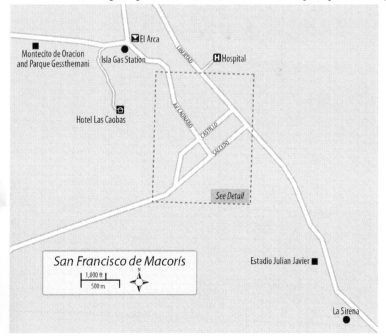

San Francisco de Macorís
1,000 ft
500 m

To Río San Juan: RD$140; 2hrs; 7:30am, 9am, 1pm, 2pm, 3:30pm.

Guaguas

To Santo Domingo: RD$180; 3hrs; 6am-5pm; 3hrs; C/ Castillo across from Caribe Tours.

To La Vega: RD$70; 1 hr; 6am-6pm; Av. 27 de Febrero and C/ Castillo.

To Nagua: RD$100 in front, RD$50 in back of a pickup truck; 1.5hrs; 7am-6pm; C/ La Cruz and José Reyes at Parque Peña Gómez

To Santiago: RD$100; 1.5hrs; 7am-6pm; C/ 27 de Febrero, across from the Fortaleza

San Francisco de Macorís (Detail)

INFO

Medical Attention
The public **Hospital Vicente de Paul** is at C/ Cristino Zeno and C/ Luperón (588-2327), and the respectable **Farmacia San José** is at C/ San Francisco and C/ Billini.

Communication
Biblioteca Municipal is a decent library with free internet for an hour, at C/ Colón and C/ Castillo. **Codetel** has variable hours, but has the best and fastest computers. You'll have to introduce yourself to the man at the desk, and sign your name; internet is free. The glass-walled center is on Av. Los Mártires next to the park, across from El Patio restaurant. The **Post Office** is on C/ Ing. Guzmán Abreu by C/ Libertad.

Banks
Branches of **Banco Popular** are located on C/ El Carmen by C/ Castillo and at La Sirena, There's also a **BanReservas** on Av. 27 de Febrero and C/ Papi Olivier.

Grocery Stores
Supermercado El Palacio sells a wide selection of food and other necessary supplies in a bi-level store downtown. There's also a food court serving slushies along with average rice and beans, and upstairs is an above-average selection of Dominican china and glassware. *Av. 27 de Febrero and C/ Padre Billini*

The enormous **La Sirena** superstore has a branch just outside town, accessible by *carro público* along Av. Libertad going east out of the city. If you need to stock up on anything, this is the place. Look out for the friendly giant walking pencil with a leaden smile. *Carretera Nagua-San Francisco Km 2*

The outdoor, block-long *mercado público*, filled with fresh, local produce and wares, is located at C/ Castillo and C/ Libertad.

Gas
The **Isla Gas Station** is at C/ Caonabo and the highway to Villa Tapia.

Police Station
Find the **police station** at C/ Castillo and C/ Salomé Ureña, a few blocks past the Caribe Tours.

EAT

El Tanque El Tanque is a dinner and late-night spot with decent wood-oven pizza and live music, from blues to jazz, in the evenings. It doesn't get crowded until late, when it's possible to catch a glimpse of the twenty-somethings out on the town. *RD$150-300; 4pm-late; C/ Castillo and C/ Gaspar Hernández*

Tu Quipe Cheap and tasty Mexican, though you wouldn't know by the name. The little spot features repose-friendly couches and festive wall art. *RD$50-75; C/ Salome Ureña and C/ Gaspar Hernandez*

Panadería Moya Newly remodeled, Panadería Moya is a sweet bakery with an extensive selection of breads, desserts, and cakes, along with a shiny coffee bar. It's also an affordable, enjoyable place for a *plato del día* or a typical Dominican breakfast. Free Wi-Fi. *RD$50-300; 7am-10pm; Av. 27 de Febrero and C/ Billini*

El Polo A favorite with both locals and foreigners, El Polo serves a variety of breakfast dishes, sandwiches, juices, and coffee drinks in a relaxed, café-style atmosphere. This eatery also has a very nice bakery section, with an array of donuts, crepes, cookies, cakes, and other goodies. *RD$100-300; 7am-10pm Mon-Sat 7am-12pm Sun; C/ Restauración and C/ El Carmen*

 El Patio El Patio is the most creative restaurant in San Francisco de Macorís, boasting an inventive menu and tables under an open-air roof. A clever, comfortable seating scheme includes plush couches, mismatched booths, and a swing set. The unique environment is bested only by the fantastic menu featuring salads, Mexican food, pizzas, pastas, burgers, steaks, fish, and sushi, as well as potent frozen margaritas (try the passion fruit). Free Wi-Fi. *RD$125-500; 12pm-12am; 6 Av. Los Mártires at C/ Castillo; 244-1394*

SLEEP

Hotel Líbano The rooms here are basic and Spartan, but certainly passable, especially given that they come with TV, A/C, and hot water. Líbano is nothing fancy, but works as an economical, downtown hotel. *RD$900-1500; 26 C/ Mella by Parque Duarte; 588-2419*

Hotel Las Caobas Hotel Las Caobas sprawls into the low plains on the edge of the city past an affluent housing development, replete with a swimming pool, poolside bar/restaurant, tennis courts, a track, and a casino. The 50 rooms are spacious, comfortable, and clean – someone clearly took the time to make them look nice. Importantly, the A/C units have significant cooling strength. Next door at the San Diego Campo Club, the Dominican Republic has hosted the Davis Cup. *RD$1550; Via Penetracion Sur in Urbanización Almanzar, look for a sign on C/ Caonabo; 290-5858; hotellascaobas@yahoo.com*

Rancho Don Lulu A self-described "ecotourism center," Rancho Don Lulu is rustic and simple, but a wonderful way to stay in the Macorís area without being in the city – this is where to temporarily live the *campo* experience. The family that runs Rancho Don Lulu is warm and welcoming, and encourages guests to take meals with them in the communal dining space. They live nearby, and love to talk about the history and environment of the hillside on which they reside. In fact, this may feel more like a home stay than anything else. *RD$400 and up; Located on the highway at the base of Loma Quita Espuela.*

DO

Catedral de Santa Ana
At the time of publication, the Cathedral was undergoing large-scale structural renovation. When finished, its Gothic revival architectural should be on full display. *Across from Parque Duarte.*

Montecito de Oración, Parque Gesthemani
Just east of the city is a small Catholic retreat center featuring a pretty, whitewashed chapel. The park area, with impeccably manicured grounds, is open to the public for picnicking and general outdoor fun, and is a nice place to get away from the noise of the city. Interestingly, lying down is not permitted, and an employee will scold you for doing so. Spiritual meditation is one thing, but taking a nap (or other lying-down activities) is a different animal. *One and a half kilometers on the highway to Villa Tapia. Catch a carro público along that highway or a guagua heading to Villa Tapia or Cenoví, which leaves from C/ San Francisco at C/ Padre Billini.*

Parque Los Mártires
Placid by day, this park comes lively by night. It can get exciting here, but you might not want to stick out too much at a place like this. However, it is a good way to

experience local nightlife flavor, especially with the university student population. There is also a movie theater right behind it, showing films you probably saw already. *Av. Antonio Guzmán and Carretera Las Cejas*

Estadio Julian Javier

The beloved Gigantes baseball team (San Francisco Giants – get it?) plays here in the Winter League at this enormous party of a concrete cavern. Games are lively, and even rowdy, so bring both your rally cap and party hat. *Tickets RD$30-60; C/ Libertad; www.gigantesdelcibao.com*

☑ Loma Quita Espuela

"Remove-Spur Mountain" is so named because of the damage the thick brush did to boot spurs of early settler-cowboys, who apparently missed the beauty of the forest for the unforgiving vegetation. It is the tallest mountain in the eastern Cordillera Central at 942 meters (3090 feet) above sea level. In 1990, a local NGO called Fundación Loma Quita Espuela was founded for the preservation of the unique ecosystem and natural beauty of the mountain, as well as the 73-square-kilometer scientific reserve that was created to protect it. It receives funding from ice cream giant Helados Bon and the German international development organization, GTZ, among others. The Foundation also acts as a liaison with local communities on the mountain, working to improve infrastructure and service provisions to the small villages across the area. Members of the communities participate in the decision-making process of the foundation in an effort to encourage community activism and ownership over the conservation and tourism efforts.

The park is home to dozens of plant, reptile, fish and other species, many of which are endangered. The only two mammal species endemic to the country live here as well. The park's mountainous expanse juxtaposes terraced cacao farms with one of the few cloud forests on the island. Because of the intense rainfall that the area receives, 61 streams and rivers find their source within the reserve, providing Macorís and the valley its drinking water.

To experience the mountain on foot, the foundation provides guided hikes to the summit, which take about three hours. At the top, a small shrine to the Virgin Mary greets visitors next to a creaking observation tower that affords sweeping views of the valley, when clouds do not obscure the scene. The Foundation guides are accommodating and informative, though tours are only given in Spanish. The excursion also includes an excellent *comida típica* lunch and a dip in two small pools at the base of the mountain. A more relaxed tour of the surrounding cacao farms is also available for those less altitude-inclined. Wear hiking boots or sturdy shoes, lest the brush mess with your footwear. *RD$300 per group up to 15 people; park entrance by itself is RD$20 for Dominicans and RD$50 for foreigners. Reservations are recommended, but not mandatory. The park is located 15 kilometers north of San Francisco up C/ Castillo, which is not paved the entire way. Public transport in the form of a pickup truck leaves from C/ Castillo by C/ Libertad infrequently 7am-5pm (RD$40).*

The Fundación Loma Quita Espuela office is located next to Hotel Las Caobas in Urbanización Almánzar at C/ Luis Carron and Av. del Jaya; 588-4156; http://www.flqe.org.do/; flqe@verizon.net.do

Cibao

NIGHTLIFE

Disco Terraza Yudul This is the chosen venue for famous Dominican and international musicians when they come to town, especially after its elaborate refurbishment in 2008. Buy tickets early and rent a table near the front for the best view. On days without shows, it is still a fun venue to party with the locals. Wear your Dominican best, because sandals are not getting you in. *RD$100-1000 cover if there is an artist; Av. Antonio Guzmán*

El Arca A typical Dominican car wash and definitely a local favorite, El Arca is a great place for sharing jumbos of beer and all sorts of bachata, merengue, salsa, and reggaeton music. The dance floor is dark and the air is thick, so bring some dancing shoes. *Av. Caonabo, to the right of the gas station*

Cordillera Central

The beaches might give the Dominican Republic its fame, but the craggy interior gives the country its heart. These mountains dare climbers to scale their rocky summits, and the crashing waterfalls beckon swimmers with refreshing dips and sweeping vistas. Far from the crowds, heat, surf, and sun, the Cordillera Central is worlds apart from the valleys below. Thrill-seekers scramble up the slopes to take advantage of incomparable outdoor activities, from river rafting to spelunking. More leisurely pursuits abound as well, from wooded hikes to horseback riding. The two major population centers in the region – Jarabacoa and Constanza – are laid-back *pueblos* with a relaxed high-altitude attitude, and act as gateways to the adventures beyond. All activity leads up to the cloud-scraper itself: Pico Duarte, the tallest mountain in the Caribbean. There are no disappointments in this part of the country, just the lush, rugged mountains, and the opportunities that lie ahead.

Jarabacoa

Vibrant, cool, and filled with charm, the mountains around Jarabacoa are speckled with enchanting villages, beautiful scenery, and perfect spots for outdoor adventure. Jarabacoa, the largest town in the Cordillera Central, is home to almost 30,000 people, not including the rush of wealthy Dominicans and foreigners who regularly flock to weekend getaways in the area. Despite being a major destination for domestic tourism, the town maintains an intimate and friendly atmosphere since the majority of visitors spend the day curled up by the fire or enjoying the area's outdoor activities. With three major rivers nearby, Jarabacoa is home to an array of sports like white-water rafting, kayaking, canyoneering, biking, and hiking. The Río Jimenoa courses downhill nearby, bestowing Jarabacoa with two immense waterfalls: Salto de Jimenoa I and II, both of which flow into gorgeous swimming holes. The steep mountains also provide excellent launch points for hang gliding, not to mention awe-inspiring views of the Cordillera Central.

HISTORY

The valley's settlement began as a refuge for people fleeing invading armies, including Taínos from the Spanish and Dominicans from Haitian incursions. After independence, the state built a military outpost here. A city has now grown up around the gorgeous setting, fertile agricultural lands, and burgeoning domestic and international tourism industry.

High in the hills, Jarabacoa is progressive in its approach to alternative energy sources and sustainable agriculture. Boasting numerous organic greenhouses and organic coffee farms, including that of Dominican-American author Julia Alvarez, Jarabacoa's farmers work toward environmentally friendly agricultural methodology. In the most remote of villages, many houses have solar panels. In addition, families use excess heat expended from cooking on wood-burning stoves to warm bath water.

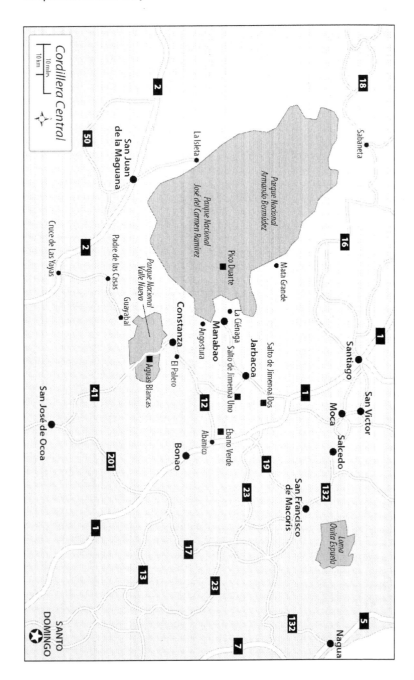

TRANSPORT

Caribe Tours

To Santo Domingo/La Vega: RD$280/RD$75; 3hrs/1 hr; 7am, 10am, 1:30pm, 4:30pm; 574-4796; C/ Independencia at C/ José Duran)

Guaguas

To La Vega: RD$100; 6am-6pm; 1 hr; C/ Independencia across from Caribe Tours

To Constanza: RD$150; 2hrs; 8am-4pm; C/ Paseo de los Profesores near the Shell station.

To La Ciénaga: RD$120; 1.5hrs; 8am-2pm; C/ Obdulio Jimenez by C/ 16 de Agosto

Around Jarbacoa

Motoconchos cost RD$20.

Taxis run RD$100-150 for trips within town. Try Taxi El Salto at C/ Colón in front of Club de Leones (574-2909/2929).

Rental Cars

Anyolino Rent-a-Car is on C/ Paseo de los Profesores (574-6878/969-0614). **Francis Rent Car** is located at Km 2 Federico Vasilis (highway to Jimenoa, by the bridge; 574-2981).

INFO

Medical Attention

Farmacia Independencia is on C/ Independencia (574-6306) and **Farmacia San Miguel** is on C/ Obdulio Jiménez leaving town on the way to Manabao (574-7272/6969/6536).

Communication

Find **Centro de Copiado y Papelería** for internet services at C/ Independencia and C/ Duarte (8am-8pm, closed 12pm-2pm) and the **Post Office** on C/ Independencia a block north of Caribe Tours.

Banks

Banco Popular is at 39 Av. Independencia near C/ Leonardo Jiménez, catty corner to Caribe Tours. There is a **Banco León** on C/ Duarte across from the Parque Central.

Gas

There is **Shell** station on C/ Obdulio Jimenez (highway to Constanza), an **Esso** when entering town from La Vega on C/ Independencia, and an **Isla** on C/ del Carmen (highway to Manabao).

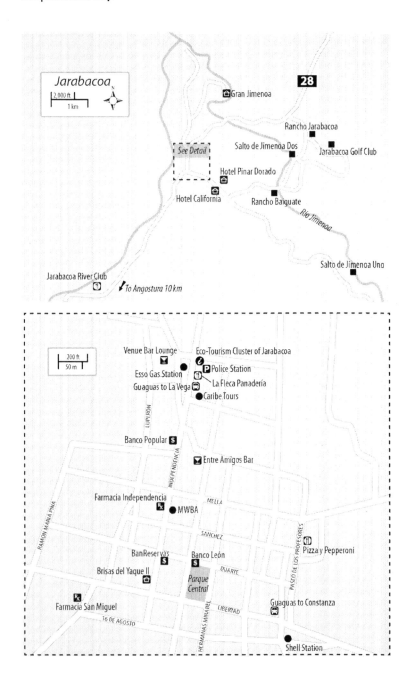

Jarabacoa

2,000 ft
1 km

Gran Jimenoa

28

Rancho Jarabacoa

Salto de Jimenoa Dos

Jarabacoa Golf Club

See Detail

Hotel Pinar Dorado

Hotel California

Rancho Baiguate

Río Jimenoa

Salto de Jimenoa Uno

Jarabacoa River Club

To Angostura 10 km

Venue Bar Lounge

Eco-Tourism Cluster of Jarabacoa

Police Station

Esso Gas Station

La Fleca Panadería

Guaguas to La Vega

Caribe Tours

LUPERON

Banco Popular

INDEPENDENCIA

Entre Amigos Bar

RAMON MARIA PINA

Farmacia Independencia

MELLA

MWBA

SANCHEZ

PASEO DE LOS PROFESORES

Pizza y Pepperoni

BanReservas

Banco León

Brisas del Yaque II

DUARTE

Parque Central

Farmacia San Miguel

LIBERTAD

Guaguas to Constanza

HERMANAS MIRABEL

16 DE AGOSTO

Shell Station

Grocery Stores

A number of grocery stores are located on C/ Independencia, such as **Supermercado Jarabacoa.**

Tourism Info

The **Eco-Tourism Cluster of Jarabacoa** office is great stop for information on activities, businesses, and cultural events in Jarabacoa. Members of the Cluster, which consist of local business and eco-tourism outfitters, work together to promote sustainable tourism in Jarabacoa. *45B C/ Independencia (next to Forestry Office) across from the Esso Gas Station; 574-6699; infoclusterjarabacoa@gmail.com; jarabacoard.com*

Visit the government's **Tourism Office** for sparse information. For the latest local happenings, check out the newspaper at www.diariojarabacoa.com. *C/ del Carmen and C/ Galan; 9am-5pm*

EAT

La Fleca Panadería Flaky croissants and crusty artisanal breads are among the specialties of this cute café as well as sinful desserts and savory finger foods. *RD$75-120; 574-4811; Located on C/ Independencia near the Caribe Tours stop and across from Esso Gas; lipebeltran@htomail.com; www.laflecajaraba.com*

Pizza y Pepperoni A family-owned Italian mainstay for ten years, this casual open-air restaurant serves hand-tossed thin-crust pizzas and desserts such as strawberry cheesecake and Oreo pie. *RD$210-680; C/ Paseo de los Profesores next to Anyolino Rent-a-Car; 574-4348*

Jarabacoa River Club Located on a precipice overlooking the River Yaque del Norte, the resort's restaurant serves mountain-inspired specialties like the dark and flavorful guinea hen al vino and soul-warming soups and stews. Afterwards, take a dip in the club's five pools or head to the bar and concert space on the weekends for dancing and occasional live music. *RD$385-725; 4km on highway toward Manabao, club is on right side; 574-2456 or 501-3020; www.jarabacoariverclub.com*

Aroma de la Montaña For a 180-degree view of the valley of Jarabacoa and the mountains that surround it, head to this upscale restaurant at the Jamaca de Dios hotel. Try the select cuts of meat or the chicken aroma, but be sure to save room for the fine desserts: savory apple caramel tart and the trance-inducing brownie packed with chocolate chips, coconut, almonds, and rum. *RD$170-990; Located in Jamaca de Dios hotel near the village of Pinar Quemado on the road to Manabao; 829-452-6867/6878; www.aromadelamontana.com*

SLEEP

Cabins

To truly enjoy the natural beauty of Jarabacoa, rent a cabin hidden in the mountains through one of the following community organizations or tourism companies.

Ramírez Tours Owned by the energetic Jarabacoa native Altagracia Ramírez, this small company is a wonderful resource for those interested in renting short- or long-term cabins. In business since 1996, Señora Ramírez also offers ideas about excursions and other tourism services in the area. *36 Av. La Confluencia; 574-6604; 399-6748; U.S. phone: 347-827-2824; Ramíreztours4@gmail.com; http://digitalsdesigns.com/Ramírez/*

◪ **Angostura** A community organization, supported by national and international funding, provides rustic eco-lodges in the remote village of Angostura. The three environmentally friendly lodges sleep six people, and the bathrooms are connected to a biodigestor that powers the complex. The lodges do not have kitchens, but there is a communal kitchen and restaurant. The organization offers hiking, horseback riding, and whitewater rafting excursions. In addition, trained guides, who are certified and registered with the National Park, lead Pico Duarte tours that begin at the La Ciénaga trailhead. The center provides transport to and from the trail, a half-hour drive away. (The project was nearing completion at the time of publication. Contact for prices and more details.) *Approximately three kilometers south of Manabao; contact Marite at 910-7520 or Inocencia at 829-539-8753*

Sonido del Yaque This hotel's unpretentious and reasonably priced cabins are scattered around the community of Los Calabazos along the River Yaque del Norte. In 1997, the La Nueva Esperanza community group solicited funds from various NGOs to build these six cabins and a restaurant that dishes up campo-style meals. Attractions include community-use greenhouses, hiking trails, and excursions to the river. *RD$400 per cabin; RD$550 cabin and all meals; in village of Los Calabazos on the road to Manabao; 829-727-7413; 829-846-7275; sonidodelyaque@gmail.com; www.sonidodelyaque.com; or contact the Tourism Cluster*

Jamaca de Dios This gorgeous and finely manicured compound is geared towards wealthy Dominicans escaping to weekend homes, but the property does have a few romantic cabins for the one-time visitor with lofted ceilings, slate bathrooms, and an extraordinary view. At the time of research, this vacation complex, whose name translates as God's Hammock, was also constructing a gym, basketball and tennis courts, and a hotel. *RD$2700 weekdays, RD$3500 weekends for 4-person lodge; RD$4,500 weekdays, RD$6,000 weekends for 3-bedroom cabin; 20 minutes on the road to Manabao; 829-452-6867/6878; www.jamacadedios.com; Amenities: hot water, fridge, fan, satellite TV, Jacuzzi and deck, coffee bar, included breakfast*

Ecotourism

As a developing country, the Dominican Republic grapples with environmental degradation as a serious issue for the long-term health of its people and land. While the majority of the DR's forest coverage is long gone, the government has taken steps to protect the remaining areas in places like the Cordillera Central. For example, there are campaigns here to end trash burning (the most common form of waste disposal) as well as teaching environmental science in schools. Especially in this part of the country, ecotourism has become an important focus in bringing in funds to protect sensitive areas from continued damage. Visitors to this region are likely already interested in outdoor, environmentally friendly activities, so ecotourism is the logical next step.

While definitions of ecotourism may vary, the goal of ecotourism is to bring visitors to enjoy and learn about natural surroundings, while maintaining and protecting them, and without leaving a damaging footprint. At organizations like Angostura, the local community is intimately involved, so as to bring together the people and the land on which they live. Some sites, for examples, use biological waste as a fuel or as compost for gardens that feed guests and Dominicans; and tiny, non-intrusive hydroelectric plants supply electricity for small villages. Others may have small farming plots to grow native and local plants best suited to the area. As more visitors patronize such places, Dominicans may be more inclined to work at and support such organizations, which in turn can better protect the environment. The Dominican government is currently partnering with international organizations like USAID to promote ecotourism and sustainable tourism under the Dominican Sustainable Tourism Alliance. As visitors, we can all support such organizations. For additional discussion, see Responsible Tourism on page 63. *Written with the assistance of Marite Pérez.*

Los Tres Corazones French owner Catherine rents cabins for all budgets and group sizes, as well as tourism and hiking services. Some of the cabins are located on the property of the Dominican General Guzman, where the only sound is the gurgle of the River Yaque del Norte. Private footpaths explore the property for an invigorating morning hike. *RD$1000-2000; 910-4321; catherinethis@hotmail.com*

Hotels

Hogar Hotel Ligia Piña This is the most economical place in town, but still manages to be both safe and clean. Owner Lidia is said to be selling the hotel, which has a nice back patio garden. *RD$400-500; 574-2739; 34 C/ Mella; 574-2739*

 Gran Jimenoa Living up to its tagline of "a hidden paradise," the resort of Gran Jimenoa is certainly the most luxurious in the valley, with an impressive collection of orchids, impeccable landscaping, and excellent service. Though all of the impeccable rooms feature large windows, ask for one of the spacious rooms facing the Río Jimenoa to enjoy the view and sound of its powerful beauty. Make sure to eat at the hotel restaurant, and sit at the deck dramatically set over the waters below. A hanging bridge crosses the river to additional activity spaces. *RD$1,225-14,900 per room; Av. La Confluencia, Los Corralitos; 574-6304/4345; hotel.jimenoa@codetel.net.do; www.granjimenoahotel.com; Amenities: hot water, A/C, fan, TV, Wi-Fi, computers with internet, pool, Jacuzzi, restaurant, spa, game room, sauna, conference rooms, karaoke bar, heliport, included breakfast*

Pinar Dorado A Jarabacoa institution in need of a slight bit of remodeling, Pinar Dorado is conveniently located in the forested hills above town, striking the perfect balance of peace and convenience. Owned by Rancho Baiguate (see Do), it is close enough to town to arrive on a taxi or motorcycle without paying too much, and is nicer than the busy, crowded options in Jarabacoa itself. Head to the hotel's restaurant, **La Guajaca**, for Dominican country classics like *asopao de pollo* (chicken stew with rice) or decadent inventions like *pechuga wicha*, a chicken breast topped with ripe plantains, tomato, and cheese in pesto. *RD$ 825-2270; 1km on the Jarabacoa-Constanza highway, turn left at sign for Pinar Dorado; 574-2820/4098; pinar_dorado@hotmail.com; Amenities: TV, telephone, A/C, hot water, Wi-Fi*

Brisas del Yaque II Located in the center of town, Brisas del Yaque II is a less-than-quiet escape to the mountains. It works, however, for those without their own vehicle, as it is within walking distance of restaurants and businesses. *RD$1500-2900; 13 C/ Independencia; 574-2100; hotelbrisasdelyaque@hotmail.com; Amenities: AC, TV, hot water*

Rancho Baiguate An eco-lodge offering rustic yet quite comfortable rooms for up to four people. (see Do for more details and contact info) *RD$1360-2450 per person; Amenities: hot water, Wi-Fi, fan, included meals*

DO

◩ Salto de Jimenoa Uno

This first waterfall on the Río Jimenoa is hidden in the forest, only accessible via a good hike through the woods. The walk, mostly downhill through lush forest, finally opens up into a clearing with this 60m-high waterfall plunging into a refreshing swimming hole below. The hike through the hills takes up to two hours, not including time lounging at the sandy banks of the Río Yaque along the walk. The entrance fee directly supports the community members of Salto de Jimenoa who serve as guides for the trail. This is the prettier, though less accessible, of the two Jimenoa falls. *RD$100 foreigners, RD$50 Dominicans; 7 kilometers on the highway toward Constanza next to a restaurant; (motoconcho RD$80-100; taxi RD$250); 271-8580; 829-828-7708; interpretesdelasmontanas.7@hotamil.com*

Salto de Jimenoa Dos

The hike to these 40-meter-high falls is much easier, including crossing a few narrow hanging bridges surrounded by verdant woodlands. The short walk the ends at the stunning waterfall and bathing area. *RD$100; 5 kilometers on the highway to La Vega, go right at the fork with well-marked signs*

Red de Productos Naturales (REDPRONA)

In 2000, a Spanish ceramic artist began to teach women in the villages around Jarabacoa how to make various crafts. The women's skill level has improved tremendously and they now sell their products in their own communities, the Tourism Cluster's Office, and as far as Centro León in Santiago. One of their primary products is replicas of Taíno pottery. They also create handmade jewelry made from natural materials and *macutos* (traditional bags) from burlap sacks. Stop by the Tourism Cluster office to speak with them about visiting Los Marranitos, where the workshop is located. *Tourism Cluster Office; 574-2121; 829-886-8272*

Moto Caribe

For the motorcycle enthusiast, expeditions starting in Jarabacoa are the perfect way to experience the rugged side of the country. Tours range from 4 to 11 days and cover the Southwest (Ocoa to Barahona) or Northeast (Jamao to Samaná) or a combination of both, entirely on Suzuki bikes. Safety is a priority for this American-owned company: each trip is followed by a van so that non-riders can tag along in a trailer full of first aid supplies, tools, and an extra motorcycle. Costs include food, gas, hotel, beach equipment, and airport transport. *Prices begin at US$1,400 per person; U.S. office: 856-343-0100x102; rcooper@motocaribe.com; www.motocaribe.com*

Rancho Jarabacoa

With over 20 years of experience, this adventure outfitter is known for its informative and well-regarded guides. Besides white-water rafting, highlights include rappelling on rock walls reaching 46m in height, and cliff jumping off an 18m waterfall. Other outdoor activities include hang-gliding, horseback riding, tubing, canyoneering, and hiking excursions to places like Pico Duarte. Prices vary, but include food. *Located next to the golf course; 222-3202; ranchojarabacoa@hotmail.com*

Rancho Baiguate

In business since 1975, this company run by the Rodríguez-Ros family offers a multitude of adventure sports while maintaining strong ties to the environment and surrounding communities. Nearly all of its employees are from Jarabacoa, and the ranch has implemented environmentally friendly practices, utilizing solar panels, a natural water filtration system, and a biological waste facility. Although the ranch is all-inclusive, selling packages that include room, board, and activities, it also offers a la carte activities, like rafting, rappelling, horseback riding, hiking, mountain biking, canyoneering, and a zip-line obstacle course. Those looking to summit Pico Duarte might consider the package hike here, which includes all the necessary food, hiking, and camping gear, led by experienced, multilingual guides. Begin your Rancho Baiguate morning in the Papillon Garden featuring more than 20 butterfly species – magical in the early morning hours. *Prices range widely depending on the package, and most include gear and food, US$50 for rafting and rappelling, US$225-1000 for Pico Duarte; 2 kilometers on the highway to Constanza, turn left at the dirt road at the cemetery and almost 1 kilometers later turn right for* *complex entrance; 574-6890, from the U.S. 646-727-7783; rancho.baiguate@verizon.net.do; reservas@ranchobaiguate.com; www.ranchobaiguate.com*

Hang-Gliding with Tony Fly

Soar above the Cordillera Central in the good hands and gear of trained professionals. There are several jumping sites spread across the Jarabacoa area, and when conditions aren't good in the hills, Tony Fly can take gliders farther afield for the perfect jump. The organization also offers rafting and rappelling tours. *Prices vary widely depending on the duration and number of people; 848-3479; 915-5319; flyingtonyjarabacoa@gmail.com; www.paraglidingtonydominicanrepublic.com*

MWVA

A small art school, café, and cultural center with local artisanal crafts for sale, this is the place to meet up with creative locals. Stop by for exhibitions of painting, sculpture, photography, film, and music. On Friday and Saturday, there are cultural activities, including live music, starting after 6pm for free or minimal cover. *19 C/ Independencia at C/ Duarte; 574-7055; mwvagaleriadearte@hotmail.com; Open Mon-Fri until 6pm.*

Jarabacoa Golf Club

For the golf-inclined, visit this 36-par, nine-hole course measuring almost 3,000 meters in length. Club and cart rentals, as well as caddy services, are available at the country's only golf course in the mountains. Bring the racket to hit some high-altitude tennis balls, and then eat at the casual restaurant for lunch or dinner. *RD$900 for 9 holes, RD$500 cart rental; 8am-7pm; Take the highway to Salto de Jimenoa and veer left at sign for Piedra Blanca and the Salto de Jimenoa at "El Quatro" (Km 4); 441-1940; www.jarabacoagolfclub.com*

Festivals in Jarabacoa

Jarabacoa celebrates a number of festivals where artists, musicians, and businesses from Jarabacoa gather. Among them are Festival de Arte Medio Ambiente (Environmental Art Festival), Festival de los Flores (Flower Festival) and La Fería Ecoturística (Ecotourism Fair). Each of these occurs annually. Check with the Tourism Cluster (see INFO), the Dominican Tourism Board (www.turismocdct.org/jarabacoa.html), or your hotel for the exact dates.

Jarabacoa Gold Company

The Spanish did not discover much gold in the DR, but this company has struck it rich offering gold tours, where visitors pan, find, and keep their treasures. Tours include a hike to the stream, equipment, and lunch. Another popular package goes to the Ramírez Coffee Factory, in operation since 1943, where guides describe coffee harvesting and processing. The company also offers rafting, tubing, paragliding, canyoneering, and hiking excursions. *US$45-85 gold tour, US$6 coffee tour; Located in town at Km 1 of the road to Jumunuco; 838-4653; Jarabacoagold@yahoo.com; open 7am-6pm; www.jarabacoagold.webs.com/; reservations required)*

NIGHTLIFE

Weeknights in Jarabacoa are quiet, but on weekends spots such as **Entre Amigos Bar y Karaoke** on the corner of C/ Paseo de los Profesores and C/ Independencia and **Venue Bar Lounge** at the entrance of town to La Vega offer some nightly diversion.

Constanza

The craggy peaks of the Cordillera Central cascade down into the highest populated mountain valley in the Dominican Republic – Constanza. Its people live in what at first glance, might resemble an alpine village dropped onto this tropical island, sitting at 1,300 meters (4,264 feet) above sea level. Arriving in town on the back of a pickup truck, descending on the winding road out of the hills and into the city, might herald one of the best views in the country on public transportation.

Agriculture is a source of income, pride, and beauty for Constanza, noted in the perfectly manicured rows of green that encircle the town. Visitors will immediately notice the cool, fresh air infused with pine and burning wood from chimneys. Because of the chilly temperatures that drop as low as 5°C (41°F) in the winter, local farmers are able to grow crops unusual for the island such as roses, apples, garlic, and strawberries. Stop by one of the many greenhouses surrounding town to see rows of exotic flowers and strawberry patches. Another Constanza specialty seen for sale in the small wooden stands lining the highway is *rábano*, a starchy root particular to the area that is most commonly boiled and mashed.

Perfect for the outdoor enthusiast, Constanza boasts challenging hikes, natural attractions, and adventure sports. The paths through the Ébano Verde Scientific Reserve are cool and lush, often blanketed by thick fog in the morning. The tallest waterfall in the Antilles, Aguas Blancas, is located nearby, whose astoundingly cold temperature sends a shock to the system. Farther into the mountains beyond Aguas Blancas is the Valle Nuevo Scientific Reserve, where a Trujillo-era pyramid marks the geographic center of the island. Across the city of Constanza are relics of distinct ethnic enclaves, once part of Trujillo's campaign to both "whiten the race," and also introduce diverse agricultural techniques to the region. The four enclaves include La Colonia Japonesa, Húngara, Kennedy, and Española. While the Hungarians of Colonia Húngara and the Americans of Colonia Kennedy are long gone, descendents of the Japanese and Spanish settlers still maintain strong identities.

TRANSPORT

Constanza is accessible via four highways, though only the first is really accessible for all vehicles. The most convenient, and best-maintained, runs to El Abanico,

Juan M. "Johnny" Tactuk

Entrepreneur, community leader, and father, Johnny Tactuk is known in Constanza and beyond for his warm personality and encyclopedic knowledge. Born to a Dominican mother and Lebanese father in 1949, Johnny learned the art of diversifying investments from his father, evidence of which can be seen in the multiple modest businesses that he owns. An entire block of C/ Duarte in Constanza is home to Johnny's framing store, television studio (the broadcast center of Constanza's channel 18), computer/television repair shop, and the pizzeria/event space Antojitos D'Lauren.

As a community leader, Johnny is as equally multi-faceted. He was involved in infrastructure improvement on the highways that access Constanza, and in the re-opening the city's airport. He is also a member of the Civil Defense and supports the Firefighter Station, which bears the name of his father. Besides his own five children, Johnny also raised six more, a testament to his community spirit.

which is located on Highway Duarte just north of Bonao. The second most commonly traversed joins with Jarabacoa, but can become impassible after rains. The other two require 4WD, an experienced driver, and at least one spare tire. One leads to San José de Ocoa through Valle Nuevo, and the other to Padre de las Casas, located in the province of Azua.

Nearly all transport leaves from the entrance of town, located on C/ Luperón. The stop (called "La Parada") is by the Isla gas station and a park home to a Founding Fathers monument. *Guaguas* also run constantly back and forth to El Abanico (RD$150; 8am-4pm), on Highway Duarte. The stop in Constanza is at La Parada, while the stop in El Abanico is located on the western side of Highway Duarte next to the Abanico bridge. Once at the highway, you can hop on any *guagua* going north or south.

To Santo Domingo: RD$300; 5am, 9am, 12pm; 3hrs; the lines are called **Linea Cobra** (539-2119), **RR Express** (539-1100), and **Expreso Constanza** (539-2134)

From Santo Domingo: RD$300; 5am, 12pm and 3pm; **Linea Cobra** is at197 C/ San Martin (732-7099) and **Expreso Constanza** at 30 C/ Juan José Duran near the corner of San Martín (565-1223).

To La Vega: RD$200; 5am; La **Linea Princesa** (539-2415)

To Santiago: RD$250; 5am-2pm; Take **Linea Junior** (539-2177; lineajunior@hotmail.com)

Air

Constanza also has a small airport, Aeropuerto Expedición 14 de Junio, utilized by private charters and domestic flights. The **Tourism Police** (539-3020) and **Hidalgo Rent a Car** (829-204-5290) are located at the airport. *The airport is located on the left side of Av. Luperón when entering Constanza; 539-2820*

INFO

Medical Attention

For 24-hour attention, the public **Hospital Principal** is located on the main road heading into town (539-2420), but it is better to visit the private **Centro de Especialidades Medicas Titi**, located on C/ Rufino Espinosa between C/ Salomé Ureña and C/ 27 de Febrero (539-3345).

The pharmacies include **Farmacia San José** with locations at the Parque Central (corner of C/ Miguel Abreu and C/ Salomé Ureña) or C/ Luperón (539-2516) or **Farmacia Díaz Quezada** (539-2020), located across from the *Mercado*.

Communication

Centro de Llamadas & Internet Plaza Dorada is on C/ Luperón by C/ Deligne; 539-2337.

Banks

Constanza has nearly all of the major banks. Find the **Banco León** at C/ Abreu and C/ Duarte, and **Banco Popular** (539-3502), **BanReservas** (at C/ Miguel Andrés Abreu; 539-2798) **BHD,** all located on Av. Luperón. The **Western Union** is on C/ Duarte by C/ 27 de Febrero (539-3253).

Cordillera Central

Gas

On Av. Luperón, find the **Shell** (539-2727) and **Isla** stations (539-2548), and an **Esso** station on the corner of C/ Sánchez and C/ Ureña (539-2477). When passing through Tireo, the community before reaching Constanza, there is a **Texaco**.

Grocery Stores

To stock up before your trip to Valle Nuevo or to make a quiet cabin dinner, head to **Supermercado El Económico** (C/ Luperón by the Isla; 539-2323; 8am-8pm), or visit the outdoor *Mercado* at C/ 14 de Junio and C/ Gratereaux (7am-6pm). For late night purchases, **Supermercado Centro** is open until 11pm (C/ Rufino Espinosa; 539-2327).

Tourism Info

Both the **Office of Tourism** (C/ Duarte between C/ Matilde Viñas and C/ Salomé Ureña; 539-2900; osita1415@hotmail.com) and the **Tourism Cluster of Constanza** (located at the airport on Av. Luperón; 539-1022; www.turismocdct.org/constanza.html; clusterecoturistico@constanza.com.do) are excellent resources for tourist information – some of the best tourism offices in the country.

EAT

Antojitos D'Lauren Antojitos D'Lauren tosses up Constanza's signature vegetarian pizza, which comes topped with every vegetable grown in the region, including broccoli and cauliflower. The restaurant also has two event spaces, one of which is used for bachata dance contests on Saturday night. *RD$220-400; 8am-9pm; 15 C/ Duarte; 539-2129/3839; osita1415@hotmail.com; delivery available*

El Comedor de Luisa At midday, this popular eatery is packed with loyal clients hankering for Luisa Duran's famous *moro de habichuelas verdes* (green beans and rice stew) and the *tres golpes* dessert. *RD$100; 12pm-2pm, 7pm-9pm; C/ Antonio García between C/ Viñas and C/ Salomé Ureña*

Lorenzo's Restaurant y Pizzeria Lorenzo's runs the most varied menu in town, with everything from pizza to chop suey to Constanza specialties like roasted goat or *conejo al vino* (rabbit sautéed in red wine). Because Constanza is a major producer of garlic, a common style for meat or seafood dishes is the delicious *al ajillo*. Enjoy the view of the mountains – painted on the wall. *RD$125-500; 8am-11:30pm Sun-Thu, 8am-1am Fri-Sat; 83 C/ Luperón; 539-2008; Lorenzo_s@codetel.net.do*

Aguas Blancas Restaurant Aguas Blancas has a monopoly on Constanza-style gourmet, combining local products to make exquisite dishes like cream of *rábano* soup or guinea hen *al vino* for probably the tastiest food in town. A must try are Doña Emilia Caceres' inventive desserts, such as the carrot, passion fruit, or strawberry flan. Behind the restaurant, there is a small, plain hotel, in case delicious food must be within shouting distance. *RD$120-350; 10am-10pm; 54 C/ Rufino Espinoso; 539-1561*

Esquisiteces Dilenia Specializing in oven-roasted lamb and *dulce de fresa*, this restaurant is oozing with rustic charm from its exposed pine walls to its cabin-inspired furniture and locally grown flowers adorning every table. See Sleep section for information about Dilenia's Hotel. *RD$200-360; 10am-10pm; 7 C/ Gaston F. Deligne, by Banco Popular; 539-2213*

SLEEP

 Alto Cerro With options for all budgets, including luxurious villas, standard hotel rooms, and camping spaces, this resort situated on the mountainside is far enough from the center of town to enjoy the peace and fresh air of the high mountain valley. Each villa feels like an alpine cabin, boasting a balcony to enjoy one of the best views of the Constanza surroundings. The bilingual staff at this wonderful hotel is gracious, and an excellent resource for the many activities available in and around the hotel. On-site activities and amenities include an exotic garden, fire pit, barbecues, zip line, soccer field, basketball court, gym, spa, and horseback riding. *US$20-43; 2km on the highway to La Vega, across from the airport; 539-1553/1429; reservas@altocerro.com; www.altocerro.com; Amenities: TV, phone, Wi-Fi, fridge, stove kitchen in villas, hot water, generator, mini-market, restaurant, electric plant*

Rancho Guaraguao Up in the mountains of Constanza, the 4WD-necessary road arriving at the ranch rewards the traveler with a stunning view of the valley. Guaraguao offers various styles of cabins, from naturally treated wood to brightly painted houses like those found in villages throughout the country. It is also possible to camp on-site. If you get bored here (which you should not), there is always the on-site mechanical bull to kick around. *RD$2000-5000; 227-1105; follow green and white signs to the left when entering Constanza; reservas@ranchoguaraguao.com; www.ranchoguaraguao.com; Amenities: hot water, TV, telephone, some with kitchen, chimney, pool, Jacuzzi, restaurant, bar, snack bar, gym, horseback riding, kid's play area, picnic area*

Cabañas Villa Pajón Located in the Valle Nuevo national park, this stunning, remote getaway has scattered seven cabins for two to eight people equipped with a kitchen, living room, dining room, and a wood-burning chimney. Horses are available for exploring the trails and streams of around the property, which has been run by the Guzman family for four generations. The cabins lack electricity, but do have hot water, and gas lamps and stoves. *RD$2,000-4,000 Nov-Apr, RD$1600-3000 May-Oct; located in Valle Nuevo, head past La Colonia Japonesa on the highway to Ocoa for 20km; 563-6209; info@villapajon.com; http://ecoturismo.com.do/eco-hoteles/villa-pajon.html; Amenities: hot water, deck with grill, bathrooms, fully stocked kitchen*

Rancho Constanza This creatively named pine lodge located just outside of town offers single rooms and suites with kitchenettes and balconies that overlook peach trees and green fields surrounding the hotel. A six-person cabin featuring a full-sized kitchen is also available. *RD$1200-2900; 7 C/ Duarte in Colonia Kennedy; 539-2930; Amenities: Wi-Fi, hot water, fridge, TV, balcony, meal packages available*

Exquiteces D' Dilenia Hotel-Restaurant Behind Dilenia's restaurant are no-frills cinderblock rooms, but they are quiet, inexpensive, and conveniently located at the entrance of town. *RD$700 single, RD$1200 double; 7 C/ Gaston F. Deligne; 539-2213; Amenities: hot water, TV*

Hotel San Ramón San Ramón is the cheapest deal in town with rooms starting at RD$150. Occasional blackouts and undependable hot water plague the hotel, but this family-owned site is very wallet-friendly for the backpacker set. *RD$150-400; 36 C/ Libertad; 539-2146; Amenities: hot water, some rooms with TV*

DO

Aguas Blancas

This cascading set of waterfalls is located at an altitude of 1680 meters (5512 feet) above sea level, is the highest in the Caribbean basin, and according to the locals, the coldest on the island, with an average temperature hovering at 10°C. The first section drops 53 meters (174 feet) in height and the second, 38 meters (125 feet). The waterfall is set on a glistening rock wall. There are bathrooms on the premises, though swimming is not recommended because of the temperature. A new trail about two kilometers long is set to open in early 2012 that runs from the base to the upper falls, which were previously inaccessible. There are several *miradores*, or lookout points, along the way offering spectacular views of the entire area. *Located near the small village of El Convento, 14 kilometers on the road into Valle Nuevo*

La Pirámide y el Monumento a Francisco Caamaño Deñó

The Egyptians are not the only ones who built pyramids. Located in Parque Nacional Valle Nuevo, this tall stone structure marks the geographical center of Hispaniola. Built by Trujillo, the pyramid is the probably last thing the unsuspecting traveler would imagine in this remote park. On the other side of the highway is the monument to Francisco Caamaño Deñó, hero of the 1965 uprising to defend the democratically elected government of Juan Bosch. Attempting to lead another revolt against the Trujillo dictatorship, he was captured and executed at this spot in the mountains. *44 kilometers on the road into Valle Nuevo*

Francisco Caamaño Deñó

Tucked away among the pines of Valle Nuevo is a small iron cross commemorating the violent and untimely death of Francisco Caamaño Deñó, a forgotten revolutionary patriot active during the restive post-Trujillo era. In 1963, after Trujillo's death, Juan Bosch was chosen as president in the first free elections in a generation – but was soon overthrown by conservative military forces supported by the American invasion of 1965. Caamaño Deñó led the armed resistance loyal to Bosch, called the *Constitucionalistas* because of their adherence to the Constitution that had called for the 1963 elections. These forces were weak, however, in the face of the American-supported Dominican military under the new President, Joaquín Balaguer (see History section, p12). The *Constitutionalistas* lost their fight, and Caamaño Deñó sought exile. In 1973, he returned to the Dominican Republic with plans to spur an uprising against the iron-fisted Balaguer regime. His revolution was not to be, however, as Balaguer's forces assassinated the rebel leader on February 16, 1973.

Ébano Verde

A verdant scientific reserve with winding trails, Ébano Verde is perfect for a daylong excursion. To access the park entrance, drive about an hour on the highway to Abanico. After passing the community of La Palma, look for La Virgen, a small chapel with candles in honor of the Virgin Mary. Once there, the walk to the beginning of the trail is about two kilometers uphill to the cell towers, at which point begins a five and a half kilometer hike down the fern and ebony covered slopes. The reserve is home to over 80 species of orchids, 20 of which are endemic, and is blanketed by the brilliant green of ferns and lichen. There are a number of bridges crossing small streams throughout the forest, which all feed into El Arroyazo ("huge stream") – providing a refreshing reward at the end of the hike. There is also a visitor's center and museum about the reserve funded by Fundación Progressio.

From El Arroyazo, it's about a two kilometer walk to the highway, where it is possible to hop on a truck heading towards La Virgen to retrieve your car, or catch a ride in the opposite direction back toward Constanza, if you'd arrived in public transport. Wear long pants and sturdy shoes, and be aware of cool temperatures in the morning hours. Visits should be arranged through Progressio (565-1422; fund.progressio@codetel.net.do) or Constanza's Tourism Office.

La Ruta del Valle

This driving or biking route through the communities around Constanza provides a glimpse into the daily life of Constanceros. Start off the tour with one of Doña Bensa's delectable *dulces de coco* found at the *colmado* at the entrance to the community of El Palero. From there, pass through a number of farming villages where men and women can be seen tending to the rich abundance of cold-weather crops like cabbage, potatoes, and chayote. The fields of hunter green beet leaves and electric green carrot shoots are cradled in the descending mountains covered with coniferous splendor. Bring your camera and go before midday when the morning dew still glistens on the crops. Other stops include exotic flower greenhouses and strawberry patches of Purama's greenhouses (539-2219; 829-222-8109; purama@codetel.net.do) as well as the intoxicating rose gardens of Vivero El Valle (C/ Antonio Abud Isaac; 539-3185). This self-guided tour is sponsored by the Office of Tourism in Constanza.

Piedra Letreada
Multiple Taíno carvings adorn the side of a massive boulder measuring 20 meters wide and seven meters high. Anthropologists believe that this was a stop along a trail used by Taínos to travel from one coast to the other. It is the only mark of the Taíno civilization in the region. Take a walk 100 meters behind the rock to see a small set of waterfalls that cascade into pretty pools. *Located in La Valle de la Culata, take the road 20 kilometers in the direction of Arroyo Arriba and La Culata*

Safari Constanza
This company offers group excursions with meals included for up to 14 people to the major attractions of Constanza including Aguas Blancas, La Pirámide, Valle Nuevo, and Ebano Verde. *7 C/ Duarte; 829-426-7100; 910-5550; osita1415@hotmail.com*

La Ruta de la Ciguapa
This 40 kilometers trail is made for the expert mountain biker looking for challenging pine-covered peaks and slopes of the Cordillera Central. Allow at least a half-day for the ride. The tour is run by Carlos Brea of MTB Dominicana, a mountain biking club. Bike rentals are available. *For more information contact Carlos Brea 829-719-4363; carlitosbreaj@gmail.com; mtbdominicanadventure.blogspot.com*

Ciguapa
The ciguapa is a fascinating mythological creature of Dominican folklore. The story is probably an amalgamation of Taíno and African roots that took on unique characteristics on the island. Ciguapas have human female qualities, except with hairier bodies and backwards-facing feet to help them escape. They are said to lure traveling men into the forest with their enchanting powers, and then leave them for dead. Looking a ciguapa in the eye means almost certain capture. Many Dominicans, especially in rural, forested regions, claim to have seen these elusive beings.

La Ruta de La Fresa & Reserves
A family-friendly bike trail for all skill levels with stops at the picturesque strawberry gardens. Alto Cerro (see Sleep) and Constanza's Tourism Office offers this excursion.

The province of La Vega encompasses two Scientific Reserves (**Ebano Verde** and **Valle Nuevo**) and two National Parks (**José del Carmen Ramírez** and **José Armando Bermúdez**). For more information on trails, camping, and attractions in Valle Nuevo, see Ocoa (p315), and regarding José del Carmen Ramírez and José Armando Bermúdez, see the following section.

NIGHTLIFE

Constanza is a quiet town but when there's party, it's juiced to the last *bachata*. On weekends, a mostly male crowd congregates around the **Café Bar Moe** (Corner of C/ Duarte and C/ Salomé Ureña) at the outdoor liquor shack. **Kapioca Bar** (841-4188)

Cordillera Central

on the main road into town Luperón also can be lively on weekends, but don't expect an all-out bash except during Easter week, Christmas and *Patronales*.

José Armando Bermúdez & José del Carmen Ramírez

Parque Nacional José Armando Bermúdez was the first National Park to open in the Dominican Republic, established in 1956 to protect the country's natural heritage from human encroachment and damage. Together, the parks cover nearly all of the rugged Cordillera Central, with Bermúdez to the north and Ramírez to the south. Through the parks, the country's highest and longest mountain range continues west into Haiti, known there as the Massif du Nord. The Cordillera Central houses the nation's (and the Caribbean's) three highest peaks, including Pico Duarte, the tallest mountain in the Caribbean basin at 10,138 feet (3,087m). The other two are close by: La Pelona (3,087m) and La Rucilla (3,049m). Twelve rivers, critical to the health of the environment and people, are born here, including both the Río Yaque del Norte and Río Yaque del Sur. These waters supply almost 80% of the Dominican population, as well as a significant area of Haiti. The mountains that form the park's backbone are over 60 million years old, remnants of a long-dormant volcanic chain that has left these high, jagged peaks filled with endemic flora and fauna seen nowhere else on the island. The parks also receive the highest amount of rainfall in the country, at more than three meters a year – which also leaves the southwest in a significant rain shadow.

Because of the parks' unique microclimate, there are no palm trees. The most commonly found tree in the area is the Hispaniolan Pine, and is the only tree found above 2,100 meters (6,890 feet). A large majority of the 32 birds endemic to the island can be found here, 13 of which are threatened or endangered. Look out for rare birds including the Bay-breasted Cuckoo, Hispaniolan Crossbill, Hispaniolan Parakeet (*cotorra*), and various doves, crows, warblers, and woodpeckers. Migratory birds are also found in the area, including Bicknell's Thrush – which, like many Dominicans, move back and forth between Hispaniola and the Northeast United States. The elusive and endangered Hispaniolan solenodon and Hispaniolan hutia officially inhabit these piney forests, but are rarely, if ever, spotted. Wild boars, however, introduced by the Spanish colonists, tend to nose around. Temperatures in the parks are much cooler than in the rest of the island. Especially in higher elevations, night readings drop below freezing, and during the day temperatures may struggle to reach 10°C (50°F) even during the summer.

Pico Duarte

Though any walk through the National Parks is a beautiful alternative to the dense heat of the rest of the island, it is the allure of Pico Duarte that draws intrepid climbers to the chilly heights of the Cordillera Central. There was some controversy over the tallest spot in the land, remaining unresolved until just recently. Pico Duarte's mile-distant sister peak La Pelona was finally measured to be just two meters shorter than Duarte. Though thousands of hikers summit Pico Duarte each year, the mountain was first climbed only in 1944, as part of the country's centennial celebrations. Refusing to be outshone, Rafael Trujillo had Pico Duarte rechristened after himself; the name returned to its original state after Trujillo's death.

There are several ways to hike the mountain. Hiking is best in the winter months, when it is drier – but also colder. Be prepared for wet weather, however, as during any season it is liable to rain, especially in the afternoons. It is therefore recommended to reach the peak soon after sunrise, before the rain and clouds come, obscuring the summit view and making climbing difficult. Note that in April and May, these rains become especially strong, making the trails impassable. Also, during the Christmas and Semana Santa holidays, groups of up to 100 people trek at the same time, creating an unpleasant experience. It is best to avoid the mountain over these weeks.

You should also check in with the ranger stations at all of the trailheads to give notice that you are entering the park. There is a park entrance fee of RD$150, usually covered by the pricing of an organized hike.

The five major routes are listed below. It is best to arrive at these communities the night before, and then set out early in the morning. There are several campsites scattered through the parks, most with fireplaces, kitchens with stoves, bathrooms, and running water. You must bring your own sleeping gear (remember that temperatures can drop to freezing at night).

LA CIÉNAGA

The shortest and most popular route leaves from La Ciénaga, outside of Jarabacoa, where a loose group of guides leads tours to the peak.

This trail is 23 kilometers (14 miles) to the top, with a 2275-meter (7,500-foot) change in elevation, taking two to three days to complete. This hike is not technically challenging, though there are some steep areas. Because this route is the most popular, it can get extremely muddy. Treading of multiple mules a day can make the trail almost impassable in certain spots.

Three lodges along the trail are the best options for sleeping. The biggest lodge, La Compartición, has fire pits and bathrooms with running water. All of the cabins are recently renovated, but it is also possible to camp along the trail instead.

Slightly off this trail is a beautiful valley called **Valle de Tétero**, a worthy side trip that adds an extra day to the hike. The valley is composed of a strikingly flat, grassy field bordered on two sides by a river with a waterfall and tranquil pools, surrounded by the steep mountains. Unlike in the dense forest, the sun penetrates the treeless field, making it a fascinating home to many birds, and a nice place to relax and take advantage of the mountain air. Usually, groups will visit the valley on the way down from the summit.

The first day on this trail, hikers pass through a rainforest valley, eventually winding along a high ridge, and then back into the forest at the source of the Yaque del Norte and Yaque del Sur rivers. Hikers will spend first night at La Compartición, at the base of the summit, which they then reach early on the second morning by sunrise. It is then possible to descend the mountain, visit Valle del Tétero, or spend the evening again at La Compartición, and descend the next day.

To arrange a visit, email picoduartelacienaga@gmail.com, which is checked about once a week, or call 869-7648. One of the lead guides is Chano, who has been working with hikers for several years, and is the guide of choice for Peace Corps volunteers. Though he does not lead tours very often anymore, his nephew Abelito has taken up his mantle, and can be contacted at 829-992-0071. Reservations are

Cordillera Central

recommended, though it is possible to simply show up at La Ciénaga and hope that there are guides available.

Transport

From Jarabacoa, catch the *guagua* on the Manabao/La Ciénaga route. If you are coming in on Caribe Tours, walk straight out of the station until you see a sign with an arrow pointing to the right that says La Ciénaga. Cross a small bridge and turn left, where there will be a line of pickup trucks on the left hand side of the road. At the stop, make sure the truck you get on is going to La Ciénaga and not just Manabao, which is only halfway up the hill to the trailhead. The first La Ciénaga truck leaves around 11am, and the other leaves between 2pm and 3pm (RD$100; 1hr). Ask the driver to drop you off at the Armando Bermúdez park office and the Park Guard who works in the office can assist you in getting a local guide from the Association.

Prices

Groups of three to nine should expect to pay at least RD$2000 per day for guides, mules, and park entrance fee. Two or more guides are required for groups larger than three, and an additional is required for larger groups. Two mules are required for groups of two or more.

MATA GRANDE

Mata Grande is a small mountain village sitting on the northern edge of the national park, outside the city of San José de las Matas.

The walk to the visitor center, where it is possible to sleep the night before beginning the hike is about an hour's walk from town; simply follow the signs to the Visitor's Center or ask the guide. The Visitor's Center is quite new and very nicely situated alongside a mountain stream on the edge of the park. The building is large and had electricity and running water at the time of research.

The trail from Mata Grande is 48 kilometers to the peak, and is a more challenging approach than La Ciénaga, taking four to six days to complete with an elevation change of more than 2200 meters. Fewer hikers ascend this way, resulting in a less abused trail and more panoramic vistas.

A standard trip from Mata Grande has hikers spending the first night at a lower elevation, at the confluence of two mountain rivers. On the second day, hikers walk through the Bao Valley, and will pass by the La Pelona peak, which they can also summit. Hikers reach the top of Pico Duarte on the third day, and usually spend the night at the base of the peak. Additional days can be taken at the Valle de Tétero. A popular alternative is to begin at Mata Grande and descend through La Ciénaga, allowing hikers to see both sides of this trail, and arrange a somewhat easier exit down the mountain on public transportation. Of course, hikers can also descend back to Mata Grande, or through the other routes.

To get in contact with the guides association phone the head guide, Antonio Fernández, or Toño, at 829-293-5551. Upon arrival in Mata Grande, you can arrange for your guide to meet you at the bus, or you can ask for him once you're there – it's a small community.

Transport

From Santiago: Monday to Saturday, two *guaguas* leave from corner of C/ Boy Scouts and Valerio at 9:30am and 3:00pm. (RD$150, 2 ½hrs).

From Mata Grande: *Guaguas* leave Monday-Saturday at 7am and 1pm for Santiago.

Prices

Prices in Mata Grande are slightly lower, but as with La Ciénaga, guides and mules are required for any hike. There is a minimum of two guides per group.

1-3 hikers: RD$1650/day
4-5 hikers: RD$2000/day
6 hikers: RD$2650/day
7-9 hikers: RD$3000/day
10 hikers: RD$3350/day

LOS CORRALITOS, CONSTANZA

The trail that leaves from outside Constanza is much less developed than the previous two hikes, and takes about six days to traverse. Some claim it to be the best overall route, as it passes through areas of both parks, as well as Valle del Tetero. The trail is 43 kilometers (27 miles) in length, with an absolute rise of about 549 meters (1,800 feet), but there are several valley dips, increasing the total altitude hiked. Unlike from La Ciénaga and Mata Grande, there is no established community-based guide association here. The trail is more challenging, and should only be done by experienced hikers.

Transport & Prices

Interested visitors should stop by the tourism office in Constanza before setting out. The trailhead is officially at Los Corralitos, reachable by taxi or motorcycle. It is possible, and recommended, to hire guides and mules there. Many hikers depart directly out of Constanza, where local operators offer inclusive hiking packages. One of these is Ecoturísmo de Montaña Constanza (RD$5,000 per person; 22 C/ Luperón; 829-801-7199, ecoturismoconstanza@gmail.com). For transport information, see Constanza (p290).

SABANETA

This is probably the most difficult trail, and can take at least a week to hike. Hikers use this trail most commonly on the way down, after beginning from La Ciénaga or Mata Grande. The trek runs 48 kilometers (30 miles) and rises just less than 2,600 meters (8,500 feet). The trailhead is in Sabaneta, outside of San Juan de la Maguana, at the large dam. Because the route begins from the south, the trail runs through an entirely different landscape. The trail is almost unknown across the country – hikers probably won't meet anyone else while hiking. Hikers spend the first night around Alto de la Rosa, the next night at Macutico, and summit the third day, spending that night at la Compartición.

Transport

Again, more information can be found in San Juan de la Maguana, at the local Tourism Office. It is best to contact the central Tourism Office in the capital at 688-0793 for more information, or visit the office on C/ Máximo Gómez once in San Juan de la Maguana (p325) There is a very infrequent *guagua* to Sabaneta with variable times and prices.

Cordillera Central

LAS LAGUNAS

The trail out of Las Lagunas is run by a guides group called Aguimora, based in the village of Padre de Las Casas. The trail is 54 kilometers (34 miles) long, and will take about six days, with an altitude rise of about 2,100 meters (6,900 feet). As with Sabaneta, the trail is difficult, and should be planned beforehand by a call or visit with the Ministry of Tourism. This trail begins in an area full of small ponds and streams, giving it the name of Las Lagunas. Like the trail out of Constanza, this one actually traverses directly through the previously mentioned, and highly recommended, Valle del Tetero.

Transport & Prices

To get to Padre de las Casas, turn off the Azua-San Juan de la Maguana highway at Cruce de Las Yayas. Twenty kilometers (12 miles) down the road is Padre de Las Casas. At the next village, Guayabal, take a left to arrive at Las Lagunas. There is *guagua* service from Azua, through Padre de las Casas. Prices are variable depending on the number of hikers and days hiked, beginning at around RD$2,000/day.

FOOD

Often as part of the deal, guides will cook breakfast and dinner at the campsite (if your hike takes you to a campsite), but you must bring food for the trail. Hikers usually accompany their guides to the local *colmado* and buy food for the group, guides included. *Colmados* in this area stock only the most basic of foodstuffs, like rice, beans, salami, and chicken, which is good for the first night – carrying a chicken farther than that is not advisable. On good days, it is also possible to pick up cans of tuna, bananas, and Gatorade. Campsite breakfast includes hot chocolate, coffee, and bread. Again, bring lots of granola bars or other snacks to eat on the trek during the day. A final word about food: be sure to seal and pack everything very well. On your author's trip, when crossing a creek, one of the mules got into the bread supply, tearing into half the loaf in the middle of the water. We're sure the mule appreciated it, but the bread would have been tastier had the hikers eaten it. Each guide and guide group has different rules regarding food, so make sure to discuss this first before setting off. As for water, bring a water bottle and purification tablets. There are many spots at which to refill your bottle, most of which are potable.

Packing List

Sleeping bag

Sleeping mat

Warm/quick-dry clothes

Hiking shoes/boots

Tennis shoes/sandals

Flashlight

Water bottle (there are a number of potable water sources on the trail, including rivers and springs)

Toilet paper

Rain jacket

Plate, cup, spoon

Large plastic trash bags in which to wrap packs if, or when, it rains

The South

Overlooked and underappreciated by many of the millions of visitors that arrive in the country each year, El Sur, as it is referred to locally, is the hidden gem of the Dominican Republic. This sprawling and vibrant region offers astounding geographic variety and biodiversity: the cool, coniferous mountains of the Sierra de Ocoa, the dusty, arid lands around Azua, the turquoise waters of Barahona's pebble beaches, and the humid forests in the Sierra de Bahoruco. Don't leave without purchasing some larimar – a blue semi-precious stone found nowhere else in the world but the hills of the Sierra de Bahoruco – and be sure to sample the local culinary favorites, such as *chenchen* (a moist, salty cornmeal bread), found in places like San Juan de la Maguana. Environmentalists swoon over the abundant wildlife found at Lago Enriquillo, the Caribbean's largest saltwater lake, and birdwatchers find their mecca in Puerto Escondido. The flourishing coral reefs around Bahia de las Aguilas are perfect for divers, and beachgoers love the isolated, white sand beaches of this starkly beautiful National Park.

The roads in the South are not in terribly good condition, making a four-wheel drive vehicle a good investment if renting a car. In general, however, the region is well connected by public transportation. The greatest draw of the South is the warmth and humility of its people, virtually unaffected by the ills of unsustainable tourism. The South's relative inaccessibility and lack of government attention have left room for something of a silver lining in the growth of more sustainable forms of development. Environmentally aware eco- and agro-tourism companies and community-based cooperatives are popping up throughout the region. These movements will hopefully allow the South to pass by the disruptive tourism booms and crashes seen in other parts of the country, while protecting its cultural and environmental heritage.

San Cristóbal

The province of San Cristóbal, home to over 220,000 inhabitants, is comprised of a variety of microclimates in its small area, from the cool and humid coffee-carpeted mountains in the north, to the sunny, stone-dotted beaches of Palenque and Najayo in the south. Manmade creations such as the well-stocked Valdesia Dam attract fishing fanatics, but all visitors can marvel at the resplendent mountain views along the small village byways. A number of cave systems including the Cuevas de Pomier (or Borbón), covered in pictographs, offer glimpses of the indigenous civilizations' way of life. While adventurous travelers will see the great potential throughout the province, the city of San Cristóbal requires a bit more imagination. Famous for being the birthplace of Trujillo, the city is a tangled mess of motorcycles and *guaguas*, destroying pleasant strolls in their wake. There are, however, a few interesting sights: Trujillo's mansions, El Cerro, and the abandoned Casa de Caoba. These paired with a decadent meal at Aubergine (pg 306) make for the perfect day trip from Santo Domingo, as San Cristóbal is less than an hour's drive from the capital.

The South

TRANSPORT

From Santo Domingo: RD$70; 6am-8pm; 45min; *Guaguas* (Rutas A and B) leave from Parque Enriquillo along C/ Duarte and from Parque Independencia along C/ Bolivar. Both Ruta A and B pass through the center of San Cristóbal.

From Santo Domingo to Palenque: RD$100; 7am-6pm; 1hr; *Guaguas* to Palenque run along C/ Bolívar in Gazcue, but originates from Parque Enriquillo.

From San Cristóbal to Palenque: RD$40; 7am-6pm; 20min; The *parada* for Palenque in San Cristóbal is on C/ Padre Borbón across from Parque Radhamés.

El Mercado de San Cristóbal: Prices vary; *Guaguas* leaving from San Cristóbal towards La Toma, Las Cuevas de Pomier, La Colonia, Cambita, Los Cacaos and many other small towns and villages leave from the lively *Mercado Público*. Ruta A or B will drop you off at the entrance to the *mercado*, where it's possible to ask a local where specific *parada* locations are within the *mercado*.

Motoconchos around town start at RD$20 a trip.

INFO

Medical Attention
Unless it's an absolute emergency, head to Santo Domingo for medical attention. As a last resort, the public **Hospital Juan Pablo Piña** is at 42 C/ Santomé and C/ Presidente Billini (528-3098). For pharmacy necessities, **Farmacia Gladys Rosa** is on the corner of C/ Dr. Brioso and Padre Ayala (528-3291).

Communication
On C/ Sánchez near the corner of C/ General Cabral is an **internet café**. The **Post Office** is located at 188 Av. Constitución (528-1176; 910-6038).

Banks
There are numerous full-service banks in the center of town including a **Banco Popular** (corner of Av. Constitución and C/ Palo Hincado; 528-4335), a **Banco BHD** (corner of Av. Constitución and C/ Salcedo; 528-6262) and a **Banco León** (corner of Av. Constitución and C/ Dr. Brioso; 476-2000/ 200-8242). All are open Monday to Friday, 8:30am to 4pm and Saturday 9am to 1pm.

Police
The local station of the **Policia Nacional** is found on Av. Constitución & C/ Sánchez.

Gas
There is an **Esso Gas Station** across from Parque Radhamés along C/ Padre Borbón, as well as an **Isla Gas Station** continuing a few meters west past the Mercado Modelo on C/ Padre Borbón.

Grocery Stores
For the largest selection of food and many other items, **La Sirena** is located on Carretera Sánchez Vieja and Los Padres (338-0909).

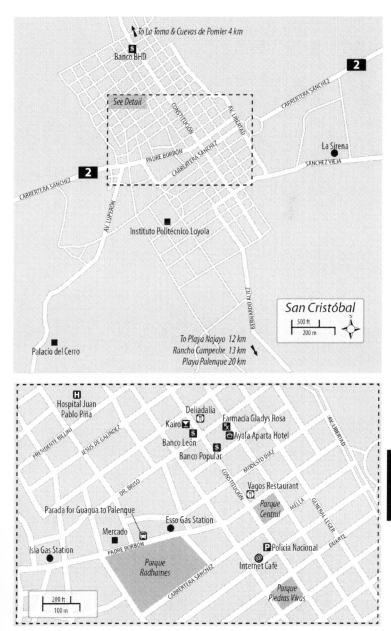

EAT

 Aubergine Jutting out from a mountainside overlooking the peaks and valleys of San Cristóbal, this avant-garde restaurant fuses Asian, German, and other flavors to create a multi-layered journey for the taste buds. Try any of the German chef's ever-changing inventions with exotic meats or one of the namesake dishes, such as fried eggplant roulettes topped with *chili con carne*, a terrific blend of Mexican and Thai. The desserts are equally imaginative: white chocolate avocado ice cream topped with eye-catching fresh strawberry sauce and poppy seeds. *RD$280-780; La Colonia Km 6 ½ past Cambita en route to Los Cacaos; 374-1382, 729-9364; harald@codetel.net.do; www.aubergine.com.do. For public transport either take a carro público (RD$40; 15min) to Cambita from the Mercado in San Cristóbal, and then a motoconcho (RD$100; 15min) to the restaurant or take a guagua (RD$50; 30min) going to Los Cacaos, which also leaves from the Mercado. Tell the cobrador to leave you at Aubergine (where the German is – "donde el aleman") in La Colonia.*

A Local Favorite

Eggplant is a favorite side dish in Dominican cuisine, often in the form of *berenjena guisado* (eggplant stewed in vegetables and spices). The fruit, however, originated in India, unlike its close biological cousins the tomato and potato, which are endemic to the Americas.

Vagos Restaurant A white-linen establishment with bright modern art, this is among the only upscale restaurants in town with international offerings such as grilled shish kabobs, large salads, and a variety of pastas. *RD$185-750; Av. Constitución & C/ Padre Borbón; 528-5400*

Fela's Place Formerly a San Cristóbal institution called Pepe Rosón, it was known for delicious, steaming *pasteles en hoja*. The current owner, Fela, has kept this tradition alive, while adding other Dominican favorites like a filling *mofongo*, and, of course, *la bandera dominicana*. *RD$100-200; 55 C/ General Leger; 288-2124*

Delidalia An air-conditioned oasis amidst the roar of *motos*, this bakery offers a large selection of both sweet and savory baked goods, such as guava-filled turnovers, carrot cake, *tres leches*, and paninis. Though there are two locations, the one with the larger selection and more pleasant atmosphere is located on Av. Constitución. *RD$ 20-200; 105 Av. Constitución; 528-7886*

SLEEP

Due to its proximity to Santo Domingo, San Cristóbal has not been able to maintain any hotels worth mentioning. If stuck, head to the **Ayala Aparta Hotel** with fans and cold water. When they ask you for how many hours you want the room, say *"para amanecer,"* meaning the whole night.

Ayala Aparta Hotel *RD$300-500; 110 C/ Padre Ayala near corner of C/ Dr. Brioso; 528-3040; Amenities: A/C, fan*

 Rancho Campeche An ecological ranch near the beaches of Najayo and Palenque, Rancho Campeche offers a rare camping opportunity. Immense and peaceful, the property is home to a number of farm animals, as well as caves and hiking trails. The owners, Gina Gallardo and Xiomara Fortuna (an internationally recognized world music singer), offer cultural tours, such as "Santo Domingo Raíces," of the surrounding communities with glimpses into daily life, religion and music. The site provides a quality restaurant, pool, and importantly, bathrooms with showers. *RD$300 for camping, RD$400 for camping space with tent and mattress; 3 meals, RD$1100; Contact before arriving: 686-1053, 889-5661; ranchoelcampeche@yahoo.com; www.ranchocampeche.com. From Santo Domingo, after passing San Cristóbal along the southern highway, turn south towards the coast and the community of Duveaux (signaled by a white and black smokestack lettered with "Caei"). Drive through the sugarcane fields, up into the hills, through Duveaux, until reaching El Limón, where there is sign for Rancho Campeche. By public*

transport, take any guagua caliente heading further southwest than San Cristóbal and ask to be dropped off at Ingenio Caei (RD$140). Then take a motoconcho to Rancho Campeche (RD$150).

DO

Cuevas de Pomier (Cuevas de Borbón)

Located 12 kilometers (7.5 miles) north of San Cristóbal, the 57 caves that make up this complex were declared a protected area in 1996 to prevent damaging limestone quarrying. The main draw here is the endangered cave art by Igneri, Carib, and Taíno indigenous groups, rediscovered by British consul and anthropologist Robert Schomburg more than 60 years ago. This is one of the highest concentrations of prehistoric cave art in the Caribbean, which the public can observe firsthand in the five caves currently open for display: La Sala de los Grandes Edentados, La Cueva del Puente, La Sala de la Penumbra, La Sala de los Grandes Bloques, and La Sala de Boinayel. In times of drought, the Taínos congregated in La Sala de Boinayel, named after the god of rain, and pleaded that Boinayel cry, wetting the earth with his tears. The first cave that visitors enter is La Sala de los Ententados, which refers to the group of mammals called Endentata (including sloths and anteaters) which are classified by their lack of front incisors and molars. A number of skeletons belonging to these animals were found by the professor and spelunker Dato Pagan, leading to the cave's name: "The Room of the Endentata." Of the pictographs on display, one of particular interest is what appears to be a man mounted on an animal, referring to the legend of a Taíno man who raised and tamed a dolphin to the point at which it would respond to its given name, Anon, and cart the man around the Caribbean Sea. *US$5; Take the road to La Toma from Highway 2 and continue past La Toma for about 6 kilometers (3.7 miles). In public transport, take a guagua to La Toma from El Mercado and then a moto from there.*

Before the Taínos

The Igneri people were an earlier Arawak-related indigenous group that originally populated present-day Venezuela. They eventually migrated in canoes to the Antilles, including Hispaniola. Later, the Igneri would become displaced by Taíno and Carib populations.

Palacio del Cerro

This five-story garish edifice was originally built for Trujillo in 1949, but the dictator never occupied it despite the ornate interior's liberal usage of Italian marble, numerous rooms for entertaining and repose, and 18 bathrooms. After years of looting, the building underwent significant renovations and many of the rooms were restored to their original flashiness. A few points of interest include the room meant for Trujillo's daughter Angelina, in which the walls and ceiling are covered with brimming baskets and vines of roses, and the room designed for Trujillo, adorned by heavy crown molding and walls almost entirely made of windows overlooking San Cristóbal. A small chapel with a mural by Spanish painter José Vela Zanetti (1913-1999) of a Dominican country fiesta is both a source of beauty and historical intrigue. Focusing on the faces of the dancers, the viewer notices their solemn expressions, an affront by the painter to Trujillo, expressing the fear and repression felt by the people during his reign. The building is now used as a training school for penitentiary employees, but offers free, guided tours to the public. *From the Parque Central, take Avenida Luperón west until Isla Gas Station, then turn left up the hill. El Cerro will be on the left.*

The South

José Vela Zanetti

To see more of Vela Zanetti's murals reminiscent of the pastoral scenes of Diego Rivera, head to the **Instituto Politécnico Loyola** (C/ 19 de Marzo b/w 18 de Agosto and Araujo). An exile of the Spanish Civil War, Vela Zanetti shared his talent throughout the Americas. One of his most celebrated murals, "La Lucha del Hombre por la Paz" (Man's Fight for Peace) is in the headquarters of the United Nations in New York City.

La Casa de Caoba

Named appropriately, this once grandiose home built for Trujillo in 1940 was made entirely of *caoba* (mahogany), but now is nothing more than a pillaged and abandoned haunting ghost of glory. Nearly all the mahogany and ornate décor have been stripped and the surviving furniture was moved to El Cerro. All that remains is an eerie sensation and a couple squatters, who will give an informal tour. *Located on a hill off the road to La Toma. The turn-off is an unmarked rocky dirt road best identified by asking a motoconchista or a local.*

La Toma

Established as the first reservoir in the Americas in the 1520s, this swimming hole (now made of poured cement) is great for experiencing how locals relax on weekends by throwing back cold ones and blaring *bachata*. *Located 6 kilometers (3.7 miles) north of San Cristóbal. When nearing San Cristóbal from Santo Domingo on Highway 2, take the exit for La Toma and follow signs. In public transport, take a guagua leaving for La Toma from the Mercado in San Cristóbal.*

Parque Piedras Vivas & Iglesia Nuestra Señora de la Consolación

This pleasant park is on the former site of one of Trujillo's residences. It is built from stones brought from distinct regions of the country, giving rise to the name "*Parque Piedras Vivas*" or Live Stone Park. Find the mustard neo-colonial church of Nuestra Señora de la Consolación bordering the park. The church features vibrant biblical murals splashed across the center chamber walls. *Av. Constitución and C/ General Cabral*

BEACHES

Playa Najayo

During the week, Najayo affords a quiet and convenient respite. For a livelier atmosphere, join the weekend crowd rolling in from San Cristóbal and Santo Domingo in SUVs packed tight with passengers and libations. Be careful when

---

A Scenic *Moto* Ride through Cane Country

For a picturesque *moto* ride (about 20 minutes) and an alternative route to the beaches of Palenque and Najayo, take this meandering, hilly road through the sugar cane fields of Ingenio Caeí and quaint rural communities like Duveaux, which eventually opens up to the coast.

To arrive at this road by public transportation, ask the *cobrador* to let you off at "*la parada del Ingenio Caeí.*" When a black and white smokestack lettered with "*Caeí*" appears in the middle of a sugarcane field, the stop is quite close. At the *parada*, tell the least pushy *motoconchista* to take you to either Playa Najayo or Palenque. Don't pay more than RD$300 and be prepared to negotiate the price.

entering the water, because there is a prickly rock shelf, and the waves can be strong. There are a few food shacks along the beach, all with essentially the same menu of whole fried fish on a bed of golden *tostones*.

Playa Palenque

A few kilometers west of Najayo is Palenque, which tends to be more raucous than its neighbor. Similarly styled fried fish shacks serve up a Presidente beer *bien fría* here as well. *Both beaches are accessible through public transportation by picking up a guagua at the stop for Palenque near the Mercado Modelo in San Cristóbal (see Transport). For Najayo, simply ask the cobrador to let you off at Playa Najayo, or stay on until the last stop for Palenque.*

Festival de Sainagua

This animated annual music festival has showcased *palo* and other forms Afro-Caribbean music for more than 35 years. Cultural heritage comes alive through the contagious rhythms of the Atabales (p329) groups of Villa Mella or the Guloyas of San Pedro de Macorís (p119), whose festive costumes and dances mesmerize viewers.

> For **nightlife** in San Cristóbal, **Kairo** at 160 C/ Constitución is a popular dance club on weekends (no cover).

Located just outside San Cristóbal, the Festival de Sainagua occurs over an entire late November weekend, so the best option for overnight stay is Rancho Campeche. Perhaps best of all, the performances are free. *To arrive using public transport, take the guagua from San Cristóbal's Mercado to Palenque and ask the cobrador to leave you in Sainagua, located after the large cemetery on the right.*

Bani

Named after a prominent Taíno cacique under Caonabo (p327), Baní means "abundant water" in Taíno, though the city sits at the edge of the driest part of the country. The city was formally established in 1764, when the Spanish Capitán Manuel de Azlor y Urries purchased land in what is now the community of Cerro Gordo. During the Haitian occupation, General Dessalines burned the town to the ground in 1805, but the industrious townspeople rebuilt the city within five years. Since then, the province in which it lies, Peravia, has grown steadily, with a population now numbering around 200,000. *Banilejos* (residents of Baní) proudly proclaim their home as the town of liberators and poets, including Enrique Montaño and Pedro Landestoy Garrido. Among the most famous Banilejos is Generalísimo Máximo Gómez y Báez (1836-1905), who originally served in the Dominican army when it was under Spanish control during the re-annexation of the 1860s. Gómez left for Cuba and soon began to conspire with Cuban revolutionaries for independence from Spain. Gómez, together with José Martí, fiercely and successfully fought the Spanish for Cuba's independence, which the U.S. eventually granted in 1902 following the Spanish-American War.

Baní is also known for its tremendous diversity and production of mangos. The season's pinnacle is celebrated during the Feria del Mango, which takes place every June. Salt is another major product from the area, extracted from the mines by the beach in

> Interestingly, the majority of Baní's expats have congregated around Boston, Massachusetts.

Las Salinas. Remittances from the numerous *Banilejos* in the U.S also have a large role in bolstering the local economy. The fruits of *Banilejos'* labor abroad can be seen especially on the way to Playa Los Almendros, where cement mansions line the road.

TRANSPORT

From Santo Domingo: *Expresos* RD$100; *calientes* RD$85; 5am-8pm every 20 minutes; 1hr; depart from Parque Enriquillo. It is also possible to hail the *guagua* anywhere along its route, which runs up C/ Bolívar through Gazcue and passes through Pintura before leaving the city.

To Santo Domingo: *Expresos* RD$100; *calientes* RD$85; 5am-8pm every 20 minutes; 1hr; *parada* located slightly west of the Parque Central on C/ Billini.

To San José de Ocoa: RD$50; hourly 7am-7pm; 30min; *parada* on Carretera Sánchez just west of the Parador Baní

To head farther southwest: All *guaguas* heading southwest pass along Carretera Sánchez, which becomes C/ Máximo Gómez in town. You can hail any *guagua caliente* along this road. Those heading to Barahona (or farther) often make a stop at the Parador Baní at the town's exit along Carretera Sánchez, where you can also hop on.

INFO

Medical Attention
Santa Ana Farmacia is located the corner of Calles Billini and Mella in Plaza II Valera-Guzmán (380-2525). For emergencies, head to **Grupo Medico Baní** on C/ Santomé and C/ Billini (346-4444).

Communication
Terabyte Internet Café is located one block south of the park (522-4622) and a **Call Center** is located on C/ Duvergé near C/ Máximo Gómez.

The **Post Office** is located at 18 C/ Canela Mota (522-3480/906-0028) or for faster shipping, **FedEx** services are available in the tourist agency, Turinter (Calles Billini and Mella in Plaza II Valera-Guzmán; 522-5363).

Gastón Fernando Deligne

The greatest poets often draw inspiration from personal suffering, and Gastón Fernando Deligne is no exception. After Deligne was orphaned at a young age, the Catholic priest, Francisco Javier Billini, raised Deligne and ensured that he received a quality, private education in Santo Domingo. Following his graduation from high school, Deligne dedicated himself to the art of letters, spinning out poetry often referred to as *poesía sicológica* or psychological poetry for his often-heavy themes and ability to venture into the human psyche, particularly the feminine mindset. Examples of this cerebral talent can be seen in such poems as, "Confidencias de Cristina." Despite his success among the authoritative Dominican publications of the 19th and early 20th century including "Letras y Ciencias" and "La Cuna de América," Deligne committed suicide in 1913 after years of enduring complications from leprosy.

Banks

Banco Popular has two locations in the center of town (corner of C/ Máximo Gómez and Duarte or 22 C/ Billini; 522-2225). There is also a **BanReservas** at 32 C/ Sánchez near C/ Ntra. Señora de Reglas (522-3801) and a **Banco León** on C/ Sánchez and Mella (476-2000). All are open Mon-Fri 8:30am-4pm and Sat 9am-1pm.

Gas Stations

A **Texaco Gas Station** is located on the main highway when entering town if coming from Santo Domingo. There is also an **Isla Gas Station** at the edge of town on the corner of Carretera Sánchez and Gastón Fernando Deligne.

Grocery Stores

For **groceries**, head to the **Super Market Pueblo** on the corner of C/ Duvergé and C/ Máximo Gómez.

EAT

The *comedores* of Baní are the best bet for a delicious and cheap meal, as sit-down restaurants are rare. Try the very popular **Comedor Lucelis** (RD$100) located at 57 Máximo Gómez, where Doña Magalis also sells *arepas* and hot chocolate from her bright blue cart across the street. Alternately, try **La Esquina D' Kelvin** (RD$100-150; corner of C/ Santomé and C/ Sánchez), serving up absurdly large sandwiches overflowing with such combos as pulled chicken or pork with gouda cheese, which should be paired with Baní's favorite flavor of *batida*, mango.

D'Santia Panadería-Repostería A rather posh gem, this bakery/café offers savory, mini-pitas stuffed with pulled chicken salad, along with sweets like glistening chocolate donuts and custard cake topped with fresh fruit. Everything is fresh and made daily on the premises; pair your treat with creamy *batidas* and a hot, sweet espresso. *RD$30-150; C/ Duarte across from Cineteatro Vaganiona, just south of the Parque Central; 522-6583/346-8640*

D' Leonel Empanadas For a cheap and delicious snack, head to this empanada stand offering the best variety of fillings in town. *RD$30-100; Corner of Fabio Herrera and 16 de Agosto*

Pollo Rey A rest stop for *guaguas* heading farther south, this popular eatery offers an abundance of aromatic fried chicken, as well as home-style Dominican favorites like *mangú* topped with liberal helpings of fried salami, onions, or eggs. Sweet treats, coffee, and fresh fruit are also available. *RD$ 70-200; Corner of Carretera Francisco del Rosario Sánchez and C/ Gastón Fernando Deligne; 522-9000*

Las Tres Rosas

Nearly 70 years ago, Señorita Elena Virginia Mejía Lujo and her sister Carmen began a humble business selling *dulce de leche* out of their small, wooden home. Señorita Elena started the business out of necessity, tasked with raising her younger brother, and later, his children. Lucia Virginia Mejía de Ruíz, niece and current co-owner with her husband and son, always refers to her aunt as Señorita (not Señora) because throughout her 105 years on earth, Elena never married. Today, Las Tres Rosas operates a factory that supplies its three locations across the area, in Baní, Paya, and Escondido. All of these offer the same delightful variety of classic and harder to find *dulces* such as *leche con limón* (milk with lemon candy) or *dulce de cajuil* (cashew fruit candy). Stop by the original house where Señorita Elena cooked up the first batch, located just north of the Parque Central at 18 Calle Duarte (522-3694).

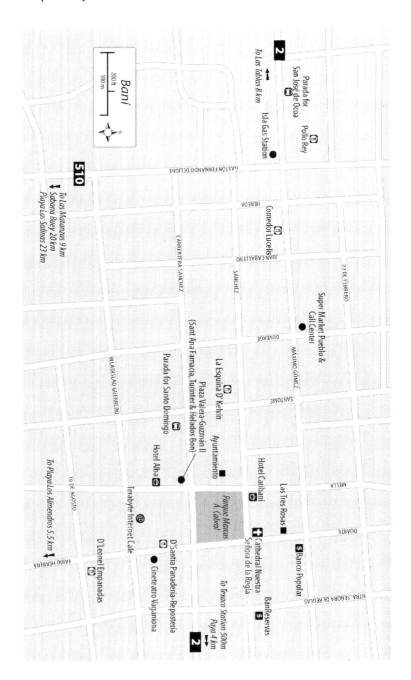

Baní

200 ft
100 m

N

2
To Las Tablas 8 km
Parada for San José de Ocoa
Pollo Rey
Isla Gas Station

GASTÓN FERNANDO DELIGNE

HEREDA

Comedor Lucelis

JUAN CABALLERO

SÁNCHEZ

CARRETERA SÁNCHEZ

510
To Las Matanzas 9 km
Sabana Buey 20 km
Playa Los Salinas 23 km

27 DE FEBRERO

Super Market Pueblo & Call Center

DUVERGE

MÁXIMO GÓMEZ

SANTOMÉ

La Esquina D'Kelvin
(Sant Ana Farmacia, Tuinter & Helados Bon)
Plaza Valera-Guzmán II

Parada for Santo Domingo

WLADISLAO GUERRERO

Ayuntamiento

Hotel Alba

Hotel Caribani

Las Tres Rosas

MELLA

Parque Marcos A. Cabral

16 DE AGOSTO

Terabyte Internet Café

To Playa Los Almendros 5.5 km

FABIO HERRERA

D'Leonel Empanadas

D'Santia Panadería-Repostería

Cineteatro Vaganiona

Cathedral Nuestra Señora de la Regla

DUARTE

Banco Popular

BanReservas

NTRA. SEÑORA DE REGLAS

To Texaco Station 500m
Playa 4 km

2

SLEEP

Staying overnight in Baní is less than desirable, as the majority of the options are of the unsavory motel variety. In a pinch, try **Hotel Caribani**, which is one of the few that does not have an "afternoon rate" and does have important comforts like A/C and hot water. *RD$1200-1600; 12 C/ Sánchez; 522-3871/3872/3873; hotelcaribani@gmail.com*

For a more economical option, try **Hotel Alba,** a no-nonsense place with two beds per room, TV, and cold water only. *RD$600-1000; C/ Mella b/w Guerrero and Billini; no phone number*

DO

Parque Marcos A. Cabral (Parque Central)
The social center for town, the Parque Central is bordered by such local monuments as the *Ayuntamiento* (City Hall), adorned with murals, and the recently restored Cathedral Nuestra Señora de la Regla. The cathedral, whose design dates back to the late 1920s, is built on the same site where the original colonial church was constructed in the late 1680s during the reign of the Spanish King Carlos II. Various shops surround the park, including the heavenly air-conditioned Helados Bon/Yogen-Früz joint and a couple internet cafés. These businesses keep the park constantly abuzz, along with vendors peddling shoe shines to men taking a break from work or tiny coffees to older women bragging to each other about their children in *Nueba Yol* (New York).

Feria de Mango
Though not the most fertile region, Baní has managed to come out on top in mango production and marketing. Each year in June, Baní, the self-proclaimed "mango capital" of the country, hosts the *Feria de Mango* (the Mango Fair) in honor of the popular crop of sweet, fleshy, and bright-orange fruit. During mango season, the air is fragrant with its thick tropical aroma, and neighbors give sackfuls to local children. Hundreds of varieties of mangos are grown on the island, and many can be sampled at the fair. The country exports almost US$5 million of mangos annually.

Playa Los Almendros
Only five minutes from the center of town, this grey-sand beach was undergoing a much-needed makeover at the time of research, involving beautification efforts like planting trees and creating a small park. Just before arriving to the beach, there are a few establishments (serving fried fish and *moro*) such as **Villa Cana**, which is a popular spot for dancing on Mondays after 6pm, and **Villa Eloa**, which also offers hourly cabañas for the other kind of dance. *To arrive, take Calle Fabio Herrera (the continuation of C/ Duarte) all the way south to Playa Los Almendros (also known as Playa Baní); RD$50-60 motoconcho*

Playa Las Salinas/Salt Mines
On the way to Las Salinas are a series of sand dunes, known as **Las Dunas**, whose unusual beauty is worth a photo. Located approximately 25 kilometers (16 miles) from the center of Baní, Las Salinas Beach is not the best the South has to offer, but it is a relaxing place to cool off from the hot Southern climate. From the beach, blinding white piles of salt, harvested from the surrounding salt flats, shimmer under

the South's unobstructed sun. The manager will gladly let visitors take back a handful of this crucial condiment and local moneymaker.

To get to Las Salinas, head southwest toward the coast on Carretera Máximo Gómez. Pick up this highway by turning left at the Isla Gas Station located on the highway leading out of Baní heading west (Parador Baní is on the right). Drive to the end of the road and turn right and pass through the towns of Villa Sombrero and Matanzas. Keep going until the coast and follow signs for Las Salinas.

You can also pick up a *guagua* (RD$80; 20min; hourly 7am-6pm) at the *parada* located a few blocks south of *El Mercado Público*.

In the town of Las Salinas, hotel and restaurant options are limited, but there is one establishment that is well worth the trip. **Hotel Salinas** is a splendid option for a relaxing day trip or even a weekend getaway from Santo Domingo. All 35 rooms are adorned with bright white linens that contrast the dark wooden furniture, and though they come with A/C, the ocean seen from the bedroom windows provides a refreshing breeze. The hotel draws both a wealthy Dominican crowd and windsurfing fanatics, who have been visiting the hotel since it held a windsurfing competition in 1988. Offering a private beach, pool, glamorous chaise-lounges, and a dock with a gazebo, Las Salinas Hotel creates an exclusive atmosphere without breaking a traveler's budget. *RD$2000-3000; Puerto Hermosa; on the right on the main road through Las Salinas; 866-8141, 310-8141; hotel_salinas@hotmail.com, www.hotelsalinas.net; Amenities: A/C, hot water, TV, restaurant/bar, pool, boat dock*

Los Corbanitos

Faded fishing boats are a bather's only company at this beach known for its mangroves and the diverse sea life that seeks shelter among the gnarled roots. With few rocks or coral reefs to obstruct the swimmer's path, these waters are warm and inviting (albeit somewhat difficult to find due to lack of signage on the poor dirt road leading to the beach). The striking arid surroundings contrast dramatically with vibrant blue sea, but this isolated vista is in danger: The Lemca Group has plans to convert the beach into a massive luxury resort with multiple hotels, a port, villas, condominiums, a golf course, and a helipad for those who find the 23 kilometers (14.3 miles) from Baní or 88 kilometers (54.7 miles) from Santo Domingo simply too far to drive. *Turn left at the Isla Gas Station located on the highway (Carretera Máximo Gómez) leading out of Baní heading west (Parador Baní is on the right). Drive to the end of the road and turn right at the fork (just past the community of Los Tumbaos). The entrance to Corbanitos is through the town of Sabana Buey.*

La Gallera de las Matanzas

A culturally authentic experience, but not for the weak-stomached, this famous cockfighting ring in the nearby town of Las Matanzas brings in competitors from across the region. While the venue generally attracts only men hoping to win big, it occasionally fills with a more equally gendered crowd swaying its hips when there are live merengue or bachata acts. By playing the curious foreigner card, newcomers might be able to get tickets for seats in the first few rows. Otherwise, take in the views from the balcony of sweaty, red-faced men as they roar at their *gallo* (rooster) to win them money. Try to decipher the multitude of hand gestures being thrown through the air used to place bets, while sharing a bottle of rum with your neighbor. Watch as grown men cry over the loss of their *gallo*, which is not only their treasured pet, but often a crucial source of income *To get there, take Carretera Máximo Gómez west and then ask a local where the gallera is located (streets are unmarked).*

Mirador de Manaclar

For an outstanding view, head up to the Mirador de Manaclar, a lookout point, where the vista pans across the Las Salinas and Los Corbanitos beaches, and the Bahía de Ocoa, along with the town of Baní, and the twinkling lights of San Cristóbal at night. *There is no public transport, so find a motoconcho with a good-sized motor (100cc or more) from the Fortaleza. In a private vehicle with four-wheel drive, head down C/ Duvergé through Villa Guera until reaching the sign for La Montería (left) and Manaclar (straight). Continue straight until reaching the cell towers.*

El Santuario San Martín de Porres

Located in the sleepy village of Las Tablas, the locals claim that each rock in this sanctuary was placed by the hands of a local man from Las Matanzas over the course of thirty years. The mysterious man built the sanctuary in honor of San Martín de Porres (1579-1639), a biracial Catholic saint who dedicated his life to the poor and humble, and was known for his embracing attitude towards all humans and animals, even rodents. The monument for the saint consists of a mount made of stones with a chapel at its crux. The stone altar is covered with candles, a painting of San Martín de Porres, and crucifixes. On the perimeter are living quarters (currently uninhabited) and a gazebo used for community meetings. While this is not worth going out of the way to see, it is a charming and tranquil spot at which to stop after a day at Las Salinas Beach. At the top of the mount, there is a delightful view of the ocean, mountains, and the desert surrounding Baní. *Using public transport from Baní, take the Las Tablas guagua and ask to be left at El Santuario de Las Tablas*

"Pa 'lla" of Baní: the Sweets of Paya

Don't leave the province of Peravia without trying the sweets made by **Las Tres Rosas** or **Las Marías**, located next to each other along the highway in Paya, a small town just east before Baní. Savor the original *dulce de leche* or mouthwatering *coco tierno con leche* (tender coconut with milk), found in the refrigerated section.

San José de Ocoa

After winding around empty mountain curves deeper and higher into the Sierra de Ocoa, what seems like a road to nowhere opens up into the quaint mountain town of San José de Ocoa. Untainted by commercial tourism, Ocoa has maintained a tranquil pace of life, where there is always extra rice and beans for the unexpected guest and time for a piping hot *cafecito*. Fray Bartolomé de las Casas, known for denouncing the enslavement of the Taínos, made the first written reference to San José de Ocoa in the 16th century when he described the then sparsely-populated Taíno province of Maniey. The region became known as El Maniel in the early 17th century when runaway slaves, or *cimarrones*, took refuge there. This population was eventually wiped out thanks to the combination of measles, smallpox, and the military campaign under Juan Villalobos to capture runaway slaves in the 1660s.

The second settlement came in the early 19th century, when a young man from Baní named Andrés Pimentel fled to Ocoa with his lover to escape her family's disapproval of their courtship. Others followed their lead, founding a municipality in

1858, but it was not until 2000 that Ocoa was officially declared a province. Ocoa continues to be a rural haven for its 60,000 inhabitants, who live primarily off small-scale agricultural production. The most common crops are avocados and potatoes, which blanket the ridges and valleys surrounding town.

Cimarrones

Coming from the Spanish word for "wild," *cimarrón* was a term used by Spanish colonists and their descendents to refer to runaway African slaves in Dominican Republic. Seeking refuge from the shackles of slavery, cimarrones chose mountainous hideaways like the Sierra de Ocoa to form communities where they could live freely. The terminology has carried over into the current century, used by Dominicans, often self-referentially, to refer to those who live outside the constraints of traditional societal rules. Among the modern *cimarrones* are several underground artists and musicians, who reject the status quo of society that they believe promotes political corruption and repressive conformity.

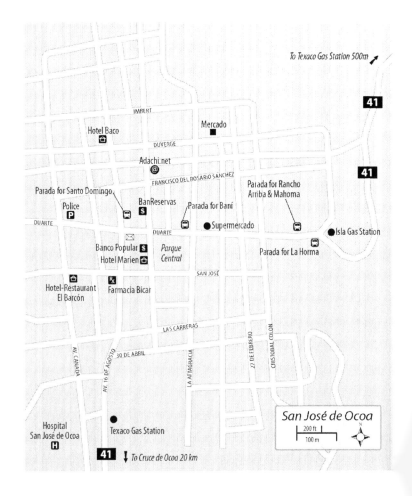

TRANSPORT

San José de Ocoa is located 23 kilometers (14 miles) north Highway 2, along Highway 41.

From Santo Domingo: *Caliente* RD$130, *expreso* RD$140; 4am-6pm every 20 minutes; 2.5hrs; from C/ Bolívar near Parque Independencia.

To Santo Domingo: *Caliente* RD$130, *expreso* RD$140; 4am-6pm every 20 minutes; 2.5hrs; *parada* just off the Parque Central on C/ Duarte, next to the Supermercado.

To continue further South: Take the Santo Domingo *guagua* to El Cruce de Ocoa (30 minutes south of Ocoa), then wait for the corresponding *guagua* heading west. *Guaguas* won't stop unless you wave them down, so when you see yours approaching, be sure to wave vigorously!

To Baní: RD$60; 6am-6pm every 30 minutes or when full; 30min; mini-vans located on the north side of the park (C/ Duarte)

To Rancho Arriba: RD$100; Safari-style jeeps make three daily trips (two on Sunday) leaving from the stop east of the Parque Central on C/ Duarte: Mon-Sat: 6am, 8:30am, 11am; Sun: 6am, 8:30am or later; 2hrs

To Piedra Blanca: From Rancho Arriba, *guaguas leave for* Piedra Blanca, the connection point to the Cibao, but an overnight stay in Rancho Arriba is required because these *guaguas* only leave in the early morning (RD$90; 7am; 2hrs). Buses depart from the big *colmado* in the center of Rancho Arriba, but be sure to ask around because they are not well marked and do not run a fixed route through town. This loop definitely covers the road less traveled, and offers a fascinating and scenic alternative route to the north instead of through the capital – but just be sure to have a very flexible schedule.

To La Horma (along the Ocoa-Constanza highway): RD$50; 11am, 12:30pm, and 4pm pickup truck (arrive 30 minutes early to ensure a seat in the cab – otherwise, it's a tough trip in the back); 1hr; *parada* located at La Cafetera Americana near the Isla Gas Station. Ask for Zapata, a friendly character, who is always at the *parada* and therefore knows which drivers came down the mountain that day and when they are leaving.

To Valle Nuevo and Constanza: RD$350; up to 4hrs; At the time of research, safari jeeps ran bi-weekly trips from Ocoa to Constanza leaving at sunrise from C/ Duarte, east of the Parque Central. The route has been suspended in the past due to poor road conditions and lack of demand, so ask around town to see if the jeep is making trips that week and on which days.

Within Ocoa: Hire a *motoconchista* to go anywhere within town (RD$20) and to many of the surrounding villages. To neighboring municipalities like Sabana Larga (there is also a *guagua* for Sabana Larga that runs along C/ Duarte heading east), a ride will cost about RD$50 and trips to the surrounding villages run RD$150-350.

INFO

Medical Attention

Hospital San José de Ocoa (558-2372) is a public hospital with limited resources that should only be used for emergencies only. (C/ Canada; next to the Escuela Pública, near corner of C/ María Asunción). **Farmacia Bicar** is on the corner of C/ 16 de Agosto & C/ San José.

Communication

The most reliable internet café, **Adachi.net**, in town is located two blocks north of the Parque Central on the corner of C/ Andrés Pimentel and C/ Luperón. The **Post Office** is at the corner of C/ Duarte and C/ 16 de Agosto across from the *guagua* stop to Santo Domingo.

Banks

Both the **Banco Popular** (#83; 558-2215) and **BanReservas** (#61; 558-2096) are located on C/ Andrés Pimentel near the Parque Central and are open Mon-Fri 8:30am-4pm and Sat 9am-1pm.

Police

The **Destacamento Policial** is located on the corner of Av. Juan Pablo Duarte and Av. Canada (558-2211).

Gas Stations

Coming into town, there is a **Texaco** (C/ 16 de Agosto, by C/ Sor. María Asunción) and when leaving town towards Sabana Larga there are two gas stations (including an Isla) along C/ Duarte.

Grocery Stores

There are three grocery stores in Ocoa, each carrying a similar selection. One is located one block to the west and the other a block to the east of the Parque Central on Calle Duarte. Both are open Monday to Saturday from 9am to 6pm and on Sunday from 10am to 2pm. **Supermercado Ocoa** is located four blocks east of the Parque Central on Calle Duarte and has extended hours on Sundays.

EAT

Surrounding the park are a few food options including **Hotel Marien** serving traditional Dominican fare (RD$100-250; corner of C/ San José and C/ Pimentel). For lighter options, try the sandwich joint on the park's east side, offering no-frills grilled ham and cheese sandwiches and fresh fruit smoothies (RD$30-150).

> **Hotel Baco** Serving up inexpensive Dominican food, this hotel-restaurant always has a generous *plato del día* as well as a hearty ham and cheese or Cuban sandwich. During the season, try *guandules guisados* (stewed pigeon peas) with rice and stewed chicken. Wash it down with the deliciously original oatmeal carrot juice, or fresh-squeezed cherry juice. *RD$100-150; Corner of C/ Duvergé and C/ 16 de Agosto; 558-2368*

SLEEP

> **Hotel-Restaurant El Barcón** Centrally located and reasonably priced, this hotel has modest, tidy rooms with simple but bright decorations and a restaurant that is open all day. *RD$400-1200; Corner of C/ Canada and C/ San José; Amenities: A/C or fan, hot water, TV*

Hotel Baco While the rooms are small and dim, this budget hotel is located on a quiet street allowing for a restful night. Plus, it has that oh-so refreshing oatmeal-carrot juice drink downstairs. *RD$400-600; Corner of C/ Duvergé and C/ 16 de Agosto; 558-2368; Amenities: A/C, fan, hot water, TV*

Rancho Francisco This serene enclave surrounded by broad trees and set along a babbling stream is certainly the most comfortable accommodation in Ocoa. Cool off in either the guests' private pool or mix it up with the locals in the larger pool open to the public. The hotel's restaurant offers a variety of local specialties, ranging from fried chicken to stewed goat. If luck has it, a visit to Rancho Francisco will coincide with one of the live merengue or bachata bands that perform here regularly. *RD$1000-1500 for a room and RD$200-400 for the restaurant; located 1km south of Ocoa on Highway 41; Amenities: A/C, fan, TV, restaurant/bar, two pools, dance hall*

DO

El Parque Central
Vines wrap around mature trees, children chase each other in the central gazebo, and neighbors gather on the shady benches to catch up on the latest gossip or the previous evening's baseball games in this small, pleasant green refuge in the center of town. Vendors selling *frío frío* (shaved iced with syrup), coffee, snacks, and pirated DVDs hang out around the perimeter. There are also two ice cream shops (**Helados Bon** and **Nestlé**) so that visitors can enjoy a coconut *paleta* (ice pop) while chatting with an *Ocoeño*.

Mercado (El Reguero)
Located on Calle Duvergé, this Thursday-only outdoor market is full of housewares, shoes, and clothing from *pacas* (huge bundles of clothing donated from North America) that reach the hands of vendors through mysterious ways. While the majority of it is junk, this market provides an interesting perspective as to where some clothing donations end up, as well as good practice for negotiating skills in Spanish.

Ocoa-Constanza Scenic Highway

Traversing the Sierra de Ocoa into Cordillera Central, this tremendous rocky dirt highway steers through the agricultural villages of La Horma, then wanders among the conifers of the Valle Nuevo National Park (p320), eventually reaching Constanza's (p290) high valley perch.

The views begin as arid, grassy plains outside Ocoa, then the vistas change into the green hills speckled with brightly painted wooden homes of La Horma, and finally lofty, pine-covered peaks of Valle Nuevo and Constanza come into view. Natural wonders like the Antilles' tallest waterfall, **Aguas Blancas** (p293), and perpetually fog-covered ridges punctuate the route, adding to the majestic feel of this exciting mountain ride.

The entire trip is approximately 90 kilometers (56 miles), but hurricane season in the DR occasionally gives the route an unplanned reconstruction, carving out sides of mountains and making deeper cuts into the already curvy road. Therefore, plan for at least four to five hours for the trip from Ocoa to Constanza, if it is possible at all, in order to take in the sights.

The South

What a Reguero!

In Spanish, the word *reguero* has a number of official meanings, including "trail" and "small stream." However, colloquially, it has also taken on the significance of "mess" or "disorder." For example, the famous children's book Curious George Cleans Up is translated into Spanish as *Jorge El Curioso Limpia el Reguero*, or "Curious George cleans up the mess." Locals have therefore given a sly nickname to their weekly market.

Presa de Jigüey

La Presa (dam) is not recommended for actual swimming, but the challenging road to get there offers some excellent views of Ocoa (four-wheel drive is required). Pack a picnic and enjoy the water views, while talking up some local fishermen. *To arrive in a private vehicle, head northwest along C/ Duarte/Highway 41 for about 2 kilometers (1.2 miles) until reaching the sign for Presa de Jigüey, at which point turn right and continue for another 16 kilometers (10 miles) along this bumpy dirt road until reaching the dam.*

Charco de Mancebo

A favorite local spot to cool off, this waterfall and connected lake provide great swimming year-round. There's also a 3.7-meter (12-foot) cliff jump to add to the fun. *To get there, ask a motoconchista at the parada for El Pinar to take you to the Río de Mancebo, then go upriver from the road until reaching the falls.*

Charco de La Ciénaga

This cool swimming hole also has an impressive 4.6-meter (15-foot) cliff jump, but only during the rainy season, which starts in the spring and can last until early fall. *Take note, there are many villages called La Ciénaga in the province of Ocoa, and across the country for that matter – the name means "swamp," of which apparently there are many. Be sure to specify to the motoconchista that you want "La Ciénaga de Los Corozos" (not, say, La Ciénaga de Naranjal). After arriving at La Ciénaga, go downriver to find the waterfall. There are also some excellent mountain hikes in this area, but they are not marked, so it's best to go with someone from a nearby village as a guide.*

Parque Nacional Valle Nuevo

Known among hyperbole-happy locals for having sub-freezing temperatures, Parque Nacional Valle Nuevo (also known as Parque Nacional Juan Bautista Pérez Rancier) offers spectacular hiking and mountain biking for the outdoor adventurer. Covering an area of 910 square kilometers (351 square miles) across the four provinces of La Vega, San José de Ocoa, Monseñor Nouel, and Azua, this expansive area is the source of various rivers that breathe life into the South, including the Blanco, Banilejo, Cuevas, Grande, Nizao, Ocoa, and Tireíto. Experienced mountain climbers often prefer the peaks of Valle Nuevo, because of the lack of infrastructure and foot traffic, as compared to the areas around Constanza and Jarabacoa. The highest peak in the park is Alto de la Bandera at 2,842 meters (9,324 feet), though the park also boasts a number of other challenging heights, including Loma del Macho and Tetero de Mejía.

Daytime temperatures generally stay cool, running in the 60s or 70s Fahrenheit (16-20°C), perfect for outdoor sports. Temperatures can reach as low as 41°F/5°C, even as locals claim otherwise. These pine-covered ridges have inspired tall tales of explorers freezing to death after getting lost in a "third dimension" that supposedly leaves anyone who enters utterly disoriented. Dehydration and/or too much Brugal is the more likely explanation, but the exaggerated storytelling that this area has provoked is reflective of its remote location and dense forests, home to moss-covered rocks, curling ferns, and towering pines.

TRANSPORT

The best and generally only way to access Valle Nuevo is in a private vehicle with four-wheel drive, or a mountain bike either from San José de Ocoa or Constanza (See Transport in San José de Ocoa, p315, and Constanza, p290). Valle Nuevo is located 14 kilometers (8.7 miles) from Constanza and about 75 kilometers (46.6 miles) from Ocoa along the Antonio Duvergé Highway, also known as Highway 41. Trujillo completed this highway connecting Ocoa and Constanza in 1950, but not even a patch of asphalt remains after numerous hurricanes and landslides have nearly reclaimed the road back to nature. The highway is muddy and mountainous, especially if coming from Ocoa, so only experienced mountain bikers and four-wheel drivers should attempt this road.

EAT

Arrive well-stocked because there are no places to buy food or water once in Valle Nuevo.

SLEEP

Camping in Valle Nuevo

There are few restrictions on camping locations, though many people tend to camp near the flat clearing that surrounds La Pirámide. For more privacy, take some time to explore the offshoots of the Constanza-Ocoa highway through Valle Nuevo. There are a few hidden camping-friendly clearings among the pines where lumber companies had their way with the land before Valle Nuevo was declared a protected area.

The Secretary of Environment recently built cabins equipped with bunk beds, a bathroom, and a kitchen to meet the growing interest and need for lodging in the park. Talk to rangers upon arrival about overnight stays, and be sure to bring a sleeping bag adequate for the chilly temperatures.

For additional information on where to Eat and Sleep, and what to Do, see Constanza (p290).

Azua

Azua was founded in 1504, very early on in the colonial game. Like many Dominican cities, Azua's trajectory has followed a tragic arc and its history is littered with progress, hope, and disaster. Precious metals, including gold, were discovered soon after its establishment, but boom times were short. Instead, sugarcane farming and processing became Azua's principal industry, and still stands as an important economic foundation for the entire region. Pirates, a mainstay in 16th century Caribbean waters, plundered and pillaged this coastal town several times. An

The South

earthquake in 1751 leveled Azua, causing the inhabitants to move farther inland to its current location flanked by the Sierra de Ocoa.

Azua was set ablaze three times by Haitian forces: first, when the newly independent Haitian army invaded the Spanish colony in 1805; again, as the Dominican army soundly defeated the retreating Haitian forces on March 19, 1844, a decisive battle in the War for Independence; and lastly, during an unsuccessful invasion attempt in 1849. Unsurprisingly, little survives from before the middle of the 19th century. Though not very wealthy, the city still presents a pleasant atmosphere around its lively central square, which was cleaned and refurbished for its quincentenary celebrations in 2004.

TRANSPORT

Caribe Tours is located on the corner C/ Fátima and Emilio Prud'Homme (521-5088).

To Santo Domingo: RD$190; 7:15am, 7:30am, 10:45am, 11:15am, 2:45pm, 6:15pm, 6:30pm; 2.5hr

From Santo Domingo: RD$190; 6:30am; 9:45am; 10:15am; 1:15am; 1:45pm; 2pm; 5:15pm; 5:30pm; 2.5hr

To Barahona: RD$60; 6:15am, 9:45am, 1:45pm, 5:15pm; 1hr

To San Juan de La Maguana: RD$60; 6:30am, 10:15am, 2:00pm, 5:30pm; 1hr

Local Guaguas

To San Juan and Barahona: RD$100; every 30 minutes 5:40am- 6pm; 1hr; leave from C/ Bartolomé between Calles Duvergé and Emilio Prud'Homme

To Santo Domingo (ASODEMA): RD$160; every 30 minutes 5am-6pm; 2.5hrs; leave from C/ Miguel A. Garrido and C/ Duarte

Within Azua: *Motoconchos* provide transport around Azua for RD$20 a ride.

INFO

Medical Attention

Farmacia de la Cruz Catáro (521-5232) is located at the corner of Calles 19 de Marzo and 27 de Febrero. For absolute emergencies, the public Hospital Simón Strideis is located on C/ Marcos Medina between Av. Mella and C/ 27 de Febrero. Otherwise, seek medical attention in Santo Domingo (p78).

Communication

KMel Internet Café and call center is located a block north of Parque Duarte on C/ Colón (521-3929). The Post Office is located at the corner of C/ Vicente Noble and Emilio Prud'Homme (522-2436/910-1874).

Banks

Banco Popular is on the corner of C/ Duarte and 19 de Marzo (521-3400) and Scotiabank is at 29 C/ Colón and Emilio Prud'Homme (521-3495).

Police

The Police Station is located at Highway Sánchez and C/ Enriquillo at the east entrance of town.

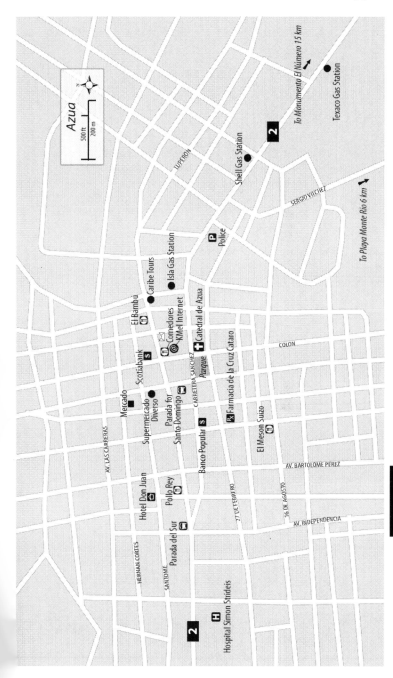

Azua

500 ft
200 m

To Monumento El Número 15 km

Texaco Gas Station

TUPERÓN

Shell Gas Station

2

SERGIO VILCHEZ

Police

To Playa Monte Río 6 km

Caribe Tours

Isla Gas Station

El Bambú

Comedores

KMel Internet

Catedral de Azua

COLON

Scotiabank

Parque

Farmacia de la Cruz Cataro

Mercado

Supermercado
Diverso

Parada for
Santo Domingo

CARRETERA SANCHEZ

Banco Popular

El Mesón Suizo

AV. LAS CARRERAS

AV. BARTOLOME PEREZ

Hotel Don Juan

Pollo Rey

27 DE FEBRERO

16 DE AGOSTO

AV. INDEPENDENCIA

HERNAN CORTES

SANTOME

Parada del Sur

2

Hospital Simon Strideis

The South

Gas

There are a handful of gas stations located on Carretera Sánchez that bisects the city.

Grocery Stores

Supermercado Diverso This grocery store offers the largest selection in town and is located in front of the *Mercado. 74 C/ Miguel A. Garrido, near corner of C/ Emilio Prud'Homme; 521-5917*

EAT

There are a number of inexpensive restaurants (RD$100-200) serving the traditional *bandera dominicana*, such as the basic **Comedor D' Yulay** on Calle Colón, a block north of Parque Duarte. **El Bambú** (C/ Emilio Prud'Homme) has a variety of Dominican fare with a little more ambiance, offering *sancocho* and fried fish under a palm-thatched roof. For quick service and variety, try one of the many eateries with fried chicken, *víveres*, and *plato del día* dishes located along Carretera Sánchez when entering town from the south. Or try **Pollo Rey** (81 C/ Emilio Prud'Homme), a fast food chain with branches across the South serving much-loved fried and oven-roasted chicken, as well as wraps, sandwiches, french fries, and *tostones*. This "chicken king" is a popular rest stop on the drive south for its hot coffee and sparkling clean bathrooms. For more formal service, **El Mesón Suizo** (below) is one of the only restaurants of its kind in town.

    El Mesón Suizo Named for the owner, who is a Swiss-trained chef, this is the only sit-down restaurant in town boasting award-winning cuisine. Specialties include fish in the Monte Río style, smothered in decadent tomato-based seafood sauce, as well as goat prepared in coconut milk. *RD$325-575; Corner of C/ 19 de Marzo and C/ 16 de Agosto; 710-7807/521-4016; mesonsuizo@hotmail.com*

SLEEP

If you want to stay the night in the South, skip Azua and find a place in Baní (p309), Barahona (p332), or San Juan (p325). Azua, unfortunately, hosts rather dismal sleeping arrangements rented on an hourly basis. One of these is appropriately named **Hotel Don Juan** after the legendary Latin lover. *RD$500; 37 C/ Santomé and C/ Nicolas Mañon; 521-3339/2337; Amenities: A/C, fan, TV*

    Alternately, try the **Casa Club Mesón Suizo** offered through the restaurant, **Mesón Suizo**. The hotel was still in development at the time of research, but had completed five rooms, all with A/C, hot water, and breakfast included for RD$1050. Contact Mesón Suizo for details.

DO

El Mercado
A labyrinth of narrow passages with stalls full of fruits, vegetables, meat, the outdoor market is located at the corner of C/ Santomé and C/ Armando Aybar.

Magueyal de Azua
Head toward San Juan de la Maguana to see Magueyal de Azua, where locals enjoy a refreshing dip in the Río Yaque del Sur, as well as the sulfurous waters after crossing the river (4WD required) past the marble quarry Explomarca. *Coming from the south, the turn-off is located shortly after passing the "Quince de Azua" meaning*

Kilometer 15 of Azua. Turn left down the dirt road after the sign for the Hydroelectric Plant of Magueyal as well as a number of fruit and veggie stands.

Monumento El Número

Located atop a hill outside of Azua on the road to Baní, the monument commemorates the heroes of the Batalla El Número on April 19, 1849, part of the Dominican War of Independence. Azua was the site of one of the first major battles in the war in March of 1844, mere days after the cry of independence from Haiti on February 27 (see History, p12). The Dominican forces under General Pedro Santana defeated a larger and better-armed Haitian military. The war raged on for at least another five years until the Dominican army won a set of decisive battles in 1849, including Batalla El Número, quietly remembered on this site.

The monument itself requires a bit of imagination and an appreciation of history to enjoy; otherwise it's best to leave it for the history buffs and patriots.

Playa Monte Río

Located just outside Azua and accessible by car or *motoconcho*, this gray beach is neither the cleanest nor the prettiest that the South has to offer. It is quite convenient, however, and offers a few restaurants, such as **La Rueda**, serving just the basics: fried seafood, *la bandera dominicana*, and beer. *When entering Azua from Baní on Highway 2/Carretera Sánchez, turn left on C/ Sergio Vilchez marked by a sign for Playa Monte Río*

San Juan de la Maguana

Visitors to San Juan are often pleasantly surprised as flat expanses of rice fields surrounded by green patchwork hills transform into this very pretty and well-maintained town. A statue of the Enriquillo, the last famous Taíno *cacique*, brother of Caonabo (p327), greets those entering the city from his colorful mosaic throne, modeled after the island of Hispaniola that his people used to inhabit. The main streets are broad, clean, and orderly, boasting architectural gems like the grand white Ayuntamiento on Avenida Independencia. Green spaces, a rare sight in the South, are found throughout the residential neighborhoods lined with arcing trees. Like many colonial cities, San Juan's center is the Parque Central, whose focal point is the impressive pink and white San Juan Bautista Cathedral, topped with green cupolas.

Visible signs of San Juan's appreciation for the arts and history begin well before entering the city. Twenty-two Taíno culture-inspired statues mark each kilometer preceding the city from the east. Toward the exit of town for Juan Herrera at La Rotonda, a mural depicting Caonabo and his wife, Anacaona, amongst their Taíno community in El Corral de los Indios, provides a splash of color and visual history. The recently completed provincial campus of La Universidad Autónoma de Santo Domingo has captivating murals and mosaics adorning its façade.

San Juan played an important role in the Dominican War of Independence due to its proximity to the border. Here, General José María Cabral y Luna led his troops to victory in the decisive battle of Santomé in 1855 that marked the end of the war. Since the Spanish conquistador Diego Velázquez founded Villa San Juan in 1503, San Juan de la Maguana has occupied three separate locations, one of which is the present town of **Las Matas de Farfán** (p331), located northwest of the city.

The South

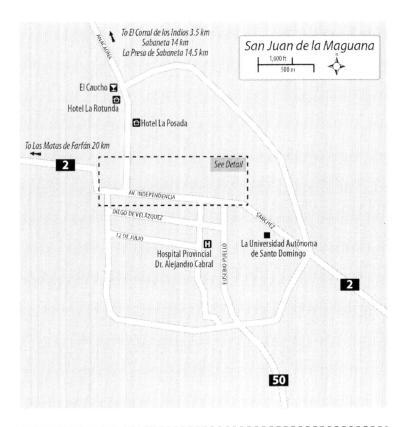

To El Corral de los Indios 3.5 km
Sabaneta 14 km
La Presa de Sabaneta 14.5 km

ANACAONA

San Juan de la Maguana

1,000 ft
500 m

El Caucho
Hotel La Rotunda

Hotel La Posada

To Las Matas de Farfán 20 km

2

See Detail

AV. INDEPENDENCIA

DIEGO DE VELÁZQUEZ

12 DE JULIO

SÁNCHEZ

Hospital Provincial
Dr. Alejandro Cabral

H

EUSEBIO PUELLO

La Universidad Autónoma
de Santo Domingo

2

50

200 ft
100 m

San Juan Bautista Cathedral

GENERAL CABRAL

El Bocconcino

Hotel El Detallista

Pizzería Leonel

SANTOMÉ

ANACAONA

Internet Café

Comedor
Bienvenida

TRINITARIA

Farmacia Central

Parque
Central

Restaurant Espía

AV. INDEPENDENCIA

Banco Popular

19 DE MARZO

Hotel Maguana

Texaco
Gas Station

La Bella Cascada
Night Club

DUARTE

BanReservas

Policía Nacional

P

CARRETERA SANCHEZ

Transporte del Valle

Pizzería Suany

AV. 16 DE AGOSTO

Ayuntamiento

Tenguerengue
Transport

Skylight

CAPOTILLO

DR. CABRAL

SÁNCHEZ

El Rincon Mexicano

Hotel Areito

WENCESLAO RAMIREZ

Gemenet Internet Café

About 300,000 people live in the province of San Juan, half of whom make the provincial capital city of the same name their home. Agriculture in the form of rice farms and cattle ranching has been the mainstays of San Juan's economy since the 17th century, and they continue to thrive on the fertile expanses of land in the province.

TRANSPORT

The following companies offer routes to Santo Domingo, with stops at El Quince de Azua, the city of Azua, and the villages along the way. (Caribe Tours stops in Azua only.) In order to head farther south, take bus lines called Tenguerengue or El Valle to the major intersection called "Quince de Azua" (marking Km 15 on the highway out of Azua) and then wait for *guaguas* heading to Barahona, Pedernales, La Descubierta, or other cities.

Caribe Tours is located at the corner of C/ Dr. Cabral & Temis (557-4520).

To Santo Domingo: RD$260 (with a stop in Azua, 1hr); 6:30am, 10:15am, 1:45pm, 5:30pm; 3hrs

From Santo Domingo: RD$260; 3hrs; 6:30am, 10:15am, 2:00pm, 5:30pm

Transporte del Valle is at 40 C/ Duarte near Av. Independencia. The bus stop in Santo Domingo is located on Av. Duarte between Independencia and 16 de Agosto. *RD$250; 3hrs; RD$100 for El Quince de Azua; 45min*

Tenguerengue Transport is on the corner of C/ Independencia and C/ Eusebio Puello, at the entrance of the city. *Guaguas* leave every 30 minutes and *expreso* buses leave every 45 minutes between 3am and 7pm. The stop in Santo Domingo is near the intersection of Av. Duarte and C/ Ana Valverde. *RD$250; 3hrs; RD$100 for El Quince de Azua; 45min; 902-8698; 767-1444; 772-2757*

To get around town, *motoconchos* start at RD$20 a ride.

Caonabo and Anacaona

Though Caonabo and Anacaona were destined to fall to the Spanish conquerors, conditions conspired to make their descent fast, hard, and violent. Caonabo, the *cacique* of much of the central part of the island of Hispaniola (called Maguana), supposedly had a hand in the destruction of the fort at La Navidad (see page 12) that Columbus had constructed in 1493. His wife, Anacaona, who was likely the only female *cacique*, ruled southern Hispaniola (called Jaragua) after the death of her brother, Bohechío, at the hands of the Spaniards. The siblings had met with Columbus several times, setting up uneasy agreements. After the finger was pointed at Caonabo for the loss of La Navidad, Spanish forces captured him and shipped him to Spain, but he died on the sea voyage. Anacaona then became the *cacique* of both Maguana and Jaragua. Anacaona, said to mean "golden flower," ruled her large territory for a brief flicker. Around 1503 (the date is uncertain) Nicolás de Ovando invited her and several other indigenous leaders to another meeting, at which his troops summarily executed most of their guests, including Anacaona. Her family was survived by a nephew, Enriquillo, who led a successful rebellion in 1534 (see page 13).

Both Haitian and Dominican cultures have immortalized and mythecized the three caciques, especially Anacaona. She is seen as a beautiful queen, first recognized by Bartolomé de las Casas in his account of the brutalization of the indigenous population. The Haitian author Edwidge Danticat also wrote a novel about her story.

INFO

Medical Attention

The public **Hospital Provincial Dr. Alejandro Cabral** (C/ Juan Pablo Piña and Diego de Velázquez; 557-2268) is centrally located, but should only be used for absolute emergencies as conditions and supplies cannot be guaranteed. **Farmacia Central** is located on C/ Doctor Cabral and Trinitaria.

Banks

Banco Popular is located at 49 C/ Anacaona near C/ Independencia (557-2370). **BanReservas** is at 47 Av. Independencia and is open Mon-Fri 8am-5pm, Sat 9am-1pm (557-2230).

Communication

There is an **internet café** near Tenguerengue's *parada* on the corner of Santomé and Doctor Cabral or **Gemenet** internet café is located on C/ Doctor Cabral and C/ Capotillo. The **Post Office** (906-0032) is at 31 C/ Mella.

Police

The **Policía Nacional** is located on Carretera Sánchez between C/ Doctor Cabral and C/ Maríano Rodríguez.

Gas Stations

There are gas stations located on Av. Independencia and one on Av. Anacaona heading towards Juan de Herrera/Sabaneta.

Grocery Stores

There are two supermarkets in San Juan, one called **Supermercado Yenni** (138 Wenceslao Ramírez) and the other is part of a commercial center called "**El Detallista.**" This commercial center also has a hotel, a restaurant, a pharmacy, and a **Banco Popular**.

EAT

For an isolated town far from Italian influence, San Juan dining culture includes an unusually high amount of pizzerias, allowing for a number of affordable and tasty dinner options. Mexican eateries have also become a popular trend in San Juan's restaurant scene, but *comedores* serving Dominican standbys maintain a strong presence. A town built around its agriculture, there is little room for big city pretenses. So regardless of the restaurant, the atmosphere is casual, the portions are generous, and the prices are reasonable.

For an Italian pizza and pool party combination, head to **El Bocconcino** (pool entrance RD$100, at C/ Trinitaria near El Detallista) or try **Pizzería Leonel**, the favorite pizza spot among locals, on C/ Duarte in front of the park and cathedral. Because pizza isn't a midday food, it is served only after 6pm. Also serving pizza along with *criollo* favorites, **Suanny** (C/ Anacaona & 16 de Agosto) is conveniently located next to the delightful ice cream shop, **Helados Bon**.

A few additional eateries are:

El Rincón Mexicano This Mexican restaurant is far from authentic, but tasty nevertheless. Because it is only open for dinner, it does not serve beans because Dominicans are adamant that legumes are only a midday food. Try the nachos served with fresh salsa and guacamole or the fajitas, which are big enough to share. *RD$150-600; C/ Capotillo and C/ 27 de Febrero*

Comedor Bienvenida Sample the San Juan's signature product – rice – at this *plato del día* joint. *RD$120; C/ Santomé between Calles Colón and Mella*

Restaurant Espía Another San Juan take on Mexican, Restaurant Espía's specialty is *gringas*, a magical concoction of tortilla and cheese resembling quesadillas. A *plato del día* is also served at lunch to keep the locals happy. Conveniently located next door is **Bar Espía,** a large nightclub with karaoke and plenty of room to dance. *RD$150-500; Av. Independencia between C/ Meriño and C/ Sánchez.*

SLEEP

Hotel Maguana Built in 1947 to accommodate Trujillo during his visits to the province, this is the classiest act in town, complete with a bar and restaurant with a large Sunday buffet. The hotel also has a "snack bar," which is more of outdoor watering hole perfect for mingling, especially on Thursdays, when the hotel offers live music. *RD$900-1600; 72 Av. Independencia; catty corner to the Ayuntamiento; 557-2244/9293/3010; Amenities: A/C, TV, telephone, restaurant/bar, Wi-Fi, room service, laundry service*

Hotel Areito With the same rates as Hotel Maguana, this smaller hotel is a close second in terms of amenities and the comfort of its rooms. Although breakfast is not included, it's tasty and reasonably priced (RD$50-160). *RD$900-1500; corner of C/ Mella and Capotillo; 557-5322/2045; Amenities: A/C, fan, TV, restaurant*

Hotel El Detallista is terribly convenient as it is located within a shopping complex that houses a supermarket, pharmacy, sandwich/juice shop, and bank. The rooms themselves are not remarkable, but are clean and air-conditioned. *RD$900-1600; corner of Trinitaria and Eusebio Puello; 557-1200/9256/9258; Amenities: A/C, TV*

Hotel La Rotonda For more economical options, try Hotel La Rotonda where rooms start at RD$375. The second floor boasts a breezy common area surrounded by trees, but it's next to El Caucho Bar and across the street from the *gallera* so unless you are a heavy sleeper, it might not provide the best night's rest. *RD$375-1000; 142 Av. Anacaona near La Rotonda; 557-4042/Lili (manager) 982-8548; Amenities: A/C or fan, TV, hot water*

Hotel La Posada As a last resort, there is the dreary Hotel La Posada, which is a two story compound surrounding a dusty parking lot, but with a convenient *comedor* next door for breakfast. *RD$300-750; 83 Av. Anacaona; 557-2296; Amenities: A/C, fan, some with TV*

DO

Fiestas de Palo

This example of syncretism is a source of pride for inhabitants of San Juan. The name, Party of Sticks, comes from the percussion instruments that are central to these spiritual gatherings that last until the wee hours of the night. Also referred to as *atabales* or *gagá*, the parties are in honor of a family or community's patron saint, based on the Catholic calendar. For this reason, Fiestas de Palo are common around the 21st of January, Día de la Altagracia, during Patronales in June, as well as in September for El Día de las Mercedes and El Día de San Miguel. As musicians beat out addictive rhythms that leave hips and feet defenseless, bottles of rum are passed while participants sing along to songs in honor of the saints. The scale of these parties vary greatly, as some families hold private get-togethers in their homes, while entire communities like Juan de Herrera take the music and dance to the streets. During a Fiesta de Palo, a number of personalities manifest themselves through the

The South

dancers, such as Santa Marta, known as the Dominator, known for her ability to tame snakes, or the flirtatious and jovial Anaisa, saint of love, money, and luck.

La Presa de Sabaneta

A popular spot, especially on the weekends, for tilapia fishing and general merriment. Both functional and beautiful, this dam is a great place to pass a peaceful afternoon overlooking the placid waters of the dam surrounded by the rolling hills of San Juan. Vendors sell fresh fried fish, straight from their nets. *Take Sabaneta guagua leaving from Av. Anacaona.*

El Corral de los Indios

Before the arrival of the Spaniards, the Taínos conducted ceremonies in this expansive field, marked today by an unremarkable circle of bowling ball-sized rocks. Some claim this circle marks the true geographical center of the island (and not La Pirámide of Valle Nuevo, p294). Regardless of geography, El Corral de los Indios did mark the cultural and governing center of the island for the Taínos, from where indigenous leaders like Caonabo and Anacaona ruled the island. They used this space to hold both spiritual and logistical meetings, drawing upon the advice of the gods. Elders also used the space to interpret important historical events through dance and song, thereby passing along the knowledge to the next generation. There have been talks for many years about constructing a monument on the grounds, but until that time, the site continues to be used as a soccer and baseball field. *Located on the main road (Av. Anacaona) from San Juan to Juan de Herrera. To get there go to the parada for Juan de Herrera located on Av. Anacaona in San Juan. Take a carro público (RD$25) towards Juan de Herrera, the Sabaneta guagua (RD$25) or a motoconcho (about RD$50) and ask to get off at El Corral de los Indios marked by a squat red wall surrounding the field.*

Nightlife

Skylight is a nightclub a notch above the rest and is therefore pricier. It has a nice ambience created by the "*culto*" crowd that frequents it. It's located on left as you are entering San Juan from El Quince de Azua, before the gas station.

A large open-air hang-out shaded by grand old trees, **El Caucho Bar** (C/ Anacaona near La Rotonda, next to Hotel La Rotunda) is a great spot for grabbing a relaxing beer with the locals.

Fiestas Patronales

Celebrated annually from June 15 to 24, Patronales in San Juan takes on all of the usual forms of evening mass, excessive drinking, and the parade of the Queen of Patronales. The celebrations in San Juan take on particular flair including jet-skiing competitions on the Presa de Sabaneta, roasting a goat underground, and the intriguing ritual of a woman in her first pregnancy cutting another women's hair in the belief that this will encourage the hair's abundant growth.

El Castillo de Maríano Sánchez

More peculiar than impressive, this unfinished modern-day castle is a landmark of the San Juan painter Maríano Sánchez's early success in Europe. The naked cement structure evokes an "if Disney went bankrupt" vibe, but despite its lack of windows or paint, the artist inhabits the central part, and may even let you enter after some art talk. *Located in an area of town where streets are poorly marked, if at all. Ask a local where the "Castillo de Maríano Sánchez" is.*

Pico Duarte from San Juan

Due to the popularity of climbing Pico Duarte from the northern routes, few know that Pico Duarte is actually located in the province of San Juan as part of the Parque Nacional José del Carmen Ramírez. Due to lack of infrastructure and the degree of difficulty, the routes from San Juan are less frequented. The main route starts in **Sabaneta**, accessible by public transport from San Juan. The hike to reach the peak takes three days with stops at the shelters in Alto de la Rosa on the first day, Macutico on the second and Pico Duarte on third. Other routes also start in **Maguana Arriba** or **Los Fríos de Arroyo Cano.** For more information, see Pico Duarte on page 296.

SURROUNDING TOWNS IN THE PROVINCE OF SAN JUAN

Las Matas de Farfán

Las Matas de Farfán, founded in 1780, was the former site of the city of San Juan. Today, it is a small town with a few attractions, like the historic **Iglesia de Santa Lucia**, Trujillo's presidential mansion, and Patronales in the days preceding December 13 in honor of Santa Lucia. The **Trapiche de Bobito Adames** is also worth a visit to try their *raspadura*, a puckering sweet and solid *dulce de leche* wrapped in dried banana leaves. *Located about 25 kilometers (16 miles) west of San Juan along Highway 2/Carretera Sánchez.*

Elías Piña

Officially named Comendador, this surprisingly verdant border town and provincial capital is commonly referred to by the name of the province, Elías Piña. Less than an hour's drive from San Juan, Elías Piña boasts a few attractions and is worth a day trip from San Juan. The best days to visit Elías Piña are Monday and Friday, when the town comes alive with vendors in the Haitian-Dominican market.

While in town, grab lunch at **Restaurant La Fuente** (30 C/ 27 de Febrero; 527-0297), a cute *comedor* with the best *plato del día* in town, made with love by Adelaida Díaz, the owner, and her family. The restaurant/bar **Rancho Bar Sussy** attracts locals in search of reprieve from the hot sun with its small but clean pool (along Carretera Sánchez just before entering town). Overnight options are pretty sub-standard, so it's best to return to San Juan after a day of exploring. But in a pinch, there is a hotel above the *ferretería* (hardware store) on the main road through town (RD$600-800; 527-0144; A/C, fan).

On the border between Elías Piña and the Haitian town of Belladère is the Cachiman Fort, a former stronghold used by immigration officials, but today the spaces within its crumbling walls are essentially abandoned. *To get there in private vehicle from San Juan, head northwest along Highway 2/Carretera Sánchez, passing Las Matas de Farfan. Elías Piña is the last town before the border on Highway 2/Carretera Sánchez about 50 kilometers (31 miles) from San Juan. In public transport, there are guaguas (RD$400) that leave regularly from Santo Domingo (parada near C/ Duarte and Av. 27 de Febrero) and Comendador (parada across from Plaza Duarte) from 5am to 6pm every 30-60min Both pass through San Juan.*

Crossing into Haiti via Elías Piña

One of the smaller crossing points into Haiti, Elías Piña is a sleepy though surprisingly verdant border town with access into Haiti. Be aware that only the Dominican side currently stamps passports. This may create problems for travelers down the road when flying out of either Haiti or the DR because they will not have a stamp entering or leaving Haiti. The Dominican side charges US$20 to cross, while the Haitian side does not have an official fee at this crossing, but be ready to bribe difficult border officials on both sides. There is no official public transport into Haiti from Elías Piña, but there is a lot of traffic in both directions on market days (Monday and Friday), though hitching a ride with vendors comes with a substantial amount of headache and insecurity.

Barahona

The town of Barahona hugs the Caribbean coast at the foot of two small mountain ranges, the Sierra de Bahoruco and Sierra de Neyba. Barahona's origins date back to 1802, when families installed themselves along the Río Biran to exploit the valuable lumber found in the surrounding hills. Today, the area is known for the rich coffee grown in these same slopes (and, thankfully, not for a thriving tree trade). Sugarcane, however, was responsible for the tremendous growth Barahona experienced during the sugar boom era of 1918 to 1960, when the industry flourished. Much of the historic architecture in Barahona, such as the Ayuntamiento, built in 1935, the Cathedral Nuestra Señora del Rosario, built in 1948, and the Arco de Triunfo at the city's entrance, were built during this period of prosperity.

Today, with a provincial population of nearly 180,000, Barahona represents a new Dominican South that is banking on a nascent and growing tourism industry. The surrounding coastline provides some of the most beautiful and remote beaches in the country, ranging from tough, pounding waves and pebbled shores to crystal clear waters and smooth, soft sand. These beaches serve as the foundation for the growth of tourism, but various other opportunities present an equally strong draw. The fascinating larimar stone mines are located nearby, and the endless possibilities for outdoors adventure in the surrounding hills overflowing with biodiversity. These exciting and underdeveloped areas provide excellent opportunities for exploration and partnership with local communities to promote responsible and environmentally friendly tourism.

TRANSPORT

Caribe Tours (524-2313) is located at 4 C/ Anacaona.

To Santo Domingo: RD$270; 6:15am, 9:45am, 1:45pm, 5:15pm; 3.5hrs

From Santo Domingo: RD$270; 6:15am, 9:45am, 1:45pm, 5:15pm; 3.5hrs

To Azua: RD$125; 6:15am, 9:45am, 1:45pm, 5:15pm; 1hr

To Santo Domingo and Azua in a *guagua*: RD$260/RD$110; hourly 6:25am-6pm; 3.5hrs; The Sindicato de Transporte Barahona-Santo Domingo (SINCHOMIBA) *parada* is located at 4 Av. Casandra Damirón across from la Plazoleta Duarte (524-2449).

Barahona is a transport hub for towns big and small around the South. The majority of the *guaguas* leave about every 30 minutes from 7am to 6:30pm. There is a plethora of small tattered *guaguas* that leave from the following streets, most of which are concentrated around the *Mercado*:

Calle Luís F. del Monte: Polo, Tamayo, Neyba

Calle María Montez: Jimaní, Duvergé

Calle 30 de mayo: Paraíso, Ciénaga, Enriquillo

Calle Uruguay: Pedernales, Oviedo

Calle Padre Billini: Cabral, Vicente Noble, Canoa, Peñon, Fundación, Pescadería, Las Salinas

Taxi

Sindicato de Transporte Taxi (SINTRATAXI) is located at 11 C/ Uruguay (524-3003/4003/4004).

Aeropuerto Internacional María Montéz (BRX)

Named after the world-famous Dominican actress María Montez, the airport is essentially closed, with the exception of a few chartered flights, due to anticipated rush of tourism that has yet to hit the South with full force. *One kilometer north of Barahona on Carretera Cabral; 524-4144*

INFO

Medical Attention

Centro Médico Regional is located on C/ José Francisco Peña Gómez and C/ Carlos Mota (524-2470).

There are multiple pharmacies in town including, **Farmacia Ana Isabel** (C/ Padre Billini; 524-2034) and **Farmacia Mendez** (C/ Jaime Mota b/w María Montez and Billini).

Communication

The **Centro de Internet** is on the corner of José Francisco Peña Gómez and Francisco Vázquez. The **Post Office** is at 34 C/ Nuestra Señora del Rosario (906-0058). For calls, **El Centro de Llamadas Terreno** is at 27 C/ Nuestra Señora del Rosario (524-3262).

Prosperity Begets Arts and Culture

The early 20th century marked a period of prosperity in Barahona, producing several cultural icons. María Montez, born in 1912 and known as "the Queen of Technicolor," is recognized as being one of the greatest stars of her era. After starring in 26 films in both Hollywood and Europe, she is certainly one of the most famous Dominicans of the early 20th century. The singer and dancer Casandra Damirón, born in 1919, brought merengue and other Dominican rhythms to an international audience. She also performed across Europe and the Americas. Since 1984, Premios Casandra, the Dominican Republic's equivalent to the Oscars, has honored her name.

Visual artists such as the photographer Juan Pérez Terreno, famous for his picture of a Dominican confronted by an American soldier's automatic weapon during the U.S. intervention of 1965, also helped to place Barahona on the map as a cradle of culture. Another *Barahonero*, Ramón Oviedo, lit up the Dominican art scene with his vibrant and abstract paintings. Today, Barahona continues to offer cultural opportunities and diversity, seen in the colorful participants of Los Diablos (devils) and Los Pintaos (p337) in Carnaval celebrations.

The South

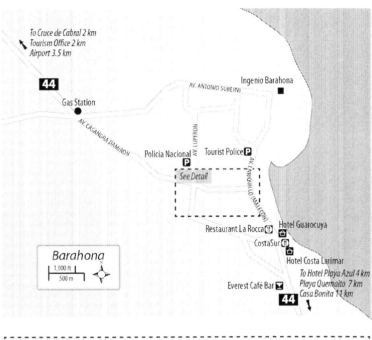

To Cruce de Cabral 2 km
Tourism Office 2 km
Airport 3.5 km

44

Gas Station

AV. CASANDRA DAMIRON

AV. ANTONIO SUBERVI

Ingenio Barahona

Policia Nacional

AV. LUPERON

Tourist Police

See Detail

AV. ENRIQUILLO (MALECON)

Restaurant La Rocca

Hotel Guarocuya

CostaSur

Hotel Costa Larimar

Barahona
1,000 ft
500 m

Everest Café Bar

To Hotel Playa Azul 4 km
Playa Quemaito 7 km
Casa Bonita 11 km

44

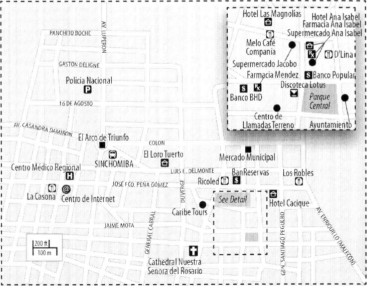

Hotel Las Magnolias

PANCHITO BOCHE

AV. LUPERON

GASTON DELIGNE

Policia Nacional

16 DE AGOSTO

AV. CASANDRA DAMIRON

El Arco de Triunfo

COLON

El Loro Tuerto

Centro Médico Regional

SINCHOMIBA

LUIS E. DELMONTE

JOSE FCO. PEÑA GOMEZ

La Casona   Centro de Internet

JAIME MOTA

GENERAL CABRAL

DUVERGE

Caribe Tours

200 ft
100 m

Cathedral Nuestra
Senora del Rosario

Hotel Ana Isabel
Farmacia Ana Isabel
Supermercado Ana Isabel

Melo Café
Compania

D'Lina

Supermercado Jacobo

Farmacia Mendez

Banco Popular

Discoteca Lotus

Banco BHD

Parque
Central

Centro de
Llamadas Terreno

Ayuntamiento

Mercado Municipal

BanReservas

Ricoled

Los Robles

See Detail

Hotel Cacique

GEN. SANTIAGO PEGUERO

AV. ENRIQUILLO (MALECON)

Banks

Conveniently located near the Parque Central, **Banco Popular** is on the corner of C/ Jaime Mota and Padre Billini and **Banco BHD** is on C/ Jaime Mota between Montez and Billini). **BanReservas** is on C/ Peña Gómez between Billini and María Montez.

Police

Politur (tourist police) is located on Carretera Batey Central (524-3650/3573), and the **National Police** is on C/ Prolongación Luperón and C/ 16 de Agosto (524-2373/2937).

Gas

There are multiple gas stations throughout the city that can be found along the Barahona-Paraíso highway, as well as a **Gas Station** located on Av. Casandra Damirón Km 2.

Grocery Stores

The best supermarkets are located within a block of each other by Calles Billini and Anacaona: **Supermercado Jacobo** and **Supermercado Ana Isabel**.

Tourism Office

The **Ecotourism Cluster** of the Province of Barahona can be a helpful source for fun and sustainable tourism options. The tiny information center is located at the Cruce de Cabral, Carretera Barahona-Santo Domingo, but its hours of operation are unpredictable.

An excellent alternative tour operator is ■ **Vainita Ecoturísmo**, run by young and enthusiastic Dominicans. With strong environmental and social business ethics, these guides support locally based projects and natural attractions that directly contribute to area communities. Vainita Ecotourism organizes a variety of personalized trips to both well-known and undiscovered destinations, including the coffee lands of Polo and the crocodile-filled waters of Lago Enriquillo (p346). They also specialize in cultural activities, such as the Festival del Café in Polo. *Prices vary, starting at RD$1000; no office; 829-717-2090; vainitaecoturismo@gmail.com; Facebook: Vainita Ecoturísmo.*

El Plátano

Approaching Barahona, gargantuan bunches of plantains adorn the roadside stands. A bountiful source of endless sexual jokes owing to their enormous size, Barahona plantains are highly sought after for anyone passing through the area. For Dominicans, failing to bring your family a *rácimo de plátano* (plantain bunch) after a trip to Barahona is unforgiveable. Not only are they impressive in size, but they also have a unique texture and flavor that plantain connoisseurs praise nationwide. The greatest producers of this provincial moneymaker are the municipalities of Vicente Noble and Jaquimeyes.

The South

EAT

For a cheap yet quality meal, head to the Parque Central across from the Ayuntamiento for delicious baked or fried chicken and *tostones* from the late night food truck (RD$100 and up; dinner only). The restaurants around the park generally serve classic Dominican fare, while the ones by the water on the *malecón* serve slightly more diverse offerings.

D'Lina This Barahona staple located just east of the Parque Central offers a delicious *plato del día* (RD$150) to the business crowd, as well as seafood, sandwiches, and passable pizza. *RD$ 150-400; C/ 30 de Mayo and Anacaona; 524-3681; open all day*

La Casona In terms of variety and price, La Casona is home to the best *plato del día*. *RD$110-160; C/ José Fco. Peña Gómez near C/ Francisco Vázquez; 524-1524; lunch only*

Ricoled Owned by a first generation Lebanese-Dominican, this pleasant outdoor patio shaded by umbrellas and plants offers Dominican favorites such as *mofongo* or conch shell with *tostones*, or lighter fare like the moist and tasty shredded chicken sandwich. *RD$75-395; Corner of C/ José Fco. Peña Gómez and María Montez next to the Centro Sírio Libanés; 524-6377; open all day*

Café Melo This restaurant serves rare (in these parts) American-style breakfasts like pancakes and french toast, as well as delicious cheese and egg sandwiches perfectly paired with Melo's locally grown coffee. *RD$60-200; C/ Anacaona b/w Billini and María Montez; breakfast and lunch only*

Los Robles Los Robles sells a variety of Dominican food, as well as favorite American knockoffs like pizza, pasta, and hamburgers. Located on the *malecón*, it has a lively atmosphere with neon lights and loud music. *RD$250-500; Av. Enriquillo near Nuestra Señora del Rosario; 524-1629; 11am-11pm (later on weekends)*

La Rocca Also located on the *malecón*, this brightly painted restaurant effortlessly mixes a family feel with a touch of class, as the interior designer opted for wooden furniture covered by linen instead of the common plastic chairs and tables. The fare is similar to that of all restaurants along the waterside, with an emphasis on seafood dishes that feature octopus *a la vinegreta* and grilled fish. *RD$80-500; Malecón; 11am-11pm (later on weekends)*

CostaSur A French-owned restaurant/disco, CostaSur adds an international touch to the other Dominican-style seafood options with a wide variety of pastas and soups. *RD$120-350; 18 Av. Enriquillo (malecón); 11am-11pm (later on weekends)*

SLEEP

Hotel Cacique This is the cheapest option in town and, for that reason, generally full of Dominicans passing through, and people in Barahona for business. The rooms are small and come with a queen-sized bed, cable TV, and either a fan or A/C. *RD$350-1250; 2 C/ Uruguay; 524-4620*

El Loro Tuerto Though the prices are a little high considering the small size of the rooms and the average prices of the other hotels within the city, this small hotel has the charm to make up for it (and the name, too – it means "one-eyed parrot"). The hotel's bar/café is housed in a red historic home, where the walls are covered with modern Haitian and Dominican art, including pieces from the surrealist Goico. Each hotel room is decorated with little more than a Frida Kahlo reproduction. *RD$1300-1500; 33 C/ Luís E. Delmonte; 524-6600; 909-2262; Amenities: A/C, breakfast available (RD$150), bar, Wi-Fi, generator, laundry-service; info@lorotuerto.com; www.lorotuerto.com*

Hotel Ana Isabel Located on a busy corner, this hotel balances comfort and cost with larger rooms and all the necessary amenities. *RD$928-1392; corner of C/ Billini and Anacaona; Amenities: A/C, fan, TV, mini-fridge, generator, and inverter*

Hotel Las Magnolia A small, centrally located hotel with clean rooms that is generally frequented by Dominican professionals. Conveniently located across the street from Melo's Café, a hot coffee and stack of pancakes is just a hop across the street. *RD$1000-1800; 13C/ Anacaona; 524-2244/5311; Amenities: A/C, TV, phone, generator, inverter*

Hotel Guarocuya In the late 1950s, this was the choice hotel of Trujillo, whose indelible legacy now includes a once-luxurious suite that bears his name. Today, little remains of the hotel's former grandeur; the last renovation looks like it took place when the dictator was still in power. *RD$1300-3500; Av. Enriquillo (malecón) near C/ Duarte; 524-4121; Amenities: A/C, TV, restaurant, fridge, casino*

Hotel Costa Larimar Costa Larimar is Barahona's nicest option, featuring bright, tastefully appointed rooms. Though the hotel does offer all-inclusive packages, the restaurants on the *malecón* offer equal quality and selection for lower prices. The highlight is the hotel's private and pristine beach, though for the saline-averse, there is always the pool. *RD$2110-5480; malecón; 524-1111/5111; costalarimar@codetel.net.do; www.hotelcostalarimar.com; Amenities: A/C, fan, hot water, TV, phone, restaurant/bar, hotel safe, balcony*

DO

Nightlife

La vida nocturna in Barahona is centered on the *malecón*, where there are discos, *colmadones*, and lively terraces, all perfect for socializing. A newer and slightly more upscale venue for tropical music is **Discoteca Lotus**, across from the Parque Central on C/ Padre Billini. For a more casual night out, **The Big Tree Liquor Store** (Highway Paraíso, across from *malecón*; 524-7239) has a seating area near the *malecón*, made for mingling and people watching. **Everest Café Bar** (corner of Carretera Paraíso and Av. Enriquillo) mixes the casual outdoor experience with bar and food service, accompanied by occasional live music. Everest also incorporates the truly and uniquely Dominican tradition of drinking while your car is being washed.

Patronales

Every year during the nine days leading up to October 9, Barahona celebrates its patron saint, Nuestra Señora del Rosario, with daily mass, dancing, and drinking. This particular *patronales* has origins dating back to the 1870s, with the installment of the first Catholic priest in Barahona, named Francisco Antonio Jannarelli, making it the party that never ends.

Melo Café Companía

Started by Américo Melo, a patriarch of Barahona, this substantial coffee company continues to be family-owned and run. Here, coffee beans are dried and packed for both local and international distribution to such destinations as Japan, Belgium, and Italy. While there are no organized tours, the owners are friendly and always willing to take a moment to explain the company's history as well as how the bean ends up in a smooth, strong *cafecito*. *16 C/ Anacaona; 707-0610 (Rafael Melo)*

Carnaval

While similar to Carnaval festivities celebrated across the DR involving the contagious devilish spirit and copious amounts of alcohol consumed, Barahona's Carnaval distinguishes itself with its unique personalities. One in particular is **Los Pintaos**, participants who paint themselves head to toe in a solid color combined with splatters of color à la Jackson Pollack. Los Pintaos are famous for their depiction of the cycle of life, which follows the birth of a child into adulthood. Even the baby used in this theatrical production is entirely painted. The Carnaval action plays out every weekend in February.

The South

OUTSIDE OF BARAHONA

Continuing further west, the striking **Playa Quemaito** is only a 15-minute ride (RD$30 on *guagua*) from Barahona. A coral reef breaks the waves out in the sea, calming the waters that lap the sand. Quemaito has two distinct sections, a white-pebble expanse dotted by sea grape trees and more frequented by the public, and the more dramatic strip of sand buttressed by white and orange cliffs that strike a magnificent and stark foil to the turquoise ocean. The beach is accessible through the main road by turning left on an unmarked dirt road after passing signs for Casablanca and Hotel Quemaito. There is also access for guests of the following two hotels, which have constructed stairs down the steep drop from the cliffs to the beach.

Sugarcane Industry in Barahona

Sip on a *cafecito* or a *jugo natural* in any given place in the Dominican Republic, and taste the sweet riches brought to the Dominican economy from the once-mighty cane industry. Beginning in the early 19th century, sugarcane became a cash crop in several regions across the island, particularly in the East and South. The sugar industry in Barahona arose following World War I as sugar prices skyrocketed, prompting the American West India Sugar Finance Corporation to try to gain market share by growing cane in the Dominican Republic.

In 1956, Trujillo began to nationalize the *ingenios* (sugarcane refineries) across the country, which all eventually fell under the Consejo Estatal del Azúcar (CEA or State Sugar Council). By the mid-1980s, the CEA dissolved and the price of sugar crashed, owing to a number of factors including cheaper production in other countries and the rise of sugar beet farming. To avoid tremendous debt, the government began to lease out the *ingenios* to foreign corporations under contracts of more than 30 years, the time supposedly needed to see a return on their investment. Today, a company called Consorcio Azucarero Central runs Ingenio Barahona, managed by the Guatemalan Campoyo family.

Though the modern sugar industry does not compare to the golden era of the mid-20th century, sugar production continues to play a significant role in regional economies across the country. Ingenio Barahona, for example, employs up to 3,000 people, depending on the season, investing over US$530,000 in Barahona's workforce.

The working and living conditions of the cane cutters, however, continue to be inexcusably substandard, despite international criticism. Though the situation varies throughout the *bateyes* (the name for communities of cane cutters), typical living arrangements involve multiple workers crammed into dark barracks that may not have direct access to latrines. The communities receive little or no basic services like running water, electricity, transportation, or healthcare, and are often quite isolated.

Find out more by watching the controversial documentary narrated by Paul Newman called "The Price of Sugar," which follows a priest's struggles with the Dominican government and surrounding communities to increase the rights of sugar cane workers. The book *Peripheral Migrants: Haitians and Dominican Republic Sugar Plantations*, by Samuel Martínez, provides an academic and thoroughly disheartening descriptions of Haitian cane cutters' journeys from Haiti to the Dominican Republic, as well as what they encounter once they arrive in the *bateyes*.

Sleep

Hotel Playa Azul Located about a five-minute drive west of Barahona, this French-owned hotel is surrounded by peacock-filled gardens ending in cliffs that drop into the ocean. The white tiled rooms are spacious, air-conditioned, and equipped with firm mattresses and pristine bed linens. Patrons of the restaurant can spend the day at Playa Azul's private pool and beach, while sampling the French-inspired seafood dishes like the shrimp crêpe. The restaurant also offers a wide variety of French wines and international liquors. *RD$1500-3200 for rooms; RD$150-450 for restaurant; Carretera Barahona-Paraíso, Km 7; 424-5375/204-8010; playaazulbarahona@hotmail.com; amenities: A/C, fan, hot water, TV, restaurant/bar, Wi-Fi, generator, pool, private beach, parking*

Casablanca Dinner at Swiss-owned Casablanca (also known as el Campo Suizo) is worth the splurge. Suzanne Knapp, the warm and whimsical owner, prepares meals in the French *table d'hôte* style, in which guests reserve dinner in the morning and the proprietor purchases everything fresh that same day. A three-course meal with impeccable service and presentation runs about RD$700-1,000.

On top of that, Casablanca is also a proper hotel. The rooms are simple, but the beds are nice and the only sound that can be heard is the crickets in the wildflower meadow surrounding the hotel. Impromptu fishing trips can also be arranged through the local artist/fisherman, Biembo, who is always buzzing around the property, helping Suzanne maintain it. *US$45-70; 471-1240; 829-714-9646; www.hotelcasablanca.com.do*

Casa Bonita After admiring the craftsmanship of the larimar artisans (see the following section), head up the hill to Casa Bonita, a former family vacation home transformed into a boutique luxury hotel in 2004. At the time of research, the hotel was undergoing significant expansion to construct 12 suites, each with its own plunge pool, in addition to the existing 12 rooms. The hotel's massage and yoga pavilions are located alongside a babbling brook and zip lines cut through the lushly forested hillside on which the complex is perched. The hotel, which continues to be owned and run by the same Dominican family since its establishment, also has a large infinity pool and a white-linen, open-air international restaurant. Casa Bonita's breezy and terraced eatery emphasizes the use of local products, such as seafood caught in the region, coffee from the Polo region, and produce from the on-site organic garden. *US$195-280; Km 17 Carretera de la Costa, Bahoruco; U.S. toll-free: (800) 961-5133; DR tel: 540-5908/ 476-5059; info@casabonitadr.com; www.casabonitadr.com; Amenities: A/C, hot water, restaurant/bar, Wi-Fi, pool, zip-line, horseback riding, yoga, massage*

LARIMAR MINES

The world's only source of larimar is right here, in the hills past the community of **El Arroyo**. Organized tours of the mines are offered through COOPDECI of La Ciénaga (p340). It is also possible to check out the mines without official guides, though it is best to do it with the organization. If you do not have access to an all-terrain vehicle, arrive at the Isla Gas Station before 7:30am to catch a bola with mine workers that load onto trucks headed for the mines. To visit the mines in private vehicle (four-wheel drive only), take a detour off the Sierra de Bahoruco road that goes from Barahona to Pedernales to reach Los Checheses and Las Filipinas, two adjacent communities. After seeing these damp, dark, and narrow passages, visitors gain a new appreciation for the final product.

⬛ Larimar Artisans Workshops

To purchase larimar straight from the artisans, head further west to their workshops near the entrance of Casa Bonita, where artisans grind, shape, and polish larimar, then place it in sterling silver settings. Darker tones of blue with fewer white veins are considered to be more precious, and therefore will be more expensive than the lighter varieties. Though you might need to negotiate a bit, the prices are far more reasonable than those found in the tourist centers in Santo Domingo, and interacting with the artists themselves is much more pleasant and informative than street hawkers in the city. In addition, purchasing the jewelry here means that proceeds go to the artisans, instead of middlemen.

⬛ La Ciénaga

This small community located just west of Barahona is spread along the beach and has received significant domestic and international support to develop community-based eco-tourism in the area. After years of hard work, COOPDECI (Cooperación para el Desarollo de La Ciénaga – Cooperative for the Development of La Ciénaga) now offers a number of sustainable tourism products. One local favorite is the delicious De Mi Siembra brand of marmalades, made from tropical fruit grown by the co-op. Stop by COOPDECI's office to peruse artisan jewelry made from cow horns, shells, and coconuts. The co-op also offers homestays with a family in La Ciénaga, eco-tours, and delicious *campo* cooking at its open-air restaurant overlooking the ocean. *COOPDECI's office is located on the left along the Barahona-Paraíso highway when entering La Ciénaga; 560-3560, 539-7568; www.guanaventuras.com*

Paraíso

The largest town between Barahona and Enriquillo, Paraíso is a good place to refuel or spend a tranquil night on the southern coast. Children crack open beach almonds on the white sand as fishermen haul in the daily catch. Life in Paraíso moves at a slower pace, allowing the visitor to enjoy some of the area's challenging hikes or simply lounge on the beach. Surfing is also possible here and at nearby beaches like **Ojeda**.

Larimar

The famous blue stone called larimar is found nowhere else in the world but the few hills in which it is mined in the Sierra de Bahoruco. Father Miguel Domingo Fuertes Loren, a Spanish priest, was the first to discover this semi-precious stone in the early 1900s. Despite this tremendous find, the Dominican Ministry of Mining denied Father Miguel's request to mine larimar in 1916. Locals continued to find the naturally polished stone in the banks of the Río Bahoruco, due to the natural tumbling motion that the currents created against the river gravel. It was not until 1974 that Miguel Méndez and Peace Corps Volunteer Norman Rilling rediscovered larimar. Méndez named the stone after a combination of his daughter's name, Larissa, and the Spanish word for the sea, "mar."

Larimar is a type of pectolite, a volcanic rock with major components of calcium and sodium. The stone's captivating hues of blue, ranging from a light sky blue with hints of green to a deep cerulean, are a result of cobalt being partially substituted for calcium, unique to larimar in the pectolite family.

TRANSPORT

All *guaguas* heading west and east pass through the town's main road, Calle Ana Ima Tejada. There, flag down any *guagua caliente* originating farther southwest to head east to **Barahona**, or take the Paraíso *guaguas* that leave every 30 minutes from the stop on Ana Irma Tejada (RD$80). To head west, simply flag down one of the *guaguas* heading to **Enriquillo**, **Oviedo**, or **Pedernales**.

Motoconchos are also available for transport around town (RD$15) and to nearby beaches such as Los Patos (RD$50).

INFO

Medical Attention

There is a small hospital in town for emergencies, but it's best to head to a private clinic, such as Clínica La Magnolia in Barahona (p332) if possible. A **pharmacy** is located on the corner of C/ Ana Irma Tejada and Arzobispo Nouel.

Communication

Clásico Digital internet Café is located on C/ Gastón Deligne near C/ Jisiaca (829-889-0217; 243-1102).

EAT

Despite being "paradise," Paraíso's food options are limited to the hotel restaurants (See the following listings for **Hotel Kalibe** and **Hotel Paraíso**). For a delicious and cheap sandwich (RD$40), try the red *colmado* located on the main road through town.

SLEEP

Hotel Kalibe Hotel Kalibe is a family-owned hotel with clean, spacious rooms. The hotel's restaurant offers very reasonably priced seafood, including lobster, all of which comes straight from the waters of Paraíso. The hotel also sells artisanal goods crated by the local women's association, like jewelry and dolls made from plantain leaves. To contact the women's group directly, call 243-1445. *RD$800-1300; Restaurant: RD$150-450; C/ Arzobispo Merino; 243-1192; Amenities: A/C, fan, hot water, TV, generator, inverter, pool*

Hotel Paraíso During research, Hotel Paraíso was undergoing renovation; it should have a fresh layer of paint and new A/C units by publication. The hotel also has one of the few restaurants in town, which offers Dominican staples with a sprinkling of Italian options. *RD$750-1000 (Prices subject to change after renovation); Corner of Luperón and C/ Gregorio Matos, across from the beach; 243-1080; Amenities: A/C, fan, TV, pool*

DO

Besides swimming and the occasional surf at Paraíso's beach, there is little more to do except relax. There is some great hiking through the pastures and coastline, but the trail is unmarked and crosses through private property. Because of this, it's best to consult the budding eco-tourism association of Paraíso. *For tours and prices, contact Rubi Rosa: 829-891-3559; rubirosa44@hotmail.com; Spanish only.*

> **Nightlife** is centered on the *colmados* and the only *discoteca* is located on C/ Arzobispo Nouel near the Parque Central.

The South

Surfing on the Southern Coast

The sleepy southern coast is no Puerto Plata – and for many, it is best kept that way. The major surf spots in the DR are concentrated in the north, with big waves and bigger crowds. However, the beaches around Bahoruco, including Los Patos, Paraíso, and Ojeda, maintain a quiet reputation as isolated gems in Dominican surfing. Swells here are lower than in the north, at about three feet, but they can run at least three times that height under certain conditions. As on the north coast, the best time to surf is before noon, when the wind goes sideward (onshore). The Dominican Surfing Association held official surfing championships in Bahoruco in 2009 and 2010 to showcase the consistent and quality conditions in the region.

Los Patos

A small community nestled astride a forested hill, the main attraction at Los Patos is the chilly, mountain-fed river that empties over a series of stone pools and finally into the ocean at the beach. The pools create a lovely bathing area, whose banks are lined by small fish fry shacks shaded by almond trees. On the weekends, Los Patos fills with raucous bathers, but weekdays are generally quiet, allowing the native jumping fish to emerge and frolic. The white pebble beach and stunning ocean water is enticing, but exercise caution, as the waves can be powerful, and the sea floor drops abruptly.

EAT

For lunch, Playa Los Patos has a number of beach shacks serving up a hearty meal of fried fish, *moro*, *tostones*, and avocado, starting at only RD$150. On the main highway, **Hollywood Pica Pollo** (open all day) serves up fried chicken and *tostones* starting at RD$60, and a *plato del día* for RD$150. For a sandwich and a beer, **Hollywood Cafetería**, located just down the road in a palm-thatched pavilion, offers lively atmosphere and a gorgeous view of the varying bands of blue sea.

For dinner, the restaurant at **Hotelito Oasis Italiano** (see Sleep) spins out Dominican-Italian fusions like conch shell with polenta aside pizzas and pasta.

SLEEP

On a hill overlooking Los Patos beach, **Hotelito Oasis Italiano** provides a laid-back, comfortable atmosphere at reasonable prices. Owned by an Italian-Dominican couple, this is the best option for accommodations by the beach. The spot nearly guarantees 24-hour water and electricity thanks to its three generators and solar panels. Wake up to the scent of the sea mingled with freshly baked bread, served with homemade banana preserves, fresh-squeezed juice, and heady Dominican coffee. *RD$1200-2000 w/ breakfast; info@lospatos.it; www.lospatos.it; Amenities: A/C, fan, hot water, TV, restaurant, fridge, pool*

During research, another hotel was under construction by Italian owners Katherine and Conrado. Though the hotel is sure to offer an excellent view of the water, it is located on the main coastal highway next to the Hollywood Pica Pollo, so it may be a bit noisy.

As a last resort, **Hotel Carmen Iraisa** (829-926-0826) is located in an unfortunate looking home on the coastal highway just between Hollywood Pica Pollo and Hollywood Cafeteria.

Cachote

Located in the mountains north of Paraíso, visitors are attracted to the cool temperatures, clean air, and fog-shrouded peaks of this hidden community far from the pebbly beaches below. Its welcoming nature and the invigorating hikes through the surrounding wooded ridges leave visitors refreshed and relaxed. Getting there, on the other hand, is a bit more of a challenge, as it requires four-wheel drive and well-steeled nerves. It's best to go with a local who knows the roads or organize a trip through **COOPDECI** or **Vainita Ecoturísmo** (p335).

For overnight stay in Cachote, try the ◪ **Centro Ecoturístico Cachote**, which has three communal cabins that fit up to 35 people, as well as a camping area and restaurant. On-site activities include trails through the cloud forest, horseback riding, and guided tours. For more information, visit La Sociedad Ecológica de Paraíso's (SOEPA) website at www.soepa.org.

Polo

This cool mountain community was built around coffee production, but is known for (and named after) a fascinating phenomenon: **El Polo Magnético**. Community members claim that magnetized iron ore mines below the town's surface are behind this natural oddity, which causes a car in neutral or any round object like a water bottle to seemingly ascend the hill on its own. The attraction received so much attention that the government constructed an alternate highway skirting the town because of the volume of visitors who stop to see what actually is an optical illusion known as a Gravity or Magnetic Hill. The surroundings, which obstruct the horizon of the slightly downward slope, cause the road to appear like a upward slope, because the viewer does not have a point of reference to accurately determine the direction of angle. If you are in the area, try it for yourself on the highway between Las Auyamas and Polo marked clearly by a sign with "Polo Magnético." On the way there, stop by the shallow natural pool called **La Represita**, for a *chapuzón* (dip), in the community of **El Guayuyo**. *Polo is accessible through Barahona via Route 44 (2.5 kilometers) until reaching the fork between Route 44 and 46, at which point you will turn left towards Route 46 in the town of Cabral and continue for about 22 kilometers until reaching El Polo Magnético. Or if coming from farther southwest, Polo is also accessible via the small coastal town of Enriquillo, along an unofficial highway (meaning an all-terrain vehicle is a must) that is best traversed with a local.*

Reserva de Biósfera Jaragua-Bahoruco-Enriquillo

UNESCO declared this area as the Reserva de Biósfera Jaragua-Bahoruco-Enriquillo in 2002, making it the first on the island to hold this internationally recognized status. When UNESCO first began the Man and Biosphere Program (MAB) in 1971, the focus was to designate areas for research and environmental conservation, but the program evolved in the 1990s to encompass zones that demonstrated sustainable human interaction with the environment, as well as income generation and poverty reduction. The region included in the Reserva de Biósfera Jaragua-Bahoruco-Enriquillo was able to demonstrate these characteristics through the Ministry of Environment's diverse and long-term efforts to provide employment opportunities

The South

for residents while preserving natural resources. The Ministry's many contributions include training locals in sustainable agriculture practices, and supplying guides with the tools and education needed to create an ecotourism industry, with the greater goal of establishing a sustainable balance between man and nature.

The Biosphere Reserve is tremendous in size, spanning the provinces of Barahona, Bahoruco, Independencia, and Pedernales, and including a marine zone surrounding the coast for a total of 5,770 square kilometers (2,228 square miles). The three National Parks encompassed within the Biosphere Reserve are Lago Enriquillo, Sierra de Bahoruco, and Jaragua, each of which offers dramatically different climates, flora, and fauna. Lago Enriquillo, the largest lake within the Antilles, is hypersalinic, creating an ideal environment for such intriguing reptiles as the American crocodile and iguanas. The Sierra de Bahoruco, tucked away at higher elevations, is known for its unusually high concentration of orchid and birds. Though the Sierra de Bahoruco is the shortest mountain chain in the Dominican Republic, it is home to the one of the highest elevations on the island (Loma Alto del Toro at 2,367 meters or 7,766 feet), causing the vegetation and temperature to change dramatically as visitors ascend its steep ridges. The Parque Nacional Jaragua covers the extreme southwestern tip of the Dominican Republic, and is home to pine-covered geological depressions, caves, and stunning white-sand beaches adorned with cactuses instead of palm trees. Each of these National Parks are discussed in detail in the sections that follow, as well as the cultural offerings of towns and villages that surround them.

On the way to Lago Enriquillo

There are two highways that skirt the perimeter of Lago Enriquillo. The first is Highway 46, which runs along the south side of the lake and connects through the town of Duvergé. The other route is Highway 48, which passes through a number of quiet villages before reaching the north side of the lake. If heading from Barahona to La Descubierta, Highway 48 is the shorter route. But because the two highways form a loop around the lake, either provides access to the town. If heading to Jimaní, Highway 46, through Duvergé, is more direct. *Note: If asking for directions, using the numbers of the highways is probably useless, as the locals use the town names, not highway numbers, for points of references.*

Cabral

Exiting Barahona towards the northwest, Highway 46 passes through the town of Cabral. During the year, this is an unremarkable place, but during Easter weekend, the town comes alive with the country's last Carnaval celebration of the year. Bands of locals dress up as *Cachuas*, dancing devils with bright paper mâché masks in search of *Los Civilies* (civilians). Armed with rope whips, the *Cachuas* spare no mercy as they intimidate and give their opponents *fuertazos* (whippings). While they do not intentionally whip innocent bystanders, it's always best to keep a safe distance, as these rituals are accompanied with a generous amount of rum, setting loose a fascinating and sometimes disturbing diabolic manifestation in the participants. After two straight days of debauchery, the event ends on Monday with the burning of the traitor Judas, known as *Júa*, brought down from the town's obelisk.

◪ LAGUNA CABRAL

Continuing northwest along Highway 46, a sign for **Laguna Cabral** (also called **Laguna Rincón**) is clearly marked. At Laguna Cabral, guides certified by the

Ministry of Environment offer boat tours. There are also a few trails near the lake, including the **Boquerón Trail**, which is an uphill climb of about 5 kilometers (3 miles). The trek rewards visitors with a spectacular view of the Laguna Cabral and the surrounding countryside, covered with sugar cane and other green fields. With 65 square kilometers (25 square miles) in surface area, Laguna Cabral is the largest freshwater lake in the Caribbean. The lake is home to exotic aquatic birds like flamingos, spoonbills (*cucharetas* in Spanish), and others from farther afield like North American migratory ducks. Freshwater turtles, rhinoceros iguanas, and tilapia can also be spotted in and around the lagoon. To enjoy the highest volume of wildlife and to avoid the scorching afternoon sun, arrive to Cabral in the early morning. *RD$50 National Park entrance fee; RD$3,500 for boat that holds up to 18; For tours, contact a National Park guide (Spanish only): William Baez (829-428-6368), Raffy (903-8027; raffy.552@hotmail.com) or Orlando (829-523-8467), or contact La Sociedad Ecológica de Cabral y Grupo Tinglar (524-1575). Proceeds directly support the community and the maintenance of this Scientific Reserve*

La Zurza

Near Cabral in the community of **Canoa** is **La Zurza**, a steamy sulfurous pool that reaches up to 42°C (108°F). Though it tends to smell of rotten eggs caused by the sulfur dioxide gas that it emits, sulfurous pools have been used for centuries for their medicinal properties that range from treating skin conditions, such as dandruff and eczema, to pain relief from sore muscles and even arthritis. *Entrance is free; Take the old road to the la mina de marmol (marble mine) about 2 kilometers from Canoa.*

La Lista & Las Salinas

After Cabral is the tiny village of **La Lista**, known for handmade rocking chairs. In case one of these chairs will not fit in your suitcase, the artisans make miniature versions as well (though these are less enjoyable after a week of rice and bean lunches). While admiring the fine craftsmanship, try the *bombones*, a dense cake-like treat made of molasses and coconut baked in an iron pot over a wood fire. Continuing on from La Lista, the highway passes the turnoff for **Las Salinas**, where bright white piles of salt from the nearby salt mines shimmer in the sunlight. *La mina de yeso* (plaster mine) is also a major source of income for the community of Las Salinas. Amidst these long stretches of arid low-growing vegetation, look out for the seemingly incongruous wetland and palm grove emerging from the sand.

Neyba

The *cruce* (intersection) where Highway 46 splits into Highway 46 and 48 (via Highway 535) marks the turnoff for Duvergé and Neyba. As the sign denotes, continue straight for Duvergé, or make a right for Neyba (also spelled Neiba). The region around this city is best known for its large-scale production of grapes. Try the syrupy-sweet wine, a local favorite, or if the calendar reads November, stick around for the Feria de la Uva (Grape Festival). Started in 2009, the Feria draws crowds from across the country to see where and how the grapes are grown and harvested, and then made into wine. The festival has a particularly important social impact, as it gives value and recognition to the unique economic and cultural offerings of this oft-

The South

overlooked region. Traditional music such as *palo* and *gagá* liven the festivities and of course, wine is sold by the gallon. For more information on visiting, contact **Vainita Ecoturísmo** (p335).

With the exception of the carefully maintained trees found in Neyba's central square, the semi-arid climate gives rise to little more than low-growing vegetation and a variety of cactus. The beauty of these surroundings is most concentrated at sunrise and sunset when the plants' silhouettes are cast against pink, purple, and orange sorbet skies.

Parque Nacional Lago Enriquillo

The best way to access this National Park is through the small town of **La Descubierta**. A welcome oasis bubbling with natural springs surrounded by empty desert, La Descubierta offers humble but convenient overnight options to experience the exceptional wildlife of Lago Enriquillo, best in the early morning.

TRANSPORT

All *guaguas* leaving La Descubierta pass by the Parque Central, making it the best place to wait for transportation.

To Santo Domingo: RD$300; 6am-6pm every 30-60mins; 4hrs; *Guaguas* that originate in Jimaní pass through La Descubierta by El Cuartel (military post) on C/ Gastón F. Deligne, and then the Parque Central of La Descubierta. There is also one *guagua* that leaves from Jimaní at 2am, arriving in La Descubierta about 30 minutes later.

From Santo Domingo: RD$300; 6am-6pm every 30-60mins; 4.5hrs; *Guaguas* leaving for Jimaní stop at Pintura in Santo Domingo and pass through La Descubierta. Alternately, take Caribe Tours or a *guagua* to Barahona, then see below.

To Barahona: Take a *guagua* heading to Santo Domingo and get off at Vicente Noble (RD$60; 1.5 hours); then take the *guagua* from Vicente Noble to Barahona (RD$50; 7am-5pm every 30min; 30 min). Alternatively, hail a *guagua* to Neyba and then in Neyba, take another to Barahona.

From Barahona: *Guaguas* leave for Vicente Noble (RD$50; 7am-5pm every 30min; 30 min) on C/ Padre Billini and for Neyba on C/ Luís del Monte (every 30min 7am-6:30pm). Then, take the connecting *guagua* to La Descubierta. Tip: Leave early to ensure getting a *guagua* in Vicente Noble or Neyba, as they depart infrequently and often stop running early in the afternoon.

INFO

Medical Attention

Try to avoid wrestling with a croc while out on the lake, because the closest hospital is in Barahona (p332). **Farmacia Fellita** is located on C/ Primera, Barrio Nuevo (905-6144).

Communication

There is a free government **Internet Center (CTC)** funded by the First Lady's Office on C/ Cuarta in Barrio Nueva, but the service is unreliable. For a slightly faster and more dependable connection, pay RD$15 for 30 minutes at **Glowicom** on C/ Billini and Juan Polanco.

Grocery Stores

Plaza Lili is the only supermarket in town, but, in good fashion, it has the added bonus of a convenient *cervecería* (beer store) directly above it. *C/ Luperón at C/ Billini*

Cacique Enriquillo

Lago Enriquillo is named for Cacique Enriquillo, a Taíno military ruler and nephew of Anacaona and Caonabo (p327). The lake would have fallen under his family's concern, and it was by its banks that he signed a peace treaty with the Spaniards after over ten years of successful rebellion. After the Spanish army eliminated most of his family, he was raised by monks, who converted him to Catholicism and baptized him as Enriquillo. After toiling on a Spanish estate, he, his wife, and several hundred followers fled to the mountains of the South. Enriquillo displayed acuity in guerilla warfare against the larger but slower Spanish military. Finally, around 1533, he signed a peace treaty with the Spanish court, which granted the group nominal freedom from Spanish control and title to their land. Enriquillo died soon after, and his followers could not defend themselves after the fall of their leader. The Spanish moved in, and the last Taíno stronghold faded away.

EAT

In **Las Barías** natural springs park, there are a couple of simple outdoor restaurants proffering local staples and cold beer. They are among the only places to eat throughout the day, but like the park, they close at dusk. In the evening, the only option is the restaurant at **Hotel La Iguana** (see Sleep), which is open all day and serves a very affordable dinner, starting at RD$125. Call ahead and ask if they can make *maíz cortado*, a La Descubierta specialty made with fresh corn simmered in meat and spices.

SLEEP

La Descubierta contains handful of reasonably priced hotels, each with different strong points. **Hotel La Iguana**, located on the main road coming into town, has one of the few restaurants in town actually open all day (RD$300-400; C/ Billini; 958-7636/301-4815). Another is **Mi Pequeño Hotel**, located just off the Parque Central at 26 C/ Padre Billini. It is located near the disco, so unless you are planning on dancing until dawn, a quiet night's rest here might be challenging (RD$400-500; 762-6329). Conversely, **Hotel El Lago** is located in a charming historic home on a quiet street. The rooms are simple, but the ornate, century-old tile floors and pleasant common area decorated with family photos and paintings put this establishment at a notch above the rest. Complimentary bread and coffee are available in the morning (RD$400-500; C/ Deligne near C/ Billini).

The South

Lago Enriquillo

The Taínos originally called this lake Hagüey Gabon, meaning "Great Spring," but it was later renamed after the last great Taíno leader. Lago Enriquillo, the largest lake in the Caribbean, was declared a National Park in 1996. The lake is located at about 40 meters (131 feet) below sea level, granting it the title of lowest point on Hispaniola. This low elevation, high evaporation rate, and irregular freshwater intake all contribute to its hypersalinic content. Millions of years ago, the lake was united with Lake Azuey, located across the border in Haiti near Jimaní, but an earthquake created a permanent land division that has separated the bodies of water ever since.

Lago Enriquillo Tours

Through the ◪ **Asociación de Guías Ecoturísticas de Lago Enriquillo** (Association of Ecotourism Guides of Lake Enriquillo), there are a number of tour options and trails in and around the lake. In order to truly experience the diversity of species that the area has to offer, take the boat tour. It's best to come with a group to lower the price of the boat, though guides are happy to take out any number of visitors as long as their costs are covered. The tour explores the zones where crocodiles emerge amidst the occasional fisherman trolling for his dinner, while tropical birds flutter across the lake's surface. Early morning is the best time to visit the lake, both to avoid the afternoon heat and to increase your chances of spotting a croc, as this is when they feed.

Another stop is **Isla Cabritos**, named after its former use as goat range – the only island in the world situated below sea level within a lake. Here, find the common rhinoceros iguana living alongside Ricord's Iguana, an endangered species that exists only on this tiny lake-locked island and in Parque Jaragua. While the rhinoceros iguanas waddle freely throughout the park grounds and seem almost tame, it would be best not to feed them. The hundreds of species of birds in the park also take refuge among the rocks, mangroves, and dry forest vegetation. There are two other islands in the lake, occasionally accessible by foot when the lake experiences drought: Isla Barbarita and Islita.

The American Crocodile

A notoriously reclusive breed, the American crocodile is rarely seen by humans, compared to its more aggressive relatives from the Nile and Australia. Found throughout Florida, the Caribbean, and from southern Mexico through Central America into Venezuela, the American crocodile is identified by the narrow snout and visible fourth tooth when its jaw is shut. Consuming a variety of wildlife from fish and crabs to reptiles and small mammals, these crocs can grow from 2.1 meters (7 feet) to 6 meters (20 feet) in length and anywhere from 68 kg (150 lbs.) to 205 kg (450 lbs.) in weight. Lago Enriquillo's brackish waters full of fish and waterfowl provide the perfect habitat for the American crocodile to thrive. The lake also provides plenty of alcoves at the water's edge for the females to lay their eggs, which take two to three months to incubate.

La Azufrada

La Azufrada was once a sulfur pool, but after Hurricane Noel in 2007, the water level of the lake rose, submerging the pool. Currently, the area around the former pool serves as the National Park's administrative offices and as a dock for lake tours. *Park Admission RD$100; Boat Tour RD$3,500 for up to 10 passengers*

Las Caritas

Taínos took refuge among these caves and left behind a number of carved faces representing gods. Las Caritas (the Little Faces) is located on the right side of the highway, just before the National Park's Administrative Offices at La Azufrada. Admission to the caves is free.

Trails

The Association of Ecotourism Guides of Enriquillo Lake also offer hikes around the lake and community of La Descubierta. One includes a short trail to the banks of the lake where crocodiles leave their nests. Tours can quietly observe baby crocodiles bobbing to the surface under their mother's watchful, glaring eye. Another trail, **Yesos de Relámpago**, starts at **Las Barías** (below) and passes through both a humid and dry forest unique to the park.

Contact the **Association of Ecotourism Guides of Lake Enriquillo** for tours and information. *Located at the National Park office at La Azufrada just before entering La Descubierta along Highway 48; 880-0871 or 829-930-0141; adenaurys@hotmail.com; www.enriquillo.com*

Balneario Las Barías

Crystalline and shockingly frigid pools fed by subterranean rivers provide welcome relief from the dry heat and baked earth of La Descubierta. *Free entrance; open in the daytime; located across from Parque Central in the center of town.*

Fever Night Discoteca

The sum of all nightlife in town, this dance club is open on weekends only, except during Semana Santa and Patronales (June 17-24) when it is open all day, every day. *C/ Padre Billini and C/ Cabral*

Boca de Cachón

Located 18 kilometers (11 miles) past La Descubierta en route to Jimaní, this refreshing watering hole is a true oasis. The natural spring is popular on weekends with locals rolling up in jeeps with *mambo violento* blasting, but during the week, there often is not a soul in sight.

Parque Nacional Sierra de Bahoruco

The National Park Sierra de Bahoruco spans the provinces of Independencia, Pedernales and Barahona with a surface area of 1,090 square kilometers (421 square miles). Pines, juniper, mahogany, and wind trees (identified by their small leaves that are constantly fluttering, causing the mountainsides to seemingly shimmer) provide homes for the park's tremendous bird population, including the green parrot, the palm chat, and the white-winged dove. This is an orchid enthusiast's utopia, as the National Park is home to 52 percent of the world's orchid species.

The park is accessible from its north end through Puerto Escondido, near the town of Duvergé, or from the south from Pedernales via the international highway. Puerto Escondido is certainly the more feasible of the two options, as the highway from Pedernales is in terrible condition. The routes vary greatly in climate and scenery, and so seasoned drivers of all-terrain vehicles with healthy senses of adventure may want to attempt both.

The South

Duvergé

The town of Duvergé is nothing to get excited about, but it serves as a jumping off point for **Puerto Escondido**, a small agricultural community spread along a mountaintop savanna. Puerto Escondido is the last inhabited patch of land before entering the northern end of the Parque Nacional Sierra de Bahoruco.

TRANSPORT

From Santo Domingo: RD$270; 7am-6pm; 4hrs; *guaguas* leave from Parque Enriquillo

From Barahona: RD$100; 7am-6pm every 30min; 1hr; *guaguas* leave from *El Mercado*

To Santo Domingo: RD$270; irregularly 5am-3pm and sometimes in the middle of the night; 4hrs; near Parque Central

To Puerto Escondido from Duvergé: RD$50; public transport is a bit scarce but exists. One pick-up truck leaves Duvergé between 7am and 7:30am, and then leaves Puerto Escondido either at 11am, 12pm, or 1pm, depending on the whim of the driver; 1hr

Getting to Puerto Escondido by Private Vehicle

The ideal way to arrive is in a private vehicle with 4WD, or with a tour such as Tody Tours (p353). When entering the town of Duvergé, pass a Shell Gas Station and BanReservas on the left. Turn left on Calle Nuestra Señora del Carmen and continue straight. The paved road will shortly change into a dirt road lined with trees and wooden homes. Finally, pass the hydroelectric plant and look for a sign for "Embalse Las Damas," at which point, again turn left. Continue uphill for at least a half hour, until the mountains spread into a savanna. Puerto Escondido is clearly marked by the Ministry of Environment's sign.

INFO

For medical attention, the nearest clinic is in Barahona (p332). In Duvergé, there is a **pharmacy** at Calle Duarte and Jhon F. Kennedy (Dominican spelling), which is catty corner to an **internet café**. Just before entering Duvergé from the east, there is an **Isla Gas Station** on the main highway through town, as well as a **Shell Station** after entering.

EAT

Dining in Duvergé is limited to the *colmados* and a few simple, no-frills eateries, all with prices under RD$150. One block west of the Fortaleza on the main road (C/ Duarte), there is a popular place for fried chicken and mashed potatoes. For snacks, take a gander at the *colmado* or try **Rachel's Pastelería** for great empanadas, both located on the main road.

If planning a trip to Puerto Escondido or Reserva de la Biósfera Jaragua-Bahoruco-Enriquillo, be sure to stock up on food and water in Barahona, because there are no grocery stores in Duvergé or Puerto Escondido.

SLEEP

In Puerto Escondido, simple lodging is available in both the visitor center at the entrance of the Reserva de la Biósfera Jaragua-Bahoruco-Enriquillo, as well as the cabins at Villa Barrancoli located on the actual trail (Contact Tody Tours, p353, for more information on accommodations here). The visitor center in Puerto Escondido offers dormitory style bunk beds, a bathroom, and a small kitchen that occasionally has gas for the stove. However, don't forget to carry along a sleeping bag, mosquito repellant, food, and water.

If there is no other option, find the hourly cabaña called **Hotel D'Amor** – notice the subtle symbol of a giant heart in the driveway – when entering the town. A restless night is guaranteed on the hotel above disco **La Casona,** next to the basketball court on the main road (Duarte). There is also another motel a block to the right of the Fortaleza, called **Hotel Ana** where *muchachos* take their girlfriends to get lucky. Again, don't count on Duverge's hotels for cleanliness or a good night's sleep.

Vengan a Ver

Just to the west of Duvergé is the village of Vengan a Ver, which translates roughly as "everyone come see." Supposedly, at one time, this area was full of agricultural wealth, though now the unsuspecting traveler could easily pass it by unnoticed.

DO

The Parque Nacional Sierra de Barohuco, Northern Side: Biosphere Reserve Jaragua-Bahoruco-Enriquillo

This protected area located deep in the Sierra of Barohuco is home to at least 28 (though expert opinions vary) of the 32 endemic species of birds in the Dominican Republic, and is therefore something of a bird watcher's paradise. This unusual concentration of bird species is just one facet of the incredible biodiversity found in the dry, mixed, and humid forests that form this biosphere. The pockets of ecosystems and microclimates are also home to such plant species as the *criollo* pine (Pinus occidentalis) and colorful orchids.

Unless you are an avid birder and individualist, this park is best enjoyed with a guide. Find informational tours with the National Park of the Sierra de Bahoruco, with headquarters located at the entrance of Puerto Escondido. A few recommended guides include Habisa Perdomo (809-862-8518), Rafael del Jesús Polanco (849-816-2657), and Yokely Pérez (809-251-0388). Tody Tours (p353) also offers quality guided tours.

The South

Antonio Duvergé

Though the town named in his honor does not have much character, General Antonio Duvergé led an interesting life. Born in 1807 in Puerto Rico of Spanish and French descent, Duvergé moved with his family to the Dominican Republic early in life. In 1844, he joined the La Trinitaria independence movement led by Juan Pablo Duarte. Duvergé led several successful battles in the southern and western regions alongside General Pedro Santana. Later, after Santana assumed authoritarian power as President, Duvergé coordinated an attempt to overthrow his regime. The movement failed, and Duvergé was caught and executed in 1855. Though killed in ignominy, he is recognized today for heroism and leadership in the fight for independence.

La Placa & El Aguacate Trails

The highway running past Duvergé along the Dominican-Haitian border is a naturalist's delight because it leads to these two magical trails. After passing through the savannah of Puerto Escondido, find the entrance to **La Placa**, a three-kilometer (two-mile) hiking trail where the great majority of endemic and resident birds can be seen and heard. Early mornings, around 5am to 7am, and then again in the evening, around 4pm to 6pm, are the best times to hear the birdsong, when 30 different species come to socialize and search for food. The forest floor is covered with a thick blanket of green where amateur naturalists can find a white snail striped with black and orange, found only on this part of the country. Spanish moss hangs from low-growing trees that envelop the trail. Creamsicle-colored butterflies flutter among the trees, especially the *cañafistol*, which shoots off vibrant yellow blooms. A visitor's cabin and camping sites are available at the trail's entrance, allowing for easy access to an early morning trek or departure. Don't forget bug repellant and binoculars!

Continuing on past La Placa, the road worsens significantly, leading to **El Aguacate**, a border stronghold from the Trujillo era. Sections of the road consist of large rocks and when it rains, the road becomes impassable. Only a highly skilled, all-terrain driver should attempt the trail. El Aguacate is the convergence point of a protected area called Charco Azul, which covers approximately 280 square kilometers (174 square miles), and the Sierra de Barohuco. It is also the site of a Haitian-Dominican produce market on Tuesday and Friday. The name comes from the acres of avocados that are grown throughout the region.

Ascending from El Aguacate, the climate and vegetation change from humid to coniferous forest, covered with ferns and bright lichen. The air is cool and infused with the smell of pine. The road continues along the Dominican–Haitian border, offering vantage points of the dramatic differences in vegetation between the two countries. On Haiti's side, the hills are brown, ragged, and completely stripped of green, while the Dominican side remains lush and dense thanks to protective and reforestation measures over the past several decades. The Ministry of Environment's maintains a post at **El Zapoten** to prevent deforestation, and partners with Haitian workers in an effort to reforest the area and improve awareness.

The next sign of civilization is at **Loma de Toro**, where a tower offers a jaw-dropping view of Lago Enriquillo to the east and Haiti to the west, as well as the surrounding rolling mountains of thick piney forest. The tower is only accessible by foot, so leave the car at the base of the short trail, which is adorned with agave and wild orchids.

Continuing by vehicle down towards **Los Arroyos** are the first houses after hours of driving. The road continues to be in astoundingly poor conditions, despite it being a major transit route for agricultural products like taro root from the area. As the road nears **Pedernales**, it will pass over **Río Bonito**, and by multiple cascading pools perfect for a cool dip.

Rabo del Gato Trail

Turning left at sign for the Jaragua-Bahoruco-Enriquillo Biosphere Reserve from Puerto Escondido is the **Rabo del Gato Trail** measuring approximately 1.5 kilometers (2 miles). Running along the trail is Río La Ciénaga, providing a cool breeze and a pleasant gurgle throughout the hike. The trail is home to a number of aquatic birds, such as migratory ducks and the Caribbean Coot. A lookout tower serves as a perfect vantage point to spot the Hispaniolan parrot, Hispaniolan Trogan, or the Broadbilled Tody, which inhabit the semi-humid forest.

Tody Tours

Owned by former Peace Corps volunteer and naturalist Kate Wallace, this company offers ambitious tours across the country for the true bird lover. A typical bird-watching tour covers the bird sanctuary of Puerto Escondido in the Sierra de Barohuco, Cabo Rojo in Parque Jaragua, Cachote in the South, and Los Haitises in the East. *US$200 per day for a group of 4 plus food, vehicle rental, and accommodation; 105 Calle José Gabriel García, Zona Colonial, Santo Domingo; 686-0882; katetody@gmail.com; www.todytour.com.*

Pedernales

The last stop in the South before Haiti, Pedernales is a small town with about 10,000 hardy souls. As a border town, Pedernales hosts a vibrant international market, attracting bargain-hunting locals and visitors taking in the frenzied atmosphere. The town has all the basic amenities, including decent hotels and restaurants, and provides a convenient base to explore the magnificent surrounding natural attractions. The top sites nearby include Bahía de las Aguilas, El Hoyo de Pelempito, and several islands off the coast that offer excellent scuba-diving opportunities.

TRANSPORT

From Santo Domingo: RD$400; hourly 5am-3pm; 6hrs; leave from Parque Enriquillo and Pintura

To Santo Domingo: RD$400; hourly 5am-3pm; 6hrs; Parque Central

INFO

Medical Attention

The private **Clínica Diaz-Pérez** is located on C/ Duarte next to the Juzgado de Instrucción. For 24-hour attention, the public **Hospital Doctor Elio Fiallo** is also located on C/ Duarte. For pharmacies, head to **Farmacia San Elías** (57 C/ 16 de agosto (524-0262) or **Farmacia & Tienda Jabbour** (1 C/ G.F. Deligne; 524-0514).

Communication

Free internet is available at the **Indotel** on C/ Duarte or at the **CTC** office on C/ Duvergé inside the provincial government building. For the most dependable access, there is also an internet café on C/ Duarte across from the Juzgado de Instrucción.

Banks

A **Banreservas** is located on C/ Duarte and C/ 27 de Febrero next to Supermercado Ravelo.

Grocery Stores

Supermercado Yuné is the best supermarket in town and also has a pharmacy (Corner of C/ Genaro Pérez Roche and C/ Socorro Pérez Cuevas). **Supermercado Ravelo** on C/ Duarte and 27 de Febrero next to BanReservas is another option.

For fresh produce, the open-air *Mercado* is located on the corner of C/ Genaro Pérez Roche and C/ Socorro Pérez Cuevas.

Tourist Info

The Ministry of Environment's office in Pedernales is an excellent spot for information on all that Parque Jaragua has to offer as well as directions, contacts and current prices. The office is located on 1 C/ Libertad at the entrance of town just after the propane station on the left. They is always someone at the office, but for maps and detailed information, it's best to arrive during normal business hours (Mon-Fri 9am-5pm; 524-0363).

EAT

For seafood, **Oleo Mendez Restaurant** (8 Antonio Duvergé, Barrio Alcoa; RD$150-500; 524-0416) and **Restaurant King Crab Café** (C/ Coronel Rafael Fernández, Barrio Miramar; 256-9607; RD$150-500) are both reasonably priced, plating regional specialties like conch shell *al ajillo* or grilled lobster. Also see **Rancho Típico Restaurant** (p356) in Bahia de las Aguilas.

SLEEP

Doña Chava This family-owned hotel offers rustically decorated rooms with balconies overlooking a tropical garden, which provides a peaceful place to relax and socialize with fellow travelers. Breakfast is available in the hotel's restaurant, which is open all day. *RD$400-750 and RD$110 for breakfast; 5 C/ Segunda, Barrio Alcoa; 524-0332; www.donachava.com; marinojos@yahoo.es; Amenities: A/C, fan, hot water, restaurant, bar, internet*

Oleo Mendez Hotel Oleo Mendez's welcoming budget hotel pays homage to a grandmother's aesthetic, brimming with ruffled comforters and silk flowers. *RD$450-1,000, RD$120 for breakfast; 8 C/ Antonio Duvergé, Barrio Alcoa; 524-0416; Amenities: A/C, TV, restaurant; contact@pedernales-online.info; http://www.pedernales-online.info/oleo_mendez_hostal_pedernales.htm*

Hotel Villas del Mar Tucked at the end of a quiet street past the baseball field, Villas del Mar offers a green space with hammocks and outdoor showers perfect for washing scuba gear alongside its pool and restaurant. All rooms come with air conditioning, but are a tad small and certainly plain. *RD$1,000-1,500, RD$115 for breakfast; 524-0448; contact@pedernales-online.info*

Sur Caribe Sur Caribe offers kitchenettes in some rooms, giving guests the ability try their hand at some of the region's seafood recipes. If that plan fails, the onsite restaurant can soothe any cravings for marine delicacies after a day of lounging by the hotel pool or on the public beach just down the road. *RD$1,000-1,500; C/ Duarte, 524-0106; Amenities: A/C, hot water, restaurant, pool*

Hotel Carolina Small and inexpensive, Hotel Carolina is an efficient operation of clean cement rooms geared towards budget travelers. *RD$400; 77 Av. Mella; 524-0181*

DO

El Mercado Internacional

Every Friday, thousands cross the border from the Haitian town of Anse-à-Pitre, bringing pots, plastic, and produce to join Dominican vendors in the largest international market in the South. This is the spot to head for dirt-cheap clothing and alcohol, among other items, as well as to take part in a fascinating cultural experience as customers are pushed and pulled though the bustle of trans-national commerce.

◪ AGUINAPE

A resource for all natural attractions in Parque Jaragua is AGUINAPE (Asociación de Guías de Naturaleza de Pedernales, Association of Nature Guides of Pedernales), which offers guided tours of all the natural attractions of the area including Bahia de las Aguilas, El Hoyo de Pelempito, and local waterfalls and rivers. Trained guides also offer cultural tours of Banano, a Haitian village just a quick walk from the border, where visitors can experience Haitian culture, food, and dance without having to deal with immigration fees and hassle. *Contact for prices; 2 C/ Duarte; Base Militar; 829-659-1523; 214-1575; amaurisfp@hotmail.com; aguinape@yahoo.es*

Nightlife

Nightlife in Pedernales is difficult to find outside of major holidays like Carnaval, when the festive folk of the city dressed in bright costumes take to the streets. Semana Santa, Patronales (January 13-21), and the Fiesta de las Mercedes (Sept 24) also draw spirited crowds. On weekends, there are two discos with the usual merengue and bachata hits: **Beri Disco** in front of the Parque Central on C/ Duarte and **Gasoline Disco** at the end of C/ Duarte near the Isla Gas Station.

BEACHES

Bahía de las Aguilas

The beach at **Bahía de las Aguilas** is completely untouched, save for a high, palm-thatched pavilion providing a shady eating area. The natural white sand and shallow, calm waters make this beach perfect for swimming or just wading around while contemplating the unruly shrubbery and shimmering horizon. With 8 kilometers (5 miles) of coastline, there is plenty of room to spread out as Bahia de las Aguilas is rarely overrun with visitors (except during Easter and other major holidays). Be sure to bring plenty of sunscreen, repellent, water, food, and supplies, because there are no places to buy anything after arriving.

Part of the **Parque Nacional Jaragua**, Bahia de las Aguilas is representative of the park's predominantly arid terrain, covered with cactus and sparse vegetation, such as the Bayo Hondo tree. It is distinguished, however, as it descends into sparkling layers of blue ocean.

When approaching Pedernales from Oviedo, the turnoff for Bahía de las Aguilas is clearly marked along the highway. If traveling without a private vehicle, either take a *motoconcho* or hire a *guagua* or truck for groups with SINCHOMIPE, the local truck drivers' association (524-0117).

◪ Boats to Bahia de las Aguilas

For boat trips to Bahia de las Aguila, contact **ASOTUR** (President Victor Ferrera: 707-5462 or 501-6016; or Jesus Turbis: 507-2294) to plan group trips. Alternately, just show up at Las Cueva, and there are always a number of fishermen who can take out passengers. Prices are generally uniform across the various associations and businesses, but a little negotiation may be necessary. The boat captain will drop passengers off as early as 8am, and then return at the agreed-upon time, or, by default, before 6pm when Bahia de las Aguilas closes. The National Park entrance fee is RD$50 for nationals and RD$100 for visitors. *Boat Prices: 1-5 people: RD$1,500-1,800 for boat; 6-12 people: RD$2,200 for boat; 12-15 people: RD$150 per person.*

The South

Cabo Rojo & Las Cuevas

Popular with locals especially during Semana Santa, **Cabo Rojo** is the first beach en route to Bahia de las Aguilas. The large port and trucks coming in and out of the Andino Cement Factory tarnish the beach's natural beauty, but it does have some shallow coral reef and spectacular red starfish hidden in the seaweed past the tip of the port. At the time of research, the Secretary of the Environment had multiple projects in action to beautify the beach.

The official park entrance is located at **Las Cuevas**, a settlement named for the immense rock shelf where many of the local fishermen lived as recent as early 2010. Not without a mighty struggle, the Secretary of the Environment was able to remove the zinc-sided shantytown thrown together under the cave after it constructed brightly painted houses for the former inhabitants, which they now own. Living with a government that is known for its empty promises, the fishermen and their families were reasonably suspicious, but after the big move to their new homes, everyone appears to be content.

At Las Cuevas, there are a few short trails along the cliffs overlooking the beach. These paths allow hikers to observe local flora and fauna and stare out at the insanely beautiful views of the ocean. Cerulean blue and golden-brown lizards sunbathe on the rocks, and birds hop from one cactus flower to the next. From Las Cuevas, a number of boat companies offer trips to the beach at Bahia de las Aguilas. The ride to this beach passes cactus–studded paprika-and-gold cliffs, set against the turquoise sea.

EAT

The only eating establishment nearby is at **Rancho Típico Restaurant** in Las Cuevas, where the game is outstanding local seafood. The owner utilizes the phrase "*del mar a la mesa*" – from sea to table – because he buys from the local fishermen, who catch it in the same waters that provide a lovely view from the table. *RD$200-600; Las Cuevas; 474-3408; 753-8058; cuevadelasaguilas@hotmail.com; www.cuevadelasaguilas.com*

SLEEP

It is illegal to camp in Bahia de las Aguilas due to lack of proper waste management associated with overnight stays. Disallowing camping also protects the vulnerable Carey turtle, which nests and hatches on the beach's shores before making the journey out to sea. Pedernales (p353) offers the most convenient sleeping options.

OTHER ATTRACTIONS IN PARQUE NACIONAL JARAGUA

Laguna Oviedo

Before reaching Pedernales is the small settlement of Oviedo. Laguna Oviedo, a few kilometers from the town, is a hypersalinic lake, fed by subterranean rivers originating in the Sierra de Bahoruco that mix with local saltwater channels. Covering 28 square kilometers (17.3 square miles) of the park, the lake is punctuated by small cays, full of limestone outcroppings and mangroves that have adapted to the high salinity content of the water. Like at Lago Enriquillo, the lake's hypersalinity is due to the rapid rate of evaporation from high temperatures and low humidity. Resident fauna include flamingos, seagulls, and rhinoceros iguanas. Laguna Oviedo is best in the early morning, when the sun is not as strong and there are greater possibilities to observe various species of endemic birds. Of the fish species found in the lake, the introduced tilapia is among the most important for the local fishing economy. *For more information, visit La Asociación de Guías de Oviedo. Tours are RD$2,000, which includes a boat captain and guide. Contact Pablo Felíz: 829-889-7586; Pablitofelizj2001@yahoo.es.*

Las Cuevas de las Abejas & Los Pozos

Between Oviedo and Pedernales, there are a number of fascinating caves in Parque Jaragua with Taíno carvings of faces known locally as **Las Caritas** (not to be confused with Las Caritas of La Descubierta). Along the same route is **Los Pozos**, a series of six underground reservoirs, popular for cave scuba diving and cooling off from the heat.

The entrances for both are unmarked, so it's best to head to the Ministry of Environment in Pedernales for more information, or go with one of the local guide associations, such as AGUINAPE (p355).

Islands of Parque Jaragua

Parque Jaragua provides some of the best scuba diving in the country, especially around the islands of Los Frailes and Isla Beata (contact scuba outfitters in Santo Domingo to arrange dives, p107). Unlike other coastal regions of the Dominican Republic, the isolated waters of Parque Jaragua are almost guaranteed to be people-free, which translates to healthier corals and abundant wildlife. The coral reefs in Parque Jaragua offer an unrivaled rainbow of undersea colors, from fire orange to deep violet to neon blue. They provide a wonderful habitat for vibrant sea life with inventive names like the parrot fish, angel fish, and the invasive lion fish, deemed a threat to endemic species.

Parque Jaragua also contains several must-see islands. **Isla Beata** is the largest, which Columbus thought so strategic that he stopped there on three of his four American journeys. The island became a hot potato, tossed between pirates and colonial authorities, and later hosted an enormous salt mine. The island has several microclimates, and makes for a field day for the amateur herpetologist, as it is home to the tiniest reptile species in the world – the cornuta iguana. There is an ongoing architectural dig to retrieve Taíno artifacts, and a small fishing community makes its home on the island.

Twelve kilometers to the southeast are the islands of **Alto Velo**, known for its significant bubby and gull populations, and tiny **Piedra Negra**. Alto Velo is equipped with hiking trails, and both make for excellent dives. These islands also provided important navigational cues for colonial mariners. In the 19th century, American and Dominican enterprises mined the enormous reserves of guano on the island, deposited by thousands of seabirds. Lastly, find **Islote Los Frailes** about 17 kilometers to the west of Isla Beata. This coral atoll derives its name from the white peaks of guano that appear like hooded monks from the distance. These islands are difficult to reach, so contact AGUINAPE (p355) or negotiate with the fishermen at the entrance to Bahía de las Aguilas for tours.

Hoyo de Pelempito

Located in the Sierra de Bahoruco, miners discovered this remarkable geological depression with depths of up to 700 meters (about one half mile). From its various heights, the site offers excellent hiking and bird watching, and is a cool respite from the hot temperatures in the desert of Parque Jaragua. Descending from the summit,

The South

temperatures can drop 15°F (9°C), and have been known to reach freezing in the winter. There is an adjacent visitor's center for more information on the formation's geology and ecology. *Before reaching Pedernales from the southeast, turn north at the Cruce de Cabo Rojo and take the Carretera del Aceitillar for 34 kilometers (21 miles) until reaching El Hoyo de Pelempito.*

Jimaní

Jimaní is one of the principal crossing points for international trade and transport between the Dominican Republic and Haiti. This border town is bleak and arid, but covers the most basic needs. The January 2010 earthquake in Haiti brought thousands of international aid workers to Jimaní, turning it into an impromptu base camp. The activity transformed this once-sleepy border crossing into an unlikely international settlement. Following the earthquake, the town was used as a hub for sending supplies into Haiti, as well as a center for critical medical attention with tents covering open spaces and convoys filling the streets. Jimaní was previously in the news in the sodden aftermath of Hurricane Noel in October 2007 when the town was inundated, and again in May 2004 when flash flooding washed away over half the town's buildings and 700 people died. Today, brightly painted rows of government-funded housing, built to replace the victims' homes, dot the road toward the border. Look out for the starkly magnificent dusty yellow hills against the reflective blue waters of Lake Azuey that abuts the international highway.

TRANSPORT

From Santo Domingo: RD$350; 7am-6pm; 6hrs; *guaguas* to Jimaní leave Santo Domingo every hour or take a guagua to Barahona (p332) and hop on a van to Jimaní, which leaves from C/ María Montez near Barahona's *Mercado* (RD$120; 2.5hrs)

Caribe Tours Buses en route to Port-au-Prince also make a stop in Jimaní, but seats are generally reserved only for those making the complete trip to Port-au-Prince.

To Santo Domingo: RD$350; 7am-6pm; 6hrs; *guaguas* leave every hour from C/ 27 de Febrero near C/ Sánchez.

Border Crossing

Interested in crossing the border into Haiti? Given the choices, Jimaní is the most convenient location for longer-term trips, especially those looking to arrive at Port-au-Prince as this is where the Santo Domingo to Port-au-Prince route run by Caribe Tours enters Haiti. For Cap Haitien, it is best to cross in the north at Dajabón. There is not much to see directly on the Haitian side, as the border regions in both countries are hardscrabble plots of dry earth. Crossing the border might be more interesting at larger towns like Ouanaminthe, from Dajabón. The Haitian twin across from Jimaní is adroitly called Malpasse ("bad passage"). There is not terribly much to experience beyond the border crossing frenzy and the divergent conditions between each side. For more information on crossing into Haiti, see p47.

INFO

Medical Attention

In case of an absolute emergency, the public **Hospital Provincial Independencia** is located on the corner of Av. Gaspar Polanco and C/ Duarte.

Communication

The **Post Office** is located on C/ 19 de Marzo (906-0033). There are two internet cafés, **Clari Papelería** at 30 C/ Duarte and another on C/ 19 de Marzo.

Banks

There is a **BanReservas** at 37 C/ 19 de Marzo and C/ Gaspar Polanco (248-3354; Mon-Fri 8am-5pm, Sat 9am-1pm).

Gas

There is a gas station on Av. 19 de Marzo near the border crossing into Haiti.

EAT & SLEEP

Hotel Jimaní This hotel became the hotspot for international aid workers following the earthquake in Haiti, as it is one of the few to offer clean rooms and dependable electricity and water. The restaurant offers the typical rice, beans, and salad with your choice of meat at midday, followed by fried meat and *tostones* or french fries at night. *RD$900; 2 C/ 19 de Marzo, 248-3139; Amenities: fan, restaurant, pool*

DO

Jimaní is not much of a destination. An agreeable place to pass the afternoon is the **Parque Central**, where locals catch up while relaxing on the shady benches (corner of Av. 19 de Marzo and C/ Restauración). In terms of sights, Trujillo built a large home here (as he tended to do in all provinces), which now serves as an administrative building at the local military outpost. The bright blue waters of **Azuey Lake** provide a stunning contrast to the chalky cliffs on the other side of the international highway. The lake is especially beautiful at sunrise and sunset when jagged silhouettes punctuate the water's edge.

Spanish Language Reference

LIST OF COMMON SPANISH WORDS

Sí – Yes

No – No

Por favor – Please

Gracias – Thank you

Perdón – Sorry

Disculpe – Excuse me

De nada – You are welcome

Perdón; Con permiso – Excuse me

Un momento – Just a second

Está bien; Muy bien – Okay

Buenos días – Good morning

Buenas tardes – Good afternoon

Buenas noches – Good night, Good evening

Señor – Sir

Señora – Madam

Señorita – Miss

Arriba – up

Abajo – down

Tengo hambre/sed – I am hungry/thirsty

¿Cómo? – What did you say?

¡ Ayuda! – Help!

No entiendo – I don't understand

¿Me ayuda? – Can you help me?

Estoy perdido/a – I am lost

Hola – Hello

Adiós – Goodbye

¿Cómo está? – How are you?

Pregunta – Question

COMMON SPANISH PHRASES

¿Habla inglés/español? – Do you speak English/Spanish?

¿Cómo se dice _____ en español? – How do you say_____ in Spanish?

No hablo español – I don't speak Spanish

Más despacio, por favor – Slower please

¿Cómo se llama? – What's your name?

¿De dónde es? – Where are you from?

¿Dónde está ____? – Where is____?

¿Cuándo? – When?

¿Cuánto? – How much?

¿Quién? – Who?

¿Por qúe? – Why?

¿Cómo? – How?

¿Qué? – What?

¿Qué hora es? – What time is it?

Son las 3 – It is 3 o'clock.

FOOD GLOSSARY

arepa - fried corn balls

asopao - sancocho made with rice

berenjena - eggplant

camarones - shrimp

carne - meat

carne de res - beef

cerdo - pork

chicharrón-fried pig fat/skin

chivo - goat

coconete - coconut bread-cake

dulce - literally "sweet," it is a dessert, usually in bar form, made with milk and sugar, and usually with some fruit filling

frío frío - shaved ice with syrup

guandules - pigeon peas (in season around February)

jugo - juice

maíz - corn

mofongo - balls of fried plantain, usually with chicharrón

mondongo - intestines

moro - rice and beans cooked together. Officially called "moro y cristianos" meaning "Moors and Christians"

pastel en hoja - a sort of tamale, made from boiled and mashed plantain or yucca stuffed with meat, vegetables or cheese then wrapped in plantain leaves and steamed

pescado - fish

pica pollo - Dominican-style fried chicken

pollo - chicken

sancocho - hearty, slow-cooked stew with lots of meat and vegetables

tostones - twice-fried green plantains

tres leches - a moist cake made with three types of milk

DAYS OF THE WEEK

lunes – Monday

martes – Tuesday

miércoles – Wednesday

jueves – Thursday

viernes – Friday

sábado – Saturday

domingo – Sunday

COLORS

amarillo – yellow

azul – blue

blanco – white

dorado – gold

gris – grey

morado – purple

naranja/mamey – orange

negro – black

rojo – red

rosa – pink

verde – green

GLOSSARY OF TERMS IN BOOK

In addition to important conversational words, there are many everyday words that make appearances in this book, words that are particular to the Dominican Republic. It will be good to familiarize yourself with them, as they are useful in getting around the country.

arena – sand

ayuntamiento – central municipal building, or city hall

bahía – bay

banco – bank

batey – barracks on sugarcane plantations, usually housing for male Haitian migrant workers. Many bateyes have transformed from barracks into entire villages, as the workers have stayed for multiple generations. Conditions in these villages are poor, lacking many basic services.

bien fría – very cold – usually used to describe beer

cacique – Taíno head of government

café/cafecito – coffee, "little coffee," a colloquial term for coffee that usually connotes coffee in a relaxing setting with conversation

calle (C/) – street

carro público – public car, a form of public transportation in major cities

cobrador – fare-taker on the bus

colmado/colmadón – general store; it often sells alcohol and can serve as a bar or center of social gathering in afternoon and evenings

comedor – cafeteria

criollo – Dominican in nature

dáme – give me

discoteca – nightclub

expreso – express bus (as opposed to voladora)

fábrica – factory or workshop

frontera – border

gallera – cockfighting ring

guagua – bus, usually minibus, often in poor condition

guapo – angry or handsome

ingenio – sugar mill

langosta – lobster

jeepeta – SUV

llego la luz – literally "the lights arrived," it means that the electricity has come back

malecón – seaside boardwalk

mercado – outdoor market

moto/motoconcho – motorcycle taxi

(moto)conchista – motorcycle taxi driver

muchacho/muchacha – boy/girl

palos – sticks, short for Fiesta de Palo, or a festive and usually religious drumming party with percussion-heavy music, singing and dancing.

panadería – bakery

parada – bus stop

perico ripiao – a type of merengue that is fast-paced, uses various percussion instruments and an accordion, and is popular in the country side

plato del día – plate of the day. A meal served at midday, usually at a reduced price and including rice, beans, a protein and another side such as salad.

presa – dam

Se fue la luz – literally "the lights left," it means the electricity has gone out

tiguere – a cunning, street-smart man, or gangster. Can have both positive and negative connotations.

una fría – a cold one, i.e., beer

vaina – stuff, a derivative of the word "vainita," string beans

valle – valley

vida – life

voladora/caliente – guagua makes lots of stops